Canadian Social Policy

Canadian Social Policy

Issues and Perspectives

Fifth Edition

Anne Westhues and Brian Wharf, editors

Wilfrid Laurier University Press acknowledges the financial support of the Government of Canada through the Book Publishing Industry Development Program for our publishing activities. This work was supported by the Research Support Fund.

Canada Council for the Arts Conseil des arts du Canada

Library and Archives Canada Cataloguing in Publication

Canadian social policy : issues and perspectives / Anne Westhues and Brian Wharf, editors. — 5th ed.

Includes bibliographical references and indexes.
Issued also in electronic formats.

ISBN 978-1-55458-359-1 (paperback).—ISBN 978-1-55458-409-3 (pdf).—
ISBN 978-1-55458-410-9 (epub)

1. Canada—Social policy. I. Westhues, Anne II. Wharf, Brian

HN107.C355 2012 361.6'10971 C2011-906139-2
C2011-907334-X

Cover design by Blakeley Words+Pictures. Text design by Angela Booth Malleau.
Cover photograph by Iva Zimova/Panos Pictures.

Chapter 7, by Yves Vaillancourt, appeared earlier, in French, as a working paper for the Laboratoire de recherche sur les pratiques et les politiques sociales (LAREPPS) at the Université du Québec à Montréal.

Waterloo, Ontario, Canada
www.wlupress.wlu.ca

This book is printed on FSC® certified paper and is certified Ecologo. It contains post-consumer fibre, is processed chlorine free, and is manufactured using biogas energy.

Printed in Canada

To the many students we have taught and learned from

Contents

Preface to the Fifth Edition

Social policy shapes the daily lives of every Canadian citizen. It should reflect what a majority of Canadians believe are just approaches to promote health, safety, and wellbeing. Too often, front line service deliverers such as social workers, nurses, and teachers observe that policies do not work well for the most vulnerable groups in society—people with diasbilities, single mothers, older Canadians, recent immigrants, racialized minorities, indigenous peoples, people with serious mental health issues, or people who are gay or lesbian. In this book, we introduce front line workers to what social policy is, who makes it, and how it can be changed. We hope that promoting an understanding of these often complex processes will empower front line workers to advocate for change that leads to a more just Canadian society.

Much has changed in this edition. Noteworthy is that Brian Wharf has joined me as co-editor. I have had the pleasure of working with Brian in the Canadian Association of Social Work Educators over the years, most closely when he succeeded me as president of the association. Like most people who have taught community practice or child welfare courses in social work programs in Canada, I had used Brian's books and admired his commitment to a commuity-based approach to program and policy development. I had never had the opportunity to write with him, though, so I welcomed the opportunity to collaborate. Sadly, Brian passed away on August 11, 2011. He remained engaged in the work of this book until just days before his death, when I received an inquiry about how the editorial work was going.

Brian's influence on this book is substantial. In addition to the more routine editorial work, he provided creative suggestions about how to reorganize the introductory section of the book. You will first see the fruits of these suggestions in Parts I and II. Here the reader is introduced to basic concepts as well as to the contested definitions of social policy and the concepts of political ideology, interest groups, policy scale, and policy purpose. The policy-making process at the federal and provincial orders of government is outlined. Four new or substantially revised chapters now outline or analyze the following: how policy can be influenced by citizens outside of government (Chapter 4, Wharf-Higgins and Weller); an indigenous approach to policy making that is grounded in traditional teachings (Chapter 5, Saulis);

an analysis of how, in spite of a commitment to eradicate racism, it is reproduced by the structures created to prevent it (Chapter 6, Mullings); and the uniqueness of the policy-making context in Quebec (Chapter 7, Vaillancourt). Chapters 5, 6, and 7 will help those teaching social policy to meet the CASWE accreditation standards that require curriculum content to promote an understanding of oppressions pertaining to Aboriginal peoples (CASWE, 2008, SB 5.10.13 and SM 5.7.8), francophones (SB 5.10.14 and SM 5.7.9), and racial minorities (SB 5.10.3 and SM 5.7.6).

In Part III, leading authors in Canadian social policy explore twelve current social policy issues. They define the policy problem and its key concepts. They then discuss who is experiencing the problem, identify the social values the problem is threatening, and discuss the efforts that have been made to address it—for example, legislation, program development, and education and advocacy. The research is reviewed regarding the problem's causes and the gender, class, and ethnoracial considerations necessary to understand how to address it. The chapters on single motherhood (Chapter 8, Lessa), child poverty (Chapter 9, Hunter), risk assessment in child welfare (Chapter 10, Callahan and Swift), mental health policy (Chapter 12, Nelson), people with disabilities (Chapter 14, Dunn), caring for older adults (Chapter 15, Neysmith), social policy pertaining to sexual orientation (Chapter 16, O'Neill), immigration policy (Chapter 17, George), and health care (Chapter 19, Burke and Silver) have all been thoroughly updated with respect to statistical data, current policy, and research and policy analyses since 2006. Three new chapters have been added to this section that address issues that appear often in the media: one on parental leave policies (Chapter 11, Evans); another on violence within the youth criminal justice system (Chapter 13, Finlay); and a third on social housing policy (Chapter 18, Grant and Munro).

In the final chapter, we return to our argument that social workers have a responsibility grounded in their Code of Ethics to advocate for more socially just policies. We explore how front line workers in the human services can advocate for changes in organizational policies that will benefit the people they support, and show how they can link with professional associations to advocate for change at the municipal, provincial, and federal levels.

While our primary audience is social workers and social work students, we hope that citizens who want to be informed about current policy debates and how policy is made will continue to find this a useful resource. The book will be a success if it encourages even one citizen to take action after reading it. We hope there will be many more.

Acknowledgements

Once again I want to thank each of the authors involved in this project for agreeing to be part of it, and for writing with passion and clarity about policy issues and processes. I particularly want to thank the authors who have stayed on for three editions of the book. Together we are educating the next generation of social workers and other helping professionals as policy analysts and advocates for social policy change. To those who have written chapters for the first time, thank you for helping us keep the book focused on current issues, and on innovative approaches to policy analysis. My thanks are also extended to the many students in social policy classes I have taught for challenging my thinking and engaging me in discussions that are now reflected in the chapters I have authored.

My warmest appreciation is extended to the staff at Wilfrid Laurier University Press for agreeing to take *Canadian Social Policy* to a fifth edition. You continue to be the consummate professionals, attending to the many details that are required to put an edited book together. My special thanks to Ryan Chynces for his enthusiastic support of the project and to Rob Kohlmeier for his amazing capacity to keep a project moving as scheduled without making an editor feel pressured. I appreciated your support and encouragement. On the technical side, I extend my thanks to compositor and designer Angela Booth Malleau, to production manager Heather Blain-Yanke, and to cover designer Gary Blakeley for the sleek design and the many decisions taken to yield an attractive, readable book. Leslie Macredie once again made it easy to provide the information she needed to market the book and has done an admirable job of highlighting its strengths.

My last words of appreciation are for Ken Westhues, my life partner, for his openness to many consultations about wording and process throughout this lengthy project.

Part I

Introduction

Becoming Acquainted with Social Policy

1

Anne Westhues

Social policy shapes our daily lives as social work practitioners and as citizens. It identifies what a majority of Canadians accept as legitimate public issues at a given moment in history—that is to say, the issues for which we see the state having responsibility rather than individuals, families, or communities. Social policy also gives direction to how the majority—as represented by the government of the day—believes these issues should be dealt with. Social workers, along with other professionals who deliver front line services—nurses, teachers, and police officers, for instance—are hired to implement these policies. Social workers have a responsibility, as reflected in the Canadian Association of Social Workers *Code of Ethics* (2005), to advocate for social policies that "uphold the right of people to have access to resources to meet basic human needs; that ensure fair and equitable access to public services and benefits; for equal treatment and protection under the law; to challenge injustices, especially those affecting the vulnerable and disadvantaged; and to promote social development and environmental management in the interests of all people" (CASW, 2005, p. 5). This means we are guided as a profession by a value base or ideology that is often described as a commitment to the promotion of greater social justice.

Following the Second World War, we saw a broadening of areas where Canadians were willing to make collective statements through social policy about the kind of society we wanted to create. Where once we saw violence against women and children as private matters to be dealt with by the family, for instance, we now have taken a position, reflected in the Criminal Code of Canada (1985) and in child welfare legislation in every province, that violence against women is not acceptable and that children may not be physically or emotionally abused. Where once we accepted structural inequalities for women and racialized groups, we now have a Charter of Rights and Freedoms (1982) and human rights legislation in every province that commit to equal treatment of marginalized groups. This process of defining and redefining our vision of what we want to be as a society is ongoing. There are supporters and there are critics for every policy decision taken, reflecting the variety of interests and values within any society. New issues emerge and are addressed as demographic, economic, and political realities change, and as

Defining Social Policy

individuals and peoples come to understand their realities differently than in the past, and to dream of a more just future.

My purpose in this chapter is to summarize the debate about what is meant by the term *social policy* and offer a definition that is inclusive of a broad range of human services, that recognizes the link between economic policy and social policy, and that highlights the important role values and ideology play in shaping policy decisions. I also explore the concept of *policy analysis*, reviewing the influences of both values and evidence in shaping policy. The concept of *ideology* is explored, and an analysis is made of how the major political parties in Canada can be characterized ideologically. Finally, the concept of *interests* or *interest groups* is explored.

Defining Social Policy

There is agreement that public policy covers all areas in which governments make decisions: the economy, immigration, transportation, international relations, the military, the environment, health care, education, and social services, for instance. There has been a long-standing debate within the literature, however, as to what is meant by the term "social policy." The central issue that frames this discussion is what is included in the domain of social policy. Does it encompass only those areas that have been described as "social care," like child welfare, counselling and supports for older adults? Does it include related human services like education and health care, or an even broader range of what some consider economic policies like labour legislation, decisions about budget deficit reduction, or free trade agreements? Does it include only decisions made with respect to the allocation of rights and resources by governmental bodies, or does it also include decisions made by not-for-profit organizations or by non-governmental collectivities like unions? Is the role of policy analysts that of detached, dispassionate observers, or do they have a responsibility to advocate for value-based positions? While the debate may sometimes seem esoteric, the position taken on it defines the range of policy issues that one believes social workers have a responsibility to be informed about, and on which the profession has an ethical obligation to try to effect change.

Canadian authors have tended to emphasize a broader rather than a narrower definition of social policy. Yelaja (1987, p. 2), for instance, offered this definition: "Social policy is concerned with the public administration of welfare services, that is, the formulation, development and management of specific services of government at all levels, such as health, education, income maintenance and welfare services." In the same vein, Miljan (2008, p. 150) says, "Many of the most expensive activities carried out by the state in advanced capitalist societies are associated with the area of social policy. These functions include public education, health care, publicly subsidized housing, and the provision of various forms of income support to

Defining Social Policy

such segments of the population as the unemployed, the aged, and the disabled." She goes on to explain that this area of policy is associated with what is commonly called "the welfare state": interventions intended to moderate the market economy with a view to "promoting the wellbeing of individuals, families or groups on the grounds of fariness, compassion or justice" (p. 150). This broader definition recognizes an unequivocal linkage between social policy and economic policy and is reflected in the writing of Canadians like Armitage (2003); Graham, Swift, & Delaney (2009); Lightman (2003); and McKenzie & Wharf (2010). As we have shifted into a global economy over the past thirty years, it has become clear that social policy can no longer be discussed in a meaningful way without understanding the economic context of policy decisions.

Parallel to the shift in thinking more globally has been an increased emphasis on understanding how policy relates to practitioners locally. Pierce (1984) suggests that there are eight levels at which social policy shapes the work of front line practitioners such as social workers. These include the three levels of government—federal, provincial, and local—that political scientists like Pal (2006) and Miljan (2008) identify as the domain of public policy. Pierce also suggests that what Flynn (1992) calls "small scale policy systems" like social service organizations and professional associations be included as policy-making levels. This reflects his understanding that an integral part of practice is the development of operational policies that define how a service user will experience a framework policy that is set at a larger-system level: for instance, "minimum intervention" into the lives of families with children, "normalization" for people who have disabilities, or a commitment to equity for marginalized groups.

Pierce (1984) also includes the family and the individual practitioner as system levels relevant to understanding social policy. He argues that decisions made by the individual practitioner when implementing policy define how service users experience both social services and the social policies that shape those services. Every worker has some discretion with regard to how he or she interprets policy. For instance, a social assistance worker may choose to accept fewer contacts with employers as acceptable job search activity because the person receiving benefits has been ill, or not. Or a worker determining the eligibility for a child care care subsidy may choose to advise an applicant who is ineligible because of savings to reduce those savings. How the worker chooses to act in these two instances sends a very different message to service users about the social policies affecting their daily lives. Similarly, decisions taken by a family with respect to the amount and types of care they are willing to provide to an older family member or a child with a disability will influence how the person needing care feels about the care they receive.

Flynn (1992) reinforces the importance of this broader perspective of social policy for social work practitioners. He argues that policy shapes and delineates what the practitioner does, how he or she relates to the service user, and the manner in which discretion is allowed or exercised. Furthermore, he argues that understanding how policies at the agency or even individual level affect what the practitioner may or must do, and how they can be changed, is a way to empower practitioners.

So how do I propose to use the term "social policy"? I build upon Pal's (2006, p. 2) definition of public policy: "a course of action or inaction chosen by public authorities to address a given problem or interrelated set of problems." Then I both broaden and narrow his definition. I broaden it by including in the definition of "public authorities" managers and front line service deliverers at the various levels of government and in social service organizations who make decisions that define the way service users experience policy. Unlike Pal, I do not see these service deliverers as merely "policy takers" (2006, p. 2), or as implementers of the directions defined by others, but rather as people who have some discretion in the way they work within broader policy guidelines. I believe it is through this exercise of agency that that policy and practice are connected (McKenzie & Wharf, 2010) and that organizational and social structures are changed (Giddens, 1979; 1984). These displays of agency, like all policy decisions, reflect a particular set of values, or ideology. Then, borrowing from Flynn (1992), I narrow the definition to include only a subset of the issues than are addressed in public policy, the issues that "deal with human health, safety or well-being."

When all of these considerations are incoporated into my definition of social policy, it reads as follows: *Social policy is a course of action or inaction chosen by public authorities to address an issue that deals with human health, safety, or well-being. These public authorities include those who work directly with service users, bureaucrats working in international organizations and at all levels of government, and elected officials. Policy decisions at the international and governmental levels reflect the values acceptable to the dominant stakeholders at the time that the policy decision is taken. Decisions taken by front line workers may reinforce the intent of these policy decisions, or may resist it when they are understood to be inconsistent with the values of the front-line professionals.*

Defining Policy Analysis

Another issue that draws conisderable discussion in the literature is the role of the policy analyst. Mirroring the debate in the social sciences about whether positivist, constructivist, critical theory or particpatory approaches are most appropriate for policy studies research today (Howlett & Lindquist, 2007; Orsinis & Smith, 2007), the question is often framed as whether the role of the policy analyst is to provide "neutral" information to decision makers that will help them make more informed decisions, or whether the analyst also has a responsibility to engage in advocacy grounded in his or her values with his or her analyses (Friedmann, 1987; Paquet, 2009). In recent literature, this disucssion has been reconceptualized as whether policy analysis should be more "rational"; more "argumentative" or value-based; or more participatory, engaging in processes that give voice to people who are usually absent in the policy debates (Howlett, 2009; Howlett & Linquist, 2007; Pawson, 2006). I take the position that policy analysis is necessarily value-based and ought also to be evidence based and participatory. I understand evidence to include both qualitative and quantitative data, and the experiences and opinions of citizens to be as relevant as demographic data or cost-effectiveness analyses in shaping policy.

If social policy is action taken to address a given problem, policy analysis is "the disciplined application of intellect to public problems" (Pal, 2006, p. 14) to produce values- and evidence-based arguments that help decision makers choose a policy alternative that is likely to have more positive outcomes than policy that is based solely on values or evidence. In his earlier work, Pal differentiates between academic policy analysis and applied policy analysis, which is the domain of social work practitioners. He suggests that the academic is concerned primarily with theory, explanation, understanding how policy came into being, and attempts to retain some impartiality in making the analysis. By contrast, he suggests that the practitioner is more interested in specific policies or problems than in theory, in evaluation rather than explanation, in changing policies, and in advocating for the interests of consumers of service (Pal, 1992, p. 24). The recent resurgence of interest in evidence-informed policy making has led to an acknowledgment of the limited policy analysis capacity at all levels of government (Howlett, 2009). To engage academics in conducting more policy-relevant research to fill this gap, academic funding bodies such as the Social Science and Humanities Research Council (SSHRC) now place a greater emphasis on the policy relevance of a study as a criterion for funding it.

Limitations of Policy Analysis

Limitations of Policy Analysis

It is important to be mindful that for all its promise of improving the well-being of Canadian citizens, policy analysis as an area of practice has limitations. A primary consideration is that the process may be exceedingly slow. Even at the organizational level, to change policy may take a year or longer from when a concern is identified until a new policy has been implemented. If the local, provincial, or federal governments are the focus of change, it is likely to take even longer. This means that a commitment to effect change must be a long-term one.

Second, efforts to make changes in policy can be highly resource intensive. It takes time, policy analysis capacity, and money to raise awareness about an issue. The more complex and controversial the issue, the more the resources will be required. It is essential to learn to build coalitions, to create

Limitations of Policy Analysis

organizations where none exist to advocate for an issue, and to identify and link with existing ones that might share your concern and have evidence to share that may help you build your case. It may also be necessary to raise funding to support your policy change initiatives. This means that a commitment to effect change is an opportunity to develop a set of social work skills that are commonly associated with community development practice.

Third, even with the investment of considerable resources, it may not be possible to effect changes that are consistent with social work values at a particular time in history because of the ideology of the party forming the government. An example would be the mandatory work requirement introduced for social assistance recipients in a number of provinces in the mid-1990s. While most social workers support the development of job training opportunities for people on assistance, requiring people to work in return for benefits is in conflict with our belief that receipt of social assistance is a right, albeit one coupled with a responsibility to provide for oneself when possible. Abundant data show that the great majority of people work when given the opportunity. Job readiness programs offered by the various levels of government in Canada have typically been oversubscribed (Snyder, 2000). In spite of this empirical evidence, the belief persists that people on assistance are lazy and need to be coerced to accept work. As long as a government in power holds this belief, and refuses to alter it in light of evidence to the contrary, efforts to change workfare policies are unlikely to be fruitful. This means that a commitment to effect change may not always be successful in the short term and can be a source of considerable discouragement if a longer-term perspective is not maintained.

Fourth, for the policy analyst working within an organization or at some level of government, it is essential that there be a clear understanding between the policy analyst and the employer regarding which kinds of political activity are acceptable. Traditionally, the role of a government employee was defined as that of a rational, apolitical analyst. Partisan political activity was not only discouraged but could be grounds for dismissal. While that has now changed, there may still be limits on what is allowed. An employee at the local government level may be free to engage in efforts to change provincial legislation with respect to the regulation of social workers, for instance, but not to lobby his or her member of the Legislative Assembly to withdraw the mandatory aspect of the workfare program. This means that choosing to engage in advocacy requires a careful assessment of one's work environment and clear communication about the boundaries on political activity.

Finally, policy analysis skills and tools are not yet sufficiently developed to ensure that issues of "difference" are systematically and fully considered when social policy is made. It is only in 1995 that the Government of Canada committed to review all public policy initiatives from a gender perspective (Status of Women Canada, 1998). Evidence of the utilization of a gender-based analysis can be found on various government websites now, but a recent review by the Auditor General of Canada found that, notwithstanding this commitment, only one ministry—Northern and Indian Affairs—was actually committed to conducting gender analysis on all policy issues, had assigned responsibility for these analyses, provided training to ensure that policy analysts had the skills to conduct the analysis, and had a system in place to monitor their progress with this commitment (Auditor General of Canada, 2009).

Ideology

Summary

In sum, policy analysis is a form of research that is intended to improve policy outcomes by informing decision makers about the magnitude of an issue of public concern, articulating possible approaches to defining an issue, and identifying a range of possible solutions to the issue. Policy analysis addresses technical questions such as what is the unemployment rate of immigrants, but to do so must first define what is meant by "unemployment" and "immigrant." Is a person only considered unemployed if he or she is actively seeking employment, for instance, or are people who have become discouraged and who have stopped looking for work also unemployed? Is an immigrant a person who was born outside Canada but now lives here, or are we concerned with "recent immigrants," people who have come to live here in the past five years? While the evidence generated from research is an essential aspect of policy analysis, ideology is an equally important aspect of the policy-making process and can lead decision makers to disregard the evidence generated by academics and advocacy groups (Geddes, 2010). The values associated with various ideological positions are explored in the next section, and connections made between political ideology and the major political parties in Canada.

Ideology

Ideology is a set of beliefs about how the economy should be structured, what kind of governance we should have, and the social values that should define our society. We typically associate ideology with political parties (whether conservative, liberal, or social democratic), but ideology is also generated by social movements such as the women's movement (feminist), the human rights movement (human rights, anti-oppression), and the anti-globalization movement (social justice for less developed nations, including democratic decision making and an equitable share of world resources). Professional ideologies can also shape our world view. Mullaly (2007) identifies humanism and egalitarianism as the fundamental values of the social work profession. He deconstructs what these overarching values mean in relation to the economy, political beliefs, view of social welfare, and practice principles for social workers. While he acknowledges that there is variation in beliefs among professionals, he concludes that, with respect to the economy, social workers support government intervention, believe that social priorities should dominate economic decisions, and support an equitable distribution of society's resources. Politically, we believe in participatory democracy and we see the purpose of social policy as the promotion of equality and a sense of community or social cohesion. The practice principles consistent with this ideology are articulated in the CASW *Code of Ethics* and include treating people with respect, enhancing dignity and integrity, facilitating self-determination and self-realization, accepting differences, and advocating for social justice.

Mahon argues that the ideologies most evident in social policy debates in Canada can be categorized as belonging to the "liberal" family (Mahon, 2008). By this she means that all of the major political parties support an economy based on markets rather than a socialist, centrally planned economy. Furthermore, individuals and their families are expected to retain a key role in the provision of social care and financial support—a value often described as independence—supplemented by state supports. These state supports are expected to be more or less generous depending on which variation of liberalism one supports. Mahon suggests that four variations capture Canadian political ideologies: classical liberalism, social liberalism, neoliberalism, and inclusive liberalism.

The primary value of classical liberalism, more commonly known as conservatism, is *freedom,* defined as "the ability to pursue one's self-interest free from the interference of the state (a negative freedom)" (Mahon, p. 343). The state's role from this perspective is to protect private property and to foster an economy that supports "orderly relations of [market] exchange" (p. 343). The purpose of social policy is to assist the deserving poor and reinforce the work ethic among those expected to provide for themselves. Deserving poor would be defined as those who need financial or other supports through no fault of their own; for example, people who are developmentally delayed. Classical liberals are fiscal conservatives, preferring balanced budgets and low levels of government debt. They are also typically social conservatives, resisting policies that encourage social and cultural change (Jost et al., 2003). This resistance may be particularly strong when fundamentalist religious beliefs are part of an individual's belief system and when policies are understood to have a moral aspect (Zafirovski, 2009), examples being abortion, euthanasia, and stem cell research. Social conservatives value traditional gender roles, with women working in the home and men as the primary breadwinners (Mahon, 2008). If women are not engaged in the workforce outside the home, they will be available to provide care to children, elders, and others who may require support, consistent with traditional practices. This opens a range of policy solutions that are not available if women are expected to be engaged in the labour force outside the home.

By contrast, social liberalism (Mahon, 2008) or reform liberalism (Mullaly, 2007) focuses on the *positive freedoms* of opportunity and personal

Ideology

development. The role of the state is to create conditions for all to develop to their full potential, a perspective consistent with social development theory (Midgley & Conley, 2010). Social policies supported by people with this world view would involve measures to counteract the impact of market forces, for example, unemployment insurance or universal health insurance. Social liberals support a mix of policy options: those that encourage individual responsibility, such as Registered Retirement Savings Plans and Registered Education Savings Plans, which provide variable benefits based on individual contributions; universal programs such as the Old Age Security demogrant, which provides the same benefit to all who are age sixty-five or more; and the top-up of these state benefits, with market provisions such as individually purchased disability insurance or supplemental health insurance for health services not covered by the state program.

Mahon (2008), who has made comparative analyses of social policy in Canada and Sweden for some years, argues that the line between a social liberal and a social democratic perspective is fine, defined most clearly by the generosity of benefits rather than by the scope of services the state should provide. Mullaly (2007) concurs that this describes the actual policy positions taken by parties in Canada associated with social democratic ideologies. However, he argues that social democrats are more likely than social (reform) liberals to generate structural solutions to social policy issues. Concern about insufficient saving for retirement might lead social liberals to recommend that employers be required to provide a retirement benefit such as matching the RRSP savings of their employees. Social democrats are more likely to recognize that average- and low-income Canadians do not benefit from RRSP programs because their lower earnings make it difficult for them to save for retirement. Hence, social democrats would be more likely to support raising the adequacy of the benefits under universal programs such as Old Age Security, or labour-force-related programs such as the Canada Pension Plan. Social liberals and social democrats are less likely to be social conservatives than classical liberals or neoliberals; they are also more likely to support policies that foster the equality of the sexes, including equal pay for women and men, equitable pay for work that is primarily provided by women, and state provision of child care so that women who choose may participate in the labour force (Zafirovski, 2009). Social liberals and social democrats are also more likely to support policies that encourage inclusion of marginalized groups, such as people with disabilities, recent immigrants, people who are minoritized racially or by sexual orientation, and older adults.

Neoliberalism, the third variation of liberalism conceptualized by Mahon, is associated with the globalization of a market economy and is generally acknowledged as the primary influence on all public policy today, including social policy (Gilbert & Terrell, 2005; Harvey, 2005; Teeple, 2000). The values supported by neoliberals include maintenance of free markets;

privatization of pubic goods such as health care, water, and education; cost-effective delivery of public services by contracting out jobs such as cleaning to minimize labour costs; and promotion of public–private partnerships for public goods such as the building of facilities such as roads and hospitals. Harvey (2005) adds that neoliberals mistrust democracy, preferring a form of governance that privileges corporations and the most elite classes. Neoliberals believe that government should be as small as possible, providing few services directly and with little regulation.

The position with respect to gender roles is less clear in neoliberalism than in classical or social liberalism. When combined with social conservatism, policy positions are taken that reassert the traditional "male breadwinner model." In the purer neoliberal form, women's primary role is not mother but labour force participant (Neysmith et al., 2005). They believe that the resulting child care needs should be met through the private sector rather than through state provision of child care or individual child care subsidies. Subsidies to businesses may be supported, however, in the belief that quality, accessible child care would help business attract female employees with young children, and that the productivity of these employees would be enhanced by reliable child care.

Mike Harris, the Premier of Ontario from 1995 to 2002, characterized this ideological perspective, and during his regime cut government expenditures by reducing the number of employees in the public service. This meant there were fewer water inspectors, for instance. A high-profile effect of this cutback was the failure to observe irregularities in the testing of the water supply in a small community, Walkerton. The subsequent contamination of the water with *E. coli* resulted in the death of seven residents and the illness of many more. The impact on health care costs was many times the savings generated by the reduction in staff cuts, and the effects on peoples' daily lives continue, and are immeasurable.

Mahon's final category is inclusive liberalism, which she characterizes as social liberalism plus fiscal conservatism. Encouragement of labour force participation is central to social policy under inclusive liberalism, as are related training programs to develop individual capacity. Social policy is understood to be a form of investment to empower individuals to take their place in the market and in civil society (p. 345), that is, an investment in human capital and in democracy. The discourse of social investment has become increasing evident in federal and provincial policies as the impact of the low birth rate on the labour force pool in Canada becomes evident and as policies are generated that attempt to maximize the productivity of labour force participants (Cameron & Stein, 2000).

Summary

The overarching goals evident in social policy debates are grounded in the ideologies of the various political parties and social movements. Whether you believe that social benefits should be provided to all citizens through a universal program or targeted to those most in need depends on whether you understand all citizens to be at risk, or only a subgroup, such as those with low income (Gilbert & Terrell, 2005). Whether you believe that the state should intervene to redistribute wealth depends on whether you think it is fairly distributed through the play of the market or needs to be adjusted to ensure that the needs of all citizens are met. Whether you believe the state should ensure protection of civil and political rights for all depends on how inclusive is your conception of democracy. Finally, whether you believe that women and children deserve to live free from coercion and the threat of physical and emotional harm or that this is a private family matter depends on whether you believe that the state should assume a role in ensuring the protection of women and children or that this should be the responsibility of family and community members. In the next section, we explore how these ideological beliefs relate to the major political parties in Canada.

Connecting Ideology to Political Parties

Connecting Ideology to Political Parties

The three major political parties in Canada are the Conservative Party of Canada, the Liberal Party of Canada, and the New Democratic Party of Canada (NDP). In the 2011 federal election, the single-issue Green Party attracted 3.9 percent of the vote and the Bloc Québécois 6.4 percent of the vote compared to 39.6 percent for the Conservatives, 30.6 percent for the NDP, and 18.9 percent for the Liberals (Elections Canada, 2011).

The values the Conservative Party aspires to uphold in their policies, according to their constitution, are as follows: a balance between fiscal accountability, progressive social policy, and individual rights; a sovereign and united Canada; rule of law; equality of all Canadians; freedom of the individual, including freedom of speech, worship, and assembly; belief in a federal system of government, including strong provincial and territorial governments; equal status for English and French; freedom to pursue enlightened and legitimate self-interest within a competitive economy and to enjoy the fruits of one's labour; freedom to own property; and acceptance of Canada's obligations among the nations of the world (Conservative Party of Canada, 2008).

This party would have been characterized as classical liberal by Mahon in the past but neoliberal today because of its promotion of a globalized economy. Its perspective with respect to the role of government in providing social services is "residual" (Wilensky & Lebeaux, 1958)—that is, it believes that public provision of social services should be minimal. Family and the community as expressed through the actions of the many not-for-profit or nongovernmental organizations that constitute civil society should be encouraged to provide social services rather than the state. A residual perspective means that it is not necessary for government to have a vision of

Connecting Ideology to Political Parties

what "well-being" looks like for Canadians, nor to plan and develop a system that supports achievement of this vision. Rather, funding for programs is allocated on an ad hoc basis, often in response to the lobbying of interest groups or stakeholders. The resulting approach to planning has been described as "muddling through" (Lindbloom, 1959).

A review of the New Democratic Party of Canada website (http://www.ndp.ca) shows that the primary value it aspires to represent in its social policy is justice—social and environmental. Equal opportunity, inclusivity, and universal programs are also values evident in its discussion of social policy. The constitution of the Saskatchewan New Democratic Party states its purpose as "to promote through political action and other appropriate means the establishment of a co-operative commonwealth in which the principle regulating production and exchange will be the supplying of human needs and not the making of profits" (New Democratic Party of Saskatchewan, 2010).

While the federal NDP does support a market economic system, its members are comfortable with a greater role for government through regulation of the market in the interest of protecting labour and reducing social and economic inequality. They support a broader range of social programs and more generous program funding than either the Liberals or the Conservatives. Higher tax rates for both individuals and corporations are the preferred mechanism for generating the revenues needed to fund their policies. The ideology of the NDP is usually identified as social democratic (Mullaly, 2007), though fitting best with Mahon's category of generous social liberals. Its orientation to social policy is consistent with a social development perspective—that is, each person should be supported to pursue the development of his or her full capacity.

The primary value the Liberal Party of Canada aspires to represent in its policy, according to its constitution, is "the dignity of each individual man and woman" (Liberal Party of Canada, 2009). Additional guiding values it identifies are individual freedom, responsibility, and human dignity in the framework of a just society; political freedom in the framework of meaningful participation by all persons; a commitment to the pursuit of equality of opportunity; enhancement of Canada's unique and diverse cultural community; recognition that French and English are the official languages of Canada; the preservation of the Canadian identity in a global society; and that all citizens should have access to full information concerning the policies and leadership of the party. This party would have been characterized by Mahon as social liberal traditionally, and as inclusive liberal more recently because of the emphasis in its current policies on employment, training to develop capacity, and social investment in programs "to empower individuals to take their place in the market and in civil society" (Mahon, p. 345). Its perspective with respect to social welfare services would be characterized as "institutional" (Wilensky & Lebeaux, 1958). This means that it believes that public provision of social services will always be required and that it is prudent to develop a national or provincial vision of what "well-being" would look like in Canada, then to plan and develop a system of programs and services that support the achievement of this vision.

Summary

It is important to note that within each political party there is probably as much variation as there is *between* parties in the values of individual party members. While some of this variation can be explained by how important balanced budgets and the size of the government debt are to a member (i.e., how fiscally conservative they are), perhaps more variation can be explained by the member's degree of social conservatism. Social conservatives are also likely to be fiscal conservatives, but this is not always the case. Some of the variation may be explained by the social location of individual voters, which tells us about the power or influence of individuals in society. In the next section, brief mention is made of the variety of interests that attempt to influence policies.

Interest Groups

A benefit of a democratic state is that citizens are given the opportunity to communicate their preferences on policy issues. The most basic way in which this is done is by voting for the party that puts forward the platform that is most consistent with one's own ideology and interests. It is not surprising that a vice-president of a large corporation experiences the world differently than a young mother in receipt of social assistance. This experience of the world defines one's understanding of it, one's definition of a "social issue"/problem, and the solutions that one believes are reasonable. I was struck by this variation recently when watching a panel on the CBC news discuss the growing concern about the inadequacy of most Canadians' retirement savings. The economist with a background in the banking industry defined the problem as an individual one and proposed solutions that called for individual action to increase savings. The economist with a background in the labour movement, by contrast, defined this as a social problem and called for a change in social policy that would ensure more adequate payments through public pensions.

While interests can be multiple, and sometimes conflicting, they can be organized under the concepts of class, gender, and racialization. All of these categories share the capacity to differentiate the power to influence policy. Class is defined by one's place in the economy. In today's economy, class position is defined by whether you are an owner or an investor in a company, by whether you are a manager within the company, or by whether you are engaged in production of goods or the provision of services. Income level might be another way of categorizing people as belonging to different classes. Gender is generally understood to be male or female, but for some policy issues being transgendered would represent a distinct interest, or policy preference. Racialization refers to the privileging of people who are white and of European origin relative to Canadians with other skin colours or countries of origin. Other interest groups commonly referred to in policy analyses include taxpayers, the public interest, faith-based communities, and age cohorts.

While, once again, there may be as much variation within an interest group as between groups, a particular policy issue may reinforce a politics of identity and bring together people who would not normally share a common position. Policy related to eliminating sexual harassment may galvanize support from women across class, ethnoracial, and age categories, for example.

Conclusion

In this chapter I have argued that social policy is pervasive, affecting the well-being of all Canadians, and that social policy addresses a broader array of policy issues than social welfare services. I have also argued that the interplay of research-generated evidence and ideology is utilized when defining whether a social issue is of sufficient concern to warrant public intervention. Whether the balance of influence rests with evidence or ideology varies from one political party to the next and within the culture of a particular party at different points in time. This culture is heavily influenced by the current leader of the party. Researchers who produce evidence that is inconsistent with the ideology of the governing party may be ignored. Interest groups that do not share the ideology of the governing party may be discounted. The ideology of the governing political party will shape the policy alternatives that are given serious consideration and ultimately selected. This does not mean that advocacy should be discontinued when the values of the governing party are inconsistent with those of a group such as social workers. It does mean that advocacy should take a different form—for example, a focus on public education rather than direct lobbying of government. Al Gore, with his educational program about the impact of global warming, is an example of how this educational approach can be used to raise public awareness among the general citizenry when the governing party is not prioritizing a policy issue.

In this chapter we have explored the concepts of *social policy, policy analysis, ideology,* and *interests*. In the next chapter we explore the range of *purposes* that give focus to policy: strategic, legislative, program, operational. We also explore the *dimensions or scale* of policy and the division of responsibilities among the various levels of government with respect to who makes, who funds, who delivers, and who monitors policy. Finally we review the range of forms that policy can take, or the *policy instruments* that policy makers can choose from to implement a policy goal.

References

Armitage, A. (2003). *Social welfare in Canada* (4th ed.). Don Mills, ON: Oxford University Press.

Auditor General of Canada. (2009). Report of the Auditor General of Canada to the House of Commons. Chapter 1. Gender-Based Analysis. Retrieved from http://www.oag-bvg.gc.ca/internet/English/parl_oag_200905_01_e_32514.html

Cameron, D., & Stein, J.G. (2000). Globalization, culture, and society: The state as place amidst shifting spaces. *Canadian Public Policy, 26* (supp. 2), S15–S34. Retrieved from http://www.jstor.org/stable/3552569

Canadian Charter of Rights and Freedoms. (Part I of the Constitution Act, 1982). In RSC, 1985. Retrieved from http://laws-lois.justice.gc.ca/eng/Const

CASW (Canadian Association of Social Workers). (2005). *Code of ethics*. Retrieved from http://www.casw-acts.ca/practice/codeofethics_e.pdf

Conservative Party of Canada. (2008). Conservative Party of Canada Constitution. Retrieved from http://www.conservative.ca/media/20090205-Constitution%20-e.pdf

Criminal Code of Canada. In RSC, 1985. c. C-46. Retrieved from http://laws-lois.justice.gc.ca/PDF/C-46.pdf

Elections Canada. (2011). 2011 general election: Preliminary results. Retrieved from http://enr.elections.ca/National_e.aspx

Flynn, J.P. (1992). *Social agency policy: Analysis and presentation for community practice*. Chicago, IL: Nelson-Hall.

Friedmann, J. (1987). *Planning in the public domain: From action to knowledge*. Princeton, NJ: Princeton University Press.

Geddes, J. (2010, August 9). Why Stephen Harper thinks he's smarter than the experts on everything from the census to climate change, taxation and crime. *Maclean's*. Retrieved from http://www2.macleans.ca/2010/08/09/cracking-eggheads

Giddens, A. (1979). *Central problems in social theory: Action, structure, and contradiction in social analysis*. Berkeley, CA: University of California Press.

Giddens, A. (1984). *The constitution of society*. Berkeley, CA: University of California Press.

Gilbert, N., & Terrell, P. (2005). *Dimensions of social welfare policy* (6th ed.). Toronto, ON: Pearson.

Graham, J., Swift, K., & Delaney, R. (2009). *Canadian social policy: An introduction* (3rd ed.). Toronto, ON: Pearson Prentice Hall.

Harvey, D. (2005). *A brief history of neoliberalism*. Toronto, ON: Oxford University Press.

Howlett, M. (2009). Policy analytical capacity and evidence-based policy making: Lessons from Canada. *Canadian Public Administration, 52*(2), 13–175.

Howlett, M., & Linquist, E. (2007). Beyond formal policy analysis: Governance context, analytical styles, and the policy analysis movement in Canada. In L. Dobuzinskis, M. Howlett, & D. Laycock (Eds.), *Policy analysis in Canada: State of the art* (pp. 86–115). Toronto, ON: University of Toronto Press.

Jost, J.T., Glaser, J., Kruglanski, A.W., & Sulloway, F.J. (2003). Political conservatism as motivated social cognition. *Psychological Bulletin, 129*(3), 339–375. doi: 10.1037/0033-2909.129.3.339

Liberal Party of Canada. (2009). Constitution. Retrieved from http://www.liberal.ca/party/documents/

Additional Resources

Lightman, E. (2003). *Social policy in Canada.* Don Mills, ON: Oxford University Press.

Lindbloom, C.E. (1959). The science of "muddling through." *Public Administration Review, 19,* 79–88.

Mahon, R. (2008). Varieties of liberalism: Canadian social policy from the "Golden Age" to the present. *Social Policy and Administration, 42*(4), 342–361. doi: 10.1111/j.1467-9515.2008.00608.x

McKenzie, B., & Wharf, B. (2010). *Connecting policy to practice in the human services* (3rd ed.). Toronto, ON: Oxford University Press.

Midgley, J., & Conley, A. (2010). *Social work and social development: Theories and skills for development social work.* Toronto, ON: Oxford University Press.

Miljan, L. (2008). *Public policy in Canada: An introduction* (5th ed.). Toronto, ON: Oxford University Press.

Mullaly, B. (2007). *The new structural social work.* Toronto, ON: Oxford University Press.

New Democratic Party of Saskatchewan. (2010). Constitution. Retrieved from http://www.saskndp.ca/assets/File/constitution/constitution2010.pdf

Neysmith, S., Bezanson, K., & O'Connell, A. (2005). *Telling tales: Living the effects of public policy.* Halifax, NS: Fernwood Publishing.

Orsinis, M., & Smith, M. (Eds.) (2007). *Critical policy studies.* Vancouver, BC: UBC Press.

Pal, L. (1992). *Public policy analysis: An introduction.* Toronto: Nelson Canada.

Pal, L. (2006). *Beyond policy analysis: Public issue management in turbulent times* (4th ed.). Toronto, ON: Thomson Canada.

Pawson, R. (2006). *Evidence-based policy: A realist perspective.* London, UK: Sage.

Paquet, G. (2009). *Crippling epistemologies and governance failures.* Ottawa, ON: University of Ottawa Press.

Pierce, D. (1984). *Policy for the social work practitioner.* New York, NY: Longman.

Snyder, L. (2000). Success of single mothers on social assistance through a voluntary employment program. *Canadian Social Work Review, 17*(1), 49–68.

Status of Women Canada. (1998). Gender-based analysis: A guide for policy-making. Retrieved from http://www.swc-cfc.gc.ca/pol/gba-acs/index-eng.html

Teeple, G. (2000). Globalization and the decline of social reform. Halifax, NS: Garamond Press.

Wilensky, H., & Lebeaux, C. (1958). *Industrial society and social welfare.* New York, NY: Free Press.

Yelaja, S.A. (1987). *Canadian social policy* (Rev. ed.). Waterloo, ON: Wilfrid Laurier University Press.

Zafirovski, M. (2009). From the "most fateful" to the "most fatal" social force? Conservatism and democracy reconsidered. *International Journal of Sociology and Social Policy, 29*(7/8), 330–357. doi: 10.1108/01443330910975669

Additional Resources

The Campbell Collaboration and the Cochrane Collaboration are two initiatives that support the writing of meta-analyses, or syntheses reviews of what we know in relation to particular areas of practice. These reviews are understood to be helpful in guiding both evidence-based practice and policy making. You can

Additional Resources

access their Web pages at http://www.campbellcollaboration.org and http://www.cochrane.org. The Campbell Collaboration addresses questions that are more within the domain of social welfare / social services; and the Cochrane Collaboration focuses more on health and mental health issues.

The Canadian Council on Social Development (CCSD) is a non-governmental, not-for-profit organization that was founded in 1920. Our mission is to develop and promote progressive social policies inspired by social justice, equality, and the empowerment of individuals and communities. We do this through research, consultation, public education, and advocacy. Our main product is information. Our sources of funding include research contracts, the sale of publications and memberships, and donations. Visit http://www.ccsd.ca.

The Caledon Institute of Social Policy is a social policy think tank, established in 1992. It is a private, non-profit organization with charitable status. It is supported primarily by the Maytree Foundation, located in Toronto. Caledon is an independent and critical voice that does not depend on government funding and is not affiliated with any political party. Caledon welcomes charitable donations from individuals and organizations and occasionally undertakes contract projects for governments and non-governmental organizations on the basis that such work advances Caledon's research agenda; but such projects do not define it. Visit http://www.caledoninst.org.

The Canadian Centre for Policy Alternatives offers an alternative to the message that we have no choice about the policies that affect our lives. We undertake and promote research on issues of social and economic justice. We produce research reports, books, opinion pieces, fact sheets, and other publications, including *The Monitor*, a monthly digest of progressive research and opinion. People need to know that there are workable alternatives. We work hard to make sure that progressive ideas and research make it into the hands of citizens, activists, and the media. Visit http://www.policyalternatives.ca.

The C.D. Howe Institute is a national, non-partisan, non-profit organization that aims to improve Canadians' standard of living by fostering sound economic and social policy. The institute began life in 1958 when a group of prominent business and labour leaders organized the Private Planning Association of Canada to research and promote educational activities on issues related to public economic and social policy. The PPAC renamed itself the C.D. Howe Research Institute in 1973. Visit http://www.cdhowe.org.

The Federal–Provincial Relations and Social Policy Branch is a branch of the Department of Finance Canada that provides policy advice to the minister on federal–provincial financial relations and social policy issues and their economic and fiscal implications. It also administers the major federal–provincial transfer programs. Visit http://www.fin.gc.ca/branches-directions/fedprov-eng.asp#FPRD.

The Fraser Institute is an independent non-partisan research and educational organization based in Canada. It conducts peer-reviewed research into critical economic and public policy issues, including taxation, government spending, health care, school performance, and trade. Visit http://www.fraserinstitute.org/about-us/overview.aspx.

The Government Organization Act of 1969 established the National Council of Welfare as an advisory group to the Minister of National Health and Welfare. Since the reorganization of federal government departments in 1993 (and again in 2004), the council has advised the Minister of Social Development. The council's mandate is to advise the Minister in respect of any matters relating to social welfare that the minister may refer to it for its consideration or that the council considers appropriate. The council's reports tend to focus on income security and poverty, and include annual updates of various poverty lines. Visit http://www.ncw.gc.ca/h.4m.2@-eng.jsp

Policy.ca is a Canadian non-partisan resource for public discussion of issues in Canadian public policy. This site consists of a constantly growing database of online public policy research publications, as well as information on policy organizations, institutes, and researchers. This unique clearinghouse for public policy is carefully managed and updated to provide users with a balanced review and examination of current developments in public policy. Visit http://www.policy.ca.

Social Policy in Ontario (SPON) is a website designed as a tool for public reporting about social programs in Ontario. It aims to inform the public about current issues relating to social programs and policies in Ontario; spotlights current news articles that have relevance to social policy in Ontario; informs the public of Canada's obligations as a signatory of the UN Covenant on Economic, Social and Cultural Rights; and promotes informed critical analysis and public participation in the development, assessment, and enhancement of social programs. Visit http://www.spon.ca.

Videos

Inside Job. (2010). Directed by Charles Ferguson. Oscar-winning documentary about the worldwide economic meltdown of 2008. It illustrates what globalization of the economy means and shows the power held by financial industry elites in influencing economic policy.

Who Makes Social Policy and How

Part II

The Policy-Making Process

2

Anne Westhues and Carol Kenny-Scherber

In this chapter, we explore two considerations beyond ideology that shape the policy-making process. The first is the *dimension* or *scale* of policy. Which order of government is responsible for policy in the area of concern? Is it the federal, provincial, or municipal government, or some mix of the three? Are there international agreements that specify principles that must guide the policy? Are there court rulings that clarify the intent of the policy and that are binding on legislatures and the organizations delivering the programs? Or is the policy a responsibility of the organization charged with implementing it (i.e., with providing the services)? The second is the *purpose* of the policy. Is it strategic, legislative, program policy, or is it operational policy? We then review the policy-making process in a Westminster-style democracy, which is the form of democracy institutionalized in Canada's constitution and in the federal and provincial governments.

Policy Scale

Canada is a federal state with a democratic government. A federal state means that more than one level of government may be responsible for public policy. The concept of *scale* refers to various levels having some responsibility in specific policy areas. In a democratic state, citizens have a say in who will represent their interests in the governance of the country. Policy making is a core function of governance.

The Federal, Provincial/Territorial, Municipal, and Organizational Scales

The "divided sovereignty" (Van Loon & Whittington, 1976) embedded in the British North America Act (1867)—and since 1982 in the Constitution Act—refers to how responsibility for public policy has been established in Canada. The federal government has jurisdiction for some areas of policy and the provinces and territories for others. With regard to social policy, the provinces are responsible for "the establishment, maintenance and management of public and reformatory prisons in and for the provinces" (Constitution Act, 1982, Section 92.6) and for "the establishment, maintenance and management of hospitals, asylums, charities, and eleemosynary

Policy Scale

institutions" (Constitution Act, 1982, Section 92.7). While it is generally agreed that the intention of the legislation was to limit the role of the provinces and to create a strong federal government, judicial interpretations of the legislation over time have limited the role of the federal government in the development of social policy. This division of responsibilities has created friction between the federal and provincial governments with respect to who has the authority to make legislation and develop new social programs, who is responsible for funding the programs, who is responsible for delivering the programs, and who is responsible for monitoring the quality of services delivered. These conflicts gave rise to legal challenges to clarify the intention of the constitution at various times in history, and in 1999 to the Social Union Framework Agreement, which defines the process by which the provinces and territories will work with the federal government to develop social policy.

Depending on the policy area of concern, the federal government may play a greater or lesser role. The federal government has no jurisdiction in the area of child welfare, for example. This means that it cannot pass legislation that will directly shape the provision of child welfare services, though it may influence child welfare policy and programs by providing federal funding for designated child welfare services. This is known as the exercise of "spending power." By contrast, the federal government has jurisdiction over legislation pertaining to young people in trouble with the law—currently the Youth Criminal Justice Act—because criminal justice is its responsibility.

The Canada Assistance Plan was the mechanism for flowing federal funds to the provinces for social services from 1966 to 1996. It allowed the federal government to match provincial spending on approved social services, including child welfare, a policy choice known as cost sharing. This federal–provincial agreement was replaced in 1996 with the Canada Health and Social Transfer, legislation that still allows the transfer of federal funds to the provinces, but now in the form of block grants. This meant that the provinces had more control over how federal funds were allocated within the "envelopes" of health, education, and social services than they had under the previous legislation. In 2004 the Canada Health and Social Transfer was split into two pieces of legislation: the Canada Health Transfer and the Canada Social Transfer (Department of Finance, 2010). This separation of funding transfers into one for health and the other for post-secondary education, social assistance, and social services was intended to protect the funding for education and social services from being redirected to health care services while maintaining automomy for the provinces to spend as they chose within these broad envelopes.

Local governments (municipal and regional) have a limited policy jurisdiction with respect to social services in all provinces in Canada (Graham, Phillips, & Maslove, 1998; Tindal & Tindal, 1984). Their primary areas of responsibility include land use, water, roads, libraries, and recreation. In

Policy Scale

most provinces they do not deliver any social services and so have no legislative jurisdiction or any reason to set policy within the strategic, program, or operational areas. This is a good fit with the capacity of local governments to collect the revenues needed to fund services because the primary revenue-generating instrument of local governments is property taxes and user fees (Manitoba Regional Plannning Advisory Committee, p. 79). Property taxes are among the most regressive forms of taxation. A person who has lived in his or her home for many years may have a valuable property but limited income. For example, a retired person may have lived in her home for twenty years during which time its value has escalated, and hence the property taxes are higher. At retirement her income is likely to be less than when she was employed, however, so increases in property taxes threaten her ability to remain in her home.

Municipalities in Ontario and Nova Scotia carry responsibility for funding and delivery of some social services. During the period of the Canada Assistance Plan, municipalities in Ontario provided 20 percent of the funding for socal assistance, the province 30 percent, and the federal government 50 percent. When the neoliberal Mike Harris became Premier of Ontario in 1995, his government increased the local governments' share of funding to 50 percent for social assistance, long-term care, and child care subsidies. Their share for social housing and community health increased to 100 percent (Melchers, 1999). This downloading of provincial repsonsibilities created pressure on municipal governments to increase property taxes and resulted in large budget deficits in many municipalities. The Liberal McGuinty government came to power in 2003 promising to review the municipal responsibilities for funding (Government of Ontario, Association of Municipalities of Ontario, & City of Toronto, 2008). As a result of this review, the province has resumed responsibility for full funding of social assistance programs, paralleling the funding structure for social assistance in other provinces.

Finally, administrative policy can be made at the organizational level, which has a profound impact on how service users experience the intent of legislation or programs developed provincially or federally. Organizations implementing these programs may be voluntary community organizations led by a commuity board of directors or profit-making organizations.

The International Scale

Before the shift to a more global economy and a more global perspective in the 1980s (Cameron & Stein, 2000; Collier, 1995; Harvey, 2005; Teeple, 2000), social policy was usually discussed in a national context. The generosity of the safety net that a country provided was understood to be related to its level of industrialization, its level of affluence, and the extent to which the nation's cultural values supported assuming public responsibility for the well-being of its citizens (Moscovitch & Drover, 1981). The shift to global capitalism has generated agreements between Canada and other countries

Policy Scale

that have a considerable influence on our social and economic well-being, however. For example, following the Free Trade Agreement between Canada and the United States in 1989 and the North American Free Trade Agreement between Canada, the United States, and Mexico in 1992, economic and political pressures mounted to "harmonize" social policy in all three countries. While ideally that may have meant that American and Mexican social policy would come to look like Canadian social policy, the safety net that was so carefully woven over a period of fifty years or more in Canada is gradually being weakened, coming to look more like its less sturdy American cousin. The worldwide crash of the economy in 2008 and subsequent discussions about the development of international guidelines for lending practices by the G20 nations leave little doubt that Canadian economic and social well-being is intertwined with the well-being of other countries worldwide and that no nation can set policy unilaterally that will protect it from the effects of decisions taken outside its borders.

International policy may be set through bilateral or multilateral agreements such as free trade legislation, or through administrative agreements between Canada and individual countries about issues such as child abduction or child migration through international adoption. International policy may also be made by international organizations such as the United Nations or the more recently formed World Trade Organization (WTO). Developed out of the Uruguay Round of the General Agreement on Tariffs and Trade (GATT) talks in 1995, this body defines public policy in areas such as the environment, genetically modified food, and labour rights as part of its mandate to regulate international trade (Cameron & Stein, 2000; Shrybman, 1999). Structural adjustment programs that promote a neoliberal policy environment are a common condition required by the WTO before it will lend money to poor countries. These plans typically divert government spending from health and social services, open these sectors to investment by people hoping to make a profit, and create barriers to accessing what had been public services without user fees (Hossen & Westhues, 2011).

Some international agreements are legally binding—for instance, laws pertaining to the conduct of war and the transfer of people charged with serious criminal activities across national boundaries. The International Court of Justice and the International Criminal Court, located in The Hague in the Netherlands, have been created to hear such cases. Agreements such as the UN Convention on the Rights of the Child (1989) and the UN Declaration of the Rights of Indigenous Peoples (2007), while not legally binding, also shape social policy initiatives in Canada. Article 8 of the Convention on the Rights of the Child, for instance, says that "State Parties undertake to respect the right of the child to preserve his or her identity, including nationality, name and family relations as recognized by law without unlawful interference" (UN, 1989). This entitlement, which Canada agreed to by becoming a signatory to the convention, has implications for child welfare policy and practice. If a child has a right to maintain his or her identity, Canada must now attempt to ensure that information is gathered on the child's background and that there is a mechanism for passing this information to the child at some specified age, in both non-identifying and identifying forms. If custody rulings made in Canadian courts are to be honoured, authorities in other signatory countries have a responsibility to repatriate an abducted child to the custodial parent in Canada. Becoming a signatory to the Declaration of Rights of Indigenous Peoples in 2010 committed Canada to protect a broad range of Aboriginal rights, among them self-government and protection of Aboriginal culture. It remains to be seen if signing this treaty will speed resolution of long-standing issues such as disputed treaty rights.

Court Rulings

The approval of the Charter of Rights and Freedoms in 1982 has had an enormous impact on how social policy is made in Canada, especially with respect to contentious issues that are grounded in widely varying beliefs about what constitutes moral behaviour, and appropriate gender relations, race relations, and opportunities for people with disabilities. The ensuing use of the courts to establish Charter rights has given rise to what has been labelled "the counter-majoritarian difficulty"—that unelected judges now have the power to overrule the decisions of elected officials (Barker, 2010, p. 3). "Judical interpretive supremacy"—that is, the assumption that judical rulings are the final say on interpretation of policy—threatens democracy by placing such power in the hands of unelected officials (Barker, 2010, p. 3).

Two broad solutions are discussed in the literature. One is to limit judical rulings to matters that protect the procedural requirements of democracy. The other is to permit the courts a wide scope for rulings, but to retain the authority of elected officals to overrule court decisions. One argument in favour of the latter suggests that interpretive power should be shared among the executive, legislative, and judical branches of government and that enduring constitutional principles will emerge through a series of exchanges (rulings, challenges of these rulings) among the three branches of government, not through any single ruling. Another argument is that legislatures can have final say with respect to policy by using Section 33 of the Charter (the notwithstanding clause) to override judical interpretations of rights or impose "reasonable limits" on those rights. While this unresolved debate continues, with enormous implications for who makes social policy in Canada, the federal and provincial parliaments remain the primary centres for the development of policy in pursuit of greater social justice.

Summary

To summarize, the issue of scale is relevant in Canada because three tiers of government may play a role in policy development: federal, provincial,

Policy Purpose

and local. Operational policy may also be made at the organizational level or through court rulings intended to clarify the intent of the law. It is important to maintain an awareness of scale when analyzing social policy because it identifies the institutional players who will have to be engaged if policy is to be changed.

Policy Purpose

Four areas of responsibility for policy making are negotiated among these institutional players. Who defines the vision for an area of policy (strategic thinking)? Who approves legislation (legislative)? Who specifies the program guidelines, including eligibility criteria, type of services provided, funding, and responsibility for service delivery (program)? And last, who specifies the administrative policies and procedures that facilitate implementation of the program (operational)? We call these the purposes of policy. As Figure 2.1 shows, policy may be made with all of these purposes at the federal and provincial scales, and with all but the legislative purpose at the municipal and organizational scales.

Strategic social policy involves the development of a vision to improve the well-being of vulnerable groups such as children, women, recent immigrants, people with disabilities, older adults, and indigenous peoples. The vision may be global, for a nation, for a region within a nation, or for the geographic area served by a social service organization. Strategic policy is future focused and is summarized in an aspirational statement. The UN

Figure 2.1 Intersectionality of Scale and Purpose in Social Policy

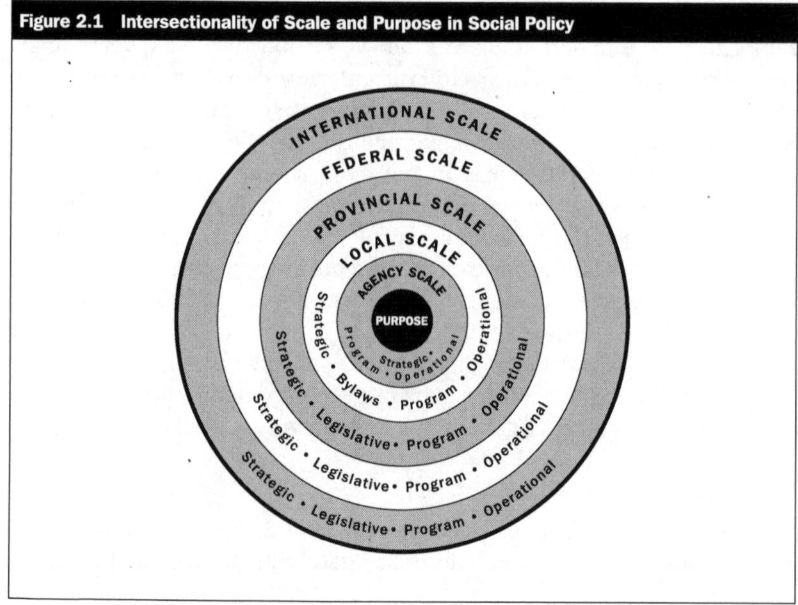

Declaration of the Rights of the Child is an example of strategic policy. It is set at a high level of abstraction and inspires policy development at the national, provincial, municipal, and organizational scales, but it cannot be enforced in the same way as legislation.

Legislative policy includes bills or acts passed by the federal House of Commons and the Senate as well as by the provincial and territorial Legislative Assemblies. It includes regulations, directives, and guidelines that are intended to facilitate the implementation of legislation. All legislation, regulations, and administrative orders of the federal government can be accessed through the Department of Justice website at http://laws.justice.gc.ca/eng. A list of provincial and territorial websites is provided under Additional Resources at the end of this chapter.

Program policy involves defining program objectives, the service delivery structure, the implementation plan, and data gathering requirements for monitoring and evaluating the program. This area of policy is sometimes called program planning (Kettner, Moroney, & Martin, 2008). It can often be found on ministry websites and is usually specified in funding agreements between the ministry funding a program and the organization selected to deliver it. Program policy is to be applied uniformly in all sites delivering a particular program.

Operational or administrative policy includes decisions that are required to implement the program and may vary from one site to the next: hours of operation, procedures that service providers and service users are to follow, human resources policies, and forms to be completed to monitor services. A ministry may not require a daily log, for example, but an organization may require one to facilitate communication among staff.

Table 2.1 uses the example of supervised access centres in Ontario to illustrate how these four policy purposes interrelate at each policy scale. The figure illustrates how policy becomes more specific as it moves from strategic, to legislative, to program and then operational policy. Supervised access centres are a relatively new service intended to facilitate contact with a non-custodial parent when there is concern about the safety of the child or the custodial parent. The centres may also help determine if the non-custodial parent is abusing drugs or alcohol (Ontario Ministry of the Attorney General, 2005).

The Policy-Making Process

So how are all of the decisions about policy made? Making social policy can be a simple process or can be full of twists and turns, depending on the scope and complexity of the issue being addressed. In its simplest form, new policy can be announced in a news release by a minister or the prime minister, through a budget decisison or through a court ruling. Even these less complex processes may not be without their intrigue, however. An example is the September 28, 2010, ruling by Justice Susan Himel of the Ontario

Table 2.1 Policy Purpose by Scale for Supervised Access Centres in Ontario

INTERNATIONAL **Strategic** UN Declaration of the Rights of the Child	• Article 3: Best interest of the child shall be the primary consideration. • Article 5: State parties shall respect the responsibilities, rights, and duties of parents. • Article 9: Child shall not be separated from his or her parents against their will, except where such separation is necessary for the best interest of the child. • Article 12: Views of child shall be given due weight, depending on age and maturity of child. • Article 19: Protection of the child from all forms of violence.
FEDERAL **Legislative** Divorce Act of Canada, 1985 Department of Justice	• **Section 16(10):** "The child of the marriage should have as much contact with each spouse as is consistent with the best interests of the child and, for that purpose, shall take into consideration the willingness of the person for whom custody is sought to facilitate such contact."
PROVINCIAL **Legislative** Ontario Children's Law Reform Act, 1990 Ministry of the Attorney General	• **Part III, Custody, Access, and Guardianship** The purposes of this Part are, 19(a) to ensure that applications to the courts in respect of custody of, incidents of custody of, access to and guardianship for children will be determined on the basis of the best interests of the children; • **Rights and responsibilities** 20.(2) A person entitled to custody of a child has the rights and responsibilities of a parent in respect of the person of the child and must exercise those rights and responsibilities in the best interests of the child. • **Duty of separated parents** (4a) Where the parents of a child live separate and apart and the child is in the custody of one of them and the other is entitled to access under the terms of a separation agreement or order, each shall, in the best interests of the child, encourage and support the child's continuing parent–child relationship with the other. R.S.O. 1990, c. C.12, s. 77 • **Access** (5) The entitlement to access to a child includes the right to visit with and be visited by the child and the same right as a parent to make inquiries and to be given information as to the health, education and welfare of the child. R.S.O. 1990, c. C.12, s. 20(5) • **Best interests of child** 24.(2) The court shall consider all the child's needs and circumstances, including, a) the love, affection and emotional ties between the child and, (i) each person entitled to or claiming custody of or access to the child, (ii) other members of the child's family who reside with the child, and (iii) persons involved in the child's care and upbringing; b) the child's views and preferences, if they can reasonably be ascertained; c) the length of time the child has lived in a stable home environment; d) the ability and willingness of each person applying for custody of the child to provide the child with guidance and education, the necessaries of life and any special needs of the child;

Table 2.1 Policy Purpose by Scale for Supervised Access Centres in Ontario

	e) the plan proposed by each person applying for custody of or access to the child for the child's care and upbringing; f) the permanence and stability of the family unit with which it is proposed that the child will live; g) the ability of each person applying for custody of or access to the child to act as a parent; and h) the relationship by blood or through an adoption order between the child and each person who is a party to the application. 2006, c. 1, s. 3 (1); 2009, c. 11, s. 10.

PROGRAM POLICY
Supervised Access
Ontario Ministry of Attorney General
http://www.attorneygeneral.jus.gov.on.ca/english/family/supaccess.asp
	Objectives of Supervised Access
	• To provide a safe, neutral and child-focused setting for visits between a child and non-custodial parent or other family member.
	• To ensure the safety of all participants, including staff.
	• To provide trained staff and volunteers who are sensitive to the needs of the child.
	• To provide reports of factual observations about the participants' use of the service.
	• "Safety measures include but are not limited to the following:
	  • staggered drop-off and pick-up hours;
	  • client arrival and departure supervised by staff and/or volunteers;
	  • staff or volunteers must monitor children at all times during visits;
	  • staff or volunteers arrange for parents to be escorted to their cars by police if there is a safety concern;
	  • there is always staff available as back up to the volunteers;
	  • develop and maintain a close liaison with the local police;
	  • security checks of volunteers and staff are always conducted before employment; and
	  • the outdoor play area, if there is one, is enclosed and directly attached to the premises."

ORGANIZATIONAL Dalhousie Place http://www.execulink.com/~bdsupacc/home.html	**Operational policies and procedures** • fees • drop-off and pick-up procedures to prevent parent contact • cancellation of visits • informing when late • scheduling procedures • guests who may visit with child • meals and snacks • clean-up • breakage • medications • washroom procedures • cameras, cell phones, and electronic equipment • physical punishment • appropriate language • speaking about other parent • substance abuse • loitering

The international, federal, and provincial legislative analysis in this table was drawn from an unpublished paper by Danielle Ritsema, "Supervised Access Centres," presented at Wilfrid Laurier University, November 25, 2010.

Superior Court that sections of the Canadian Criminal Code pertaining to prostitution are unconstitutional under the Charter of Rights and Freedoms. Acknowledging that prostitution is one of the thornier social issues in Canadian and other societies, she argued that the criminalization of running a brothel, communicating for the purposes of prostitution, and living off the avails of prostitution forces people who engage in this line of work to choose between their liberty rights and their personal safety. Because it is one of the thornier social policy issues, this ruling raised concerns for as many citizens as cheered the ruling, and because this ruling had implications for the law in all provinces and territories, Rob Nicholson, Canada's Minister of Justice and Attorney General, proceeded to appeal it. At time of publication, no decision had been reached on the appeal.

The process by which these elected bodies engage in making legislative policy is described in the section that follows. It is essentially the same process at the federal and provincial/territorial levels of government, except that legislation requires approval of the House of Commons and the Senate nationally but only the legislative assembly provincially and territorially. Whether policy is being made nationally or federally, the process creates many opportunities for citizens to actively influence public policy. This section describes the policy-making functions within political parties, governments, and state bureaucracies and outlines the opportunities they provide for citizens to contribute to the policy process. These opportunities are summarized in Table 2.2.

The Political Party Phase

For a number of reasons, provincial and federal political parties have not made much genuine effort to develop in-house policy capacity (Cross & Young, 2006). The two most significant reasons are that, for parties not in power, it is difficult to keep supporters politically active between elections; and for the party in power, the policy process is highly confidential and contained mostly within the caucus and the Cabinet. Weak policy capacity within political parties has contributed to the growing influence of interest groups and independent think tanks (Baier & Bakvis, 2001; Cross & Young, 2006). The vision and strategies of political parties are usually determined by some combination of the party leaders, the executive, and the members. The opinions of individual members, especially Cabinet members, have an important bearing in formulating party positions, but this occurs behind the scenes and has little bearing on the House and its committees (Cross, 2004; White, 1997). Party leaders enjoy a dominant position and in most cases are able to impose their views on the party. In fact, almost nothing that occurs in the legislature can be understood except through the lens of the party and the leader.

The 2000 Study of Canadian Political Party Members found that an important motivation for becoming a member of a political party was to

Table 2.2 Opportunities for Participation

ENVIRONMENT	INTERVENTIONS	INFLUENCE ON POLICY
POLITICAL		
Election campaign	• Voting, pamphlet distribution, public contact on issues, discussion with candidate	• Extremely minimal, influence dependent on election outcome
Ridings association executive member	• Networking, volunteer on riding and regional policy committees, informal discussion with party members and MPPs, representation at policy conventions	• Collective outcome, encourage MPP to carry messages to caucus, coalition building, lobbying MPPs and executive
Executive position	• Strategy planning, local candidate selection, contact with Cabinet members at conventions/ meetings	• Highest influence, access to backroom, lobbying caucus; only big issues discussed at Cabinet
ADVOCACY/ ADVISORY		
Citizen initiated	• Contact with politician/ bureaucrat on single issue, individual problems	• Extremely minimal, usually self-interest
Issue orientation	• Local, requires ongoing lobbying, media publicity; goal is to have politician take up the cause	• Can achieve or avert specific decisions; little influence on policy
Pressure group	• Membership in larger organization, staffed through donations, internal specialized policy expertise, confrontation, and/or lobbying	• Degree of influence determined by prestige, power, contacts; multiple accesses to system
Advisory group	• Invited expertise, subgovernment, interface with bureaucracy	• Continuous discrete influence; change in government may be detrimental
PROFESSIONAL		
Individual worker	• Contact with politician/ opposition/bureaucrat on single policy impact, letter writing, lobbying on change status, advocates for service user	• Contribution to policy stew, builds foundation for ongoing contacts with politicians, opposition, and bureaucrats, contributes from practice field
Agency representative	• Agency identifies client and organization issues, approach fits organization's decision models, coordinated through agency, letter writing, media, meetings, lobbying	• Build linkages to advisory group status, perceived as advocate for agency, networks with similar agencies
Association	• Builds coalitions across practice fields, educates membership, meetings and lobbying, position papers, presentations, briefings	• Facilitates policy discussion across practice fields and agencies, adds credibility to expert input, ongoing input to policy process

influence party policy on a particular issue. A great majority of respondents expressed dissatisfaction with their opportunities to exercise influence, however, agreeing with the statement that the party should do more to encourage local associations to discuss public policy (89 percent) and that regular party members should play a greater role in developing the national election platform (73 percent) (Cross & Young, 2006). Some parties, as a means of building grassroots support, engage in more participatory methods to develop their party platforms. The resolutions adopted at their policy conventions form the basis of party policy and direct the activities of the executive and the caucus of the New Democrats, the Bloc Québécois, and the Conservative Party of Canada, for example (Cross, 2004). The Liberal Party convenes periodic national policy development conventions—its Thinker's Conference in 2010 was the most recent instance. Liberal leaders, however, are not bound by the policy resolutions approved at such conventions. Regardless of the process and degree of inclusiveness, a party runs on a platform shaped by these conventions, and if elected, that strategic policy gives direction to the government's policy agenda for the next four years.

The Pre-legislative Phase

In Westminster-style parliaments the Cabinet and bureaucracy make many critical decisions out of the public eye during the pre-legislative phase. Westminster government, as found in Canada and its provinces, is centred on ministers who are individually and collectively responsible to the House of Commons for the policies and programs of government. In the traditional Westminster model, ministers lead departments staffed with career civil servants, who provide the minister with background on policy issues as well as with policy analyses that they understand to reflect both the ideology of the governing party and the public interest. Each minister is also supported by political staff, whose job it is to advise the minister of his or her party's politics as well as its policy preferences. The pillars of the Westminster system are *responsible government* (i.e., accountability to citizens), *a loyal opposition, party discipline*, and *ministerial responsibility* (Forsey, 2010; White, 1989).

Although a great number of policy issues arise in addition to those identified in the election platform of the party that forms the government, many initiatives are rejected, significantly revised, or ascribed such a low priority that they fall off the policy agenda. Policy advisers work in an environment fraught with dynamic tensions: political versus administrative responsibility for policy development, centralized versus coordinated models of development, and, finally, closed versus participative design models. These tensions are more evident with a minority government than with one that has a clear majority, as we have seen since 2006 with the Harper governments.

Internal policy units, producing analysis and advice for ministers and senior public servants, are located in the central agencies and throughout the line ministries. At the federal level, these agencies include the Prime Minister's Office, Cabinet, and the Ministry of Finance. The central agencies oversee the functions of government policy approval and coordination, fiscal planning, fiscal approval, and government human resources planning. As information-seeking and processing groups, they are concerned with policy development, program planning and design, liaison, research, and evaluation.

In addition, policy groups act as gatekeepers to the system by screening and reducing the demands made on ministries and their deputies. In some groups, "firefighting," whether intended or not, dominates and may even prevent the development of planning and evaluation roles. Other constraints and considerations include insufficient resources (time, staff, position classifications, and facilities), difficulties in recruiting and retaining qualified personnel, the inexperience of some advisers, the absence of relevant data, and technical problems in the use of analytic methods (Meltsner, 1976). The policy strategy is determined through an interactive process between the policy groups and their clients: the minister, senior management, and members of the immediate policy network.

Understanding the dynamic tensions within the bureaucracy begins with the policy–administration dichotomy (Doern & Phidd, 1988). The crux of the tension is the bureaucracy's need to be sensitive to the political objectives and constraints of the governing party, while initiating policy ideas and "massaging" policy proposals. During the drafting of Cabinet documents and memoranda, staff-level advisers attempt to bring the right nuance of meaning, provide the best supporting data, and develop the most cost-effective options while maintaining the integrity of the minister's policy vision. Advisers engage in constant discussions "up the tube" to the minister through the deputy and across ministerial lines and central agency officials. Frequently, there is also contact with interests outside the government and with other levels of government. Ideally, the end product of this iterative process is a polished Cabinet document.

Bureaucracy staff intent on ascertaining the political acceptability or feasibility of a policy must evaluate whether it generates support for the particular political party that will propose it. One question becomes key: In the current environment, what solution is most likely to attain the policy goals? The technical skills that analysts bring to the process are set into this framework and define the methodologies, selection of data, analysis tools, evaluation criteria, and selection of options for determining the choice of directions. As Faludi and Voogd (1986) note, one can accept as a given that ideological political and moral factors will be part of the policy and planning process, but that does not rule out using rationality as a decision-making rule. Rationality is the pragmatic way for policy advisers to negotiate the recognition of diverse political values, recruitment of political support, and accommodation of contradictory goals and objectives. Analysts become adept at the language of rationality and its application in well-prepared arguments to position problems, goals, and potential solutions within the ideology of the party forming the government (Fisher, 1980).

From a policy perspective, the result of rights talk and cultural pluralism is that stakeholders expect to be consulted on public decisions. Putting this expectation into practice raises issues of managing public expectations of what will become of their advice. For the policy analyst, consultations are another source of information and advice contributing to the policy "stew"; however, those who are consulted want to see their contributions reflected. Considering the range of stakeholder views, this is not possible. In practice, policy advisers seek a balance between competing interests while keeping the government's vision central.

At the end of the pre-legislative phase, legislation is drafted for the approval of the minister. Approval follows discussion and debate in the House of Commons and Senate (legislative assembly provincially), the most visible locations of social policy-making.

The Legislative Phase

In debating the issues of the day, Parliament brings new problems to public attention, educates the public about those problems and possible solutions to them, and enables voters to assess the positions of the political parties. The House of Commons and the Senate legitimize support for federal government policy by providing legal authorization for laws and government spending; they also encourage people to accept measures that they dislike, by fostering the perception that decisions made by their elected representatives reflect public opinion and public involvement as central elements (White, 1997). A brief description of the activities of the House follows.

Formal executive authority is vested in the Crown's representative, the Governor General (the lieutenant-governor provincially), but exercised by the premier and the ministers of the Executive Council (Cabinet). Ministers are accountable to the House of Commons (legislative assembly provincially) for their exercise of executive authority, which entails initiating legislation and administering public affairs. The Speech from the Throne, read by the Governor General at the opening of a parliamentary session, details the government's policy agenda. Any subsequent budgets during the session present the financial estimate for the new and ongoing policy initiatives and identify the funding sources for these initiatives.

Legislation is introduced to the House in the form of public bills (which are introduced by a Cabinet minister) and private bills (introduced by any other member of legislature). Government bills are the end product of processes of consensus building within Cabinet, between Cabinet and caucus, and between senior administrators and political advisers. Once a government bill is introduced to the legislature, it is expected to pass, with the full support of the caucus, barring opposition stalling, shifting government priorities, being held up in committee, or the legislation dying on the order paper when the House dissolves. Party discipline and the tendency of the electoral system to produce majority governments, combined with the considerable resources of the governing party, create a solid and predictable block of support for government initiatives. A minority government requires consultation with the leaders of the parties that do not form the government and often that concessions be made to these leaders for bills to pass.

At the introduction of new legislation, the Speaker of the House moves that "leave be given to introduce the bill entitled [bill named] and the same to be read for the first time" (White, 1989). The member's brief statement explaining the bill's principles is followed by a vote on whether to accept the bill for future debate. If accepted, it is assigned a number, printed, and scheduled for second-reading debate several days later. This allows MPs time to study the proposed bill and the opposition parties to caucus on it. The second-reading debate is the opportunity for the MPs to make statements on the principles of the bill. Following the debate, a unanimous vote of all members present in the House will enable a bill to bypass the committee stage and be ordered for third reading. Other bills receiving a majority vote are referred to committee. A listing of bills currently under discussion, their stage in the approval process, and the actual text of the proposed legislation are available on the Parliament of Canada website (http://www.parl.gc.ca/common/index.asp?).

The decision about whether to send a bill to the committee of the whole (House of Commons) or a standing committee (e.g., Human Resources, Skills, and Social Development and the Status of Persons with Disabilities) is made by the minister introducing the bill, usually in consultation with the House leaders. Besides reviewing and amending proposed legislation, with their all-party representation standing committees also conduct special inquiries into proposed policy changes that are not associated with a particular bill. Tradition expects that standing committees will hold public hearings, call expert witnesses, hear directly from ministry staff, and accept submissions and oral presentations from private citizens and stakeholder groups (Docherty, 2005; White, 1989). The committee also has the option of calling for public hearings before its clause-by-clause treatment or holding public hearings on specific clauses. Since meetings are less formal than House sittings and MPs engage in real discussions among themselves and with witnesses, committees offer much greater scope for influencing policy. This depends, however, on the extent to which the government members are open to advice and the degree to which committee members set aside partisan differences rather than attempting to score political points. Committee discussion of an issue often brings it to the attention of the media and raises public concern, which may force the government to modify a policy (White, 1997). Amendments may also be generated from the bureaucracy's interpretation of the public's concerns about the bill. Once the work of the Standing

The Policy-Making Process

Figure 2:2 The Legislative Process in Canada

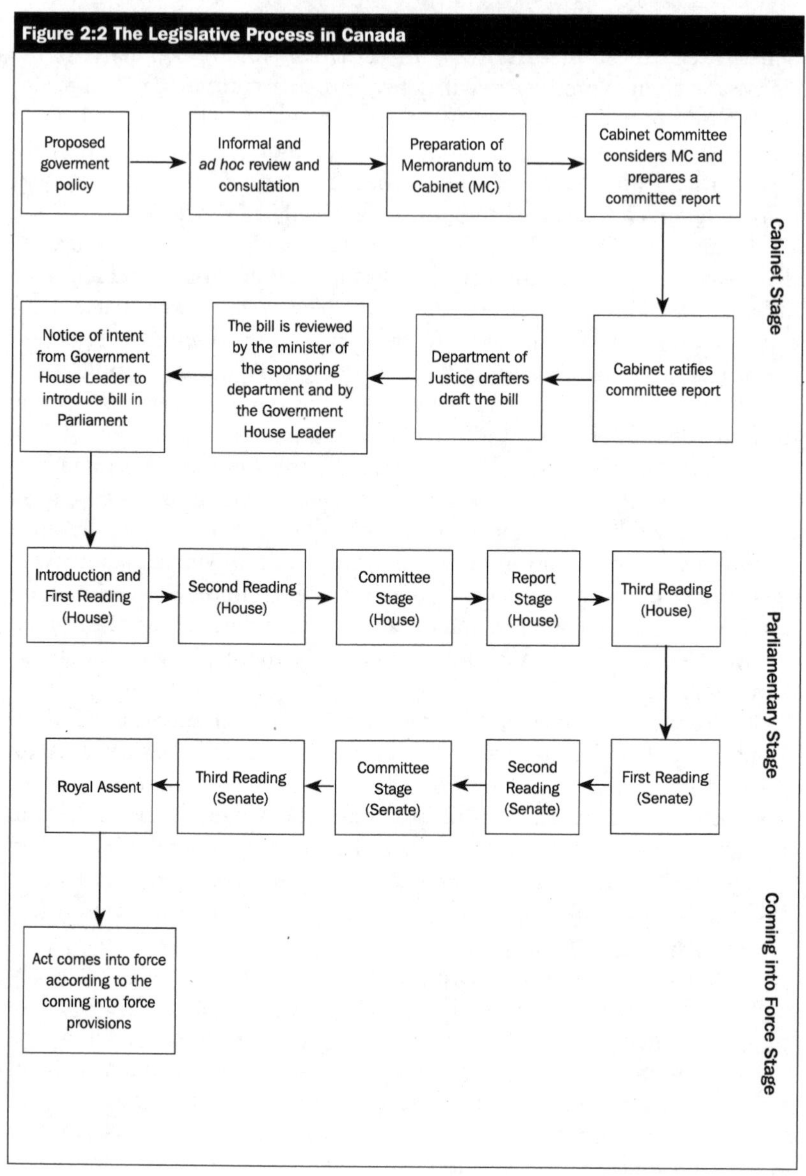

Committee is completed, the amended bill is returned to the House. Making a presentation to a Standing Committee and networking with government staff assigned to support the process provides an opportunity for citizens to use their expertise to reframe the problems and present concrete solutions for changes. Individual and professional credibility can and does affect the recommendations developed by the Standing Committee. Making formal presentations is one venue for professionals such as social workers to inject social knowledge into the process.

At third reading the bill is voted on by the members without debate, or it may be returned to the Standing Committee with instructions to make specific amendments. Following third reading, the bill is referred to Senate and the process of first, second, and third readings is repeated (Barnes, 2009). When both the House of Commons and the Senate have approved the bill, it receives Royal Assent from the Governor General (or the lieutenant-governor, for provinces/territories). That person has the constitutional authority to withhold Royal Assent, but in practice this does not occur. Royal Assent and proclamation dates are set by the Cabinet. The most common reason for delaying implementation is to allow the bureaucracy to put the administrative machinery in place. This process is summarized in Figure 2.2.

Almost all government bills contain a crucial provision authorizing the government to issue legally binding *regulations* that set out details of the policy without requiring any approval from the legislature. The consequence is that vast areas of policy making do not come under the scrutiny of elected members (Docherty, 2005; White, 1997). This is a serious weakness in the legislature's ability to hold the government accountable.

Summary

This chapter has explored the concept of dimension, or scale, and explained its relevance to the development of socal policy in Canada. We also explored the concept of policy purpose and illustrated the intersectionality of the two concepts using the example of policy pertaining to supervised access programs. We then provided an overview of the legislative policy-making process in Westminster-style governments and of the system of government federally and provincially in Canada. In the next chapter, we review approaches to policy analysis.

References

Baier, G., & Bakvis, H. (2001). Think tanks and political parties: Competitors or collaborators? *Canadian Journal of Policy Research, 2*(1), 107–113.

Barker, D. (2010). *Not quite supreme: The courts and coordinate constitutional interpretation.* Montreal, QC, and Kingston, ON: McGill–Queen's University Press.

Barnes, A. (2009). The legislative process: From government policy to proclamation. Ottawa: Library of Parliament. PRB 08-64E. Retrieved from http://www2.parl.gc.ca/Content/LOP/ResearchPublications/prb0864-e.pdf

References

Cameron, D., & Stein, J.G. (2000). Globalization, culture, and society: The state as place amidst shifting spaces. *Canadian Public Policy, 26*(Suppl. 2), S15-S34. Retrieved from http://www.jstor.org/stable/3552569

Collier, K. (1995). Social policy versus regional trading blocs in the global system: NAFTA, the EEC, and "Asia." *Canadian Review of Social Policy, 35*(1), 50–59.

Constitution Act. (1982). Retrieved from http://laws-lois.justice.gc.ca/eng/Const/page-11.html#anchorsc:7

Cross, W.P. (2004). *Political parties.* Vancouver, BC: UBC Press.

Cross, W., & Young, L. (2006). Are Canadian political parties empty vessels? Membership, engagement, and policy capacity. *IRRP Choices, 12*(4), 14–28.

Dalhousie Place. (2009). Brantford and District Supervised Access Centre. Haldimand-Norfolk Supervised Access Centre. Retrieved from http://www.execulink.com/~bdsupacc/home.html

Department of Finance. (2010). *Canada Social Transfer.* Retrieved from http://www.fin.gc.ca/fedprov/cst-eng.asp

Divorce Act. R.S.C., 1985, c. 3 (2nd Supp.). Retrieved from http://laws-lois.justice.gc.ca/eng/acts/D-3.4

Docherty, D.C. (2005). *Legislatures.* Vancouver, BC: UBC Press.

Doern, G.B., & Phidd, R. (1988). *Canadian Public Policy: Ideas, Structure, and Process.* Scarborough, ON: Nelson.

Faludi, A., & Voogd, H. (1986). *Evaluation of complex policy problems.* Delft, Netherlands: Delftsche Uitgevers Maatschappij.

Fisher, F. (1980). *Politics, values, and public policy.* Boulder, CO: Westview Press.

Forsey, E.A. (2010). How Canadians govern themselves (7th ed.). Retrieved from http://www.parl.gc.ca/About/Parliament/SenatorEugeneForsey/Home/Index-e.html

Government of Ontario, Association of Municipalities of Ontario, & City of Toronto. (2008). Provincial-municipal fiscal and service delivery review. Retrieved from http://www.mah.gov.on.ca/Page181.aspx

Graham, K.A., Phillips, S.D., & Maslove, A.M. (1998). *Urban governance in Canada: Representation, resources, and restructuring.* Toronto, ON: Harcourt Canada.

Harvey, D. (2005). *A brief history of neoliberalism.* Toronto, ON: Oxford University Press.

Hossen, A., & Westhues, A. (2011). The medicine that might kill the patient: Structural adjustment and its impacts on health care in Bangladesh. *Social Work in Public Health* (in press).

Kettner, P., Moroney, R., & Martin, L. (2008). *Designing and managing programs: An effectiveness-based approach* (3rd ed.). Thousand Oaks, CA: Sage Publications.

Manitoba Regional Planning Advisory Committee (2003). A partnership for the future: Putting the pieces together in the Manitoba capital region. Final Report of the Manitoba Regional Planning Committee. Retrieved from http://www.gov.mb.ca/ia/pdf/cap_partner/fulldoc.pdf

Melchers, R. (1999). Local governance of social welfare: Local reform in Ontario in the nineties. *Canadian Review of Social Policy, 43*(2), 29–57.

Meltsner, A. (1976). *Policy analysts in the bureaucracy.* Berkeley, CA: University of California Press.

Moscovitch, A., & Drover, G. (1981). *Inequality: Essays on the political economy of social welfare.* Toronto: University of Toronto Press.

Ontario Children's Law Reform Act. R.S.O. 1990, chapter c. 12. Retrieved from http://www.e-laws.gov.on.ca/html/statutes/english/elaws_statutes_90c12_e.htm

Ontario Ministry of the Attorney General. (2005). Supervised access. Retrieved from http://www.attorneygeneral.jus.gov.on.ca/english/family/supaccess.asp

Shrybman, S. (1999). *A citizen's guide to the World Trade Organization.* Ottawa, ON: Canadian Centre for Policy Alternatives and James Lorimer.

Social Union, News Release. (1999, February 4). A framework to improve the social union for Canadians: An agreement between the Government of Canada and the governments of the provinces and territories, February 4, 1999. Retrieved from http://www.socialunion.gc.ca/news/020499_e.html

Teeple, G. (2000). Globalization and the decline of social reform. Halifax, NS: Garamond Press.

Tindal, C.R., & Tindal, S.N. (1984). *Local government in Canada* (2nd ed.). Toronto, ON: McGraw-Hill Ryerson.

UN. (1989). Declaration of the Rights of the Child. Retrieved from http://www.un.org/cyberschoolbus/humanrights/resources/child.asp

UN. (2007). Declaration on the Rights of Indigenous Peoples. Retrieved from http://www.un.org/esa/socdev/unpfii/en/declaration.html

White, G. (1989). *The Ontario legislature: A political analysis.* Toronto: University of Toronto Press.

White, G. (1997). The legislature: Central symbol of Ontario democracy. In G. White (Ed.), *The government and politics of Ontario* (5th ed.) (pp. 71–92). Toronto, ON: University of Toronto Press.

Addtional Resources

Additional Resources

Legislative and Parliamentary websites
Alberta. Online at http://www.assembly.ab.ca
British Columbia. Online at http://www.legis.gov.bc.ca
Manitoba. Online at http://www.gov.mb.ca/legislature/homepage.html
New Brunswick. Online at http://www.gov.nb.ca/legis/index.htm
Newfoundland and Labrador. Online at http://www.gov.nf.ca/hoa
Northwest Territories. Online at http://www.assembly.gov.nt.ca
Nova Scotia. Online at http://www.gov.ns.ca./legislature
Nunavut. Online at http://www.assembly.nu.ca/english/index.html
Ontario. Online at http://www.ontla.on.ca
Prince Edward Island. Online at http://www.gov.pe.ca/leg/index.php3
Quebec. Online at http://www.assnat.qc.ca/eng/indexne3.html
Saskatchewan. Online at http://www.legassembly.sk.ca
Yukon. Online at http://www.gov.yk.ca/leg-assembly
Canada. Online at http://www.parl.gc.ca

Approaches to Policy Analysis

3

Anne Westhues

In Chapter 1, I drew on Pal's definition of policy analysis—"the disciplined application of intellect to public problems" (2006, p. 14)—to produce evidence- and values-based arguments that help decision makers choose a policy alternative that is expected to have more positive outcomes than policy that is based solely on evidence or solely on values. In this chapter I review what is meant by evidence-based, values-based, and participatory approaches to policy analysis. While none of these approaches consider only evidence, only values, or only input from people affected by a policy, each privileges its preferred kind of knowledge. McKenzie and Wharf's (2010) integrated model of policy analysis, which synthesizes the three approaches, is then reviewed. I argue that a strengths-based integrated policy analysis model that gives equal weight to evidence, values, and the experiential knowledge garnered through the input of people most affected by a policy is consistent with the belief system of the social work profession. I then explore what this would look like in practice.

The policy analysis movement that developed in Canada during the 1960s is grounded in the belief that better policy outcomes can be achieved by applying "systematic evaluative rationality to the development and implementation of policy options" (Dobuzinskis, Howlett, & Laycock, 2007, p. i). This position challenged the practice of developing policy and programs based on a privileging of political ideology, often favouring the interests of elites. The evidence-based, values-based, and many participatory approaches to policy analysis are guided by a problem-solving model—that is, by a belief that a general consensus can be reached on what constitutes a social problem, and that a solution in the form of policy can be generated that will ameliorate the problem. While more participatory approaches have begun to create a space for the input of people most affected by policy, a problem-solving approach often leads to an analysis that focuses on individual behaviour or community dysfunction rather than service delivery or structural barriers (Chapin, 2011; Payne, 2011).

The strengths-oriented approach that has evolved most recently begins the policy development process with an analysis of the strengths and goals of service users and seeks to remove structural barriers that prevent people from achieving these goals. The purpose of social policy is therefore to support individuals and communities in achieving the goals that would allow them to maximize their potential, not to ameliorate problems (Chapin, 2011; Payne, 2011).

The problem-solving and strengths-oriented approaches vary on several other important points. First is regarding the extent to which they privilege empirically generated knowledge rather than experiential knowledge. Second is regarding whether they understand the analyst to be a neutral party, providing advice representing "the public interest," or to be an advocate for a particular interest group or ideology. Third is regarding the extent to which the analyst believes that all affected interests should be directly engaged in policy design and evaluation. These differences mean that the change theory underlying the models differs and that the range of activities in which the analyst engages varies across models. These differences are summarized in Table 3.1 and explored in the discussion that follows.

Table 3.1 Approaches to Policy Analysis: Basic Beliefs

	Evidence-Based model	Values-Based Model	Participatory Model	Strengths-Based Integrated Model
Type of knowledge privileged	Systematically gathered, qualitative or quantitative (positivist or post-positivist)	Reasoning deduced from clearly stated principles/values (subjective)	Experiential knowledge (constructivist)	A mix of systematically gathered data, reasoning, and experiential knowledge (realist)
Role of analyst	Neutral; public interest; analyst is expert	Advocate; analyst is expert	Facilitator of process; affected interests are expert	May be all three at different points in the analytic process
Role of affected interests	Indirect input, through participation in research studies	May be involved in defining principles/values guiding analysis, but usually are not	Direct, through consultation, presentations at public meetings	May be indirect or direct
Activities/skills	An emphasis on analytic skills	An emphasis on deductive reasoning	An emphasis on interactional skills	Analytic, interactional, and reasoning
Change theory	Elitism: policy analysts and researchers guide change	Pluralism: group interests are contested, most persuasive has greatest influence on policy	Principle of affected interests: those most affected should have the greatest influence	Strengths orientation: people have the capacity to find the best solutions to their individual and community problems. Policy analysts need to design processes that allow these solutions to emerge.

Evidence-Based Policy Analysis

Evidence-Based Policy Analysis

Howlett and Lindquist (2007, p. 105) characterize the dominant policy style in Canada from 1960 to 1980 as rational. They argue that it was guided by a post-positivist epistemology, though others characterize it as positivist (Durning, 1993). Policy analysts were positioned as experts who offered neutral advice to policy makers that they believed reflected the public interest, and engaged in attempts to influence policy directions through claims to expertise in research and policy analysis. Research findings from economic, political, and social studies were utilized to design policy and programs, to monitor their development, and to evaluate their impacts. Recent innovations in the rational model are being proposed under the rubric of "evidence-based" policy analysis (Banks, 2009; Pawson, 2006).

As noted in Table 3.1, the type of knowledge that is most valued by evidence-based policy analysts is systematically gathered data, whether qualitative or quantitative. This may include demographic data or the results of a needs assessment to determine the preferences within a community, constituency, province, or nationally in the problem definition phase. Opinion polls may be utilized to assess the degree of public concern about an issue, census data to establish demographic changes, and/or longitudinal studies such as the National Longitudinal Survey of Children and Youth (NLSCY) (Statistics Canada, 2010) to understand factors that influence social, emotional, and behavioural development over time. The research literature may be reviewed to assess what is known about how to most effectively and efficiently intervene to achieve a policy goal. In analyzing these data, the policy analyst is influenced by studies that are judged to be more rigorous by traditional positivist standards: representative sampling for surveys or randomized control groups for evaluations of interventions; utilization of outcome measures with good reliability and validity; and researchers who are "outsiders" to program and policy development, and hence understood to be impartial. While consultations may occur with the citizens affected by the proposed policy or program changes, it is not an essential part of the process for policy analysts working from this perspective (Pawson, 2006).

Meta-Analysis and Synthesis Reviews

Pawson (2006) argues that the first phase of evidence-based policy analysis in the 1960s was grounded in a belief that social science research generally, and evaluation research more specifically, could generate knowledge that would direct policy makers to policy positions that were more likely to achieve their identified goals. Evaluation research has failed to influence policy making, he argues, because it occurs only after policy and programs have been developed, and it is difficult to feed research findings back into the policy-making and program development process. Furthermore, after fifty years, we know that research findings about the effectiveness of a particular

Evidence-Based Policy Analysis

policy or program are often based on small, non-randomized samples; that outcomes are measured using different tools from one study to the next; and that findings are sometimes contradictory. What, then, is a policy analyst to recommend?

Pawson argues that it is the *collective* evidence that should guide policy making rather than any particular study. In many policy areas there are a sufficient number of studies to synthesize our current research-based knowledge, and this synthesis can be used to guide policy and program development. New tools have been developed to synthesize the findings of multiple studies, often evaluations, of a specific program or policy. These tools are known as meta-analyses (Lipsey & Wilson, 2001; Littell, Corcoran, & Pillai, 2008) or as synthesis reviews (Cooper, 1998; Littell et al., 2008). Meta-analyses are approached quantitatively: an effect size is calculated that assesses the magnitude of the impact of an intervention compared to no intervention to an alternative way of providing a service, or to an alternative policy. These analyses require that the research design used include a control group, preferably one that was randomly assigned. Needless to say, this excludes many quantitative studies from consideration, and qualitative research is not utilized in this approach. The Cochrane Collaboration (http://www.cochrane.org/cochrane-reviews) and the Campbell Collaboration (http://www.campbellcollaboration.org) are examples of organizations that sponsor reviews of health policy and programming that privilege more positivist research. The critiques of this approach to policy analysis include that it is ahistorical, that it does not use qualitative data, and that the concept of effect size is of limited help in guiding policy and program developers regarding what works, for whom, under what conditions (Pawson, 2006).

More recent systematic review models have attempted to address these critiques. Pawson's well-developed model achieves this by proposing that the purpose of a synthesis review is to refine the middle-range theory of programs that have positive impacts instead of focusing—as has traditionally been done—on the nature and size of the impacts of an intervention (pp. 76, 93). Middle-range theory articulates the generative mechanism of the policy or program; the traditional question "Does it work?" is transformed into "*What* is it about this kind of intervention that works, for *whom*, in what *circumstances*, in what *respects* and *why*?" (p. 94).

Pawson describes his epistemology as realist, by which he means that it takes a post-positivist perspective that "steers a path between empiricist and constructivist accounts of scientific explanation" (p. 17). This is to say that it favours neither quantitative nor qualitative research and recognizes the importance of context in understanding the impact of an intervention. Context includes aspects of the organization delivering a service as well as the community or communities where it is delivered and individual characteristics of people using the service. His emphasis on context reflects the understanding that social policy and programs are not "treatments" aimed at "subjects"; rather, they are "complex systems thrust amidst complex systems" (Pawson, p. 168).

In a policy context, change mechanisms are called policy instruments, and Bemelmans-Videc, Rist, and Vedung (2003) argue that there are only three choices: carrots, sticks, and sermons. Sticks describe options where no choice is offered about expected behaviour. A legislative example is the Safe Schools Act in Ontario, which set mandatory consequences for violent behaviours such as one child assaulting another. The 2009 change in regulations that means a passport is now required to cross the Canadian border is another "stick," as are municipal bylaws regarding the safety and appearance of buildings.

Carrots entice citizens to engage in desired behaviours, by remunerating them; or to discontinue undesirable behaviours, by depriving them of material resources, usually through fines or through taxation. An example of policy encouraging behaviour is the tax credit announced in the 2011 federal budget for involving children in sports activities. The various provincial and federal "green" programs that provide a rebate if devices such as energy-saving furnaces are purchased is another. Parking tickets are an example of a financial penalty for engaging in behaviours that the state wants to discourage.

Sermons, the third policy instrument, include intellectual and moral appeals to encourage desired behaviour. Public service announcements about getting your children involved in activities that will promote better health and fitness are an example of this policy instrument, as are warnings on cigarette packages about the health risks of smoking.

While Pawson champions the utility of evidence-based policy, and believes that it can influence the policy direction that is taken, he acknowledges that "evidential truths are partial, provisional and conditional" (pp. 175–176). He concludes that in the final analysis, politics "will always trump research" (p. 175). Politics is another way of talking about ideology, values, and values-based policy analysis, which I explore next.

Values-Based Policy Analysis

In contrast to the evidence-based approaches to policy analysis, which have traditionally promoted an understanding of policy analysis as "objective" or "value-free," values-based approaches explicitly identify and advocate for the values that guide decision making among possible policy alternatives. Values disagreements can occur over questions of who counts (standing), what counts (criteria), or how much different individuals and criteria count (weights) (Robert & Zeckhauser, 2011). Values-based approaches are sometimes described as normative or prescriptive in the literature (Pal, 2006; Robert & Zeckhauser, 2011).

Evidence-based approaches to policy analysis encourage the policy analyst to think of him or herself as a neutral agent, able to provide advice to any

Values-Based Policy Analysis

political party that forms the government, with a view to enhancing the public interest. The rationality guiding this work is understood to be *instrumental*, that is, about identifying more efficient and effective means to achieve the policy ends determined by the political party in power. This approach assumes not only that decision makers have well-thought-through policy goals at a higher level of abstraction where they are unlikely to be contested—social and environmental justice, for example—but also that they have thought about the mid-level principles that are consistent with implementing these higher-order ethical values in a particular policy context. Thatcher (2004) argues that in practice, decision makers often have *unfinished preferences* about policy goals and that the role of the policy analyst is to help them sort out the full range of goals they would like to achieve, including those that are contradictory. This process of discernment can be achieved through what Rawls (1971) calls *reflective equilibrium*, where lower-level beliefs and values are brought into harmony with higher-level ideals.

In contrast to policy analysts working in the public service, people engaged in policy work for a political party or in advocacy on behalf of a social movement or interest group do not attempt to consider all interests that constitute the public interest. Rather, they quite deliberately and transparently advocate for the interests they represent and for a vision that they believe will generate greater social justice and well-being for that interest group. This is to say that they are "political" in the sense of attempting to empower a preferred interest group or groups. Deductive reasoning from a specified set of principles or values is utilized in this approach to analysis, and the policy-making process is understood to be contested, with a range of interest groups using persuasion to convince policy makers to support their recommendations.

The Canadian Association of Retired Persons (CARP) is an example of an interest group that is explicitly values-based in its analysis of policy issues. Its vision is stated thus: "a society in which everyone can live active, independent, purposeful lives as they age." Their overarching policy goal of "enhancing the quality of life for all Canadians as we age" is refined in their vision statement through the use of the descriptors *active*, *independent*, and *purposeful*. This policy goal is to be achieved through "advocating for social change that will bring financial security, equitable and timely access to health care, and freedom from discrimination"; through "ensuring that the marketplace serves the needs and expectations of our generation and providing value-added benefits, products and services to members"; and through "building a sense of community and shared values among our members."

The values-based approach to policy analysis is *transparent* with respect to the interests that CARP supports and through the policy goals it intends to achieve. CARP draws on research evidence and consultations with older adults when useful to persuade policy makers, but it makes no attempt to use these data in an impartial way. Policy analysts remain the experts in this approach, deciding which systematically gathered and/or experiential knowledge to utilize in their analysis. The values-based (Williams, 2007) or value criteria (McKenzie & Wharf, 2010) approaches to policy analysis were developed to counter the positivist influences that dominated the policy sciences from the 1960s to the 1980s—influences that failed to acknowledge the influence of values in policy analysis.

Values that might be considered in all analyses include the effectiveness of a policy program, its cost-effectiveness in achieving its goals, the political feasibility of alternatives, and technical feasibility. Technical feasibility addresses questions such as whether there are sufficient numbers of people with the necessary training to implement an alternative (McKenzie & Wharf, 2010). Values specific to the policy issue may also be identified. Child care activists have consistently advocated for quality, affordable, accessible child care, for instance. Values such as empowerment, self-determination, and social inclusion are typically considered by social work professionals as well.

A criticism of values-based approaches is that they may allow ideology or values to filter evidence or the preferences of people affected by the policy to such an extent that the policy alternatives selected are based on assumptions that cannot be demonstrated as true. A recent example is the "law and order" policy stand taken by the Harper Conservatives with respect to longer prison terms as a disincentive for crime. The weight of the research evidence is that longer prison terms do not reduce crime rates (Gendreau, Goggin, & Cullen, 1993). Harper's former chief of staff, Ian Brodie, explained in a panel discussion at McGill University that they support lengthening prison terms anyway because "voters tend to side with Conservatives when they argue with 'sociologists, criminologists, defence lawyers and Liberals' about prison terms" (Geddes, 2010, August 16).

Participatory Policy Analysis

Participatory approaches to policy analysis (PPA), like participatory action research, value experiential knowledge over systematically gathered evidence or deductive reasoning from clearly stated principles or values. The primary role of the policy analyst is facilitation; this person engages all of the affected interests in a discussion about how a policy issue should be defined and possibly addressed. He or she still carries a responsibility for interpreting and synthesizing the ideas provided by the people most affected by an issue, but it is expected that the resulting interpretations will be verified with citizens who have participated in the process. People who are considered "affected interests" under this approach are expected to provide input directly, through focus groups, consultations, or public meetings, rather than indirectly, through participation in research studies. These tenets of the participatory model, first outlined by Laswell in 1948, are intended to promote a more democratic society.

A Strengths-Based Integrated Model for Policy Analysis

Howlett and Lindquist (2007) argue that participatory approaches to policy analysis have evolved in response to the two main critiques of the rational, evidence-based approaches: that they are not sufficiently democratic, and that they yield poor advice to policy makers because they fail to examine the policy context adequately. While all PPA approaches promote greater engagement with the citizens affected by a policy decision, there is variation in the extent to which the policy analysis remains in the hands of the policy analyst, or is taken on by the citizens themselves. In the variation that Durning (1993) calls "providing analytic inputs through PPA," stakeholders are consulted and provide information and opinions, which the policy analyst then transforms into advice for decision makers. By contrast, in the variation called "stakeholder policy analysis", the policy analyst forgoes his or her expert role and delegates responsibility for the policy analysis to engaged citizens. All PPA approaches provide more opportunity for affected interests to define the policy issue and to generate possible solutions. Thus, these approaches not only allow for the explicit identification of principles or values to guide the policy recommendations, but also ensure that the values guiding policy are those of the people most affected by the decision.

The critique of PPA is that it is difficult to engage the most marginalized groups in society in public discourses. They may experience language barriers to participation when meetings are held in English. They may carry a class or gender identity that prevents them from engaging in public discourses. The success of PPAs depends on the skill of the policy analyst when engaging these disenfranchised communities and when providing supports, such as interpreters, to ensure that all voices are heard.

A Strengths-Based Integrated Model for Policy Analysis

In the discussion so far, it is evident that each of the three policy analysis approaches has strengths and weaknesses. Two models have emerged recently in the social work literature that attempt to capture the strengths of all three. One is called an integrated value-critical model for policy analysis (McKenzie & Wharf, 2010), the other a strengths-based approach to policy analysis (Chapin, 2011). In this section, I review these two models, then propose a strengths-based integrated approach to policy analysis that draws from both. Integrated approaches to policy analysis incorporate both the content factors of the evidence-based approach and the process factors of the participatory approach. They are explicitly values-based and lend themselves well to special lenses such as gender-based analysis (Status of Women Canada, 2007; Callahan, 2010). They differ from the models already reviewed in that they give equal weight to evidence, values, and participation in developing policy and programs.

The end product of McKenzie and Wharf's model is a recommendation with respect to policy and program design. They identify five stages: problem

A Strengths-Based Integrated Model for Policy Analysis

identification and goal specification, identification of value criteria, assessment of alternatives, feasibility assessment, and recommendation of a policy or program alternative (2010, pp. 100–106). Chapin adds implementation and evaluation to her conceptualization of the policy development process, emphasizing that policy and program development continue after a recommendation is made and are ongoing after a policy or program has been implemented. She names her phases as follows: define needs, goals, and barriers; formulate policy alternatives; make claims based on right to self-determination and social justice; identify opportunities and resources necessary for people to meet their goals in partnership with clients; formulate policy goals; develop and implement the policy/program; and evaluate outcomes (Chapin, 2011, p. 15).

The problem identification stage draws heavily on evidence such as demographic data, research findings, and primary data collection through needs assessments. Chapin encourages using the language of needs and goals rather than problems to promote a more strengths-oriented analysis. Both models encourage direct participation by engaging key stakeholders such as service users, service providers, and funders at this stage and all others.

Citing a professional responsibility to consider issues of social justice in policy analysis and program development, McKenzie and Wharf (2010) argue that the values that will be drawn on to select an alternative to recommend should be stated explicitly during this stage of the process. Values such as efficiency and effectiveness are used by policy analysts routinely. Additional values specific to the issue under consideration need to be discerned and may focus on process (e.g., the form of consultation with the affected interests) or on expected outcomes (e.g., equality of outcomes between vulnerable groups and the majority population). Professional social work values and political ideology can be drawn on to formulate these value criteria, or a more participatory approach may be utilized to define the value criteria. Chapin identifies social justice as a value to be considered by social workers in *all* policy analyses and defines it as "the equitable distribution of societal resources to all people as well as equity and fairness in the social, economic and political spheres" (p. 2).

In the next stage, assessment of alternatives, research evidence is drawn on to generate possible solutions. While some research may be available about service user experiences and preferences, this stage presents another opportunity for the policy analyst to consult with current and potential service users, service providers, and funders. Only alternatives that promise to achieve the specified policy goal should be retained for a systematic analysis of how consistent they are with the value criteria specified. Chapin refers to this as "claims-making."

The next stage in McKenzie and Wharf's model is feasibility assessment. They indicate that this is particularly relevant for program and operational

A Strengths-Based Integrated Model for Policy Analysis

policy. Three aspects of feasibility should be considered: financial, technical, and political. Financial feasibility requires an assessment of whether potential funders are likely to support the policy alternative. Technical feasibility means that questions are raised about whether there are people with the necessary training to implement the alternative. Political feasibility is an assessment of whether policy makers are likely to support the alternative, and also whether the staff tasked with implementing a policy or delivering a program are likely to implement it as intended. Chapin calls for a deeply participatory process at this stage of the analysis—that is, for collaboration with the people most likely to use a service or to be affected by a policy decision.

The final stage for McKenzie and Wharf is a policy or program recommendation. The recommendation is justified by its expected capacity to achieve the identified policy goal(s) as well as by its consistency with the value criteria articulated. This analysis may take the form of an assessment of strengths and weaknesses of each alternative considered and would be formulated in relation to the consistency of the approach with the specified value criteria. Chapin recommends that consensus-based decision making be utilized in order to reach agreement on what to recommend. Both Chapin (2011) and Payne (2011) argue that a strengths-oriented approach to social work practice generates ideas about how to develop policies, programs, and practices that celebrate the capacities of individuals and communities, and that maximize opportunities for developing their potential.

A strengths-based integrated model consists of the tasks and activities outlined in Table 3.2. In this model, policy and program development is conceptualized as consisting of three primary tasks: policy/program design, policy/program implementation, and policy/program evaluation.

Table 3.2 A Strengths-Based Integrated Approach to Policy and Program Development

Tasks	Activities
Policy/program design	• Generating a values-based vision of a society that encourages people to engage in caring relationships and maximize their opportunities • Specifying principles/values to guide decision making about policy and program development • Specifying policy goals that incorporate these principles/values • Generating policy and program alternatives that might achieve the policy goals • Specifying the logic of the policy/programs/interventions (logic models) to assess whether they hold the promise of achieving the policy goals • Recommending alternatives that maximize consistency with the agreed-on principles/values
Policy/program implementation	• Implementation planning • Implementing the preferred option through one or more interventions
Policy/program evaluation	• Monitoring the implementation of the intervention(s) • Evaluating the impacts of the policy • Confirming or revising policy or program goals • (Re)assessing the need for the policy (or program)

A Strengths-Based Integrated Model for Policy Analysis

Participatory processes that engage the people most affected by the proposed policy or program are integral to all three of these tasks. Policy/program design involves generating a values-based vision of a society that encourages people to engage in caring relationships and to maximize their opportunities; specifying principles/values to guide decision making about policy and program development; specifying policy goals that incorporate these principles/values; generating policy and program alternatives that might achieve the policy goals; specifying the logic of the policy/program interventions to assess whether they hold the promise of achieving the policy goals; and recommending the alternative that maximizes consistency with the agreed on principles/values. Policy/program implementation involves drawing on research-based evidence and the experiences of service users and service providers when planning how the program will operate. It also involves the work of putting the new policy/program in to operation. The final task, policy/program evaluation, consists of monitoring the implementation of the intervention to assess whether it is consistent with what was planned; confirming or revising policy/program goals in light of experience with operating the intervention; and reassessing the need for the policy/program periodically.

The commitment to a strengths-based approach to policy development means that policy analysts and policy makers acknowledge the capacity of citizens to find the best solutions to individual and community problems (Saleebey, 2006). In the case of social policy, this means they will be particularly interested in engaging the people most affected by a policy or most likely to use a program being developed. The policy analyst is therefore charged with designing processes that will allow these solutions to emerge rather than serving as an expert whose responsibility is to generate recommended solutions to social issues. solving the problems him or herself.

Conclusion

Claudia Scott (n.d.) tells us that in a more contested policy environment, "high quality policy analysis and advice is critical to good governance" (p. 1). She refers to this as "value-adding" policy analysis. She goes on to describe an approach to policy analysis that incorporates policy frameworks which make the value assumptions of the argument transparent, which utilize research evidence to support recommendations, and which foster "a robust and engaged polity" (p. 2). The strengths-based integrated approach outlined above is a value-adding approach to policy analysis in this sense. It differs from evidence-based, values-based, or participatory approaches in that it does not privilege any one of these essential inputs into the policy-making process; rather, it attempts to balance and value each equally.

Skills Required for Policy Analysis

Skills Required for Policy Analysis

Whether policy analysis is a primary job responsibility or a secondary one, the skills required can be conceptualized as falling into two categories: process (Rothman & Zald, 1985), interpersonal (Tropman, Erlich, & Rothman, 1995), or interactional skills (Perlman & Gurin, 1972); and task (Rothman & Zald, 1985), intellectual (Tropman, Erlich, & Rothman, 1995), or analytic skills (Perlman & Gurin, 1972). Table 3.3 outlines the analytic *and* interactional skills required at each stage in the policy development process. The analytic skills identified draw heavily from an earlier article by Pancer and Westhues (1989).

In addition to the general skill of thinking analytically, or reasoning, at the initial stage of policy design, when the problem is defined or the vision articulated, analytic skills are needed in two areas: values analysis, and generating evidence through needs assessment. To complete a values analysis, the analyst must know how to conduct opinion polls or to cull useful information from opinion polls conducted by others; carry out key informant interviews; use participatory techniques like the nominal group technique, the Delphi technique, focus groups, and community forums; and do preference scaling. To complete a needs assessment, the analyst has to know how to identify and interpret social indicators; carry out surveys; and use the group approaches identified above.

Interactional skills required at this critical first stage of policy design include the following: leadership skills in setting up a process that will allow the exchange of ideas on the issue; the ability to create a safe environment so that people feel they can express their feelings about the issue; facilitation skills, to ensure that all stakeholders have an opportunity to participate in constructing the problem; active listening skills, to ensure that the nuances of different stakeholder perspectives are not missed; skills in working with people who differ in terms of culture, racialization, class, gender, sexual orientation, and ability; public speaking skills, if one is going to advocate for a particular policy position; and the ability to write clearly and concisely, whether one is playing the role of neutral internal policy analyst at some level of government or that of community-based advocate.

At the next stage of policy design—agreeing on policy or program goals—analytic skills are again needed in two areas: goal formulation and priority setting. When goals are being formulated, it takes skill to carry out surveys, conduct community forums, and rate goal characteristics. Procedures like the Q-sort, paired comparisons, multi-attribute utility measurement, and decision theoretic analysis can be used to set priorities. To support the analytic tasks, interactional skills that permit the analyst to engage stakeholders in the process of reaching consensus on goals are needed, as well as skills in clarifying, brokering, and mediating. If the analyst is acting as an advocate, she or he will also need to be skilled in persuasion. Again, competence in working across differences is needed to ensure not only that marginalized

Skills Required for Policy Analysis

Table 3.3 Skills Required at Each Stage of Policy Development

STAGE IN POLICY DEVELOPMENT	ANALYTIC SKILLS	INTERACTIONAL SKILL
Defining the Problem	**Values Analysis** • opinion polls • key informant interviews • group approaches (nominal group technique, Delphi, community forum) • preference scaling **Needs Assessment** • social indicators approaches • surveys • group approaches	**Leadership** • creating a safe environment • ensuring participation • active listening • public speaking • clear, concise writing
Agreeing on Goals	**Goals Analysis** • *Goal formulation*: surveys, community forums, rating of goal characteristics • *Priority Setting*: estimate—discuss—estimate procedure, Q-sort, paired comparisons, multi-attribute utility measurement, decision-theoretic analysis	**Engaging People in Process** • clarifying intent • brokering • mediating • persuading
Identifying Alternatives	**Policy Logic Analysis** • review of theories of causation • review of outcome evaluations in policy area • concept development	**Sharing Knowledge** • facilitating
Choosing an Alternative	**Feasibility Study** • investigation of funding sources • cost–benefit analysis • cost-effectiveness analysis • price analysis • administrative feasibility assessment	**Sharing Knowledge** • facilitating • guiding
Implementing the Policy	**Implementation Assessment** • Gantt charts • milestone charts • PERT–CPM networks	**Information Gathering** • manufacturing commitment
Evaluating the Policy	**Process** • collection of data from information systems • peer review ratings • client satisfaction surveys **Outcomes** • experimental approaches • quasi-experimental approaches • single case design • client satisfaction surveys • social impact assessments	**Sharing of Expertise** • safe environment • ensuring participation in developing design • communication of results

Skills Required for Policy Analysis

groups are included in these processes but also that their preferences, if not the same as those of the majority, are taken into account.

Policy logic analysis, a variant of program logic analysis (Rush & Ogborne, 1991), can be used to facilitate the identification of policy alternatives that, in light of a specified theory of causation of the identified problem, could be expected to achieve the policy goals agreed upon. A review of any outcome evaluations of these policy alternatives would identify empirical evidence, which could either support the implementation of a particular alternative or suggest that it would not, in fact, achieve the anticipated outcomes. Theory often precedes practice, so another skill required by the analyst is the ability to discern the implications for practice of a particular theoretical perspective for policy development. The interactional skills required at this stage include being able to summarize and share knowledge in a way that is both interesting and concise, and the ability to facilitate discussion to generate alternative ideas.

Feasibility studies provide information that assists in choosing among policy alternatives. Assessing feasibility includes determining whether funds would be available for the various alternatives; completing cost–benefit or cost-effectiveness analyses on each alternative; completing a political feasibility assessment using a technique such as PRINCE (Probe, Interact, Calculate, Execute); and assessing the administrative feasibility of the alternatives. Good skills in presenting information in an interesting and concise way are required at this stage as well. In addition, the analyst must be able to draw on facilitation and sometimes conflict resolution skills to generate a consensus about which alternative to recommend.

At the implementation stage, an implementation assessment permits the analyst to identify how much time would be required to implement the alternative selected, which jurisdictions would need to be involved, and which approvals are required. Pressman and Wildavsky (1973) alerted us to the importance of this stage when they discovered that many policies never have their intended effects because they fail to make it through the long string of decisions necessary for the policy to be implemented. Analyzing these approval processes beforehand and identifying potential blocks will provide greater assurance that the policy will be implemented with fidelity (Wandersman et al., 2008). The primary interactional skills required at this stage are the ability to gather information on complex systems and to generate commitment on the part of service providers to the new policy alternative, so that it will, in fact, be implemented as intended.

Finally, any policy must be systematically evaluated to assess what has happened in light of its intended effects. Process evaluation includes a review of who has been served, for what reasons, and what service they have received. Peer reviews are made of cases to determine whether defined standards of care have been met. Client satisfaction surveys assess whether consumers received the expected service, whether they were served in a timely fashion, and whether they found it helpful. Outcome evaluations may focus on individual goals or program goals and are intended to assess the extent to which the changes that are intended to occur for the service user have, in fact, occurred. The interactional skills required of the policy analyst as evaluator include sharing his or her knowledge about how evaluations may be designed, creating a feeling of safety with respect to the evaluation, ensuring that all those affected by the evaluation participate in its design, engaging service deliverers in the data collection process, and communicating the results of the research to all those involved.

Conclusion

Social workers have come to accept the development of social policy as an essential component of our work as professionals. While the prospect of trying to change legislation, the vision of an organization, or agency policy with respect to service delivery may seem daunting, our successes in these efforts not only provide us with an opportunity to develop a complementary set of skills to those we use as clinicians but also teach us that it can be done. Whether we choose to focus on issues at the international, federal, provincial, local, or organizational level, our efforts improve the well-being of individual clients, build a sense of community, and empower us as individuals and as a profession. Ultimately, the values we promote, infused throughout social policy, will shape and give definition to a more just and inclusive Canada.

References

Banks, G. (2009). *Evidence-based policy making: What is it? How do we get it?* (ANU Public Lecture Series, presented by ANZSOG, 4 February). Canberra, Australia: Productivity Commission. Retrieved from http://www.pc.gov.au/speeches/cs20090204

Bemelmans-Videc, M-L., Rist, R.C., & Vedung, E. (2003). *Carrots, sticks, and sermons: Policy instruments and their evaluation.* Somerset, NJ: Transaction Publishers.

Callahan, M. (2010). Chalk and cheese: Feminist thinking and policy-making. In B. McKenzie & B. Wharf (Eds.), *Connecting policy to practice in the human services* (3rd ed.) (pp. 166–180). Toronto, ON: Oxford University Press.

Chapin, R. (2011). Social policy for effective practice: A strengths approach (2nd ed.). New York, NY: Routledge, Taylor, and Francis Group.

Cooper, H. (1998). *Synthesizing research* (3rd ed.). Thousand Oaks, CA: Sage Publications.

Dobuzinskis, L., Howlett, M., & Laycock, D. (Eds.). (2007). *Policy analysis in Canada: The state of the art.* Toronto, ON: University of Toronto Press.

Durning, D. (1993). Participatory policy analysis in a social service agency: A case study. *Journal of Policy Analysis and Management, 12*(2), 297–322. doi: 10.2307/3325237

Geddes, J. (2010, August 16). Cracking eggheads. *Maclean's*. Retrieved from http://www2.macleans.ca/2010/08/09/cracking-eggheads

References

Gendreau, P., Goggin, C., & Cullen, F.T. (1993). The effects of prison sentences on recidivism. User report 1993-3. Ottawa, ON: Public Works and Services Canada. Retrieved from http://www.prisonpolicy.org/scans/e199912.htm

Howlett, M., & Linquist, E. (2007). Beyond formal policy analysis: Governance context, analytic styles, and the policy analysis movement in Canada. In L. Dobuzinskis, M. Howlett, & D. Laycock, D. (Eds.), *Policy analysis in Canada: The state of the art* (pp. 86–115). Toronto, ON: University of Toronto Press.

Laswell, H.D. (1948). *Power and personality.* New York, NY: Viking Press.

Lipsey, M.W., & Wilson, D.B. (2001). *Practical meta-analysis.* Thousand Oaks, CA: Sage Publications.

Littell, J.H., Corcoran, J., & Pillai, V. (2008). *Systematic reviews and meta-analysis.* Toronto, ON: Oxford University Press.

McKenzie, B., & Wharf, B. (2010). *Connecting policy to practice in the human services* (3rd ed.). Toronto, ON: Oxford University Press.

Pal, L. (2006). *Beyond policy analysis: Public issue management in turbulent times* (4th ed.). Toronto, ON: Thomson Canada.

Pancer, S.M., & Westhues, A. (1989). A developmental stage approach to planning. *Evaluation Review, 13*(1), 56–77.

Pawson, R. (2006). *Evidence-based policy: A realist perspective.* Thousand Oaks, CA: Sage Publications.

Payne, M. (2011). *Humanistic social work: Core principles in practice.* Chicago, IL: Lyceum Books.

Perlman, R., & Gurin, A. (1972). *Community organizing and social planning.* New York: John Wiley and Sons.

Pressman, J.L., & Wildavsky, A.B. (1973). *Implementation.* Berkeley, CA: University of California Press.

Rawls, J. (1971). *A theory of justice.* Boston, MA: Harvard University Press.

Robert, C., & Zeckhauser, R. (2011). The methodology of normative policy analysis. HKS Faculty Research Working Paper Series RWP11-004. John F. Kennedy School of Government, Harvard University. Retrieved from http://dash.harvard.edu/bitstream/handle/1/4669672/RWP11-004_Robert_Zeckhauser.pdf?sequence=1

Rothman, J., & Zald, M.N. (1985). Planning theory in social work community practice. In S.H. Taylor & R.W. Roberts (Eds.), *Theory and practice of community social work* (pp. 125–153). New York, NY: Columbia University Press.

Rush, B., & Ogborne, A. (1991). Program logic models: Expanding their role and structure for program planning and evaluation. *Canadian Journal of Program Evaluation, 6*(2), 95–106.

Saleebey, D. (2006) *The strengths perspective in social work practice* (4th ed.). Boston: Allyn and Bacon.

Scott, C. (no date). Value-adding policy analysis and advice: New roles and skills for the public sector. Wellington, New Zealand: Institute of Policy Studies, Victoria University of Wellington. Retrieved from http://ips.ac.nz/publications/files/fd16d0a4683.pdf

Statistics Canada. (2010). National longitudinal study of children and youth. Retrieved from http://www.statcan.gc.ca/cgi-bin/imdb/p2SV.pl?Function=getSurvey&SDDS=4450&lang=en&db=imdb&adm=8&dis=2

References

Status of Women Canada. (2007). An integrated approach to gender-based analysis. Retrieved from http://www.swc-cfc.gc.ca/pol/gba-acs/guide/2007/index-eng.html

Thatcher, D. (2004). Value rationality in policy analysis. Unpublished manuscript. Retrieved from http://www.fordschool.umich.edu/research/pdf/Value_Rationality_in_Policy_Analysis.pdf

Tropman, J.E., Erlich, J.L., & Rothman, J. (Eds.). (1995). Tactics and techniques of community intervention (3rd ed.). Itasca, IL: F.E. Peacock.

Wandersman, A., Duffy, J., Flaspohler, P., Noonan, R., Lubell, K., Stillman, L., & Saul, J. (2008). Bridging the gap between prevention research and practice: An interactive systems framework for building capacity to disseminate and implement innovations. *American Journal of Community Psychology, 41*(3–4), 171–181. doi: 10.1007/s10464-008-9174-z

Williams, R. (2007). Evidence-based and values-based policy, management, and practice in child and adolescent mental health services. *Clinical and Child Psychology and Psychiatry, 12*(2), 223–242. doi: 10.1177/1359104507075926

Influencing Policy from the Outside:

Are Citizens Game Changers or Sidelined?

4

Joan Wharf Higgins and Fay Weller

The objective of this chapter is to explore the various ways in which citizens are engaged directly in influencing policy and, more broadly, social change. The principle of citizen participation, and right to participate in the policy processes within government, are accepted as cornerstones of democracy (Aulich, 2009). Arnstein (1969) famously likened participation to eating spinach, since "no one is against it in principle because it is good for you" (p. 216). While relatively few citizens are able to take advantage of the more direct and demanding opportunities to successfully shape public policy (Callahan, 2007; Martin, 2008), individuals in the corporate sector strenuously lobby governments to enact policies that will advance their interests. Other citizens also engage in lobbying activities, either individually or collectively; and some citizens engage in social change activities outside government processes. We take the position that citizen participation in social change is crucial to a healthy and socially just society (Bowen, 2008; Denhardt & Denhardt, 2000) and that opportunities for engagement should be expanded and/or revised to be more inclusive and effective.

This chapter provides an overview of recent literature on individual and collective citizen participation, as well as citizen-initiated actions directed primarily at societal rather than local levels. While the benefits to individuals participating in local opportunities are important and have been documented (e.g., Attree et al., 2011; Bowen, 2008; Callahan, 2007), this chapter describes the impacts or outcomes of involvement more broadly. The topics covered range from environmental processes and policies, to broad social welfare policies, to consumer actions, health policies, and social change or revolution; the topics *not* covered include those addressed in other chapters: mental health, homelessness and housing, disabilities, and immigration policies. The impact of technology on citizen participation is reviewed, and so is the role of education. Coverage focuses on the Canadian literature, complemented by experiences from the United States, Britain, and the Nordic countries between 2005 and 2011. Efforts prior to 2005 were included only if the material was fundamental to subsequent thinking.

For the purposes of this chapter, we define social change as the alteration of mechanisms within the social structure that influence how citizens live their lives (e.g., mechanisms related to social services, health, education, or the environment). We believe that the policies that define society's structures need to reflect the lives and values of the citizens they affect, not just those who are in positions of power. This belief arises from empirical evidence that policies are far more effective when the citizens they impact have been involved in shaping social change (Callahan, 2007; McKenzie & Wharf, 2010; Ravensbergen & Vanderplaat, 2010; Wharf Higgins, 2002). We also recognize that while the onus is on government to include the range of voices, there is a corresponding responsibility on the part of citizens to engage in ways they feel will influence change most effectively.

What is the motivation behind citizen participation? Bowler, Donovan, and Karp (2007) discovered that in sixteen affluent democracies (including Canada), the engagement in citizen participation was driven by a distrust of government and by a belief that citizens have a duty to keep a watch on government. The following sections will describe the range of ways in which citizens participate in influencing social change, including (a) individual or collective engagement with government-initiated processes, (b) citizen-initiated processes aimed at influencing government policies, and (c) citizen-initiated processes aimed at changing government or economic policy from outside the realm of government-sanctioned processes.

Government Processes for Engaging Citizens

The processes that governments use to engage citizens reflect the underlying ideology of the government in power and the era in question. Nikolas Rose (2000) describes how the 19th century saw the gradual incorporation of the social realm into the responsibilities of government, equal to and linked with the economic realm. By the middle of the 20th century, "the social state would have the role of shaping and coordinating the strategies that would oblige all sectors and social interests, no longer antagonists, to work towards and facilitate social progress" (2000, p. 157).

However, by the 1980s this way of governing started to change as neoliberal ideology influenced governments throughout North America and Europe. Neoliberalism emphasized the separation of social needs from economic ones so as to make social goals subservient to government's role of ensuring that the mechanisms of the free market were running smoothly (Rose, 2000). These ideological changes have had repercussions in terms of government's approach to engaging citizens in social change.

Citizen as Consumer of Government Services

Consistent with the move toward conducting government as a business, the description (and often treatment) of citizens who are using government

Government Processes for Engaging Citizens

services becomes "consumer," "user," "patient," and "client." Many government processes for engaging citizens over the past two decades have reflected practices from the corporate world, in which citizens are consumers (Blomgren Bingham, Nabatchi, & O'Leary, 2005). These tools fail to provide opportunities for citizens to influence change. Moreover, this way of thinking about citizens has resulted in decreased opportunities for citizen participation and in the use of questionable survey results to justify policy shifts being promoted by the government in power.

Almost fifteen years ago, Graham and Phillips (1997) reflected on government's democratic deficit and the role that the notion of "consumers as citizens" has played in fostering distrust of government among Canadians. The concerns raised by Graham and Phillips mirror those in a more recent analysis of "user participation" in the United Kingdom (Bochel et al., 2008). Both studies reflect on the limited possibilities for change in policy and practice that are currently provided by consumer input tools. And both speak to the need for a more radical approach to the policy process, one that is grounded in co-governance, with citizens setting the course, checking that the course is the right one, and "*occasionally ... sharing the helm*" (Graham & Phillips, p. 270; our italics).

These concerns echo those expressed by Dutil et al. (2007), who highlight how surveys and electronically based services decrease citizen empowerment and democratic interactions between citizens and government. They describe how e-government is reshaping relationships: as public servants begin to view citizens as faceless "market-inspired customers," government's reliance on meaningful (and time-consuming) engagement strategies decreases. Dutil et al. highlight the need for governments to broaden their perspective and deepen their participatory processes to encourage active, deliberative involvement from "citizens"—in contrast to "consumers" responding to questions on a survey.

Canada's Citizens First Surveys[1] have positioned this country as "a recognized leader in the field" (Howard, 2010, p. 66). Yet an analysis of the methodology, results, and implementation of those surveys has brought to light that they are substantially biased, resulting in findings that tend to support private sector models of delivery. Howard has described how these findings are shaped through the structuring of questions, the exclusion of certain questions because they cannot be addressed at the managerial level, and the low response rate. Finally, Howard describes how the process itself promotes a passive view of the role of citizens in official decision making.

Citizen Advisory Committees

A common form of citizen participation practised by governments at all levels is advisory committees, comprised of citizens representing specific constituencies and/or specialists in the field of interest. While there is some

Government Processes for Engaging Citizens

evidence that decisions are influenced by advisory committees, there are also concerns related to representation, authority, and autonomy.

For example, Parkins and Davidson (2008) analyzed the effectiveness of Alberta's Forest Advisory Committees in terms of political representation and group autonomy. They discovered, as had others in earlier studies (Church et al., 2002; Knaap, Matier, & Olshansky, 1998; Wharf Higgins, 1999; Wharf Higgins et al., 1999), that while the committees appeared to reflect diverse interests (youth, environmentalists, recreational interests, the forestry industry, and clergy), most of the people at the table were white, middle-class men, well educated, well spoken, and well off. The same representation is to be found on the National Council of Welfare, one of the last remaining active advisory groups to the federal government. Six of its nine members are white, middle-class men; four of those men have strong links to traditional Christian organizations, and the other two have strong links to the business world (National Council of Welfare, 2010).

Notwithstanding the profile of their members, Parkins and Davidson (2008) found the influence of advisory committees to be extremely limited. This finding echoed that of Knaap et al. (1998) from a decade earlier. However, even in the context of strong state and corporate interests, the opportunity for critical discourse arose in one of the three committees studied, which led Parkins and Davidson to conclude that "[there exists] the potential for deliberative autonomy and public spiritedness despite privileged interest" (p. 193).

Consultation and Partnership

Consultation and partnership activities share many of the same challenges and opportunities as citizen advisory groups. For example, the British initiative boldly labelled "the Big Society" aims to broaden citizen engagement (Scott, 2011). As Scott notes, the goal of what is fondly known as "BS" appears to be persuading community development sectors to carry out voluntarily work that used to be done and paid for by governments. Acknowledging the extent to which the initiative is highly manipulative and uses both moral persuasion and ideological consent to mould responses by citizens, he also describes the process as an opportunity to transform the Big Society initiative by "relocating the point of origin to communities" (p. 136).

Closer to home, and an example of relocating citizen input, is a Vancouver initiative that engaged citizens in the creation of indicators for sustainability (including social, environmental, and economic). Here, the process of deliberating over which indicators to use enabled citizens to challenge the government's priorities regarding what was important and needed to be measured. It also provided those citizens with an opportunity to monitor the City's ongoing work (Holden, 2009).

Another example of effective community–government collaboration supports the potential for influence to move from the local to affect broader

Government Processes for Engaging Citizens

policy change. A mobile drop-in for, and run by, sex workers on Vancouver's Downtown Eastside was established in response to a partnership among sex workers, researchers, and representatives from the three levels of government (Janssen et al., 2009). Building on the relationships formed through this initiative, sex workers together with government representatives called for changes to federal laws to support legal brothels and sex-worker cooperatives (Lee, 2007). While there are many examples of official consultation processes that have created frustration and distrust of governments rather than providing opportunities for actual citizen engagement (Abelson & Gauvin, 2004; Read & Maslin-Prothero, 2011), the creation of relationships with decision makers, so that one can use one's right as a citizen to access information and answers, nevertheless opens spaces for citizens to influence change.

Deliberative Democracy

In 1980, Jane Mansbridge coined the term "deliberative democracy," contrasting it with adversarial democracy. She describes the former—it has also been called "communal democracy"—as a deliberative process that assumes common interests among citizens, rather than a divisive one that assumes conflicting interests (Mansbridge, 1990). Parkins and Davidson (2008) summarize the criteria for effective deliberative democracy as follows: "opportunity for participation by all citizens; the tendency among all participants to be open about their true intentions; critical assessment of all assertions and validity claims through orderly exchange; expression of the merits of arguments in terms of the common good; willingness to listen and respect others; and yielding to the better argument" (2008, p. 179).

Johnson (2009) offers case studies of two government bodies and one large not-for-profit organization implementing deliberative democracy practices in Canada aimed at influencing policy consistent with these criteria. The recommendations were implemented in only one of the three cases. In the other two, the intermediary policy makers within the government or institution vetoed the recommendations arising from the engagement with citizens. Thus, despite implementing processes that hold true to the deliberative intent, outcomes may still reflect the views of the powerful few.

Case in point: The establishment of the Citizens Assembly in British Columbia to deliberate on electoral reform and identify options for it was a form of deliberative democracy at the provincial level. However, the premier was using the deliberative democracy process to sidestep disagreement with the concept of electoral reform from within his caucus. This exemplifies the danger that "deliberative mechanisms may be used to co-opt and suppress dissenting opinions or to provide a false sense of legitimacy to decisions that were actually taken with little or no views of the public" (Flinders & Curry, 2008, p. 374).

The use of information and communication technologies to increase civil society's capacity is discussed in Smith, Bellaby, and Lindsay's (2010) examination of neighbourhood-level deliberative democracy, as well as by de Moor (2010), who advocates the use of intermedia communities. De Moor's rationale is premised on the need to include civil society in the discussion of "wicked problems" and on the effectiveness of using intermedia to create informational public documents co-authored by a range of stakeholders. De Moor defines wicked problems as crosscutting, "complex, situated and interrelated" (p. 279) issues that must be resolved by both government and citizenry (Aulich, 2009). Here, de Moor uses the examples of globalization and (un)sustainable development, including the process established regarding logging in Clayoquot Sound.

Nancy Roberts (2004) describes a range of experiments in direct citizen participation. She concludes that citizens need to be engaged in wicked problems (echoing de Moor, 2010) and that increased deliberative democracy is the most effective approach. However, as with other opportunities for citizen participation, there are many hurdles to a successful process, which requires the following: effective representation; institutional commitment to implement the results of the deliberations; assurances that the process is not being used to sidestep disagreement within a governing body; and participants who are free from institutional restrictions so that they can freely voice their opinions.

Citizen-Initiated Engagement in Government Processes to Influence Social Change

A primary means to influence environmental policies is through environmental assessment processes of the sort required for corporate and government activities. While there are opportunities to influence decisions through these processes, restrictions related to ease of access and extent of engagement affect the extent of that influence. Mitchell's (2006) account of "the Citizen Submissions on Enforcement Matters," a trilateral institution established by Canada, the United States, and Mexico as part of the North American Agreement on Environmental Cooperation (http://www.naaec.gc.ca/), describes how an environmental assessment process restricted access for many citizens. Difficulties that relate to finding the information regarding the submissions process, and to the knowledge required in order to complete the application process, impeded participation.

Broadening the context, scope of opportunities, and time frame to be involved in environmental assessments has been suggested as one solution (Hunsberger, Gibson, & Wismer, 2005). For Sinclair, Diduck, and Fitzpatrick (2008), the key is increasing citizen knowledge through engagement in environmental assessments; conducting ongoing monitoring and assessment; and improving citizens' understanding and behaviour, as well as that of the broader community, with the goal of encouraging a more sustainable lifestyle.

Citizen-Initiated Engagement in Government Processes

Legal Systems

There has been less success in using the courts and government commissions to challenge the rights of governments and multinational corporations that are creating health problems or destroying the environment. This is because the rights of corporations are embedded in our legal system. As Bakan (2004) notes, corporations' legally defined mandate is to pursue their own interests relentlessly, regardless of the often harmful consequences to others. The following stories have some positive elements regarding the effectiveness of citizens who challenge actions by corporations; however, the obvious power of corporations and governmental support of their rights underpin both stories.

A newspaper article titled "Court victory for citizen participation" (*The Gazette,* 2010) is as much about corporate power as it is about citizen participation. The article describes how a landfill in Quebec was producing poisonous gas that far exceeded WHO standards and that was lethal enough to kill anyone who approached the landfill. A couple who lived nearby complained to the corporation, which launched a $1.25 million lawsuit against the couple for complaining. Fortunately, Quebec has an anti-SLAPP (Strategic Lawsuits against Public Participation) law in place, and the court tossed the lawsuit out. Quebec is the only province to have this type of protection in place for its citizens.

The negative health impacts of sour gas from petroleum development galvanized a number of communities in Alberta to fight back against oil companies. Evans and Garvin (2009) describe how citizens attended public hearings and provided evidence of health problems resulting from the sour gas. The Alberta Utilities Commission still proceeded in granting the right to drill for one of the corporations, though it did attach eighteen conditions—which have not yet been met. The interveners won in the second case, and the right of the corporation to drill in the proposed area was turned down.

Collective Action by Community Organizations and Practitioners

There is a long history of advocacy for social change by community organizations in the social and environmental fields. These organizations work alongside practitioners, who witness on a daily basis the negative impacts of government policies. The Caledon Institute of Social Policy (Community-Government Collaboration on Policy, 2009; Leviten-Reid, 2009; Torjman, 2009) has identified specific examples of strategies that have been initiated at the local level by non-governmental organizations, practitioners, and businesses to bring about social policy change at the provincial or federal level in twelve communities across Canada. The means employed in each case has been the Vibrant Communities initiative (http://www.vibrantcommunities.ca/g2.php). Five years of advocating for change by the Hamilton Round Table saw an increase in tax dollars going to address poverty; this resulted in

6,000 fewer citizens living below the low-income cut-off (Hamilton Roundtable for Poverty Reduction, 2011; Leviten-Reid, 2009). Other examples include "Vibrant Calgary" advocacy efforts to establish a living wage for city employees and to acknowledge living wage employers, and Victoria's "Quality of Life Challenge," with its established community sustainability indicators to monitor and measure quality of life for its citizens.

Using the Olympics to Influence Policy

There is also potential for citizen engagement in mega-events such as the Olympics. This engagement can have positive *or* negative outcomes. For example, the Bid Book for the 2010 Vancouver Whistler Winter Olympics included the Inner City Inclusive Commitment Statement, a series of pledges related to housing, economics, civil liberties, employment, and access agreed to by the host country, the province, and the city (Frankish, Kwan, & Van Whynsberghe, 2010). These commitments had been developed by the provincial and city governments, working with the residents of Vancouver's inner-city neighbourhoods. Not surprisingly, in their analysis of what was promised versus what transpired, Frankish et al. noted concessions and trade-offs. When budgetary restraints arose, the commitments were viewed as expendable; when opportunities for disagreement with governments' actions arose, community meetings ceased. Frankish et al. indicate that some steps were taken by the governments involved, including efforts related to housing and low cost access to the events.

Mega-events are not staged for the purpose of righting the wrongs in our society; however, event organizers may *appear* to be supportive of addressing those wrongs if doing so will help them stage a relatively protest-free event. While there is evidence that some positive actions were taken as a result of the 2010 Winter Games, it remains unclear whether issues related to housing, employment, and health services would have been tackled during the relevant time period if, say, Salzberg had won the 2010 bid. Activists challenging the 2010 Olympics raised this question and others; we will be discussing their actions in more detail later in this chapter.

Social Change through Actions Outside Government

As suggested in the preceding sections, there are many actions that citizens take outside of government to bring about social change.[2] We will attempt to understand the implications and the impact of both consumer action and civil action, considering individual and collective action as well as the links among technology, education, and civil action. We will also consider the creation of alternative spaces in which social change can be realized and the extent to which those spaces stretch beyond the local.

Social Change through Actions Outside Government

Consumer Action

Neoliberal ideology within governments has placed the success of the economy as the top priority for policies and funding. Those priorities encompass international trade and corporations' right to profits. Proposed approaches to challenging these priorities and the hegemony of capitalism include escaping from the consumer culture that supports the economy or consuming in non-capitalist markets (Arnould, 2007).

Arnould (2007) explores the implications of escaping the market versus consuming within those spaces that are not capitalist in nature in order to change the market economy. He suggests that it is possible to change the market by buying from local small businesses, attending flea markets and swap meets, and purchasing fair trade products. Such actions are based on the common good rather than self-interest (Schudson, 2007). For Lamla (2008), however, actions by consumers who do not understand the complicated relationship between consumer behaviour and markets' responses are problematic. Communication regarding that relationship, and opportunities for consumerism with the non-capitalist market, are seen as a crucial complement to effective consumer action by both Lamla and Arnould.

Gibson-Graham (1996) suggests that by recognizing and avoiding products that involve exploitation, we may be able to bring about social change. For example, various initiatives have sprung up to support changed consumer behaviour, including no-shopping days (or weeks), social enterprise products, local and fair trade, and farmers' markets.

Civil Action

With pictures and reports of civil uprising during the Jasmine Revolution[3] consuming media outlets during the first two months of 2011, we have vivid depictions of recent civil action. In this section we explore the rationale for citizen engagement outside government processes and attempt to understand the dynamics of collective action.

Sorensen and Sagaris (2010) analyzed three cases of citizen action at the neighbourhood level that succeeded in stopping government actions. The Canadian example describes citizens' opposition to an expressway that would have gone through their downtown Toronto neighbourhood. "Strong durable organizations with expertise, institutional memory, and neighbourhood self-governance capacity" (p. 297) were the characteristics that enabled the neighbourhood coalition to establish these citizens' rights to the city, thereby blocking construction of the expressway.

Another example of collective action in Canada happened at the 2010 Winter Olympics. Earlier in this chapter we described how some citizens worked with the municipal and provincial governments to develop inner-city inclusive Olympic statements. In addition, a range of groups engaged in activities outside the government realm to challenge the corporate agenda of the Olympics. Boykoff (2011) describes their activities as including peaceful protests (except for one incident); alternative news forums featuring a range of perspectives from those against the Olympics; and a radio show featuring readings by and discussions with activist poets. When the radio station was shut down by Industry Canada early in the games, the show was streamed online. Boykoff notes that the activism generated real results: "Numerous activists I spoke with stressed that the creation of the Olympic Tent Village was not merely a symbolic act, but a material victory too: because of the action, approximately eighty-five people secured housing through the City of Vancouver and BC Housing" (2011, p. 53).

Collective action that challenges governments' decisions can succeed at the local level, as the Toronto example demonstrates, and at the national level, as witnessed by the uprisings in the Arab world. However, to change socio-structural beliefs with the goal of altering social structures requires a capacity for collective action as well as an ability to communicate the need for the change to the larger public.

Education, Technology, and Civil Action

A theme that runs through many of the preceding discussions is the importance of information and education for citizen participation. Whether it is understanding the link between consumer behaviour and sweatshops (Lamla, 2008) or gaining a thorough understanding of sustainability principles when participating in environmental assessments (Sinclair et al., 2008), there appears to be agreement on the importance of citizen education in influencing social change. Schnack (2008) discusses the importance of understanding participation in education in terms of co-determinance to help people reflect on meanings, not merely to provide them with facts, in order to realize "alternative futures in more informed and democratic ways" (Huckle & Sterling, 1996, p. 3, cited by Schnack, 2008).

An example of reflective activism in a post-secondary setting is described by M'Gonigle and Starke (2006). During a multiyear activist project at the University of Victoria, students challenged the development plan established by the university authorities, demanding a more sustainable approach to campus planning than that being implemented by the adminstration. Unfortunately, the forest that the students were attempting to protect was bulldozed to make way for another building. Questioning the disconnect between the actions of university administrators and the democratic ideals being taught on campus, M'Gonigle and Starke challenge universities to act on their potential to foster progressive social change and be locations for models of local and global innovation.

Technology has been playing a role in civil actions; this was evident during the recent overthrow of the Egyptian government. Gladwell (2010) critiques the idea that technology is solely responsible for recent citizen actions in the Middle East, pointing out that face-to-face social interactions were central to the Civil Rights movement in the United States. Schuler (2010) calls for local face-to-face connections combined with effective uses of technology, arguing that community Internet networks increase civic intelligence—a core capacity if citizens are to participate knowledgeably and influence social change. He reflects on the coming together of local groups with others around the world through shared values and commitments: "The organizational structure of global civic intelligence becomes a vast network of people and institutions all communicating with each other and sharing information, knowledge, hypotheses, and lessons learned. This network is necessarily composed of dissimilar institutions and individuals who cooperate with each other because they share values and commitments to similar objectives" (2010, p. 297).

Creating Alternative Spaces

Magnusson (2011) encourages us to consider being political within the local everyday spaces in which we are engaged and, in that way, influencing broader social change. Massey (2005) describes the concept of an accumulation of localisms, in which the spaces we create at local levels, together with other local spaces, generate global social change. An example is the Transition Town movement, in which a community in Great Britain in 2006 started working toward less reliance on fossil fuel. Interest developed among other communities carrying out similar activities, and this led to the creation of the Transition Network. By March 2011, more than 352 communities in 31 countries had signed on to the network (Transition Network, 2011). Similarly, Paul Hawken (2007) provides an inspiring description of the accumulation of localisms around the world. He describes how citizens are rising up to change social policy, and how this is bringing about a profound transformation of human society—one that has remained, however, under the radar of the media and politicians. Schuler (2010) echoes Hawken's findings, noting that the number of transnational groups focused on environment and social justice issues counts in the thousands and is growing exponentially each year.

Summary and Conclusions

What do we know about influencing policy from outside government? It is clear that the mechanisms established by government bodies to meaningfully engage citizens remain weak. These mechanisms effectively leave citizens on the sidelines with little hope of bringing change about. Another grave concern is the lack of policy changes arising from the engagement process when these changes would run counter to economic interests or those of entrenched powers. Surveys, advisory groups, community–government partnerships, and deliberative democracy processes are usually aimed at achieving results or inputs that are consistent with a government's position. However, there is evidence that even within those processes, opportunities do arise for citizens to engage in deliberative rather than responsive processes, to challenge the dominant discourse, and to create spaces for alternative ways of understanding or approaching issues. This may also be true for both legal action and engagement in environmental impact assessments; although both tend to be defensive in nature, they provide opportunities for broader public awareness about issues such as corporate rights. Stronger and more effective citizen participation processes are required, with citizens using these opportunities to open up the discourse to alternatives that reflect people's lived experiences.

A strong theme in the literature is education that builds capacity for civic engagement. The 2010 Olympics provided us with insights into the "sidelining" nature of government–citizen participation processes aimed at influencing mega-events. At the same time, civil action demonstrated how such events can become spaces for democratic engagement, in which a range of groups have the opportunity to converge and unite in challenging the rhetoric of governments and corporations involved in mega-events. Finally, the concept of creating local spaces—for example, by taking back communities and culture, as is being done by First Nations—and the rise of a global accumulation of local spaces, as depicted by Hawken (2007)—provide hope that places will develop in which policy can be shaped from the outside, thus enabling citizens to lead social change.

Notes

1 *Citizens First* are surveys asking Canadians across the country what they thought about the delivery of public services, what expectations they held, and what they saw as the priorities for improvement. The surveys were carried out in 1998, 2000, 2002, 2005, and 2008.

2 Although an important form of social change, it is beyond the scope of this chapter to address whistle-blowing. As an act of revealing harmful, dishonest, or illegal activities, allegations can be made within or outside public, not-for-profit, and private sector organizations to media, law enforcement bodies, or corporate/government authorities. The most recently publicized whistle-blowing is probably Julian Assange and his WikiLeaks not-for-profit media organization (http://wikileaks.org), which released secret Pentagon documents on the Afghan and Iraqi wars.

3 The Tunisian Revolution, in which popular protests forced President Zine El Abidine Ben Ali out of the presidency in late 2010 and early 2011, was called "the Jasmine Revolution" by many media organizations, and was the impetus of the Arab Spring. Action in Tunisia was closely followed by protests in Algeria, Yemen, Jordan, Syria, Bahrain, Iraq, Mauritania, and Libya.

References

Abelson, J., & Gauvin, F. (2004). *Transparency, trust, and citizen engagement.* Ottawa, ON: Canadian Policy Research Networks.

Arnould, E.J. (2007). Should consumer citizens escape the market? *The ANNALS of the American Academy of Political and Social Science, 611*(96), 96–111. Retrieved from http://ann.sagepub.com/content/611/1/96.full.pdf+html

Arnstein, S.R. (1969). Ladder of citizen participation. *Journal of American Institute of Planners, 35,* 216–224.

Attree, P., French, B., Milton, B., Povall, S., Whitehead, M., & Popay, J. (2011). The experience of community engagement for individuals: A rapid review of evidence. *Health and Social Care in the Community, 19*(3), 250–260. Retrieved from http://onlinelibrary.wiley.com/doi/10.1111/j.1365-2524.2010.00976.x/pdf

Aulich, C. (2009). From citizen participation to participatory governance in Australian local governance. *Commonwealth Journal of Local Governance, 2,* 44–60. Retrieved from http://utsescholarship.lib.uts.edu.au/epress/journals/index.php/cjlg/article/view/1007

Bakan, J. (2004). *The corporation: The pathological pursuit of profit and power.* New York, NY: Free Press.

Blomgren Bingham, L., Nabatchi, T., & O'Leary, R. (2005). The new governance: Practices and processes for stakeholder and citizen participation in the work of government. *Public Administration Review, 65*(5), 547–558. Retrieved from http://onlinelibrary.wiley.com/doi/10.1111/j.1540-6210.2005.00482.x/pdf

Bochel, C., Bochel, H., Summerville, P., & Worley C. (2008). Marginalised or enabled voices? User participation in policy and practice. *Social Policy & Society, 7*(2), 201–210. Retrieved from http://journals.cambridge.org/action/displayFulltext?type=1&pdftype=1&fid=1779784&jid=SPS&volumeId=7&issueId=&aid=1779776

Bowen, G. (2008). Analysis of citizen participation in anti-poverty programmes. *Community Development Journal, 43*(1), 65–78. doi: 10.1093/cdj/bsm011

Bowler, S.D., Donovan, T., & Karp, J. (2007). Enraged or engaged? Preferences for direct citizen participation in affluent democracies. *Political Research Quarterly, 60*(3), 351–362. Retrieved from http://prq.sagepub.com/content/60/3/351.full.pdf+html

Boykoff, J. (2011). The anti-Olympics. *New Left Review, 67,* 41–59. Retrieved from http://www.newleftreview.org/?issue=301

Callahan, K. (2007). Citizen participation: Models and methods. *International Journal of Public Administration, 30*(11), 1179–1196. Retrieved from http://pdfserve.informaworld.com/622349_770885140_781773276.pdf

Church, J., Saunders, D., Wanke, M., Pong, R., Spooner, C., & Dorgan, M. (2002) Citizen participation in health decision-making: Past experience and future prospects. *Journal of Public Health Policy, 23*(1), 12–32. Retrieved from http://www.jstor.org/stable/3343116?origin=crossref

Community-Government Collaboration on Policy. (2009). *Collaboration on policy: A manual developed by the Community-Government Collaboration on Policy.* Ottawa, ON: Caledon Institute of Social Policy.

de Moor, A. (2010). Reconstructing civil society with intermedia communities. *AI & Society, 25*(3), 279–289. Retrieved from http://www.springerlink.com/content/mh673115768vu748/fulltext.pdf

References

Denhardt, R.B., & Denhardt, J.V. (2000). The new public service: Serving rather than steering. *Public Administration Review, 60*(6), 549–557. Retrieved from http://onlinelibrary.wiley.com/doi/10.1111/0033-3352.00117/pdf

Dutil, P.A., Howard, C., Langford, J., & Roy, J. (2007). Rethinking government-public relationships in a digital world: Customers, clients or citizens? *Journal of Information Technology and Politics, 4*(1), 77–90. Retrieved from http://www.jitp.net/files/v004001/JITP4-1_Rethinking_Government_Dutil_et_al.pdf

Evans, J., & Garvin, T. (2009). You're in "oil country": Moral tales of citizen action against petroleum development, Alberta, Canada. *Ethics, Place and Environment, 12*(1), 49–68. Retrieved from http://pdfserve.informaworld.com/472250_770885140_910322762.pdf

Flinders, M.C., & Curry, D. (2008). Deliberative democracy, elite politics, and electoral reform. *Policy Studies, 29*(4), 371–392. Retrieved from http://www.informaworld.com/smpp/ftinterface~db=all~content=a906881762~fulltext=713240930

Frankish, J., Kwan, B., & Van Whysnberghe, R. (2010). "Two solitudes": The 2010 Vancouver Olympics and inner city inclusivity commitments. Canadian Institute for Health Information. Retrieved from http://www.cihi.ca/CIHI-ext-portal/pdf/internet/frankish_en

The Gazette (2010, August 7). Court victory for citizen participation. *The Gazette.* Retrieved from http://proquest.umi.com.ezproxy.library.uvic.ca/pqdweb?index=0&did=2105433231&SrchMode=1&sid=1&Fmt=3&VInst=PROD&VType=PQD&RQT=309&VName=PQD&TS=1301065319&clientId=3916

Gibson-Graham, J.K. (1996). *The end of capitalism (as we knew it).* Cambridge, UK: Blackwell Publishers.

Gladwell, M. (2010). Small change: Why the revolution will not be tweeted. *The New Yorker.* Retrieved from http://www.newyorker.com/reporting/2010/10/04/101004fa_fact_gladwell?currentPage=2

Graham, K.A., & Phillips, S.D. (1997). Citizen engagement: Beyond the consumer revolution. *Canadian Public Administration, 40*(2), 255–273. Retrieved from http://onlinelibrary.wiley.com/doi/10.1111/j.1754-7121.1997.tb01509.x/pdf

Hamilton Roundtable for Poverty Reduction. (2010). Community champion, Mark Chamberlain ends term as Chair of Hamilton Roundtable for Poverty. Hamilton, ON. Retrieved from http://www.hamiltonpoverty.ca/docs/news_and_reports/2010/mark-chamberlain-announcement.pdf

Hawken, P. (2007). *Blessed unrest.* New York, NY: Viking Press.

Holden, M. (2009). Community interests and indicator system success. *Social Indicators Research, 92*(3), 429–448. Retrieved from http://www.springerlink.com/content/3081112731831146/fulltext.pdf

Howard, C. (2010). Are we being served? A critical perspective on Canada's Citizen's First satisfaction surveys. *International Review of Administrative Sciences, 76*(1), 65–83. Retrieved from http://ras.sagepub.com/content/76/1/65.full.pdf+html

Huckle, J. (1996) Realizing sustainability in changing times. In J. Huckle & S. Sterling (Eds.), *Education for sustainability* (pp. 3–17). London: Earthscan.

Hunsberger, C., Gibson, R., & Wismer, S. (2005). Citizen involvement in sustainability-centred environmental assessment follow-up. *Environmental Impact Assessment Review, 25*(6), 609–627. Retrieved from http://www.sciencedirect.com/science?_ob=MImg&_imagekey=B6V9G-4FBN79F-1-1&_cdi=5898&_

user=1007916&_pii=S0195925504001763&_origin=browse&_zone=rslt_list_item&_coverDate=08%2F31%2F2005&_sk=999749993&wchp=dGLzVlz-zSkzk&md5=f4dd58de211eb4956f52a0c163749d5d&ie=/sdarticle.pdf

Janssen, P.A., Gibson, K., Bowen, R., Spittal, P.M., & Peterson, K.L. (2009). Peer support using a mobile access van promotes safety and harm reduction strategies among sex trade workers in Vancouver's downtown eastside. *Journal of Urban Health: Bulletin of the New York Academy of Medicine, 86*(5), 804–809. Retrieved from http://www.springerlink.com/content/q6120q43n3kq554l/fulltext.pdf

Johnson, G.F. (2009). Deliberative democratic practices in Canada: An analysis of institutional empowerment in three cases. *Canadian Journal of Political Science, 42*(3), 679–703. Retrieved from http://journals.cambridge.org/action/displayFulltext?type=1&pdftype=1&fid=6375424&jid=CJP&volumeId=42&issueId=&aid=6375416

Knaap, G.J., Matier, D., & Olshansky, R. (1998). Citizen advisory groups in remedial action planning: Paper tiger or key to success? *Journal of Environmental Planning and Management, 41*(3), 337–354. Retrieved from http://pdfserve.informaworld.com/117878_778084902_713676467.pdf

Lamla, J. (2008). Consumer citizen: The constitution of consumer democracy in sociological perspective. *German Policy Studies, 4*(1), 131–166. Retrieved from http://www.spaef.com/file.php?id=909

Lee, J. (2007, November 12). Coalition pushes for legal brothel. *The Vancouver Sun.* Retrieved from http://www.canada.com/vancouversun/news/story.html?id=0057e9b8-1503-499c-9268-7610a233f121

Leviten-Reid, E. (2009). *Comprehensive strategies for deep and durable outcomes.* Ottawa, ON: Caledon Institute of Social Policy.

Magnusson, W. (2011). *Politics of urban: Seeing like a city.* New York: Routledge.

Mansbridge, J. (1990). Democracy and common interests. *Social Alternatives, 8*(4), 20–25.

Martin, G.P. (2008). "Ordinary people only": Knowledge, representativeness, and the publics of public participation in health care. *Sociology of Health & Illness, 30*(1), 35–54. doi: 10.1111/j.1467-9566.2007.01027.x

Massey, D. (2005). *For space.* London, UK: Sage Publications.

McKenzie, B., & Wharf, B. (2010). *Connecting policy to practice in the human services.* Don Mills, ON: Oxford University Press.

M'Gonigle, R., & Starke, J.C. (2006). Minding place: Towards a (rational) political ecology of the sustainable university. *Environment and Planning D: Society and Space, 24*(3), 325–348. Retrieved from http://www.envplan.com/epd/fulltext/d24/d3104.pdf

Mitchell, R.E. (2006). Environmental actions of citizens: Evaluating the Submission Process of the Commission for Environmental Cooperation of NAFTA. *Journal of Environment and Development, 15*(3), 297–316. Retrieved from http://jed.sagepub.com/content/15/3/297.full.pdf+html

National Council of Welfare (2010). *Council members.* Retrieved from http://www.ncw.gc.ca/m.2mbers@-eng.jsp.

Parkins, J.R., & Davidson, D.J. (2008). Constructing the public sphere in compromised settings: Environmental governance in the Alberta forest sector. *Canadian Review of Sociology, 45*(2), 177–196. Retrieved from http://onlinelibrary.wiley.com/doi/10.1111/j.1755-618X.2008.00009.x/pdf

References Ravensbergen, F., & Vanderplaat, M. (2010). Barriers to citizen participation: The missing voices of people living with low incomes. *Community Development Journal, 45*(4), 389–403. doi: 10.1093/cdj/bsp014

Read, S., & Maslin-Prothero, S. (2011). The involvement of users and carers in health and social research: The realities of inclusion and engagement. *Qualitative Health Research, 21*(5), 704–713. doi: 10.1177/1049732310391273

Roberts, N. (2004). Public deliberation in an age of direct citizen participation. *American Review of Public Administration, 34*(4), 315–353. Retrieved from http://arp.sagepub.com/content/34/4/315.full.pdf+html

Rose, N. (2000). Governing liberty. In R. Ericson & N. Stehr (Eds.), *Governing modern societies* (pp. 141–176). Toronto, ON: University of Toronto Press.

Schnack, K. (2008). Participation, education, and democracy: Implications for environmental education, health education, and education for sustainable development. In A. Reid, B. Jensen, J. Nikel, & V. Simovska (Eds.), *Participation and learning* (pp. 181–196). Bath, UK: Springer.

Schudson, M. (2007). Citizens, consumers, and the good society. *The ANNALS of the American Academy of Political and Social Science, 611*, 236–249. Retrieved from http://ann.sagepub.com/content/611/1/236.full.pdf+html

Schuler, D. (2010). Community networks and the evolution of civic intelligence. *AI & Society, 25*(3), 291–307. Retrieved from http://www.springerlink.com/content/u2135830h434g677/fulltext.pdf

Scott, M. (2011). Reflections on "The Big Society." *Community Development Journal, 46*(1), 132–137. Retrieved from http://cdj.oxfordjournals.org/content/46/1/132.full.pdf+html

Sinclair, J., Diduck, A., & Fitzpatrick, P. (2008). Conceptualizing learning for sustainability through environmental assessment: Critical reflections on 15 years of research. *Environmental Impact Assessment Review, 28*(7), 415–428. Retrieved from http://www.elsevier.com/wps/find/journaldescription.cws_home/505718/ description#description

Smith, S., Bellaby, P., & Lindsay, S. (2010). Social inclusion at different scales in the urban environment: Locating the community to empower. *Urban Studies, 47*(7), 1439–1457. Retrieved from http://usj.sagepub.com/content/47/7/1439.full.pdf+html

Sorensen, A., & Sagaris, L. (2010). From participation to the right to the city: Democratic place management at the neighbourhood scale in comparative perspective. *Planning Practice & Research, 25*(3), 297–316. Retrieved from http://pdfserve.informaworld.com/362878_770885140_927092814.pdf

Torjman, S. (2009). *Community roles in policy.* Ottawa, ON: Caledon Institute of Social Policy.

Transition Network. (2011). *Initiatives by numbers.* Retrieved from http://www.transitionnetwork.org/initiatives/by-number.

Wharf Higgins, J. (1999). Citizenship and empowerment: A remedy for citizen participation in health reform. *Community Development Journal, 34*(4), 287–307. Retrieved from http://cdj.oxfordjournals.org/content/34/4/287.full.pdf+html

Wharf Higgins, J. (2002). Participation in community health planning. *Encyclopedia of Public Health, volume 3* (890–891). New York, NY: Macmillan Reference.

Wharf Higgins, J. Vertinsky, P., Green, L.W., & Cutt, J. (1999). Using social marketing as a strategic approach to understanding citizen participation in health reform. *Social Marketing Quarterly, 5*(2), 42–55. Retrieved from http://pdfserve.informaworld.com/725560_770885140_921724933.pdf

Indigenous Wholistic Healing Social Policy:

Rethinking, Reframing, and Re-presenting Policy Development for Indigenous People

5

Mac Saulis

I asked a former colleague of mine, who is known as a policy wonk, what he thought of the conclusion that the average *Indian*[1] in Canada perceives policy wonks as having "wonky." ideas. I have always known that to be a policy wonk in Canada is to be viewed as a member of a rather exclusive club. I have not seen too many Aboriginal people in this group, and even fewer Aboriginal policy wonks writing from their traditional indigenous perspective. I thought it might be good to begin this chapter by presenting the indigenous world view and the meanings of concepts such as *wholistic, healing, ceremonies,* and others associated with this distinctive world view, along with the implications of those concepts for social policy analysis. As an indigenous scholar myself, I have found engaging in "my people's world view" a very liberating experience, even though it is not well supported by existing social policy and social welfare paradigms.

For the past five years I have been delivering a new Master of Social Work program that is entirely rooted in the indigenous world view. It has been a very powerful experience for me and for all who are associated with the program as faculty, staff, Elders, or students. We have had many non-indigenous people in this program, and they have engaged in learning the Indigenous-based Wholistic Healing process alongside the indigenous students who attend. The mutual growth is very discernable, even though the character of the growth is distinctively different between the two groups. Indigenous students very clearly appreciate that their heritage, knowledge, and world views are being valued equally with non-indigenous world views—this, at a mainstream Faculty of Social Work at a very mainstream university. It is just as clear that non-indigenous students appreciate a program of study that focuses on indigenous healing, health, and wellness as an approach to social work as opposed to an illness-focused program. They come to conclude that the indigenous-based Wholistic Healing approach to people and the world they live in is valid. The validity accorded the indigenous world view through this Master of Social Work program is helping undo the ongoing colonialism that for centuries has devalued, rejected, and delegitimized indigenous world views to the benefit of mainstream ones.

What has been the battleground that has resulted in the active devaluation of the indigenous world view? And why has that battle continued for so long? Is there an end in sight to it, and who will finally lend credence to the indigenous world view and allow the healing it represents to exist and thrive within society? I can't wait to see who is named with this power to give blessing to this indigenous world view and approach. The battleground has been colonialism, and it is the lingering effects of colonialism that have sustained the devaluing effect.

The lingering effects of colonialism are well stated in the following quote:

> The essence of the colonial relationship, as Canadian policy essayist Peter Puxley explains, is that the colonized are "unilaterally defined by the other." The colonizer then cannot accept "any move toward real autonomy on the part of the colonized." And any such move is either "ignored, defined as unacceptable, or reprimanded, depending on the degree of institutionalization of the relationship." With some exceptions, the colonial forces attacking Native peoples in Canada have not been military, but rather, have been institutional, through economic, religious, educational, legislative, and media systems. Not surprisingly, the colonial relationship between White and Native peoples is profoundly institutionalized, and has grown more so with time. One of the indices of such systemic control is the extent to which Native peoples have been defined outside of themselves, and when they seek to change this definition, meet opposition in many forms. (LaRocque, 2010, pp. 68–69)

Here, LaRocque is explaining with great eloquence not only that colonialism is a historic artifact but also that it exists to this day and is having an impact on the lives of both Native people and non-Native people because both are locked into the harmful effects of this *relationship*. Present-day colonialism exists not only in Canada's institutions but also in the very intimate aspects of the social relationship between indigenous citizens of Canada (our homeland) and the rest of Canadian society. This colonialism is so powerful that even new immigrants to Canada learn to engage with indigenous people in the same way that lifelong Canadians always have. In some ways it is scary that diverse, new Canadians learn to marginalize indigenous Canadians and that they learn it so quickly. Hope rests in new relationships that are built on the valuing of indigenous world views, in the ideas that grow from this process, and in the contributions that indigenous knowledge can make to problems that society faces.

Two choices made by Canada long ago about Status Indians (Indians registered on Band lists as defined by the Indian Act) have affected perceptions of the value of those people. These two persistent views in policy have been as follows:

1. Room must be made for settlers, and it must be ensured that the lands given to the settlers cannot be reverted to the original inhabitants. This has always been a disturbing policy for indigenous peoples, because it implies that the settlers are here to stay and that they own and can exploit the land that agents took for them.
2. Canada will formulate, adopt, and administer a policy for Indians. This implies that decisions can be made from afar, usually by non-indigenous peoples, without a need to consult the indigenous people themselves or to show concern about the implications. Significant here is that use of evidence or facts and figures is sufficient to determine the right direction. The evidence that is trusted, however, is gathered in ways that are valued by mainstream academics; evidence generated by the Indians themselves is suspect.

The Beginning (of Liberation)

In a previous edition of this book I quoted a passage from Paulo Freire's *Pedagogy of the Oppressed,* in which he presented a challenge to the oppressed (me) to engage in a process of liberation. This quote has given me the strength, determination, and spiritual energy to engage my own indigenous teachings so that I might be able to show the oppressor that what I represent in this world is valuable and non-competitive with their own knowledge. We need to embrace a new relationship between us, a relationship characterized by equality and respect. I learned some time ago that I need to be the source of learning and liberation for my non-Native relative. That my indigenous world view helps them embrace a new humanity so that they can help Creation be stronger and not hurt and destroy it. Because their world view is to exploit nature, they leave the care of Creation to others. Their position as oppressor, exploiter, and user of Creation means that they do not take care of Creation and that others (not really named or identified) take care of it instead.

The following quote reminds me of each occasion when I go to reserves and communities and I meet ordinary people who are assumed to know very little of any value, in relation to the great scholars in the academy, or the policy wonks, or the intellectuals, who get their degrees and accolades from writing the knowledge that these ordinary people give to them via research. I feel tremendous pressure to try and understand what these ordinary people are saying because my social location in the academy is so different than theirs, but really I am simply, in the end, one of them. I feel valued by them and challenged to comprehend the indigeneity of their thoughts and reference points about the world. I ask myself, "How did life get so complicated that the only real reference is in books?" Freire seems to express the same insight:

The Beg[illegible] (of Liberation)

> In his intonations, his labourer's syntax and rhythm, the movements of his body, his hands of an orator, in the metaphors so common to popular discourse, he called the attention of the educator there in front of him, seated, silent, sinking down into his chair, to the need, when speaking to the people, for the educator to be up to the understanding of the world people have. An understanding of the world which, conditioned by the concrete reality that in part explains that understanding, can begin to change through a change in concrete reality. In fact, that understanding of the world can begin to change the moment the unmasking of concrete reality begins to lay bare the "whys" of what the actual understanding had been up until then. (Freire, 1994, p. 26)

I have decided to embrace my inner indigenous identity in order to be strong enough to stand with this knowledge and world view as though it were as valid as any I might encounter in the rest of the world. So I begin by defining myself as the first step toward liberation. I offer the following definition of indigenous:

Indigenous refers to the people and their world view prior to contact with non-indigenous and usually European peoples. It refers to the social, political, economic, and spiritual expression of their world view and in respect to their relationship to Creation. It refers to their heritage of healing, medicines, language, ceremonies, and relationships—in essence, their society.

This definition was first offered to me by Stan Wilson, a renowned indigenous educator, who also offered an understanding that "indigegogy" is an educational approach that flows from this indigenous definition. With this definition, he gave me a sense of liberation and freedom to be myself as a university professor, thus reinforcing the power of words. Words can set you free or they can bind you and imprison you, and their function within the ongoing colonial process is well noted.

This definition offers a view of the indigenous world as a fully functional society with well-established institutions. Indigenous people had (and still have) ways of dealing with issues facing their populations, such as poverty, hunger, homelessness, landownership, environmental challenges, and civil society. They had (and still have) functional policies on diversity and multinationalism, on settlement of immigrants, and on how to allocate resources to save lives. They had policies and a bureaucracy, and civil servants—usually in the form of clans and natural helpers—Elders, medicine carriers, teachers, and judges. They had ways of dealing with gender issues. But under colonialism all of these were deemed—along with the people who performed all of these roles—to be inferior to the practices of the dominant group. Nonetheless, these norms and roles are discernible in the remnants of knowledge that exist today. So this definition is important to the work of relearning and revaluing indigenous knowledge, if for no other reason than to understand the value and importance of life.

What Is Wholistic Anyway? (Rethinking)

What Is Wholistic Anyway? (Rethinking)

The core component of the indigenous world view is the notion of wholistic. My own journey to fully comprehending this notion has been long. As with most other indigenous teachings, the reflexive (understanding and rethinking the world) and reflective processes (showing it in my own life) necessary to engage the teachings are time consuming and are linked to the process of rehearing the teachings over and over again, and retelling them over and over again. The indigenous oral educational approach requires this type of rehearing and retelling, and an ancillary outcome of this process is the building of a relationship between teacher and learner until the two are the same. I am both teacher and learner, and I replicate the process with others.

A common representation of the four wholistic directions is the diagram presented here. It shows the mental, spiritual, emotional, and physical aspects of the wholistic perspective. We could view the wholistic elements to be as follows:

- Mental: This is what you know. It is what information you need in order to understand the phenomenon you are experiencing. It is an orderly, logical, and rational consideration of the experience that is taking place.
- Spiritual: This is the aspect of what you are experiencing that is non-physical and unconscious in nature. It is the understanding we have of the world that is rooted in belief and faith, and it influences the present beyond our control. The simplest expression of the spirit is in prayer. The most sophisticated expression of this spirituality is in the outcome of relationships and in the tangible impact that relationships have on us.
- Emotional: This is the feeling element of the wholistic consideration. How do we experience the world through our feelings, and how do we feel as a result of our experiences? There is a full range of emotions from the very worst to the very best, from the easily described to the impossible to describe.
- Physical: This is the aspects of reality that are tangible and perceivable within our senses. Physical reality is constructed and discernible through our senses.

The basic conceptualization of wholistic is that of the four parts and the middle, as seen in the diagram below. In this conceptualization there are four aspects of every person's life: the mental, the spiritual, the emotional, and the physical. As such it is important for every person to be nurtured in all of these areas so that the centre—that is, the person/you/self—will be strong. In this wholistic world view, the social welfare responsibility of society is to ensure that every person has enough resources that they will be nurtured wholistically. Within this wholistic world view, society is ordered in such a way that the community helps nurture its people through intimate relationships. These community people nurture their immediate and extended families; in turn, the families nurture their community and their society. But within the indigenous world view, this nurturing does not stop at the societal level—it continues on to the world, and to the universe, and our relationships extend to all of these levels. Therefore, persons who act in a nurturing way within themselves help keep Creation strong because there is a direct connection between each person and Creation.

Within this indigenous wholistic world view, how do you view the plight of others? You view their suffering as your own suffering and their joy as your joy, and the natural social welfare impulse is to nurture and help. Thus the fundamental motivation of social policy is to articulate this desire to nurture people within society and to offer them help. Freire offers this understanding of society within a wholistic world view: "We have the holistic concept of society being one, that the Universe is one. People, trees, and water and history are all merged. In Native American visions, they're all related. They have the vision but they know history. The Holistic concept is the oldest tradition we actually have in terms of history" (Leonard, 1993, p. 137).

Within the indigenous wholistic world view and traditions, social policy is created in order to nurture all people in their mind, spirit, and emotions and in their physical needs. In the expression and manifestation of society's social welfare, this is not an option, but a given. Social policy, then, is an expression of the commitment to sustaining the health of the mental, spiritual, emotional, and physical environment, because society can only be sustained by the health of each of these areas of society and its people. Social welfare programs that flow from the social policy will unfold themselves at

Figure 5.1 The Medicine Wheel

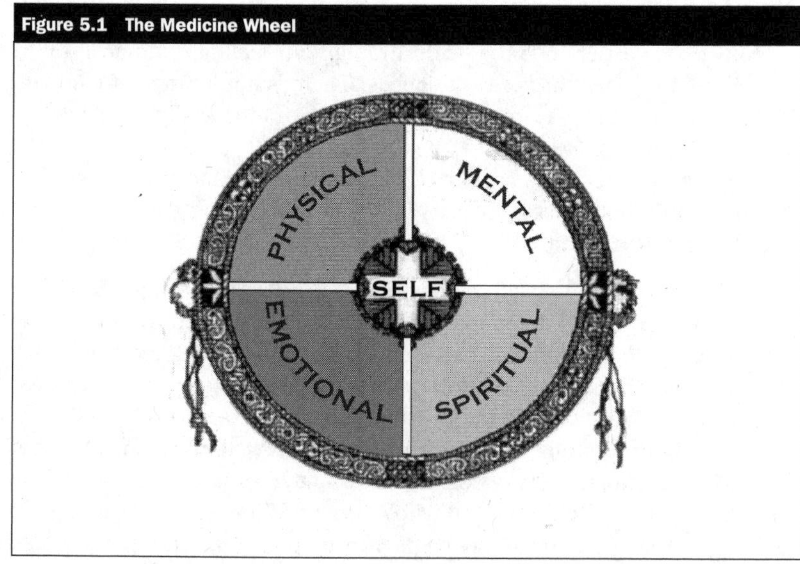

all levels of society, from the individual to the universe. This seems to be explaining what a wholistic approach means rather than engaging in the argument about which kinds of knowledge are to be valued.

Indigenous World View and Healing (Reframing)

Indigenous World View and Healing (Reframing)

How are people viewed in a society that embraces the indigenous wholistic world view? People are viewed as the most valuable element of society, that if we value them in this way then we ought to create a civil society that creates a context where these valuable entities can thrive. This context happens to be both the Earth and the Universe, the epistemological and the ontological, the temporal and the spiritual. It is important to note here that the social order we are speaking of in the indigenous world view does not make distinctions between genders of people, races of people, ages of people, or social locations of people. This is a very important element of the indigenous world view: a person is a person no matter their gender, race, age, or social location. In a society grounded in the indigenous world view, the following primary values would guide social policy:

Non-judgmental. We would not judge the person. We would extend this perspective to their life circumstances as well. Considering the prevalence of social ills in the lives of people generally and indigenous people specifically, we would view them—in most contexts where there are challenges—as normal and ordinary. Only through this perspective could we establish a social policy perspective that would foster trust and mutual respect for the society we live in. It would also motivate us to seek to keep this society strong and vibrant for future generations.

Unconditional acceptance. That is, we would unconditionally accept the person who is living in our society as well as that person's circumstances. Acceptance expresses the indigenous Wholistic Healing world view. Being unconditionally accepted is a wholistic experience for the person or group.

Wholistic valuing of people. People are to be valued for their presence in the world. Indigenous traditions and culture teach us that the Creator values all people equally. The indigenous-based Wholistic Healing world view tells us that each of us has a mind and intelligence to understand our world (North). Each of us has a spirit and connection to the world we see and to the spirit world, which is the world we can't see (East). Each of us has feelings and emotions that are affected by our interaction with the world we live in and the relationships we have (South). And each of us has a physical body and physical needs and deserves those things that sustain life (West).

All people deserve all of these things to preserve their life. Our indigenous cultural values (the values we express in our daily lives) guide the approach we demonstrate in our social work practice toward people, and we characterize these behaviours as the conditions required for people experiencing respectful wholistic interactions.

Outcomes of Indigenous-Based Wholistic Healing Social Policy

Outcomes of Indigenous-Based Wholistic Healing Social Policy

What we seek as outcomes of our indigenous-based Wholistic Healing social policy process and the social welfare programs that flow from these policies, are the following:

Hope—for a better future for all people and for the communities and societies where parents and their children live. This is because it is their health and the expression of healthy relationships that keeps the community functioning well alongside all other aspects and dimensions of Creation.

My own teacher/Elder Danny Musqua made two profound gestures to me that fostered hope in my own life, while I was learning the fundamentals of indigeneity as well as how to express my own indigenous nature. He came to my office one day and said very succinctly, "Hey little brother, Creator eh!" and walked away, leaving me shocked and confused. This was a profound gesture in two ways. One, that he thought I was worthy and competent to share with me this succinct piece of indigenous knowledge. And two, that he thought I was capable and responsible enough to comprehend its meaning. Through the reflexive and reflective process embedded in the indigegogical learning approach, I was able to fathom this profound thought and the shorthand it represented to present the sum of our world view.

The second gesture was when he came up to me while we were at a large gathering and said to me, "The before and the before and the before and the beyond and the beyond and the beyond, little brother." He repeated this at one of our culture camps for our graduate students. This profound thought is rooted in respect for our ancestors and in our need to be conscious that Creation extends far beyond earthly bounds.

For our social policy and social welfare programs to fulfill our hopes as outcomes of our societal efforts, we need to have a historical appreciation of our indigenous inheritance, as well as the vision to go beyond ourselves. This vision we extend to other people whom we work with and who are equally as indigenously capable as we are or even more so. We bring them (and ourselves) to these lofty understandings as societal outcomes rooted in the social policy we create and in the social welfare programs we exhibit. Their hopefulness makes more real our hopefulness and the hopefulness of society and Creation!

Belief—in our ability to be healthy parents, grandparents, families, and communities and together to help keep Creation strong.

I learned about belief from the lack of belief that indigenous people have in themselves. I had shared this experience and saw it as a consequence of all of the historical and structural ills that have been cast on us by Canadian society and its institutions. How could we believe in ourselves when all indications of our value as people were absent? The challenge I faced was, How do I help people who have profound inheritances of devaluation? I started with myself, and whatever I learned I shared among the people I worked with. The most important aspects of my understanding came from my work

Outcomes of Indigenous-Based Wholistic Healing Social Policy

in child welfare on reserve, where my efforts to establish *Indian Way* child welfare conflicted fundamentally with the purposes of child welfare in the mainstream settings I had known. Through *Indian Way* I wanted the Indian people I encountered to learn to believe in themselves and value their own abilities to "naturally" be nurturing, loving, and caring to their children. I wanted to help people learn skills of loving that they had not experienced in the public institutions that administered services to them or in the residential school settings to which they had been sent. It was hard work, but it succeeded, and I learned the value of the Indian world view and, after that, the indigenous world view. Social policies and the social welfare programs that flow from it can be loving expressions for the people who experience them and for the society that provides them.

Faith—in own abilities, in our relationships with other people, in the future, and in our place within a caring, loving, and supportive community. This reflects the kind of community that the Creator has taught us to have.

I learned indigenous knowledge that spoke of various dimensions of the world around us and that articulated aspects of the world which we can see and which we cannot see. An example of this is knowledge about the Creator, ceremonies, medicines, and community—knowledge that requires us

Figure 5.2 Expected Outcomes from an Indigenous-Based Wholistic Healing Approach to Social Policy Development

This diagram represents the relationships among the three outcomes and the social welfare programs emerging from social policy within the indigenous-based Wholistic Healing world view.

to have faith. My own life experiences began to be informed by these teachings, and I began to see outcomes in life that are affected by aspects of the world we cannot see. These outcomes resulted in hope and belief in what might be possible if I used these teachings in my work. In essence, they became part of my bundle of tools and skills. I saw the changes that could occur in me and in the lives of people and communities I worked with when faith was part of the context in which this work took place. When I focused on spirit and spirituality, I visited these aspects of life more frequently.

Essential Indigenous Teachings: (Re-presenting)

Existing social policies are informed by various teachings that emerge from the Western economic and political social order. These teachings, like the indigenous teachings I present here, manifest themselves in processes, institutions, functions, and programs that emerge from policy making. They establish how people who live in that society view the world, how they view community, and how they view other people.

In my own language, which is the repository of my own indigenous heritage, there is a single word for person: *mowsawin*. That word implies no gender, no race, no nationality, and no class distinction. That word also implies that each person has a spirit and that he or she is part of Creation and has value. It also implies that if you engage a *mowsawin,* that person deserves the best we have to give them. And when it comes to social welfare measures, that person will be supported on the basis of being a "valuable human." This indigenous meaning of *mowsawin* has long been demonstrated in Canadian history, whenever the original people of Canada encounter strangers, whom they welcome and treat as valued humans.

The following indigenous teachings underpin the indigenous world view about people and our relationship to Creation.

Teaching 1: The Creator exists and influences your life. The presence of the Creator and the knowledge that flows from the Creator have meaning in this world—both the world you see (physical and conscious) and the world you can't see (the unconscious, instinctive, intuitive, spiritual, universal).

Teaching 2: There is only one Creation, of which all things are a part. There is a single relationship among all elements of Creation, and the fundamental element of this relationship is respect. Respect for all things in the physical and non-physical world allows us to learn from all things in Creation and allows us to provide a place for all things in Creation and to seek the gift that all things carry.

Teaching 3: Creation provides all living things with what they need to sustain life. This teaching, along with appreciation for all things in Creation, is most clearly expressed in the wide variety of indigenous Creation stories. Indigenous languages contain the "spirit" of this respect for life. Creation stories provide insights into man's total reliance on all other segments of Creation.

Essential Indigenous Teachings: (Re-presenting)

Teaching 4: The purpose of life is to keep all other segments of Creation strong and healthy. This can be achieved by the relationships humans have and build with all other segments of Creation. Human life is a single wholistic entity that has four parts: mental (the mind), spiritual (the essential source of energy and connection to Creation), physical (the body and physical world), and emotional (feelings, intuitions, instincts, which are unlike those of any other animal in Creation).

This wholistic reality helps us to understand the knowledge that comes to us and to work at receiving it. Sometimes, the source of knowledge is physical and discernable; other times, it comes to us in non-physical ways. An example is when we engage in ceremony and acknowledge that we are opening ourselves to non-physical teachers.

Teaching 5: We are community people and we are responsible for the community so that it can be there for us when we need it. Our relationships with other people are directed at keeping community with people and keeping our relationships strong so that we can achieve the larger purpose of keeping Creation strong.

The nature and purpose of relationships is contained in this understanding of what relationships are for. We can easily see the fundamental impact of being respectful to people, to animals, to plants, to water and earth, and to our ancestors (the people who have gone before us), who carried wisdom based on their experiences.

Teaching 6: Medicines and ceremonies are given to us by the Creator in order for us to use them to keep strong both ourselves and others with whom we share Creation. We were given ceremonies so that we could build relationships and a community with those with whom we share ceremonies.

We have been given medicine and ceremonies so that we can communicate with our ancestors, who pass on to us the purpose of life and the wisdom of their life experience. With medicines and ceremonies we keep Creation strong and help heal illness in Creation. Illness is a wholistic reality, just as health is wholistic, and healing is the process of moving from illness to health.

Forgiveness is built on love and respect and is the ultimate expression of health, for it provides freedom from the burden of hate and resentment.

Teaching 7: There exists a light side and a dark side to Creation, but this does not imply good and bad; rather, it means that we learn from the simultaneous presence of these two sides. People often categorize their experiences as good or bad and then assess their own value as people based on the nature of their life or on how others might view their experiences. The things we learn from our experiences are more important than whether we are good or bad based on what has happened to us. This teaching helps us reframe the nature of people's lives and the value of what they experience in the context of their lives.

Linking the Teachings to the Social Policy-Making Process

Linking the Teachings to the Social Policy-Making Process

The social policies that emerge from these teachings, and their expected outcomes, were articulated earlier in this chapter and underpin the indigenous-based Wholistic Healing social policy process. The policy wonks who centre themselves in the usual world view and in the research and analyses required to bring their findings to life in programs and bureaucracies will arrive at very different policies than the ones we seek in this indigenous world view. The results will aspire to a different society than the one we have now—one that we as indigenous people know we need in order to have a strong, vibrant, and healthy Creation that sustains all living things. The notion of better or worse will not be applied to this social order—it will just "be."

The guiding principle behind indigenous-based Wholistic Healing social policy is that the concern for us shown by the Creator is the same kind of concern we need to express for humans and their society in the policies we develop. The intention of society in providing social welfare measures must be to sustain a Creation that is good for its citizens.

There is only one Creation. That teaching will serve as a powerful reminder as we develop indigenous-based Wholistic Healing social policy. The health of Creation is directly related to the health of those who reside within Creation. None of us can escape the duty of working to keep Creation viable and healthy. As we become preoccupied with acquiring wealth and possessions, we forget that the source of both is exploitation. A consequence of colonialism that we indigenous people live with every day is the history of exploitation and our (wholistic) "condition" of poverty. Illness, displacement, marginalization, and devaluation are indicative of the ultimate consequence for all humans, even the rich and powerful, in a Creation that cannot support human life. I think the animals that have a respectful non-exploitive relationship with Creation will survive and thrive in the midst of the human demise. This offers us hope that we can turn the tide if we take up our responsibilities.

The teaching that Creation provides all we need to sustain life is important to the development of indigenous-based Wholistic Healing social policy, for if we destroy the life-sustaining elements of Creation, we jeopardize our own lives. Creation provides wholistically the things we need in our lives, the knowledge, the spiritual awareness and processes, the emotional support, and the physical requirements of life. The preservation and nurturing of these need to be reflected in the social policy we create. And these teachings need to be lived out in the institutions, programs, and bureaucracies that flow from the policies.

The teaching that the purpose of our lives is to keep Creation strong is a call to action for all human beings to engage in living out this purpose. It is not in the hands and efforts of one group, or one gender or class or race of people, or one people of a certain spiritual belief and practice, to engage in this work. It is not natural for some groups in society to do this work so that all others can be sustained. It is the responsibility of all people all over this earth. Social policy can reflect that all of society has committed itself to this work and that all of society takes up this responsibility. Society can commit all of its political, economic, social, cultural, and traditional resources to this most important of all tasks for human life.

Linking the Teachings to the Social Policy-Making Process

The teaching that we are all one community and that our responsibility is to keep community strong and vibrant so that it can sustain its residents' lives reflects the common understanding about what community means in the lives of humans. We all long to be in a community that is supportive, loving, and nurturing and that feels like our home. Our community in an indigenous sense would provide us, our children, and our families with a wholistically loving and caring place, one where we belong without having to qualify for membership. Wholistic communities provide us with our mental, spiritual, emotional, and physical needs. Indigenous-based Wholistic Healing social policy would reflect the intention to support and sustain community.

The teaching that Creation provides us with medicines and ceremonies reflects that we have in our midst the ways to be healthy—that we do not have to manufacture medicines to address our wholistic needs. We have the knowledge, the spirit, the emotions and feelings, and the physical capacity to seek the medicines and to undertake the ceremonies that would result in our wellness and healing. Indigenous-based Wholistic Healing social policy would acknowledge the full range of medicines that exist in society and invest in discovering them, not for profit but for the well-being of all humans. There would be no competition among perceived valuable and marginal medicines, between those created by science and those that naturally occur and can be prepared by natural medicine carriers. Many indigenous medicine carriers have been devalued by science and scientists in favour of manufactured and synthetic medicines.

The teaching that there are two sides to reality—the light side and the dark side to Creation—challenges us to take lessons from the things that happen in our world. From this teaching we need to learn and address the consequences of both sides and to seek to reduce or eradicate the elements that underpin the events in our world that threaten Creation.

The notions of society that are presented in such ideas as social capital, social economy, and even the idea of civil society imply that society needs to understand the light- and dark-side consequences for humans of the economic, political, and social aspects of the present order. They also recognize the need for human relationships and the value of these in both economic and non-economic terms. We remind ourselves of our inherent human responsibility to one another and of our inherent consciousness of community. Often it occurs to me that these notions also remind us that we have forgotten how to care for one another and that we know we lose something when we marginalize such notions in our day-to-day consciousness.

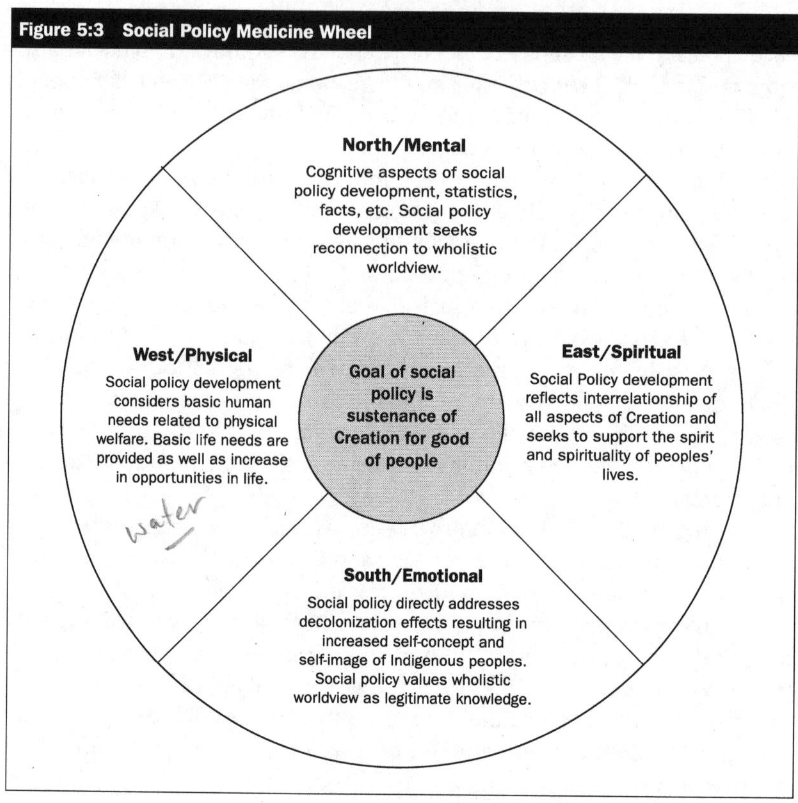

Figure 5:3 Social Policy Medicine Wheel

Social Policy Medicine Wheel

One of the most powerful indigenous teachings is that of the Medicine Wheel. The Medicine Wheel as adapted in the following diagram depicts an indigenous-based Wholistic Healing social policy process. The goal of this process is to meet the wholistic needs of all the world's people so that Creation is nurtured and sustained. The Medicine Wheel thus represents the four sides of Creation and the sustenance of the centre.

Conclusion

In this paper I have explored an indigenous-based Wholistic Healing social policy approach. This process values all people and is good for Creation, thus making possible the presence of an ongoing humanity on Earth.

The vision offered by the indigenous world view of valuing people and the unique nature of their worlds in social policy and in the associated social welfare programs, bureaucracies, and agencies is realizable. That this vision could be wholistic in nature is also possible. It would require society to be concerned for the humans that inhabit this world.

Questions for Reflection

Undoing the effects of colonialism will need a dramatically new approach rooted in a process that seeks a very different outcome for Aboriginal people by valuing their history and nature. This dramatic new approach would be guided by indigenous-based Wholistic Healing ideals. The very different outcome would be the valuing of indigenous people, but whatever is done using this new dramatic approach would be good for all human beings.

Note

1 An Indian, according to the Indian Act, is a person who pursuant to the Indian Act is registered or eligible to be registered as an Indian (Indian Act RCS 1985 Canada), resulting in the designation of these individuals as Status Indians.

References

Bird, J., Land, L., & Macadam, M. (2002). *Nation to nation: Aboriginal sovereignty and the future of Canada.* Toronto, ON: Irwin Publishing.

Freire, P. (1994). *Pedagogy of hope: Reliving the pedagogy of the oppressed.* New York, NY: Continuum Press.

LaRocque, E. (2010). *When the Other is me.* Winnipeg, MB: University of Manitoba Press.

Leonard, P.M. (1993). *Paulo Freire: A critical encounter.* London, UK: Routledge.

Additional Resources

Kenny, C. (2004). *A holistic framework for Aboriginal policy research.* Ottawa, ON: Status of Women Canada.

Royal Commission Report on Aboriginal Peoples. (1996). *Volume 2: Restructuring the relationship.* Retrieved from http://www.ainc-inac.gc.ca/ap/pubs/rpt/rpt-eng.asp

White, J., & Bruhn, J. (2010). Aboriginal policy research: Exploring urban landscapes, Volume VIII. Toronto, ON: Thompson Educational Publishing.

Questions for Reflection

1. When you reflect upon the notion of an indigenous Wholistic world view, does it make sense to you that you are also a person who is wholistic in nature; that you have intelligence, that you have a spirit, that you have emotions and feelings, and that you have a physical presence?

2. When you think of the function of social welfare in a civilized and a just society, does it make sense that the concerns of humans ought to be the focus of your social welfare policy? That this concern should be the foundation of social policy?

3. When you reflect on the impact of a history of injustice, oppression, and marginalization, on a given group of people, does it seem to you that social policy and programs hold the possibility of undoing the intergenerational effects of this history?

Racism in Canadian Social Policy

6

Delores V. Mullings

Canada is known as a safe country, one of the best places in the world to live, with a high standard of living, democratically elected governments, strong social programs, and a sense of pureness in character (Frideres & Gadacz, 2005; Lawrence, 2002). Canada was the first Western country to enact a multiculturalism policy (the Canadian Multiculturalism Act, 1985) and has an international reputation as a tolerant country that has strong human rights policies and that respects cultural differences (Frideres & Gadacz, 2005). A comparative analysis of Canada and the United States results in the U.S. receiving more criticism for what is perceived as discriminatory policies in the treatment of people who are marginalized (Mendes, 1995). In truth, Canada compares well to many other countries in the area of human rights policies and practices. But if we peel back the layers in Canada, we will quickly find historical and contemporary atrocities committed against various groups.

Canadians routinely deny and obscure slavery (Tulloch, 1975), the internment of Japanese Canadians in camps (Oikawa, 2002), the refusal to extend Aboriginal peoples the right to vote (Moss & Gardner-O'Tool, 1987), the invasion of places frequented by lesbians and gays (Canadian Lesbian and Gay Archives, 1981), the barring of Jewish and racialized people from Canada (Satzewich, 1991), and the sterilization of people with mental disabilities (Grekul, Krahn, & Odynak, 2004). Human rights violations and subhuman conditions in Canada are not the usual picture the nation presents to the world, so taking up the issue of racial discrimination in Canada is unsettling, to say the least.

This chapter discusses racism in Canadian social policy and calls into question the effectiveness of the Canadian Human Rights Commission and the Canadian Human Rights Tribunal in combatting employment discrimination of "visible minorities," who are defined under the Employment Equity Act as "persons, other than Aboriginal peoples, who are non-Caucasian in race or non-white in colour" (Employment Equity Act, [S.C. 1995, c. 44]). Various human rights policies and institutions are summarized and discussed, and an example of a resolved Canadian Human Rights Tribunal case is used to demonstrate how institutional racism is reproduced in the human rights process.

Canadian Human Rights Policies and Structures against Discrimination

Canadian Human Rights Policies and Structures against Discrimination

The Canadian Charter of Rights and Freedoms (the Charter) and the Canadian Human Rights Act (CHRA) are known as the pillars of human rights policies in Canada, while the Canadian Human Rights Commission (CHRC, the Commission) and the Canadian Human Rights Tribunal (CHRT) are the structures responsible for ensuring compliance with those policies. Canada has implemented policies and structures to combat racism, but are they effective? In spite of the good intentions behind our human rights policies, there is mounting evidence that these policies have not significantly reduced discrimination. If we have policies designed to reduce human rights violations, why do research, government statistics, and personal testimonies continue to show that discrimination remains in all areas of Canadian life?

Canadian Charter of Rights and Freedoms

The Canadian Charter of Rights and Freedoms was enacted in 1982, but the equality rights section of the Charter, Section 51(1), was not implemented until 1985. That section offers broad and sweeping rights under the constitution to Canadian citizens and residents so that "every individual is equal before and under the law and has the right to the equal protection and equal benefit of the law without discrimination and, in particular, without discrimination based on race, national or ethnic origin, colour, religion, sex, age or mental or physical disability." Under the Charter, the federal government acknowledges and promises certain rights, duties, and entitlements while agreeing not to interfere with individuals' self-expression. Similarly, individuals have the right to "claim non-interference from the government" (Charter, 1985). The rights and entitlements correspond with the constitution and are governed by the legal system. Therefore, if the government violates an individual's rights, the courts have the legal mandate to force the government to uphold its duties under the Charter. These include freedom of association; the right to vote, move to, and live anywhere in Canada; freedom from arbitrary imprisonment; equal protection under the law; and access to government services in both English and French language (Charter, 1985).

The aftermath of the G20 Summit held in Toronto in June 2010 provides an example of how the Charter works. During the summit, hundreds of Canadian citizens and residents were arrested, harassed, and detained while peacefully protesting (Makela, 2010; Puscas, 2010). Various groups, agencies, and individuals have called for a public inquiry; charges have been filed against the Toronto Police Services Board (the arm of government responsible for enforcing the law) for violating individuals' civil rights to peaceful assembly and for arbitrary imprisonment (CBC News, 2011). Charter rights may be limited under certain conditions such as national security, and under those circumstances residents and citizens can be detained or imprisoned without full disclosure. The Anti-Terrorism Act (2001), which authorizes law enforcement officials to arrest and detain persons deemed a security risk, is an example of such a limitation (Canada, 2008). The Charter is the supreme law of Canada and takes precedence over all other laws, policies, and legislations.

Canadian Human Rights Policies and Structures against Discrimination

Canadian Human Rights Act

The Canadian Human Rights Act (CHRA) is federal anti-discrimination legislation intended to ensure equality of opportunity for all Canadians so that they may fully participate in Canada "as members of society, without being hindered in or prevented from doing so by discriminatory practices based on race, national or ethnic origin, colour, religion, age, sex, sexual orientation, marital status, family status, disability or conviction for an offence for which a pardon has been granted" (Canadian Human Rights Act, 1985, s.2). Since its proclamation in 1977, the act has gone through several changes. Most recently, in 2008, Section 67 of the act was repealed by Bill C-21, which amended it to extend to First Nations people the right to bring complaints against the federal government in cases where the Indian Act pertains. The CHRA remains a foundation of Canada's human rights legislation and is administered by the Canadian Human Rights Commission. Bakan and Kobayashi (2000) argue that the CHRA is implemented passively; it is structured in a way that forces individuals to bring their complaints to the appropriate body to seek redress and also, until recently, has not considered strategies to address institutional discrimination. Nonetheless, the CHRA is an important piece of legislation that works to reduce discrimination.

Employment Equity Act

The Employment Equity Act (EEA) was a response to the *Report of the Commission on Equality in Employment* (Abella Report, 1984) tabled by Judge Rosalie Abella. That report documented persistent discrimination in employment for some groups of Canadians. It recommended strong government-mandated programs and policies to reduce employment discrimination for four designated groups: Aboriginal people, people with disabilities, "visible minorities," and women in the federal government, federal agencies, and federally regulated agencies. This fourth category includes the Canadian Forces, the RCMP, the Treasury Board, the Public Service Commission, airlines, and banks (Employment Equity Act [S.C. 1995, c. 44]). The EEA, enacted in 1986, promised to reduce systemic employment discrimination and to create equity in the workplace for designated groups. Specifically, the EEA stated that "no person shall be denied employment opportunities or benefits for reasons unrelated to ability and, in the fulfillment of that goal, to correct the conditions of disadvantage in employment" (Employment

Equity Act [S.C. 1995, c. 44]) experienced by members of the four designated groups. The EEA also recognized that achieving equity means providing accommodation and attending to difference, to minimize discrimination (Employment Equity Act [S.C.1995, c. 44]).

Ten years after the Abella Report and the enactment of the EEA, the evidence demonstrated that members of the four designated groups still experienced employment discrimination (Agócs, 2002). In 1995, the policy was reviewed; in 1996, Employment Equity Programs (EEPS) were introduced; and in 2003, guidelines were provided to help employers recruit, select, train, and promote members of the designated groups to better reflect Canadian society (Auditor General, 1998). Although agencies are mandated to submit annual reports documenting their compliance with the EEA and EEP, there is no accountability mechanism; many employers do not submit reports, and there is no consequence for failure to submit reports (Agócs & Burr, 1996). The system and its processes remain dysfunctional, and members of the designated groups continue to pay the price of employment discrimination. The EEA gives the CHRC powers to conduct reviews of agencies in order to document and monitor their compliance, but this too has been a failure (Agócs, 2004; Bakan & Kobayashi, 2000). "Visible minorities" and others in the designated groups continue to experience employment discrimination in the federal government and in the larger Canadian society. When their rights are violated and they seek redress from the CHRC, they encounter racist human rights processes.

Structures Charged with Administering Human Rights Policies

Canadian Human Rights Commission

The CHRC (instituted in 1977) administers the CHRA and is responsible for ensuring compliance with the EEA. The Commission, therefore, is responsible for resolving complaints based on discrimination in all federal jurisdictional matters. Individuals who have experienced discrimination may file a complaint with the Commission under Section 7 or 14 of the CHRA. The complaint filtration process takes a specific form:

1. At the *preliminary assessment* stage, the Commission identifies the best way to resolve the situation without invoking a formal process; discusses with the parties the pertinent issue raised; and explains the next steps and the potential process the complaint could take. At this point the Commission determines whether the complaint falls under its jurisdiction (e.g., complaint based on race). If the complaint does not fall within its jurisdiction, it is referred elsewhere. If the complaint merits moving forward, it may be referred to the Commission.

Structures Charged with Administering Human Rights Policies

2. *Alternative dispute resolution,* which involves mediation either before or after the complaint is formally filed, may result in conciliation—that is, resolution of the dispute without resorting to a formal procedure.
3. When a full *investigation* of the complaint is conducted, a settlement may be approved, the complaint may be dismissed, or a referral may be made to the Tribunal if it is understood to be a particularly complex case or new grounds for discrimination.
4. The final step is *conciliation* and *resolution,* where the parties agree on a settlement (CHRC, 2001, p. 6).

In exceptional cases, complaints are referred to the Canadian Human Rights Tribunal. The ineffectuality of the CHRA is demonstrated in the CHRC process: the individual is required to bring his/her own complaint forward and is responsible for providing evidence similar to what is required in a court of law to substantiate the case. Furthermore, complainants have no authority in the process and are bound by the Commission's decisions. The Commission does have provisions allowing it to initiate a complaint when institutional discrimination has occurred, but it rarely employs these because it lacks the resources (Hucker, 1997), large-scale investigations are expensive, and it is expected that cases will be processed in short time frames.

Canadian Human Rights Tribunal

The Tribunal was instituted in 1977. In 1996, Parliament expanded its role to include responsibility for adjudicating cases filed under the EEA. With the agreement of both the complainant and the respondent, the CHRC refers cases to the Tribunal that are complex and legally complicated, often dealing with emerging human rights concerns (CHRT, 2002). The Tribunal is similar to a court of law, but some of the judicial pomp and pageantry are suspended in the adjudication process, which gives the appearance of less formality. The Tribunal maintains a stance of impartiality, and the evidentiary requirements are somewhat less stringent than for a trial. Either a panel of three or a single adjudicator hears the case and makes a decision based on the following guidelines:

A complaint is customarily brought under Section 7 or Section 14 of the Canadian Human Rights Act, which makes it a discriminatory practice to refuse to continue to employ an individual, or to differentiate adversely in relation to an employee in the course of their employment on a prohibited ground of discrimination. In cases based on the prohibited grounds of discrimination as mentioned earlier, similar to a court of law, "the burden of proof" is on the complainant who has to establish a "prima facie case of discrimination," following which the respondent has to "provide a reasonable explanation" for the alleged behaviour (*Ontario Human Rights Commission v. Etobicoke,* [1982] 1 S.C.R 202 at 208, as cited by CHRT, *Chander and Joshi v. Department of National Health and Welfare,* [1995] pp. 16–18).

Examination of Institutional Racism in Canada

Establishing a prima facie case is one of the major differences between a court proceeding and the Tribunal adjudication process. The respondent also needs to provide a reasonable explanation for why the decision alleged to be discriminatory was made. And herein is a significant flaw in the process: discrimination may occur, but if there is an explanation that the adjudicator finds reasonable, the Tribunal may accept it and rule against the complainant. To mitigate this limitation, the Tribunal uses the concept of "subtle scent of discrimination" in complaint cases (*Chopra v. Dept. of National Health and Welfare* [2001], 40 C.H.R.R. D/396 [CHRT]) to determine whether discrimination has occurred in a subtle way. Unfortunately, many adjudicators are unable to recognize the more subtle aspects of racial discrimination, in part because they tend to be white and from mainstream Canadian cultural backgrounds.

Examination of Institutional Racism in Canada

This discussion takes a one-dimensional approach in choosing to discuss only racism while disregarding intersecting social locations such as gender, ability, and sexual orientation. Charges associated with racism are generally filed using the triad of anti-discriminatory grounds of race, colour, and national or ethnic origin. I use the term "visible minority" simply to mimic the language of the government and policies, but where possible I use the term "racialized" to make visible the inherent marginalization and lived experiences of those who are identified by physical features and characteristics. Similar to the policies, this chapter broadly discusses "visible minorities" as one category without acknowledging that racialized people have different experiences based on their histories of colonization and imperialism, which means that different groups are stereotyped and racialized differently. Regardless of their histories, all groups of racialized people in Canada have encountered racism through a phenomenon that Essed (1991) terms "everyday racism." A common form of everyday racism is avoiding contact with racialized people. Racism is widespread and is located in all aspects of human life, including social institutions, judicial and educational institutions, and individual relationships and interactions.

Racism continues to flourish because of personal biases and ignorance, but most significantly because of institutional policies, programs, and practices. Initially, scientific rationality was used to justify racism; that is, it was suggested that Aboriginal and racialized peoples were inherently inferior to non-racialized people (Winant, 2000). The term "race" is ambiguous and objectionable in that it segregates groups based on physical features such as skin colour, facial structure, and hair texture, which results in fixed and linear racial categorizations such as "red," "yellow," "black," and "white" (Dei, Karumanchery, & Karumanchery-Luik, 2004; Lopez, 1995). There is no scientific merit in these categorizations, of course, but the results have

Examination of Institutional Racism in Canada

allowed Western society to create a hierarchy—with "white" at the top—to distinguish those termed "civilized" from those labelled "barbaric" (Banton, 1977; Dei, 1996; Omi & Winant, 1993). This historical hierarchy has privileged "white" cultures to the extent that Western social structures, norms, policies, literature, medicine, education, and so forth are based on the principles and perspectives of "whites." More recently, social incongruence and difference have been used as a justification for categorizing different groups of racialized people; that is, racialized people are seen as socially different from non-racialized people (Thobani, 2007). The Canadian Race Relations Foundation (1992) defines racism as "a set of ideologies and beliefs that implies, justifies, and asserts the superiority of one social group over another on the basis of physical and cultural characteristics" (1992, p. 7). In this context, institutional racial discrimination results when these beliefs and ideologies are embedded in our social structure and benefit some while disadvantaging Aboriginal and racialized people (Fleras & Elliot, 2007). This process of systemic or institutional discrimination allows a climate of racial discrimination to flourish in Canada.

In spite of various policies against discrimination, institutional racism is inherent in Canadian society and is especially prevalent in the labour market, educational institutions, law enforcement, and the criminal justice system. For example, education plays a significant role in an individual's ability to find employment that is enjoyable and financially satisfying. On average, racialized people, including those born outside Canada, have higher levels of education than non-racialized ones (Canadian Race Relations Foundation, 2000; Galabuzi, 2006). However, even with university education, racialized groups are persistently unemployed or underemployed in low-paying labour sectors; they are also less likely than non-racialized people to hold managerial and professional positions and are therefore underrepresented in higher income brackets (Canadian Race Relations Foundation, 2000; Galabuzi, 2006; Pendakur & Pendakur, 1998; Pendakur, Mata, Lee, & Dole, 2000). When they are employed in management, executive, or professional positions, they face particular barriers in career advancement, which include "perceived unfair career advancement processes, lack of access to informal networks, and stereotyping in the workplace" (Giscombe, 2008, p. 2); lack of role models; and the need to work harder and be judged by higher standards and expectations than non-racialized colleagues (De Zwart, 2005). Other stereotypes suggest that some groups are lazy, make incompetent managers, are poor communicators, have attitude problems, and are oversensitive (Das Gupta, 1996). Some employers identify a lack of "fit" with their corporate environment; and racialized women feel the need to adjust their behaviour, communication style, and character to feel more accepted (Giscombe, 2008). All groups generally report feeling that close identification with their racial group was a barrier to becoming part of workplace social networks. Racialized people born outside Canada have the added burden of a non-Canadian accent, discredited professional skills, and unrecognized educational attainment, which further marginalizes and ghettoizes them (Li, 2001; Reitz, 2001). Given the various policies and structures to mitigate against racism, how do we account for the level of racial discrimination evident in Canadian society? I will be exploring this question with a discussion of racism in human rights processes.

Racist and Discriminatory Human Rights Process

Racialized people are disadvantaged in the redress-seeking process at the Commission and the Tribunal. These processes require concentrated and exhaustive time and can be extremely costly. As well, the backlog at the Commission, although much smaller since 2002, when a streamlined process was implemented, is still a problem. The Commission has full jurisdiction over the cases and is the only body that decides how cases are resolved. At both the Commission and the Tribunal, many cases are dismissed on procedural matters such as lack of sufficient evidence. Some complainants are not aware of the evidentiary requirements to substantiate their cases and so do not maintain a record of their experiences. Sometimes they have no witnesses to substantiate their claims. In addition, Commission representatives have multiple roles in that they must provide guidance when investigating, mediating, promoting human rights, and providing education. Commission representatives are responsible for Employment Equity audits of employers, for monitoring employers who have been audited, and for working with employers to prevent discrimination. Many complaints cases originate from federal agencies, which places the Commission in a conflict; it must provide the services mentioned and still deal with complaint cases coming from government agencies and possible ones that have been audited or are being monitored for compliance with the EEA. More significantly, many of the representatives, commissioners, and adjudicators are not Aboriginal or racialized people and are not politically conscious or aware of how pervasive racism is or how to identify and address it in its more subtle forms. The statistics the Commission produces with respect to the filtering of cases demonstrate this clearly.

A CHRC study published in 1992 found evidence of institutional racial discrimination at both the federal level and the provincial level. At the federal level, 36 percent of cases based on race were dismissed, compared to 20 percent of all other complaints. At the provincial level, Nova Scotia, for example, dismissed 17.2 percent of race-based complaints and only 4.5 percent of other complaints (Canadian Human Rights Commission, 1992, cited by Sangha & Tang, 2003). In 1999 the Commission began to separate complaint cases by ethnicity, race, and colour. In 1998–99, 334 complaints cases were filed based on race, colour, and national or ethnic origin. Only 27.5 percent (92) of these cases were resolved: through early resolution (9),

Racist and Discriminatory Human Rights Process

settlement during investigation or conciliation (17), an alternative redress mechanism (65), or referral to the Tribunal (1). The remaining 72 percent (242) were not dealt with because they were determined to be filed too late or without purpose (5); the complaint was dismissed for lack of evidence (56); the complainants withdrew or abandoned the complaint or the claim was made outside the jurisdiction of the commission and did not warrant a referral to the Tribunal (19); or the complaint was discontinued because the complainant did not wish to pursue the complaint or no link could be established between the allegations and a prohibited ground (162). The startling figure of more than 70 percent of race-based cases going unresolved means that a large majority of individuals who found the courage to file a complaint of discrimination on this ground were turned away without redress.

Mohammed (2000) conducted a study on behalf of the British Columbia Human Rights Commission in which she reviewed 71 complaints cases based on race (37) and sexual harassment (34). The findings revealed a significant difference in the successful resolution and settlement of the cases: 53 percent of sexual harassment complaint cases were successfully resolved and 56 percent were settled. In contrast, only 3 percent of race-based cases were successfully resolved and 3 percent were settled. In another study, 16 race-based employment-related complaints cases filed by individuals and resolved between 1995 and 2005 at the CHRT were analyzed (Mullings, 2009). Although adjudicators acknowledged racism and the use of racially derogatory terms to describe complainants in their place of employment (Baptiste, [2005]; Brooks, [2005]; Hill, [2003]), they still fully dismissed 10 of the 16 complaint cases. This trend continues in other areas where institutional racism is practised. Another trend is the CHRC's referring large numbers of complaints to the Tribunal, as demonstrated in 2003, 2005, and 2010 with 195, 119, and 191 referrals respectively. Perhaps this indicates the complexities of complaint cases that require more expertise than is available at the Commission.

Aside from the increase in referrals to the Tribunal and dispute resolution, nothing has changed with respect to handling of cases. The CHRC reported the following statistics for 2010: received 1,435 potential complaints, accepted 853 complaints, referred to alternative redress 166 complaints, approved 177 settlements, dismissed 139 complaints, and referred 191 complaints to the CHRT (CHRC 2010). The additional 180 cases were not accounted for in the Commission's report. The largest number of potential cases (582) were not heard and 139 were dismissed, so at least 721 complainants did not receive resolution after contacting the CHRC.

The government prides itself on offering Canadians a place to seek justice when their human rights have been violated. As discussed earlier, the CHRT is one of the institutions charged with ensuring that justice is served when a complaint is brought to the quasi-judicial court. A fundamental flaw with this system is the belief that racism is abnormal in Canadian society.

Racist and Discriminatory Human Rights Process

A further barrier to receiving a fair hearing is that when racialized people bring their concerns to these institutions seeking redress, they are asked to rely on and trust non-racialized, mostly white male policy makers who do not understand the complexities of racism. The Tribunal adjudicators and chairs are almost exclusively drawn from the legal system, with the majority being judges and lawyers; this means that the perspective from which they adjudicate the cases is based on their training and education as lawyers and judges. Furthermore, members can serve for a very long time at the Tribunal in various capacities, often moving from adjudicator to vice-chair and chair. The chair of the Tribunal is responsible for the overall administration of the agency, hears cases, assigns members, designates chairs for proceedings, and determines the number of adjudicators—either one or three—to hear each case. The vice-chair has planning and administrative responsibilities and acts on behalf of the chair in his or her absence. Two adjudicators, both non-racialized, served a combined thirty-three years at the Tribunal in various roles, and both made controversial rulings on race-based cases up to the final year they served at the Tribunal. Generally, having extensive job experience is a plus. However, in the case of the Tribunal adjudicators, it is a minus because the same individuals continue to view evidence in race-based complaint cases the same way year after year, in spite the Tribunal's acknowledgment of systemic racism and their own acknowledgment of individual instances of racism in some cases. These individuals are stakeholders in the criminal justice system, a system that continues to document disproportionate racial profiling, overrepresentation of Aboriginal and racialized Canadians in the prison system, and criminalization of racialized people (Ontario Human Rights Commission, 1995, 2003; Royal Commission on Systemic Racism in the Ontario Criminal Justice System 1992–1995, 1995). I understand that the cornerstones of our justice system are objectivity and neutrality and that both are needed. However, the adjudicators, who are mostly white and male, do not appear to understand the pervasiveness of everyday racism, how it is manifested, and how it affects racialized people. They are therefore unable to fully appreciate the complexities of race-based complaint cases.

Adjudicators have scapegoated and stereotyped racialized complainants by accusing them of being oversensitive, difficult, bitter, not team players, and unlikable (Canadian Human Rights Tribunal: *Batiste v. Correctional Service of Canada*, 2005a; *Brooks v. Department of Ocean and Fisheries*, 2005b; *Chander and Joshi v. Department of National Health and Welfare*, 1995). Eyewitnesses are needed to substantiate complainants' cases, and where there are no witnesses, the adjudicators often support the respondents. An example of this dynamic occurred when Keith Norton wrote a dissenting opinion in *Chander and Joshi*, in which he disagreed with the ruling of the other two adjudicators, who had rendered a decision in favour of the complainant.

Challenging Institutional Racism

Norton opined: "A finding would have been simpler if there had been any independent corroboration of the one piece of evidence suggesting an overt indication of such discrimination—namely, the statement attributed to Dr. Gadd allegedly reported by Dr. Kapitany to Dr. Joshi that 'those two browns' won't be selected" (1995, p. 24).

More glaring is the way that adjudicators have interpreted experiences of racism. In *Batiste,* chairperson Mactavish heard testimony that co-workers and supervisors had used racial epithets and racially derogatory names to address and describe the complainant in the workplace but suggested that the issues raised in the complaint had "absolutely nothing to do with the colour of her skin." And in *Hill v. Air Canada* (Canadian Human Rights Tribunal, 2003), adjudicator Groarke suggested that Mr. Hill had issues with "respecting authority" and that these had caused most of his problems in the workplace. In fact, Mr. Hill felt that he and other racialized employees had been marginalized in the workplace by being assigned to work in areas that provided little opportunity for skills development, and that they had been assigned menial tasks and the dirtiest and most difficult jobs in the engine shop. These observations parallel the themes that Mullings (2009) identified, which include *constructing a guilty complainant, normalizing racism,* and *accepting negative descriptions and categorization of complainants.* To further demonstrate the systemic nature of racial discrimination in the adjudication process, I will discuss a specific case.

Challenging Institutional Racism

Dr. Chopra filed a complaint with the CHRC in 1992, and it was referred to the Tribunal. The CHRC identified differential treatment based on his race, colour, and national or ethnic origin. He had worked for Health Canada for more than thirty years and had been denied promotion. The Tribunal dismissed his complaint, so he applied to the Federal Court of Canada under Section 18.1 of the Federal Court Act. The Federal Court set aside the Tribunal's decision, and this gave the Commission and Dr. Chopra the opportunity to introduce evidence of systemic discrimination in the department, which the Tribunal adjudicators had previously disallowed. The case was subsequently reopened and heard at the Tribunal. In 2001, Tribunal adjudicator Hadjis ruled in favour of the complainant, agreeing that he had suffered racial discrimination. In spite of this finding, he did not support the full compensation requested by Dr. Chopra. His arguments to justify the only partial remedy included an assessment that Dr. Chopra had not tried hard enough to excel, had not applied for other jobs as an avenue to promotion, had not tried hard enough to get along with colleagues, and had a poor attitude at work.

In 1997 the Tribunal officially recognized the pervasiveness of systemic racial discrimination in the federal public service. This recognition came after the National Capital Alliance of Race Relations initiated a complaint against the federal public service and other federal agencies, including Health Canada, the Public Service Commission, and the Treasury Board. The Tribunal found that the federal government and its agencies had discriminatory hiring, promotion, recruiting, and selection practices toward "visible minorities." These practices had resulted in underrepresentation of "visible minorities" in management; for example, of the 119 managers in Health Canada in 1992, only one was a "visible minority." The Tribunal also found that the career progress of "visible minorities" was blocked at the lower end of the entry process, that they were unlikely to serve on selection boards, and that senior management saw them as "culturally different within HC [Health Canada] and ... not considered suitable for management and [therefore] they were not offered information on training opportunities" (2001, p. 29). The Tribunal recommended a program to increase the recruitment, selection, and retaining of racialized persons in managerial positions in the Federal Public Service. Some of the recommendations were adopted in a federal government action plan (Treasury Board of Canada Secretariat, 2000) by the *Task force on the participation of visible minorities in the federal public service.*

However, in 2006, Maria Barrados, the president of the Public Service Commission of Canada (PSC), reported a persistent gap in the representation of "visible minorities" in the public service and voiced concerns that "general recruitment is not keeping up with the growing proportion of 'visible minorities' in the population." She said she was "concerned with the lack of progress in appointing 'visible minorities' into the executive group" (Barrados, 2006, para. 10). She further noted that in 2004, eighteen departments had 280 potential vacancies of which eight were targeted for "visible minorities"; yet only six of the 254 appointments that year were "visible minorities." While there has been some progress in the public service and an attempt to change the "chilly climate" for racialized people, the 2010 public service annual report documents the continued underrepresentation of "visible minorities" in the federal government and federally regulated agencies (Public Service Commission, 2009–2010). It does, however, show that in 2008–9 and 2009–10 there was an increase in the number and proportion of "visible minorities" in external appointments. This means that racialized people from the general public or those who are employed in government organizations are appointed a public service position under the Public Service Employment Act. However, the gap in attaining managerial positions remains, and the proportion of racialized people in such positions in the public service is below their workforce availability.

System Failure

The previous sections described policy measures that the Canadian government has implemented to deal with discrimination in general and with racial discrimination in employment in particular. Their implementation, however, has not been effective in addressing institutional racism, which the data show is subtly embedded in the social structures of Canadian society and in the operations of the Human Rights Commission and the Human Rights Tribunal. Critics suggest that human rights programs and policies are implemented passively, without political commitment and without an understanding of institutional racism (Bakan & Kobayashi, 2000). Furthermore, the policies and the people charged with implementing them tend to adopt a liberal, colour-blind attitude (Aylward, 1999; Freeman, 1995). The failure of these policies to achieve their intended outcomes signals the need for a change from the stand that impartiality is possible to one that acknowledges the role that social location plays in how we understand social processes. Policies, programs, and procedures intended to create equity for racialized people must adopt a perspective that focuses on race and racism (Aylward, 1999; Delgado & Stefancic, 2007; Mendes, 1995; Razack, 1998).

Mullings (2009) found that white, male adjudicators and white females to a lesser extent used *power-legitimizing practices* that tended to produce rulings that supported respondents rather than complainants. These included *constructing a guilty complainant, normalizing racism,* and *accepting negative descriptions and categorization of complainants.* She also found the use of case law to determine the outcome of complaint cases to be problematic. If an adjudicator uses past cases that are similar to current cases to make a ruling, changes in the ethnoracial makeup of Canadian society will not be considered; new understandings of social phenomena will not be drawn on in reaching a decision; and new social policy goals will not be realized. Case law, after all, had been used to support the Tribunal's initial decision to dismiss Dr. Chopra's case. Alyward (1999) notes that race-based litigation in Canada is limited partly by possible ignorance or fear among non-racialized lawyers, who either do not understand how to legally deconstruct such cases, or who believe in the myth of objectivity, or who fear that such arguments may disadvantage their clients "because of the courts' unacceptance or hostility towards these arguments" (1999, p. 83). It is clear that other means of adjudicating raced-based complaint cases are needed.

Recent Changes

The Tribunal has undergone some changes in the hope of improving the complaint process and providing more support to complainants who are disadvantaged both in the process and through life circumstances that may affect their ability to pay for legal services. A review of the Tribunal's website offers insight into some of its recent changes. Shirish P. Chotalia was

Recent Changes

appointed the new chair of the Tribunal in November 2009 after serving as a commissioner with the Alberta Human Rights Commission and an adjudicator with the CHRT. Ms. Chotalia is an academic and lawyer who has taught, published, and litigated in the areas of human rights, immigration, and employment.

In 2009, the Tribunal enhanced the mediation process with emphasis on evaluative mediation and case assessment and have concluded that the changes have reduced case backlogs and resulted in 70 percent settlement before trial of those who chose this process. Ms. Chotalia is emphasizing evaluative mediation, which is a process modelled after settlement conferences, during which judges help the parties identify weaknesses in their cases and offer an opinion on what a judge or jury may say (Riskin, 1994). More recently, prehearing case management has been introduced, which aims to offer the parties an opportunity to discuss aspects of their cases and is particularly useful to complainants who do not have legal representation or are disadvantaged.

On a more practical level, the Tribunal has committed its operations to transparency. This is demonstrated by easily accessible documentation, including biographical information, roles, and status of all Tribunal members. Furthermore, there was a stakeholder consultation in January 2011 during which individuals, groups, and community organizations were given the opportunity to voice concerns about the Tribunal. The chairperson, in her report, promises to "explore other innovative ways to provide an effective and efficient process, one that gives parties timely access to justice and brings Canada closer to the truly diverse, equal, and fair society our citizens deserve" (CHRT, 2009) and to consult with stakeholders on future changes. Indeed, the changes identified are positive, and this statement seems to suggest that Canadian citizens have yet to truly experience equity and fairness.

These changes provide hope, but we must be cautiously optimistic about the actual differences that may result when complainants bring their cases to the Tribunal. It is too early to assess the impact of these changes for racialized Canadians, and we must remember that the Tribunal members remain similarly drawn from the legal profession, that the majority are still non-racialized people, and that after a case is resolved, complainants who are financially disadvantaged still have no recourse but to accept the Tribunal's judgment because they cannot afford the high cost of litigation through the federal court system up to the Supreme Court. In addition, mediation seems to be a preferred process of the Tribunal to resolve cases. I have documented that adjudicators do not understand the complexities of racism and how to approach the various levels of discrimination that are presented to them in such cases. Therefore, the mediation process is not necessarily barrier free or non-discriminatory, so resolving cases mostly though mediation does not mean that issues of racism have been acknowledged or sufficiently addressed. Evaluative mediation is concerned with legal fairness rather than with the needs and interests of those who believe they have experienced discrimination, and the process is attorney driven (Riskin, 1994). Therefore, the emphasis on evaluative mediation may not serve the best interests of complainants. Further research is necessary to review the resolved cases both through mediation and trial to determine what, if any, changes have actually taken place.

Conclusion

This paper has focused exclusively on racial discrimination in employment, particularly in the federal public service. Where does social work fit into this issue? Well, social workers constantly encounter racialized people who are affected by racial discrimination. These encounters include individuals, their families, and their children as consumer survivors; patients in hospitals and long-term care institutions; and caregivers and receivers in home care programs; as well as individuals working in school offices, child welfare agencies, churches, community centres, prisons, and classrooms. The trauma of racial discrimination cannot be minimized; everyone closely involved with survivors of this violence is affected. The OHRC (2003) has documented the effects of racial profiling. James and colleagues (2010) have documented the health and social consequences of racial discrimination for African Canadians; these include mental stress, psychological trauma, anxiety, sense of alienation, feelings of dehumanization, worry and concern for their children, and loss of self-esteem. The long-term impact of racial discrimination cannot be denied; social workers must be cognizant of these experiences and work within their mandate to provide service using a critical race approach.

References

Abella, R. (1984). *Equality in employment: The report of the commission on equality in employment.* Ottawa, ON: Supply and Services Canada.

Agócs, C. (2002). Canada's employment equity legislation and policy, 1987–2000: The gap between policy and practice. *International Journal of Manpower, 23*(3), 256–276. doi:10.1108/01437720210432220

Agócs, C. (2004). Surfacing racism in the workplace: Qualitative and quantitative evidence of systemic discrimination. *Canadian Diversity / Diversite Canadienne, 3*(3), 25–28.

Agócs, C., & Burr, C. (1996). Employment equity, affirmative action, and managing diversity: Assessing the differences. *International Journal of Manpower, 17*(4/5), 30–45. doi: 10.1108/01437729610127668

Anti-Terrorism Act. (S.C. 2001, c.41). Retrieved from http://laws.justice.gc.ca/en/showtdm/cs/A-11.7

Auditor General of Canada. (1998). *Report on the Canadian Human Rights Commission.* Ottawa, ON: Minister of Public Works and Government Services.

Aylward, C. (1999). *Canadian critical race theory.* Halifax, NS: Fernwood Publishing.

References

Bakan, A., & Kobayashi, A. (2000). *Employment equity policy in Canada: An interprovincial comparison*. Ottawa, ON: Status of Women Canada.

Banton, M. (1977). *The idea of race*. Boulder, CO: Westview Press.

Barrados, M. (2006). Conference on visible minorities in the federal public service (Atlantic Region). Speaking notes. Public Service Alliance. Retrieved from http://www.psc-cfp.gc.ca/spch-disc/2006/2006-02-20-eng.htm

Canada. (2008). Keeping Canada safe. Ottawa, ON: Public Safety Canada. Retrieved from http://www.securitepublique.gc.ca/prg/ns/le/cle-en.asp

Canadian Lesbian and Gay Archives. (1981). *Victories and defeats: A gay and lesbian chronology—1964–1982*. Retrieved from http://www.clga.ca/Material/Records/docs/flitchro/81.htm

Canadian Human Rights Act (R.S.C., 1985, c. H-6). Retrieved from http://laws.justice.gc.ca/en/H-6/index.html.

Canadian Human Rights Commission. (1999). *Annual report*. Ottawa, ON: Public Works and Government Services Canada.

Canadian Human Rights Commission. (2001). Annual Report 2002. Ottawa, ON: Minister of Public Works and Government Services. Retrieved from http://www.chrc-ccdp.ca/publications/reports_archive_rapports-en.asp

Canadian Human Rights Commission. (2010). Annual report. Ottawa, ON: Public Works and Government Services Canada. Retrieved from http://www.chrc-ccdp.gc.ca

Canadian Human Rights Tribunal. (1995). *Chander & Joshi v. Department of National Health and Welfare*. Retrieved from http://www.chrt-tcdp.gc.ca

Canadian Human Rights Tribunal. (2001). *Chopra v. Dept. of National Health and Welfare*. Retrieved from http://www.chrt-tcdp.gc.ca

Canadian Human Rights Tribunal. (2002). Jurisdiction. Retrieved from http://www.chrt-tcdp.gc.ca/index_e.asp

Canadian Human Rights Tribunal. (2003). *Hill v. Air Canada*. Retrieved from http://www.chrt-tcdp.gc.ca

Canadian Human Rights Tribunal. (2005a). *Batiste v. Correctional Service of Canada*. Retrieved from http://www.chrt-tcdp.gc.ca

Canadian Human Rights Tribunal. (2005b). *Brooks v. Department of Ocean and Fisheries*. Retrieved from http://www.chrt-tcdp.gc.ca

Canadian Human Rights Tribunal. (2009). Annual Report. Retrieved from http://chrt-tcdp.gc.ca/NS/pdf/annual09-e.pdf

Canadian Race Relations Foundation. (1992). Acknowledging racism. Retrieved from http://www.crr.ca

Canadian Race Relations Foundation. (2000). *Unequal access: A Canadian profile of racial differences in education, employment, and income*. Ottawa, ON: Canadian Council on Social Development.

CBC News. (2011). G20 lawyer wants charges filed against police. Retrieved from http://www.cbc.ca/news/canada/toronto/story/2011/02/11/g20-lawyer-police628.html

Das Gupta, T. (1996). *Racism and paid work*. Toronto, ON: Garamond Press.

Dei, G.J.S. (1996). *Anti-racism education: Theory and practice*. Halifax, NS: Fernwood Publishing.

Dei, G.S., Karumanchery, L., & Karumanchery-Luik, N. (2004). *White power, white privilege. Playing the race card*. New York, NY: Peter Lang Publishing.

Delgado, R., & Stefancic, J. (2007). Introduction. In R. Delgado & J. Stefancic (Eds.), *Critical race theory: An introduction* (pp. 1–6). New York, NY: NYU Press.

De Zwart, F. (2005). The dilemma of recognition: Administrative categories and cultural diversity. *Theory and Society, 34*(2), 137–169. doi:10.1007/s11186-005-6234-3

Employment Equity Act (S.C. 1995, c. 44). Retrieved from http://laws-lois.justice.gc.ca/eng/acts/E-5.401/page-1.html#h-2

Essed, P. (1991). *Understanding everyday racism: An interdisciplinary theory.* Newbury Park, CA: Sage Publications.

Fleras, E., & Elliot, J.L. (2007.) *Unequal relations: An introduction to race, ethnic, and Aboriginal dynamics in Canada.* Toronto, ON: Pearson Education Canada.

Freeman, R. (1995). Legitimizing racial discrimination through antidiscrimination laws: A critical review of Supreme Court doctrine. In K. Crenshaw, N. Gotanda, G. Peller & K. Thomas (Eds.), *Critical race theory: The key writings that formed the movement* (pp. xi–xii). New York, NY: New Press.

Frideres, S.J., & Gadacz, R.T. (2005). *Aboriginal peoples in Canada* (7th ed.). Scarborough, ON: Pearson Education Canada.

Galabuzi, G.E. (2006). *Canada's economic apartheid: The social exclusion of racialized groups in the new century.* Toronto, ON: Canadian Scholars' Press.

Giscombe, K. (2008). *Career advancement in corporate Canada: A focus on visible minorities—Workplace fit and stereotyping.* Toronto, ON: Catalyst Canada & Diversity Institute in Management and Technology.

Grekul, J., Krahn, A., & Odynak, D. (2004). Sterilizing the "feeble-minded": Eugenics in Alberta, Canada, 1929–1972. *Journal of Historical Sociology, 17*(4), 361–384. doi:10.1111/j.1467-6443.2004.00237.x

Hucker, J. (1997). Antidiscrimination laws in Canada: Human rights commissions and the search for equality. *Human Rights Quarterly, 19*, 547–571. doi:10.1353/hrq.1997.0028

James, C.E., Este, D., Thomas-Bernard, W., Benjamin, A., Bethan, L., & Turner, T. (2010). *Race and well-being.* Halifax, NS: Fernwood Publishing.

Lawrence, B. (2002). Rewriting histories of the land: Colonization and indigenous resistance in Eastern Canada. In S. Razack (Ed.), *Race, space, and the law* (pp. 21–46). Toronto, ON: Between the Lines.

Li., P.S. (2001). The market worth of immigrants' educational credentials. *Canadian Public Policy, 27*(1), 23–38. Retrieved from http://www.jstor.org/stable/3552371

Lopez, I.J. (1995). The social construction of race. In R. Delgado (Ed.), *Critical race theory: The cutting edge* (pp. 159–168). Philadelphia, PA: Temple University Press.

Makela, F. (2010). Open letter calling for an inquiry into alleged violations of civil liberties during the Toronto G20 Summit. Faculty of Law, University of Sherbrooke. Retrieved from http://www.g20justice.com/files/let-toews-G20-en.pdf

Mendes, E. (Ed.). (1995). *Race discrimination: Law and practice.* Toronto, ON: Carswell.

Mohammed, A. (2000). *The investigation of race complaints at the BC Human Rights Commission.* Vancouver, BC: BC Human Rights Commission.

Moss, W., & Gardner-O'Toole, E. (1997). Aboriginal people: History of discriminatory laws. Depository Service Program. Government of Canada. Retrieved from http://dsp-psd.pwgsc.gc.ca/Collection-R/LoPBdP/BP/bp175-e.htm#CIVIL ANDPOLITICAL RIGHTS

Mullings, D.V. (2009). The paradox of exclusion within equity: Interrogating discourse at the Canadian Human Rights Tribunal. (Doctoral Dissertation). Retrieved from http://proquest.umi.com/pqdweb?did=1850215841&sid=1&Fmt=2&cl%20ientId=27850&RQT=309&VName=PQD&cfc=1 http://proquest.umi.com/pqdweb?did=1850215841&sid=1&Fmt=2&cl ientId=27850&RQT=309&VName=PQD

Oikawa, M. (2002). Cartographies of violence: Women, memory, and the subject(s) of the "internment." In S. Razack (Ed.), *Race, space, and the law* (pp. 11–98). Toronto, ON: Between the Lines.

Omi, W., & Winant, H. (1993). On the theoretical status of the concept of race. In C. McCarthy & W. Crichlow (Eds.), *Race identity, and representation in education* (pp. 3–10). New York, NY: Routledge.

Ontario Human Rights Commission. (1995). *Commission on systemic racism in the Ontario criminal justice system.* Toronto, ON: Queen's Printer.

Ontario Human Rights Commission. (2003). *Paying the price: The human cost of racial profiling.* Toronto, ON: Queen's Printer.

Ontario Human Rights Commission. (n.d.). *Racial discrimination, race, and racism.* Fact Sheet. Retrieved from http://www.ohrc.on.ca/en/resources/factsheets/race/view

Pendakur, K., & Pendakur, R. (1998). The colour of money: Earnings differentials among ethnic groups in Canada. *Canadian Journal of Economics, 31*(3), 518–548.

Pendakur, R., Mata, F., Lee, S., & Dole, N. (2000). *Job mobility and promotion in the federal public service.* Strategic Research and Analysis, Canadian Heritage and Research Directorate, Public Service Commission.. Retrieved from http://www.tbs-sct.gc.ca/res/dwnld/jmp-eng.pdf

Public Service Commission. (2009–2010). Annual report. Public Service Commission of Canada. Retrieved from http://www.psc-cfp.gc.ca/arp-rpa/2010/rpt-eng.pdf

Puscas, D. (2010). G20 police repression press conference. G8/G20 Breakdown. Retrieved from http://www.g20breakdown.com/2010/06/g20-police-repression-press-conference-video

Razack, S. (1998). *Looking White people in the eye: Gender, race, and culture in courtrooms and classrooms.* Toronto, ON: University of Toronto Press.

Reitz, J.G. (2001). Immigrant skill utilization in the Canadian labour market: Implications of human capital research. *Journal of International Migration and Integration / Revue De l ;Intégration et de la Migration Internationale, 2*(3), 347–378. doi:10.1007/s12134-001-1004-1

Riskin, L. (1994). Mediator orientations, strategies, and techniques. *Alternatives to the High Cost of Litigation, 12*(9), 111–114. doi:10.1002/alt.3810120904

Royal Commission on Systemic Racism in the Ontario Criminal Justice System 1992–1995. (1995). *Report of the commission on systemic racism in the Ontario criminal justice system.* Toronto, ON: Queen's Printer.

Sangha, D., & Tang, K. (2003). Race discrimination and the human rights process. Paper presented to Canadian Critical Race Conference, May 2, 2003, University of British Columbia, Vancouver, Canada. Retrieved from http://edocs.lib.sfu

.ca/ccrc/html/CCRC_PDF/RaceDiscriminationAndTheHumanRightsProcess%28DaveSangha&Kwong-leungTang%29.pdf

Satzewich, V. (1991). *Racism and the incorporation of foreign labour: Farm labour migration to Canada since 1945*. London, UK: Routledge.

Thobani, S. (2007). *Exalted subjects: Studies in the making of race and nation in Canada*. Toronto, ON: University of Toronto Press.

Treasury Board of Canada Secretariat. (2000). Embracing change in the federal public service. Task Force on the Participation of Visible Minorities in the Federal Public Service. Retrieved from http://www.tbs-sct.gc.ca/pubs_pol/hrpubs/tb_852/ecfps-eng.asp

Tulloch, H. (1975). *Black Canadians: A long line of fighters*. Toronto, ON: NC Press.

Winant, H. (2000). Race and race theory. *Annual Review of Sociology, 26*, 169–185.

The Quebec Model of Social Policy, Past and Present

7

Yves Vaillancourt

From the outset, we could ask the following question: Why is there a special chapter on Quebec social policy in a book on social policy in Canada? After all, in Canada's federal system, is Quebec not just one province among others in a whole comprising 10 provinces and three territories? If there is a special chapter on Quebec, why not chapters on Ontario, British Columbia, Nova Scotia, and the other provinces?

The question is a delicate one, and it is not our role to answer it in the editors' place. For our part, we accepted the invitation to write a chapter on Quebec's social policies, not only because they have a specific shape,[1] but above all because this specificity derives from the fact that Quebec, in addition to being a province within Canada's federal system, is also a nation and a national state. That is why, from a certain point (the 1960s), Quebec's specificity led to the emergence of a truly Quebec model of social policy. But that model would evolve from the 1980s to the 2010s.

To our mind, the Quebec difference, in terms of social policy, stems largely from the existence of the Quebec nation, its vulnerability, and its resilience in a Canadian and North American context. We are referring to the fragility of the French language and culture, which have long been under threat and have given rise through history to various forms of nationalism, some more defensive and traditional, others more aggressive and modern. Clearly, the history of social policy in Quebec is shorter than that of the Quebec nation. Indeed, it stretches over slightly more than a century, while that of the Quebec nation began more than four centuries ago (Quebec City was founded in 1608).

One cannot define social policy without referring to intervention by the state (or public authorities at the local level). It is possible to have social protection measures *without* state intervention, such as initiatives developed in the past or present by the churches, private corporations, foundations, associations, and so on, to offer financial or other support to individuals, families, and groups exposed to certain social risks. But for social measures to become social policy in the true sense, there has to be intervention by public authorities. This intervention takes two main forms: first, that of fostering monetary transfers aimed at enhancing income distribution; and second, that of providing collective services (education, health care, social services, public transit, housing) to make them available on a universal basis (to the entire population) or on a selective basis (to part of the population).

Within the conceptual framework used in this chapter, state intervention is analyzed on the basis of its interfaces with family, market, and the third sector, as well as the specific configurations stemming from them. The state intervenes in social policy in the general interest. In a broad theoretical perspective, it is important to take into account not only interaction between the state and the market, but also the involvement of families (domestic economy) and the third sector (social and solidarity economy) (Jetté, Lévesque, et al., 2000; Lévesque, 2003; Vaillancourt & Tremblay, 2002; Vaillancourt, Caillouette & Dumais, 2002; Vaillancourt, 2003, 2010; Proulx, Dumais & Vaillancourt, 2006; Jetté & Vaillancourt, 2011).

We base our analysis on Esping-Anderson (1990, 2008), while differing from him on one point. This Scandinavian researcher, in reviewing welfare state social policy, distinguishes three types of configurations: liberal, corporatist, and social democratic. In so doing, he is interested in the interactions among three groups of players, namely, the state or public sector, the market or private sector, and the family or domestic economy. In that context, the purpose of state intervention through social policy is to rein in market logic (decommodification) and excessive emphasis on family responsibility (defamilialization), which primarily affects women. But, unlike Esping-Anderson, we also take into account the participation of the third sector or the social and solidarity economy. In that regard, we draw on the theoretical contributions of European researchers who are interested in the role the third sector plays in democratic social policy reform, albeit without undervaluing state intervention (Lipietz, 1989; Defourny & Monzon Campos, 1992; 6 & Vidal, 1994; Laville, 1994, 2011; Lewis, 1999; Defourny, Develtere & Fonteneau, 1999; Laville & Nyssens, 2001; Evers & Laville, 2004; Lévesque & Thiry, 2008).

In this chapter, we point to three great moments in the history of social policy in Quebec, taking the Quiet Revolution and the Castonguay reform (1960–1980) as benchmarks.

I. Pre-1960: Distrust of the State

During this period between the end of the 19th Century and the start of the Quiet Revolution, a number of social policies appeared in Quebec. While they had a distinct character, they did not constitute a Quebec model for social policy, because they were too defensive. In fact, intervention by the state in Quebec was undervalued by the dominant groups in civil society and by successive governments.[2] This distrust concerned both the provincial and the federal state, and stemmed from the dominance of a type of nationalism that was traditional, defensive, and subservient to the Catholic Church.

Pre-1960: Distrust of the State

Traditional Nationalism Under the Guardianship of the Church

In the Quebec of the period, civil society was strongly influenced by the Catholic Church. Ultramontane and subject to the directives of the Vatican and the bishops, the Church made a conservative interpretation of its social doctrine. It maintained a special relationship with the population, more than 80 percent of whom were French Canadian and Catholic. The French language and the Catholic faith, while shared by French Canadians outside Quebec, were seen as the two pillars of the nationalism prevalent in Quebec at the time. In the traditional nationalistic vision, the Quebec state was seen as being at the service of the English Canadian and American economic elites. The French-speaking economic elites were unable to become more prominent and remained confined to the margins. In that context, the elites of the Quebec nation turned toward the Church and its networks (including parishes, religious communities, and charitable and social agencies) to compete with the provincial state in several areas of collective life, notably education, health care, culture, and social services, and indeed in certain facets of economic life. The Catholic Church, with its parishes and religious communities, was something of a "junior state" controlling an impressive number of institutions, networks, and activities. It also controlled some components of social movements (labour unions, cooperatives, farmers, feminists, and so on).

Anti-Statism in Quebec and the Rest of Canada

Until the Second World War, distrust of the interventionist state was not exclusive to Quebec. It also arose from the ideology of economic liberalism that was dominant at that time in Canada as a whole and in capitalist countries on the international scene. But in Quebec, the distrust of the state specific to the ideology of economic liberalism was combined with another distrust, stemming from traditional nationalism. From the late 1930s onward, however, a time when the federal state and some provincial states—Saskatchewan, British Columbia, and Manitoba—were becoming more interventionist with respect to social and economic development, the distrust of the state that dominated in Quebec stood out more on the Canadian scene. In other words, the anti-statism prevalent in Quebec became more of an element of differentiation from the moment that the socialist, Keynesian, Beveridgean, and social democratic visions of the Commonwealth Co-operative Federation (CCF) type gained less ground in French-speaking Quebec than in English-speaking Canada. In Quebec, social democratic progressive visions existed, but these were in competition with the traditional nationalist vision. In fact, the Quebec nationalist movement, in the context of the 1930s crisis, developed a more reformist, corporatist-type social project, which included social policy reforms. One of these involved a French-style family allowance proposal that aimed, for large families, to complement the "family wage" and alleviate the poverty associated with the costs of maintaining and educating children (Lebel, 1931; École sociale populaire, 1934; Angers, 1945). Compared with those advocated by social democratic leaders in English Canada,[3] the corporatist reforms were more in line with the Bismarckian model than the Beveridge model (Majnoni d'Intignano, 1993). In the Bismarckian model, state intervention is sifted through "intermediary bodies" on the boundary between civil society and the state. This gives the impression that state intervention is "softened" and is less offensive to anti-statists (Lévesque, 2007; Pelletier & Vaillancourt, 1975; Vaillancourt, 1988, 2010).

Reticence Toward Federal Social Policy

A significant portion of the social policies appearing in Quebec prior to 1960 were directly or indirectly impelled by the federal government. Noteworthy among direct interventions were Unemployment Insurance in 1940, the Family Allowance in 1944, and Old Age Security in 1952. As to indirect intervention by the federal state, this often took the form of cost-sharing programs.[4] In the face of these federal initiatives, Quebec was often the province that waited the longest before taking advantage of them and signing agreements. Thus, Quebec waited until 1936 before joining the program of assistance for the elderly aged 70 and over adopted by the federal government in 1927; until 1956 before joining the disabled persons assistance program adopted by the federal government in 1954; and until 1959 before joining the Unemployment Assistance program launched by the federal government in 1956 (Guest, 1980, pp. 145–147; Vaillancourt, 1988). On the other hand, during the 1930s crisis, Quebec was as quick as the other provinces in embarking on cost-sharing programs—those jointly funded with the federal government and municipalities—in order to help the unemployed. This breach of the principle of state non-intervention was legitimized by the idea that such intervention was temporary and would disappear once the crisis was over (Pelletier & Vaillancourt, 1974, 1975).

Faced with direct and indirect federal intervention, Quebec showed reticence. The dominant elites in the government and civil society, in particular during the time of Duplessis's Union Nationale (1936–39 and 1944–59), were critical of the federal initiatives and the texts underpinning them—Rowell-Sirois, 1940; Davidson, 1943; Cassidy, 1943; Marsh, [1943] 1975—for having centralizing intentions, abusing the division of constitutional responsibilities, and taking their inspiration from Anglo-Saxon culture. In short, for not respecting Quebec's national uniqueness with respect to language and religion (Minville, 1939; Bouvier, 1943a, 1943b, 1943c, 1944; Angers, 1945, 1955; Poulin, 1955; Tremblay Commission, 1956). Despite this reticence, Quebec would eventually accept the federal intervention, which, after all, was funded by its taxes and catered to social problems also being experienced by Quebec citizens.

Pre-1960: Distrust of the State

The Timidity of the Social Policy Initiated by the Quebec State

During these years, Quebec was not content to react defensively to federal social policies. It was in no hurry to develop original programs that would belong fully to Quebec. Moreover, when it did so, it sought terms and conditions that reduced state intervention. Let us look at three examples.

First, the social insurance program for those injured at work, launched in 1909, provided for an intermediate structure—the Workmen's Compensation Board—which, in line with the Bismarckian model, constituted a buffer between the state and civil society.

Second, the Public Assistance Act, launched in 1921 and amended several times through to 1970, placed strong limits on state intervention by providing provincial and municipal financial support for third-sector institutions—primarily of a religious nature—that offered health and social welfare services within institutions to poor people in need. During the 1950s, with the increase in needs and costs, financial participation and regulation by the state would grow, and this would pose the question of the autonomy of third-sector organizations.

Third, the Needy Mothers Assistance Act, launched in 1937, represented the dissemination and adaptation in Quebec of a model introduced in the preceding years in most other provinces of Canada. Here, state intervention in assistance for poor people was legitimized insofar as it concerned people who, while not deemed incapable of working, were not obligated to enter the labour market. That is what prompted Premier Duplessis, in adopting the act in 1937, to say: "We want mothers to stay at home to mind and bring up children rather than dispersing them throughout the province" (Duplessis, quoted in Vaillancourt, 1988, p. 276).

Preparing the Way for the Quiet Revolution in Civil Society

In short, aside from the brief episode of the Godbout government, the Quebec governments of the period, particularly those led by Duplessis for 20 years, were quite simply uninterested in developing a genuine system of social policy in Quebec. They were not even concerned with implementing some of the labour and social reforms promoted by the corporatist nationalist movement. Against the backdrop of the rise of capitalist industrialization, urbanization, and the resulting social problems for the working classes, government timidity and inaction in social development meant that families, the third sector, and the market were squeezed together in an untenable situation. The third sector associated with the Catholic and Protestant Churches and the Jewish community was exhausted. At the end of the 1930s crisis, economist Esdras Minville—himself a representative of the traditional nationalist current—summed up the limitations of a system of social protection in which requests were referred to religious-based third-sector institutions associated with the Catholic Church: "The institutions were overwhelmed, and were unable, even by making countless appeals for private charity, to meet needs, develop their establishments or perfect their equipment to keep pace with progress in science, public health and social services" (Minville, 1939, p. 55).

During the period from 1945 to 1960, traditional nationalism began to lose way with the rise of a new nationalism that was more modern, independent of the Church, and open to state intervention. In fact, the Quiet Revolution was being prepared in several areas in civil society. That is what happened in particular in the labour union movement, both with the Catholic Workers Confederation of Canada (*Confédération des syndicats catholiques du Canada* [CTCC]) under Picard and Marchand and with the *Fédération des unions industrielles du Québec* (FUIQ); in Laval University's Faculty of Social Science under Georges-Henri Lévesque; in social economy networks with the debate on non-religious-based cooperatives sparked by the creation in 1939 of the *Conseil supérieur de la coopération* (CSC); in specialized Catholic action movements such as the *Jeunesse étudiante catholique* (JEC) and *Jeunesse ouvrière catholique* (JOC); in established publications such as *Le Devoir* and new ones such as *Cité Libre;* and in annual get-togethers such as those held by the *Institut canadien des affaires publiques* (ICAP) in the 1950s (Trudeau, 1956; Rocher, 1960; Vaillancourt, 1988; Clavette, 2005).

II. Quebec Model—Version 1 (1960–1980): The Entrepreneur State

As we have just seen in Part I, prior to 1960 Quebec gave the impression of being a passive recipient of social policy. During the 1960s and 1970s, it would take social policies in hand proactively and take responsibility for their implemention. Using a distinction made by Gilles L. Bourque (2000) in his research on the evolution of Quebec's industrial policy from 1960 to 2000, we will be talking of "Version 1" of a Quebec model in which the Quebec state acted as an "entrepreneur" in the development of social policy from 1960 to 1980. This will allow us to use "Version 2" of the Quebec model to analyze the emergence of a state that is more of a "partner" of civil society in certain social policy reforms introduced during the 1990s and 2000s.

A New, Modern Nationalism

This period is characterized by the rise and supremacy of a new, modern nationalism, which affirmed its independence from the Church and valued intervention by the Quebec state in economic, cultural, and social development. Without causing traditional nationalism to disappear, this new nationalism would become predominant in civil society and have a determining impact on successive governments' orientations. It was a feature first of all of the Liberal government of Jean Lesage, who held power from June 1960 to the summer of 1966 with the slogan *Maîtres chez nous* (masters in our own house), and implemented several significant reforms within a short period, including Quebec's implementation of hospital insurance (from January 1961 onward), the introduction of school family allowances for 16- and 17-year-olds (also in 1961), and the establishment of the Quebec Pension Plan (QPP) and the Quebec Deposit and Investment Fund (*Caisse de dépôt et placement*) (in 1965). Astonishingly, during the Union Nationale (UN) governments from 1966 to 1970, public policy, such as the Quebec Family Allowance program adopted in 1967, was often in line with the new nationalism, even if the UN's discourse continued to draw on the vocabulary of traditional nationalism. During the 1970s, the new nationalism marked the actions of Robert Bourassa's Liberal government (1970–76)—particularly when Claude Castonguay was Minister of Social Affairs (1970–73)—and even more so those of René Lévesque's Parti Québécois government, which came to power in 1976. Under pressure from civil society, which was secularizing and becoming more pluralistic, and from social movements, which were becoming more radical, all governments of the time put forward social policy reforms that contributed to the emergence of a Quebec welfare state of a more social democratic hue,[5] to use Esping-Anderson's typology.

Quebec Model—Version 1 (1960–1980): The Entrepreneur State

The Boucher Report and the Social Assistance Reform

The Boucher Report, published in 1963, was very representative of the vision of the welfare state that reflected the evolution of Quebec social policy throughout the period. The Boucher Committee[6] had been struck in 1961 to look at increases in the cost of targeted assistance programs—those aimed at the elderly, the blind, the disabled, needy mothers, the unemployed, and so on—following the introduction of the Unemployment Assistance program in 1960, against a backdrop of economic recession. The committee's mandate included not only financial assistance—welfare cheques—but also assistance in kind for eligible poor individuals within third-sector institutions in the health and welfare field recognized by Quebec's 1921 public assistance legislation, which was still in effect in the 1960s.

Among the recommendations of the Boucher Report, let us underscore the following six: (1) Quebec must abandon its obsolete conception of the "residual state" whereby the state is authorized to intervene only as a last resort, on the grounds that private charity can be left to do the rest; (2) the Quebec government must build an "overall economic and social policy whose components are coordinated and coherent" (Boucher Committee, 1963, p. 214); (3) "the Quebec government should explicity recognize the principle whereby any individual in need is entitled to assistance from the state, regardless of the immediate or remote cause of that need" (p. 215, recommendation 7); (4) categorial assistance laws and the Quebec Public Assistance Act must be replaced by a "general social assistance legislation" (p. 215–216); 5) administration of the new assistance system following the reform is to be the responsibility of well-trained officials and to be taken on by "government public services themselves" and not by third-sector agencies

(p. 220); and (6) "the Quebec government should continue and intensify its efforts to have the Government of Canada withdraw from joint assistance programs and compensate, through a broadening of taxation fields, for the increased costs that would ensue for Quebec" (p. 216, recommendation 14).

As we have pointed out elsewhere (Vaillancourt, 2003), many of the Boucher Report's recommendations concerning social assistance were inspired by ideas and reforms developed elsewhere in Canada and the world over the previous 20 years. But the uniqueness of the Boucher Report was twofold. First, it valued the role of the Quebec state as coordinator and operator of an overall reform of social policy, and of social assistance in particular. Second, it offered the Quebec government a specific strategy for acting with regard to federal cost-sharing programs in areas of provincial jurisdiction, such as social assistance. This was the opting-out option implemented by the Quebec government over the following years (Morin, 1972; Vaillancourt, 1991, 1994). This strategy was to yield "temporary" results beginning after the spring 1964 federal–provincial conference, at which Pearson's federal government, placed on the defensive with respect to the Canada Pension Plan (CPP), agreed in principle to withdraw from hospital insurance programs and other federal cost-sharing programs in the area of social assistance in return for the transfer of some 20 personal income tax points. But this withdrawal was seen as an "interim arrangement" that would become permanent only after 1970, following a transition period. At the time, Quebec was pleased. Except that, in the following years, the federal government would ensure that opting out never became permanent (Vaillancourt, 1991, 1994).

As to the reform leading to comprehensive social assistance, it took place less quickly than expected. In fact, it was implemented gradually from 1963 to 1970. While the new general law was launched only in May 1970 under the Bourassa government, the administrative reforms were initiated starting in 1964 and 1965, with the creation of local and regional administrative centres for social assistance. Over time, these centres were to become branches—following the Beveridge model—of the Quebec state.

The Castonguay-Bourassa Reforms

Claude Castonguay's name is associated with several reforms that were planned or implemented by the Quebec government during the 1960s and 1970s. He started out as an adviser to the Lesage government in the federal–provincial tug of war concerning the choice between the Canada Pension Plan developed in Ottawa and the pension plan developed in Quebec City. The Quebec plan was chosen in April 1964, although the federal government subsequently managed to do damage control by negotiating harmonization between the two programs. Since that time, the two programs have existed side by side, similar in every point—the QPP for Quebec and the CPP for the rest of Canada (Guest, 1980, pp. 150–152; Morin, 1972; Bryden, 1974; Banting, 1987; Vaillancourt, 1991).

Quebec Model—Version 1 (1960–1980): The Entrepreneur State

From 1966 to 1973, Castonguay's leadership was associated with his responsibilities as chair of a commission of inquiry on health and social welfare—which included income security issues—and as an influential minister in the first Bourassa government, from 1970 to 1973. Many believed his influence was strong enough that he was able to draw up reform projects and then implement them. But that is only partly true. Following is a brief summary of Castonguay's achievements:

1. The health insurance reform initiated in fall 1970, which carried out the recommendation for universal health insurance made in Volume 1 of the commission's report in the fall of 1967 (Castonguay Commission, 1967), and was in line with the cost-sharing program implemented by the federal government in 1968. Here, Quebec was merely catching up with most of the other provinces, which had already joined Medicare.
2. The comprehensive social assistance reform proposed by the Boucher report, drafted by the UN governments from 1966 to 1970 and implemented by the Bourassa–Castonguay government in fall 1970.
3. The reform of the health and social services system launched with Bill 65 in the fall of 1971 (Quebec, 1971). On the Canadian scene, this reform stands out as a social innovation for four reasons: (a) it promoted the objective of universality in social services as well as health services; (b) it opted for an integrated approach bringing health and social services together in a single system at the Quebec national, regional, and local levels;[7] (c) for the coordination and distribution of services at the regional and local levels, it built on state public organizations and no longer on third-sector organizations, as was the case under the Quebec public assistance plan;[8] but it also provided these organizations with a structure of democratic governance that made room for participation by users, practitioners, and local and regional communities; and (d) it created, for integrated front line services, local community services centres (CLSCs), taking its inspiration from the UK's Seebohm Report. CLSCs were innovative bodies mandated to provide preventive as well as curative services and to promote community development (Armitage, 1975, pp. 165–169).
4. The income security reform that introduced an integrated, comprehensive social policy. The foundations of this reform lay in the three parts of Volume V of the report (Castonguay Commission, 1971a, 1971b, and 1971c). While these 800 pages were published only in 1971, their orientations and recommendations were familiar to Castonguay and his colleagues as early as 1970. The integrated approach advocated publicly by Castonguay was based on the links among three pillars for combating family poverty: (a) a higher minimum wage; (b) universal family allowances, indexed to the cost of living, taxable, and substantially increased; and (c) a guaranteed income program to supplement the incomes of the working poor.

The reform proposals attributed to Castonguay inspired, albeit unevenly, the three succeeding governments in Quebec City during the 1970s, namely, the first and second Bourassa governments (1970–73 and 1973–76) and the first Lévesque government (1976–81). They were well received in progressive networks interested in Canadian social policy, notably, by NDP provincial governments in Manitoba, British Columbia, and Saskatchewan. In terms of their social content, they also held an attraction for some politicians and senior officials in the federal government, especially between 1972 and 1974, when Trudeau's minority Liberal government was forced to ally itself with the NDP. That in turn required it to be more open to social policy reforms. But even while Quebec's reform plans were exerting a certain attraction in Ottawa and other provincial capitals, some of their aspects were heightening intergovernmental tensions. Among other things, the universality of social services promoted in Volume VI of the report (Castonguay Commission, 1972a and 1972b) cast an unflattering light on the highly selective approach taken by the Canada Assistance Plan (CAP) (Vaillancourt, 1991, 1992). Furthermore, the income security reforms proposed in Volume V of the same report and the idea of substantially increasing family allowances tolled the death knell for the selective Family Income Security Plan (FISP) proposed in the Blue Book of Minister John Munro (1970) and his deputy, Joe Willard. But what most bothered people was that Quebec was not content with pleading for a comprehensive, integrated social policy. In the wake of the Boucher Report, it was also arguing that Quebec City, not Ottawa, should be responsible for this integrated policy.

Early in 1973, Castonguay and the Quebec government seemed jolted when the federal Department of Health and Welfare, under the newly appointed minister Marc Lalonde and his deputy Al Johnson, offered Quebec and the other provinces an alternative plan for reforming social security in Canada. Astutely, with respect to income security this plan borrowed several elements from Castonguay's, notably with regard to family allowances, which it proposed to triple, and to a guaranteed income for the working poor. There was, however, one significant difference: the federal government, not the Quebec government, would implement the reform (Lalonde, 1973). At the time, Quebec reacted well to the new proposals in Lalonde's Orange Book, and the federal government reformed the Family Allowance in 1974.

Then, under the second Bourassa government, Quebec, with a less than coherent strategy, took part in federal–provincial discussions on the Social Security Review, which ran from 1973 to 1977. This process would begin in euphoria and end in disappointment (Vaillancourt, 1991, 1992).

The First Lévesque Government's Social Democratic Reforms

When one looks at the evolution of social policy in Canada during the second half of the 1970s, one notes, both with the federal government and with

Quebec Model—Version 1 (1960–1980): The Entrepreneur State

provincial governments other than Quebec's, the end of the period of growth of the welfare state and the start of a period of crisis and transformation of welfare state social policies (Jetté et al., 2000). But when one observes what happened in Quebec over the same period, one notes the advent of a final wave of social democratic social policies. In short, if the *Trente Glorieuses*[9] arrived later in Quebec than elsewhere in Canada—in 1960, not 1945—they ended later, in 1980, not 1976.

In hindsight, the first Lévesque government was highly proactive in making significant additions to Quebec's welfare state social policies. Among these initiatives, we will mention merely the following:

1. The Youth Protection Act, adopted in 1977 and implemented from 1979 onward, which recognized children's rights and expressed Quebec's desire to develop a less punitive approach with respect to young people in difficulties (Quebec, 1977).
2. An act to secure the rights of handicapped people, adopted in 1978, which led to the creation of the *Office des personnes handicapées du Québec* (OPHQ) in 1979 (Boucher, Fougeyrollas & Gaucher, 2003).
3. The creation of a public auto insurance plan in 1978, which introduced the principle of no-fault insurance for people injured in car accidents.
4. The adoption of a first public homecare policy in 1979, in which the state was the key link, even if greater value was being given once again to the contributions of community and voluntary organizations (MAS, 1979).
5. The adoption of occupational health and safety legislation, which acknowledged the importance of prevention and created the Occupational Health and Safety Board (*Commission sur la santé et la sécurité au travail*) in 1979.
6. The introduction in 1979 of a family allowance program for handicapped children.
7. The introduction in 1979 of a support program for community organizations—*Programme de soutien aux organismes communautaires* (PSOC)—which constituted an embryonic public policy for recognizing and supporting community organizations interfacing with the Quebec state in health and social services (Jetté, 2008).
8. The adoption in 1979 of a new Quebec policy with respect to daycare centres, which reflected a preference for not-for-profit centres and led to the creation of the child care services bureau, *Office des services de garde à l'enfance* (Vaillancourt & Tremblay, 2002, p. 40).

Finally, the implementation of the Castonguay reform in the health and social services field continued with the construction, in the late 1970s and early 1980s, of new public long-term institutional care centres representing 5,200 new places, and the decision to lift the moratorium on the development of new CLSCs that had been in place since 1975. By 1980, there were 100 or so CLSCs.

Conclusion

The social policy system in Quebec at the end of the period was quite close to a social-democratic-type welfare state. In that system—Version 1 of the Quebec model—the Quebec state played the role of key link, even if several important pieces came directly from the federal state or were influenced by the indirect federal intervention. The state acted most often as the planner, contractor, funder, regulator, administrator, and distributor of cheques and services. This yielded a system that we have occasionally called the *social étatiste* system. For instance, with the reforms in social assistance and the health and social services system, the organizations administering the new policies on a regional or local basis were public, totally financed from public funds, using public sector officials and practitioners and accountable to the Quebec state. Thus, in Version 1 of the Quebec model, the Quebec state in the programs it controlled—just like the federal state in those it controlled (Unemployment Insurance, the federal Family Allowance, Old Age Security, and so on)—gave the impression of being the sole player. This made it look as though agents from the third sector and the private sector were no longer present as they had been before the Quiet Revolution and as they would be once again from the 1980s onward. In fact, they were still there, albeit on a smaller and more discreet scale.

III. Quebec Model—Version 2 (1980–2010): The State as Partner

Crisis and Transformation of the Welfare State

As we mentioned earlier, because of the social democratic social policy thrust supported by the PQ government during René Lévesque's first mandate, the welfare state crisis erupted four or five years later in Quebec than elsewhere in Canada. But when it did arrive in 1981, the shock waves in the government and civil society—especially in social movements—were many and brutal. The crisis took the form of a series of socio-economic and socio-political shocks stemming from a variety of simultaneous factors: the defeat of the Yes side in the May 1980 referendum; the unilateral (i.e., without Quebec) patriation of the 1982 constitution; the 1981–82 economic recession, which led to an increase of more than 25 percent in social assistance clientele and costs; the dramatic increase in public debt and deficits in Quebec and elsewhere; and so on.

In the progressive literature on social policy in Quebec and the rest of Canada, the word "crisis" has been overused to analyze what happened in the 1980s, and indeed in the 1990s and 2000s. For our part, in the research we have conducted collectively at CRISES (*Centre de recherche sur les innovations sociales*) and LAREPPS (*Laboratoire de recherche sur les pratiques et les politiques sociales*) since the second half of the 1980s, we have got into the habit of talking not only of crisis but also of transformations. In so doing,

Quebec Model—Version 2 (1980–2010): The State as Partner

we have departed from many pessimistic analyses that interpret the crisis and the policy transformations associated with it as always and only a series of reversals and losses. In our view, the crisis also created opportunities for *improving* certain social policies. We do not subscribe to the idea that all governments in Quebec since the early 1980s[10] have painted themselves into a corner in the development of neoliberal policies. On the contrary, we contend that the economic and social policies adopted have been plural and have featured various types of logic. That is the context in which we view the emergence of a Version 2 of the Quebec model over the past three decades (Bourque, 2000; Jetté et al., 2000; Lévesque & Thiry, 2008; Bouchard & Hudon, 2008; Jetté, 2008; Côté, Lévesque & Morneau, 2009; Klein et al., 2010).

Characteristics of the New Quebec Model

In this new development model, the old social policies that have been transformed and new ones that are arising are hybrids in the sense that they are marked by interactions that often vary, from one policy to another, among neoliberal regulation, "neo-welfarist" regulation, and solidarity-based regulation. The first takes its inspiration from market logic (competition), the second from state logic (redistribution), and the third from the logic of the social and solidarity economy (cooperation).[11] The interlacing of these three logics has given rise to various configurations and policies. Among the configurations conferring their mark on the renewed Quebec model, we find the following characteristics: (1) a reaffirmation of the importance of the state, but less a Beveridge-type and more a partnership-oriented type (Noël, 1996; Lévesque, 2003) that is more open to participation by civil society, in particular third-sector players, in turn implying an openness to policy decentralization; (2) a placing of value on forms of governance of public organizations in regions and local communities that make room for citizen participation; and (3) participation by third-sector players not only in the implementation but also in the democratic co-construction of policy (Vaillancourt, 2009, 2011; Jetté & Vaillancourt, 2011). The new model implies a rediscovery of the third sector and its participation in the development of new, innovative interfaces with the state, the market, and the domestic economy. After all, in Quebec as in the rest of Canada, the third sector has existed as long as social policies have existed. For instance, in social policy concerning disabled people in Canada, third-sector organizations have played a major role in supporting individuals and families for the past 80 years (Rioux & Prince, 2002, p. 17). Thus, the issue in the new Quebec model of social policy has less to do with the quantitative weight of the third sector and more to do with the quality of the relations among the third sector, the state, the market, and families. Now, this quality opens up the possibility for third-sector players to avoid solely instrumental relations and to enter into truly partnership-based relationships with the state (Proulx, Bourque & Savard, 2007; Jetté & Vaillancourt, 2011).

Quebec Model—Version 2 (1980–2010): The State as Partner

Our analysis of the evolution of the new model during the 30 years being considered here can be summarized as follows, taking into account the successive governments.[12]

Preparations for the New Model (1981 to 1994)

Some preparations began from 1981 to 1985 under the PQ government's second mandate, even if the arrival of the crisis took that government by surprise, destabilized it, and placed it on the defensive. This led to the abandonment of the social democratic momentum of the first mandate, and above all to the government-ordered reopening of public sector workers' collective bargaining agreements and wage cuts ranging from 12 to 20 percent (Piotte, 1998, pp. 188–189). On the social policy front, four initiatives were noteworthy: (1) the decision to complete the universal network of CLSCs, which had been constantly challenged since 1975, with the result that the number of CLSCs rose from 100 to 150 between 1980 and 1985; (2) the decision to place value once again on the contributions of voluntary and community organizations in areas such as mental health, violence against women, and support for the elderly and handicapped; (3) the decision to launch employability programs to support the labour market entry of young people under 30 who were on on social assistance (this initiative would stimulate the development of community organizations in the field of support for the employability of socially vulnerable individuals); and (4) the endorsement by the government of *À part égale*, a visionary policy concerning handicapped people developed by the OPHQ in close dialogue with the disability community (OPHQ, 1984; Boucher, Fougeyrollas & Gaucher, 2003; Boucher in Vaillancourt, Caillouette & Dumais, 2003).

With Bourassa's return to power in December 1985, many analysts predicted that the government would switch to neoliberal policies. This appeared to be confirmed in the summer of 1986, when three ministerial think tanks delivered reports proposing that the government move in the direction of privatization and deregulation. These proposals encouraged the Quebec state to act like private enterprise—so much so, in fact, that there was talk at the time of the "Provigo state," by which was meant management of the state carried out in the same way as management of a private company such as Provigo. But the Bourassa government did not follow these recommendations (Bourque, 2000). Over the years, it sometimes adopted centre-right policies—in particular in 1988 with its reform of social assistance (known since as income security), which reintroduced differential treatment for those able and unable to work. But it also occasionally adopted centre-left policies that, on reflection, contributed to the renewal of the Quebec model. We are thinking here of the decisions to implement certain progressive recommendations from the Rochon Report (1988), notably those reaffirming the role of the CLSCs and advocating recognition of and support for community organizations. The Bourassa government, with the Côté reform and Bill 120, both launched in the early 1990s, also followed the Rochon Report—and the Harnois Report on mental health—in emphasizing the decentralization and regionalization of public health and social services networks by making their decision making and advisory structures more democratic (Jetté, 2008).

The Emergence of a New Generation of Policies (1994–2003)

In our view, the most fertile period for innovative public policies in Quebec was between 1994 and 2003 under the Parizeau, Bouchard, and Landry governments. The October 1996 Summit on the Economy and Employment is often mentioned in the literature as a high point in the planning, structuring, and implementing of new public policies that would continue over the next 15 years. However, care must be taken not to fall into the trap of focusing solely on what transpired during that three-day summit. The decisions made there and at the previous summit in January 1996 must be analyzed in a way that takes into account the struggles and debates that occurred in civil society in the years leading up to those meetings (Lévesque, 2007; Vaillancourt, 2010). Among other things, the tone of the deliberations that culminated in the fall 1996 summit was largely established during the women's Bread and Roses March of the spring of 1995. It also went back to the strategic alliance that was forged in fall of 1995 between the sovereigntist political parties (PQ and Bloc Québécois) and progressive social movements, which were strong supporters of the Yes side in the 1995 referendum and which argued that a closer relationship should be encouraged between the Quebec national state and progressive social policies.

A New Generation of Progressive Public Policies

In our research and writings over the past 20 years, we have looked at many tangible cases of new social and socio-economic policies that point to the rise of a new model of social and economic development in Quebec. We have often said that these new policies had to emerge and be sustained in a difficult social and political environment which made their existence difficult. Two constraints in particular come to mind: on the one hand, the neoliberal restructuring of federal policies carried out by the Chrétien–Martin government in 1994 and 1995 with respect to social housing, Employment Insurance, and social transfers to the provinces (Vaillancourt, 1996, 2003); and on the other hand, the zero deficit policy for Quebec's public finances adopted in early 1996 by the Bouchard government. At the outset, this policy was supposed to run for four years, but in fact it was successfully completed in three. It was largely improvised, and it led to adverse consequences by imposing drastic cutbacks and the early termination of doctors and nurses, which then helped derail the health and social services reforms carried out by Minister Jean Rochon. That said, we will mention, without going into any

Quebec Model—Version 2 (1980–2010): The State as Partner

great detail,[13] a number of examples of policies specific to Version 2 of the Quebec model.

1. The AccèsLogis housing policy, which led between 1996 and 2011 to the development—with the support of the provincial housing corporation (*Société d'habitation du Québec*)—of 23,000 new social housing units, most of them administered by third-sector players, namely, housing not-for-profit organizations and cooperatives (Vaillancourt & Ducharme, 2001; Vaillancourt, 2009; Bouchard & Hudon, 2008).
2. The policy of recognizing and supporting autonomous community organizations that would maintain an interface with the Quebec state and influence the design of several social policies. This policy, developed since the 1970s for community organizations in the health and social services field, was broadened in 2001 to all community organizations. It has affected 5,000 organizations in 25 areas of activity. It recognizes the principle of funding for three years at a time, and it distinguishes between two sorts of funding—with respect to an organization's overall mission, and with respect to specific projects (Jetté, 2008).
3. The Parizeau government's decision, from 1994 and 1995 onward, to institutionalize the previously experimental Carrefours Jeunesse Emploi (CJE). These youth employment centres are third-sector organizations working in association with the public sector network toward the labour market entry of young people (Assogba, 2000; Shields, 2006, 2010).
4. The launch, at the 1996 Summit on the Economy and Employment, of a new social policy on the family, which includes the goal of developing a nearly universal network of 200,000 daycare centre places for children under six, with preference given—though not exclusively—to daycare centres run by the third sector, and with the price of places paid by parents set at $5 per day per child (Briand, Bellemare & Gravel, 2006; Gravel, Bellemare & Briand, 2007; Lévesque, 2011; see also Box 1). The family policy includes a Quebec parental insurance plan to enhance the parental leave provided under federal employment insurance. But this reform, which required the negotiation of an arrangement with the federal government, was achieved only in January 2006 under the Charest government.
5. A local and regional development policy, also launched in 1996, that has led to a network of 100 or so local development centres—public organizations rooted in local communities with public sector funding (from the province and municipalities)—which use a democratic governance structure open not only to elected municipal representatives but also to prominent people in local community organizations who have expertise in local development (Comeau et al., 2001).
6. Support for a network of domestic help social economy enterprises (EESADs). This was announced at the Summit on the Economy and Employment in 1996 and led to the development over the following two or three years of 100 or so enterprises providing home housekeeping

Quebec Model—Version 2 (1980–2010): The State as Partner

services, primarily to the elderly but also to regular households and handicapped individuals (Vaillancourt & Jetté, 2009; Jetté & Vaillancourt, 2011).

7. Recognition of the social economy and of 20 or so specific social economy projects. This recognition was given by the government at the Summit on the Economy and Employment and was subsequently renewed. It has led among other things to the support provided by the Quebec state to the *Chantier de l'économie sociale* (Task Force on the Social Economy), which, with the *Conseil québécois de la coopération et de la mutualité* (CQCM), represents one of the two national social economy umbrella organizations in Quebec (Favreau, 2006, 2008; Lévesque, 2007; Vaillancourt, 2010).
8. The anti-poverty and anti-social-exclusion policy adopted unanimously in the National Assembly in December 2002, having been prepared in the preceding years through a vast mobilization of civil society and an impressive public debate. We see this policy as a fine example of the democratic co-construction of public policy, which has enabled it to survive the change of government in the spring of 2003 (Government of Quebec, 2002; Noël, 2003; Godbout & St-Cerny, 2008; Aubry, 2010; Vaillancourt, 2012).
9. With respect to discourse, it is possible to note points of convergence in the recent evolution of policies concerning people with disabilities. In Quebec as in the rest of Canada, the emphasis is on the empowerment and social participation of individuals who for all too long have been "absent citizens" in the construction of public policies concerning them in Quebec and Canada (Prince, 2009). But when one compares the English Canadian literature with Quebec writings in this field, one sees two differences. First, Quebec writings turn spontaneously toward the Quebec state (Boucher, Fougeyrollas & Gaucher, 2003; Vaillancourt, Caillouette & Dumais, 2002; Proulx, Dumais & Vaillancourt, 2006; Archambault, Dumais & Vaillancourt, 2011), whereas Canadian writings turn spontaneously toward the federal state (Torjman, 2001; Rioux & Prince, 2002; Prince, 2002). Then, in Quebec more than in Canadian writings, there is an openness to partnership-based participation by community organizations in the construction and implementation of post-welfare-state social policy (Archambault, Dumais & Vaillancourt, 2011; Aubry, 2010; Proulx, Dumais & Vaillancourt, 2006).

We could go on with other examples,[14] but the number and variety of those we have given are sufficient foundation for the analysis to which we shall be returning in our conclusion.

Under the Three Charest Governments: Continuity and Breaks

Still later, from 2003 to 2011, under Jean Charest's three governments, public policies typical of the new Quebec model were maintained, especially in social housing (Bouchard & Hudon, 2008; Vaillancourt, 2009) and the fight against poverty and exclusion (Aubry, 2010).[15] But some of these policies were reconfigured to bring them into line with the dominant current on new public management, which subordinated the principles of cooperation specific to the social and solidarity economy to the principles of competition specific to the market economy (Jetté & Goyette, 2010; Jetté & Vaillancourt, 2011). The rules governing public bodies in health and social services and in local and regional development have been altered in ways that have lessened participation by civil society players, reinforced upward reporting, and fostered a shift toward recentralization (Bourque, 2008; Vaillancourt & Jetté, 2009). The gains made by the social economy in daycare centres have been weakened through a policy that is more favourable to private, for-profit child care centres. That same policy is in no hurry to create new places despite growing demand (Briand, Bellemare & Gravel, 2006; Lévesque, 2011). The privatization of health and social services has become a more prominent subject of public debate and has made particular progress in residential care services for the frail elderly (Béland, Contandriopoulos, Quesnel-Vallée & Robert, 2008; Castonguay, 2008; Fournier, 2011; Ménard, 2005).

Conclusion

This chapter on Quebec social policy is one among many in a collection about Canadian social policy more generally. Several chapters in this volume focus on direct and indirect federal initiatives that have an impact in Quebec and the rest of Canada. Taking this into account, this chapter has emphasized the initiatives of the Quebec state and in doing so has made passing reference to federal initiatives. In other papers (Vaillancourt, 1988 and 1996; Vaillancourt et al., 2004; Vaillancourt & Thériault, 2009), we have often examined in detail social policies stemming from the federal state. To summarize: in Quebec as in Ontario, Manitoba, Nova Scotia, and so on, today as in the past, social policies are the outcomes of intervention by two levels of government of the sort that is unavoidable within the framework of Canadian federalism, namely intervention by both the federal and the provincial governments. With Quebec, however, there is one difference, which we pointed out in the introduction and considered on various occasions in this chapter. That difference is that the Quebec state is not merely a provincial state, it is also a national state—that is, a state to which the Quebec nation has historically felt the need to turn in order to defend and affirm its identity and future. This helps explain why, in Quebec's political culture, the social stakeholders who wish to develop and enhance social policy turn first toward their provincial and national state, and not toward the federal state,

Box 1 Characteristics of Quebec Policy on Child Care Services

A policy adopted in 1997, after 45 years of struggle by the women's movement, labour unions, not-for-profit child care centre groups, etc., to establish a "universal, no-charge network" of daycare centres.

A policy that from 1997 to 2005 aimed for an increase from 55,000 to 200,000 child care places for children aged 0 to 5 at a cost of $5 per day per child. This cost was raised to $7 per day in 2003.

A policy which meant that by 2011, 214,804 places were being offered in a plural system using three sorts of suppliers: (a) 1,000 Centres de la petite enfance (CPEs)—not-for-profit daycare centres under the social and solidarity economy (82,671 places; 38.5 percent of supply); (b) 646 subsidized commercial daycare centres (40,626 places; 18.9 percent); and (c) 14,700 individuals responsible for child care services in a family setting, supervised by 163 coordinating offices reporting to CPEs or third-sector organizations (91,607 places; 42.6 percent).[a]

A policy built on mixed funding: 15 percent from citizen-users (the $7 per day per child from parents); 85 percent from public funds, equivalent to $1.8 billion in 2009–2010.

A policy distinguished by the fact that most of the 40,000 employees of CPEs and family child care centres are women and are heavily unionized. The type of labour unionism practised over the years has helped improve working conditions and raise service quality standards.

A policy that recognizes the CPEs' democratic governance, which is based on the participation of 7,000 parent and employee volunteers on boards of directors.

A policy in which CPEs and the principles of cooperation and reciprocity specific to the social and solidarity-based economy play a structuring role with respect to overall daycare services, including those provided by family child care centres and subsidized commercial daycare centres.

A policy that calls upon social regulation and quality standards co-constructed over the years by the Quebec state and civil society stakeholders, including CPE groups and their allies in social movements.

A policy that has supported the education of children under 6 and has increased women's labour market participation.

A policy whereby services are regularly evaluated by Quebec's statistics bureau (Bureau de la statistique du Québec). These evaluations highlight the fact that the services provided by CPEs are of higher quality than those delivered by family child care services and subsidized commercial daycare centres; they also underscore that the quality of the services provided by family child care services is higher than those delivered by subsidized commercial daycare centres.

[a] We are not including here the 346 unsubsidized commercial daycare centres, which offer 17,824 places (Lévesque, 2011, p. 15).

Source: Lévesque (2011); http://www.aqcpe.com/CPE/CPE-chiffres.

when they seek to have a national policy—for instance, on combating poverty, or on family social policy, social housing, and so on.

It is equally relevant to talk of Quebec's uniqueness in Canada and North America. That is what we have done in our review of a century of social policy, paying attention to the shifting boundaries that divide states from markets, the third sector, and families. To that end, we have distinguished three main periods, observing that the first (up to 1960) was marked more by government inaction on social policy, and that the most progressive initiatives were launched between the 1960s and the 2010s. This is why we have reserved the term "Quebec model of social policy" for the five decades beginning in 1960.

During the first period (1910–60), under the sway of traditional nationalism, which was subservient to the Catholic Church, Quebec fell behind with respect to social policy development. This nationalism, coupled with a corporatist vision, led to a distrust of the state which affected the provincial as much as the federal state. Until the late 1930s, anti-statism was not a feature solely of Quebec; economic liberalism, which advocates *laissez-faire*, had led to anti-statism in Canada as a whole. Then after the Second World War, the federal government embraced Keynesian policies and sought to develop new social programs that would regulate the economy besides playing a humanitarian role. Here, distrust of the state helped make Quebec's posture more distinctive. Faced with the rise of capitalist industrialization and the resulting social problems, Quebec—especially under the Duplessis governments (1936–39 and 1944–59)—was characterized by timidity and inaction with respect to social policy, and by an eagerness to criticize the federal government's programs and interventions. The defensive nationalist discourse of Quebec's elites in government and civil society delayed but did not prevent new federal programs, such as Unemployment Insurance, family allowances, Old Age Security, and so on. Furthermore, when the Quebec state did intervene, it did so "backwards," by targeting—most often with regard to social assistance—groups viewed as unfit to work or as not required to work, such as the disabled, the elderly, and mothers in need. The Quebec state was reluctant to intervene in problems resulting from the limitations of free markets. Individuals, families, and the third sector were called upon to take up the slack in the name of mutual assistance and Christian charity. But over the years, their social responsibilities became overwhelming and their mission impossible. On their own, the third-sector organizations of this period were unable to ameliorate the weaknesses of the market economy or the absence of a social state.

During a second period (1960–80), with the rise of a new, more modern nationalism, Quebec was increasingly interested in using the state to take charge of the development of its social policy and economic development. Distrust of federal intervention persisted, but distrust of intervention by the Quebec state disappeared. For Quebec's social policy, this was a period of both catching up and innovation. It saw the emergence of "Version 1" of a Quebec model in which the state behaved as an entrepreneur. In choosing the Beveridgian rather than the Bismarckian route under the influence of the philosophy advocated in the Boucher and Castonguay Reports, the state promoted social policy reforms in which it nationalized third-sector organizations, such as family social services in the 1950s, and kept for itself the roles of planner, operator, administrator, funding provider, supplier, and evaluator.[16] Unlike what was advanced in the mid-1930s in certain reform proposals in line with the more proactive component of

Conclusion

the corporatist movement[17]—proposals then forgotten under the Duplessis governments—state interventionism in social policy did not encourage the participation of stakeholders from civil society and the labour market. This interventionism led to progress with regard to the redistribution of income and access to collective services; it also contributed to the rise of a modern public administration, attentive to citizens' rights and seeking greater territorial equity in the various regions of Quebec. But it also led to a degree of centralization and bureaucratic standardization, particularly in the social assistance reforms that were gradually implemented in 1964–65. Quebec during this period signed on to federal cost-sharing programs, such as hospital insurance and Medicare. Above all, it innovated by developing its own programs, such as the Quebec Pension Plan, its family allowance, a network of local community service centres (CLSCs), automobile insurance, and so on. Building on compliance with the areas of constitutional jurisdiction set aside for the provinces, it fought for the repatriation with fiscal compensation of federal cost-sharing programs developed in preceding decades—for instance, in the fields of social assistance and health insurance. It went further by seeking to broaden its constitutional responsibilities so as to become the key link in an integrated social policy system. But since the federal government already held that ground and wanted to control social policies carried out from Ottawa, federal–provincial tensions and struggles began to appear from 1963 onward concerning the control of social policy. The new Quebec nationalism, espoused both by federalist political parties (such as the Liberal Party and the *Union nationale*) and by a sovereigntist political party (the Parti Québécois), encouraged the Quebec people and its governments to see the Quebec state as their national state. Over that period, the enhancement of the state's role in social development went hand in hand with recognition of the market's inability to self-regulate. It also led to shelving the participation of the association-based and cooperative third sector in the conceptualization and implementation of social policy, even while new generations of community and voluntary organizations emerged that were concerned with preserving their autonomy from the Church and the state and were involved in the promotion of social innovation.

Over a third period (1980–2010), in a context marked by the globalization of neoliberal ideas and the crisis in the welfare and Fordist state, transformations were seen that, for Quebec's social policy, represented possibilities for moving backward, but also opportunities for advancing in the direction of more inclusive, democratic social policies. In that context, the mid-1990s saw the emergence of a new generation of progressive public and social policies, which we have called "renewed social democratic" policies (Doré, Lapierre, Lévesque & Vaillancourt, 2009), and the appearance of new configurations in terms of the interfaces among the state, the market, the third sector, and families. To illustrate that, we described the context in which these new policies of the Quebec state emerged under PQ governments from

1994 to 2003. We then briefly gave nine examples of these policies, in the areas of family policy, recognition of the social economy and community organizations, local development, daycare centres (CPEs), and social housing, for instance. By way of illustration, we looked in greater detail at the characteristics of one of these exemplary policies—namely, the policy on child care services (see Box 1). We emphasized the fragility of these innovative initiatives, and mentioned that they were representative not of the whole but of only part of the social policy reforms developed during the period. We specified that they cohabited with other more neoliberal policies also emerging from Quebec governments (under the PQ and the Quebec Liberal Party)[18] and, of course, the federal governments of Chrétien and Martin (Liberal) and Harper (Conservative), such as the Employment Insurance reform of the 1990s and 2000s and the withdrawal of federal joint funding in the development of new provincial social housing programs since 1994. We acknowledged that the progressive policies appearing since 1995 had been sorely tested while nevertheless showing resilience over the past eight years of Charest government. Overall, we stated that these policies had proven to have a lasting and structuring effect for 15 years or so, and we pointed to the existence of a "Version 2" of the Quebec social policy model.

In this renewed Quebec model, there are characteristics such as the following five: (1) a conception of the social state that is more of a partner and is able to accommodate participation by stakeholders from civil society and the labour market in both the design and the implementation of public policy, involving "co-construction with public authorities" at the local, regional, national, and international levels (Laville, 2011, pp. 70–71; Vaillancourt, 2012); (2) funding, often mixed, coming mainly, but not totally from the public purse, as in the case of child care services; (3) participation by third-sector or social and solidarity based economy organizations in the administration and delivery of certain collective services of public interest, meaning that third-sector organizations have made gains, unequal from one policy to another, in terms of their ability to impose themselves as true partners of the state, "by refusing not only the market society, but also the instrumentalization of the social and solidarity economy permitting it to become equivalent to a public sub-service" (Laville, 2011, p. 90); (4) making use of certain public agencies (such as health and social service centres and local development centres) or third-sector organizations (such as housing cooperatives and NPOs), which intervene in local communities and receive substantial public funding, while maintaining governance structures open to the participation of stakeholders from local communities and civil society;[19] and (5) the struggle of stakeholders from the third sector of the social and solidarity based economy to participate in a plural economy where it is possible to go beyond a dual reductionism, where the economy is reduced to the market economy and politics is reduced to representative democracy, implying the attainment of a better balance among the principles of competition specific to the market economy, the redistribution specific to the public economy, and the reciprocity specific to the social and solidarity based economy (Laville, 2011, pp. 36–40; Jetté & Shields, 2010, pp. 203–214).

NOTES

This chapter was translated by David Llewellyn.

1 We postulate that in the 12 Canadian provinces and territories other than Quebec, there are also specific, original social policies. This does not prevent all the provinces and territories from having a number of points in common, since the same social policies from the federal state are applied more or less the same way across Canada.

2 We make an exception for the Liberal government of Adélard Godbout, who put forward several social policy reforms from 1939 to 1944. These reforms were curtailed or abandoned with the return of the Union Nationale government of Maurice Duplessis, who remained in power from 1944 to 1959 (Vaillancourt, 1988: chapter 3; Clavette, 2005).

3 We are thinking for example of the social-democratically oriented English Canadian intellectuals who, from the 1930s onward, drew up the social policy reform plans subsequently implemented by the federal government and some provincial governments, including Tommy Douglas's CCF government, in power in Saskatchewan from 1944 to 1960.

4 Cost-sharing programs were also called *conditional grants*. In these programs, the federal government offered the provinces the opportunity to sign agreements with it and share the costs of these provincially administered programs, provided the provinces complied with Canada-wide standards set by the federal government.

5 The radicalization of social movements took place during the second half of the 1960s and during the 1970s in the labour union movement, the co-operative movement, the women's movement, the student movement, international solidarity groups, and community organizations. It led to a reinforcement of the social democratic and Marxist and even Marxist-Leninist currents from 1973 to 1980. Paradoxically, it boosted on the left, with reference to statism, both higher demands on the state and a new distrust of the state (Lévesque, 2007; Vaillancourt, 2010).

6 Claude Morin (1972), a close adviser of Premier Lesage, was a member of the committee and drafted a substantial part of the report. He would become deputy minister in the new Ministry of Federal-Provincial Affairs in the summer of 1963 and would play an important role in the negotiations concerning social policy issues up to the 1971 Victoria Conference. He would be Minister of Intergovernmental Affairs in the PQ government from 1976 to 1981.

7 Integration was not anticipated in the commission's reports but was decided on by the Bourassa government.

8 The Castonguay Commission in a short document devoted to the question had been particularly severe concerning the possibility of resorting to private, for-profit organizations in the health and social services field (Castonguay Commission, 1970). Paradoxically, three decades later, Castonguay's name would be associated with privatizaton of the health care system (Castonguay et al., 2008).

9 The "*Trente Glorieuses*" ("Thirty Glorious Years") is an expression commonly used by French-language authors to refer to the Golden Age of the welfare state from 1945 to 1975.

10 These governments were the following: the second PQ government, headed by René Lévesque and Pierre-Marc Johnson (1981–1985); the Quebec Liberal Party (PLQ) governments headed by Robert Bourassa and Daniel Johnson Jr. (1985–1994); the PQ governments headed by Jacques Parizeau (1994–1995), Lucien Bouchard (1996–2000),

and Bernard Landry (2001–2003); and the PLQ governments headed by Jean Charest (2003–2011).

11 For a more in-depth presentation of this theoretical perspective, see Vaillancourt, 2003, pp. 162–168.

12 The emergence and evolution of the new development model are attributable to contributions from both civil society players and the labour market and government.

13 For more detailed analyses of these cases, see Jetté & Vaillancourt, 2011; Proulx, Bourque & Savard, 2007; Proulx, Dumais & Vaillancourt, 2006; Vaillancourt & Tremblay, 2002; and Vaillancourt, 2003, 2010, and 2012.

14 Among other possible examples, some, such as the universal medical drug insurance program introduced in 1998 and the evolution of housing policy for the frail elderly during the 1990s and 2000s, could underscore the fact that some policies are leaning toward a closer partnership between the state and the private sector than between the state and the third sector. This is borne out by the reports of government task forces that encourage the Quebec government to open health and long-term care policies up more to private sector participation (Castonguay, 2008; Ménard, 2005).

15 Available evaluations of the outcome of the fight against poverty and exclusion reveal that this struggle has been a success for families with children, but a failure for single individuals. A large part of the reason for the failure to improve the latter's socio-economic situation lies in the political refusal of governments of the past three decades to make any significant increase in the social assistance scales of single individuals deemed to be capable of working (Brochu, Makdissi & Taohan, 2011; Noël, 2011).

16 In fact, the Beveridgian vision of the role of the state advocated in the Boucher Report (1963) in Quebec was quite closely harmonized with the vision seen a few years earlier in such federal documents as the Marsh Report (1975).

17 We are thinking here of certain proposals in the *Action libérale nationale* (ALN) platform in which Duplessis pretended to be interested in 1935 and which he rapidly forgot when he became premier in a majority government from 1936 to 1939 and from 1944 to 1959 (Pelletier & Vaillancourt, 1975).

18 We are thinking, for instance, of the evolution of the long-term institutional care policy for the frail elderly during the 1990s and 2000s.

19 This perspective of stakeholders' participation in the co-construction of public policy led to a post-welfare state vision of social policy in which citizen users, taken individually and collectively, are not only recipients but also co-constructors of social policy.

References

6, P., & Vidal, I. (Eds.) (1994). *Delivering welfare. Repositioning non-profit and co-operative action in Western European welfare states.* Barcelona, Spain: Centro de Iniciativas de Economía Social.

Angers, F.-A. (1945). Les allocations familiales fédérales de 1944. *L'actualité économique*, 21, 228–262.

Angers, F.-A. (1955). *La sécurité sociale et les problèmes constitutionnels*, Annexe no 3 du rapport de la Commission Royale d'Enquête sur les Problèmes Constitutionnels. Québec: Province de Québec, Volumes I et II.

Archambault, L., Dumais, L., & Vaillancourt, Y. (2011). *Reducing poverty and promoting social participation? Benefits and limitations of measures for the activation of employment and occupational integration services for people with disabilities in Québec.* Winnipeg, MB: Council of Canadian with Disabilities, Social Policy—Disabling Poverty, Enabling Citizenship CURA Research Report.

Retrieved from http://www.ccdonline.ca/en/socialpolicy/poverty-citizenship/income-security-reform

Armitage, A. (1975). *Social welfare in Canada.* Toronto, ON: McClelland and Stewart.

Assogba, Y. (2000). *Insertion des jeunes, organisation communautaire et société. L'expérience fondatrice des Carrefours jeunesse-emploi au Québec.* Sainte-Foy, QC: Presses de l'Université du Québec.

Aubry, F., in collaboration with Plamondon, C. (2010). *The Québec Act to Combat Poverty and Social Exclusion: How does it tackle the situation of people with disabilities?* Study conducted for the Community University Research Alliance "Disabling Poverty and Enabling Citizenship." Winnipeg, MB: Council of Canadians with Disabilities. Retrieved from http://www.ccdonline.ca/en/socialpolicy/poverty-citizenship/quebec-law-poverty-exclusion

Banting, K. (1987). *The welfare state and Canadian federalism* (2nd ed.). Kingston, ON & Montreal, QC: McGill-Queen's University Press.

Béland, F., Contandriopoulos, A.-P., Quesnel-Vallée, A., & Robert, L. (Eds). (2008). *Le privé dans la santé. Les discours et les faits.* Montréal, QC: Presses de l'Université de Montréal.

Beveridge, W. (1942). *Social insurance and allied services.* New York, NY: Macmillan.

Bouchard, M.J., & Hudon, M. (Eds.). (2008). *Se loger autrement au Québec.* Montreal, QC: Éditions Saint-Martin.

Boucher Committee (or Comité d'étude sur l'assistance publique). (1963). *Rapport.* Québec, QC: Gouvernement du Québec.

Boucher, N., Fougeyrollas, P., & Gaucher, C. (2003). Development and transformation of advocacy in the disability movement of Quebec. In D. Stienstra & A. Wight-Felske (Eds.), *Making equality. History of advocacy and persons with disabilities in Canada* (pp. 137–162). Toronto, ON: Captus Press.

Bourque, G.L. (2000). *Le modèle québécois de développement: De l'émergence au renouvellement.* Sainte-Foy, QC: Presses de l'Université du Québec.

Bourque, D. (2008). *Concertation et partenariat. Entre levier et piège du développement des communautés.* Québec, QC: Presses de l'Université du Québec.

Bouvier, É. (1943a). De Beveridge à Marsh, *Relations*, 28, 87–90.

Bouvier, É. (1943b). Accepterons-nous le Plan Marsh? *Relations*, 30, 144–147.

Bouvier, É. (1943c). Centralisation et unité nationale, *Relations*, 33, 231–235.

Bouvier, É. (1944). Un projet d'allocations familiales, *Relations*, 44, 202–205.

Briand, L., Bellemare, G., & Gravel, A.-R. (2006). Contraintes, opportunités et menaces de l'institutionnalisation: le cas des centres de la petite enfance. In P.-A. Lapointe & G. Bellemare (Eds.), *Innovations sociales dans le travail et l'emploi, Recherches empiriques et perspectives théoriques* (pp. 185–207), Quebec, QC: Presses de l'Université Laval.

Brochu, P., Makdissi, P., & Taohan, L. (2011). Le Québec, champion canadien de la lutte contre la pauvreté? In INM (Ed.), *L'État du Québec 2011* (pp. 91–102). Montréal, QC: Boréal.

Bryden, K. (1974). *Old age pensions and policy-making in Canada.* Montreal, QC, and Kingston, ON: McGill-Queen's University Press.

Cassidy, H.M. (1943). *Social security and reconstruction in Canada.* Toronto: Ryerson Press.

Castonguay, C. (or Commission of Inquiry on Health and Social Welfare). (1967). *Rapport. Volume I: L'assurance-maladie.* Québec, QC: Gouvernement du Québec.

References Castonguay, C. (or Commission of Inquiry on Health and Social Welfare) (1970). *Rapport*. Volume VII, III: *Les établissements à but lucratif*. Québec, QC: Gouvernement du Québec.

Castonguay, C. (or Commission of Inquiry on Health and Social Welfare). (1971a). *Rapport. Volume V: La sécurité du revenu*, tome I. Quebec, QC: Gouvernement du Québec.

Castonguay, C. (or Commission of Inquiry on Health and Social Welfare). (1971b). *Rapport. Volume V: La sécurité du revenu*, tome II. Quebec, QC: Gouvernement du Québec.

Castonguay, C. (or Commission of Inquiry on Health and Social Welfare). (1971c). *Rapport. Volume V: La sécurité du revenu*, tome III. Quebec, QC: Gouvernement du Québec.

Castonguay, C. (or Commission of Inquiry on Health and Social Welfare). (1972a). *Report, Volume VI: Social Services*, tome I. Quebec, QC: Government of Quebec.

Castonguay, C. (or Commission of Inquiry on Health and Social Welfare). (1972b). *Report, Volume VI: Social Services*, Tome II. Quebec, QC: Government of Quebec.

Castonguay, C. et al. (2008). *En avoir pour son argent. Des services accessibles aux patients, un financement durable, un système productif, une responsabilité partagée*, Rapport du Groupe de travail sur le financement du système de santé. Québec, QC: Gouvernement du Québec.

Clavette, S. (2005). *Les dessous d'Asbestos*. Québec, QC: Presses de l'Université Laval.

Comeau, Y., Favreau, L., Lévesque, B., & Mendell, M. (2001). *Emploi, économie sociale, développement local*. Quebec, QC: Presses de l'Université du Québec.

Côté, L., Lévesque, B. & Morneau, G. (Eds.). (2009). *État stratège et participation citoyenne*. Québec: Presses de l'Université du Québec.

Davidson, G.F. (1943). The future development of social security in Canada. *Canadian Welfare*, 18*(7)*, 2–5 and 26–32.

Defourny, J., & Monzon Campos, J.L. (Eds.). (1992). *Économie sociale (entre économie capitaliste et économie publique) / The third sector (Cooperatives, mutual and nonprofit organizations)*. Bruxelles, Belgique: Centre international de recherche et d'information sur l'économique, sociale et cooperative (CIRIEC) and De Boeck Université.

Defourny, J., Develtere, P., & Fonteneau, B. (Eds.). (1999). *L'économie sociale au Nord et au Sud*. Paris, France & Bruxelles, Belgique: De Boeck Université.

Doré, M., Lapierre, M., Lévesque, B., & Vaillancourt, Y. (2009). Le renouvellement de la social-démocratie au Québec: Un chantier qui s'impose plus que jamais. In *Chantier pour une social-démocratie renouvelée*. Retrieved from http://www.eve.coop/social_democratie_15_mai_2009.pdf

École sociale populaire (ESP) (Ed.). 1934. *Le programme de Restauration sociale expliqué et commenté*. Montréal, QC: ESP, nos. 239–240.

Esping-Andersen, G. (1990). *The three worlds of welfare capitalism*. Cambridge, UK: Polity Press.

Esping-Andersen, G. (2008). *Trois leçons sur l'État-providence*. Paris, France: Seuil.

Evers, A., & Laville, J.-L. (Eds.) (2004). *The third sector in Europe*. Cheltenham, UK: Edward Elgar.

Favreau, L. (2006). Social economy and public policy: The Quebec experience. *Horizons*, *8*(2), 7–15.

Favreau, L. (2008). *Entreprises collectives. Les enjeux sociopolitiques et territoriaux de la coopération et de l'économie sociale.* Quebec, QC: Presses de l'Université du Québec.

Fortin, S., Noel, A., & St-Hilaire, F. (Eds.) (2003). *Forging the Canadian Social Union: SUFA and beyond.* Montreal, QC: Institute for Research on Public Policy (IRPP).

Fournier, J. (2011, 14 juillet). Détérioration des services aux personnes âgées. *Le Devoir.*

Godbout, L., & St-Cerny, S. (2008). *Le Québec, un paradis pour les familles? Regards sur la famille et la fiscalité.* Quebec, QC: Presses de l'Université Laval.

Government of Quebec (2002). *RSQ, c, L-7: An Act to combat poverty and social exclusion.* Quebec, QC: Quebec Official Publisher.

Gravel, A.R., Bellemare, G., & Briand, L. (2007). *Les centres de la petite enfance. Un mode de gestion féministe en transformation.* Québec, QC: Presses de l'Université du Québec.

Guest, D. (1980). *The emergence of social security in Canada.* Vancouver, BC: UBC Press.

Jetté, C. (2008). *Les organismes communautaires et la transformation de l'État-providence. Trois décennies de coconstruction des politiques publiques dans le domaine de la santé et des services sociaux.* Quebec, QC: Presses de l'Université du Québec.

Jetté, C., & Goyette, M. (2010). Pratiques sociales et pratiques managériales: Des convergences poissibles? *Nouvelles pratiques sociales, 22*(2), 25–34.

Jetté, C., Lévesque, B., Mager, L., & Vaillancourt, Y. (2000). *Économie sociale et transformation de l'État-providence dans le domaine de la santé et du bien-être. Une recension des écrits (1990–2000).* Sainte-Foy, QC: Presses de l'Université du Québec.

Jetté, C., & Shields, G. (Eds.) (2010). *Le développement de l'économie sociale au Québec.* Montréal, QC: Éditions Saint-Martin.

Jetté, C., & Vaillancourt, Y. (2011). Social economy and home care services in quebec: co-production or co-construction? *Voluntas: International Journal of Voluntary and Nonprofit Organizations, 22*(1), 48–69.

Klein, J.-L., Fontan, J.-M., Harrisson, D., & Lévesque, B. (2010). L'innovation sociale dans le contexte du "modèle québécoi." *The Philanthropist, 23*(3), 93–104.

Lalonde, M. (1973). *Document de travail sur la sécurité sociale au Canada.* Ottawa, ON: Gouvernement du Canada.

Laville, J.-L. (Ed.). (1994). *L'économie solidaire: Une perspective internationale.* Paris, France: Desclée de Brouwer.

Laville, J.-L. (2011). *Agir à gauche. L'économie sociale et solidaire.* Paris, France: Desclée de Brouwer.

Laville, J.-L., & Nyssens, M. (Eds.) (2001). *Les services sociaux entre associations, État et marché. L'aide aux personnes âgées.* Paris, France: La Découverte / MAUSS / CRIDA.

Lebel, L. (1931). Les allocations familiales et les hommes d'affaires. *L'Actualité économique,* janvier.

Lévesque, B. (2003). Fonction de base et nouveau rôle des pouvoirs publics: vers un nouveau paradigme de l'État. *Annals of Public and Cooperative Economics, 74*(4), 489–513.

References Lévesque, B. (2007). Un siècle et demi d'économie sociale au Québec: Plusieurs configurations en présence (1850–2007). Montréal, QC: CRISES, ENAP and ARUCES. Retrieved from http://www.crises.uqam.ca.

Lévesque, B. (2011). L'institutionnalisation des services québécois de garde à la petite enfance à partir de l'économie sociale: un processus qui s'échelonne sur plusieurs décennies. Montréal: CRISES, No ET1105. Retrieved from http://www.crises.uqam.ca.

Lévesque, B., & Thiry, B. (2008). Conclusions. Concurrence et partenariat, deux vecteurs de la reconfiguration des nouveaux régimes de la gouvernance des services sociaux et de santé. In B. Enjolras (Ed.), *Gouvernance et intérêt général dans les services sociaux et de santé* (pp. 227–261). Brussels, Belgium: P.I.E. Peter Lang.

Lewis, J. (1999). Reviewing the relationship between the voluntary sector and the state in Britain in the 1990s. *Voluntas. International Journal of Voluntary and Nonprofit Organizations, 10*(3), 255–270.

Lipietz, A. (1989). *Choisir l'audace. Une alternative pour le XXIe siècle.* Paris, France: Éditions La Découverte.

Majnoni d'Intignano, B. (1993). *La protection sociale.* Paris, France: Éditions de Fallois.

Marsh, L.C. [1943] (1975). *Report on social security for Canada 1943.* Toronto, ON: University of Toronto Press.

Ménard, L.J. et al. (2005). *Pour sortir de l'impasse: la solidarité entre les générations.* Rapport du Comité de travail sur la pérennité du système de santé et de services sociaux du Québec, QC. Québec: Gouvernement du Québec.

Ministère des Affaires sociales (MAS). (1979). *Les services à domicile.* Québec, QC: MAS.

Minville, E. (1939). *La législation ouvrière et le régime social dans la province de Québec.* Ottawa, ON: Gouvernement du Canada.

Morin, C. (1972). *Le pouvoir québécois ... en négociation.* Montréal, QC: Boréal.

Munro, J. (1970). *Income security for Canadians.* Ottawa, ON: Department of National Health and Welfare.

Noël, A. (1996). Vers un nouvel État-providence? Enjeux démocratiques. *Politique et sociétés, 30,* 3–27.

Noël, A. (2003). Une loi contre la pauvreté : La nouvelle approche québécoise de lutte contre la pauvreté et l'exclusion sociale. *Lien social et politiques, 48,* 103–114.

Noël, A. (2011). Une lutte inégale contre la pauvreté et l'exclusion sociale. In Institut du Nouveau Monde (inm) (Ed.), *L'État du Québec 2011* (pp. 103–110). Montréal, QC: Boréal.

Office des personnes handicapées du Québec (OPHQ) (1984). *À part ... égale. L'intégration sociale des personnes handicapées: un défi pour tous.* Québec, QC: Gouvernement du Québec.

Pelletier, M., & Vaillancourt, Y. (1974). *Les politiques sociales et les travailleurs. Cahier I: Les années 1900 à 1929.* Montréal, QC: À frais d'auteurs.

Pelletier, M., & Vaillancourt, Y. (1975). *Les politiques sociales et les travailleurs. Cahier II: Les années 1930.* Montréal, QC: À frais d'auteurs.

Piotte, J.-M. (1998). *Du combat au partenariat. Interventions critiques sur le syndicalisme québécois.* Montréal, QC: Éditions Nota bene.

Poulin, G. (1955). *L'assistance sociale dans la Province de Québec, 1608–1951*. Annexe no 2 au Rapport de la Commission Royale d'Enquête sur les Problèmes Constitutionnels. Québec, QC: Gouvernement du Québec.

Prince, M.J. (2002). Designing disability policy in Canada: The nature and impact of federalism on policy development. In A. Puttee (Ed.), *Federalism, democracy and disability policy in Canada* (pp. 29–77). Montreal, QC, & Kingston, ON: McGill-Queen's University Press.

Prince, M.J. (2009). *Absent citizens. Disability politics and policy in Canada*. Toronto, ON: University of Toronto Press.

Proulx, J., Bourque, D. & Savard, S. (2007). The Government-third sector interface in Quebec. *Voluntas: International Journal of Voluntary and Nonprofit Organizations, 18*(3), 293–307.

Proulx, J., Dumais, L., & Vaillancourt, Y. (2006). *Les services aux personnes ayant des incapacités au Québec: Rôle des acteurs et dynamiques régionales*. Montréal, QC: Cahier du LAREPPS no 06-12, UQAM.

Québec (1971). Loi sur les services de santé et les services sociaux. In *Lois du Québec, 1971*. Québec: chapitre 48.

Québec (1977). Loi sur la protection de la jeunesse. In *Lois du Québec, 1977*. Chapitre 20.

Rioux, M.H., & Prince, M.J. (2002). The Canadian political landscape of disability: Policy perspectives, social status, interest groups and the rights movement. In A. Puttee (Ed.), *Federalism, democracy, and disability policy in Canada* (pp. 11–28). Montreal, QC & Kingston, ON: McGill-Queen's University Press.

Rocher, G. (1960). Ambiguïtés et fonction de l'initiative privée dans le bien-être social. *Service social, 9*(2).

Rochon Commission (or Commission d'enquête sur la santé et les services sociaux). (1988). *Rapport*. Québec, QC: Gouvernement du Québec.

Rowell-Sirois Commission (or Commission royale des relations entre le Dominium et les provinces). (1940). *Rapport, 3 vols*. Ottawa, ON: Gouvernement du Canada.

Shields, G. (2006). *Dynamiques partenariales dans le champ de la main-d'oeuvre (1996–2003). Le défi d'une nouvelle gouvernance québécoise impliquant les organismes communautaires d'insertion*. Montréal, QC: LAREPPS, UQAM.

Shields, G. (2010). Le renouvellement de la politique sociale de l'emploi par la contractualisation avec les organismes communautaires québécois. In C. Jetté & G. Shields (Eds.), *Le développement de l'économie sociale au Québec* (pp. 117–139). Montréal, QC: Éditions Saint-Martin.

Torjman, S. (2001). Canada's federal regime and persons with disabilities. In D. Cameron & F. Valentine (Eds.), *Disability and federalism. Comparing different approaches to full participation* (pp. 151–196). Montreal, QC, & Kingston, ON: McGill-Queen's University Press.

Tremblay Commission (or Commission royale d'enquête sur les problèmes constitutionnels). (1956). *Rapport*, 4 volumes. Québec, QC: Gouvernement du Québec.

Trudeau, P.E. (Ed.) (1956). *La grève de l'amiante*. Montréal, QC: Les Éditions du Jour.

Vaillancourt, Y. (1988). *L'évolution des politiques sociales au Québec, 1940–1960*. Montréal, QC: Presses de l'Université de Montréal.

Vaillancourt, Y. (1991). Un bilan québécois des quinze premières années du Régime d'assistance publique du Canada (1966–1981): la dimension constitutionnelle. *Nouvelles pratiques sociales, 4*(2), 115–146.

Vaillancourt, Y. (1992). Un bilan québécois des quinze premières années du Régime d'assistance publique du Canada (1966–1981): La dimension sociale, *Service Social, 41*(2), 19–48.

Vaillancourt, Y. (1994). Quebec and the federal government: The struggle over opting out. In D. Glenday & A. Duffy (Eds.), *Canadian society. Understanding and surviving in the 1990s* (pp. 168–189). Toronto, ON: McClelland and Stewart.

Vaillancourt, Y. (1996). Remaking Canadian social policy: A Québec Viewpoint. In J. Pulkingham & G. Ternowetsky (Eds.), *Remaking Canadian social policy. Social security in the late 1990s* (pp. 81–99). Halifax, NS: Fernwood Publishing.

Vaillancourt, Y. (2003). The Quebec model in social policy and its interface with Canada's Social Union. In S. Fortin, A. Noël, & F. St-Hilaire (Eds.), *Forging the Canadian Social Union: SUFA and beyond* (pp. 157–195). Montreal, QC: Institute for Research on Public Policy (IRPP).

Vaillancourt, Y. (2009). Social economy in the co-construction of public policy. *Annals of Public and Cooperative Economics. Annales de l'économie publique, sociale et coopérative, 80*(2), 275–313.

Vaillancourt, Y. (2010). Social economy in Quebec and Canada: Configuration past and present. In J.J. McMurtry (Ed.), *Living economics. Canadian perspectives on the social economy, co-operatives, and community economic development* (pp. 57–104). Toronto, ON: Emond Montgomery Publications.

Vaillancourt, Y. (2012). Third sector and the co-construction of Canadian public policy. In V. Pestoff, T. Brandsen & B. Verschuere (Eds.), *New public governance, the third sector, and co-production.* London, UK, & New York, NY: Routledge.

Vaillancourt, Y., Aubry, F., Kearney, M., Thériault, L., & Tremblay, L. (2004). The contribution of the social economy towards healthy social policy reforms in Canada. A Quebec viewpoint. In D. Raphael (Ed.), *Social determinants of health: Canadian perspectives* (pp. 311–329). Toronto, ON: Canadian Scholars' Press.

Vaillancourt, Y., Caillouette, J., & Dumais, L. (Eds) (2002). *Les politiques sociales s'adressant aux personnes ayant des incapacités au Québec: Histoire, inventaire et éléments de bilan.* Montréal, QC: LAREPPS / ARUC-ES / UQAM.

Vaillancourt, Y., & Ducharme, M.-N., in collaboration with R. Cohen, C. Jetté & C. Roy (2001). *Social Housing—A key component of social policies in transformation: The Quebec experience.* Ottawa, ON: Caledon Institute of Social Policy. Retrieved from http://caledoninst.org

Vaillancourt, Y., & Thériault, L. (2009). Social economy, social policy, and federalism in Canada. In A. Gagnon (Ed.), *Contemporary Canadian federalism. Foundations, traditions, institutions* (pp. 330–357). Toronto, ON: University of Toronto Press.

Vaillancourt, Y., & Tremblay, L. (Eds.) (2002). *Social economy, health, and welfare in four Canadian provinces.* Halifax, NS: Fernwood Publishing.

Current Social Policy Issues

Part III

Single Motherhood in the Canadian Landscape

Postcards from a Subject

8

Iara Lessa

As enduring and controversial as the welfare system itself, the single mother is a popular image in Western societies. She may be seen as a threat to the assumptions of the traditional family; or as a promise of women's independence from male control; or even as posing a challenge to the universalization of the wage worker subject. She, nevertheless, has been central to the discussions about the future of the national social welfare system, the public management of a future society, and the socialization of its members. In 2006, women headed approximately 13 percent of all census families in Canada, constituting 80 percent of all lone-parent families (Statistics Canada, 2006a). Although single mothers come from a variety of social locations and life circumstances, through many processes their social identity becomes essentialized as mothers raising children alone, and at different times social policies have interpreted, valued, and addressed their contributions to society differently.

In this chapter I discuss how the women referred to as single mothers have assumed this position of importance in Canadian social policy. This discussion calls attention to the nature of single motherhood and its relationship with social welfare, and focuses on the ways in which society problematizes certain population groups and makes them the object of collective provision. This chapter's conceptual underpinnings can be situated in a body of literature inspired by Foucault's work and loosely called governmentality for its interest in exploring the contexts in which government of self and others takes place (Dean, 1999; Rose, 1999). The chapter starts with a classification of the various issues associated with single mothers to arrive at a rather broad definition of this group. It then proceeds to examine the several policy periods that contributed to shape and define single motherhood in Canada. It concludes with a discussion of contemporary issues associated with single mothers and neoliberalism.

Defining Perspectives

Defining Perspectives

The term "single or lone mother" gained currency during the 1960s, consolidating within one group the war widow with young children, the deserted mother, the divorced mother, the separated or married mother with absent husband, the displaced homemaker, the battered wife, the adolescent mother, and multiple other characterizations of many women's lives, which had been, throughout the twentieth century, the focus of particular social policies and strategies. This large group of mothers, independent of their class, race, religion, sexual preference, country of birth, abilities, or any other descriptor, became defined by one sole aspect of their lives: the absence of a father in their family unit. In the United States the term is highly racialized through an association with African Americans, and in western Canada, Pulkingham, Fuller, and Kershaw (2010) suggest an association with Aboriginal groups. In general, throughout the Western world, single motherhood is linked to various social concerns, and addressing those concerns has made the lives of poor women raising children alone the subject of public scrutiny and attention.

The social organization of Western societies and the functioning of their capitalist economic systems assume an ideal family unit comprising the male breadwinner, dependent wife, and children. Shaped according to specific class, race, gender, and heterosexual assumptions, this ideal is core to the production and reproduction of resources (Lessa, 2008). Families that deviate from it, such as the one constituted by the woman who is raising children alone, are considered incomplete and problematic. Single mothers become the feared others, outside the idealized norm, problematized through reference to social expectations regarding the family's private responsibility for maintenance, care, and upbringing of its children (Gordon, 1994). They invoke a variety of tightly woven social traditions, values, and judgments both echoed and fuelled by professional and scientific discourses that cast this group of women as a social problem (Harding, 1993a, 1993b). The problems they seem to represent are as diverse as the many individual portraits of single mothers themselves. Those problems seem, nevertheless, to converge around three general arguments—individual characteristics, structural circumstances, and moral imperatives (Seccombe, James, & Walters, 1998)—which, although not mutually exclusive, characterize the common discourses regarding single motherhood.

A first set of arguments sees single motherhood as a problem characteristic of particular groups, such as African Americans in the United States, who, as argued by Amott (1990), were forced into a tradition of family separations under slavery. This association persists even though in 1996, African Americans constituted only 36 percent of welfare recipients (Seccombe et al., 1998, p. 850). In Canada a group of single mothers that is highly problematized is teenage single mothers. Dryburgh (2007) documents that there has been a decline in teen pregnancy in the past decade. This group is usually

Defining Perspectives

single and is described as unprepared for the physical and social aspects of motherhood and as doomed to dependency on state support, despite evidence to the contrary (Davis et al., 1999; Lessa, 2006). They are commonly pathologized (Horowitz, 1995) and are portrayed in the media as deviant and as symbols of the decline of social order and discipline (e.g., Hewlett, 1986; Schamess, 1990). As part of these arguments some authors have proposed that single motherhood has integrated certain families, which have developed sets of "sub-cultural" (Seccombe et al., 1998) or "underclass" (Leung, 1998) values as a result of living for prolonged periods in social marginalization. Therefore, single-mother families are not only a problem for the present but also a reminder of the exponential growth of these problems, which have intergenerational consequences for the future. Some arguments have proposed that offspring from single-mother families are "more likely to drop out of school, be unemployed, and themselves form mother only families than are children who grow up with two parents" (Garfinkel & McLanahan, 1986, pp. 11–12).

The structural argument invokes the prevalence of poverty and associated stresses among single mothers (Lero & Brockman, 1993; McDaniel, 1993). Although not all single mothers are poor, a large group of the poor are single mothers. Resting on feminist and political economy explanations, authors using this argument (Kitchen, 1992) discuss the structural barriers to women obtaining stable, well-paid jobs; the demands of contemporary standards of living that require, most often, two incomes per family; the domestic division of labour; and women's disadvantaged situation in the labour market. Consequently single mothers are associated with low income, housing difficulties, and dependence on state support (Milar, 2000). Single mothers' poverty is also seen as significantly affecting their children's academic, behavioural, and emotional situation (Polakow, 1994), as well as being a risk to adolescents' health and adaptation (Judge & Benzeval, 1993). These arguments are variously explained by a combination of less parenting time, extreme stress and duress, absence of a father figure, an impoverished living environment, and less than adequate housing (Amato, 1999; Gringlas, 1995).

The third set of general arguments—the moral arguments—proposes that fatherless families are a problem to the institution of the family, threatening to break down and disorganize this basic unit of society (Morgan, 1995). In the United Kingdom, Green (1993, p. vi) suggests that the traditional family is the foundation of freedom because in it children "learn voluntary restraint, respect for others and sense of personal responsibility." Reflecting the deep patriarchal roots of Western society, single-mother families, in this argument, embody the fears and concerns about the changes in the family and the relationships between the genders (see discussion in Eichler, 1997). In this sense lone mothers are portrayed as a growing threat to the foundations of liberal societies and constitute the preferred target for groups advocating the return to traditional ways (Richards, 1997). Single motherhood, thus, has been used as one of the reasons to attack sex education, divorce laws, abortion, obscenity, homosexuality, and contraception (Somerville, 1992).

These understandings of single motherhood as a problem for social organization have made this group of women the focus for welfare state policy intervention. In the liberal regime of state welfare (Esping-Andersen, 2006) single mothers embody a particularly conflicting combination of social roles: they are responsible for children's upbringing and socialization, but, at the same time, they are also responsible for supporting the family. In other words, they are mothers and workers or caregivers and breadwinners (Evans, 1992). On one side, as mothers nurturing the future generation, they should be supported in order to adequately carry out their social reproduction functions. On the other, they must be socially discouraged in order to dampen the numbers of those entering single motherhood and to limit the costs to the system. Ellwood (1988) has argued that availability of financial and other benefits tends to encourage single parenthood and consequently just increases the problem. More conservative commentators have charged that the support of single mothers is a disincentive to marriage and family life (Gilder, 1982; Murray, 1984) and actually causes single motherhood (Richards, 1997). As Fraser and Gordon (1994) have demonstrated, despite arguments to the contrary, single mothers have become intrinsically linked to negative interpretations of social dependency. To map the nature of what we call single mother is, hence, to touch on the very processes that constitute the complex set of relations and interactions embedded in the implementation of social care—the welfare system and our society as a whole.

I propose that we approach single motherhood as an assemblage of ideas, knowledges, expectations, beliefs, judgments, and assumptions about women raising children without a male partner. This assemblage represents relations of power; that is, it represents ways of acting upon these women that bring about relations among individuals. Some women become socialized into single motherhood through a series of rationalities and practices directed at poor women raising children alone but also aimed at the well-being of the population of a nation as a whole. As such, single mothers are not a given, ahistorical, or universal. They are located in a specific time and place, in constant change, and profoundly bound to collective values, social policies, and practices.

Thus, discussing single motherhood in Canada necessarily involves reviewing the policies that help create a variety of power relations to produce a concrete group of women who, despite their various circumstances, represent a challenge to the social ethics of care. This discussion involves not only the actual policies but also their motivations and intentions, as well as the contexts and practices that help translate those into actions. The next sections examine the policies addressing single motherhood in

Canada organized into three broad periods to inform the discussion of contemporary policies and understandings. The starting point is not *who* single mothers are or *what* their needs are but *how* they were made to be; *how* it became thinkable to support mothers in their child-raising activities; and what forms these practices took.

The Importance of Mothers' Caring Work

The Importance of Mothers' Caring Work

While single motherhood is not specific to any economic class, it is primarily the poor mothers who became a social concern and in need of financial support. Support to mothers constituted, both in Canada and in the United States (Gordon, 1994; Mink, 1998), the first direct public financial aid for a group. Until early 20th century, there was no concerted social policy addressing women who raised children without a male partner; rather, there was a series of traditions and conventions with old roots undertaken by individuals, institutions, organizations, and local governments. In Britain, the Poor Laws called for different treatment for widows, deserted, and unmarried mothers, and these traditions, although not implemented throughout Canada, influenced charitable approaches to these women during the 19th and early 20th centuries until the introduction of Mother's Allowance legislations by the provinces after the First World War.

Many factors contributed to the widespread acceptance of supporting poor mothers. Across the Western nations in the late 19th and early 20th centuries, paid motherhood was one of the reforms advocated by the women's movement (among other demands were women's suffrage, birth control, sexual freedom, child welfare, labour reform, and civil rights) (Comacchio, 1999). Paid motherhood was proposed as a way of preventing the dissolution of family ties and attending to the plight of dependent poor children. It stressed the importance of enabling women to dedicate themselves to child socialization. As articulated at the time, these arguments implied support for a gender division of labour, with the male worker being paid a family wage; and a definition of motherhood according to English, white, middle-class heterosexual standards of what constitutes care, cleanliness, and family (Little, 1995).

By the First World War in Canada, crime, disease, infant mortality, and the growth of slums became increasingly associated with the instability of the family and support for motherhood received widespread sanction. Suffragists, such as Nellie McClung, argued for greater appreciation of women's maternal qualities and more humane values, while Leacock, for example, emphasized female weakness, questioning women's ability to support themselves and their families on their own (Strong-Boag, 1979). Mothers' Allowance legislation in Canadian provinces was also influenced by events during the 1914–18 war: the images of poor widows and their children popularized the need for the propagation of a physically and morally fit generation to inherit the nation. Examples of public interventions were provided by the implementation of the mothers' aid programs in some of the American states and, as well, by support provided by the Canadian Patriotic Fund to wives of soldiers abroad and local experiments by Local Councils of Women providing for poor widows.

Mothers' Allowance (1916–1964)

Mothers' Allowance was the first instance of provincial governments accepting responsibility for the welfare of a specific group of people and committing themselves to their support (Struthers, 1994). Manitoba (in 1916) was the first province in Canada to pass legislation granting an allowance to poor widows. By 1920 the western provinces and Ontario had similar legislation in place, and by the 1950s all provinces had some form of support for these mothers (Little, 1998). Particularly important is the fact that provinces and municipalities were paying mothers without means of support to stay at home to look after their children. They were, thus, supporting caring work and family life, and recognizing the importance and value of motherhood and its effects on a healthy citizenry. From the onset, as we shall see next, allowances were characterized by restricted domestic supervision, categorical eligibility, rigorous moral requirements, and meagre financial support.

The Mothers' Allowance programs were modelled on the English, Protestant charitable initiatives of women's organizations and social service leaders characterized by stringent eligibility criteria and by the normalization of their own values. While supporting poor mothers, women in these organizations also saw for themselves a role in the public world defined by a career in family management, and developed professional tools to "direct" mothers of the lower classes, whom they regarded as deviant and distressed. They initially supported primarily poor widows with at least two dependent children, but gradually the eligibility criteria were extended to include various categories of excluded poor mothers alone: wives of incapacitated men, deserted women, foster mothers, mothers with only one child, divorcees and officially separated mothers, wives of criminals in prison, and unmarried mothers, as well as previous residents of other provinces and immigrants. These sequential enlargements of eligibility criteria were the result of struggles by the excluded group and their allies (social workers and women's groups). This process of negotiation left its mark on the program by simultaneously maintaining its categorical nature and increasing the total number of beneficiaries. By the 1960s most provinces did not place restrictions on the causes of single motherhood, but arguments regarding fathers' or male partners' responsibility for their families continued to be important mechanisms for excluding some mothers from benefits.

Under the allowance, mothers were subjected to strict tests of destitution and thriftiness, as well as ongoing moral investigations and supervision

Mothers' Allowance (1916–1964)

regarding motherhood expertise, household management, and moral fitness (Strong-Boag, 1979). The programs incorporated an understanding of individual circumstances of the families, but imposed on them a grid of moral values and priorities addressing healthy habits, children's upbringing, satisfactory home environment, budgeting and management, and moral fitness (Lessa, 1999). In so doing they defined the indicators of good motherhood, shaping them according to the class, race, religion, and sexual identity of investigators and administrators.

The type and amount of support varied, but provinces were constantly concerned with cost containment and only reluctantly accepted responsibility for the well-being of the families. Resulting from advocacy and from recognition of the inadequacy of benefits, some in-kind and tagged benefits—medical and dental assistance, support for fuel and winter clothing, and, in some cases, emergency funds—were incorporated into the allowance as a discretionary practice. The programs were unequivocally residual and partial, and even by the most modest standards, they never provided enough to raise a family. Financial support, reflecting a fear of discouraging industriousness, in addition to strict regulations and low ceilings, assumed initially that the mothers would supplement any money they received with approved work. However, the major supplementation to Mother's Allowance only came with the postwar Family Allowance, a universal benefit established by the federal government in 1944 (Kitchen, 1987).

Parallel with the process of building the Canadian post–Second World War welfare state, transfer of federal funds for provincial social programs became contingent on the employable–unemployable dichotomy (Hum, 1987). As a result, a focus on work gradually came to dominate the discourse of Mothers' Allowance programs, eroding their initial valuing of caring activities. Consequently mothers raising children alone were recast under this dichotomy: rather than being seen as important to the nation because of their motherhood role, they came to be seen primarily in relation to their participation in the labour market. Their motherhood duties, until then understood as a necessary job, were reinterpreted as an obstruction to entering the labour force. In earlier periods, the Mother's Allowance beneficiary was prompted to work to supplement the allowance; in the postwar period she gradually become a category of the unemployable because of her family responsibilities. Mothers' Allowance ceased to be an enabler for the ability to raise children with employment supplementation and supervision, and became essentially a provision attending to a deficiency that impeded full-time employment (Lessa, 1999).

Family Benefits under the Canada Assistance Plan (1966–1996)

Family Benefits under the Canada Assistance Plan (1966–1996)

The introduction of the Canada Assistance Plan (CAP) in the mid-1960s is a marker for the consolidation of the transformations in social policy approaches to poor women raising children alone: women were above all workers. Women had begun to re-enter the labour force in large numbers, but many of them had become, in fact, "unemployable" not only because of motherhood obligations but also because of their lack of paid work experience, limited skills, the cumulative effect of living in poverty for years, and the structural results of devaluing traditional women's jobs. While some of these trends also affected married women; in the two-parent family, the mother's income from work was but a complement to her husband's. Within the families of women raising children alone, earnings from work were the sole source of support, and when they supplemented the allowance, these earnings were controlled and deducted from the benefit received.

CAP captured and crystallized a change in the understanding of the importance of motherhood in a new legislation. Under the CAP umbrella, provincial Mother's Allowance programs were integrated into the national system of welfare, consolidating a number of federal and provincial programs—Unemployment Assistance, Old Age Assistance, Blind Person's Allowance, Disabled Person's Allowance, and Mothers' Allowance—into a single 50/50 cost-sharing arrangement between the governments: Family Benefits. Provincial residency requirements were dropped, and standard responsibilities were imposed on all provinces. Reflecting contemporary progressive discussions regarding poverty amidst the postwar wealth (Struthers, 1994), benefits were proposed in terms of human rights and their calculation was conditioned to a particular definition of needs. But the discourse of needs, rights, and dignity of the poor, however promising, carried only a rhetorical weight. The support provided by the provincial programs was below the poverty line in all provinces and was constantly eroded by inflation and the high cost of shelter. Added to the regulation not only of home life but also of the type and hours of work, the program failed to transform poor single mothers into self-sufficient workers and made women raising children alone the main image of the newly discovered feminization of poverty.

CAP emphasized employability, which constituted, perhaps, its most striking legacy for single motherhood. Provincial governments experimented with a number of different training and support programs, varying from education advice to significant supports for voluntary participation in employment schemes (Snyder, 2000). By the end of the 1980s, these programs occupied an increasingly central place in the government agenda in an attempt, as discussed by Evans (1996), to transform the single mother into a worker modelled after the ideal of the independent male breadwinner. They overlooked the structural forces that locked women into low-paying jobs, and in fact, few poor mothers could escape poverty even with full-time employment. These women were in a weak position in the marketplace due

Family Benefits under the Canada Assistance Plan (1966–1996)

to their low salaries, the devaluation of professions and tasks traditionally performed by women, and the declining number and quality of entry-level jobs. In addition, unaffordability of child care made it impossible for women to work for the low wages offered to the abundant pool of unskilled labour with diminishing chances for improvement through training, individual mobility, or collective bargaining. While employment constituted a banner of the women's movement and has substantially improved the lives of middle-class professional mothers, their sisters raising children alone in poverty found in the banner of employment just another mechanism for transferring the responsibility for structural inequalities onto them.

Under CAP, preventive services and employment training also received federal cost sharing, and the social services sector expanded enormously through the provision of personal services to poor mothers. Provided primarily by a variety of dispersed, private, not-for-profit agencies, these social services posed integration and coordination challenges, and their dissociation from the Family Benefits drove a wedge between the financial and personal needs of poor mothers (Lessa, 2004). These services integrated home visiting by caseworkers, further disseminating the supervisory and moral surveillance activities of Mother's Allowance (Little, 1994). In particular, Little (1998) points out, as the number of divorced mothers increased with the Divorce Act of 1968, the lives of women raising children alone were scrutinized, their contacts with men carefully monitored, and cohabiting mothers became the target of extreme regulations. To these structural changes, additional barriers to poor mothers' ability to care adequately for their children were added by professional discourses about the requirements of child development, the increased costs in standards of living, and consumption of goods (Callahan, 1991).

These circumstances—hopeless poverty, intrusiveness of benefits, the individualistic nature of preventive services, and the changes in child-rearing practices—combined to establish a common set of individual characteristics attributed to mothers receiving services funded under CAP: low self-esteem, anxiety, guilt, and inability to manage their families under increasingly demanding child care requirements. They were increasingly seen, under the influence of neoconservative arguments, as difficult to employ, incompetent learners, and unable to keep a job for a lengthy period. Despite the failure of the employment programs, as of the mid-1980s, work requirements grew increasingly mandatory and the amount of time women could stay on benefits was reduced. In addition, the universal Family Allowance, which since the Second World War had complemented Mother's Allowance, was replaced in 1993 by the Child Tax Benefit, which privileged those in employment. After many changes, CAP was finally eliminated in 1996 and replaced by the Canada Health and Social Transfer (CHST).

Despite these many legacies, CAP gave women who raise children alone the legal right to benefits, which although rhetorical, contributed to help empower mothers (as well as other groups) to demand dignity and adequate living standards (Evans, 1996). CAP installed a different language for the category of women raising children alone: the discourse of rights to benefits based on needs. Its emphasis on employment helped associate single motherhood with structural gender inequities and made single mothers into a political category (May, 2010). The mothers' own understanding of themselves and their situation was also radically changed from the supplicant and grateful widow of the early twentieth century. Single mothers, living in public housing projects; receiving benefits as a single category of unemployable for family reasons; and being bombarded with professional and media discourses that harmonized their predicaments, gained a sense of group identity and became the centre of gender discourses. They achieved priority in public housing waiting lists (Lessa, 2002), consultation status in support services, a voice in the movements against injustices and inequality, and leadership roles in organizations and campaigns (McKeen, 2001). Their image became the symbol of social inequity and a catalyst for struggles regarding the issues of social citizenship and the right to form an independent household without the risk of poverty, violence, or marginalization (Orloff, 1993).

Neoliberalism and Workfare: The Worker Single Mother

The end of CAP belongs to the political landscape of economic globalization and the neoliberalism regime installed in the late 20th century (Graefe, 2007). At its core is an emphasis on individual responsibilities and market rewards through labour force participation that has brought radical changes to the workings of the welfare state (Mahon, 2008; Starke, 2006). A programmatic, systematic, and paradigmatic retrenchment of postwar consensus (Rice & Prince, 2000) has radically changed the aims of supporting those who, through no fault of their own, find themselves disadvantaged in society. As it refocused the welfare architecture, the state came to see its role as that of manager of social investment in human capital, strengthening the autonomy of families, focusing on children, and integrating marginalized groups into the labour force (Jenson & Saint-Martin, 2003; Peck & Tickell, 2002).

The CHST materialized these directions in 1996. It came in the form of federal block funds to provinces and territories for health, post-secondary education, and social assistance. Then in April 2004, the funds for post-secondary education and social assistance and services were separated under the new Canada Social Transfer (CST). These funding reorganizations, which continued the trend toward reducing federal contributions to social programs (Dunlop, 2006), resulted in a profound shift in social assistance in Canada (Saint-Martin, 2007; Olsen, 2007). The provinces were given leeway to spend federal funds without central standards and to establish their

Neoliberalism and Workfare: The Worker Single Mother

own eligibility criteria for social welfare. The effects were cuts to benefits, a redefinition of who is an employable person, and the requirement to work for a specific number of hours in a designated job for basic welfare benefits (McKeen, 2006). Support to single mothers was no longer under Family Benefits; rather, it was integrated into a social assistance program to encourage workers into the workforce: workfare.

Lone mothers, an important political category that after the CAP period became a focus of social activism, become a special target in every change made to the welfare state and also an indicator of its performance regarding children. A decade and a half later, the CHST/CST assistance rates for single mothers had experienced increases in most provinces, although these were still below increases in the cost of living. The National Council of Welfare (2011) documents that in all provinces, the rates are below the market basket measure of poverty and, except in Newfoundland and Labrador, are also below the low-income cut-off (LICO). However, consistent with the directives of the social investment state of rewarding integration into the workforce, workfare is being complemented by a series of federal and provincial refundable tax credits, such as child tax benefits and consumption and property tax credits. These are indexed to inflation and are not restricted to people who receive government assistance, so they offer financial advantages to paid employment. These credits, in 2010 in Ontario, for example, accounted for half of the income of a single parent with two children on social assistance (Social Assistance Review Advisory Committee [SARAC], 2010, p. 8). Their result has been that the numbers of single mothers joining the labour force have increased dramatically, reaching 69 percent in 2009. But despite the increase of 20 percent since 1995, lone mothers have not yet caught up with their counterparts in two-parent families at 74 percent (Statistics Canada, 2010a).

Employment earnings constituted 64 percent of total income for single mother families in 2008 (Williams, 2010) and have improved significantly, due primarily to demographic changes: female lone parents are older and better educated in Canada since the 1980s (Statistics Canada, 2008). But employment offers only limited possibilities to many single mothers, who hover around the poverty line and have the largest earning gap compared to all other employed women (Statistics Canada, 2009a). Occupying insecure, part-time, temporary, low-paying, precarious jobs shaped by deregulation and the erosion of employment relations (Cranford, Vosko, & Zukewich, 2003), some women raising children alone maintain a pattern of moving in and out of welfare, being especially overrepresented among the chronically unemployed (Statistics Canada, 2005d) and low paid workers (Statistics Canada, 2005a). Among the primary obstacles to sustained employment is the lack of access to child care (Stephenson & Emery, 2003) and various other child supports. These obstacles are barriers to entering paid employment and also to keeping it, since child emergencies are inevitable (Mason, 2003).

Mothering young children has greater negative employment impact (Ferrao, 2010) and earning disadvantage (Zhang, 2009) for single mothers than for mothers with partners.

The reliance on the job market resulted in an incidence of poverty for single mothers higher than for any other type of family: 22 percent in 2009 (Statistics Canada, 2011). While these numbers are much lower than the corresponding rate of 56 percent in 1996, single-mother families continue to have the lowest average total income of all families and, in 2009, had the lowest median net worth of any type of family in Canada (Statistics Canada, 2010b). The income data for 2007 (Statistics Canada, 2009b) show that despite the decrease in the prevalence of low incomes among female lone parents, for those who were not in the labour force, the poverty rate was still 75 percent. In summary, labour force participation brought the income of many single mothers to above the LICO, but despite this rise, the economic position of those who remained in low income, or close to it, continued to offer a bleak picture.

Housing, especially in large cities, poses particular challenges for lone mothers (Jackson, Schetagne, & Smith, 2001) who are taken to court over minor rent issues (Monsebraaten, 2005). The number of single mothers who spent 30 percent or more of their income on rent in 2006 is higher than the proportion among all renters, and in 2009 they had the lowest median total assets and net worth across all family types (Williams, 2010). One-third of all single-mother households reported food insecurity in comparison to 9 percent of people who were partners in a couple without children (Statistics Canada, 2005b; Lightman, Herd, & Mitchell, 2008). Women raising children alone seem to have a high debt rate and restricted expenditures on basic items, lack choice in housing and neighbourhood, and are unable to have things that other families take for granted, such as holidays, toys, new clothes, and sports equipment (McMullin, Davis, & Cassidy, 2002).

These conditions are accompanied by the institutionalization of demeaning everyday practices and a public discussion of the cost of single motherhood to the public purse (Breitkreuz, 2005). Such discussions define women raising children alone as incompetent mothers who produce children that are costly to society. Their treatment by social systems is permeated with suspicion, disrespect, and the utmost contempt (Power, 2005). Negative stereotypes diminish dignity and self-esteem, and lead to shame, concealment, and chronic depression. Staying married or entering a marital relationship (Lochhead & Scott, 2000), receiving spousal or parental benefits, or living with other adults (Cooke, 2009) seem to be the best guarantees against being locked in poverty.

The Category Single Mother in Contemporary Neoliberalism

How can we make sense of this paradigmatic group today? As one of the banners of feminist struggles of the late 20th century, this political category

Neoliberalism and Workfare: The Worker Single Mother

has assumed centre stage in thinking about society today. Lone mothers are used as postcard images to enforce and urge the moral imperative of employment and to further institutionalize a social organization that is dependent on the nuclear family. They constitute undeniable evidence of the need for social supports, and their standing has become a key indicator of government performance in the management of the social environment. Neoliberal initiatives have redefined the profile of this group, thus raising those engaged in the labour force above the LICO and leaving those with no market earnings in abject poverty. Yet our understanding of these two groups of single mothers is incomplete.

While not answering Lister's (1997) calls to define a new citizenship based on human rights and entitlement, the neoliberal Canadian state has raised the incomes of a large group of women rearing children alone. By and large, however, these women are precarious workers who, having their salaries complemented by government transfers in the form of tax credits, are trapped in a position just above the LICO. While in this position they continue to experience extreme hardship and everyday sacrifices (Pollack & Caragata, 2010). The movement across the LICO should be further explored. There is some indication that the not-for-profit sector's services and supports to single mothers may have played an effective role in this move, and it is particularly important to further study the effects of their flexible and targeted components.

The groups below the LICO, those not engaged in employment, are further victimized and blamed for their situation by neoliberalism. There is some suggestion that this group is becoming increasingly racialized, with Aboriginal and recent immigrant lone mothers strongly associated with high risk for low income and social exclusion (Kapsalis & Tourigny, 2002). Discussing the racialization of single motherhood in Canada, Pulkingham and colleagues (2010, p. 273) cite Aboriginal women as twice as likely to be single mothers. In 2006, 20 percent of First Nations, 17 percent of Inuit, and 14 percent of Métis women over the age of fifteen were lone parents compared to 8 percent of non-Aboriginal women (O'Donnell & Wallace, 2011). In western centres alone, the proportion of all Aboriginal households headed by a lone parent was at least double that of their non-Aboriginal counterparts, and in Winnipeg, Regina, and Saskatoon, over half of Aboriginal children lived in lone-parent families (Statistics Canada, 2005c). Aboriginal single-mother families tended to be larger and to have younger parents than non-Aboriginal ones (O'Donnell & Wallace, 2011). One-third of First Nations on-reserve children and 41 percent of those off-reserve resided with lone parents (Gionet, 2009). O'Donnell and Wallace report, however, that many people are involved in raising Aboriginal children, including extended families and community members such as elders. Furthering the suggestion of racialization, Chui and Maheux (2011) document that in 2006, 10 percent of visible-minority women aged fifteen and over were lone parents compared

References

to 8 percent for non-visible minority women: among black women this rate was 24 percent, among Latinas 14 percent, among Southeast Asian women 12 percent, and among West Asian women 10 percent. In 2006 in Canada, 11 percent of immigrant women were lone mothers, a higher proportion than those born in Canada—a pattern skewed by the high rates among women older than fifty-five (Chui, 2011). Despite their high level of education, immigrant women are less likely to be employed than their Canadian-born counterparts, but a larger proportion of foreign-born work on a part-time, temporary, or precarious job basis (Statistics Canada, 2006b, p. 224).

These are important directions for investigation of a political category that continues to be a barometer of how society addresses not only work issues—jobs, education, and training articulated with a wage policy—but also a variety of issues relating to the value of care work, the future of children, and the possibility of gender equity. Rather than holding single mothers in a never-ending struggle at the poverty level, when a category redefinition occurs it must promote women's independence, in the context of relationships of interdependence. For women raising children alone, this will signal welcome news of the ethics of collective care and social justice.

Note

Different parts of the research for this chapter were supported by a National Welfare Fellowship from the government of Canada, the Dean of the Faculty of Community Services at Ryerson University, and a SSHRC standard grant.

References

Amato, P.R. (1999). Parental involvement and children's behaviour problems. *Journal of Marriage and the Family, 61*(2), 375–385.

Amott, T.L. (1990). Black women and AFDC: Making entitlement out of necessity. In L. Gordon (Ed.), *Women, the state, and welfare* (pp. 280–298). Madison, WI: University of Wisconsin Press.

Breitkreuz, R.S. (2005). Engendering Citizenship? A critical feminist analysis of Canadian welfare to work policies and the employment experiences of lone mothers. *Journal of Sociology and Social Welfare, 32*(2), 147–165.

Callahan, M. (1991). A feminist perspective on child welfare. In B. Kirwin (Ed.), *Ideology, development, and social welfare: Canadian perspectives* (pp. 137–156). Toronto, ON: Canadian Scholars' Press.

Chui, T. (2011). *Immigrant women.* In Statistics Canada, *Women in Canada: A gender-based statistical report.* Catalogue no. 89-503-X. Retrieved from http://www.statcan.gc.ca/pub/89-503-x/2010001/article/11528-eng.htm

Chui, T., & Maheux, H. (2011). Visible minority women. In Statistics Canada, *Women in Canada: A gender-based statistical report.* Catalogue no. 89-503-X. Retrieved from http://www.statcan.gc.ca/pub/89-503-x/2010001/article/11527-eng.htm

Comacchio, C.R. (1999). *The infinite bounds of family: Domesticity in Canada, 1850–1940.* Toronto, ON: University of Toronto Press.

References

Cooke, M. (2009). A welfare trap? The duration and dynamics of social assistance use among lone mothers in Canada. *Canadian Review of Sociology, 46*(3), 179–314.

Cranford, C.J., Vosko, L.F., & Zukewich, N. (2003). Precarious employment in Canadian labour market: A statistical profile. *Just Labour,* 3(Fall), 6–22.

Davis, L., McKinnon, M., Rains, P., & Mastronardi, L. (1999). Rethinking child protection practice through the lens of a voluntary service agency. *Canadian Social Work Review, 16*(1), 103–116.

Dean, M. (1999). *Governmentality: Power and rule in modern society.* London, UK: Sage Publications.

Dryburgh, H. (2007). Teenage pregnancy. *Health Reports, 12*(1). Statistics Canada. Catalogue 82-003. Ottawa, ON: Minister of Industry.

Dunlop, J. (2006). Privatization: How government promotes market-based solutions to social problems. *Critical Social Work, 7*(2), Retrieved from http://www.criticalsocialwork.com

Eichler, M. (1997). *Family shifts: Families, policies, and gender equality.* Toronto, ON: Oxford University Press.

Ellwood, D.T. (1988). *Poor support: Poverty in the American family.* New York, NY: Basic Books.

Esping-Andersen, G. (2006). The three worlds of welfare capitalism. In C. Pierson & F.G. Castles (Eds.), *The welfare state reader* (2nd ed.) (pp. 160–174). Cambridge, UK: Polity Press.

Evans, P. (1992). Targeting single mothers for employment: Comparisons from the United States, Britain, and Canada. *Social Services Review,* 66(3), 378–398.

Evans, P. (1996). Single mothers and Ontario's welfare policy: Restructuring the debate. In J. Brodie (Ed.), *Women and public policy* (pp. 151–171). Toronto, ON: Harcourt Canada.

Ferrao, V. (2010). Paid work. In Statistics Canada, *Women in Canada: A Gender-Based Statistical Report.* Catalogue no. 89-503-X. Retrieved from http://www.statcan.gc.ca/pub/89-503-x/2010001/article/11387-eng.htm

Fraser, N., & Gordon, L. (1994). Genealogy of "dependency": Tracing a keyword of the U.S. welfare state. *Signs, 19*(2), 309–336.

Garfinkel, I., & McLanahan, S. (1986). *Single mothers and their children.* Washington, DC: Urban Institute Press.

Gilder, G. (1982). *Wealth and poverty.* London, UK: Buchan & Enright.

Gionet, L. (2009). First Nations people: Selected findings of the 2006 Census. In Statistics Canada, *Canadian Social Trends No. 87.* Catalogue no 11-008-X. Retrieved from http://www.statcan.gc.ca/pub/11-008-x/2009001/article/10864-eng.htm

Gordon, L. (1994). *Pitied but not entitled.* New York, NY: Free Press.

Graefe, P. (2007). Political economy and Canadian public policy. In M. Orsini & M. Smith (Eds.), *Critical policy studies* (pp. 19–40). Vancouver, BC: UBC Press.

Green, D.G. (1993). Editor's foreword to the second edition. In N. Dennis & G. Erdos (Eds.), *Families without fatherhood* (2nd ed.), (pp. vi–vii). London, UK: IEA Health and Welfare Unit.

Gringlas, M. (1995). The more things change: Single parenting revisited. *Journal of Family Issues, 16*(1), 29–53.

Harding, L.F. (1993a). "Alarm" versus "liberation"? Responses to the increase in lone parents—Part 1. *Journal of Social Welfare and Family Law, 2,* 101–112.

Harding, L.F. (1993b). "Alarm" versus "liberation"? Responses to the increase in lone parents—Part 2. *Journal of Social Welfare and Family Law, 2,* 174–184.

Hewlett, S.A. (1986). *A lesser life: The myth of women's liberation in America.* New York, NY: William Morrow.

Horowitz, R. (1995). *Teen mothers: Citizens or dependants?* Chicago, IL: University of Chicago Press.

Hum, D. (1987). Working poor, the Canada Assistance Plan, and provincial response in income supplementation. In J.S. Ismael (Ed.), *Canadian social welfare policy* (pp. 120–138). Montreal and Kingston, ON: McGill-Queen's University Press.

Jackson, A., Schetagne, S., & Smith, P. (2001). *A community growing apart: Income gaps and changing needs.* Ottawa, ON: Canadian Council on Social Development.

Jenson, J., & Saint-Martin, D. (2003). New routes to social cohesion? Citizenship and the social investment state, *Canadian Journal of Sociology, 28*(1), 77–99.

Judge, M., & Benzeval, M. (1993). Health inequalities: New concerns about the children of single mothers. *British Medical Journal, 306*(6879), 677.

Kapsalis, C., & Tourigny, P. (2002). *Profiles and transitions of groups at risk of social exclusion: Lone parents.* Ottawa, ON: Human Resources and Development Canada, Strategic Policy—Applied Research.

Kitchen, B. (1987). The introduction of family allowance in Canada. In A. Moscovitch & J. Albert (Eds.), *The benevolent state* (pp. 222–241). Toronto, ON: Garamond Press.

Kitchen, B. (1992). Framing the issues: The political economy of poor mothers. *Canadian Woman Studies, 12*(4), 10–15.

Lero, D., & Brockman, L.M. (1993). Single parent families in Canada: A closer look. In J. Hudson & B. Galaway (Eds.), *Single parent families* (pp. 91–114). Toronto, ON: Thompson Educational Publishing.

Lessa, I. (1999). Restaging the welfare diva: Case studies of single mothers and social policy. Unpublished PhD dissertation, Wilfrid Laurier University.

Lessa, I. (2002). Unravelling a relationship: Single motherhood and the practices of public housing. *Affilia, Journal of Women and Social Work, 17*(3), 314–331.

Lessa, I. (2004). "Just don't call her a single mother": Shifting identities of women raising children alone. *Atlantis: A Women's Studies Journal, 29*(1), 43–51.

Lessa, I. (2006). Discursive struggles within social welfare: Restaging teen motherhood. *British Journal of Social Work, 36*(2), 283–298.

Lessa, I. (2008). The changing status of women: From poverty to precarious work. In F. Turner & J. Turner (Eds.), *Canadian social welfare* (6th ed., pp. 122–134). Toronto, ON: Pearson Education Canada.

Leung, L.C. (1998). *Lone mothers, social security, and the family in Hong Kong.* Aldershot, UK: Ashgate Publishing.

Lightman, E., Herd, D., & Mitchell, A. (2008). Precarious lives: Work, health, and hunger among current and former welfare recipients in Toronto. *Journal of Policy Practice, 7*(4), 242–259.

Lister, R. (1997). *Citizenship: Feminist perspectives.* London, UK: Macmillan Press.

Little, M.H. (1994). "Manhunts and bingo blabs": The moral regulation of Ontario single mothers. *Canadian Journal of Sociology, 19*(2), 233–247.

Little, M.H. (1995). The blurring of boundaries: Private and public welfare for single mothers in Ontario. *Studies in Political Economy, 47* (Summer), 89–109.

References

Little, M.H. (1998). *No car, no radio, no liquor permit: The moral regulation of single mothers in Ontario, 1920–1997.* Toronto, ON: Oxford University Press.

Lochhead, C., & Scott, K. (2000). *The dynamics of women's poverty in Canada.* Ottawa, ON: Status of Women Canada.

Mahon, R. (2008). Varieties of liberalism: Canadian social policy from the "Golden Age" to the present. *Social Policy and Administration, 42*(4), 342–361.

Mason, R. (2003). Listening to mothers: Paid work, family life, and child care. *Journal of Children and Poverty, 9*(1), 41–54.

May, V. (2010). Lone motherhood as a category of practice. *Sociological Review, 58*(3), 429–443.

McDaniel, S.A. (1993). Single parenthood: Policy apartheid in Canada. In J. Hudson & B. Galaway (Eds.), *Single parent families* (pp. 203–212). Toronto, ON: Thompson Educational Publishing.

McKeen, W. (2001). Writing women out: Poverty discourse and feminist agency in the 1990s national social welfare policy debate. *Canadian Review of Social Policy, 48,* 19–33.

McKeen, W. (2006). Diminishing the concept of social policy: The shifting conceptual ground of social policy debate in Canada. *Critical Social Policy, 89,* 865–887.

McMullin, J.A., Davis, L., & Cassidy, G. (2002). Welfare reforms in Ontario: Tough times in mothers' lives. *Canadian Public Policy, 28*(2), 297–314.

Milar, J. (2000). Lone parents and the new deal. *Policy Studies, 21*(4), 333–345.

Mink, G. (1998). *Welfare's end.* Ithaca, NY: Cornell University Press.

Monsebraaten, L. (2005, September 27). Tenant act ruled discriminatory; Working single mother of three faced eviction Activists hail unprecedented decision. *Toronto Star,* A04.

Morgan, P. (1995). *Farewell to the family?* London, UK: Institute of Economic Affairs.

Murray, C. (1984). *Losing ground.* London, UK: Basic Books.

National Council of Welfare (2011). *Welfare incomes 2009.* Retrieved from http://www.ncw.gc.ca/l.3bd.2t.1ilshtml@-eng.jsp?lid=331&fid=27

O'Donnell, V., & Wallace, S. (2011) First Nations, Métis, and Inuit Women. In Statistics Canada, *Women in Canada: A gender-based statistical Report.* Catalogue no. 89-503-X. Retrieved from http://www.statcan.gc.ca/pub/89-503-x/2010001/article/11442-eng.htm#a13.

Olsen, G.M. (2007). Toward global welfare state convergence? Family policy and health care in Sweden, Canada, and the United States. *Journal of Sociology and Social Welfare, 34*(2), 143–164.

Orloff, A.S. (1993). Gender and the social rights of citizenship: The comparative analysis of gender relations and welfare states. *American Sociological Review,* 58 (June), 303–328.

Peck, J., & Tickell, A. (2002) Neoliberalizing Space. *Antipode, 34*(3), 380–404.

Polakow, V. (1994). *Lives on the edge: Single mothers and their children in the other America.* Chicago, IL: University of Chicago Press.

Pollack, S., & Caragata, L. (2010). Contestation and accommodation: Constructions of lone mothers' subjectivity through workfare discourse and practice. *Affilia, 25*(3), 264–277.

Power, E.M. (2005). The unfreedom of being other: Canadian lone mother' experiences of poverty and "life on the cheque." *Sociology, 39*(4), 643–660.

References

Pulkingham, J., Fuller, S., & Kershaw, P. (2010). Lone motherhood, welfare reform, and active citizen subjectivity, *Critical Social Policy*, 30(2), 267–291.

Rice, J.J., & Prince, M.J. (2000). *Changing politics of Canadian social policy.* Toronto, ON: University of Toronto Press.

Richards, J. (1997). *Retooling the welfare state.* Toronto, ON: C.D. Howe Institute.

Rose, N. (1999). Powers of freedom: Reframing political thought. London, UK: Cambridge University Press.

Saint-Martin, D. (2007). From the welfare state to the social investment state: A new paradigm for the Canadian social policy. In M. Orsini & M. Smith (Eds.), *Critical policy studies* (pp. 279–298). Vancouver: UBC Press.

Schamess, G. (1990). Toward an understanding of the etiology and treatment of psychological dysfunction among single teenage mothers: Part 1, a review of the literature. *Smith College Studies in Social Work, 60*(2) (March), 153–168.

Seccombe, K., James, D., & Walters, K.B. (1998). "They think you ain't much of nothing": The social construction of the welfare mother. *Journal of Marriage and the Family, 60*(4), 849–865.

Snyder, L. (2000). Success of single mothers on social assistance through a voluntary employment program. *Canadian Social Work Review, 17*(1), 49–68.

Social Assistance Review Advisory Council (SARAC). (2010). *Report of the Social Assistance Review Advisory Council.* Toronto, ON: Ministry of Community and Social Services.

Somerville, J. (1992). The new right and family politics. *Economy and Society, 21*(2), 100–120.

Starke, P. (2006). The politics of welfare state retrenchment: A literature review. *Social Policy and Administration, 40*(1), 104–120.

Statistics Canada. (2005a). Study: Low paid work and economically vulnerable families, 1980 to 2004. *The Daily*, April 25, 2005. Retrieved from http://www.statcan.gc.ca/daily-quotidien/050425/tdq050425-eng.htm

Statistics Canada. (2005b). Food insecurity in Canadian households, 2000/01. *The Daily*, May 3, 2005. Retrieved from http://www.statcan.gc.ca/daily-quotidien/050503/tdq050503-eng.htm

Statistics Canada. (2005c). Study: Aboriginal people living in metropolitan areas, 2001. *The Daily*, June 23, 2005. Retrieved from http://www.statcan.gc.ca/daily-quotidien/050623/tdq050623-eng.htm

Statistics Canada. (2005d). Study: Trends and conditions in census metropolitan areas: final assessment. *The Daily*, September 21, 2005. Retrieved from http://www.statcan.gc.ca/daily-quotidien/050921/tdq050921-eng.htm

Statistics Canada. (2006a). Census population. Catalogue no. 97-553-XCB2006007. Ottawa, ON: Minister of Industry.

Statistics Canada. (2006b). Women in Canada (5th ed.). Catalogue no. 89-503-XIE, p. 220. Ottawa, ON: Minister of Industry. http://www.statcan.gc.ca/pub/89-503-x/89-503-x2005001-eng.pdf

Statistics Canada. (2008). Study: Employment growth among lone mothers in Canada and the United States, 1980 to 2000. *The Daily*, March 7, 2008. Retrieved from http://www.statcan.gc.ca/daily-quotidien/080307/tdq080307-eng.htm

Statistics Canada. (2009a). Study: Earnings of women with and without children, 1993 to 2004. *The Daily*, March 24, 2009. Retrieved from http://www.statcan.gc.ca/daily-quotidien/090324/tdq090324-eng.htm

Statistics Canada. (2009b). Income of Canadians, 2007. Catalogue no. 75-202X. Ottawa, ON: Ministry of industry. http://www.statcan.gc.ca/pub/75-202-x/75-202-x2007000-eng.pdf

Statistics Canada. (2010a). Women in Canada: Paid work, 1976 to 2009. *The Daily*, December 9, 2010. Retrieved from http://www.statcan.gc.ca/daily-quotidien/101209/tdq101209-eng.htm

Statistics Canada. (2010b). Women in Canada: Economic well-being, 2008. *The Daily*, December 16, 2010. Retrieved from http://www.statcan.gc.ca/daily-quotidien/101209/tdq101209-eng.htm

Statistics Canada. (2011). Income of Canadians, 2009. *The Daily*, June 15, 2011. Retrieved from http://www.statcan.gc.ca/daily-quotidien/110615/tdq110615-eng.htm

Stephenson, M., & Emery, R. (2003). *Living beyond the edge: The impact of trends in non-standard work on single/lone parent mothers.* Ottawa, ON: Status of Women Canada.

Strong-Boag, V. (1979). "Wages for housework": Mothers' allowances and the beginnings of social security in Canada. *Journal of Canadian Studies, 14*(1), 24–34.

Struthers, J. (1994). *The limits of affluence: Welfare in Ontario, 1920–1970.* Toronto, ON: University of Toronto Press.

Williams, C. (2010). Economic well-being, women in Canada: A gender-based statistical report. Statistics Canada Catalogue no. 89 503-X. Retrieved from http://www.statcan.gc.ca/pub/89-503-x/2010001/article/11388-eng.htm

Zhang, X. (2009). Earnings of women with and without children. *Perspectives on Labour and Income, 10*(3). Retrieved from http://www.statcan.gc.ca/pub/75-001-x/2009103/article/10823-eng.htm

Additional Resources

Additional Resources

Gordon, L. (1994). *Pitied but not entitled.* New York, NY: Free Press. An exceptional analysis of single motherhood in the United States.

Little, M.J.H. (1998). *"No car, no radio, no liquor permit": The moral regulation of single mothers in Ontario, 1920–1997.* Toronto: Oxford University Press. This book provides a comprehensive description of the Mothers Allowance program in Ontario, providing extensive documentation about the lives of women raising children alone.

http://www.statcan.ca; and http://www.statcan.ca/Daily. Statistics Canada's website and *The Daily* are the most important sources of empirical data about single mothers in Canada. In addition to census data they publish periodical booklets addressing specific groups, among which single mothers figure prominently.

http://www.canadiansocialresearch.net: This site offers a comprehensive array of links to policy and discussions about children, families, and youth in Canada.

Child Poverty and the Canadian Welfare State

Garson Hunter

To address the problem of child poverty in Canada, the federal minister of Finance, Paul Martin, presented the New Canada Child Tax Benefit (CCTB) program on February 18, 1997, as part of the 1997–98 Federal Budget. The federal, provincial, and territorial governments negotiated an agreement known as the National Children's Agenda to advance the income and living standards of families with children (National Council of Welfare [NCW], 1999a). Certainly, it was with good reason that a program to address child poverty was introduced in Canada. A comprehensive household survey of twenty-three industrialized nations, based on data from the *Luxembourg Income Study*, ranked Canada's relative[1] child poverty level at seventeenth out of twenty-three industrialized nations in its 2000 report (UNICEF, 2000, p. 3) and nineteenth out of twenty-five industrialized nations in its 2005 report (UNICEF, 2005, p. 6). Canada's child poverty rate is higher than Hungary's, Greece's, Poland's, and the Czech Republic's.

In rich nations such as Canada, a high child poverty rate is a serious issue, for there is solid research that correlates lack of an adequate income with negative impacts on families and children. UNICEF's Innocenti Report Card on *Child Poverty in Rich Nations* (2000) noted this basic fact:

> Such statistics represent the unnecessary suffering and deprivation of millions of individual children. They also represent a failure to hold faith with the developed world's ideal of equality of opportunity. For no matter how many individual and anecdotal exceptions there may be, the fact remains that the children of the poor simply do not have the same opportunities as the children of the non-poor. Whether measured by physical or mental development, health and survival rates, educational achievement or job prospects, income or life expectancies, those who spend their childhood in poverty of income and expectation are at a marked and measurable disadvantage. (p. 3)

Research on child poverty in Canada demonstrates that the disadvantages for children in poor families include being more likely to grow up in substandard housing; to live in neighbourhoods with drug dealing and vandalism; to suffer health problems such as vision, hearing, mobility, and cognition impairments; and to participate less in organized sports or in arts programs (Ross, Scott, & Smith, 2000, pp. 1–2). Obviously, addressing child poverty is a serious issue. However, analyzing child poverty is not an easy task: "The political landscape is already littered with political rhetoric about children, broken promises and token efforts that provide very little real help to families or help only a minuscule number of the families who are in dire straits" (NCW, 1999a, p. 1).

The year 2000 marked the 11th anniversary of the House of Commons' unanimous resolution to achieve the goal of eliminating child poverty by the year 2000.

When discussing child poverty, we need to remember that we cannot discuss children in isolation from the economic situation of their parents. All children except those who live in an institutional setting live in some definition of a family.[2] At the Eighth Conference on Canadian Social Welfare Policy (Regina, June 25, 1997), Joan Grant-Cummings told the audience that child poverty is presented to the public as if it fell from an impartial sky to settle among us as a gentle rain. She reminded them of the obvious: poor children live in poor families. Any attempt to separate poor children from their poor families is a circuitous diversion from the class and gender issues of child poverty. Therefore it is useful to examine child poverty within the larger milieu of Canadian poverty.

Commenting on overall poverty in Canada, the Organisation for Economic Co-operation and Development (OECD) made the following observations in its 2008 report on Canada (OECD, 2008):

- After 20 years of continuous decline, both inequality and poverty rates have increased rapidly in the past 10 years, now reaching levels above the OECD average.
- In the last 10 years, the rich have been getting richer leaving both middle and poorer income classes behind. The rich in Canada are particularly rich compared to their counterparts in other countries–the average income of the richest 10 percent is US $71,000 in purchasing power parities[3] which is one third above the OECD average of US $54,000.
- Canada spends less on cash benefits such as unemployment benefits and family benefits than most OECD countries. Partly as a result, taxes and transfers do not reduce inequality by as much as in many other countries. Furthermore, their effect on inequality has been declining over time.
- Over the past 10 years poverty (meaning people who live on less than half the median incomes) has increased for all age groups, by around 2 to 3 percentage points to an overall rate of 12 percent.

The OECD report on Canada describes an environment of socio-economic disparities that are growing without a corresponding increase in social spending to mitigate the imbalance—what could be considered a policy of social disengagement on the part of Canadian governments. Rapidly increasing poverty, income inequality, and social spending in Canada below the rate in most other OECD nations provides the economic context for understanding child poverty in Canada.

How Child Poverty Is Defined and Measured

This chapter examines how child poverty is measured and defined. It also discusses who the poor are; what causes child poverty; what political, social, and economic factors are involved; and what social policy measures have been taken to address child poverty. Finally, it suggests social policies to address child poverty in Canada.

How Child Poverty Is Defined and Measured

Canada actually has no official poverty line, and there is no general agreement in Canada regarding what constitutes poverty (Fellegi, 1997). On the issue of poverty lines, Ternowetsky (2000) comments: "We have come to understand, for example, that even the concept of poverty is elusive. It is difficult to define, hard to measure and it is seemingly impossible to obtain a level of agreement on what it means to be poor in Canada" (p. 1). Poverty is a political issue, especially in Canada since the House of Commons resolution to eliminate child poverty. Canada is also a signatory to the UN Convention on the Rights of the Child, in which Article 27 speaks directly to the material needs of children and the obligations of parents and governments to meet those needs. UNICEF's Innocenti Report Card on *Child Poverty in Rich Nations* (2005) has an section titled "Canada: Children Still Waiting," which focuses on Canada's commitment to end child poverty by the year 2000. The report discusses how Canada continues to use and develop different poverty lines, concluding that "Canada's target year 2000 came and went without agreement on what the target means, or how progress towards it is to be measured, or what policies might be necessary to achieve it" (p. 21). The debate about child poverty in Canada has become a debate about "duelling poverty lines." One way to avoid dealing with poverty is for governments to continually challenge how it should be measured. So this chapter will spend some time exploring the substance of the poverty line debate. Figure 9.1 illustrates the incidences of child poverty in Canada from 1989 to 2009.

In reporting child poverty numbers, the media and most advocacy organizations rely on Statistics Canada's low-income cut-off (LICO),[4] which is the most common unofficial poverty line used in Canada. The LICO calculation is a relative measure of poverty. It measures relative deprivation based on income compared to a defined community standard. Relative measures of poverty place deprivation in a societal context; "in other words, people's experience of hunger and poverty is directly related to the societies in which they live and the standards of living which are customarily enjoyed" (Riches, 1997, p. 10). LICO is based on the average family or individual expenditures

How Child Poverty Is Defined and Measured

Figure 9.1 Percentage of Child Poverty in Canada 1989–2009; Using LICO Before-Tax, LIM, LICO After-Tax, and MBM

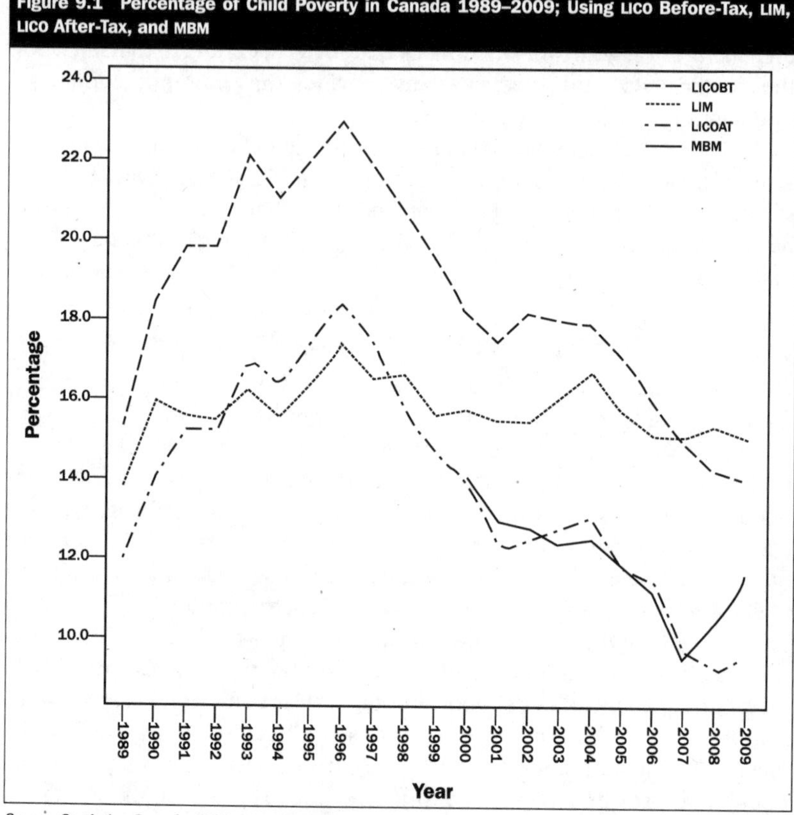

Source: Statistics Canada. Table 202-0802—Persons in low-income, annual, CANSIM (database) for 1989–2008 data; and Income in Canada 2009. Catalogue no.:75-202-XWE for 2009 data.

for food, shelter and clothing: "The LICOs represent levels of gross income where people spend disproportionate amounts of money for food, shelter and clothing. Statistics Canada has decided over the years—somewhat arbitrarily—that 20 percentage points is a reasonable measure of additional burden" (NCW, 1999b, p. 3).

Most income data from Statistics Canada contain one of two base years: the 1986 base or the 1992 base. Using the 1986 base, the average Canadian family spent 36.2 percent of its gross income on food, shelter, and clothing; therefore, with the addition of 20 points, low-income Canadians spent 56.2 percent or more on these necessary items. If the 1992 base is used, then a low-income Canadian spent 54.7 percent or more on these necessary items (NCW, 1999b, p. 3). When LICO is used to measure the child poverty rate, family size and differences in costs of living (by size of community) are both taken into account.

How Child Poverty Is Defined and Measured

A number of criticisms have been raised about LICO since it was developed in 1961. Perhaps the most common is that although it is widely used, it is not a poverty line. The political nature of the debate about poverty was not lost on Statistics Canada when it commented that it was partly due to the government commitment to eliminate child poverty that the LICO measure was placed under a great deal of public scrutiny (Webber, 1998, p. 7).

Statistics Canada, which produces the LICO data, entered into the debate about using LICO as a poverty measure. "At the heart of the debate," it reported, "is the use of the low income cut-offs as poverty lines, even though Statistics Canada has clearly stated, since their publication began over 25 years ago, that they are not" (Fellegi, 1999, p. 36). As well, "Statistics Canada continues to correct media commentary that portrays low income estimates as a measure of poverty. The Agency often repeats that they are not intended as such" (Webber, 1998, p. 9). Statistics Canada argues that LICO is not actually a poverty measure; rather it is a measure of low income. However, a reading of Poduluk's writing indicates that at least to her, as the developer of LICO, low income and poverty are synonymous.[5] No distinction is made between low income and poverty in her work, and the terms are often used interchangeably.

Another important concern with the LICO measure is that in recent years, expenditures on necessities have risen less rapidly than incomes; that is, people are spending, on average, less of their yearly income on necessities. As the amount of family income spent on necessities declines, low-income cut-off levels rise. For example, in 1961 when the LICO measure was developed, the average family expenditure on necessities was roughly 50 percent of pre-tax income. With the 20 percentage points added to the average, low income was defined as families who spent 70 percent or more on necessities. As incomes have increased and the average ratio of expenditures on necessities as a proportion of income has decreased, low-income cut-off levels have risen. The most current rebasing (1992) of the LICO measure—calculated on the average family expenditures on necessities—has been established at 35 percent of pre-tax income. When the 20 percentage points are added to that average, low income is defined as families who spend 55 percent or more on necessities. The decline from 70 percent of income spent on necessities to be considered low income in 1961 to 55 percent of income spent on necessities to be considered low income in 1992 has caused concern (Kerstetter, 2000, pp. 6–8).

LICO's developers were aware that their poverty measure was relative and that the level at which people would be considered poor would climb over time. Commenting on the issue, Poduluk (1968) wrote: "It is because poverty is a relative concept that poverty or low income does not diminish as much as might be expected in view of the real income growth of a country. The extent of change can be evident only if contemporary standards are applied to the income structure of an earlier day" (p. 183).

Explaining why poverty or low income does not decrease, as would be expected in terms of income growth that is adjusted for the inflation rate, Poduluk noted: "Thus, even though the level of living of the poor improves through time, poverty never seems to be eliminated because a wide gap persists between the level of living attained by some segments of the population and those enjoyed by the majority of the community" (p. 184).

The developers of LICO also knew that the low-income rate, or poverty rate, would not remain fixed at 70 percent; rather, if the income of the majority rose over time, then the level of what was considered low income would rise as well. They believed that if the standard of the community changes, then low income should be evaluated in the context of the rising (or possibly, falling) community standard.

Statistics Canada has made a major change in how it reports low income in its publications. In its major publications used to evaluate low income, Statistics Canada now only reports after-tax LICO.[6]

Much debate has revolved around the use of LICO based on the before-tax Total Income variable and the after-tax Total Income variable to calculate low-income rates. It is an important discussion. At the essence of this argument is the poverty rate in Canada. Using LICO on the after-tax Total Income variable dramatically reduces the poverty rate. For example, if the before-tax Total Income LICO is used with the 2009 Survey of Labour and Income Dynamics (SLID) data, the poverty rate for children in 2009 is 14.0 percent; however, if the after-tax Total Income LICO is used, the poverty rate for children in 2009 falls to 9.5 percent.[7]

The argument presented by Statistics Canada for the drop in poverty rates is that using the LICO measure based on after-tax Total Income reflects the progressive income tax structure of Canada whereby the income disparity in Canada becomes more compressed (Statistics Canada, 2002, p. 135). Some contend that the after-tax method may be a truer standard of poverty than the before-tax method (Graham, Swift, & Delaney, 2009, p. 85). Others see problems with the after-tax method. For instance, the after-tax method only adjusts income for provincial and federal income taxes and not for all other taxes such as provincial sales tax, GST, HST, EI premiums, and so on (Ross et al., 2000, pp. 35–36); moreover, taxation rates vary across provinces.[8] It has also been argued elsewhere that the major problem with using the after-tax Total Income LICO is methodological (Hunter & Miazdyck, 2006). The methodological argument focuses on the additional 20 points added to average expenditures.

The LICO measure was developed when only before-tax income figures were available; therefore, Poduluk's decision to add 20 points was intended to include room for taxation. If Statistics Canada wishes to measure LICO with after-tax income, that is fine, but it is "double counting" to use income after tax and then still add 20 points as if before-tax income were still being used to measure low income. To be methodologically sound, the 20 points needs to be reduced by some amount. I would suggest that if after-tax income is used, then the 20 points should be reduced by the rate of taxation. If one-third of income is taxed, then 14 or 15 points should be added. When this is done, the after-tax LICO rate comes out to be more similar to the before-tax LICO rate.

How Child Poverty Is Defined and Measured

LICO is the most common measure of poverty, but other ones are used in Canada. Additional *relative* measures of poverty include the Low Income Measure (LIM) from Statistics Canada, the Toronto Social Planning Council measure, the Canadian Council on Social Development measure, the measure devised by the 1971 Senate Committee on Poverty known as the Croll, and the Gallup Poll measure. Others argue that provincial welfare rates are implicit poverty lines, with welfare rates serving as the minimum income a family or person should receive (Ross et al., 2000). In reporting on child poverty in rich countries, the Innocenti Report Card uses 50 percent of the national median income (UNICEF, 2005, p. 6), which is the same measure used by the OECD. There are also three *absolute* measures of poverty that are commonly used in Canada: the Montreal Diet Dispensary measure, the Fraser Institute's Sarlo poverty line, and Statistics Canada's new Market Basket Measure (MBM).

Absolute poverty measures differ from relative measures of poverty in that they are not linked to an average standard of living. Rather, these measures consider what is the absolute minimum an individual or a family needs to survive.[9] In actuality, though, absolute poverty measures are always relative because of the decisions that are made as to what constitutes an absolute minimum. How many socks, how many shoes, and how much milk to buy each year are all relative judgments, which are made by those who develop absolute poverty measures.

In May 2003, Statistics Canada introduced its own absolute low-income measure: the MBM. This measure was not produced as a result of requests from a large number of advocacy groups and researchers. Rather, it was developed in response to a 1997 request of the Federal/Provincial/Territorial Ministers Responsible for Social Services (Human Resources Development Canada [HRDC], 2003, p. 1). As an absolute measure, the MBM approach is an attempt to determine how much disposable family income[10] is required for a predetermined, specific basket of goods and services. The HRDC's MBM includes five types of expenditures: (1) food, (2) clothing and footwear, (3) shelter, (4) transportation, and (5) other household needs (e.g., school supplies, personal care products, telephone, furniture).

The MBM is calculated with a referent family, comprised of two adults (one male and one female) aged 25 to 49, and two children (a girl aged 9 and a boy aged 13). All other household configurations are calculated using a formula based on the Low Income Measure (LIM) equivalence scale. A family of four has an equivalence scale value of 2. A single person has an equivalence value of 1. Therefore it is postulated by Statistics Canada that a family of four requires twice as much income as a single adult (HRDC, 2003, pp. 34–35). The MBM then establishes thresholds, which are the sums of costs for predetermined baskets of goods and services for selected communities and community sizes across the ten provinces. Economic families that are below the MBM thresholds are considered low income.

Several issues with the MBM approach should be raised in the context of the LICO measure. First, although the MBM is considered an absolute approach to poverty measurement, it is actually a relative measure because it must be decided what constitutes a basket of goods and services. Any number of subjective opinions comprise what should and should not be in the market basket. All measures of poverty, in this sense, are relative. However, the larger problem is that the MBM approach does not account for the growing income disparity between the rich and the poor. The income and wealth of the rich recede from scrutiny when the focus is on what constitutes a reasonable MBM basket of goods and services. A relative measure of poverty has the advantage of employing *all* sources of income in its methodology; therefore, it reflects the growth of income disparity.

To illustrate why it matters to policy makers and advocates which measure is used to assess child poverty, Figure 9.1 presents the after-tax LICO, MBM, the before-tax LICO, and the LIM with their corresponding poverty rates. For 2009, the incidence of low income for children in Canada was 9.5 percent using after-tax LICO; 11.6 percent using the MBM; 14.0 percent using before-tax LICO; and 15.0 percent using LIM.[11] When poverty is discussed in Canada, the debates among activists, researchers, politicians, and the public are muddled because of differences in the various poverty measurements. The MBM is weak because of the enormous number of relative decisions that go into deciding what is an acceptable basket of goods. The LICO measure is weak because it utilizes the national *average*[12] spent on food, shelter, and clothing, adds 20 points to average family expenditures for those items, and then applies the measure across the country. LICO is an idiosyncratic measure used only in Canada. Although LIM is not without critics, the reasonable approach would be to use it, based on one-half the median income, adjusted for family size.[13] To examine poverty, this chapter adopts the LIM measure, which is the same approach utilized by the UN and the OECD. It is worth noting that the OECD, much like the UN, does not call this measure "low income"; rather, both organizations refer to this as a measurement of poverty.

Using Income Measures to Define the Condition of Child Poverty

We can see from the above figures that, using the Statistics Canada LIM measure,[14] high levels of child poverty persisted up to and including 2009 in Canada. In 1989 (the year of the declaration to end child poverty in Canada by 2000), the child poverty level in Canada was 13.7 percent. Disturbingly, the incidence of child poverty in Canada increased to 15.0 percent for the year 2009.[15] The clear and disconcerting finding from an analysis of the data is the continuous high incidence of child poverty in Canada.

A related concept to the incidence of poverty is the *depth* of poverty. Depth of poverty refers to how far below a poverty line an income falls (Ross et al., 2000, p. 103). The average low-income gap is calculated by determining the sum of all of the income amounts that are below the income cut-off level for any given category, then dividing that sum by the number of units (individuals, families). This measure is useful because it provides some idea of how much income in dollar figures is needed to raise people's income to a predetermined low-income cut-off level. However, for the 2008 data, Statistics Canada changed the measure of this concept so that it reflected a percentage of a given income cut-off. Statistics Canada now provides the aggregate low-income gap as a percentage of income.[16] Using the LIM income measure and Statistic Canada's new depth-of-poverty measure, in Canada the depth-of-poverty figure for children was 2.0 percent for 1989, and 1.9 percent for 2009.

Who Experiences the Problem of Poverty? Class and Gender Issues

Who Experiences the Problem of Poverty? Class and Gender Issues

There are four major sources of income available to people: (1) private material resources such as dividends, savings, insurance, and property; (2) employee compensation from a job; (3) family and community support; and (4) state subsidies in the form of pensions, Employment Insurance, welfare, and other income assistance. Obviously, the poor do not have private material resources for a source of income. Also, the poor either do not have employee compensation, or if they do it is barely adequate to meet basic needs. The poor often rely on family and friends for support, or on charities such as food banks, and they often rely on social income programs to survive.

The threat to working people and the poor is income insecurity. Those who can work depend utterly on securing and keeping waged labour and therefore constantly face the threat of unemployment. The unemployable who are poor, and the poor who cannot obtain decent employment, must rely on state subsidy programs. The threat to people who rely on these programs has parallels to the one that faces those who rely on waged labour: programs may be cut or eliminated, or the people who use them may be denied their services. The lesson is very clear: if you are not wealthy, you had better have a good job or a responsible government (Hicks, 1999).

Hundreds of thousands of Canadian children are poor and live in families that have no private wealth, whose breadwinners do not have decent steady work, and that are without wealthy and generous relatives or neighbours. In 2009 the highest incidence of child poverty was among female lone-parent families at 37.2 percent; in other words, 338,000 children out of the total of

Who Experiences the Problem of Poverty? Class and Gender Issues

908,602 children living in female lone-parent families, were poor.[17] Aboriginal children are especially vulnerable to poverty; almost half of them under fifteen live with a lone parent (Anderson, 2003). Aboriginal children under fifteen had a poverty rate of 47.5 percent in 2005, while the total child poverty rate for children under fifteen in Canada was 18.3 percent.[18] Economic families reporting single responses to the category of Aboriginal ancestry[19] comprised only 86,295 (or 1.6 percent) of all economic families (5,420,365), yet their poverty rate was 40,970 (47.5 percent) of the total 991,845 (18.3 percent) of the population under fifteen using the poverty measure and data in the 2006 Census.

When the data are examined for 1989, the highest incidence of poverty using LIM was among people in female lone-parent families[20] with no earner: 88.6 percent (288,000 persons of the total of 325,056 persons in female lone-parent families). That figure remained almost unchanged in 2009, with an incidence of 86.5 percent (238,000 persons out of a total of 275,144).[21] Female lone-parent families with one earner[22] had a poverty incidence level in 1989 of 38.7 percent (246,000 out of 635,658). The overall incidence of poverty for female-headed families with one earner in 2009 was 30.6 percent (276,000 out of 901,960). In 2009, the figures indicated two things: (1) the inadequacy of social income programs for the poor in bringing female lone-parent families with no earner anywhere near the internationally used poverty line; and (2) the persistence of poverty among the vulnerable children in Canada.

The group experiencing the next-highest levels of child poverty are two-parent families with children. In 1989, 87.9 percent of people in two-parent families with children and no earners were poor (131,000 out of 149,033).[23] In 2009 the incidence of poverty was 77.2 percent (183,000 out of 237,047). When employment is considered, for two-parent families with children and one earner the poverty rate in 1989 was 18.4 percent (434,000 of 2,358,696); by 2009 this rate had grown dramatically to 31.3 percent (581,000 out of 1,856,230). The obvious fact that can be gleaned from these data is that having a job does not ensure escaping poverty either for female lone-parent families or, increasingly, for two-parent families with children with one earner.

Jackson and colleagues (2000) write that Canada is experiencing an increase in wage inequality, with employment becoming polarized into streams of good jobs and bad jobs. And it is not just employment that employable people need; it is employment with a living wage that is required. Evidence from the research of Jackson and colleagues (2000) indicates that collective bargaining raises employment remuneration for union workers compared to that of non-union workers doing similar jobs. In fact, the advantage of unionization is greatest for those who would otherwise be low-wage[24] earners. The union advantage for women relating to low wages can be seen clearly in the fact that almost one-half of women who are not unionized are in low-wage employment, while less than 10 percent of women who are unionized are in low-wage employment (Jackson et al.,

Who Experiences the Problem of Poverty? Class and Gender Issues

2000, p. 101). Many factors besides wages affect the quality of life, and in that regard, many union positions also provide for holidays, sick days, dental plans, maternity leave, and occupational pensions—things that are not available to women in low-wage non-unionized employment.[25]

A Statistics Canada study sheds further light on employment and low income in Canada (Janz, 2004). Fewer than half of Canadian workers (47 percent) who had low-paying jobs in 1996 had managed to climb out of poverty by 2001. Those most likely to rise above low income were young, university-educated men in professional occupations and industries. Most often they worked full-time in large, unionized firms in Ontario or Alberta. The 53 percent trapped in low-paid work from 1996 to 2001 tended to be older women, those with high school education or less, and those working part-time for small, non-unionized organizations.

Wages are obviously important when examining characteristics of poverty. Data published by the Canadian Council on Social Development (Jackson, 2001) demonstrate that a household with a single earner working 40 hours per week for the *median salary* of $13.86 per hour is unlikely to be defined as low-income using the LICO measurement. A full-time job at or near the minimum minimum wage (low wage) is not enough to bring a single-parent family with one child above the LICOs, however. Comparative data from the 2005 Innocenti Report Card (see Table 9.1) show that countries that have succeeded in reducing the percentage of families with low wages also have lower child poverty rates (UNICEF, 2005).

Canada was reviewed in 2009 by the UN General Assembly, Human Rights Council, Eleventh Session, Universal Periodic Review. Recommendation 17 of the UN review of Canada reads "Develop a national strategy to eliminate poverty." Canada's response to the UN recommendation 17 was as follows:

> Canada does not accept recommendation 17 or the related recommendation from Ghana to develop a national strategy to eliminate poverty. Provinces and territories have jurisdiction in this area of social policy and have developed their own programs to address poverty. For example, four provinces have implemented poverty reduction strategies. The Government of Canada supports these measures, notably through benefits targeting children and seniors. These efforts are having a positive impact: low-income rates for seniors, women and children have fallen considerably in the past decade.[26]

The most significant change in programming for the poor was the elimination of the Canada Assistance Plan (CAP) 1996, which was replaced by the Canada Health and Social Transfer (CHST). In 2003, the CHST was eliminated; Medicare is now funded through the Canada Health Transfer (CHT), while welfare programming for the poor is funded, along with post-secondary education, by the Canada Social Transfer (CST).

Who Experiences the Problem of Poverty? Class and Gender Issues

Table 9.1 Child Poverty Rate and Low Wages in Rich Nations

Country (Rich Nations)	Child poverty (%)	Low wages (%)
Sweden	2.8	5.2
Finland	4.3	5.9
Belgium	4.4	7.2
Netherlands	7.7	11.9
France	7.9	13.3
Germany	10.7	13.3
Japan	12.2	15.7
Spain	12.3	19
Australia	12.6	13.8
Canada	15.5	23.7
Ireland	16.8	18
UK	19.8	19.6
Italy	20.5	12.5
USA	22.4	25

Source: *The league table of child poverty in rich nations*, UNICEF, 2000. Florence: UNICEF Innocenti Research Centre.

Poverty data compiled by Statistics Canada point to a serious contradiction between the lives of poor Canadian children and Canada's official statements about poverty to the UN Human Rights Council's Universal Periodic Review (UN General Assembly, 2009). Canada's statement about poverty to that council is not accurate. Utilizing Statistics Canada data and the international definition of poverty, Canada's benefits that are targeting children are not having a positive impact. The low-income rates for lone-parent female households and children have *not* fallen considerably in the past decade.[27]

In summary, the factors that are most important for answering the question of who is poor are as follows: the level of support from social income programs, the type of wages that can be secured in the labour market, the unionization of employment, and economic bubbles.

Neoliberalism and Child Poverty

In the realm of political discourse, the federal and provincial governments and territories have suggested that social income programs create dependency among the recipients and therefore actually harm recipients by keeping them from paid employment. The familiar argument is that people are poor because they do not have a job, and that if they are moved off welfare by supports such as the Canada Child Tax Benefit (CCTB) program and into employment, then employment will lead them out of poverty. Even writers who present themselves as progressive state that social income programs like welfare contain disincentives from taking employment and create dependency among social income program recipients:

Neoliberalism and Child Poverty

> Paradoxes of intervening in the economic life of some Canadians have long been recognized: financial assistance programs may sometimes decrease the incentive to paid work for some recipients, that is, they contain inherent labour force participation disincentives. Authors of this textbook, like other progressive observers, insist on the need for plentiful jobs offering meaningful employment and decent wages. More than any other factor, decent jobs would alleviate much of the problem of labour force participation disincentives. (Graham, Delaney, & Swift, 2000, p. 57)

Given that these and other authors suggest that creating decent jobs and meaningful employment is a way to overcome the disincentives of social income programs, should not the argument about welfare dependency be revised? Instead of creating programs such as the CCTB to help working-poor families, governments should shift their focus toward labour market disincentives to employment. Should it not be argued that it is the *labour market* that creates disincentives to employment and that the *labour market* needs to change to create meaningful employment, unionized workplaces, decent wages, and decent jobs? This would shift the focus away from the individual poor and individual solutions for poverty, toward the market system as a cause of unemployment and poverty—a cause that requires solutions based on universal social and employment policies.

Yet since the mid-1970s, the social and economic agendas of right-wing "think tanks" advocating neoliberalism have come to dominate discussions of economic and social policy. The following, which adapts to the Canadian context the main features of neoliberalism identified by Wacquant (2009a), highlights the most salient features of that ideology:

- *Economic deregulation.* Promoting "the market" as the optimal device not only for economic transactions but for organizing a whole range of human activities, including the provision of core public goods such as food, education, health care, housing, labour regulation, and environmental protections.
- *Welfare state devolution.* Intensifying the recommodification of marginal workers toward desocialized labour (removal of ideas of a living wage, job security, work benefits, pensions, labour laws, full employment). Also, international variants of workfare within a quasi-contractual relationship between the state and lower-class recipients, who are treated not as citizens but as clients required to display behavioural obligations as conditions for state aid. In Canada, the extension of marginal governmental aid (e.g., CCTB and the

numerous provincial programs delivered in partnership with the NCB) to lower-class working families not normally receiving aid has resulted in vastly extended surveillance[28] of portions of the lower class who traditionally have not received welfare benefits.

- *A mantra of individual responsibility.* Personal identity is thus moulded around the ideal of the private entrepreneur in an environment of widened competition for meeting basic human needs. At the same time, the environment exhibits widespread evasion of corporate liability and a weakening of the state's accountability in its performance of social and economic obligations.
- *Expansive, intrusive, and proactive penal apparatus.* This encompasses the disorders and disarray generated by diffuse social insecurity and deepening inequality. Disciplinary supervision of post-industrial workers reasserts the authority of the state and dampens any questioning of the legitimacy of elected officials and the political order. (p. 307)

Although government programs for the poor concentrate on employment skills (e.g., writing resumés, looking for work, developing work habits), or work discipline (e.g., being on time, being rested for work, deporting oneself properly at work), or instilling moral responsibility among the poor, the structural and cyclical nature of unemployment and poverty are not easy to ignore. The market bubbles of expansion and contraction in the economy as well as wages require attention if the issue of child poverty is going to be addressed in a serious manner using government social security programs. But Wacquant (2009a) argues that with the ascendency of neoliberalism beginning in the mid-1970s, a growing linkage has developed between workfare in the welfare state and prisonfare in the carceral state. This linkage fulfills three main interrelated functions. (1) The incarceration of the supernumerary fractions of the lowest rung of the working class, in particular the dispossessed members of stigmatized groups, which entails physically neutralizing and warehousing them. (2) The disciplining of desocialized wage work among those in the working class and in the declining and insecure middle class. This is carried out by raising the costs of strategies of escape or resistance within the illegal sectors of the street economy. (3) For the upper class and society as a whole, penal institutions serve the symbolic mission of reaffirming the authority of the state (pp. xvi–xvii). It should be no surprise that in Canada, a major feature of the Conservative Party's re-election platform in 2011 was its call for vastly increased expenditures on prisons along with truth-in-sentencing and mandatory minimum legislation—all of this during a period of declining crime rates. Canada's intensified carceral policy is similar to changes in the carceral policies in other countries that have developed modern welfare states, including the United States, which led the neoliberalism project. These policies have since been adopted by the United Kingdom, France, Germany, and now Canada.

Neoliberalism and Child Poverty

The neoliberal perspective that now dominates all political parties in Canada and the Western world defines the modern welfare state as a major offender in creating poverty. Current changes to public policy to address poverty, as viewed by their advocates, are a viewed as break from the mistakes of the old welfare state. Public policy during the modern welfare state was "passive" and based mainly on the concept of entitlement, with little to say about responsibility—that is, the state has a duty to offer assistance to citizens who have no other resources or options for support. The policy of entitlement did little to stimulate employment. Reflecting a neoliberal perspective, the OECD advocates an "active society" characterized by a wide range of reforms, which include linking cash benefits (welfare) to work-oriented incentives across a broad range of options (Gilbert, 2004).

The Scandinavian countries, Britain, Australia, New Zealand, the United States, and Canada have all embraced this perspective and developed somewhat different work-oriented welfare policies. In tandem with the transition from passive to active policies, programs have moved away from a needs-based approach (i.e., the financially destitute have a right to social benefits) to focus on the responsibilities of recipients to find work, to become self-sufficient, and to lead productive lives. The continuation of entitlement-based public policy without responsibilities is perceived as unworkable. Canada, as well as the rest of the world, we are told, must face and adjust to the new global economy: "Social programs must change to keep up with new realities—realities around a changing economy, around unmanageable public debt and around problems with the programs themselves" (Gilbert, 2004, p. 283).

In the "New Economy" welfare state, it is not material benefits that matter. What is important is a different concept, one that is thin in tangible benefits and vague in definition and that has a pleasant ring in media soundbites—social exclusion. Social exclusion (again, not poverty) has come to join welfare dependency as the enemy. The supposed wreckage to society and to the New Economy brought about by social exclusion is to be overcome through government policies of labour market inclusion. It is not the labour market that needs to change. Rather, the excluded (the poor, including the disabled) should be rendered employable in response to the shifting nature of the economy and employment. To be without employment—apparently unless one is wealthy, idle, and living in a gated neighbourhood—is to be outside the community. The idea that people on welfare and the disabled are excluded from full citizenship has its genesis in conservative ideology. Jones and Novak (1999) comment: "The primary aim of social inclusion and cohesion is therefore to bind the excluded back into the labour market as a solution to the problem. That this may result in their continuing poverty is conveniently overlooked, since it is their exclusion (whether self-imposed or structural) that is the problem rather than their poverty" (p. 188).

Neoliberalism and Child Poverty

Within the logic of active welfare state public policy, citizenship for individuals and families is defined as having a "job, [being] self-sufficient, contributing to society with access to education, health care and security" (Saskatchewan Social Services, 1999). In industrialized countries with both conservative and social democratic governments, poverty policies "are increasingly wrapped in the elaborate rhetoric of social inclusion (in the labor force), empowerment (to earn wages), activation (to find a job), and responsibility (to take the job)" (Gilbert, 2004, p. 67).

Much of the debate about welfare reform has come to focus on whether "active" programming changes should adopt a labour force attachment (LFA) model, wherein the government considers *any* employment to be better than welfare provision. Increasingly for both Canada and the provinces, the LFA approach to welfare has been the model most favoured. "Welfare has increasingly shifted from being an 'entitlement' program designed to help fight poverty, to a temporary support intended to promote individual self-sufficiency through labour force attachment strategies" (HRDC, 2000). The other model is the human resources development (HRD) or human capital development (Peck, 2001, p. 78) model, which is identified most strongly with the Scandinavian social democratic welfare states. The HRD model is, in the short term, more costly because it emphasizes education and training leading to labour force entry above the minimum wage. Over the long term the HRD model is viewed as beneficial to workers and the labour market because individual and overall wages increase with this approach.

Especially disheartening in discussions about labour force attachment versus human capital development models is the lack of any serious debate. The LFA model can be criticized for placing people in temporary, at- or near-minimum-wage employment with few if any benefits. However, the more "progressive" human capital development model is not without flaws. As noted by the economist James K. Galbraith (1998), the skills-mismatch idea distracts attention from the fact that the roots of income inequality lie in monopoly power rather than in educational deficiency (Katz, 2001, p. 352). Galbraith observes: "What the existing economy needs is a fairly small number of first-rate technical talents, combined with a small superclass of managers and financiers, on top of a vast substructure of nominally literate and politically apathetic working people" (Galbraith, 1998, pp. 34–35, cited in Katz, 2001, p. 352). Perhaps that explains why so many countries have adopted the LFA model in their "active welfare states." When the causes of poverty are examined, the lack of money and/or wealth is the simplest explanation.

Alleviating Child Poverty and the Canada Child Tax Benefit Legislation

The major piece of legislation enabling the social income transfer program in Canada designed to specifically address child poverty is the Canada Child Tax Benefit (CCTB), which is administered by the Canada Customs and Revenue Agency (CCRA) using filed income tax returns. The predecessor to the CCTB (1997) was the New Integrated Child Tax Benefit (CTB) (1993). The social income programs that existed for families with children before the CTB were the universal Family Allowance program and income-tax-based measures, including the refundable child tax credit, the non-refundable child tax credit, the equivalent-to-married credit, and the child care expense reduction. Under the Integrated CTB there were three components: the CTB, the equivalent-to-married credit, and the child care deduction. The previous non-refundable and refundable tax credits and the Family Allowance program were aggregated into the income-tested CTB. The elimination of the Family Allowance program represented a fundamental rethinking about children in Canada: children were now seen as part of the budget and expenses for family after-tax income spending (Kitchen, 2001, p. 240). Family Allowances allowed all children access to some portion of the social wage; with the CTB program, the social wage was available only to families that were economically vulnerable. The CTB program clawed back benefits as family incomes increased. Additionally, the program did not have scheduled adjustments for inflation.

In 1997 the CTB program was replaced with the CCTB legislation. The two programs are somewhat similar in their underlying values. The major difference between them is that the CCTB includes all provinces and territories, while they were not part of the federal-only CTB. The CCTB is divided into two benefits. One is the Basic Benefit, which is provided to all families with children contingent on their level of income. The other is provided under the cost-shared National Child Benefit program (NCB), a program that the federal government shares with the provinces and territories and that is intended for low-income families with children. The federal contribution to the NCB is the National Child Benefit Supplement (NCBS), which is similar to the previous Working Income Supplement (WIS) program. The WIS Program replaced the universal Family Allowance program and was a *per family benefit* provided to low-income families with children, while the NCBS is a *per child benefit* (as was the Family Allowance program) provided to low-income families with children.

The NCBS has been integrated into the basic allowance component of provincial social assistance programs in the provinces and territories (Kitchen, 2001, p. 241). The NCBS can be used to remove children from the basic allowance component of the provincial welfare rolls, with those payments now coming from the federal government's NCBS contribution to the NCB. The provincial, territorial, and First Nations contribution to the NCB is to provide programs that support low-income working families with children, whether or not the families receive welfare. Programs provided by the provinces to low-income families with children include pharmacare or dental care, child care services, a child credit for low-income families (British Columbia, Quebec), an earned income credit (Alberta), a combination of programs (Saskatchewan and New Brunswick), and early prevention programs for children at risk (Ontario). The provincial and territorial contributions to the NCB are made under a dazzling multitude of names (some having a shorter life span than others) in the various provincial/territorial and First Nations jurisdictions.[29]

The provincial savings from reduced welfare expenditures under the CCTB have been quite substantial, and these "reinvestment funds" created through provincial clawbacks of the increased federal spending under the CCTB have gone into programs that supplement low-income wages. The provincial savings on welfare expenditures due to increased federal contributions through the CCTB do not need to go to increased spending on families with children on welfare who have no other source of income—presumably the poorest children in Canada. Rather, the money can be used to fund social income programs for the working poor, as has happened in a number of provinces. Taking the funds saved by not passing on the increase in federal expenditures to the poorest families on welfare with no source of income, and using them to support families with low incomes, is entirely in keeping with the intent of the CCTB program. An Enriched Canada Child Tax Benefit will "pave the way for provinces and territories to redirect their resources towards improved child services and income support for low-income working families" (Government of Canada, 1997a, p. 2); furthermore, it will "promote attachment to the workforce—resulting in fewer families having to rely on social assistance—by ensuring that families will always be better off as a result of finding work" (Government of Canada, 1997b, p. 1).

The savings incurred by the provinces under the NCB program of the CCTB are to be directed toward children's services and income support programs for low-income families with children. Lightman (2003) writes of the NCB program that "the central intent of this change was to reward families in the low-paid workforce and, by extension, to penalize those on social assistance. In other words, the program was now structured to provide a strong work incentive; and arguably, the focus was more on work incentives than on support for children" (pp. 156–157).

Conclusion

The continuing high rates of child poverty suggest that the rewards aspect of the NCB needs closer investigation. The focus of the NCB policy initiative on the workplace attachment of the recipient is a fundamental flaw in the NCB portion of the CCTB program. If the program were designed to eliminate child poverty, benefits would increase according to the financial need of families with children (Pulkingham & Ternowetsky, 1997, pp. 206–207). There is no extra money for families whose only source of income is social assistance. Rather, the federal government has used the CCTB to alleviate some of the provincial welfare expenditures related to children in order to gain provincial support for the program.

Conclusion

An examination of the program criteria and the income effects of the "active welfare state" federal/provincial child poverty program could lead to a conclusion that the new CCTB initiative is not about reducing poverty for the poorest children in Canada. The initiative appears to be designed within the framework of citizenship theory and the policy goal of making it more attractive to work than to receive assistance. Beyond simply distinguishing between worthy and unworthy poor, the program is therefore also entrenching the poor law concept of "less eligibility." Also, the main benefactor of the CCTB will not be children; rather, the business sector will gain the most from it because the CCTB tends to subsidize low-wage labour. Research evidence indicates that the consequences of the cuts made during the 1990s to the welfare system in Canada have been to impoverish further the poor on welfare and to depress the wages of the working poor (Klein & Montgomery, 2001, p. 5).

Current job growth in Canada is mainly in the service sector, in which many jobs are low paying with no benefits (Broad, 2000). The CCTB has in effect implemented a program that could subsidize employers by distributing small income gains and limited health benefits to their employees. Clearly, some businesses cannot afford to pay high wages; however, the government could have chosen to help these workers through a more progressive income tax structure. Lower-paid workers in marginal industries and services identified through the income tax system could be taxed at a reduced rate; consistent with the principles of a progressive tax system and a desire to reduce inequality, top income earners would be taxed at a higher rate. As well, the program could be funded from a variety of taxes on business profits (Mackenzie, 1998, pp. 335–358). That way, a program to assist workers who are vulnerable to job elimination and who receive lower wages would be funded by a vertical transfer of benefits from the wealthy rather than the horizontal transfer system introduced by the CCTB program.

Under the CCTB's current structure, any business, large or small, can hire taxpayer-subsidized employees at a minimum wage, providing few or no health benefits or wage increases to them. Commensurate with neoliberal ideology, instead of using the tax system in a progressive manner to assist low-income earners, the government has decided to assist businesses by subsidizing low wages and has, therefore, firmly entrenched the concept of less eligibility and worthy and unworthy poor within the welfare system. As presently designed and delivered, the CCTB is not a children's benefit. Rather, it is an enriched Working Income Supplement (WIS) for working-poor families with children (Pulkingham & Ternowetsky, 1997, p. 206). By introducing the CCTB in its current form, governments are acknowledging that, for more and more people, the economic system will not provide a surplus and/or social wage. As a consequence, inequality of income, inequality of opportunity, and inequality of condition for the poorest in Canada will continue to grow.

Notes

1 UNICEF uses a relative measure of poverty based on households with incomes below 50% of the national median income. This measure differs from the after-tax LICO measure, which is the most reported measure issued by Statistics Canada and is based on the community average spent on essentials.

2 Statistics Canada defines a family economic unit as all occupants of a dwelling unit who are related by blood, marriage, or adoption, and couples living together in common-law relationships.

3 The OECD defines purchasing power parities (PPPs) as currency conversion rates that both convert to a common currency and equalize the purchasing power of different currencies. In other words, they eliminate the differences in price levels between countries in the process of conversion. Continuously updated data on PPP adjusted for GDP can be found at http://stats.oecd.org/Index.aspx?datasetcode=SNA_TABLE4.

4 The year 1997 is the last year that Statistics Canada produced the *Survey of Consumer Finances*, the data set that has been used on a yearly basis to examine child poverty. The *Survey of Labour and Income Dynamics* (SLID) has replaced it. There are currently strict criteria on access to the SLID data. The longitudinal nature of the SLID data has raised concerns of possible identification of respondents. Only a cross-sectional version of SLID is available to the public. When using Statistics Canada data, income can be calculated using income from either Wages and Salaries, or Total Income, including government transfers or income after tax. The researcher should identify what income variable was used in the study. In creating the data sets, Statistics Canada does not include families living in First Nations communities (reserves) and children living in institutions.

5 For more on Poduluk and the development of LICO, see Hunter & Miazdyck (2006, pp. 408–418).

6 Previously Statistics Canada provided two sets of measures in *Income Trends in Canada 1976–2006 13F0022XIE*. One set measured the ratio of "economic family" types (economic families or unattached individuals) in low income, and the other measured the ratio of "persons" (or totals) in low income. Logically, the ratios for unattached individuals did not change across these two data measures, but the ratios for economic families could have dramatic differences. For example, if we look at the overall ratio of low income in Canada using the "persons in low income" measure the result is 14.5% for 2006 (families/unattached). If we use the "families in low income" measure the result is 19.5% for 2006 (families/unattached). The "persons" data set counts *each individual* in a family, and the "family" data counts *each family* as an individual economic unit. For the 2008 data, Statistics Canada ceased producing the "family" level data. In justifying this change, Statistics Canada explains: "Because it is essential to portray the low income situation for the entire population, it is more appropriate to analyze individuals rather than families." *Survey of Labour and Income Dynamics: 2008 Survey Overview 75F0011X*.

7 Statistics Canada, *Table 202-0802—"Persons in low income families," Income in Canada 2009*, Catalogue no. 75-202-X.

8 For a more complete discussion of issues with after-tax incomes and the LICO measure, see Cotton & Webber (2000).

9 For a more thorough discussion of poverty lines in Canada, see Graham, Swift, & Delaney (2009); see also Ross, Scott, & Smith.

10 The MBM defines disposable family income as the sum remaining after deducting from the total household income the following: total income taxes paid; the personal portion of payroll taxes; other mandatory payroll deductions such as contributions to employer-sponsored pension plans, supplementary health plans, and union dues; child support and alimony payments made to another household; out-of-pocket spending on child care; and non-insured but medically prescribed health-related expenses such as dental and vision care, prescription drugs, and aids for persons with disabilities (HRDC, 2003, p. 4). As such, the MBM definition of disposable household income would appear to more closely reflect available funds than the after-tax LICO.

11 Statistics Canada, *Table 202-0802.*

12 Average scores are highly susceptible to extreme values, which greatly skew this measure of central tendency.

13 In the past, Canada's LIM calculation used a different procedure for adjusting for family size than the UN and OECD. This created problems with direct comparison. In 2008, Statistics Canada changed its equivalence factor to adjust for family size and adopted the UN and OECD method. "In order to ensure international consistency and to facilitate the calculation of adjusted family income, a new scale will now be used. From now on, adjusted family income will be obtained by dividing family income by the square root of the number of members in a family." *Survey of Labour and Income Dynamics: 2008 Survey Overview 75F0011X.* This is a welcome change as researchers have needed to generate international equivalences from the raw data files rather than using Statistics Canada's published LIM data.

14 In this report, Statistics Canada Low Income Measure (LIM) is used as the benchmark to identify poor children and their families. The data for poor children under 18 exclude those who are unattached individuals, those who are the major income earner, and those who are the spouse or common-law partner of the major income earner. In creating these survey data sets, Statistics Canada does not include families living in First Nation communities (reserves).

15 Statistics Canada, *Table 202-0802.*

16 The aggregate low-income gap as a percentage of income represents the sum of the gap of all persons in low income, divided by the sum of the family (or household) income of all persons, where the gap is the difference between the low income threshold and the family (or household) income. The type of income used depends on the selected low-income line. Total income is used for the low income cut-off before tax, after-tax income is used for both the low income cut-off after tax and the low income measure, and disposable income is used for the market basket measure.

17 As previously mentioned, starting with the 2008 data, Statistics Canada ceased producing the "family" level data in preference for "individual" level data. Therefore the incidence of child poverty when examined at the family level is not comparable to incidences produced in the past, which reflected family level data. See note 6 for more on this matter.

18 Statistics Canada, 2006 Census of Population, Catalogue no. 97-564-XCB2006001. Low-income before-tax measure of economic "families" is reported as the 2006 Census does not provide the LIM measurement or the "individual" measurement.

19 Statistics Canada cautions that when using the 2006 Census for those answering North American Indian single response, users should be aware that the counts for this item are more affected than most by the incomplete enumeration of certain Indian reserves and Indian settlements. The extent of the impact will depend on the geographic area under study. In 2006, a total of 22 Indian reserves and Indian settlements were

incompletely enumerated by the census. The populations of these 22 communities are not included in the census counts. In this report the category of multiple responses is not used because that category indicates the number of respondents who reported the North American Indian ethnic origin, either as their only response or in addition to one or more other ethnic origins. The total represents the sum of single responses and multiple responses received in the census. Respondents who reported multiple ethnic origins are counted more than once, as they are included in the multiple responses for each origin they reported.

20 Includes economic families and unattached individuals. An economic family is defined as a group of two or more persons who live in the same dwelling and are related to each other by blood, marriage, common law, or adoption. An unattached individual is a person living either alone or with others to whom he or she is unrelated, such as roommates or a lodger. This concept is different from previous reports where data for economic family was produced.

21 Statistics Canada, *Table 202-0804*.

22 Statistics Canada defines an earner as a person who received income from employment (wages and salaries) and/or self-employment during the reference year. *Income in Canada 2009*.

23 Statistics Canada, *Table 202-0804*.

24 Less than two-thirds of median income.

25 Low wages based on the before-tax LICO. To calculate the "low paid work" threshold, the appropriate LICO was divided by 52.14 (weeks/year), which provides the dollars per week needed to reach a LICO low income cut-off line in 1996. Earning at 10% above the applicable LICO low income cut-off is defined as "moving up" out of low-paid work.

26 United Nations General Assembly, Human Rights Council, Eleventh Session, Universal Periodic Review, A/HRC/11/17, 03 March 2009.

27 For a complete analysis of Canada's response to the UN regarding the increasing rates of poverty among single seniors and an analysis of poverty among women and children, see G. Hunter (2010).

28 "[T]he punitive regulation of the impoverished fractions of the new post-Fordist proletariat is effected mainly through the agency of ever-more refined and intrusive panoptic mechanisms directly integrated into programs of social protection and assistance" (Wacquant, 2009b, p. 105).

29 For further information on provincial programs, see Canada Revenue Agency, *T4114 Canada Child Benefits (including related federal, provincial, and territorial programs)*.

References

Anderson, J. (2003). "Aboriginal children in poverty in urban communities: Social exclusion and the growing racialization of poverty in Canada." Ottawa, ON: Canadian Council on Social Development. Retrieved from http://www.ccsd.ca/pr/2003/aboriginal.htm

Broad, D. (2000). *Hollow work, hollow society? Globalization and the casual labour problem in Canada*. Halifax, NS: Fernwood Publishing.

Canada Revenue Agency. (n.d.). *T4114—Canada Child Benefits (including related federal, provincial, and territorial programs)*. Retrieved from http://www.cra-arc.gc.ca/E/pub/tg/t4114

Cotton, C., & Webber, M. (2000, September). Should the Low Income Cut-offs be updated? *A summary of feedback on Statistics Canada's discussion paper*. Ottawa, ON: Income Statistics Division, Statistics Canada, Catalogue no. 75F0002MIE-00011.

References

Fellegi, I. (1997, September). *On poverty and low income.* Ottawa, ON: Statistics Canada, Catalogue no. 13F0027XIE.

Fellegi, I. (1999, December). On poverty and low income. In *Should the low income cut-offs be updated? A discussion paper.* Ottawa, ON: Income Statistics Division, Statistics Canada, Catalogue no. 75F0002MIE—99009.

Galbraith, J. (1998). *Created unequal: The crisis in American pay.* New York, NY: Simon and Schuster.

Gilbert, N. (2004). *Transformation of the welfare state: The silent surrender of public responsibility.* London, UK: Oxford University Press.

Government of Canada. (1997a). "Towards a national child benefit system." Retrieved from http://www.fin.gc.ca/budget97/pamph/childpae.pdf

Government of Canada. (1997b). "Working together towards a national child benefit system—Budget 1997." Retrieved from http://www.fin.gc.ca/budget97/child/childe.pdf

Graham, J., Delaney, R., & Swift, K. (2000). *Canadian social policy: An introduction.* Toronto, ON: Prentice Hall.

Graham, J., Swift, K., & Delaney, R. (2009). *Canadian social policy: An introduction* (3rd ed.). Toronto, ON: Pearson Prentice Hall.

Hicks, A. (1999). *Social democracy and welfare capitalism.* Ithaca, NY: Cornell University Press.

Human Resources Development Canada. (2000, March). *Reconnecting social assistance recipients to the labour market: Lessons learned.* Ottawa, ON: Evaluation and Data Development, Statistics Canada, Catalogue no. SPAH123E-03-00.

Human Resources Development Canada. (2003, May). *Understanding the 2000 low income statistics based on the market basket measure.* Ottawa, ON: Statistics Canada, Catalogue no. SP-569-03-03E.

Hunter, G. (2010, November). United Nations Human Rights Council review of Canada and Canada's response to recommendation 17. Poverty among seniors, women, and children, and income inequality in Canada and Saskatchewan. *University of Regina.* Retrieved from http://www.uregina.ca/socialwork/faculty-staff/FacultySites/HunterGarsonSite/Index.html

Hunter, G., & Miazdyck, D. (2006). Current issues surrounding poverty and welfare programming in Canada: Two reviews. In R. Blake & J. Keshen (Eds.), *Social fabric or patchwork quilt: The development of social policy in Canada* (pp. 383–418). Peterborough, ON: Broadview Press.

Jackson, A. (2001). "Low income trends in the 1990s." Canadian Council on Social Development. Retrieved from http://www.ccsd.ca/pubs/2000/lit

Jackson, A., Robinson, D., Baldwin, B., & Wiggins, C. (2000). *Falling behind: The state of working in Canada.* Ottawa, ON: Canadian Centre for Social Policy.

Janz, T. (2004, March). Low-paid employment and "moving up": 1996–2001. Ottawa, ON: Statistics Canada, Catalogue no. 75F0002MIE-No. 003.

Jones, C., & Novak, T. (1999). *Poverty, welfare and the disciplinary State.* London, UK: Routledge.

Katz, M. (2001). *The price of citizenship: Redefining the American welfare state.* New York, NY: Henry Holt and Company.

Kerstetter, S. (2000). LICOs and LIMs. In M. Goldberg & J. Pulkingham (Eds.), *Defining and measuring poverty: Prince George Forum, April 3, 2000.* Prince George, BC: Child Welfare Research Centre, University of Northern British Columbia.

References
Kitchen, B. (2001). Poverty and declining living standards in a changing economy. In J. Turner & F. Turner (Eds.), *Canadian social welfare* (4th ed.) (pp. 232–249). Toronto, ON: Pearson Education Canada.

Klein, S., & Montgomery, B. (2001). *Depressing wages: Why welfare cuts hurt both poor and working poor*. Ottawa, ON: Canadian Centre for Policy Alternatives.

Lightman, E. (2003). *Social policy in Canada*. Toronto, ON: Oxford University Press.

Mackenzie, H. (1998). Tax relief for those who really need it. In Canadian Centre for Policy Alternatives, *Alternative Federal Budget Papers: 1998* (pp. 335–358). Ottawa, ON: Canadian Centre for Policy Alternatives.

National Council of Welfare. (1999a). *Children first: A pre-budget report by the National Council of Welfare*. Ottawa, ON: Minister of Public Works and Government Services Canada.

National Council of Welfare. (1999b). *Poverty profile 1997*. Ottawa, ON: Minister of Public Works and Government Services Canada.

Organisation for Economic Co-operation and Development (OECD). (2008). *Growing unequal?: Income distribution and poverty in OECD countries*. Retrieved from http:/ / www.oecd.org/ dataoecd/ 44/ 48/ 41525292.pdf

Peck, J. (2001). *Workfare states*. London, UK: Guilford Press.

Poduluk, J. (1968). *Income of Canadians*. Ottawa, ON: Census Monograph, Dominion Bureau of Statistics.

Pulkingham, J., & Ternowetsky, G. (1997). The new Canada Child Tax Benefit: Discriminating between "deserving" and "undeserving" among poor families with children. In J. Pulkingham & G. Ternowetsky (Eds.), *Child and family policies: Struggles, strategies, and options* (pp. 204–208). Halifax, NS: Fernwood Publishing.

Riches, G. (1997). Hunger and the welfare state: Comparative perspectives. In G. Riches (Ed.), *First world hunger: Food security and welfare politics* (pp. 1–13). London, UK: Macmillan Press.

Ross, D., Scott, K., & Smith, P. (2000). *The Canadian fact book on poverty*. Ottawa, ON: Canadian Council on Social Development.

Saskatchewan Social Services. (1999). "Information: Social assistance handbook" [Brochure].

Statistics Canada (2002). *Income in Canada 2000*. Ottawa, ON: Catalogue no. 75-202 XIE.

Statistics Canada. (2006). *Census of population*. Ottawa, ON: Catalogue no. 97-564-XCB2006001.

Statistics Canada. (2008). *Income trends in Canada 1976–2006*. Ottawa, ON: Catalogue no. *13F0022XIE*.

Statistics Canada. (2010). *Survey of labour and income dynamics: 2008 survey overview*. Ottawa, ON: Catalogue no. 75F0011X.

Statistics Canada (2011). *Income in Canada 2009*. Ottawa, ON: Catalogue no. 75-202-X.

Ternowetsky, G. (2000). *Poverty and corporate welfare*. Regina, SK: Social Policy Research Unit, Faculty of Social Work. University of Regina.

UNICEF. (2000). *The league table of child poverty in rich nations*. Florence, Italy: UNICEF Innocenti Research Centre.

UNICEF. (2005). *Child poverty in rich countries 2005*. Florence, Italy: UNICEF Innocenti Research Centre.

United Nations General Assembly. (2009, March). *Report of the Working Group on the Universal Periodic Review: Canada.* Human Rights Council, Eleventh Session, Universal Periodic Review, A/HRC/11/17.

Wacquant, L. (2009a). *Punishing the poor: The neoliberal government of social insecurity.* Durham, NC: Duke University Press.

Wacquant, L. (2009b). *Prisons of poverty.* Minneapolis, MN: University of Minnesota Press.

Webber, M. (1998, May). *Measuring low income and poverty in Canada: An update.* Ottawa, ON: Statistics Canada, Income Statistics Division, Catalogue no. 98-13.

Additional Resources

Additional Resources

For a vast number of sources on social policy in Canada, including numerous references to child poverty, see the personal website of Gilles Seguin, http://www.canadiansocialresearch.net.

For resources that present neoliberal ideology on the welfare state, poverty lines, and so on, see: Paul, E., Miller, F., Jr., & Paul, J. (Eds.). (1997). *The welfare state.* Cambridge, UK: Cambridge University Press.

Back to the Present

Rethinking Risk Assessment in Child Welfare

10

Marilyn Callahan and Karen Swift

Risk assessment measures were introduced into provincial child welfare systems within the last two decades, at a time when child welfare "failures" were featured prominently in the media and when several formal reviews of child welfare systems were undertaken as a response to media coverage.[1] This trend was not limited to Canada; it also appeared in the United States, the United Kingdom, Australia, and other Euro-Western countries (Parton, Thorpe, & Wattam, 1997; Saunders & Goddard, 1998; Schene & Bond, 1989) and extended beyond child welfare to many other fields and disciplines in the human services.

The promise of risk assessment in child welfare was considerable. Among other attributes, it appeared to provide tangible evidence that governments were taking action on child protection, using tools designed to predict which children were in danger of maltreatment. It also seemed to provide a way to screen the important cases from those of less concern, thus triaging the scarce resources of child welfare.

This chapter chronicles the development and implementation of risk assessment in child welfare in Canada from the early 1990s to around 2005 and is based on research conducted in two Canadian provinces during this period (Swift & Callahan, 2009). It illustrates the willingness of those in the field of child welfare—a highly volatile and often politically risky endeavour—to adopt measures that were far-reaching and prescriptive yet were based on only modest empirical support. It speaks to the power of uncontested ideas and "policy fads"—a lesson that applies well beyond this particular example. While fascination with the original risk assessment tools has waned in the past several years, the concept of risk itself remains, and so does the next generation of risk diagnostic tools. Providing a critical assessment is often easier than proposing alternatives, but we undertake this task in the latter section of the chapter.

The Meanings of Risk

The Meanings of Risk

Risk is a ubiquitous concept, largely taken for granted as meaning "bad things might happen." While hardly a new idea—it dates at least back to the Renaissance and the development of probability laws to challenge superstition—it has found purchase in contemporary life and professional practice. We are reminded daily about the risks around us and what we should do to avoid them. Good citizens are increasingly defined as those who manage their risks. Those who cannot are viewed more and more as irresponsible and as a drain on the public purse if they need help or if the public must take action to protect itself from their activities. Attention has shifted from the "needs" of the vulnerable to the "risks" they create for themselves and others. The solutions arising from risk thinking are to shore up the commitment and skills of individuals so that they are self-managing citizens, or, to segregate them if they will not comply. This attention to individual responsibility to manage an increasing number of risks fits with neoliberal thinking about citizenship and achieving reductions in the welfare state apparatus.

Our confidence in the validity of particular "risks" is shaken regularly. We find ourselves confronted with new "scientific" facts that make old risks redundant and new risks visible. Yet we cling to the notion that risks are real, not just a computation of factors that can be measured and ducked, even as old risks fade and new ones emerge. The evidence that many risks are socially constructed and differ across time and cultures does not seem to shake our belief in their concrete existence.

Our study revealed some further thoughts on the meaning of risk (Swift & Callahan, 2009). For the most part, both social workers and parents had negative connotations about risk, which is not surprising, given that the instruments they were using to measure risk focused on a series of negative factors. But workers and parents often shifted from thinking about risk as a set of factors that could supposedly predict future behaviour or risks as real things to be avoided to identifying risk with particular individuals. "I am the risk," as one mother put it succinctly. This transference from risk factors to individuals is apparent more broadly. For instance, the activity of profiling requires us to view individuals according to a set of risk factors that are supposed to predict their behaviour. They become known as risky individuals even if they do nothing at present or in the future to merit such a label.

Furthermore, a more positive notion of risk was nowhere evident in our study. Yet daily, social workers are charged with asking their clients to take many risks: to give up a mate or a neighbourhood, or to change longstanding behaviours—all actions requiring considerable courage and daring, which is yet another meaning of risk.

Risk Assessment in Human Services

Risk assessments are instruments designed to measure risk and presumably to point to actions to avoid or mitigate risk. They often consist of a series of factors requiring that professionals and/or their clients collate evidence to provide scores, usually numerical. Those so measured often internalize these scores just as they have come to accept themselves as "the risk." "I used to be a 4 and now I'm a 2," one mother told us.

While risk assessment is prevalent in child welfare, it has also permeated the practice of other human service professionals. Ask your doctor about blood pressure pills and she might well open her computer, show you the risk factors for high blood pressure problems, weigh your factors against these, and place you in a category from low to high risk. Then you and she can discuss whether medication is required and the efficacy of different treatments. Risk assessment is so ubiquitous that we often take the assessments on our own and then hurry to a professional with our diagnosis.

A review of the literature on risk assessment across professions and fields in human services reveals many common characteristics in these instruments, although cross-disciplinary work on risk assessment is largely absent. Based on our review, we constructed a typology for comparison on several different variables (Swift & Callahan, 2009). Most striking is the degree to which risk assessment is viewed as a developmental tool, an addendum to practice, or a prescribed activity central to practice. Child welfare, along with some areas of the corrections field, provides the clearest example of risk assessment as a mandatory activity driving practice. Another significant variable is the degree to which the instrument is defensible based on empirical research. Most instruments falter in this area, with child welfare measures being no exception.

This review also illustrates the intense interest in and application of risk assessment in many different professions, including medicine, nursing, teaching, law, corrections, and psychology as well as social work. This affection for risk assessment is not surprising. Many professions besides social work face intense pressure to husband resources and to streamline their activities according to management principles. Moreover, human service professionals have always longed to put more emphasis on preventing problems rather than simply mopping up the damage afterwards. Risk assessment, with its promise to predict, appears to be a significant tool to realize this aim.

The Development of Risk Assessment in Child Welfare

In Canada, provincial rather than federal governments are responsible for health, education, and welfare, including child welfare. All ten provinces and the three territories have their own child protection legislation, as well as organizational structures designed to protect children. Although child welfare in Canada cannot be described as a single, unified system, some common traditions and understandings across the country provide the basis for describing Canadian child welfare. Generally speaking, child welfare services are residual or "last chance" services and are highly regulated.

Since its inception in the early 20th century, formal child welfare work in Canada has been driven in large measure by complaints made by individuals about particular children and parents, who are then investigated by social workers, most of whom are women (Chen, 2001; Swift, 1995a). Records suggest a strong leaning toward British moral traditions of individual responsibility, the nuclear family, and at least the appearance of propriety and morality as central to the style and direction of much child welfare work during the early period (Swift, 1995b).

The mid-20th century saw a series of changes to child welfare legislation and its focus. One in particular, the "discovery" of the battered child (Kempe et al., 1962), led to several changes, the most notable being the addition of mandatory reporting requirements in child welfare legislation. Other significant events included the release of the Badgley Report (1984) on sexual abuse of children and the introduction of the Canadian Charter of Rights and Freedoms (1982). Both of these policy influences increased attention on legal issues in child welfare and intensified relations among child protection workers, police, and the court system. At the same time, the idea of least intrusive action—always a thread in Canadian child protection practice—was encoded in protection legislation, imposing a requirement for child welfare intervention to be at the least intrusive level consonant with protecting children from harm. This stands in contrast to the approach of pioneer child welfare workers, who intervened without much compunction into the lives of families, offering advice and services wherever they deemed these necessary.

In the 1990s a series of high-profile media reports of deaths of children known to child protection authorities led to several formal reviews of child welfare (Bennet, 1998; Bridge Child Care Consultancy, 1991; Gove, 1995; Porter, 1998). These cases and subsequent reviews have prompted policy shifts in several provinces and jurisdictions (Parton et al., 1997; Swift, 2001). In general, formal reviews have occurred after a child has been killed by a parent or caregiver and have focused on the actions of individual workers and the practices and policies governing their work. As a result, recommendations emerging from these reviews have tended to lower the threshold of risk required to intervene to protect a child and also to expand definitions of abuse and neglect in order to ensure that cases are identified. For instance, changes to child welfare legislation in British Columbia included the phrase "has been or is likely to be" when defining child maltreatment, where previous legislation made no mention of future harm.[2] This inclusion in many child welfare statutes has given legislative authority for risk assessment designed to predict the safety of children. Other recommendations have included the development of training programs for child welfare workers, the installation of computer-based information systems, and tougher mandatory reporting clauses in legislation. Taken together, these changes are sometimes referred to as a "child-centred" approach. This approach stands in contrast to a "family-centred" one, where services are offered to families in need of support without a requirement for intensive investigations into their care of children.

The introduction of risk assessment measures also occurred following rapid increases in complaints to child welfare organizations, in part as a result of media coverage and formal inquiries. While not all complaints are investigated—some are deemed frivolous, out of jurisdiction, or outside the mandate of legislation—there has been a startling increase in the number of investigations that child welfare organizations carry out each year. From 1998 to 2003 this rate almost doubled, from 24.5 to 45.6 per 1,000 children, and it has held fast since (46.6 per 1,000 in 2008). In real terms, this has resulted in the number of investigations increasing from 118,552 in 1998 to 217,960 in 2008 (Canadian incidence study of reported child abuse and neglect, 2010, p. 22).

This disquieting increase in investigations came at a time when governments of all political stripes were making strenuous efforts to reduce expenditures on social programs, child welfare included. Thus risk assessment, while it promised to take seriously the goal of child protection, also offered hope that costs could be contained by limiting worker involvement to only those cases where children were likely to be harmed. It was a tall order.

Child welfare workers have always conducted assessments to determine whether individual children are safe in their homes. The most recent iteration, risk assessment, reflects a concerted attempt to change these assessments from ones governed largely by Euro-Christian values about traditional families and practice wisdom based on medical or other scientific knowledge that can meet the test of legal evidence.

Risk Assessment: A Tool and a Work Process

In child welfare, risk assessment is first and foremost "a process of predicting whether or not a child will be maltreated at some future point in time" (Jones, 1994, p. 1037). It is based primarily on actuarial rationales that make predictions of behaviour according to statistical computations of particular characteristics shared by groups within the population at large (Silver & Miller, 2002).[3] Many of these characteristics have been provided by social workers, who draw from their experience with parents and caregivers reported to child welfare. Most risk assessment instruments include measures of present safety, but all of them focus on making some prediction of future harm. Previously, child welfare investigations were largely limited to assessing the present safety of children; they did so by examining individual and family conditions as more or less unique cases.

By 2000, six of ten provinces had introduced formal risk assessment instruments in child welfare, the majority favouring the New York Risk Assessment Model (Federal/Provincial Working Group on Child and Family Services Information, 2001). While risk assessments vary in their length and rating criteria, the New York model[4] requires workers to score parents and children in two major areas: child-specific factors (age of child, number of children in home) and caretaker factors (caretaker abilities, age). Twenty-two or twenty-three items are scored on a four-point scale, with descriptors provided for each item and level. The assessment of the likelihood of risk to children is based on tallied scores for each of these items.

Administering these tools requires a substantial investment in time, including training of workers and their supervisors. Workers are urged to collect "objective" data to validate their scores, and these data are frequently obtained from files and opinions of other professionals and community workers. The risk assessment may be completed without the involvement of parents and children. These assessments are filed on computer and become part of the client's permanent record.

Risk assessment also defines a work process involving a series of stages from evaluating the initial complaint, to an immediate safety assessment, to a risk assessment and risk reduction plan. Although the process is not exactly a linear one, nonetheless the activities of each stage are outlined in detail through practice standards and agency policy. Particularly in large urban offices, each phase of the assessment may be completed by a different worker, and the file is passed from one staff member to the next. In some provinces, particularly Ontario, the time allotted to complete tasks is specified and child welfare organizations receive funding on the basis of a formula determining the amount and nature of the work completed.

The above account portrays the worker as something of a cog in a machine, carrying out various tasks according to well-defined policies and instructions. This is true in part, but it misses the point that social workers in child protection are individuals with their own histories and values shaped by their experience and education, among other things. While the documents and policies direct workers to act in specific ways and demand that workers complete paperwork to demonstrate that they have taken these actions, workers nonetheless devise their own systems for completing the work using different techniques for different occasions.

Risk Assessment: Managing Work, Protecting Children

The next section of the chapter assesses two important goals of risk assessment: its effect on the nature and volume of the work of child welfare, and its capacity to identify and protect children in need of assistance.

One of the clearest attributes of risk assessment is that it makes visible and precise the work process that social workers must undertake in child protection. There is a set pattern to the work, one that is governed by detailed policies and procedures. While these policies differ from jurisdiction to jurisdiction, there is a general consensus that risk assessment adds to the work of child protection in significant ways and for unexpected reasons.

A Screen with Few Holes

The profile of people who are reported to child welfare has remained consistent over the years. Most often, they have limited economic means and are disproportionately female single parents and women of colour (Callahan, 1994; Swift, 1995a; Trocmé et al., 2005). Poverty frequently leads to poor housing, more frequent moves, and limited social networks. Risk assessment scores parents on most of these characteristics, thus making it a self-fulfilling prophecy that poor parents who are reported will exhibit risk characteristics. Risk assessment also requires workers to fill out all items on the assessment, and therefore it is likely that further risks besides the ones named in the initial complaint will be found. It is difficult and perilous for the worker to set aside a case where at least some risks have been given high ratings.

A Powerful Instrument

Parents and caregivers reported to child welfare organizations have little opportunity to refuse to participate in the risk assessment process. Those from other cultures may be totally unfamiliar with the process and potential outcomes of investigations. Others who have been through it before know that workers will complete the risk assessment whether they cooperate or not and therefore decide that compliance is their best strategy. Risk assessment, as a "scientific instrument," makes it difficult for either parents or social workers to dispute its findings. At the same time, risk assessment makes the work process visible so that steps that social workers omit or do not undertake fully will be evident to supervisors and auditors. Workers must protect themselves.

A Complex Administrative Process

Following a comprehensive study of the Ontario Risk Assessment Model, Parada (2004) identifies three ways in which the model intensifies the work of child protection. First, it is heavily based on documentation guided by computer programs that demand completion of one screen before another can be tackled. Workers in his study, and others (Lu, 2000), report that these demands for documentation and administrative tasks are so great (up to 70 percent of their time) that little time is left over for contact with families and children. Second, the model places sharp limits on the time that can be expended on specific tasks. In the face of many steps and procedures to be undertaken and many cases waiting for attention, workers must triage their

Assessing Risk Assessment

time, focusing on the work that must be done within specific time frames (the paperwork) and putting aside optional tasks (such as relationship building with families and community members). Third, risk assessment demands constant consultation between supervisors and workers about making decisions and taking next steps. Any variations from time frames and policies also require consultations.

Finally, at least in the initial stages of the work process, risk assessment shifts workers' views of children and families: from viewing people as unique individuals to seeing them as scores on a series of risk factos (Parada, Swift, & Callahan, 2005), and this further removes workers from a sense that they are "doing social work." Taken together, shifts in practice that respond to risk assessment require social workers to view their work as a series of largely administrative tasks that must be done quickly and that are completed, not when the family or child is "helped," but when the file is turned over to the next worker or managed in some fashion. Given the disjuncture that occurs for some workers who enter social work with the intention of working with "people not paper," the work seems even more demanding.

Assessing Risk Assessment

The work of child protection has expanded, intensified, and become less like social work. This would be a justifiable outcome if children benefited from the changes. The next section of the chapter examines the evidence as to whether the expected benefits have been realized.

A search of recent literature reveals no studies demonstrating that the incidence of abuse and neglect of children has been reduced since the introduction of risk assessment measures in North America and elsewhere. The most serious form of harm to children—and the one of most concern to child protection authorities—is death, which often occurs at the hands of parents or caregivers. Over the past thirty years, there has been no significant change in the number of children killed by family members in Canada, and no pattern of change or decrease in the years since a risk assessment approach was introduced (Statistics Canada, 2005, p. 51).

As mentioned before, statistics kept by provinces showed a sharp increase in cases reported and investigated by child welfare authorities in the years immediately following the introduction of risk assessment. In Ontario, for example, the number of investigations carried out increased 23 percent from 1998 to 2004–5, from 66,759 to 82,137. The number of children in care also rose dramatically in that province, from 11,260 in 1997 to 18,830 in 2005, an increase of 67 percent (Federal/Provincial Working Group, 2001; Ontario Association of Children's Aid Societies, 2005), and that figure continued to rise until at least 2007 (Swift, 2011, p. 49).[5] In BC. the proportion of Aboriginal children in care, already very high at 31–33 percent of all children in care, jumped to 37 percent between 1998 and 2000 after the introduction

Assessing Risk Assessment

of risk assessment (Foster & Wright, 2002, p. 124), and stood at over 49 percent in August 2005 (Foster, 2007). It might seem from this increased level of surveillance and intervention that more children were rescued from dangerous situations. However, there is substantial evidence that is not the case.

In almost half of the cases reported and investigated by child welfare workers during that period, the case was "unsubstantiated," and of those cases that were substantiated, only 44 percent received any ongoing attention (Trocmé et al., 2005, p. 56). Thus we had the situation that for many of the families investigated by child welfare workers, little else occurred, at least until another complaint was lodged.

There are indications that workers make decisions based on risk assessment that could be harmful for children (Rycus & Hughes, 2003). One Ontario study showed that workers' ratings of risk have become higher as the tools have become entrenched in practice (Leslie & O'Connor, 2002) because workers feel more secure themselves rating risk levels as high. Higher ratings, of course, mean an increased likelihood that children will come into care.

Furthermore, it is not clear that children coming into care are at risk of immediate harm. The Canadian Incidence Study (Trocmé et al., 2005, p. 108) found that only 13 percent of investigated cases involved physical harm to children and in only 3 percent of these was the harm sufficient to merit treatment. It was also found that children in families designated as neglectful were more likely to be brought into care than children who had been abused (Trocmé et al., 2005, p. 114).[6] The study demonstrated in fact that in at least 40 percent of reported child protection cases, the primary issue is neglect (p. 114).

It is well established that the indicators of child neglect are very similar to those of poverty (Swift, 1995a). In cases in which poverty is a substantial issue, two things can happen. One is that poverty may be viewed by protection workers as neglect. In this case the parent, usually the mother, will be asked to address problems of deprivation that she may not have resources to correct. She will be scrutinized and supervised, but neither the agency nor the worker has the mandate to ameliorate her poverty, and children may be brought into care as a result. A study on housing by Chau and colleagues (2001) showed that for up to 20 percent of children brought into care in Ontario, one precipitating factor is lack of acceptable housing. The other possible response is that the case may be accurately assessed as poverty and closed since no resources to address this issue are available. In any event, the case-by-case nature of child welfare work ensures that issues of poverty will only become visible when an individual referral is made. Families living in communities suffering widespread poverty—for example, on First Nation reserves—will receive no attention for this issue from child protection authorities.

Assessing Risk Assessment

One of the chief attributes of risk assessment, especially the more complex kinds, is that it is "front-end loaded." That is, the intensive amount of investigative work at the front end consumes a substantial amount of the total time and resources that will be devoted to working on any given case. Furthermore, given the increase in numbers of children being brought into care, substantial child protection resources will go to supporting alternative care arrangements.[7] The drastic cuts in services and levels of income support across North America during the past decades have resulted in a context of extreme scarcity for the most vulnerable families. Child welfare workers report that many of the programs they found helpful in supporting and helping families to heal have been cut or are underfunded. Long waiting lists for existing programs mean that when children are assessed as requiring significant kinds of help, they often don't receive it because supporting programs are not available. What is available, and most often recommended, are programs to "fix" the family, for instance, parenting skills programs.

A critique of risk assessment instruments has emerged from research that challenges modernist notions of the unlimited potential of science. This research suggests that although risk assessment measures appear to be empirical instruments, there is no research-based evidence that they actually predict what they purport to (Camasso & Jagannathan, 1995; Doueck et al., 1993; Michalski, Alaggia, & Trocmé, 1996; Pecora, 1991; Wald & Woolverton, 1990). Unclear conceptualization (English & Pecora, 1994), inconsistency of operational definitions (DePanfilis, 1996), debates about appropriate definitions of "risk events," and inconsistencies among laws, policies, mission, and training (Berkowitz, 1991) have raised important questions about what is being measured. Furthermore, questions about whether risk assessment models are effectively and consistently implemented have been raised by Doueck and colleagues (1993) and Pecora (1991). Questions about conflicting expectations as to what such measures can produce (Cicchinelli, 1989), about the use of associated factors rather than causal links (Pecora, 1991), and about the actual predictive value of assessments, especially concerning the all-important issue of child death (Lyons, Doueck, & Wodarski, 1996; Trocmé & Lindsey, 1996), all arise in the literature of the 1990s, when risk assessments were introduced. Moreover, the research problems in testing these instruments are substantial. For instance, each assessment tool may contain many items, but trying to isolate how scores on the variables interact in a particular situation is extremely difficult. Does a high score (unfavourable) on alcohol and drug abuse overshadow a low score on the child's response to parent? Under what conditions? In the most wide-ranging review of the literature sponsored by the North America Resource Centre on Child Welfare, the authors examine the issues of predictability in risk assessment and state that

> the preponderance of research literature continues to raise serious questions about the reliability and validity of most of the risk assessment models and instruments currently used by child welfare agencies. In practice, many child welfare professionals are making decisions about children and families with little more accuracy than flipping a coin, while believing they are using technologies that reduce subjectivity and bias, and that increase the quality of their decisions. (Rycus & Hughes, 2003, p. 23)

Other Outcomes of Risk Assessment

If risk assessment has failed to reduce workloads and cannot be shown to increase protection to children, then it is interesting to speculate about why it persists as a policy direction in many jurisdictions in Canada and beyond. Several reports evaluating risk assessment claim that one reason for its ongoing appeal rests in its ability to protect organizations (Saunders & Goddard, 1998; Parton et al., 1997):

> Under the guise of protecting children, and even of protecting workers from potential litigation, risk assessment instruments may essentially be attempts by bureaucratic, managerialist organisations to protect themselves from blame when tragedies occur. Ill-equipped to ensure the prompt delivery of services to all those in need, organisations have adopted risk assessment instruments "in lieu of pushing political system[s] for more resources." (Wald & Woolverton, 1990, p. 504)

While this may appear cynical, there may be some truth to it. If a child is harmed or killed while under the protection of an organization, risk assessment procedures make it possible for that organization to argue that all possible actions had been undertaken to ensure the child's safety. If individual workers failed to complete the procedures as required, they could be held personally responsible for the tragedy. Risk assessments on parents have become central to the risk management plans of organizations.

For managers, risk assessment narrows and specifies the range of skills necessary for social workers and enables them to hire novices, who can quickly be trained in risk assessment processes and thinking. Given the chronic problems of social work turnover in child protection, this is no small benefit. Furthermore, risk assessment organizes the work into clear stages with specific goals, making it more possible to "contract out" portions of it. Much of the work of "risk reduction" is accomplished through contracts with profit and not-for-profit organizations, reducing the need for public employees.

Risk assessment holds some appeal for child protection workers. They state that while it has added to their paperwork and increased their vulnerability, it has also brought a welcome order to their practice (Swift & Callahan, 2009; Shlonsky & Lambert, 2007). There is a beginning and an end to their

Policy Alternatives to Risk Assessment

work. Risk assessment brings standardized practices to the chaotic work of child protection, ensuring that most workers follow the same procedures and cover the same ground in their investigations. Risk assessment instruments help social workers raise difficult matters with parents and children that they may have ignored in the past—for instance, questions pertaining to sexual abuse. Also, the scientific aura of risk assessment has helped workers make clear presentations in court, with evidence to support their statements.

For these reasons, risk assessment may be difficult to dislodge from child welfare organizations in spite of evidence that it has not fulfilled its promise. It is also difficult to challenge risk assessment because it occupies sacred turf: predicting harm to children and taking action to prevent it. To be opposed to risk assessment would appear indefensible.

Policy Alternatives to Risk Assessment

Before policy alternatives to risk assessment have a chance of consideration, some unpleasant truths must be debated widely. One of these is the vulnerability of child welfare to "scientific fads," that is, to single-solution thinking that largely ignores the evidence from practice instead of building on it. As we noted at the beginning of this chapter, the battered child syndrome of the 1960s, child sexual abuse of the 1970s, and "family violence" of the 1980s all drew attention to important facets of child maltreatment but also reified the explanation that individual family pathology is at the core of this maltreatment. These theories and the resulting policies and practices ignored the ongoing reality that most child maltreatment reports were about the neglect rather than the physical and sexual abuse of children; also, that an increasing number focused on Aboriginal families—a reality evident to this day. Theories about the *context* of child maltreatment—about factors such as poverty, the oppression of women, Aboriginal peoples, and other people of colour, and poor health, education, and housing—have never received the same attention and have never grabbed the resources of child welfare in the way that other, more sensational theories have. Theories of individual pathology heighten the focus on ferreting out these individuals for correction and punishment using forensic and legal measures. Risk assessment is a logical outcome of a long history.

Child welfare cannot solve child maltreatment, nor can it prevent tragedies from occurring, no more than physicians can prevent disease or death. But health practitioners have done a much better job of making that plain, emphasizing that the key role of public health measures is to support the work of medical practitioners. Similarly, child welfare requires rethinking, so as to put at its core child well-being policies such as family economics, support, and housing. Government policies that support child well-being, as well as the results of those policies, should be displayed regularly alongside

Policy Alternatives to Risk Assessment

any child welfare reports, in order to emphasize that child welfare is only one part of a much larger policy field.

One of the most unsettling findings from our research was the ease with which risk assessment was implemented in child welfare, without critical analysis and without professional protest. It was the latest answer to the unsolvable questions in child welfare. Few raised concerns about its lack of scientific rigour or its infringement on social work practice. Placing child welfare in the context of larger social forces and responses would make its mandate more feasible and help insulate the field from quick fixes. Risk assessment offers salutary lessons about what can happen when we do not cast a critical eye on new policy proposals.

One way to enhance critical thinking about risk assessment is to remain connected to other professions and their research and practice. Our review of the risk assessment literature in child welfare and other fields revealed that little cross-professional comparison exists. Consequently, lessons were lost that child welfare could have learned from other professions well ahead of the implementation of risk assessment.

Risk assessment is now firmly entrenched in child welfare practice in Canada, but it has lost some of its early lustre. The sharp rise in removals of children from their families has not found favour with the many governments that are introducing other policies to counteract this trend. Two of these policies are "differential response," where only some cases are investigated[8] with risk assessment tools, and "kinship care," including family group conferencing, where children are placed with extended family members rather than coming into government care. Yet these policies are not without problems, which should be addressed openly. Differential response returns some opportunities for judgment to social workers yet leaves intact the assumptions about risk assessment. Kinship care offers potential for children and their families, but it cannot be simply a measure to cut costs and offload care onto family members (Callahan et al., 2005).

Our overarching conclusion is that risk assessment has shifted the balance of child welfare efforts and expenditures so that the focus is now strongest on investigation and on out-of-home placements of children. Risk assessment has altered the fundamental tension between building a case for child protection and providing supportive services to parents, who often struggle on their own. We need to restore balance—a conclusion reached by many others, including the authors of a review of "reviews" of child deaths in many countries (Axford & Bullock, 2005). In the last section of this chapter we examine how this may be achieved and what social work perspectives could offer to the task.

Revamping Funding Policies

Funding for child welfare emanates from the Canada Social Transfer between the federal government and the provinces. This agreement places

Policy Alternatives to Risk Assessment

no demands upon the provinces about how funds should be spent, aside from some very broad parameters. Provincial governments develop funding formulas for child welfare that are often based on the number of protection investigations and children in care. In Aboriginal communities where the federal government has direct responsibility for funding, the number of children in care determines the amount of money transferred to a particular band or nation. Under these conditions, the funding in child welfare envelopes diminishes if there is a reduction in investigations and out-of-home placements—the very direction that many advocates recommend. Funding formulas that are based on the number of children in the jurisdiction hold much more promise, for they provide child welfare agencies with the resources to develop many of the key family support programs required by parents.

Transforming Some Individual Complaints into Community Actions

Legislative changes have expanded the definition of child maltreatment and have introduced and reinforced mandatory reporting clauses. Now it would be timely to acknowledge the resources that are being spent and the harm that may be done in investigating the large number of unsubstantiated complaints. Moreover, many families—particularly those reported for neglecting their children—are investigated again and again (Trocmé et al., 2005, p. 55). A more sensible course would be to provide first-level responses in communities so that those with concerns about children and their parents would have local resources to call upon. Several studies have demonstrated that meeting concrete needs (Chaffin, Bonner, & Hill, 2001) and providing other preventive resources can be the most effective approach to promoting child safety (Gambrill & Shlonsky, 2001; Gilgun, Klein, & Pranis, 2000; Wharf, 2002).

Risk assessment may be useful in this regard, when it focuses on communities at risk rather than individuals. Risk assessments have been used in institutions for the elderly to prevent falls (Haines et al., 2006); they have also been used to develop public policies to address infant mortality, with the resources targeted at communities "at risk" (Centres for Disease Control, 2006).

Nowhere is the need to transform complaints into community actions more apparent than in situations where children witness violence in their homes. Between 1998 and 2003, the rate of exposure of children to such situations increased 259 percent, from 1.72 to 6.17 substantiated cases per 1,000 children (Trocmé et al., 2005); moreover, such exposure was the second most likely type of complaint to be substantiated (after neglect). Most situations involve children witnessing violence in their home between a male person and their mother (2004, 2006). Mothers suffer double jeopardy: injury to themselves, and the potential loss of their children because they did not protect them from the sight of their beating. It is likely that changes in reporting and investigating procedures are resulting in the documentation of many more situations than before, particularly since workers in women's shelters may be required to report such situations to child welfare workers. We need imaginative responses that direct attention and resources away from reporting these incidents as our only response and *toward* approaches that offer protection and healing for mothers and children. We should build on the sparsely funded efforts of women's shelters to undertake such actions. Instead, cutbacks to these organizations have resulted in the elimination of many of their programs designed to address the effects of violence on women and children.

Policy Alternatives to Risk Assessment

In many parts of the country, Aboriginal peoples are taking charge of their own child welfare systems, although in most cases they are required to replicate the existing child welfare system and to govern themselves by existing child welfare laws. This requirement works against their long traditions of extended family and community responsibilities for child rearing. Many Aboriginal peoples and social workers are working together to find ways to shape child welfare services so that traditions are respected. At the same time, they acknowledge the loss of those traditions, as well as the limited resources that exist in many communities (Brown, Haddock, & Kovach, 2002). This should be the highest priority of child welfare at the present time, given the large numbers of children in care who are of Aboriginal origin.

Refocusing on Social Work Principles in Child Protection Investigations

A risk assessment approach places the responsibility for diagnosing the problem and recommending the solution squarely on child protection authorities—a highly disempowering process that reduces parents' motivation and ignores their knowledge. In a spirited examination of the social work shortage in the United Kingdom, Harlow (2004) argues that the incursion of managerialism into social work practice, evident by work processes such as risk assessment, is a significant force driving the predominantly female social workers out of the field and preventing others from entering. She argues that relationships with others and opportunities to make change are what attract people to social work, and that risk assessment practices sharply curtail both. In the process, parents and social workers may be disenfranchised.

In line with this analysis, Krane and Davies (2000) suggest that we return to investigations that focus on parents', children's, friends', and families' narratives about what is happening, and build bridges among these stories and our own understanding of the situation. The challenges facing parents, children, and social workers are often deeply confounding and contradictory, change at a rapid pace, and are not captured in the precise and stationary instrument of risk assessment (even if it is repeated on several occasions). Approaches to accountability that incorporate parents' and children's views of their circumstances and what they think makes a difference to their lives is indeed possible (Weller & Wharf, 2002). These are not pie-in-the-sky suggestions. The violence-against-women movement has used such methods as a staple approach. Police involved in family violence units are trained in dispute resolution based on these principles. Family group conferences offer a beginning opportunity to return these approaches to child welfare, albeit they usually occur after the investigation is well under way or indeed has been completed (Pennell & Anderson, 2005).

One of the most poignant observations of risk assessment is that it directs attention to future harm that *may* occur, thus taking the worker's gaze away from what has already happened to the child and what must be done to repair the damage (Saunders & Goddard, 1998). Too often, once immediate safety is addressed, the file is closed, even though children and parents have been through very difficult and destructive experiences. Given the possible consequences of ignoring present harm, the frailty of the science in predicting risk for children, and the finite resources available for child welfare, it seems sensible to turn our attention to the present as well as the future.

We propose a re-examination of those definitions of child maltreatment that include future harm to children. Until the field of child welfare is defined more broadly (as we suggest above) and is given more resources, phrases in legislation such as "at risk of harm" or "likely to be harmed in future" will continue to overwhelm the present system. As long as we have inadequate tools to measure that future and few resources to offer families who score high for future risk, involving them in overburdened and forensically oriented child welfare programs serves little purpose.

Conclusion

This chapter has identified risk assessment as an important and pervasive policy in child welfare and has marshalled evidence to assess how this policy addresses two of child welfare's most confounding problems: increasing workloads, and the apparent failure to protect children. On these issues, risk assessment simply does not measure up. But we also suggest that risk assessment provides a highly valued approach to redefining and reorganizing the volatile and unruly work of child welfare so that politicians, managers, and social workers can argue that they are doing what needs to be done. We also note that risk and risk assessment in child welfare are part and parcel of a larger discourse that contributes to redefining the relationship between citizens and government from one where citizens are entitled to some benefits to one where citizens are expected to manage their own risks. Moreover, risk assessment is embedded in many other human services. Given these realities, it will be a formidable task to dislodge current conceptions of risk and risk assessment.

We contend that social work responses have a great deal to offer child protection services at the present time. We do not shrink from recognizing that some children are in grave danger within their families and must be protected. We do, though, challenge the notion that the best way to protect these children is by using scarce resources trying to predict the future while paying scant attention to the present circumstances that confront these children, their families, and their neighbourhoods.

Notes

1 This chapter arises from a study on risk assessment in child welfare that aims to examine the work processes of risk assessment in two provinces—B.C. and Ontario—and how these processes affect the organization of social work and other human service professions in the social and economic conditions of globalization (Swift & Callahan, 2009). Data have been collected through a series of interviews with key informants, social workers, and parents who have experienced the risk assessment process. We also analyzed the many documents related to risk assessment in these two provinces. The study is funded by the Social Science and Humanities Research Council of Canada.

2 Section 13(1) a, b, c, and d of the Child, Family and Community Service Act (FCSA) of British Columbia, 1996.

3 At least two types of risk assessment items have been identified in child welfare: actuarial (based on research such as that used for car insurance) and consensus (based on the views of professionals about which are the most important items). However, regardless of the means of identifying variables to be assessed, all risk assessments are expected to predict future harm to children.

4 The New York Risk Assessment Model was imported almost without changes into several Canadian jurisdictions, although it was developed in a jurisdiction with a very different policy context, population, and history. By 2000, the State of New York had made significant changes to the model, reducing the number of items in the instrument because many did not predict future child maltreatment. However the original model remained in place in Canada.

5 Ontario has moved away from the New York tool, adopting a simpler risk assessment model, and has also moved from an almost total focus on risk assessment toward a "differential response model" that reduces attention to risk to some extent. Alberta's model also relies on differential response. It remains to be seen whether these shifts result in a reduction in the care population.

6 The Canadian Incidence Study reported that 11 percent of neglect investigations resulted in out-of-home placement, compared to 6 percent of abuse investigations (Trocmé et al., 2005, 58–59, 114).

7 In Ontario the budget for child welfare services has increased 56 percent since 2000, to a total of $1.174 billion In 2005. Almost exactly half this amount is allocated to substitute care.

8 Several authors question the use of risk assessment for situations based primarily on neglect where parents simply don't have the resources to care for their children (key informant; Weller & Wharf, 2002). These cases usually represent about half of the complaints coming to child welfare. In many situations risk assessment is scarcely necessary as it is obvious that continued deprivation would be harmful to children. Others also wonder about the usefulness of risk assessment in obvious and egregious cases of abuse where the outcomes are clear.

References

References

Axford, N., & Bullock, R. (2005). Child death and significant case reviews: International approaches. Dartington, UK: Dartington Social Research Unit.

Badgley, R. (1984). *Sexual offences against children: Report of the Committee on Sexual Offences against Children and Youth.* Ottawa, ON: Justice Canada.

Bennet, R. (1998). *Verdict, recommendations, synopsis, and summary of responses regarding the inquest into the death of Shanay Jami Johnson.* Toronto, ON: Ministry of the Solicitor General.

Berkowitz, S. (1991). *Key findings on definitions of risk to children and uses of risk assessment by state CPS agencies from the state survey component of the study of high risk child abuse and neglect groups.* Paper prepared by Westat, Inc., and presented to the National Center on Child Abuse and Neglect Symposium on Risk Assessment in Child Protective Services, Washington, DC.

Bridge Child Care Consultancy. (1991). *Sukina: An evaluation report of the circumstances leading to her death.* London, UK: Bridge Child Care Consultancy.

Brown, L., Haddock, L., & Kovach, M. (2002). Watching over our families and children: Lalum'utul' Smun'eem Child and Family Services. In B. Wharf (Ed.), *Community approaches to child welfare* (pp. 131–151). Peterborough, ON: Broadview Press.

Callahan, M. (1994). Feminist approaches: Women recreate child welfare. In B. Wharf (Ed.), *Rethinking child welfare* (pp. 172–209). Toronto, ON: McClelland and Stewart.

Callahan, M., Brown, L., MacKenzie, P., & Whittington, B. (2005). Catch as catch can: Grandmothers raising grandchildren. *Canadian Review of Social Policy, 54,* 58–78.

Callahan, M., & Swift, K. (2007). Great expectations and unintended consequences: Risk assessment in child welfare in B.C. In L. Foster & B. Wharf (Eds.), *People, politics, and child welfare.* Vancouver, BC: UBC Press.

Camasso, M., & Jagannathan, R. (1995). Prediction accuracy of the Washington and Illinois Risk Assessment Instruments: An application of receiver operating characteristics curve analysis. *Social Work Research, 19*(3), 174–183.

Canadian incidence study of reported child abuse and neglect. Major findings. (2008). Ottawa, ON: Public Health Agency of Canada.

Centres for Disease Control. (2006). List of publications using multistate PRAMS data. Retrieved from http://www.cdc.gov/PRAMS/References/PublicationList052006.doc

Chaffin, M., Bonner, B.L., & Hill, R.F. (2001). Family preservation and family support programs: Child maltreatment outcomes across client risk levels and program types. *Child Abuse and Neglect, 25,* 1269–1289.

Chau, S., Fitzpatrick, A., Hulchanski, D., Leslie, B., & Schatia, D. (2001). *One in five ... housing as a factor in the admission of children to care: New survey of Children's Aid Society of Toronto updates 1992 study.* Toronto, ON: Central for Urban and Community Studies, University of Toronto.

Chen, X. (2001). *Tending the gardens of citizenship: Child protection in Toronto, 1880s–1920s.* Unpublished thesis. Toronto, ON: Faculty of Social Work, University of Toronto.

Child, Family, and Community Services Act, R.S.B.C. 1996, c.46.

Cicchinelli, L. (1989). Risk assessment models: CPS agencies and future directions. In *CPS risk assessment conference proceedings: From research to practice:*

Designing the future of Child Protective Services. Burlington, VT; Washington, DC: American Public Welfare Association.

DePanfilis, D. (1996). Implementing child mistreatment risk assessment systems: Lessons from theory. *Administration in Social Work, 20*(2), 41–59.

Doueck, H., English, D., DePanfilis, D., & Moote, G. (1993). Decision-making in child protective services: A comparison of selected risk assessment systems. *Child Welfare, 72*(5), 441–452.

English, D., & Pecora, P. (1994). Risk assessment as a practice method in child protective services. *Child Welfare, 73*(5), 451–473.

Federal/Provincial Working Group on Child and Family Services Information. (2001). *Child welfare in Canada 2000.* Ottawa, ON: Human Resource and Social Development Canada. Retrieved from www.hrsdc.gc.ca/en/cs/sp/sdc/socpol/publications/reports/2000-000033/page02.shtml

Foster, L. (2007). The more things change, the more they stay the same. In L. Foster & B. Wharf (Eds.), *People, politics and child welfare in British Columbia.* Vancouver, BC: UBC Press.

Foster, L., & Wright, M. (2002). Patterns and trends in children in the care of the Province of British Columbia: Ecological, policy, and cultural perspectives. In M. Hayes & L. Foster (Eds.), *Too small to see, too big to ignore: Child health and well-being in British Columbia* (pp. 103–140). Victoria, BC: Western Geographical Press.

Gambrill, E., & Shlonsky, A. (2001). The need for comprehensive risk management systems in child welfare. *Children and Youth Services Review, 23*(1), 79–107.

Gilgun, J.F., Klein, C., & Pranis, K. (2000). The significance of resources in models of risk. *Journal of Interpersonal Violence, 15*(6), 631–650.

Gove, T.J. (1995). *Report on the Gove inquiry into child protection.* Victoria, BC: British Columbia, Ministry of Social Services.

Haines, T., Hill, K., Bennell, K., & Osborne, R. (2006) Recurrent events counted in evaluations of predictive accuracy. *Journal of Clinical Epidemiology, 59*(11), 1155–1161.

Harlow, E. (2004). Why don't women want to be social workers any more? New managerialism, post-feminism, and the shortage of social workers in social service departments in England and Wales. *European Journal of Social Work, 7*(2), 167–179.

Jones, D. (1994). Assessing and taking risks in child protection work. *Child Abuse and Neglect, 18,* 1037–1038.

Kempe, C.H., Silverman, F.N., Steele, B.F., Droegemuller W., & Silver, H.K. (1962). The battered child syndrome. *Journal of the American Medical Association, 181,* 17–24.

Krane, J., & Davies, L. (2000). Mothering and child protection practice: Rethinking risk assessment. *Child and Family Social Work, 5,* 35–45.

Leslie, B., & O'Connor, B. (2002). What are the products of the Ontario Risk Assessment Tool? *Journal of the OACAS, 46*(4), 2–9.

Lu, V. (2000, August 24). CAS to resume talks with social workers. *Toronto Star,* A1.

Lyons, P., Doueck, H., & Wodarski, J. (1996). CPS risk assessment: A review of the empirical literature on instrument performance. *Social Work Research, 20*(3), 143–155.

References Michalski, J., Alaggia, R., & Trocmé, N. (1996) *A literature review of risk assessment models.* Toronto, ON: Centre for Applied Social Research, Faculty of Social Work, University of Toronto.

Ontario Association of Children's Aid Societies. (2005). *CAS Facts: April 1, 2004–March 31, 2005.* Retrieved from http://www.oacas.org

Parada, H. (2004). Social work practices within the restructured child welfare system in Ontario: An institutional ethnography. *Canadian Review of Social Policy, 21*(1), 67–86.

Parada, H., Swift, K., & Callahan, M. (2005, June 16–18). Forging social futures: Illuminating the interaction of housing and risk assessment in child protection. Paper presented to the Canadian Social Welfare Policy Conference: Forging Social Futures, Fredericton, NB: University of New Brunswick.

Parton, N., Thorpe, D., & Wattam, C. (1997). *Child protection, risk, and the moral order.* Basingstoke: Macmillan.

Pecora, P. (1991). Investigating allegations of child maltreatment: The strengths and limitations of current risk assessment systems. In M. Robin (Ed.), *Assessing child maltreatment reports: The problems of false allegations* (pp. 73–93). New York, NY: Haworth Press.

Pennell, J., & Anderson, G. (Eds.). (2005). *Widening the circle: The practice and evaluation of family group conferencing with children, youths, and their families.* Washington, DC: NASW Press.

Porter, B. (1998). *Report on inquests into the death of children receiving services from a Children's Aid Society.* Toronto, ON: Ontario Ministry of the Solicitor General.

Rycus, J.S., & Hughes, R.C. (2003). *Issues in risk assessment in child protective services.* Policy White Paper. Columbus, OH: North American Resource Center for Child Welfare, Center for Child Welfare Policy.

Saunders, B., & Goddard, C. (1998). *A critique of structured risk assessment procedures: Instruments of abuse?* Ringwood, Australia: Australian Childhood Foundation and the National Research Centre for the Prevention of Child Abuse, Monash University.

Schene, P., & Bond, K. (1989). *Research issues in risk assessment for child protection.* Denver, CO: American Humane Association.

Silver, E., & Miller, L. (2002). A cautionary note on the use of actuarial risk assessment tools for social control. *Crime and Delinquency, 48*(1), 138–161.

Statistics Canada. (2005). "Family violence in Canada: A statistical profile." Retrieved from http://www.statcan.ca/english/freepub/85-224-XIE/free.htm

Strega, S. (2004). *The case of the missing perpetrator: A cross-national investigation of child welfare practice, policy, and discourse in cases of mother battering.* Unpublished PhD dissertation, School of Social Work Studies, University of Southampton, England.

Strega, S. (2006). Failure to protect? Child welfare interventions when mothers are being battered. In R. Alaggia and C. Vine (Eds.), *Cruel but not unusual: Violence in Canadian families* (pp. 650–690). Waterloo, ON: Wilfrid Laurier University Press.

Swift, K. (1995a). *Manufacturing "bad mothers": A critical perspective on child neglect.* Toronto, ON: University of Toronto Press.

Swift, K. (1995b). "Missing persons": Women and child welfare. *Child Welfare, 74*(3), 486–502.

Swift, K. (2001). The case for opposition: An examination of contemporary child welfare policy directions. *Canadian Review of Social Policy, 47*, 59–76.

Swift, K. (2011). Canadian child welfare: Child protection and the status quo. In N. Gilbert, N. Parton, and M. Skivenes (Eds.), *Child protection systems: International trends and orientations.* New York, NY: Oxford University Press.

Swift, K., & Callahan, M. (2009). *At risk: Social justice in child welfare and other human services.* Toronto, ON: University of Toronto Press.

Trocmé, N. & Lindsey, D. (1996). What can child homicide rates tell us about the effectiveness of child welfare services? *Child Abuse and Neglect, 20*(3), 171–184.

Trocmé, N., MacLaurin, B., Fallon, B., Black, T., & Lajoie, J. (2005). *Canadian incidence study of reported child abuse and neglect 2003 data.* Toronto, ON: Centre of Excellence for Child Welfare.

Wald, M., & Woolverton, M. (1990). Risk assessment: The Emperor's new clothes? *Child Welfare, 69*(6), 483–511.

Weller, F., & Wharf, B. (1997). *From risk assessment to family action planning.* Victoria, BC: University of Victoria School of Social Work, Child, Family and Community Research Program.

Wharf, B. (2002). *Community work approaches to child welfare.* Peterborough, ON: Broadview Press.

Parental Benefits Policy in Canada and Quebec

Sharing the Caring?

11

Patricia M. Evans

> If you want to understand what it means to be a good mother or father in a country, then look at the parental leave policy that is in place there. (Moss, 2010a, p. 131)

At a time of significant cutbacks in many social benefits, policies to enable parents to stay at home to care for their very young children have expanded remarkably. This trend is most evident in continental Europe, in countries as diverse as the Nordic states and, in the south, Greece, Italy, and Portugal (Daly, 2011). Canada is the leader in parental benefit programs in the "liberal" or "reluctant" welfare states where English predominates, and where an emphasis on individualistic and market-oriented public policy ensures that the protections offered by social programs are relatively weak (Kershaw, 2008; O'Connor, Orloff, & Shaver, 1999). Quebec carries its distinctive culture, history, and traditions into a more collectivist orientation to social policy and, in 2006, overtook the rest of Canada by introducing its own, more expansive version of parental benefits.

Parental benefit policies are particularly interesting for students of social policy because they are fashioned from normative assumptions about the following: the proper role for the state in the provision of social care; the importance attached to women's employment; and the appropriate balance to be struck in gender divisions regarding paid and unpaid work. An examination of these policies over the past decade provides a "window" onto an area of social policy that is intended to respond to dynamic changes in gender relations, labour markets, and social welfare provisions. The increasing presence of mothers with young children in paid work places the greatest pressure on governments to promote paid parental leave. Also important are a fall in birth rates, concerns about an aging workforce, and efforts to control spending in the context of slow economic growth.

Countries vary in their motives and objectives as they introduce or enhance programs for parental benefits. However, these policies are most often designed to respond to what has been termed a "crisis in care" (Daly & Lewis, 2000) or, more euphemistically, to address the problems in "work–life balance" that arise as women's paid work expands without a parallel increase in men's unpaid work (Lewis, 2006). Making it easier for parents (i.e., mothers) to combine employment with family responsibilities has been identified by the federal government as "a critical public policy issue in Canada" (Human Resources and Skills Development Canada [HRSDC], 2005, cited in Marshall, 2006), and parental benefits are viewed as part of its solution.

Policies to enable parents to stay at home to care for young children are the focus of an ever-expanding body of comparative research examining social policy through the lens of gender equality (Ray, Gornick, & Schmitt, 2010). This interest is hardly surprising, for these policies confront the central policy dilemma of how to value care without reinforcing the gendered division of labour in paid and unpaid work (Morgan & Zippel, 2003). Peter Moss and Fred Deven describe the Catch-22 nature of the dilemma: "If parental leave were equally taken by women and men, it might promote or consolidate gender equality. But to be equally taken requires gender equality to be achieved already, or to be further advanced than at present. If gender equality is not already advanced, then parental leave may retard or even reverse progress towards its achievement" (1999, cited in Ray et al., 2010, p. 199).

Parental benefits are part of the broader fabric of "social care" policies (often equated with "family" policies), which include child and elder care services, along with other programs providing supports for caregiving. They add onto the benefit entitlements that cover the period immediately following birth/adoption. In Canada, parental benefits are available to either parent who qualifies—they can be shared between them or can be taken at the same time. They are administered through the federal or Quebec governments and are separate from the provincial employment standards that ensure that people can return to their jobs.[1] While gender-neutral in terminology, parental benefits interact with a gendered division of labour, and the resulting earnings gap ensures that it is mothers, overwhelmingly, who claim them.

In 2001, parents became eligible for thirty-five weeks of benefits under Canada's parental benefits program (CPB). This change more than tripled the number of benefit weeks from the ten previously available since the program's inception in 1990. When combined with maternity/adoption benefits, a total of 50 weeks of benefits are now available to those who qualify through Employment Insurance. In 2006, Quebec introduced its own Parental Insurance Program (QPIP), which differs from its federal counterpart in some important respects. It offers more generous benefits and is the only parental benefit program outside Europe to incorporate an explicit gender equity objective in its design by adding benefits for the sole use of fathers.

Even though gender issues are fundamental to programs of social care, some argue that "as family policy has come to the fore, gender has been cast in the shade" (Daly, 2011, p. 2). This chapter examines Canada and Quebec's parental leave programs and assesses, in an international context, whether gender has indeed been left in the shade. To the extent that data are available, the discussion considers the effectiveness of the programs in Canada for addressing class and racialization, inequalities that intersect with gender but are not limited to it.

The chapter begins by considering models of policy approaches to gender and social care. This is followed by a discussion of the programs in Quebec and in the rest of Canada that compares their coverage, level of benefits, and the absence/presence of incentives to encourage the participation of fathers in parental benefits. These are the components that are used to assess the effectiveness of the two programs in counteracting systemic inequalities. Finally, reforms of the programs are suggested to improve equity objectives.

Policy Models in Gender and Care: The International Context

Governments have a variety of reasons for encouraging parents to stay home to care for very young children: to boost declining fertility rates by making it easier to combine paid and unpaid work; to foster what many regard as an optimal environment for infant care; and to relieve pressure on scarce and expensive forms of state-provided care. Increasingly, with gender equity and/or child development objectives at play, countries show an interest in increasing the involvement of fathers in the care of very young children (OECD, 2011). Depending on design, parental benefits can encourage women to return to employment or can discourage women's employment in times of high unemployment and strengthen the maternal responsibility for care (Morgan & Zippel, 2003). Different rationales for national policies reflect specific histories, the nature of interest group politics, and particular socio-demographic challenges. They also reflect more general normative assumptions about the role of the state in social care, the importance of women's employment, and the appropriate balance in gender divisions in paid and unpaid work.

To understand better these national variations, I draw upon different types of policy orientations for the treatment of gender in social care policies.[2] Most typologies classify policies by their effects on gender roles in earning and caring—that is, whether they are used to support or disrupt traditionally assigned gender responsibilities. I have adopted the classification used by Misra, Budig, and Moller (2007), whose models include these: (1) the *dual earner / dual carer* approach; (2) the *primary caregiver* orientation; and (3) the *primary worker* model. The *dual earner / dual carer* model is generally accepted as the best approach to social care to advance gender equality because it promotes a better gender balance in paid and unpaid work by strengthening women's ties to employment *and* men's ties to caregiving. Generous parental benefits and strong incentives to encourage fathers to use them are key aspects of successful policies. In addition, high-quality and affordable child care is available, and workplaces are encouraged to be "family-friendly." A recent study of twenty-one countries found that policies in Finland, Sweden, and Norway come closest to the earner/carer model: parental benefits were relatively generous, and a portion of the benefit period was reserved for exclusive use by fathers (Ray et al., 2010).

In contrast to the earner/carer approach, the primary caregiver and primary earner strategies focus on a single aspect of the equation—either caregiving or employment, but not both. In the primary caregiver approach, women's employment is discouraged through long leaves with little available alternative care. "Care" leaves may last as long as two to three years and carry little or no job protection, while benefits are usually low and paid on a flat-rate rather than an earnings-related basis. Austria and Germany are examples of this approach (Morgan & Zippel, 2003), although Germany is shifting toward shorter leaves and earnings-related benefits in an effort to increase women's employment (Lewis et al., 2008).

The last approach, the primary earner strategy, promotes both women's and men's paid work but directs little attention to their care responsibilities. For example, while employment equity policies are present and women's employment rates may be high, child care is largely left as an individual responsibility to be discharged through market-provided care. While this strategy has been evident from the beginning of parental benefit policies, it has been further strengthened by the emergence of what is often called an "adult worker" model that represents a highly individualized and gender-stripped approach. Issues of gender/work/family are subsumed under employment-driven social policies primarily geared to increase economic productivity (Lewis et al., 2008; Daly, 2011). Typically, the United States, Canada, the United Kingdom, and other "liberal" or "reluctant" welfare states are used as examples of this approach (Misra, Budig, & Moller, 2007). But is this an altogether fair classification? The United States, after all, is now the only affluent country that makes no provision for paid leave (Ray et al., 2010).[3] In contrast, Canada hosts two distinct programs that take the top two spots in this group of reluctant welfare states and even leads among others.

What model/s do the parental leave programs in Canada and Quebec reflect? What are the implications of these policies as gender intertwines with other systemic inequalities, ignored in the models sketched above? How do our programs stack up internationally? These questions are addressed in the next section.

Parental Benefits in Canada and in Quebec: An Intra-National Comparison

The design and implementation of parental benefits can have profound public policy consequences: they can encourage, or inhibit, women's employment, just as they can encourage, or discourage, men's unpaid work. Policy design can also help alleviate or consolidate income inequalities that result from class and employment disadvantages too often experienced by

Coverage: Who Has Access?

racialized individuals. The policy dimensions critical to assessing the capacity of parental benefits to either reinforce or redress inequalities of gender, class, and racialization include these: (1) eligibility criteria—how expansive/restrictive is coverage? (2) the length and level of benefits—generous or minimal? and (3) whether they are designed to encourage men to participate. These dimensions provide a guide as we explore Canada's parental benefits program (CPB) and the Quebec Parental Insurance Program (QPIP).

Canada's parental benefits ranked first for their generosity in the league of "reluctant" welfare states. However, in 2006, Quebec introduced its own stand-alone program, which surpassed the benefits available in the rest of Canada. Quebec's parental benefits policy was preceded in 1998 by a universal and low-cost child-care program. Both programs reflect the capacity of women's organizations and unions to mobilize *and* the receptivity of the Quebec government to their input (Tremblay, 2010a). In contrast, the significant extension in the length of Canada's parental benefits that occurred in 2001 has been attributed, not to pressure from social actors, but to a particular set of circumstances, including a large Employment Insurance surplus that had accumulated as a result of program cutbacks and that was subject to increasing scrutiny. In these circumstances, a significant extension to the duration of benefits was a "compellingly easy" step to take (Evans, 2007, p.121).

Quebec's program was motivated by concerns about the province's low fertility rate, which was below the Canadian average (Garcia, 2010), and by a desire to increase women's employment and fathers' involvement in childrearing (Tremblay, 2010b). It incorporates important differences regarding eligibility, income replacement, and incentives for fathers' use that make it an exception in the North American context and beyond.

The next section explores and contrasts three policy dimensions of QPIP and CPB—coverage, benefit levels, and incentives to encourage participation by fathers—and assesses how far they have reduced or redressed the inequalities of gender and class. While there are fairly good data tracking gender in the take-up and use of parental benefits, little of this information relates to education and income (a crude indicator of class), and virtually none allows take-up and use of benefits to be examined by "race."

Coverage: Who Has Access?

All income benefits are governed by explicit criteria that spell out the terms of eligibility to receive benefits. These criteria, whether generous or meagre, operate as gatekeepers to ration benefits. As Table 11.1 shows, the qualifying conditions to receive benefits under CPB and QPIP are very different. Mothers and fathers living outside Quebec must accumulate 600 hours of paid work during the previous year in order to qualify for benefits. Quebec parents qualify when they earn at least $2,000 during the previous twelve months. If

Coverage: Who Has Access?

we translate these earnings into hours by using $21.21 (the average hourly wage rate in Quebec, August 2011),[4] a Quebec parent needs to have worked only ninety-four hours to be eligible—less than one-sixth of the number of hours required for parents in the rest of Canada.

Given the QPIP's more expansive eligibility criteria, it is not surprising that a greater proportion of Quebec new mothers access maternity/parental benefits. In 2008, nine out of ten new mothers in Quebec received benefits, in contrast to only three-quarters of mothers in the rest of Canada (Marshall, 2010). Mothers who are not eligible for CPB, including those who were not employed at all or who did not have enough job hours to qualify, are not evenly distributed across the socio-economic spectrum. Women with lower levels of education, Aboriginal women, women who have recently immigrated to Canada, and single mothers are among those women less likely to be employed and to experience higher levels of unemployment (Statistics Canada, 2010b).

This is part of the broader consequences of "precarious" employment, the term used to capture the nature of paid work in the globalized economy, in which jobs are more likely to be temporary and low paid, to require non-standard hours, and to provide fewer benefits. The face of precarious employment is both gendered and racialized (Cranford et al., 2003). As a result, eligibility for and receipt of general Employment Insurance benefits is less for women than for men, less for part-time workers than for full-time

Table 11.1 Comparison of Canada's Parental Benefits and Québec's Parental Insurance 2010

	CPB	QPIP
Eligibility	600 hours of employment in last 52 weeks and 40 percent drop in earnings	$2,000 earnings in last year and 40 percent drop in earnings
Duration	35 weeks (+15 weeks paid + 2 unpaid weeks of maternity leave)	Basic: 32 weeks (+18 weeks paid maternity leave) Special: 25 weeks (+15 weeks paid maternity leave)
Benefit	55 percent earnings to maximum of $468 week Maximum insurable earnings: $44,260	Basic: 70 percent earnings to maximum $862 for 7 weeks 55 percent earnings to maximum $677 for 25 weeks Special: 75 percent earnings to a maximum $923 for 25 weeks Maximum insurable earnings: $64,000
Father-only benefits	None available	Basic: 70 percent of earnings to maximum $862 for 5 weeks Special: 75 percent earnings to maximum of $923 for 3 weeks

workers, and less for those in non-seasonal forms of non-standard employment, such as retail, where women prevail (Statistics Canada, 2010b). QPIP covers more women (and men) whose employment is fragile than CPB; moreover, Quebec students find it easier to qualify than students in the rest of Canada (Doucet, Tremblay, & Lero, 2010).

The only factor that can be expected in the future to narrow the gap in coverage under the two programs is the very recent (January 2011) extension of CPB to the self-employed; self-employed mothers and fathers in Quebec have been covered from the start. As mothers are more likely to claim parental benefits and women are also an increasing proportion of the self-employed workforce, this is a welcome change (Statistics Canada, 2010b).

Benefit Levels and Affordability

Eligibility is not the only factor influencing mothers' and fathers' access to parental benefits. Mothers are so overwhelmingly represented in parental benefits programs because their earnings are typically lower than those of fathers—an aspect that will be examined in more detail in the next section. But other factors come into play, too. Families, and the mothers and fathers in them, vary in the value they place on higher incomes, just as some will be less prepared to take time off because of the personal satisfaction they receive from their paid work, or their desire to protect career advancement. However, the amount of benefits they receive is an important consideration. Benefit levels are determined by two factors: (1) the rate of earned income that benefits replace, and (2) the cap placed on the amount of earnings that are taken into account for benefit purposes ("insurable" income). These two features determine the maximum benefit payable.

As Table 11.1 shows, parental benefits in Quebec are payable at a higher rate of income replacement, and the income considered is also capped at a higher level. As a result, the maximum payments available are considerably larger in Quebec than in the rest of Canada. Quebec parents also have some flexibility (albeit limited) in choosing more weeks with lower benefits (the "basic" option) or higher benefits for a shorter period (the "special" option). The basic option provides fifty-five weeks of combined maternity/parental/paternity benefits, most of it paid at 55 percent of earnings but some weeks at a higher rate (70 percent). The special option provides a total of forty-three weeks of maternity/parental/paternity benefits, but at 75 percent of earnings. The option is chosen at the beginning of the maternity benefit claim and cannot be changed later. Three-quarters of Quebec parents opt for the "basic" program (Quebec, 2011).

Canada's parental benefits program, in contrast, provides a single earnings replacement rate for all its fifty weeks of benefits—55 percent of insurable earnings. Although the replacement rate is identical to some of the weeks in the QPIP basic plan, because insurable earnings are higher in the

QPIP, its maximum benefit is more generous (by $200 a week). When benefits are paid at the highest replacement rate (75 percent), the maximum benefit under QPIP is nearly double the maximum available to parents in the rest of Canada.

Although the levels of benefits paid by QPIP to its claimants are very different from those available in the rest of Canada, the supplements provided to families with low incomes are identical. Both programs have become more restrictive over time. The sliding-scale supplement disappears when net household income reaches $25,921, an amount that has not increased since 1998 (Evans, 2006; updated through CEIC, 2010). As a result, every year, fewer and fewer families are eligible. In 2009, for example, the percentage of all families making Employment Insurance claims eligible for a supplement was 6 percent, down 4 percentage points from the previous year (Annex 2.13 in CEIC, 2010). Not surprisingly, its effectiveness in combating poverty has also eroded. In 1998, a three-person household with an annual income $3,600 over Canada's unofficial "poverty line" was eligible to receive a partial supplement. By 2009, in order for the same family to be eligible, its income had to fall nearly $2,000 under the poverty line.[5]

As in many other countries, little information is available about the take-up of CPB and QPIP benefits that would enable us to determine the programs' specific impacts. However, affordability is an important factor in how long parents can take off work, as well as in how the time is divided in two-parent households. As men generally earn more than women, family income will be higher in most households if the mother stays at home. But affordability reaches beyond gender. Mothers who earn less claim fewer weeks of benefits than mothers with higher earnings. As well, women whose jobs were precarious (temporary, term, contract, or casual) were five times more likely to return to their job within nine months compared to women whose jobs were permanent (Marshall, 2003).

The European Commission directs that parental benefits payable by member countries should be set at an earnings replacement rate of at least two-thirds (Moss, 2010b). All the benefits under the CPB and most of the weekly benefits provided under QPIP's basic plan are set at 55 percent and so fall well below this standard. However, under the special plan, QPIP benefits exceed the EC standard (70 to 75 percent).

Sharing the Caring

The third element in assessing the impact of parental benefits on systemic gender inequalities is the inclusion of incentives to encourage fathers to increase their involvement in the care of young children. Countries may include these incentives for reasons other than gender equity. First, increasing paternal participation in child rearing may provide optimal child development (O'Brien, 2009). Evidence suggests that fathers who take leave from employment in the early months after a child is born continue a pattern of greater involvement after returning to paid work (Waldfogel, 2007). Second, father-targeted parental benefits programs are thought to increase women's paid work, not simply by freeing up time for paid work, but also by reducing employment discrimination by more closely aligning patterns of women's and men's paid and unpaid work.

Sharing the Caring

While rationales are rarely given for *not* including specific provisions for fathers to take up parental benefits, policy neutrality is framed by maximizing "choice" to parents. However, as Arnaug Leira (1998, p. 367) explained more than a decade ago, "often couched in gender-neutral terms, parental choice does not appear as an option for fathers, because the family income would generally be dramatically reduced if fathers were to choose to stay at home with children." The OECD reported that in 2011, the wages of Canadian women who worked full-time were 20 percent lower than men's (OECD, 2011). Because the income replacement levels under CPB are especially low, it is normally more costly for families if fathers claim parental benefits.

In light of this, it is not surprising that, while both CPB and QPIP permit parents to share their parental benefits entitlement, mothers are far more likely than fathers to claim parental benefits. Outside Quebec, for example, in the last three years for which data are available (2007, 2008, 2009), fathers have represented roughly 13 percent of all new claims (CEIC, 2010). As well, when fathers do claim CPB, they claim benefits for significantly less time: in 2009, they claimed them for an average of just less than seventeen weeks, while mothers claimed nearly thirty-two weeks (CEIC, 2010).

For reasons that are also likely to reflect differences in culture and tradition, Quebec fathers are more likely to claim parental benefits. In 2005, the year before QPIP was introduced, all fathers living in Canada faced the same terms and conditions for claiming parental benefits. However, 32 percent of Quebec fathers claimed parental benefits in comparison to only 13 percent of fathers in the rest of Canada (Marshall, 2008). In 2006, Quebec fathers became eligible for paternity benefits as well as parental benefits, both paid at higher rates than in the rest of Canada. By the end of the first year of QPIP, the claim rate for Quebec fathers had increased to 56 percent, reaching 82 percent in 2008 (Doucet, Tremblay, & Lero, 2010). This remarkable increase provides a dramatic example of the impact that social policy can have on individual behaviour.

Policies can also have unintended consequences. While the proportion of Quebec fathers claiming QPIP increased dramatically, the number of weeks they claimed fell from an average of thirteen weeks in 2005 to seven weeks in 2006. Some of this drop is undoubtedly because the newly established paternity benefits attracted fathers who did not claim under the old scheme and who may be more likely than other fathers to claim benefits for short periods. But when Quebec fathers claimed benefits, three-quarters used them for five weeks or less. It is possible that creating a stand-alone program with a five-week maximum had the unintended effect of only encouraging the take-up of paternity benefits, thus shortening the length of time fathers spend away from employment. Although Quebec parents have the choice to claim benefits separately for a total of 55 weeks, it is estimated that 80 to 90 percent of fathers claiming paternity benefits use them while the mother is also at home (Garcia, 2010). If one of the objectives of paternal (and parental) benefits is to encourage fathers to take on a greater share of primary responsibility for the care of young children, then the QPIP may not appear to be very effective.

Although fathers in the rest of Canada are much less likely to take advantage of parental benefits than Quebec fathers, when they do claim CPB, they claim for considerably longer periods, and the length of their claims appears to be increasing. In 2005, fathers used an average of eleven weeks of parental benefits; by 2009, they were claiming seventeen weeks (Marshall, 2008; CEIC, 2010). But the extension of parental benefits from ten to thirty-five weeks that took effect in 2001 also carried consequences that have tended to reinforce rather than alleviate gender divisions in caring responsibilities. While more fathers claimed benefits as a result of the extension to thirty-five weeks, it also increased the gap between the time that mothers, compared to fathers, stay away from their paid work to care for their very young children. Before 2001, when fathers used parental benefits, their claims amounted to 87 percent of the length of time that mothers received benefits. By 2003, the ratio of paternal to maternal time on benefits had fallen to 61 percent (Evans, 2006), and to 53 percent by 2009 (calculated from Annex 2.9, CEIC, 2010).

In summary, a comparison of the Canada and Quebec programs demonstrates that on each of the policy dimensions examined, the program available to Quebec mothers and fathers is far superior because it offers broader coverage and more generous benefits and incorporates a period of paternity benefits that are either used by the father or are lost. But even the more progressive Quebec program has allowed the supplement available to low-income families to erode in value over time, providing less protection every year.

Lessons from Outside and Inside Canada

Although Quebec and Sweden have been grouped together in the "premier league" of jurisdictions for father-sensitive parental benefit policies (O'Brien, 2009), in all other respects, QPIP falls well behind Sweden. In 1974, Sweden became the first country to implement parental benefits (Duvander, Lappegård, & Andersson, 2010). Reflecting an earner/carer approach, Sweden's approach can be regarded as the "gold standard."

All Swedish parents are eligible: those in employment receive earnings-related benefits (80 percent of earnings up to a maximum), while others are paid at a lower, flat rate. Benefits are available for a total of 480 days (nearly

Lessons from Outside and Inside Canada

seventy weeks), sixty days of which are reserved for the exclusive use of each parent. The remaining days are divided, with half assigned to each parent; however, they can be transferred between parents with signed consent. As an added incentive to divide time at home more equally, the parent (typically the mother) who has been at home the longest receives a bonus if the other parent (typically the father) exceeds his allocation of sixty days. Benefits can be used flexibly, which is why they are counted in days instead of weeks. The benefits can be claimed as single days, in separate blocks, and used to reduce employment hours as long as a child is less than eight years old. Parents are also entitled to unpaid leave until a child is eighteen months old (Duvander, Haas, & Chronholm in Moss, 2010b).

Sweden's program meets the yardsticks that should be the measure of a good parental benefits policy: 80 percent income replacement, equal and non-transferable quotas for the use of each parent, and flexibility in the way benefits can be used (Moss, 2010a). Quebec's program comes very close to the income replacement standard, at least in the "special" plan. The duration of QPIP father-only benefits is a maximum of five weeks, leaving mothers, by default, using an extremely disproportionate share of "parental" benefits. Benefits in both QPIP and CPB must be used within the first year of a child's birth, so there is not the flexibility of the Swedish program.

The broad range of parental benefit policies across countries reflects national values, aspirations, political constraints, and policy preferences. Such policies cannot simply be exported from one country to another. However, within Canada, Quebec's program stands as a policy example that, while not perfect, is considerably better in coverage, levels of benefits, and father-targeted incentives than the program available to mothers and fathers in the rest of Canada. A reduction in the number of employment hours required for eligibility under CPB would broaden coverage and extend it to more precarious workers. Raising benefit levels, which have fallen over time, would help make parental benefits more affordable to low-income mothers and fathers.[6] Paul Kershaw (2008) argues that benefits should be paid up to a maximum of 80 percent earnings replacement and that between two and four months of benefits should be reserved for the exclusive use of fathers.

Should our examination of the programs in Quebec and the rest of Canada lead us to conclude that gender "is left in the shade"? In making a business case for improving the effectiveness of social care programs, the OECD (2011) emphasizes the importance of women's paid work for combating child poverty and for increasing economic productivity as the population ages and the proportion of those in paid work declines. However, in the absence of adequate supports for mothers and fathers in their paid work, and with an understanding of the persistence of gender inequities, a new version of the primary worker model seems to be emerging: one that reflects the entrance of the "adult worker" model for women, accompanied by increased expectations of paid work even while scant attention is given to care responsibilities. Policies in Quebec show more similarity to an earner/carer model, evident in their child care policies as well as parental benefits. By contrast, Canada's parental benefits policy makes no attempt to tilt the gender balance in favour of men's caregiving, and its child care policy has remained firmly privatized.

The current construction of parental benefits outside of Quebec implicates class and gender in ways that amplify inequalities between men and women and among women who are differently situated. Following the leadership of Quebec in parental benefits, and adopting some changes suggested in this chapter, would begin to remove gender from the shadows. This is critically important if our social policies are not to be simply "a transmission mechanism," but to challenge the inequalities embedded in social, political and economic structures (Taylor-Gooby, 1991, pp. 202–203, cited in Kershaw, 2008).

Notes

1 While there is some provincial variation in length of leaves, they approximate the length of the federal and Quebec benefit periods (see Doucet, Tremblay, & Lero, 2010). For convenience, I use the term "parental benefits" instead of "paid parental leave."

2 Many of these typologies stem from the early work of Nancy Fraser (1994). For other typologies, see, for example, Haas, 2003; Tremblay, 2010a.

3 Australia introduced paid parental leave in January 2011, a provision too recent to be included in the study reported by Ray et al., 2010.

4 See http://www40.statcan.ca/l01/cst01/labr69f-eng.htm.

5 Calculated for a family living in a metropolitan area, using after-tax low-income cut-offs. Statistics Canada (2010a). Retrieved from http://www.statcan.gc.ca/pub/75f0002m/75f0002m2010005-eng.pdf.

6 In 1996, the maximum weekly benefit was $604. See http://www.canadianlabour.ca/issues/unemployment-insurance.

References

Canada Employment Insurance Commission [CEIC] (2010). *EI Monitoring and Assessment Report 2009.* Retrieved from http://www.hrsdc.gc.ca/eng/employment/ei/reports/eimar_2010/index.shtml

Cranford C, Vosko L, & Zukewich N. (2003). Precarious employment in the Canadian labour market: A statistical portrait. *Just labour: A Canadian journal of work and society,* 3: 6–22.

Daly, M. (2011). What adult worker model? A critical look at recent social policy reform in Europe from a gender and family perspective. Social Politics, *18*(1), 1-23. doi: 10.1093/sp/jxr002

Daly, M., & Lewis, J. (2000). The concept of social care and the analysis of contemporary welfare states. British Journal of Sociology, *51*(2), 281–298. doi: 10.1080/00071310050030181

Doucet, A., Tremblay, D.-G., & Lero, D. (2010). Canada. In P. Moss (Ed.), *International review of leave policies and related research 2010* (pp. 65–73). London, UK: Employment Market Analysis and Research, Department of Business, Innovation, and Skills.

Duvander, A.-Z., Haas, L., & Cronholm, A. (2010). Sweden. In P. Moss (Ed.), *International review of leave policies and related research 2010* (pp. 223–229). London, UK: Employment Market Analysis and Research, Department of Business, Innovation, and Skills.

Duvander, A.-Z., Lappegård, T., & Andersson, G. (2010). Family policy and fertility: Fathers' and mothers' use of parental leave and continued childbearing in Norway and Sweden. *Journal of European Social Policy, 20*(1), 45–57. doi: 10.1177/0958928709352541

Evans, P. (2007). Comparative perspectives on changes to Canada's paid parental leave: Implications for class and gender. *International Journal of Social Welfare, 16*, 119-128. doi: 10.1111/j.1468-2397.2006.00450.x

Fraser, N. (1994). After the family wage: Gender equity and the welfare state. *Political Theory*, 22(4), 591–618.

Garcia, C. (2010). Analysis of the Québec Parental Insurance Plan. Retrieved from http://www.iedm.org/33500-analysis-of-the-quebec-parental-insurance-plan

Haas, L. (2003). Parental leave and gender equality: Lessons from the European Union. *Review of Policy Research*, 20(1), 89–114.

Kershaw, P. (2008). Carefair: Gendering citizenship "neoliberal" style. In Y. Abu-Laban (Ed.), *Gendering the nation state: Canadian and comparative perspectives* (pp. 203–219). Vancouver, BC: UBC Press.

Leira, A. (1998). Caring as a social right: Cash for child care and daddy leave. *Social Politics, 5*(3), 362–378.

Lewis, J. (2006). Employment and care: The policy problem, gender equality and the issue of choice. *Journal of Comparative Policy Analysis, 8*(2), 103–114.

Lewis, J., Knijn, T., Martin, C., & Ostner, I. (2008). Patterns of development in work/family reconciliation policies for parents in France, Germany, the Netherlands, and the UK in the 2000s. *Social Politics, 15*(3), 261–286. doi: 10.1093/sp/jxn016

Marshall, K. (2003). Benefiting from extended parental leave. *Perspectives on Labour and Income, 4*(3), 5–11. Statistics Canada, Catalogue no. 75-001-XPE, 15–21. Retrieved from http://www.statcan.gc.ca/pub/75-001-x/00303/6490-eng.html

Marshall, K. (2006). Converging gender roles. *Perspectives on Labour and Income, 7*(7), 5–16. Statistics Canada, Catalogue no. 75-001-XPE, 5–17.

Marshall, K. (2008). Fathers' use of paid parental leave. *Perspectives on Labour and Income, 9*(6), 5–14. Retrieved from http://www.statcan.gc.ca/pub/75-001-x/2008106/pdf/10639-eng.pdf

Marshall, K. (2010). Employer top-ups. *Perspectives on Labour and Income, 11*(2). Retrieved from http://www.statcan.gc.ca/pub/75-001-x/2010102/article/11120-eng.htm

Misra, J., Budig, M., & Moller, S. (2007). Reconciliation policies and the effects of motherhood on employment, earnings, and poverty. *Journal of Comparative Policy Analysis, 9*(2), 135–155. Retrieved from http://proquest.umi.com.remote.libproxy.wlu.ca/pqdlink?did=1279993001&sid=1&Fmt=2&clientId=27850&RQT=309&VName=PQD

Morgan K., & Zippel, K. (2003). Paid to care: The origins and effects of care leave policies in Western Europe. *Social Politics, 10*(1), 49–85. doi: 10.1093/sp/jxg004

Moss, P. (2010a). Improving the quality of childhood in the European parental leave Union: Parental leave policies. Retrieved from http://www.ecswe.org/downloads/publications/QOC-VII/Chapter5-Parental-Leave-Policies-by-Professor-Peter-Moss.pdf

Moss, P. (Ed.). (2010b). *International review of leave policies and related research 2010*. London, UK: Employment Market Analysis and Research, Department of Business, Innovation, and Skills.

O'Brien, M. (2009). Fathers, parental leave policies, and infant quality of life: International perspectives and policy impact. *Annals of the American Academy of Political and Social Science (AAPSS), 624*(1), 190–213. doi: 10.1177/0002716209334349

O'Connor, J., Orloff, A., & Shaver, S. (1999). *States, markets, families: Gender, liberalism and social policy in Australia, Canada, Great Britain, and the United States*. Cambridge, UK: Cambridge University Press.

Organisation for Economic Co-operation and Development (OECD). (2011). Doing better for families. OECD Publishing. doi: 10.1787/9789264098732-en

Québec. (2011). *Rapport actuariel du Régime québécois d'assurance parentale au 31 décembre 2010*. Québec City, QC: Conseil de gestion de l'assurance parentale. April.

Ray, R., Gornick, J., & Schmitt, J. (2010). Who cares? Assessing generosity and gender equality in parental leave policy designs in 21 countries. *Journal of European Social Policy, 20*(3), 196–216. doi:10.1177/0958928709

Statistics Canada. (2010a). Low income lines, 2008–2009. Income Research Paper Series. Ottawa, ON: Minister of Industry. Catalogue no. 75F0002M, no. 005. Retrieved from http://www.statcan.gc.ca/pub/75f0002m/75f0002m2010005eng.pdf

Statistics Canada (2010b). Women in Canada: A gender-based statistical report: Paid work. Ottawa: Minister of Industry, December. Catalogue no. 89-503-X. Retrieved from http://www.statcan.gc.ca/pub/89-503-x/2010001/article/11387-eng.pdf

Tremblay, D. (2010a). Paid parental leave: An employee right or still an ideal? An analysis of the situation in Québec in comparison with North America. *Employee Responsibilities and Rights*, 22, 83-100. doi: 10.1007/s10672-009-9108-4

Tremblay, D. (2010b). Parental leave: From perception to first-hand experience. *International Journal of Sociology and Social Policy, 30*(9/10), 532–544. doi: 10.1108/01443331011072280

Waldfogel, J. (2007). Parental work arrangements and child development. *Canadian Public Policy, 33*(2), 251–271. doi: 10.3138/cpp.33.2.251

Mental Health Policy in Canada

12

Geoffrey Nelson

The purpose of this chapter is to review and analyze mental health policy in Canada. I concentrate on adult mental health rather than children's mental health because policy initiatives and reforms across Canada have focused primarily on the adult population.

The Canadian Context

Canada is a vast, bilingual nation comprised of ten provinces and three northern territories with a population of about 34 million in 2011. Over 60 percent of Canadians reside in Ontario and Quebec, and most of them live close to the southern border with the United States. English and French are the first languages of about 57 percent and 22 percent of the population, respectively (Statistics Canada, 2005). Canada is rapidly becoming more culturally diverse, with 20 percent of the 2006 population being foreign born and 16 percent visible minorities. There are more than one million Aboriginal people (Statistics Canada, 2005).

In 1961, under Premier Tommy Douglas, the Government of Saskatchewan implemented a provincial health care system (Freeman, 1994). Five years later, in 1966, the federal government passed the Medical Care Act, which brought health care to all Canadians. The federal government has set principles (accessibility, universality, portability, comprehensiveness, government administration) and provides funding to the provinces; but planning and decision making in health care are the responsibility of the provincial governments (Goering, Wasylenki, & Durbin, 2000). Perhaps because the provinces have so much responsibility for health care, Canada is the only G8 nation without a national mental health policy. The federal government is responsible, however, for the mental health care of Aboriginal people and veterans.

Recently there have been calls for a national action plan on mental health and mental illness. Former Senator Michael Kirby led a multipronged investigation into mental health reform in Canada. The resulting report, *Out of the Shadows at Last* (Kirby & Keon, 2006), was guided by the vision of a "consumer-centred system with a focus on recovery and access to personalized care" (Kirby, 2005, p. S9). This report led to the founding of the Mental Health Commission of Canada. In the spring of 2009, that commission undertook public consultations on a mental health strategy framework (Mulvale & Bartram, 2009), which led to a final report, *Toward Recovery and Well-Being: A Framework for a Mental Health Strategy for Canada* (Mental Health Commission of Canada, 2009). That report's thrust toward a recovery orientation is consistent with the one found in other nations' policy statements (Piat & Sabetti, 2009). However, underfunding of community mental health has slowed mental health reform in Canada and other countries (Lurie, 2005; Mulvale, Abelson, & Goering, 2007). Later in this chapter, I discuss the concept of recovery.

Federal funding for health care is a contentious issue between the federal and provincial governments. The federal portion of health care funding was reduced from 42 percent to 10 percent between the mid-1970s and 2000, although it has risen under subsequent governments (Barlow, 2005). At the same time, there has been an increase in privatized health care in tandem with pressures for further privatization—trends that have been fuelled by current trends toward economic globalization, tax reduction, and reduced government spending on social programs (Barlow, 2005; Morrow, 2004b).

Within the framework of national health care, the mental health system consists of provincial psychiatric hospitals, general hospital psychiatric units, reimbursement to physicians (including psychiatrists) for mental health services, and—more recently—community mental health programs (Goering et al., 2000). Typically, these services are controlled by provincial health ministries. The provinces are moving toward decentralized, regional administration of health services, which includes the planning, decision making, funding, and coordination/integration of mental health services (Latimer, 2005). In terms of human resources, mental health specialists in private practice from disciplines other than medicine and psychiatry (psychologists, social workers, occupational therapists, psychiatric nurses) cannot receive reimbursement from government sources for mental health services. Individuals who have the financial means or supplementary private health insurance (typically through their workplaces) can obtain therapeutic services from these mental health professionals, who are private practitioners. As well, individuals can receive help from professionals from disciplines other than psychiatry who work for publicly funded agencies (e.g., hospitals, community mental health services). Historically, mental health services in Canada have been controlled by governments, by the medical profession, and, in Quebec until the 1960s, by the Catholic church (Boudreau, 1987; Simmons, 1990).

"Mental Illness" and Mental Health

"Mental Illness" and Mental Health

Since the late 1800s, the mental health field has been dominated by the biomedical perspective (i.e., psychiatry). Medical superintendents and psychiatrists have run mental hospitals and general hospital psychiatric units. As was noted earlier, only medical doctors are eligible to receive reimbursement from governments for mental health services provided in the context of private practice. With the advent of psychoactive drug treatments beginning in the 1950s, the pharmaceutical industry has become a major partner to medicine and psychiatry in the promotion of the medical model of mental illness. The Diagnostic and Statistical Manual (DSM), now in its fifth edition, is *the* tool for diagnosing mental illness. Today, in their approach to mental health issues, many mental health professionals adhere to a broad biopsychosocial framework, one that assumes there are multiple interacting causes of mental illness (e.g., genetic, biochemical, hormonal, psychological, familial, environmental, economic). However, the biological component continues to receive the strongest emphasis in both research and practice.

Both the biomedical perspective and the concept of "mental illness" as a disease have been contested. Psychiatrist Thomas Szsaz (1961) argued that mental illness is a myth and that there are no known lesions, defects, or diseases of the nervous system that underlie any of the conditions that are called mental illness. He argued that when psychiatrists label problems, they are engaging in a social act that involves value judgments. What is judged to be normal or abnormal depends on one's values and the social context. Are individuals abnormal? Or is there something wrong with the social conditions in which people live?

Questions of sexual orientation illustrate the contested nature of mental illness. Prior to 1973, "homosexuality" was included in the DSM as a mental disorder. Values and social contexts, not scientific evidence, were the reasons why homosexuality was included as a disorder—and, as well, why it was later removed from the DSM. Psychologist Paula Caplan (1995) argued that the DSM is biased both ethnoracially and in terms of gender and that it allows white, male, North American psychiatrists to decide who and what is "crazy." There have been many other criticisms of the medical model and the DSM—for example, that they emphasize deficits; that they neglect environmental conditions that contribute to mental health problems (especially poverty, racism, sexism, and homophobia); that the "stickiness" of their diagnostic labels can lead to stigma, discrimination, and negative self-fulfilling prophecies; that they foster power imbalances between psychiatrists and patients; and that they can lead to iatrogenic illnesses (problems created by professional treatments, an example being tardive dyskinesia, a disorder resulting from psychoactive drug treatment) (Cohen, 1990).

In the federal report *Mental Health for Canadians: Striking a Balance* (1988), former Minister of Health and Welfare Jake Epp distinguished between mental disorder and mental health, arguing that the two exist on separate continua. The report defined mental health broadly as "the capacity of the individual, the group and the environment to interact with one another in ways that promote subjective well-being, the optimal development and use of mental abilities (cognitive, affective and relational), the achievement of individual and collective goals consistent with justice and the attainment and preservation of conditions of fundamental equality" (Epp, 1988, p. 7). To address mental disorders effectively and to promote mental health, the report advocated reducing inequities, increasing prevention, and enhancing coping. More recently, the Canadian Institute for Health Information (CIHI) (2009) has underscored the importance of promoting positive mental health.

How widespread are mental health problems in Canada? Bearing in mind the criticisms of the DSM and of the notion that mental illness is a disease, there is epidemiological research suggesting that mental health problems in Canada, whether conceived as problems in living or as illness, are widespread (Cairney & Streiner, 2010). A survey of 36,984 adult Canadians conducted in 2002 by Statistics Canada found a one-year prevalence rate of 11 percent for any mental disorder (Lesage et al., 2006). This rate was lower than had been reported in previous epidemiological studies, perhaps because the survey did not include some common disorders (e.g., generalized anxiety disorder, specific phobias). The most prevalent disorder was depression. Lim and colleagues (2008) estimated that in 2003, the economic burden of mental health problems in Canada was $51 billion.

Mental health policy in the Canadian provinces has focused on individuals with "serious mental illness." Here, *serious* relates mainly to the illness that has been diagnosed, how disabling it is, and how long it lasts. People with *serious* mental illness typically have been diagnosed as suffering from schizophrenia, severe depression, or bipolar disorder; most of them are unemployed and have major problems coping with daily living; and generally, their problems are long-term. In contrast, those with more moderate mental health issues typically have been diagnosed as suffering from anxiety, minor mood disorder, or substance abuse; most of them are employed but have significant problems coping with the stressors of daily living; and generally, their problems are viewed as short-term or episodic. A problem in mental health policy has long been that people with moderate mental health issues are more likely to receive psychotherapy than those with more serious mental health issues (Hollingshead & Redlich, 1958). Schofield (1964) wrote that mental health professionals prefer to work with clients who are young, attractive, verbal, intelligent, successful, and female, and that many people who seek help are not mentally ill, but merely lonely and looking for friendship.

Serious Mental Health Issues

In their review of the evolution of mental health policy in Canada for people with serious mental health issues, Trainor, Pape, and Pomeroy (1997) argued that mental health policy has passed through several stages: (a) the institutional consensus, (b) deinstitutionalization, (c) community mental health services, and (d) the community process approach. In this section, we review these stages.

From Institutionalization to Deinstitutionalization

In the early 1800s in Canada, as elsewhere, people with significant mental health issues were placed in poorhouses and jails. The first mental hospital in Canada opened in 1836 in New Brunswick, and by the mid-1860s there were eleven provincial mental hospitals (Rochefort, 1992). American mental health crusader Dorthea Dix was influential in establishing some of the first institutions in Canada's Maritime provinces. Foucault (1965) and Scull (1977) argued that these institutions were developed to confine people with mental health problems who did not fit into the industrial labour market in the growing capitalist economies of Western nations. Power was vested in the hands of psychiatry, and there was a tremendous power imbalance between psychiatrists and other institutional staff, on one hand, and people who were institutionalized, on the other hand (McCubbin & Cohen, 1996). This sometimes resulted in abuse of patients, both subtle and blatant (Burstow & Weitz, 1988). One of the most egregious examples of patient abuse occurred at the Allan Memorial Institute in Montreal in the 1950s and early 1960s under the direction of Dr. Ewan Cameron. His CIA-funded research included subjecting roughly 100 patients to sensory deprivation, drugging, and massive shock treatments. In mental hospitals, patients were "out of sight and out of mind," with little chance of returning to their families and home communities. Moreover, the mental hospital was *the* mental health system for most people; few other options existed. There are a number of valuable first-person accounts as well as some historical studies from the perspective of Canadians who were patients in such settings that chronicle the many problems inherent in institutionalization (Burstow & Weitz, 1988; Chamberlin, 1978; Reaume, 2000).

There were periodic efforts to reform mental health policy and move to a more community-based approach, but until recent decades, these efforts never gained enough momentum to have an impact (Simmons, 1990). Clarence Hincks, a physician, founded what is now known as the Canadian Mental Health Association (CMHA) in 1918. Through the efforts of Hincks and other reformers, the CMHA brought to light the deplorable conditions of mental hospitals and advocated for community-based care. But it was not until much later in the century that progressive reforms took root.

Deinstitutionalization in Canada began in the 1960s. The bed capacity of provincial mental hospitals dropped from 69,128 in 1965 to 20,301 in 1981—a 70 percent reduction (Sealy & Whitehead, 2004). This change occurred in part for economic reasons: psychiatric hospitals were becoming expensive to maintain, and the development of a public welfare system provided a (very) minimal support system that enabled people with mental health problems to live in the community (Bloche & Cournos, 1990; Lewis, Shadish, & Lurigio, 1989; Scull, 1977). Recognition of the limitations of institutions, an increasing focus on human rights, and a new vision that support and treatment would be more effective in the individual's home community were other reasons for deinstitutionalization (McCubbin, 1994). In the early years of deinstitutionalization, funding was transferred to local general hospital psychiatric units rather than community mental health services. Between 1960 and 1976, the number of general hospital psychiatric beds increased sevenfold from 844 to 5,836 (Wasylenki, Goering, & MacNaughton, 1994). One of the more innovative approaches was the famous "Saskatchewan Plan," which created eight regional mental health centres in that province and which emphasized providing services in the person's home and community (Lafave & Vanden Ham, 1979).

Many discharged individuals were—and remain to this day—isolated from communities of support, often living in "psychiatric ghettos" consisting of boarding homes or other poor-quality housing. Indeed, they were often homeless (Capponi, 1992; Dear & Wolch, 1987; Rochefort, 1993). Aftercare support often consisted mainly of medication, with little in the way of psychosocial support, even though many of the problems these people face in the community are social, economic, or interpersonal (Harris, Hilton, & Rice, 1993). In their 1981 study of psychiatric aftercare in Toronto, Goering and colleagues (1984) found that six months after discharge from psychiatric facilities in Toronto, one-third of the sample had been readmitted to hospital. Another 38 percent were employed; 68 percent reported moderate to severe difficulties in social functioning; and 20 percent were living in inadequate housing.

In this context of institutional abuse and community neglect, people with mental health problems formed their own mutual aid organizations. In Vancouver, ex-patients formed the Mental Patients Association (MPA), which provided respite housing and mutual aid and which engaged in advocacy to protect the rights of people with mental health problems (Chamberlin, 1978). Inspired by the Vancouver MPA, a group in Toronto formed On Our Own, a radical anti-psychiatry group that operated a "mad market," engaged in political action (e.g., opposition to ECT and psychoactive drug use in hospitals), and produced a periodical called *Phoenix Rising* for several years (Weitz, 1984). These early self-help, social movement organizations of ex-patients set the stage for the expansion of self-help alternatives that have recently received government support.

Community Mental Health and Mental Health Reform

Reallocation of resources. Since the late 1980s, most of the provinces have pursued mental health reform. Like deinstitutionalization before it, mental health reform in Canada, and elsewhere, has been driven by governments' concerns for cost containment as well as by visions of more effective community supports for people (Fisher, 1994; Morrow, 2004b; Shera et al., 2002). Mental health reform has included efforts to reallocate resources from institutional services to community mental health supports and programs. During the late 1980s, all of the provinces except Saskatchewan spent 68 percent or more of their mental health budgets on institutional services (Saskatchewan spent 48 percent) (MacNaughton, 1991). Then, from the late 1980s to 1998, provincial spending on community mental health increased thirteenfold, from $8 million to $113 million (Sealy & Whitehead, 2004), with several provinces making significant progress in reallocating resource from hospitals to community-based services.

The creation of community mental health alternatives. New Brunswick created a Mental Health Commission in 1988, which made significant reforms. For example, it developed more than thirty self-help groups and activity centres and a variety of alternatives to hospitalization (Niles & Ross, 1992). British Columbia dramatically scaled down the number of beds in its main mental hospital and reallocated resources to community mental health services (Berland, 2001). From the late 1980s to the mid-1990s, Ontario made significant reforms. For example, it developed and funded more than fifty Consumer/Survivor Initiatives as well as a provincial umbrella organization called the Ontario Peer Development Initiative (OPDI). It also established more than ten consumer-run businesses and a provincial umbrella organization called the Ontario Council of Alternative Businesses (OCAB), as well as supportive housing options and a variety of other community-based case management and psychosocial programs (Hartford et al., 2003; Nelson, Lord, & Ochocka, 2001; Trainor et al., 1997; Trainor & Tremblay, 1992).

Beginning in the late 1990s, Ontario doubled the number of supportive and supported housing spaces, focusing on people with serious mental illness who were homeless or at risk for homelessness (Sylvestre et al., 2007). The province has also funded more than sixty Assertive Community Treatment (ACT) teams across the province (Bishop et al., 2011).

Quebec has undergone a number of major changes in recent years. For example, it has regionalized mental health services, integrated mental health services with *Centres de santé et services sociaux,* and developed more than 100 alternative supports and consumer advocacy groups (e.g., *Regroupement de ressources alternatives en santé mentale au Québec* [RRASMQ], and *l'Association des groupes d'intervention en défense de droits en santé mentale au Québec* [L'AGIDD-SMQ]), all with an emphasis on partnership between professionals and people with mental health problems and their family members in planning community supports (Boudreau, 1991; Fleury, 2005; Latimer, 2005; Mercier & White, 1994).

Community treatment and rehabilitation paradigm. But simply reallocating resources from institutions to community mental health services does not guarantee a fundamental transformation of mental health policies and services. Some institutional programs may be repackaged in the community, yielding "old wine in new bottles." Many community treatment and rehabilitation approaches have retained the character of the institutional paradigm (see Table 12.1). For example, case management and ACT teams (e.g., Stein & Test, 1980) are often professionally driven services that aim to prevent hospitalization, reduce symptoms, and promote life skills. While located in the community, programs like these have long been guided by many of the same values as the institutional approach. They function like "hospitals without walls," maintain a power imbalance between staff and clients, and use some coercive methods (Spindel, 2000). While clients are *in* the community, they are not a part *of* the community. Often they are isolated in segregated settings, such as group homes, boarding homes, and sheltered workshops.

Table 12.1 Changing Paradigms in Community Mental Health

KEY VALUES	COMMUNITY TREATMENT AND REHABILITATION PARADIGM	RECOVERY AND EMPOWERMENT PARADIGM
Health	• Emphasis on symptom reduction and prevention of hospitalization • Focus on psychosocial deficits and social skills training	• Focus on whole person • Recognition of strengths • Emphasis on recovery and quality of life
Stakeholder participation and empowerment	• Dependence on professionals • Client role • Professional as expert • Professionally prescribed treatment	• Consumer choice and control • Autonomous consumer and family organizations • Citizen role • Professional role focuses on enabling and collaboration
Community support and integration	• Professional, paraprofessional, and volunteer services • Community-based	• Self-help/mutual aid • Individualized support • Informal supports • Integration in community settings and social networks
Social justice and access to valued resources	• Group homes, halfway houses, and supervised apartments, often with many people with mental health challenges living in the same setting • Vocational training and placement • Sheltered workshops	• Independent housing chosen by residents from normal housing stock in the community, with portable and flexible support • Supported employment and education

Source: Adapted from Nelson, Lord, & Ochocka, 2001.

Approaches like ACT and psychiatric rehabilitation have been widely disseminated and adopted. Lewis and colleagues (1989) warned the mental health field about the perils of "guild innovationism" in community mental health, which benefits professionals more than service users. Planning and policy in mental health often uses the progressive language of "partnerships" among mental health professionals, individuals with mental health problems, and their family members. Researchers and activists argue that in practice, however, power imbalances between professionals and service users and family members continue to plague community partnerships and to undermine more radical reforms (McCubbin, 2009; Morin, 1992; Mercier & White, 1994). In a qualitative study of service user's participation in mental health reform in Ontario, Everett (2000) described the participation of service users as a "fragile revolution."

Empowerment and recovery paradigm. Since the 1990s, however, alternative visions and values of community mental health have been articulated both by professionals and by people who use mental health services (who refer to themselves as "consumers" or "survivors"). Some of the key themes of this emerging, alternative paradigm are empowerment, recovery, community integration, peer support, informal support, self-help, and social justice (see Table 12.1). Whereas the community treatment and rehabilitation paradigm focuses on ameliorative change (moving from hospitals to the community), this recovery and empowerment paradigm focuses on transformative or fundamental change in the values and power arrangements of mental health policy and practice (Nelson, 2010). Trainor, Pape, and Pomeroy (1997) make a similar distinction between what they call community mental health services and a community process approach.

In the United States, Patricia Deegan (1988), who is both a consumer/survivor activist and a mental health professional, introduced the idea of recovery as an alternative vision to the dominant professional view of the "chronic mental patient." One of the founders of psychiatric rehabilitation, William Anthony (1993), has further promoted recovery as the "guiding vision of the mental health service system." Deegan and Anthony, as well as others (Ralph & Corrigan, 2005; Jacobson, Provencher, & Thompson, 2009), emphasize that recovery involves movement toward a more positive quality of life. The concept of recovery stems from the voices of consumers and progressive mental health professionals; it also stems from longitudinal research that has demonstrated that many people who have experienced mental illness do, in fact, improve, with some showing a full recovery (Ralph & Corrigan, 2005). Recovery has become the rallying cry and vision for a reformed mental health system.

The National Office of the Canadian Mental Health Association's "framework for support" for people with serious mental health problems (Trainor, Pomeroy, & Pape, 1999) provides a clear idea of how empowerment recovery principles can be implemented. This framework, first conceived during the early 1980s, elaborates on the community approach (Pomeroy, Trainor, & Pape, 2002). There are several key features of the framework. First, the consumer is more than simply at the centre of the framework; that person also controls and directs the sources of support that surround him or her. Second, while mental health services are part of the framework, there is a strong emphasis on other sources of support, including family, friends, social networks, peer support, self-help, and community groups and agencies. Third, the framework includes access to the basic resources that are needed to promote a desirable quality of life, including housing, income, work, and education. Fourth, the framework asserts that while medical science and social science are valuable ways to understand mental illness, they are not the only sources of knowledge. Experiential knowledge and the knowledge of lay persons are also valuable and need to be incorporated into mental health policy and programs. Finally, implicit in the framework is a strong emphasis on the participation of mental health consumers and family members in mental health policy making, planning, and service delivery and in the creation of self-help approaches.

This framework has been highly influential and has been adopted by the governments of New Brunswick and Ontario as guides to their mental health reforms. The progressive changes that have been achieved in New Brunswick (Niles & Ross, 1992) and Ontario (Nelson, Lord, and Ochocka, 2001) point to the importance of having a framework that clearly outlines an alternative vision and values, as well as strategies for change (Carling, 1995). While vision and values are necessary in order to implement new paradigms, there are often many obstacles to implementing such practices, as Townsend (1998) found in a study of occupational therapy settings in mental health in Nova Scotia.

Incorporation of recovery and empowerment principles into community treatment and rehabilitation. Today, the lines between the community treatment and rehabilitation paradigm and the recovery and empowerment paradigms, between community mental health services and community processes, have become blurred. While there are clear examples of more traditional programs and more innovative programs, many programs are hybrids that straddle the two paradigms. This is clearly illustrated in the case of ACT programs. For example, the Pathways program in New York City uses ACT as the support component for its supported housing, and ACT staff are committed to the "practice of radical acceptance of the consumer's point of view." Also, "unlike the traditional ACT model, the Pathways supported housing program allows clients to determine the type and intensity of services or refuse them entirely" (Tsemberis & Eisenberg, 2000, p. 489). Research on ACT teams in Ontario and Quebec has shown that while clients have some concerns about ACT (e.g., conflict over medications and money), most are very satisfied with their relationships with staff and the program (Krupa et al.,

2005; Latimer et al., 2010; Redko et al., 2004). Moreover, in a study of sixty-seven ACT teams in Ontario, Kidd and colleagues (2010) reported "a moderate to high degree of recovery orientation in service provision" (p. 342). There is also a growing trend toward peer support within case management and ACT programs (Nelson & Grant, 2011), and research has found that consumer case managers achieve the same beneficial outcomes as professional case managers (Solomon, 2004). In summary, there is a growing rapprochement between ACT and recovery principles (Salyers & Tsemberis, 2007), which indicates a rapprochement between treatment/rehabilitation and recovery/empowerment approaches.

Evidence-Based Mental Health Policy and Practice

Historically, mental health policy has relied very little on research. With the advent of community mental health programs, there has been an increasing emphasis on research informing mental health policy. In 1997 the Health Systems Research and Consulting Unit of the Centre for Addiction and Mental Health completed a review of best practices in mental health for the federal government (Health Canada, 1998). The review included research evidence regarding the core services of a comprehensive mental health system, including the following: case management, ACT teams, crisis intervention, supportive and supported housing, in-patient and outpatient care, consumer self-help and consumer initiatives, family self-help, and vocational services. In Ontario, the government partnered with the Centre for Addiction and Mental Health, the Ontario Division of CMHA, and the Ontario Mental Health Foundation (a research funding organization) in the creation of a Community Mental Health Evaluation Initiative (CMHEI). The CMHEI involved a coordinated set of studies, including several with common measurement tools and assessment intervals, that longitudinally examined the effectiveness of crisis services, intensive case management, ACT, family self-help, and consumer/survivor initiatives. The results of these studies have been reported in a document titled *Making It Happen* (Ontario Ministry of Health and Long-term Care, 2004). In 2005 the Government of Ontario provided $167 million in additional funding for crisis services, intensive case management, court diversion and support, ACT, and early psychosis intervention; it also committed funding to evaluate the impacts of this Systems Enhancement Evaluation Initiative (SEEI). Academic and applied researchers were recruited to evaluate various services funded by the SEEI (George & Durbin, 2010). Similar linkages among policy makers, researchers, and service providers are being made in other provinces as well (Berland, 2001; Latimer 2005).

Moderate Mental Health Issues

Moderate Mental Health Issues

Dewa and colleagues (2003) have argued that in focusing on people with serious mental illness, mental health reform has neglected a large population of people with moderate mental health issues. They define moderate mental illness as "diagnosable, sufficiently severe to impede functional abilities, and considered to require, and could likely benefit from, mental health treatment under broadly established professional norms" (p. 45). The main types of moderate mental health problems are anxiety disorders, mood disorders, and personality disorders. These disorders cause significant distress to the individuals afflicted and to their families and social network members, and they are quite costly to society.

The previously mentioned epidemiological study of adult mental health problems in Canada (Lesage et al., 2006) found that only about 40 percent of those who were judged to have a disorder sought treatment for it from a health professional or mental health specialist. Clearly, the mental health system is not working when most of those with moderate mental health problems do not seek treatment.

Other research has shown that those experiencing mental health problems often turn to their family doctors, counsellors, or clergy for help (Kulka, Veroff, & Douvan, 1979), although people are turning to doctors less often than they have in the past (Swindle et al., 2000). Because of their training in medicine rather than psychotherapy, physicians are likely to rely on psychoactive drugs for treatment. While drug treatments can be effective for a variety of moderate mental health problems, such as anxiety or depression, many people need more than what drugs have to offer. They often need help with their marriages and families, other relationships, work-related stressors, traumatic experiences, coping and social skills, self-esteem, and a variety of complicated life problems. Clergy often have some training in counselling, but physicians, clergy, and other counsellors and helpers who are not mental health specialists typically do not have training in current evidence-based treatment approaches for moderate mental health issues.

The question then for moderate mental health issues is how to bring the most effective mental health treatments to people with mental health problems. There are now a number of well-established psychotherapeutic and pharmacological treatments for anxiety and depression (Dewa et al., 2003). Moreover, clinical researchers have developed a number of self-directed treatments that can be used by people with emotional disorders, such as anxiety and depression, including bibliotherapy, audiotape programs, multimedia computer packages, interactive voice response systems, Web-based systems, stepped-care approaches, and so on (Vincent, Walker, & Katz, 2008). There is evidence that these approaches are effective; furthermore, much of the research indicates that these approaches are as effective as traditional face-to-face professional treatment (den Boer, Wiersnia, & van den Bosch, 2004; Vincent et al., 2008). Finally, it has been shown that primary

Prevention of Mental Health Problems and Mental Health Promotion

care patients and their physicians are receptive to these treatments (Vincent et al., 2008). Shared care arrangements between mental health professionals and primary care physicians and training of physicians, clergy, and other helpers are some possible ways of bringing evidence-based treatments to people with moderate mental health problems (Dewa et al., 2003).

To reform mental health policy for people with moderate mental illness, there also needs to be a re-examination of what professionals and what treatments should be reimbursed for private practice. Since many of the most effective psychotherapeutic treatments for anxiety and mood disorders have been developed by psychologists and social workers, policy changes are needed that would tap into the resources of such non-medical professionals for private practice. Finally, as is the case with serious mental illness, policy and practice for people with moderate mental health problems should not be viewed exclusively in terms of professional treatment. Across Canada, self-help and mutual aid groups for people facing a variety of life issues have been developed (Gottlieb & Peters, 1991). There is a growing body of research attesting to the effectiveness of such groups in improving the mental health and quality of life of a number of different populations (Pistrang, Barker, & Humphreys, 2010).

Prevention of Mental Health Problems and Mental Health Promotion

The prevention of mental health problems for adults has not received a great deal of attention in Canadian mental health policy. For example, in a 1979 mental health planning report, the B.C. government based its position on prevention on an article by two American psychiatrists who asserted that mental health problems are genetically caused and thus not preventable and that there is no evidence that "mental illness" can be prevented (see Nelson, Potasznik, & Bennett, 1983). More than thirty years later, a great deal of evidence has accumulated regarding the effectiveness of prevention and promotion programs in mental health (Nelson, Prilleltensky, & Hasford, 2009). In spite of an emphasis on prevention/promotion in federal policy documents (CIHI, 2009; Epp, 1988), this has not translated into prevention/promotion policies for adults. For example, in a survey of the provinces and territories, Nelson and colleagues (1996) found that funding for prevention is very low (less than 1 percent of health budgets).

There are, however, some encouraging signs about policy related to prevention/promotion. First, the federal government created a mental health promotion unit in 1995 within its public health agency, whose mandate is to develop knowledge and policy regarding mental health promotion from a population health perspective, one that considers a broad range of determinants of mental health. Second, the provinces, with federal funding for early childhood education, have invested in prevention programs focused on preschool children, including family support and centre-based programs

(Nelson et al., 2009). Such programs can prevent later mental health problems as the children mature into their youth and adult years (Nelson, Westhues, & MacLeod, 2003). Further policy work on mental health promotion is required in order to build on these positive developments.

Class, Ethnoracial, and Gender Considerations

To what extent has an analysis of class, race, and gender been used to inform mental health policy? While social class and poverty are sometimes mentioned in mental health policy documents, actions to address the problem of poverty are lacking. In an early study, Hollingshead and Redlich (1958) found that those in the lowest social class are most likely to receive a diagnosis of *serious* mental illness, while those in the higher social classes are more apt to receive a diagnosis indicating *moderate* mental illness. This finding has been replicated many times, and poverty is clearly a major problem for people with serious mental illness as well as a risk factor for the development of mental health problems. Canadian survivor and advocate David Reville (2005) has cautioned mental health reformers not to "lose sight of the issue of poverty" (p. S65). Wilton (2004) documented the deleterious impacts of chronic poverty on the quality of life of people with serious mental illness. Moreover, he found that social assistance benefits in Ontario declined by 13 percent from 1994 to 2001 and that this decline was directly attributable to changes in government policy. People with serious mental illness who are on social assistance receive a personal needs allowance of a mere $112 per month, a sum that has not been increased since 1992. Krupa and colleagues (2005) have outlined a number of strategies that could be used to improve the employment of people with serious mental illness. There is a great need for mental health policy to be linked with income support, employment, and housing policies and programs toward the goal of poverty reduction. However, in Canada, these different policies are currently disconnected (Forchuk et al., 2007).

With regard to ethnoracial status, in the 1980s the federal government commissioned a Canadian Task Force on Mental Health Issues Affecting Immigrants and Refugees. The reports of this task force (Health and Welfare Canada, 1988a, 1988b) and a subsequent review (Beiser, 2005) found that certain aspects of the migration experience (e.g., drop in socio-economic status, language challenges, separation from family, isolation, etc.) and premigration catastrophic stress experiences (e.g., exposure to or victim of war, violence, torture, or natural disasters) are risk factors for mental health problems. The same reports underscored the importance of measures to prevent mental health problems, including language and job training programs and settlement services. Poverty, poor housing, and racial discrimination have also been found to contribute to the poor mental health of racialized groups in Canada (Access Alliance Multicultural Community Health Centre, 2005).

Class, Ethnoracial, and Gender Considerations

In their review of factors influencing people's utilization of mental health services in Canada, Beiser, Gill, and Edwards (1993) noted that treatment approaches are based on European and North American values, which are often incongruent with the beliefs of immigrants and refugees and which lead to their underutilization of mental health services. Different cultural concepts of mental illness, the strong stigma and shame associated with mental illness that exists in many cultures, racism, and language are all barriers to the use of mental health services (Beiser et al., 1993; Health and Welfare Canada, 1988b). The need to incorporate traditional healers from different ethnoracial groups and to provide training in cultural competence to mental health service providers has been reinforced in a recent community–university partnership that examined the mental health needs and experiences of culturally diverse groups in Toronto and Kitchener-Waterloo (Simich et al., 2009).

Mental health services for Aboriginal people, which are primarily the responsibility of the federal government, are a major concern. As Lafave and Vanden Ham (1979) stated: "In Canada as a whole, and Saskatchewan is no exception, services to the Indian population are abominable" (p. 14). Bennett (1982) has argued that the power loss, culture loss, residential schooling, poverty, and racism experienced by Native communities have led to a host of health and mental health problems. Schmidt (2000) has shown that geographic and economic factors pose major barriers to psychiatric rehabilitation programs in remote Aboriginal communities. A transformative approach is needed to address the mental health needs of Aboriginal people in their historical, cultural, social, political, and economic context.

A great deal of work has documented sexist practices in the mental health system. Women have historically been viewed as more irrational than men and as more vulnerable to emotional problems, and this has been linked to women's biological makeup (e.g., attributions of hysteria to a woman's "wandering uterus") (Morrow, 2007). In *Women and Madness*, Phyllis Chesler (1972) argued that women are diagnosed with disorders for overconforming or underconforming to stereotypical female gender roles. In support of this argument, Broverman and colleagues (1970) found in a study of clinicians that if women conform to traditional female qualities, they are judged as unhealthy *people*, but if they do not conform to such a role, they are judged as unhealthy *women*. As well, for many years, mental health professionals ignored many of the social stressors that disproportionately affect women, including child sexual abuse, sexual assault, rape, sexual harassment, psychological and physical violence, single motherhood, and poverty. Women from ethnoracial minorities and Aboriginal women are particularly at risk for these stressors (Morrow, 2007).

While feminist therapies and other alternative approaches have been developed that are sensitive to the gendered nature of mental health and illness, public mental health policy and programs have, for the most part, taken a gender-neutral approach (Morrow, 2007). Some notable exceptions that exemplify a women-centred approach to mental health include the Women's Mental Health and Addiction Section of the Centre for Addiction and Mental Health and the Women's Mental Health Program in the Department of Psychiatry, University of Toronto, both in Toronto. A conference in 2003 in Quebec titled Women, Psychiatry, Secondary Victimization brought the concerns of women into the mental health consumer movement, and several reports on women's mental health by the B.C. Centre of Excellence for Women's Mental Health, including a policy document on the creation of a national strategy for women's mental health (Morrow, 2004a), have also brought women's mental health concerns to the attention of practitioners and policy makers. More attention needs to be paid to how women and men with serious mental health problems view their service needs. Scheyett and McCarthy (2006) found that while women and men have many similar perceptions of service needs, women tend to place more emphasis on the need for relationships with mental health support workers to be based on caring, understanding, and mutuality.

In answer to the question about the extent to which mental health policy in Canada has been informed by an analysis of class, race, and gender, the available evidence suggests that all of these critical issues have been in the background of mental health policy. While there have been some excellent policy documents dealing with some of these considerations, there have been few strategic policy decisions in the provinces addressing issues of oppression due to poverty, ethnoracial background, and gender.

Conclusion

While there is still pervasive social stigma attached to mental health problems, some progress had been made with regard to mental health over the past fifty years. Issues of mental health and "mental illness" are now much more visible—witness the number of TV talk shows and self-help books that touch on mental health issues. Psychiatric terminology—"ADHD," "bipolar disorder," "eating disorders," and so on—has become common in public discourse. In Canada, provincial governments have made people with serious mental illness the priority in mental health policy reform. While progress has been uneven, all of the provinces have created community mental health programs and have begun to shift resources from hospitals to communities. Moreover, in many communities, mental health consumers and survivors and family members are now much more visible and active in the creation of mental health policy and the provision of community mental health services and supports.

In spite of these advances, many issues have been neglected in current policies. These neglected issues include the population of people with moderate mental health issues, supportive and supported housing, poverty, ethnoracial and gender considerations, and the need for more emphasis on prevention. To address these issues, a values-based, systems approach to policy reform is needed, since many policies and systems outside the traditional domain of mental health are important for the promotion of mental health reform (McCubbin & Cohen, 1999). In keeping with Epp's (1988) report and the recent work of the Kirby Commission (2005), social policies that promote social justice and social inclusion are needed to broaden the vision of mental health, to address the biopsychosocial factors and processes that promote or undermine the mental health of Canadians, and to further develop approaches to mental health that are community based, consumer directed, recovery oriented, and sensitive to class, race, ethnicity, and gender.

References

Access Alliance Multicultural Community Health Centre of Toronto. (2005). Racialised groups and health status: A literature review exploring poverty, housing, race-based discrimination, and access to health care as determinants of health for racialised groups. Retrieved from http://www.settlement.org/sys/whatshappen_detail.asp?anno_id=2005450

Anthony, W. (1993). Recovery from mental illness: The guiding vision of the mental health service system in the 1990s. *Psychiatric Rehabilitation Journal, 16*(4), 11–24.

Barlow, M. (2005). *Too close for comfort: Canada's future within fortress North America.* Toronto, ON: McClelland and Stewart.

Beiser, M. (2005). The health of immigrants and refugees in Canada. *Canadian Journal of Public Health, 96,* Supp. 2, S30–44.

Beiser, M., Gill, K., & Edwards, R.G. (1993). Mental health care in Canada. Is accessible and equal? *Canada's Mental Health, 41*(2), 2–7.

Bennett, E.M. (1982). Native persons: An assessment of their relationship to the dominant culture and challenges for change. *Canadian Journal of Community Mental Health, 1*(2), 21–31.

Berland, A. (2001). Mental health reform in British Columbia. *Administration and Policy in Mental Health, 29,* 89–93.

Bishop, J., George, L., Lurie, S., & Wales, R. (2011). Current developments in Assertive Community Treatment. In E.R. Vingilis & S.A. State (Eds.), *Applied research and evaluation in community mental health services* (pp. 182–210). Montréal, QC and Kingston, ON: McGill-Queen's University Press.

Bloche, M.G., & Cournos, F. (1990). Mental health policy for the 1990s: Tinkering in the interstices. *Journal of Health Politics, Policy, and Law, 15,* 387–411.

Boudreau, F. (1987). The making of mental health policy: The 1980s and the challenge of sanity in Québec and Ontario. *Canadian Journal of Community Mental Health, 6*(1), 27–47.

Boudreau, F. (1991). Stakeholders as partners: The challenge of partnership in Québec mental health policy. *Canadian Journal of Community Mental Health, 10*(1), 7–28.

References

Broverman, I.K., Broverman, D.M., Clarkson, F.E., Rosencrantz, P.S., & Vogel, S.R. (1970). Sex-role stereotypes and clinical judgements of mental health. *Journal of Consulting and Clinical Psychology, 34*, 1–7.

Burstow, B., & Weitz, D. (Eds.). (1988). *Shrink resistant: The struggle against psychiatry in Canada.* Vancouver, BC: New Star Books.

Cairney, J., & Streiner, D.L. (Eds.). (2010). *Mental disorders in Canada: An epidemiological perspective.* Toronto, ON: University of Toronto Press.

Canadian Institute for Health Information (CIHI). (2009). Improving the health of Canadians: Exploring positive mental health. Ottawa, ON: CIHI. Retrieved from http://www.cihi.ca/CIHI-ext-portal/internet/en/Search/search/search_main_en?q=exploringpercent20positivepercent20mental percent20health&client=all_results&start=0&num=10&filter=0

Caplan, P. (1995). *They say you're crazy: How the world's most powerful psychiatrists decide who's normal.* Reading, MA: Addison-Wesley Longman.

Capponi, P. (1992). *Upstairs in the crazy house: The life of a psychiatric survivor.* Toronto, ON: Penguin.

Carling, P.J. (1995). *Return to community: Building support systems for people with psychiatric disabilities.* New York, NY: Guilford Press.

Chamberlin, J. (1978). *On our own: Patient-controlled alternatives to the mental health system.* New York, NY: McGraw-Hill.

Chesler, P. (1972). *Women and madness.* New York, NY: Avon Books.

Cohen, D. (Ed.). (1990). Challenging the therapeutic state: Critical perspectives on psychiatry and the mental health system [special issue]. *Journal of Mind and Behavior, 11*(3/4).

Dear, M.J., & Wolch, J.R. (1987). *Landscapes of despair: From deinstitutionalization to homelessness.* Oxford, UK: Polity Press.

Deegan, P. (1988). Recovery: The lived experience of rehabilitation. *Psychosocial Rehabilitation Journal, 11*(4), 11–19.

den Boer, P.C.A.M., Wiersnia, D., & van den Bosch, R.J. (2004). Why is self-help neglected in the treatment of emotional disorders? A meta-analysis. *Psychological Medicine, 34*, 959–971.

Dewa, C.S., Rochefort, D.A., Rogers, J., & Goering, P. (2003). Left behind by reform: The case for improving primary care and mental health system services for people with moderate mental illness. *Applied Health Economics and Health Policy, 2*, 43–54.

Epp, J. (1988). *Mental health for Canadians: Striking a balance.* Ottawa, ON: Minister of Supplies and Services.

Everett, B. (2000). *A fragile revolution: Consumers and psychiatric survivors confront the power of the mental health system.* Waterloo, ON: Wilfrid Laurier University Press.

Fisher, D.B. (1994). Health care reform based on an empowerment model of recovery by people with psychiatric disabilities. *Hospital and Community Psychiatry, 45*, 913–915.

Fleury, M.-J. (2005). Quebec mental health services networks: Models and implementation. *International Journal of Integrated Care, 1.* Retrieved from http://www.ijic.org

Forchuk, C., Turner, K., Joplin, L., Schofield, R., Csiernik, R., & Gorlick, C. (2007). Housing, income support and mental health: Points of disconnection. *Health Research Policy and Systems, 5*, 14–20. doi:10.1186/1478-4505-5-14

References

Foucault, M. (1965). *Madness and civilization: A history of insanity in the age of reason*. New York, NY: Vintage Books.

Freeman, S.J.J. (1994). An overview of Canada's mental health system. In L.L. Bachrach, P. Goering, & D. Wasylenki (Eds.), *Mental health care in Canada* (pp. 11–20). San Francisco, CA: Jossey-Bass.

George, L., & Durbin, J. (Eds.). (2010). Moving in the right direction—Articles from Ontario's Systems Enhancement Evaluation Initiative [special supplement]. *Canadian Journal of Community Mental Health, Supplement 5.*

Goering, P., Wasylenki, D., & Durbin, J. (2000). Canada's mental health system. *International Journal of Law and Psychiatry, 23,* 345–359.

Goering, P., Wasylenki, D., Farkas, M., Lancee, W., & Freeman, S.J.J. (1984). From hospital to community: Six-month and two-year outcomes for 505 patients. *Journal of Nervous and Mental Disease, 172,* 667–673.

Gottlieb, B.H., & Peters, L. (1991). A national demographic portrait of mutual aid group participants in Canada. *American Journal of Community Psychology, 19,* 651–666.

Harris, G.T., Hilton, N.Z., & Rice, M.E. (1993). Patients admitted to psychiatric hospital: Presenting problems and resolution at discharge. *Canadian Journal of Behavioural Science, 25,* 267–285.

Hartford, K., Schrecker, T., Wiktorowicz, M., Hoch, J.S., & Sharp, C. (2003). Four decades of mental health policy in Ontario, Canada. *Administration and Policy in Mental Health, 31,* 65–73.

Health Canada (1998). Review of best practices in mental health reform. Ottawa, ON: Minister of Public Works and Government Services Canada. Retrieved from http://www.phac-aspc.gc.ca/mh-sm/pdf/best_practices.pdf

Health and Welfare Canada. (1988a). After the door has been opened. Ottawa, ON: Minister of Supplies and Services. Retrieved from http://ceris.metropolis.net/virtual percent20library/health/candian_taskforce/canadian1.html

Health and Welfare Canada. (1988b). *Review of the literature on migrant mental health*. Ottawa: Minister of Supplies and Services.

Hollingshead, A., & Redlich, F. (1958). *Social class and mental illness: A community study*. New York, NY: Wiley.

Jacobson, N., Provencher, H.L., & Thompson, A. (Eds.). (2009). Recovery in community mental health policy and services: Implementation and innovation [special issue]. *Canadian Journal of Community Mental Health, 28*(2).

Kidd, S.A., George, L., O'Connell, M., Sylvestre, J., Kirkpatrick, H., Browne, G., & Thabane, L. (2010). Fidelity and recovery-orientation in Assertive Community Treatment. *Community Mental Health Journal, 46,* 342–350. doi: 10.1007/s10597-009-9275-7

Kirby, M. (2005). Mental health reform for Canada in the 21st century: Getting there from here. *Canadian Public Policy, 31,* S5–11, Special Electronic Supplement on Mental Health Reform for the 21st Century. Retrieved from http://economics.ca/cpp/en/special2005.php

Kirby, M., & Keon, W. (2006). Out of the shadows at last: Transforming mental health, mental illness and addictions services in Canada. Standing Senate Committee on Social Affairs, Science, and Technology: Government of Canada. Retrieved from http://www.parl.gc.ca/Content/SEN/Committee/391/soci/rep/rep02may06-e.htm

References Krupa, T., Eastabrook, S., Hern, L., Lee, D., North, R., Percy, K., Von Briesen, B., & Wing, G. (2005). How do people who receive Assertive Community Treatment experience this service? *Psychiatric Rehabilitation Journal, 29*(1), 18–24.

Krupa, T., Kirsch, B., Gewurtz, R., & Cockburn, L. (2005). Improving the employment prospects of people with serious mental illness: Five challenges for a national mental health strategy. *Canadian Public Policy, 31,* S59–63, Special Electronic Supplement on Mental Health Reform for the 21st Century, retrieved from http://economics.ca/cpp/en/special2005.php

Kulka, R.A., Veroff, J., & Douvan, E. (1979). Social class and the use of professional help for personal problems: 1957 and 1976. *Journal of Health and Social Behavior, 20,* 2–17.

Lafave, H., & Vanden Ham, M.T. (1979). Mental health in Saskatchewan: A look at the past, present, and future. *Canada's Mental Health, 27*(1), 13–16.

Lakaski, C.M., Wilmot, V., Lips, T.J., & Brown, M. (1993). Canada. In D.R. Kemp (Ed.), *International handbook on mental health policy* (pp. 45–66). Westport, CT: Greenwood Press.

Latimer, E. (2005). Community-based care for people with severe mental illness in Canada. *International Journal of Law and Psychiatry, 28,* 561–573. doi:10.1016/j.ijlp.2005.08.001

Latimer, E., Farmer, O., Jenkins, A.G., & Jenkins, T. (2010). Perceived coercion, client-centredness, and positive and negative pressures in an Assertive Community Treatment program: An exploratory study. *Canadian Journal of Community Mental Health, 29*(1), 35–50.

Lesage, A., Vasiliadis, H.-M., Gagné, M.A., Dudgeon, S., Kasman, N., & Hay, C. (2006). Prevalences of mental illness and related service utilization in Canada: An analysis of the Canadian Community Health Survey. Mississauga, ON: Canadian Collaborative Mental Health Initiative. Retrieved from http://www.ccmhi.ca

Lewis, D.A., Shadish, W.R., & Lurigio, A.J. (1989). Policies of inclusion and the mentally ill: Long-term care in a new environment. *Journal of Social Issues, 45,* 183–186.

Lim, K.L., Jacobs, P., Ohinmaa, A., Schlopflocher, D., & Dewa, C. (2008). A new population-based measure of the economic burden of mental illness in Canada. *Chronic Diseases in Canada, 28,* 92–98.

Lurie, S. (2005). Comparative mental health policy: Are there lessons to be learned? *International Review of Psychiatry, 19,* 97–101. doi: 10.1080/09540260500073356

MacNaughton, E. (1991). *Community reinvestment—Vol. 2: Towards rebalancing Canada's mental health system.* Toronto, ON: Canadian Mental Health Association / National Office.

McCubbin, M. (1994). Deinstitutionalization: The illusion of disillusion. *Journal of Mind and Behavior, 15*(1/2), 35–54.

McCubbin, M. (2009). Oppression and empowerment: The genesis of a critical analysis of mental health. In D. Fox, I. Prilleltensky, & S. Austin (Ed.), *Critical psychology: An introduction* (pp. 300–316). Los Angeles, CA: Sage Publications.

McCubbin, M., & Cohen, D. (1996). Extremely unbalanced: Interest divergence and power disparities between clients and psychiatry. *International Journal of Law and Psychiatry, 19,* 1–25.

McCubbin, M., & Cohen, D. (1999). A systemic and valued-based approach to strategic reform of the mental health system. *Health Care Analysis, 7,* 1–21.

Mental Health Commission of Canada. (2009). Toward recovery and well-being: A framework for a mental health strategy for Canada. Ottawa, ON: National Library of Canada. Retrieved from http://www.mentalhealthcommission.ca/English/Pages/Reports.aspx

Mercier, C., & White, D. (1994). Mental health policy in Québec: Challenges for an integrated system. In L.L. Bachrach, P. Goering, & D. Wasylenki (Eds.), *Mental health care in Canada* (pp. 41–52). San Francisco, CA: Jossey-Bass.

Morin, P. (1992). Québec's mental health policy: A sign of hope or a false start? *Canada's Mental Health, 40*(1), 19–24.

Morrow, M. (2004a). *Mainstreaming women's mental health: Creating a national mental health strategy*. Vancouver, BC: BC Centre of Excellence in Women's Health.

Morrow, M. (2004b). Mental health reform, economic globalization, and the practice of citizenship. *Canadian Journal of Community Mental Health, 23*(2), 39–50.

Morrow, M. (2007). Women's voices matter: Creating women-centred mental health policy. In M. Morrow, O. Hankivsky, & C. Varcoe (Eds.), *Women's health in Canada: Critical perspectives on theory and policy* (pp. 355–379). Toronto, ON: University of Toronto Press.

Mulvale, G., Abelson, J., & Goering, P. (2007). Mental health service delivery in Canada: How do policy legacies shape prospects for reform? *Health Economics, Policy, and Law, 2,* 363–389. doi:10.1017/S1744133107004318

Mulvale, G., & Bartram, M. (2009). Recovery in the Canadian context: Feedback on the framework for mental health strategy development. *Canadian Journal of Community Mental Health, 28*(2), 7–15.

Nelson, G. (2010). Housing for people with serious mental illness: Approaches, evidence, and transformative change. *Journal of Sociology and Social Welfare, 37,* 123–146.

Nelson, G., & Grant, J. (2011). Consumer participation in mental health services. In E.R. Vingilis & S.A. State (Eds.), *Applied research and evaluation in community mental health services* (pp. 129–145). Montreal, QC, and Kingston, ON: McGill-Queen's University Press.

Nelson, G., Lord, J., & Ochocka, J. (2001) *Shifting the paradigm in community mental health: Towards empowerment and community*. Toronto, ON: University of Toronto Press.

Nelson, G., Potasznik, H., & Bennett, E.M. (1983). Primary prevention: Another perspective. *Canadian Journal of Community Mental Health, 2*(1), 3–12.

Nelson, G., Prilleltensky, I., & Hasford, J. (2009). Prevention and mental health promotion in the community. In P. Firestone & D. Dozois (Eds.), *Abnormal psychology: Perspectives* (4th ed., pp. 440–457). Scarborough, ON: Prentice-Hall.

Nelson, G., Prilleltensky, I., Laurendeau, M.-C., & Powell, B. (1996). The prevention of mental health problems in Canada: A survey of provincial policies, structures, and programs. *Canadian Psychology, 37,* 161–172.

Nelson, G., Westhues, A., & MacLeod, J. (2003). A meta-analysis of longitudinal research on preschool prevention programs for children. *Prevention and Treatment, 6*(December). Retrieved from http://journals.apa.org/prevention/volume6/toc-dec18-03.html.

Niles, E., & Ross, K. (1992). Putting policy in practice: Mental health in New Brunswick. *Canada's Mental Health, 40*(1), 15–19.

References Ontario Ministry of Health and Long-term Care. (2004). Making a difference: Ontario's Community Mental Health Evaluation Initiative. Toronto, ON: Centre for Addiction and Mental Health, Canadian Mental Health Association / Ontario Division, Ontario Mental Health Foundation, and Ontario Ministry of Health and Long-term Care. Retrieved from http://www.ontario.cmha.ca/policy_and_research.asp?cID=7655

Piat, M., & Sabetti, J. (2009). The development of a recovery-oriented mental health system in Canada: What the experience of commonwealth countries tells us. *Canadian Journal of Community Mental Health, 28*(2), 17–33.

Pistrang, N., Barker, C., & Humphreys, K. (2010). The contribution of mutual help groups for health health problems to psychological well-being: A systematic review. In L.D. Brown & S. Wituk (Eds.), *Mental health self-help: Consumer and family initiatives* (pp. 61–85). New York, NY: Springer.

Pomeroy, E., Trainor, J., & Pape, B. (2002). Citizens shaping policy: The Canadian Mental Health Association's framework for support project. *Canadian Psychology, 43*, 11–20.

Ralph, R.O., & Corrigan, P.W. (Eds.). (2005). *Recovery in mental illness: Broadening our understanding of wellness.* Washington, DC: American Psychological Association.

Reaume, G. (2000). *Remembrance of patients past: Patient life at the Toronto Hospital for the Insane, 1870–1940.* Oxford, UK: Oxford University Press.

Redko, C., Durbin, J., Wasylenki, D., & Krupa, T. (2004). Participant perspectives on satisfaction with Assertive Community Treatment. *Psychiatric Rehabilitation Journal, 27*(3), 283–286.

Reville, D. (2005). Mental health reform: Still saying the same thing after all these years. *Canadian Public Policy, 31*, S65–68, Special Electronic Supplement on Mental Health Reform for the 21st Century. Retrieved from http://economics.ca/cpp/en/special2005.php

Rochefort, D.A. (1992). More lessons, of a different kind: Canadian mental health policy in comparative perspective. *Hospital and Community Psychiatry, 43*, 1083–1090.

Rochefort, D.A. (1993). *From poorhouses to homelessness: Policy analysis and mental health care.* Westport, CT: Auburn House.

Salyers, M.P., & Tsemberis, S. (2007). ACT and recovery: Integrating evidence-based practice and recovery orientation on Assertive Community Treatment teams. *Community Mental Health Journal, 43*, 619–641. doi: 10.1007/s10597-007-9088-5

Scheyett, A.M., & McCarthy, E. (2006). Women and men with mental illnesses: Voicing differing service needs. *Affilia: Journal of Women and Social Work, 21*, 407–418.

Schmidt, G. (2000). Barriers to recovery in a First Nations community. *Canadian Journal of Community Mental Health, 19*(2), 75–87.

Schofield, W. (1964). *Psychotherapy: The purchase of friendship.* Englewood Cliffs, NJ: Prentice-Hall.

Scull, A.T. (1977) *Decarceration: Community treatment and the deviant—A radical view.* Englewood Cliffs, NJ: Prentice-Hall.

Sealy, P., & Whitehead, P.C. (2004). Forty years of deinstitutionalization of psychiatric services in Canada: An empirical assessment. *Canadian Journal of Psychiatry, 49*, 249–257.

Shera, W., Aviram, U., Healy, B., & Ramon, S. (2002). Mental health system reform: A multi-country comparison. *Social Work in Health Care, 35*(1/2), 547–575.

Simich, L., Maiter, S., Moorlag, E., & Ochocka, J. (2009). Taking culture seriously: Ethnolinguistic community perspectives on mental health. *Psychiatric Rehabilitation Journal, 32*, 208–214. doi: 10.2975/32.3.2009.208.214

Simmons, H.G. (1990). *Unbalanced: Mental health policy in Ontario, 1930–1989.* Toronto, ON: Wall and Thompson.

Solomon, P. (2004). Peer support / peer provided services: Underlying processes, benefits, and critical ingredients. *Psychiatric Rehabilitation Journal, 27*, 392–401.

Spindel, P. (2000). Polar opposites: Empowerment philosophy and Assertive Community Treatment (ACT). *Ethical Human Sciences and Services: An International Journal of Critical Inquiry, 2*, 93–100.

Statistics Canada. (2005). Canadian statistics—Tables by subject: Population and demography. Retrieved from http://www12.statcan.gc.ca/census-recensement/index-eng.cfm

Stein, L.I., & Test, M.A. (1980). Alternative to mental hospital treatment: I. Conceptual model, treatment program, and clinical evaluation. *Archives of General Psychiatry, 37*, 392–397.

Swindle, R., Heller, K., Pescosolido, B., & Kikuzawa, S. (2000). Responses to nervous breakdowns in American over a 40-year period: Mental health policy implications. *American Psychologist, 55*, 740–749.

Sylvestre, J., George, L., Aubry, T., Nelson, G., & Trainor, J. (2007). Strengthening Ontario's system for housing for people with serious mental illness. *Canadian Journal of Community Mental Health, 26*(1), 79–95.

Szasz, T.S. (1961). *The myth of mental illness: Foundations of a theory of personal conduct.* New York, NY: Dell.

Townsend, E. (1998). *Good intentions overruled: A critique of empowerment in the routine organization of mental health services.* Toronto, ON: University of Toronto Press.

Trainor, J., Pape, B., & Pomeroy, E. (1997). Critical challenges for mental health policy. *Canadian Review of Social Policy, 39*, 55–63.

Trainor, J., Pomeroy, E., & Pape, B. (Eds.). (1999). *Building a framework for support: A community development approach to mental health policy.* Toronto, ON: Canadian Mental Health Association / National Office.

Trainor, J., Shepherd, M., Boydell, K. M., Leff, A., & Crawford, E. (1997). Beyond the service paradigm: The impact and implications of consumer/survivor initiatives. *Psychiatric Rehabilitation Journal, 21*, 132–140.

Trainor, J., & Tremblay, J. (1992). Consumer/survivor businesses in Ontario: Challenging the rehabilitation model. *Canadian Journal of Community Mental Health, 11*(2), 65–71.

Tsemberis, S., & Eisenberg, R.F. (2000). Pathways to housing: Supported housing for street-dwelling homeless individuals with psychiatric disabilities. *Psychiatric Services, 51*, 487–493.

Vincent, N., Walker, J.R., & Katz, A. (2008). Self-administered treatments in primary care. In P.L. Watkins & G.L. Clum (Eds.), *Handbook of self-help therapies* (pp. 387–417). New York, NY: Taylor and Francis Group.

References Wasylenki, D., Goering, P., & MacNaughton, E. (1994). Planning mental health services: Background and key issues. In L.L. Bachrach, P. Goering, & D. Wasylenki (Eds.), *Mental health care in Canada* (pp. 21–29). San Francisco, CA: Jossey-Bass.

Weitz, D. (1984). "On Our Own": A self-help model. In D.P. Lumsden (Ed.), *Community mental health action: Primary prevention programming in Canada* (pp. 312–320). Ottawa, ON: Canadian Public Health Association.

Wilton, R. (2004). Putting policy into practice? Poverty and people with serious mental illness. *Social Science and Medicine, 58*, 25–39. doi:10.1016/S0277-9536(03)00148-5

Keeping Kids Safe in Custody

13

Judy Finlay

The Youth Justice Policy Context

In Canada, the institutional culture of youth justice is shaped by federal youth justice legislation, the provincial youth justice policy framework, and institutional ideology and practice. The Youth Criminal Justice Act (YCJA), introduced on April 1, 2003, emphasizes the following: the rehabilitation of youth and their reintegration into society; fair and proportionate accountability that is consistent with the greater dependency and reduced level of developmental maturity of young people; and the youth justice system as an entity separate and apart from the adult correctional system.

For more than a century, human rights have been foundational to Canadian culture and values (Denov, 2004). The YCJA respects the rights and freedoms of young people, including those set out in the UN Convention on the Rights of Children (UNCRC) and the Canadian Charter of Rights and Freedoms (the Charter). These covenants accept the need to protect children and youth; to treat them separately and differently from adults in the criminal justice system; to provide rehabilitation, not repression and deterrence, when offering judicial intervention with young people; and to consider the best interests of the child to be a guiding principle (Hamilton & Harvey, 2004; Leblanc, 2002). Furthermore, the YCJA is predicated on a narrower, more focused role for the justice system, one that recognizes the role of social, mental health, and educational services in addressing the root causes of youth crime and that identifies and prevents antisocial behaviour patterns (Bala, 2005). Less reliance on custodial sentences and the increased use of extrajudicial community alternatives requires the application of professional judgment on the part of police, probation officers, court social workers, and judges as well as the knowledge on the part of these individuals to access services on behalf of these young people. Flexibility is offered to the provinces in making policy and resource decisions. Thus, the availability of and access to the required resources to effectively fulfill the goals, requirements, and aspirations of the act ultimately depend on provincial decisions. Indeed, without the influx of resources, meeting the requirements of the act is not feasible.

In Ontario, a major influence on the youth justice system is that since 2003, young persons in conflict with the law who are sixteen or seventeen years of age have been the responsibility of the Ministry of Child and Youth Services; in other words, they were transferred that year out of the ministry that manages the adult correctional system. This strengthened the focus on the rehabilitative needs of youth in a manner that is developmentally appropriate. Furthermore, the legislative framework for the Child and Youth Services Ministry is the Child and Family Services Act (CFSA), which is responsible for child protection and children's mental health services in Ontario. Incarcerated youth should therefore be able to readily access services provided under the CFSA. However, the existing service system in that ministry is complicated, multifaceted, and fragmented, which makes it very difficult for service providers such as police, probation officers, court mental health workers, and families to navigate the system to access the required services (Finlay, 2004).

Public opinion has a strong influence on the laws and policies at the national, provincial and local levels. The level of anti-youth sentiment is currently more intense, as witnessed by the recent political campaigning during the 2011 federal election in Canada. Political parties converged on the need to address youth crime, albeit with divergent "get tough" strategies. Focus was directed at physical aggression and violence as the most socially feared and costly forms of youth crime. Changes to legislation and policy will be outcomes of this public debate.

Peer Violence among Incarcerated Youth

It is postulated that the nature and incidence of peer violence among incarcerated youth is a measurable outcome of the ideology, structure, and operations at the institutional level, which in turn reflects the legislation that regulates these (Levesque, 1996). A security-oriented organizational ideology emphasizes obedience, respect for authority, and submission to external controls (Feld, 1981). By contrast, vocational and educational goals, therapeutic models of programming, pro-social skill development, and staff/youth relationships are paramount in a rehabilitation-oriented organizational ideology (Ellis, 1997; Lescheid, Cunningham, & Mazaheri, 1997; Matthews & Pitts, 1998; Nurse, 2001). Organizational ideology in youth justice institutions exists on a continuum from security to rehabilitation.

Recent studies in Ontario have gained information from youth, offering an analysis of bullying and peer violence that goes beyond incidence, definition, and categorization of behaviour (Finlay, 2006). These studies confirm the existence of a peer subculture within custodial settings. Peer norms, roles, and social rankings organize and sustain the hierarchical arrangements that are necessary in this culture (Ireland, 1999a, 2000, 2001, 2002a, b, c, e; Roland & Idsoe, 2001). The ability to survive and adapt depends to a large extent on the youths' capacity to develop and maintain status (Connell & Farrington, 1996). Ireland (1999a) reports that power and dominance are central to peer relationships. In this context, peer cultural norms promote victimization to gain social acceptance and status (Schwarzwald & Koslowsky, 1999). Aggression is often in retaliation for challenges to reputation, in an effort to enhance status or to gain goods and services (Ellis, 1997, 1999a, 2002a; McCorkle, 1992; Palmer & Farmer, 2002). Aggression and bullying are normalized, and this forces the ranking of bullies and victims. Types of violence include the following: name calling; horseplay; the use of intimidation, coercion, or force to take away possessions such as food and clothing; the use of telephone and so on; forcing youth to "soldier," which involves one youth (the bully) demanding that another youth (the weaker) assault a third youth who is stronger; acts of degradation; physical assault; stabbings and shows of weapons; and initiations.

In my role as the Child Advocate in Ontario, I was challenged by the "top dogs" or bullies in secure youth justice settings to "do something about peer violence." These youth understood the prevalence and risks inherent in violence in institutions and the danger that it posed for each of them. They stated that it was safer on the streets than in youth justice institutions because at least there "you can get away." This led to a series of interventions by the Office of Child and Family Services Advocacy that influenced the introduction of policy across the youth justice system in Ontario related to zero tolerance for peer aggression and the introduction of programming which reinforced this policy.

The Keeping Kids Safe Study

The impact of a security- versus a rehabilitative-oriented institutional environment on youths' sense of safety related to peer-on-peer aggression was examined in a cross-Canada study called Keeping Kids Safe (KKS). The KKS study built on the report of the Youth Partners Project (YPP), a research project undertaken by the Canadian Council of Provincial Child and Youth Advocates (CCPCYA) that was released in 2005 (Finlay & Snow, 2005). The YPP report documented the experiences of young people residing in secure custody facilities in seven Canadian provinces. Provincial advocates and/or ombudspersons interviewed 148 youth. As the interview was designed to give voice to youth in secure custody facilities, the use of advocates/ombudspersons was intended to create a sense of security and an environment in which youth participants would feel safe to share and elaborate on their own experiences. Furthermore, the interview was designed to provide insight into youth perceptions on how the care and programming in various secure custody facilities addressed their basic and psychosocial needs. This information was expected to inform the development of national "standards of care" that would comply with the requirements of the UN Convention on the

The Keeping Kids Safe Study

Rights of the Child. Thus, data were collected on seven care domains: basic care, caring for young people by staff, rights of young people, programming, behaviour management, peer violence, and community and family. Note that both the YPP report and the KKS study speak solely to the experiences of males, who are the youth predominantly served in youth justice institutions in Canada.

A window into the culture of the institutional environment can be found in the voices and language of the young people. The importance of understanding and respecting the lived experiences of young people as consumers of service cannot be overstated (Covell & Howe, 2009; Johnson, 1999; Van Manen, 1997). This is particularly crucial to youth incarcerated in youth justice institutions, for these youth are more vulnerable to the global influences of political will and public opinion, and they face harsher consequences when developmental considerations are brushed aside in favour of retributive justice. How circumstances, incidents, and events are interpreted by youth in custody influences the meanings they attach to their experience as well as their behavioural responses (Peterson-Badali & Koegl, 2002). Furthermore, owing to their youth status, they are equipped with fewer tools to alleviate, intervene in, or compensate for this harsh treatment. Self-reports are often the primary sources of information for understanding the experiences of incarcerated youth. This method is considered more reliable and valid than staff or peer reports or documentation (Connell & Farrington, 1996; Davidson-Arad, 2005; Dyson, Power, & Wozniak, 1997; Elliott, Huisinga, & Morse, 1997; Finlay, 2006; Ireland, 1999a, b, 2002a, b, d; Sprott & Doob, 2005). The YPP and the KKS studies both considered youth to be "the experts of their lived experience," and their voices and participation are reflected throughout each report.

Ninety-three youth participants who were residing in four secure custody facilities in Canada provided valuable insight into their perceptions and experiences. Analysis of this information provided the basis for the KKS study. Two sets of sites were designated—*Safer* and *Less Safe*—based on institutional safety as perceived by the youths. A variation in culture across the two institutional types was evident through the descriptions of peer harassment and aggression and the concomitant coping strategies used by youth to manage the milieu. Further analysis of the data according to the youths' involvement in the child welfare and youth justice systems was undertaken.

The KKS study demonstrates that the interaction between the youths and the institutional environment acts to promote or deter safety among incarcerated youth. The peer subculture that produces a spectrum of violence (Finlay, 2006) is dependent both on the extra-custody attributes of youth that affect the youth's attitudes, beliefs, and behaviours, and on the critical influence of institutional attributes such as physical structure, program resources, staff/youth interactions, and practices of social control. The interaction between these importation factors and the institutional environment influences perceptions of safety among incarcerated youth. For example, a predisposition that includes child maltreatment and exposure to domestic violence led to the development of coping strategies that ameliorated or managed the impact of peer aggression. Importantly, the protective features of the institutional environment and the role played by staff mediated the prevalence and impact of peer aggression.

This chapter describes some of the key findings that emerged from the study and discusses their implications for institutional practice, research, and policy development in the field of youth justice.

Analysis

Less Safe and Safer Institutions

To understand the relationship between youths' perceptions of safety in youth justice institutions and their reported experiences of peer harassment and aggression within those four secure custody institutions, *less safe* and *safer* institutions were operationalized as follows. Perceptions of safety were measured by two dichotomous variables (yes/no) indicating youths' feelings of safety. Those variables were "feeling safe" and "fear of being hurt." The youths' experiences of violence were measured by thirteen dichotomous variables (yes/no) that identified the youths' exposure directly and indirectly to peer aggression. These variables included sexual harassment or assault; verbal harassment based on sexual orientation, culture, race, or special needs; meals taken by the threat of force; canteen (items such as chocolate bars) taken by the threat of force; fighting witnessed; fighting experienced; injuries sustained from fighting; group-on-one violence; threatened by a weapon; and unwritten rules promoting a prison subculture. Youths residing in youth justice institutions were reticent to disclose their own victimization by peers owing to fear of retribution or reprisals. Youths may be embarrassed by this type of disclosure owing to the humiliating nature of the violence and the circumstances surrounding the incidents (Finlay, 2006). Youths, however, will openly discuss incidents of harassment and direct aggression they have *witnessed* within the institution. Youths will sometimes openly describe episodes of peer aggression and violence in which they were the perpetrator. This is why information about their indirect as well as direct experiences of peer violence was sought from youth participants.

A cross-province comparative analysis was conducted among the four sites identified as provinces C, D, F, and G. Each institution was affiliated with one of these four provinces. The fifteen variables related to the perceptions and experiences of safety by youth participants in each of the four institutions are illustrated in Table 13.1.

Analysis

Table 13.1 Youth Perception and Experience of Safety in the Institutional Environment

Institution	C (#) %	D (#) %	F (#) %	G (#) %	Mean Score %
Perception of Safety (yes/no)					
1 Feel safe (yes)	(15) 60.0	(26) 100.0	(21) 84.0	(15) 93.7	84.4
2 Fear of being hurt (yes)	(10) 40.0	(4) 14.6	(4) 17.4	(2) 12.5	21.1
Experience/Witness (yes/no)					
3 Sexual harassment (yes)	(15) 60.0	(3) 12.0	(10) 40.0	(2)12.5	31.1
Verbal Harassment:					
4 Sexual orientation (yes)	(20) 80.0	(15) 60.0	(17) 68.0	(8) 47.1	63.8
5 Culture (yes)	(10) 40.0	(7) 30.4	(7)28.0	(3) 17.6	29.0
6 Race (yes)	(18) 72.0	(16) 61.5	(15) 60.0	(8) 47.1	60.2
7 Special needs (yes)	(16) 64.0	(8) 32.0	(12) 48.0	(5) 29.4	43.4
8 Canteen items taken (yes)	(14) 56.0	(15) 62.5	(15) 60.9	(6) 35.3	53.5
9 Meals taken (yes)	(9) 36.0	(6) 25.0	(6) 24.0	(3) 17.6	25.7
10 Fighting witness (yes)	(19) 76.0	(21) 91.3	(21) 84.0	(15) 88.2	84.9
11 Fighting experienced (yes)	(15) 60.0	(11) 44.0	(17) 68.0	(13) 76.5	62.1
12 Injuries (yes)	(14) 58.3	(10) 40.0	(18) 78.3	(12) 70.6	61.8
13 Group violence (yes)	(12) 48.0	(3) 13.0	(10) 40.0	(5) 29.4	32.6
14 Weapons (yes)	(12) 48.0	(5) 20.8	(15) 60.0	(10) 58.8	46.9
15 Unwritten rules (yes)	(25)100.0	(17) 68.0	(16) 64.0	(10) 58.8	72.7

1. n's = C (25), D (26), F (25), G (16)
2. n's = C (25), D (26), F (23), G (16)
3. n's = C (25), D (25), F (25), G (16)
4. n's = C (25), D (25), F (25), G (17)
5. n's = C (25), D (23), F (25), G (17)
6. n's = C (25), D (26), F (25), G (17)
7. n's = C (25), D (25), F (25), G (17)
8. n's = C (25), D (24), F (25), G (17)
9. n's = C (25), D (24), F (25), G (17)
10. n's = C (25), D (23), F (25), G (17)
11. n's = C (25), D (25), F (25), G (17)
12. n's = C (24), D (25), F (23), G (17)
13. n's = C (25), D (23), F (25), G (17)
14. n's = C (25), D (24), F (25), G (17)
15. n's = C (25), D (25), F (25), G (17)

The four institutions were subdivided and grouped according to feelings of safety, with institutions C and F and institutions D and G clustering with similar results. When institutions C and F were grouped, they scored above the mean score on fourteen variables. This was in contrast to institutions D and G, which, when grouped, scored above the mean score on only two variables, "feeling safe" and "witnessing fighting" (Table 13.2). Having linked youth perceptions of safety (feeling safe) with scores related to direct or indirect experiences of peer aggression (Table 13.2), the study identified institutions by type: institutions C and F were categorized as *less safe* and institutions D and G were categorized as *safer*. These two distinctive groupings were utilized to compare and contrast youth participants' responses according to their perceptions and experiences of safety. Further analysis validated the distinction between these two groups. There is a significant association between institution type (*less safe* or *safer*) and youths' feelings of safety.

Analysis

Table 13.2 Youth Perception of Safety and Experience of Peer Aggression According to the Type of Institution

	Less Safe	Safer			
	C & F Mean Score (#) %	D & G Mean Score (#) %	Total Mean Score %	Score Above Mean C & F	Score Above Mean D & G
Perception of Safety (yes/no)					
Feel safe (yes)	(36) 72.0	(41) 96.9	84.4		+
Fear of being hurt (yes)	(14) 28.7	(6) 14.0	21.1	+	
Experience/Witness (yes/no)					
Sexual harassment (yes)	(25) 50.0	(5) 12.3	31.1	+	
Verbal Harassment:					
Sexual Orientation (yes)	(37) 74.0	(23) 53.6	63.8	+	
Culture (yes)	(17) 34.0	(10) 24.0	29.0	+	
Race (yes)	(33) 66.0	(24) 54.3	60.2	+	
Special Needs (yes)	(28) 56.0	(13) 30.7	43.4	+	
Canteen items taken (yes)	(29) 58.0	(21) 48.9	53.5	+	
Meals taken (yes)	(15) 30.0	(9) 21.3	25.7	+	
Fighting witness (yes)	(40) 80.0	(36) 89.8	84.9		+
Fighting experienced (yes)	(32) 64.0	(24) 60.3	62.1	+	
Injuries (yes)	(32) 68.3	(22) 55.3	61.8	+	
Group violence (yes)	(22) 44.0	(8) 21.2	32.6	+	
Weapons (yes)	(27) 54.0	(15) 39.8	46.9	+	
Unwritten rules (yes)	(41) 82.0	(27) 63.4	72.7	+	

Youth Experience of Peer Violence

Youth who did not feel safe had their perceptions reinforced by their experiences of peer aggression within the institution. Sexual harassment or assault, threatening with a weapon, group-on-one fighting, and harassment based on special needs were the most serious forms of aggression based on their level of dangerousness or deleterious impact on the victim (Finlay, 2006). There was a significant association between these forms of aggression (i.e., sexual harassment/assault, threatened by a weapon, group-on-one fighting, harassment based on special needs) and the type of institution. There was more evidence of these extreme forms of peer aggression in the *less safe* institutions than in the *safer* institutions.

The primary objective of the qualitative analysis in the KKS study was to develop a deeper understanding of the experiences and meanings of peer aggression among incarcerated youths in youth justice institutions.

Participants in the study were grouped by two aspects of peer aggression: participants' perceptions of safety within the institutional environment (*safer* and *less safe*) and reported evidence of peer harassment and aggression by participants. In the preliminary analysis of the data, two overarching themes emerged: coping strategies used by youth to mediate the impact of peer aggression, and the role of staff in protecting youth.

Findings

Perceptions of Safety and Experiences of Peer Violence

The youth from sites perceived as *less safe* and *safer* had differing perceptions of safety and experience of peer violence within the institutions. This was illustrated through their descriptions of peer aggression, strategies for coping with that aggression, impressions of the role played by staff in protecting youth, and youth engagement by staff.

Youth participants in the *less safe* institutions were faced with the trauma of actual victimization, coupled with the stress of potential victimization. This undoubtedly had a deleterious effect on their well-being; this was indicated in their expressions of anxiety and fear. In contrast, proportionately more participants in the *safer* institutions expressed fewer fears of being hurt and a greater sense of safety. Furthermore, they offered reassurances of their safety and attributed this to proactive intervention by staff.

Youth in *less safe* institutions felt that violence was inevitable; there was no protection from violence, and they discussed escape. They worried about their personal safety and were afraid to report their fears to staff or peers as it would violate the "code" or show weakness that would attract victimization. In contrast, youth in *safer* institutions felt safe, which they attributed to staff vigilance and ability to protect them. Furthermore, youth in *less safe* institutions reported direct experience with and witnessing of peer aggression such as fights, threatening with a weapon, serious injuries, and group violence. They offered graphic examples. They spoke of seeking opportunities to assault others at times and in locations that prevented them from being detected. Getting caught carried high costs in terms of institutional sanctions such as segregation from peers or criminal charges. Youth in *safer* institutions rarely referred to fights and were more concerned about indirect violence such as "punking off" (youth taking possessions from other youth through intimidation, coercion, and force). They sought staff intervention to remedy this aggression.

With regard to the victimization of peers, youth in *less safe* institutions ridiculed or shifted responsibility for the violence to the victim. Some respondents declared that victims brought the abuse on themselves. Youth in the *safer* institutions responded with empathy and, once again, relied on staff intervention to neutralize the interaction and set boundaries.

Findings

Youths report fear of peer aggression whether they have experienced violence directly, witnessed peer aggression in the institution, or perceived violence to be a possibility owing to an alleged history of violence in that institution. Two alternative strategies are used by youth to address this fear and protect themselves. One approach is to fight back; the other is to avoid violence. Avoiding peer aggression was achieved by withdrawing from the group, presenting as tough, or leaving the environment. Youths in the *less safe* institutions described aggression directed at peers and staff; demonstrated their "tough guy" bravado; brandished weapons; and planned escapes. These youth appeared anxious and hypervigilant. Youth in the *safer* institutions presented as getting "tough" but rarely acted on this in terms of actual fighting. These youths spoke of going to their room as a self-imposed isolation from the group, or they kept to themselves to avoid altercations. They also described "numbing out" as an internalizing avoidant coping strategy (McCorkle, 1992; Ireland, 2002a). Both groups adhered to the unwritten rule or informal institutional code "no ratting." Violation of this rule led to being ostracized or victimized.

Youths in the *less safe* institutions felt that the responsibility for their own personal safety rested with them. They could not rely on staff intervention or protection. In contrast, youths in the *safer* institutions sought staff out for protection and alerted them to potentially dangerous situations. They had confidence in the staff's ability to protect them and felt that it was their role and duty. Youth in *less safe* institutions recommended improved staff supervision, whereas youth respondents in the *safer* institutions felt that staff intervened proactively and were able to predict potential violence by observing group dynamics.

Youth in the *less safe* institutions described the escalating sequence of consequences for violence or poor behaviour. Staff appeared to be anxious to escalate interventions for relatively minor infractions or to "teach a lesson." They spoke of extreme examples of the use of intrusive measures to manage and contain youth such as pepper spray, painful restraints, the use of the emergency team, and a unit lockdown. They appeared anxious about these interventions. These youth also did not resist compliance to the rules of custody etiquette (conventional rules for social behaviour within the institution). These rules related to a rigid code of behaviour that was managed through clear lines of authority between staff and youth. There was peer pressure to conform to these rules to maintain an equilibrium within the peer culture. At the same time, these youth reported manipulative means to get positive staff attention and rewards. This demonstrates overt conformity and covert deviance (Feld, 1981).

Youth in *safer* institutions, on the other hand, described less serious consequences for poor behaviour such as time-out in their room or a loss of points. They understood the routines involved in escalating an intervention and were clear on the expectations when this occurred. Youth were matter-of-fact in their descriptions of these events and circumstances. Charging as a practice to deter peer violence was acknowledged as effective. Rules for custody etiquette related to respect for others, rules of social discourse, and social conformity. Cooperation was encouraged and rewards were offered for compliance.

Youth in *safer* institutions engaged in a broad range of recreational, sports, and program activities. These activities included organized group activities such as sports and game tournaments as well as informal opportunities for staff to engage youths in dialogue such as walks, outings, and BBQs. There was no mention of watching television. Youths described staff as active and enthusiastic and valued their participation. Youths were offered rewards and incentives to encourage their interest and involvement. The most common activities for youths in *less safe* institutions were indoor games that were largely unorganized, such as television, cards, and board games.

In the *safer* institutions, youths described relationships with staff that were participatory, open, and caring. Youth received assistance and advice in their day-to-day activities and were able to negotiate the consequences of some behaviour by taking responsibility for it. This was useful in the development of skills such as problem solving and conflict resolution. They were able to be open with staff as they had relationships built on trust, respect, and mutuality. They identified staff as role models whom they would talk to about their concerns, including peer violence.

Youth in *less safe* institutions also valued staff who listened and talked to kids. They viewed staff relationships with some ambivalence and felt that relationships were not necessarily built on a principle of quid pro quo. Youth participants in both *less safe* and *safer* institutional settings spoke about the propensity for rigidity in the assignment of levels, points, and consequences by staff. (Points were assigned contingent on good behaviour, adherence to rules, or the completion of chores. The accumulation of points allowed youth to move up the level system. There were more and more privileges and opportunities for independent recreational activities of choice as youths progressed from level to level.) Some staff were viewed as harsh, authoritarian, and judgmental and as imposing overly regimented rules in a threatening manner. Youths described this as the misuse of power and control. Overall, youth participants described their perceptions of safety, their experiences of peer aggression strategies, factors that contributed to their protection, and coping strategies they used to mediate the aggression. When comparing the two sets of institutions, youth participants described their experiences differently. Table 13.1 illustrates these differences.

Kids from the Child Welfare System

Half of the youth participants in this study (51.1 percent) reported a history of involvement in the child welfare system. There was a significant association between involvement in the child welfare system and the type of institution. Youth participants who had a history in the child welfare system were more likely to report being in *less safe* institutions at the time of the interview. Furthermore, if youth participants had ever been placed in out-of-home child welfare care, they were more likely to report being in a *less safe* institution ($x^2[1] = 3.82$, $p < .045$).

In most cases, entry into the child welfare system presupposes some form of maltreatment. Therefore, in all likelihood, the youth participants in this study with child welfare involvement had a history of child maltreatment that was reported and investigated and that resulted in child welfare intervention services. Youth participants in this study with no reported history of child welfare involvement may, nonetheless, have a background of child maltreatment that went unreported. There are direct links between both child maltreatment and exposure to domestic violence and later conflict problems, which include some form of recurrent aggression and in some cases perpetration of violence (Herrenkohl, Herrenkohl, Sousa, Tajima, & Moylan, 2008). These risk factors generate pathways into the youth justice system (Sprague & Walker, 2000).

Youth participants who had a history of maltreatment had an expectation of retraumatization and were therefore anxious and hypervigilant in the environment. They had a propensity to interpret the behaviour of peers and staff as victimizing. They were reactive to the potential hot spots in the environment and described an acclimatization process following admission to the institution that was thoughtful and calculated. Youths in both the *less safe* and *safer* institutions with a history of child welfare involvement were disturbed by the nature and frequency of sexual harassment and assaults. Youths in *less safe* institutions either reported it to staff or remained silent but vigilant. Both these response patterns represent post-traumatic stress reactions of traumatized children (Grogan-Kaylor et al., 2008; Van der Kolk, McFarlane, & Weisaeth, 1996). Youths in the *safer* institutions sought staff intervention to support themselves or the victims. Youth participants with a history of maltreatment were more likely to disclose incidents or fears of sexual harassment or assault to the interviewer.

Common among traumatized youth is the reliving of the threat of trauma, the failure to feel protected, or the sense of helplessness (Van der Kolk et al., 1996). In the *less safe* institutions, in anticipation of revictimization, youth participants were defiantly provocative with staff, setting up similar dynamics as in the relationship with the abusive parent (Stone, 2002). Their provocative behaviour often resulted in alienation or retaliation from peers. In some instances they described serious injuries they, or others, sustained in these altercations. Their key coping strategy was avoidance, which was evident in their avoidant ambivalent relationship with staff. They aspired to closeness, as illustrated in their use of words "attached," "parent," or "mom," but they had difficulty approaching staff for support owing to their anxious hypervigilance. They reported relying on staff for guidance and direction.

Findings In both *less safe* and *safer* institutions, these child-welfare-involved youth were insightful, self-reflective, and introspective. They viewed the relational aspects of the institutional environment as the most important and the most challenging. More often, youth residing in *safer* institutions were offered the opportunity to confront effectively the challenging aspects of relationships with adults necessary for the building of trust. They felt safe seeking out staff guidance, and they established respectful, collaborative interactions.

Finally, youth across institution types with involvement in the child welfare system—and therefore, presumably, with a history of child maltreatment—were more likely to present with more extreme behaviours, such as self-protective strategies that were harassing or violent toward their peers, in an effort to mediate the impact of the institutional environment (McGhee & Waterhouse, 2007).

Institutionalization

Youths not involved in child welfare, who had more experience in the youth justice system as defined by the number of placements, were circumspect and prosaic in their responses. They expressed a resignation to institutional realities and a sense of powerlessness to change the inevitable risks involved. They were adverse to meaningful relationships with staff or peers and used avoidance strategies to demonstrate this ambivalence. Their conformity to the rules and regimen of the institution was at times self-serving and manipulative. Their adherence to the oppressive peer subculture and inmate code resulted in exploitation and aggressive behaviours. These youth participants, for the most part, had become institutionalized. Youth participants with no child welfare involvement fared better in the active, rehabilitative environments that were *safer*. However, their doubts persisted regarding the institution's ability to keep them safe and also regarding their relationships with staff. Indeed, it was these youths who referred to the staff as "guards." This was a clear indication that they had been institutionalized.

Finally, youth participants in *safer* institutions who had more experience in the youth justice system were more likely to feel safer because they appeared to be more familiar with the environment and the inherent risks. They felt that staff vigilance was important in promoting the safety of youths; they also felt that laying charges was an important deterrent to peer aggression. The accruing of more charges would activate anxiety among these youths owing to their history of frequent incarcerations. They were also more fearful of the powerful group dynamics. Their substantive experience in youth justice settings may account for this fear, for it meant they had greater knowledge and understanding of the centrality of these dynamics to the peer subculture. They appeared more acclimatized to the realities of the institution. Thus their previous history in the youth justice system—a history they had imported into the institution—did indeed influence their understanding of the milieu as well as the coping strategies they used to

Findings

Table 13.3 Comparative Analysis of Less Safe and Safer Institutions

Less Safe	Safer
Youth Experience of Peer Harassment and Aggression	
• evidence of extreme forms of peer aggression (group-on-one fights, threatening with a weapon, sexual assault/harassment, harassment based on special needs) • serious injuries sustained as a result of fighting • routine exposure to range of peer aggression reinforced it as part of an accepted institutional lifestyle • oppositional peer culture	• punking off is a primary form of peer aggression • evidence of threatening, coercion. and harassment • witnessing of fights reported • minimal evidence of injuries • status gained through peer subculture • protective element to peer interactions
Coping Strategies	
• avoidant strategies for self-protection similar to inmate code • avoid staff involvement • use of externalizing, aggressive strategies that are offensive and retaliatory as the primary means of self-protection • minimization through shifting responsibility or blaming the victim • AWOL as a means to escape the environment • youth conformity to custodial codes and rules • deviant methods utilized by youth to gain status and manipulate staff	• use of internalizing avoidant strategies for self-protection that are self-imposed • use of defensive tough guy bravado for self-protection • compliance to "no ratting" code • turn to staff for protection of self or others as necessary • conformed to social norms as code of behaviour • compliance to staff demands • assist peers
Role of Staff in Protecting Youth	
• inability to rely on staff for intervention in unsafe circumstances • staff turned a blind eye to forms of harassment and aggression	• staff intervene proactively to protect youth
Staff Intervention	
• the escalation of interventions by staff to the use of more intrusive measures for minor infractions or to "teach a lesson" • the overuse of intrusive measures for behavioural management, security, and social control • rigidity in the application of rules and consequences by staff	• use of rewards and incentives • pro-social role modelling • clarity in rules and expectations • escalation of intervention to the use of intrusive measures when there was a risk of injury to self or others
Program Features	
• recreational, sports and program activities are unorganized and do not require staff–youth interaction	• broad range of meaningful recreational and program activities that are organized and engage youth as active participants
Relational Features of Staff	
• ambivalent staff/youth relationships • staff viewed by youth as indifferent, unhelpful, and untrustworthy • some staff viewed as authoritarian	• formal, collaborative relationships with staff • staff viewed as caring, open, enthusiastic and trustworthy • staff promote insight, self-awareness, empathy and problem-solving

manage peer aggression. This was in the context of other mediating features of *safer* institutions.

Discussion

In the KKS study, all institutional sites surveyed served relatively the same population of youth; they also had similar mission statements, philosophy, and principles, which they articulated for public consumption; and they followed the same legislative and policy requirements and had similar procedural guidelines. It was anticipated that variability would exist in terms of the local organizational ideology and leadership and that this would be reflected in the institutional milieu or culture. Indeed, sites were separated into two groups based on scores assigned for the level of institutional safety as perceived by youth residents (*less safe, safer*). This confirms that there were variations in institutional culture evidenced through the description of peer harassment and aggression and the concomitant strategies used by youth to manage the milieu. The contrast between the two groups with regard to the role of staff in protecting and engaging youth provided further insight into what contributed to the experience of safety within the institutional milieu.

The quality of life for youth while incarcerated depends largely on the nature of their relationship with the staff. Staff/youth relationships set the tone for institutional culture, and that tone both flows from and reflects the organization's ideology. The core principles of the institutional culture, as made "visible" among the staff, are assimilated by youth and generalized in their interactions and behaviours. Staff relationships with youth function as the principal medium for interpersonal growth. A formal, collaborative, and open relationship with staff signals to youth that they can inform staff of their fears or incidents of aggression. The greater visibility of staff also contributes to reduced peer violence and a more positive peer culture. Staff response to coercion and aggression is one of the most important determinants of the nature of the peer subculture. In essence, the institutional milieu provides a system of management through relationships that can foster safety and healing in interpersonal interactions.

It is striking that youth with child welfare involvement are hypervigilant. They witness, fear, and anticipate violence and victimization at every turn while in custody, and this is what they report. In contrast, institutionalized youth without child welfare involvement know, understand, and anticipate violence but put blinders on to avoid confronting or reporting it. This leaves the reader with the following unanswered question: Who is safer—hypervigilant youths or avoidant ones? These two groups had similar perceptions of safety in the environment but their reactions, responses, and coping strategies were different. Furthermore, youth who were involved in the child welfare system were more often in the *less safe* institutions. Staff responses to these youths and their attention to creating a rehabilitative, protective

Discussion

milieu modulated perceptions of lack of safety. Like the youth they served, staff were vigilant when it came to anticipating the behaviours of youth in the institutions that the youths themselves considered to be *safer*.

This study suggests that the majority of youth who are incarcerated report a history of child welfare involvement. Nonetheless, youths who did not report such a history may have had a background of child maltreatment that went unreported. Service providers can assume, therefore, that most youth in the youth justice system suffer from adverse family backgrounds and the associated traumas.

The program policy implications are multiple. Intake assessments and plans of care need to reflect this reality. Staff who are interviewing a youth at the time of intake need to ensure that they have asked the youth directly about any history of child welfare involvement. Records are not always available at the time of admission. Further exploration may be required to determine what led to child welfare intervention, including child maltreatment or neglect or the witnessing of family violence. Plans of care can be developed in cooperation with the youth to determine the nature of the psychoeducational approaches that may be offered to assist youth in gaining an understanding of and perspective on their family history and its impact on their feelings and behaviour. Owing to a longer length of stay in secure custody settings, this type of programming is possible. Staff must be vigilant and anticipate provocative behaviours on the part of youth that replicate abuse dynamics through internalizing symptomology, externalizing behaviours, and relationship difficulties. These response patterns of victims or witnesses of abuse translate into predictable behaviours in the institutional milieu. Specialized pre-service or in-service training that acknowledges these dynamics and that offers effective assessment and intervention strategies is required. Youth with child welfare involvement present with insight and a keen self-awareness; they also solicit meaningful interactions with staff. Staff need to anticipate and honour these opportunities. To this end, further exploration is required to understand "relationship custody" and the impact of staff/youth relationships in promoting or deterring violence among youth.

Therapeutic strategies and interventions need to be in place so that child welfare authorities and residential care operators can interrupt the trajectory of youth from child welfare to youth justice systems. Community-based alternatives to incarceration, which are predicated on effectively integrating a range of services across the education, mental health, health, social services, recreation, justice, and employment sectors, are required in order to prevent entry of youth with personal and family risk factors into the justice system. A single case manager for each youth—one who has the time, resources, and ability to know and understand the youth—could navigate the appropriate service systems and negotiate the provision of services on behalf of the youth (Finlay, 2004). This model of service delivery could circumvent the inappropriate incarceration of youth with an early or current history of child maltreatment and domestic violence.

Summary and Conclusions

Returning to the original discussion of youth justice policy, it is clear that the interactions among federal and provincial legislation and policy have the ability to influence the ideology, structure, and operations at an institutional level. At the same time, however, there must be acknowledgment that public opinion influences legislative and policy directions.

With the introduction of the YCJA, Canada reaffirmed its unique position that the developmental needs of young people are to be considered in concert with meaningful consequences and the protection of society. Furthermore, in Ontario, enhanced protective opportunities for incarcerated youth have been put in place through the transfer of youth justice institutions and programs to the "children's" ministry, which operates in the context of child welfare legislation (CFSA). There is a trajectory documented herein, of youth with a history in the child welfare system moving into the youth justice system. The present circumstances in Ontario therefore allow for the capacity to effectively blend policy across legislative jurisdictions—specifically, across federal youth justice legislation and provincial child welfare legislation.

Given that a clear relationship exists between formal institutional ideology and the informal peer subculture, thoughtful consideration needs to be given to the components of the organizational structure that can effectively influence peer violence, such as the physical environment, programs, staff/youth relationships, and practices of social control that interact dynamically to create the institutional culture. The preponderance of youth from the child welfare system in these institutions behooves policy makers, first, to take into account this predisposition and provide programs and services to divert their admission in the first instance, and second, to provide institutional programming to ameliorate the perpetuation of the cycle of violence from family to institutional settings for those youth who are incarcerated.

Political context and public opinion have had a significant impact on these youth justice institutions. Recently a "law and order" approach has been introduced by the federal government and a sizeable proportion of the general public has tended to view the treatment of incarcerated youthful offenders as a necessary deterrent. This position overlooks the fact that if society tolerates violence within its institutions, it will negatively influence community and family safety in the long run. The Keeping Kids Safe study illustrates this cycle of violence. Continued research is needed that takes into account the lived experience of youth whose pathways cross a number of service sectors in order to deepen our understanding of the complex policy issues and their practice implications.

References

Bala, N. (2005). The development of Canada's youth justice law. In K. Campbell (Ed.), *Understanding youth justice in Canada* (pp. 41–64). Toronto, ON: Pearson Education.

Connell, A., & Farrington, D.P. (1996). Bullying among incarcerated young offenders: Developing an interview schedule and some preliminary results. *Journal of Adolescence, 19,* 75–93. doi: 10.1006/jado.1996.0007

Covell, K., & Howe, B. (2009). *Children, families and violence: Challenges for children's rights.* London, UK: Jessica Kingsley Publishers.

Davidson-Arad, B. (2005). Observed violence, abuse, and risk behaviours in juvenile correctional facilities: Comparison of inmate and staff reports. *Children and Youth Services Review, 27,* 547–559. doi: 10.1016/j.childyouth.2004.11.013

Denov, M.S. (2004). Children's rights or rhetoric? Assessing Canada's Youth Criminal Justice Act and its compliance with the UN Convention on the Rights of the Child. *International Journal of Children's Rights, 12,* 1–20.

Dyson, G.P., Power, K.G., & Wozniak, E. (1997). Problems with using official records from young offender institutions as indices of bullying. *International Journal of Offender Therapy and Comparative Criminology, 41*(2), 121–138. doi: 10.1177/0306624X97412003

Elliott, D. S., Huizinga, D., & Morse, B.J. (1997). Self-reported violent offending: A descriptive analysis of juvenile violent offenders and their offending careers. *Journal of Interpersonal Violence, 1*(4), 472–511. doi: 10.1177/088626086001004006

Ellis, D. (1997). *Report on youth vulnerability in secure custody facilities for young offenders.* Oakville, ON: Ellis Research Associates.

Feld, B.C. (1981). A comparative analysis of organizational structure and inmate subcultures in institutions for juvenile offenders. *Crime and Delinquency, 27,* 336–363. doi: 10.1177/001112878102700303

Finlay, J. (2004). *Snakes and ladders.* Report prepared for the Ministry of Child and Youth Services. Toronto, ON.

Finlay, J. (2006). The use of power and control by incarcerated youth. *Relational Child and Youth Care Practice, 18*(4), 33–48.

Finlay, J., & Snow, K. (2005). *Youth partners project.* Toronto, Canada: Canadian Council of Provincial Child and Youth Advocates.

Grogan-Kaylor, A., Ruffolo, M.C., Ortega, R.M., & Clarke, J. (2008). Behaviors of youth involved in the child welfare system. *Child Abuse and Neglect, 32,* 35–49. doi.org/10.1016/j.chiabu.2007.09.004

Hamilton, C., & Harvey, R. (2004). The role of public opinion in the implementation of international juvenile justice standards. *International Journal of Children's Rights, 11,* 369–390.

Herrenkohl, T.I., Herrenkohl, R.C., Sousa, C., Tajima, E.A., & Moylan, C.A. (2008). Intersection of child abuse and children's exposure to domestic violence. *Trauma, Violence, and Abuse, 9*(2), 84–99. doi: 10.1177/1524838008314797

Ireland, J.L. (1999a). Bullying behaviors among male and female prisoners: A study of adult and young offenders. *Aggressive Behaviour, 25,* 161–178. doi: 10.1002/(SICI)1098-2337(1999)25:3<161::AID-AB1>3.0.CO;2-#

Ireland, J.L. (1999b). Pro-victim attitudes and empathy in relation to bullying among prisoners. *Legal and Criminological Psychology, 4,* 51–66. doi: 10.1348/135532599167789

References Ireland, J.L. (2000). "'Bullying" among prisoners: A review of the research. *Aggression and Violent Behavior, 5*(2), 201–215. doi: 10.1016/S1359-1789(98)00031-7

Ireland, J.L. (2001). The relationship between social problem-solving and bullying behavior among male and female adult prisoners. *Aggressive Behavior, 27,* 297–312. doi: 10.1002/ab.1013

Ireland, J.L. (2002a). Bullying in prisons. *The Psychologist, 15*(3), 130–133.

Ireland, J.L. (2002b). Do juveniles bully more than young offenders? *Journal of Adolescence, 25,* 155–168. doi: 10.1006/jado.2002.0458

Ireland, J.L. (2002c). How does assertiveness relate to bullying behaviour among prisoners? *Legal and Criminological Psychology, 7,* 87–100. doi: 10.1348/135532502168405

Ireland, J.L. (2002d). Official records of bullying incidents among young offenders: What can they tell us and how useful are they? *Journal of Adolescence, 25,* 669–679. doi: 10.1006/jado.2002.0512

Ireland, J.L. (2002e). The perceived consequences of responding to bullying with aggression: A study of male and female adult prisoners. *Aggressive Behaviour, 28,* 257–272. doi: 10.1002/ab.80001

Ireland, J.L. (2002f). Social self–esteem and self reported bullying behaviour among adult prisoners. *Aggressive Behaviour, 28,* 184–197. doi: 10.1002/ab.90021

Johnson, M.N. (1999). Managing perceptions: A new paradigm for residential youth care. *Child and Youth Care Forum, 28*(3), 165–179. doi: 10.1023/A:1021939710960

LeBlanc, M. (2002). *Rehabilitation of young offenders in Quebec: 30 years of empirical research and professional intervention.* Paper presented at the Youth Criminal Justice Seminar. Université de Montréal, Canada.

Leschied, A., Cunningham, A., & Mazaheri, N. (1997). *Safe and secure: Eliminating peer-to-peer violence in Ontario's phase II secure detention centres.* Toronto, ON: Ministry of the Solicitor General and Correctional Services.

Levesque, R.J.R. (1996). Is there still a place for violent youth in juvenile justice? *Aggression and Violent Behaviour, 1*(1), 69–79. doi: 10.1016/1359-1789(95)00006-2

Matthews, R., & Pitts, J. (1998). Rehabilitation, recidivism and realism: Evaluating violence reduction programs in prison. *Prison Journal, 78*(4), 390–405. doi: 10.1177/0032885598078004003

McCorkle, R.C. (1992). Personal precautions to violence in prison. *Criminal Justice and Behaviour, 19*(2), 160–173. doi: 10.1177/0093854892019002004

McGhee, J., & Waterhouse, L. (2007). Classification in youth justice and child welfare: In search of "the child." *National Association for Youth Justice, 7*(2), 107–120. doi: 10.1177/1473225407078772

Nurse, A.M. (2001). The structure of the juvenile prison. *Youth and Society, 32*(3), 360–394. Retrieved from http://www.ncjrs.gov/App/Publications/abstract.aspx?ID=187088

Palmer, E.J., & Farmer, S. (2002). Victimizing behavior among juvenile and young offenders: How different are perpetrators? *Journal of Adolescence, 25,* 469–481. doi: 10.1006/jado.2002.0492

Peterson-Badali, M., & Koegl, C.J. (2002). Juveniles' experiences of incarceration: The role of correctional staff in peer violence. *Journal of Criminal Justice, 30,* 41–49. doi: 10.1016/S0047-2352(01)00121-0

Roland, E., & Idsoe, T. (2001). Aggression and bullying. *Aggressive Behavvior, 27,* 446–462.

Schwarzwald, J., & Koslowsky, M. (1999). Gender, self-esteem, and focus of interest in the use of power strategies by adolescents in conflict situations. *Journal of Social Issues, 55*(1), 15–32. doi: 10.1111/0022-4537.00102

Sprague, J., & Walker, H. (2000). Early identification and intervention for youth with antisocial and violent behaviour. *Exceptional Children,* 66(3), 367–379. Retrieved from http://www.freepatentsonline.com/article/Exceptional-Children/61585784.html

Sprott, J., & Doob, A. (2005). Trends in youth crime in Canada. In K. Campbell (Ed.), *Understanding youth justice in Canada* (114–134). Toronto, ON: Pearson Education.

Stone, D.T. (2002). Countertransference issues in adolescent residential settings. *Journal of Child and Adolescent Group Therapy, 11,* 147–157. doi: 10.1023/A:1014762507428

Van der Kolk, B.A., McFarlane, C., & Weisaeth, L. (1996). *Traumatic stress—the effects of overwhelming experience on mind, body, and society.* New York, NY: Guilford Press.

Van Manen, M. (1997). *Researching lived experience.* London, ON: Althouse Press.

Canadians with Disabilities

14

Peter A. Dunn

The concept of disability is socially constructed, in that people have different ideas of who is disabled or what conditions constitute a disability. These ideas change over time, location, and culture (Enns & Neufeldt, 2003; Miceli, 2010; Pothier & Delvin, 2006). In fact, some cultures, including many Aboriginal ones, do not have the term "disability" in their language (Elias & Demas, 2001; Durst, South, & Bluechart, 2006). Policy makers determine who is disabled and deserves financial and other benefits. They categorize people and limit services to individuals with certain conditions. Instead of responding to individual needs, eligibility rules are often designed to reduce costs. This leaves many, including people with multiple disabilities, ineligible for services. Canadians with disabilities are often disempowered and oppressed by social policies and programs. Unresponsive social policies have resulted in major gaps in services as well as regional differences in Canada. One of the main challenges of social policy is to respond to the needs of Canadians with disabilities in a comprehensive, just, and empowering manner (Beachell, 2011; Carpenter, Estey, & Rioux, 2010; Dunn, 2003; Rioux & Prince, 2002).

Many confront multiple oppressions in terms of environmental, economic, social, and attitudinal barriers (Baker, 2005; Council of Canadians with Disabilities, 2007; Hanes, 2010; Walter, 2010). Many individuals are marginalized and excluded from participation in Canadian society. For example, Statistics Canada (2006) indicates that roughly 55 percent of Canadians with disabilities require significantly more help with personal supports. Canadians with disabilities have been categorized, stigmatized, medicalized, and confined rather than supported in the community through self-help initiatives (Capponi, 2008; Nelson, Lord, & Ochocka, 2001).

Barriers to entering the labour force and extremely low public assistance payments have marginalized many Canadians with disabilities (Crawford, 2010). Barnes and Mercer (2010) explain that capitalism has forced many to the bottom of the labour market. In 2008 the median income of Canadians with disabilities was $19,200, with about 30 percent living in poverty (Statistics Canada, 2008). Approximately 52.4 percent were unemployed or had given up looking for work. Approximately 65 percent of working-age adults with disabilities did not complete post-secondary education because of multiple barriers in the education system.

Many people face attitudes that stress charity rather than equal rights and citizenship. Multiple forms of oppression often overlap and reinforce one another. For example, visible minorities who are disabled confront both racism and demeaning stereotypes related to their abilities. Women with disabilities have extremely low incomes (Dunn, 2003; Statistics Canada, 2008) and roughly 83 percent have been sexually abused (Bramham, 2011). Stienstra (2002) emphasizes the importance of understanding how race/ethnicity intersects with disability as well how these identities are socially constructed. Barile (2000) stresses the multiple levels of discrimination that impact individuals with a multiple-minority status. For example, Canada's policies are especially dehumanizing for immigrants with disabilities. Service providers often ignore the unique needs of individuals from different racial or ethnic groups. Usually services are not culturally appropriate; rather, there is one service for everyone (Ethno-Racial People with Disabilities' Coalition of Ontario, 2000; Stienstra, 2002).

The incidence of disability is about twice as high for Aboriginal peoples as for the general population (Human Resources and Skills Development Canada [HRSDC], 2007). While Aboriginal peoples have inclusive attitudes toward individuals with disabilities, many government responses have been oppressive. The issues are exacerbated by jurisdictional conflicts between various levels of government. Elias and Demas (2001) found that individuals with disabilities living on reserves have limited resources. Many live in substandard housing with physical barriers in their homes and cannot obtain personal supports, accessible transportation, health care, employment training, or work. Durst and Bluechardt (2004) found that individuals who moved to urban areas to obtain disability supports often live a marginalized existence.

Statistics Canada has undertaken several studies of the number of people with disabilities in Canada and the barriers they confront. It conducted Health Activities and Limitation Surveys (HALS) in 1983–84, 1986, and 1991. In 2001, 2006, and 2011, this survey was expanded to become the Participation and Activity Limitation Survey (PALS). These surveys included people with physical, developmental, and mental health disabilities. They illustrate the subjective nature of categorizing people. Statistics Canada (2006) defined people as disabled if they were limited in tasks of daily living because of long-term physical, mental, or health problems, or if they were told by health professionals that they had learning or mental health disabilities. People who use technical aids such as eyeglasses or hearing aids to eliminate their limitations were not considered disabled.

The Statistics Canada (2006) survey indicates that about 4.4 million people in Canada—14.3 percent of the population—have some form of disability. The number of people reporting a disability increased by 21.2

percent—that is, by more than three-quarters of a million people—in five years. This significant increase is attributed to the aging of the population and the increased social acceptance of reporting a disability. The rate of disability increases dramatically with age. Roughly 3.7 percent of Canadians under fifteen are disabled, 11.5 percent of those fifteen to sixty-four years old, and 43.4 percent of people aged sixty-five or older (Statistics Canada, 2006). Progressive social policies are essential to respond to these trends.

Davis (2010) explains that disability entered public discourse with industrialization in the late eighteenth century. Certain human bodies were classified as the "norm," while others were classified as deviant. People with disabilities were considered as "others" and labeled as "outsiders." Even after the waning of the eugenics movement, capitalism, racism, and patriarchy continue to promote the concept of the "normal" body. The result has been that many people reject their bodies. Everyone has limitations, and almost half the population will be classified by government agencies as "disabled" as they become seniors and encounter more serious health issues.

Disability Paradigms

How social issues are conceptualized affects the policy responses of governments (Wharf & McKenzie, 2010). For example, the grassroots efforts of the disability movement and evolving social theory have transformed our understanding of disability issues. Paradigms have shifted from a medical and rehabilitation model, to traditional services in the community, to a more critical approach based on rights as citizens, consumer control, and empowerment. These shifts have resulted in changes in policies and programs (Hanes, 2010; Lord, 2010). The following table illustrates the different concepts, values, and social policy orientations of these three paradigms.

Medical and Rehabilitation Paradigm

The medical and rehabilitation paradigm considers people who are classified as "disabled" as being deviant from the "normal body." It views disability as a sickness, focusing on the limitations of individuals, their inadequate performance of daily tasks, and their lack of compliance. People are categorized, isolated, and separated from the mainstream. They are labelled according to limitations and are considered as the "other." They are often pitied, and the existing economic and political order is not questioned. This paradigm involves medicalization, separation, and isolation, and its associated social policies emphasize institutional care, separate programs, and charity. Medical and rehabilitation practitioners are in charge. People are considered patients and are often socialized to the role of sick people (Dunn, 2003; Lord 2010).

Disability Paradigms

Table 14.1 Disability Paradigms

Paradigms	Medical and Rehabilitation Paradigm (Institutional)	Traditional Community Services Paradigm (Institutionalized in the Community)	Critical Disability Paradigm (Consumer Control)
Concepts of disability	Disability can be scientifically measured as deviant from the "normal" body	Disability is measured as lack of activities of daily living	Disability is socially constructed Stresses the social model of disability
Nature of problems	Sickness of individual and pathology	Lack of specialized care in the community	Physical, social, attitudinal, political, and economic barriers Othering and labelling Dependency on professionals
Social relations	Categorization, separation, isolation dependency, stigma, sympathy, and charity	Categorization, separation, isolation dependency, stigma, sympathy, and charity	Rights as citizens, social inclusion, social identity, independent living, and quality of life
Political and economic relations	Accept existing political and economic order	Support liberal incremental changes	Challenge ableism, capitalism, racism, sexism, homophobia, and other oppressive conditions
Policy principles	Medicalization, segregation, specialized services, and functional limitations	Professional, segregated, and specialized services One service fits all	Consumer control, self-direction, choice/ options, and flexibility/ freedom
Decision makers	Medical practitioners	Service professional providers	Consumers
Role of participants	Patient/sick role	Recipient/client role	Consumer/decision makers
Focus of social policies	Policies support more institutional care and regulation	Policies support specialized/segregated education, housing transportation, group homes, sheltered workshops, and community services	Policies support removal of disabling environments, full integration, responsive holistic services, peer supports and political rights

Note: This table radically changes and updates some of the initial concepts of G. DeJong (1981). Environmental accessibility and independent outcomes. East Lancing, MI: University Center for International Rehabilitation.

Traditional Community Service Paradigm

As people with disabilities were deinstitutionalized, they experienced in the community some of the same approaches to service provision as in institutional settings. These included categorization, separation, isolation, and stigma. McKnight and Block (2010) point out that many people have been, in essence, institutionalized within the community. Instead of being called patients, they are now called clients, but they treated in a similar manner.

Disability Paradigms

Furthermore, community programs are often unresponsive, complex, and fragmented. Service providers are concerned about the lack of specialized programs in the community and advocate for only incremental changes. In this paradigm, policies emphasize segregated and specialized services, including group homes, sheltered workshops, traditional clubhouse models, special education, and specialized transit (Dunn, 2003; Council of Canadians with Disabilities, 2005).

Many people have difficulty distinguishing between this approach and the critical disability approach, since both take place in the community. The differences are profound. One approach treats people as "others" who are segregated from the mainstream and viewed as dependent. In contrast, the critical disability approach focuses on total inclusion, citizens' rights, empowerment, consumer control, and choice. People have textured lives and participate fully in the community (Pedlar et al., 1999).

Critical Disability Paradigm

The disability movement offers an alternative analysis of the issues of disability, based on a social construction of disability. This paradigm, the critical disability approach, locates pathology not in the disabled individual but in the environment: in unprotected rights, in overdependency on relatives and professionals, and in a lack of responsive services (Hanes, 2010; Barnes & Mercer, 2010). It asserts that consumers are oppressed and emphasizes that people can live in the community and lead productive lives through self-help, peer support, advocacy, and the removal of barriers (Rioux & Prince, 2002; Walters 2010). The disability movement proposes social policies that emphasize consumer control and self-direction, choices and options, flexibility, and freedom (Lord, Snow, & Dingwall, 2005).

The critical disability approach developed in opposition to the medical model, which focuses on what they call impairments of individuals and puts doctors in charge (Hiranandani, 2005; Pothier & Delvin, 2006). Barnes and Mercer (2010) stress that individuals with disabilities do not wish charity but rather social rights and inclusion. They should be in charge of their lives and fully included in all aspects of society. Reid and Knight (2006) expose the destructive results of labelling people and emphasize the rights of individuals with disabilities to make their own decisions based on their lived experiences.

Some radical disability theorists (McRuer & Berube, 2006) argue that the critical disability approach should go further and critique the capitalistic system, which creates economic divisions in society and drives people with disabilities into poverty. The whole system should be transformed, with more discussion of how dominant and marginal bodily and sexual identities are developed and intersect. The radical theorists also critique atomistic Eurocentric thinking, recommending a more holistic approach.

Transforming Government Policies and Programs

Feminist scholars (Morris, 2001; Wendell 2006) have been critical of those who focus solely on societal barriers and propose a new synthesis. They turn the focus back on "impairment," while also acknowledging the impact of the environment. They point out that the values and negative concepts related to impairment are also socially constructed. Feminist activists believe it is important to examine women's stories about their feelings and their relation to their bodies as well as dealing with the external environment. They are concerned with the messages in society that result in women devaluing their bodies and buying into the myth that the body should be controlled. According to Miceli (2010), men in the disability rights movement often focus primarily on disabling external barriers, while women focus on both external barriers and the experiences of living with "impairment."

Transforming Government Policies and Programs

There is a growing emphasis on transforming how we think of the issues related to disability identity and creating consumer-driven models of service delivery. Consumers have established their own initiatives and developed partnerships with government organizations to develop new approaches to service delivery (Dunn, 2003; Dunn et al., 2008; Lord et al., 2005; Lord 2010).

The human service industry has moved from containing Canadians with disabilities in large institutions with health care staff to developing smaller institutions in the community with staff who reinforce dependency, submission, Eurocentric concepts, and segregated services (Nelson, 2006). For example, massive resources are still spent on group homes and sheltered workshops (Lord & Hutchison, 2007).

Nevertheless, new visions and initiatives are transforming policies and programs in Canada. Lord and Hutchison (2007) outline new pathways for inclusion based on policies guided by the voices of people, social innovations, collaboration, a power shift to citizens and their networks, and personalized supports centred on the gifts of individuals with disabilities and their communities. Nelson, Lord, and Ochocka (2001) emphasize stakeholder participation, empowerment, community support, integration, holistic programs, social justice, and access to valued resources. Lord (2010) stresses social inclusion and full citizenship for everyone with a disability. This chapter will outline specific policies that incorporate these principles. First, however, it would be useful to consider the historical context of policies and programs for Canadians with disabilities.

Historical Context

Historically, we have responded to people with disabilities in various ways. Aboriginal peoples provided supports within their nation in a collective fashion. Individuals with disabilities were not stigmatized or excluded. Often, a disability was considered a sign of "specialness" (Durst et al.,

Historical Context

2006). In contrast, early European settlers in Canada provided services in the community for people with disabilities who were considered deserving, although many ended up in poorhouses or jails. By the mid-nineteenth century, people were being moved to newly built, permanent institutions. Over time, these institutions grew in size and specialization. This period of government intervention evolved in the 1960s and 1970s into a movement toward deinstitutionalization. People were moved into the community, but often with very limited supports (Armitage, 2003).

During the period of deinstitutionalization, the disability movement gained strength and influenced government policies. The disability movement was comprised of several submovements that joined together to lobby for change. Many efforts arose from the increased awareness of social injustice brought about by the human rights movement in the 1950s and 1960s (Pedlar et al., 1999; Peters, 2004).

The Independent Living movement has had a major impact on social policies and programs in Canada. This movement began in the United States in the early 1970s with the development of three Independent Living Centers. Although many of the initial consumers had physical disabilities, the centres increasingly served people with a wide range of disabilities. The movement grew rapidly, and by the early 1990s it included several hundred centres in the United States. They lobbied for human rights, deinstitutionalization, and full participation in all aspects of society (Pfeiffer, 2003). The Independent Living movement began later in Canada but grew quickly from a few centres in the early 1980s. Independent Living Resource Centres follow four principles: consumer control, a cross-disability approach, community-based services, and the promotion of integration and full participation. Although each centre responds to the needs of its particular community, all have four common programs: information and referral, peer support, independent living/empowerment skills and development, and research and demonstration. The centres are run by and for consumers (Hanes, 2010; Lord, 2010; Walters, 2010). In 1986 the Canadian Association of Independent Living Centres (now called Independent Living Canada) was formed as a national coordinating body for the Independent Living movement; it provides training, support, networking with government and non-governmental organizations, and information dissemination. The centres have promoted a new service delivery system in which citizens with disabilities are responsible for developing and managing their own personal and community resources (Hutchison et al., 2000; Lord, 2010).

The community living movement in Canada had its roots in the 1960s as parents of children with developmental disabilities began to fight for their children's right to publicly funded education and recreation, adequate residential and vocational programs, and small residences and group homes rather than institutions. During this time, the normalization principle, emphasizing physical and social integration, was introduced from

Scandinavia. The initial segregated services such as specialized education and sheltered employment were increasingly criticized as institutionalizing people in the community. Alternatives were developed, including supported independent living arrangements, integrated education, supported employment, and participation in mainstream recreation. The focus turned in the 1990s toward quality-of-life issues, people's strengths and friendships, strong social networks, consumer empowerment, and individualized planning and funding. Rights, choices, and individual preferences were emphasized. People First, an advocacy organization of people with developmental disabilities, played a critical role in lobbying for social change. They called for an end to institutional care, group homes, and sheltered workshops (Pedlar et al., 1999).

Denton (2000) has reviewed the significant reforms in mental health over the past century. Humanitarian reforms helped shift the focus of services in institutions away from custody toward treatment. The psychodynamic/holistic approach emphasized understanding and treating the social causes of mental health problems. This was followed by the community mental health movement, which focused on community services, the prevention of long-term hospitalization, and local, accessible, integrated, and coordinated services. Prevention programs were developed for early detection, intervention, and alleviation of adverse conditions, such as poverty, that contributed to mental health problems. Community programs were developed to respond to individuals who had been discharged from institutions but who found themselves isolated and unsupported (Nelson, 2006).

Lord (2000) outlines the growth of the psychiatric consumer/survivor movement in Canada since the 1980s. This movement developed in response to people's experiences of alienation and oppression within the mental health system. The psychiatric consumer/survivor movement uses an empowerment–community integration paradigm that stresses self-help, mutual aid, peer support, and advocacy. The movement critiques approaches such as case management and clubhouses as expert-driven and segregated and as failing to respond to the social conditions faced by consumer-survivors. It proposes a model of stakeholder participation and empowerment, community support and integration, and social justice and access to valued resources. Organizations such as the National Network for Mental Health have played an active role in promoting policies based on these approaches (Everett, 2000; Nelson, 2006; Nelson, Lord, & Ochocka, 2001).

Other consumer initiatives in Canada have dealt with issues related to women, Aboriginal peoples, students, and people with hearing and visual disabilities. Provincial and national organizations have helped coordinate these efforts. For example, the Council of Canadians with Disabilities (CCD) was established as a national coordinating body that advocates for full and equal participation. This cross-disability organization argues that institutionalization, inaccessible public places, and negative attitudes have excluded people with disabilities from the mainstream of Canadian life. The CCD advocates for citizen rights, self-determination, consumer control, and equality. It has had a major impact on disability rights and service delivery systems across Canada (Beachell, 2011).

Peters (2004) points out that while the Disability Rights Movement in Canada has had some major successes, there is a long way to go. For example, disability was included in the equality provisions of the Charter of Rights and Freedoms. However, it is difficult for individuals with disabilities to litigate the removal of every barrier under this law, especially given the high costs of court challenges. Disability advocates in Ontario lobbied for the Ontarians with Disability Act and later for the Accessibility for Ontarians with Disabilities Act. The AODA has specific enforceable standards related to goods, services, accommodation, facilities, buildings, and employment in the public and private sectors (AODA Committee, 2005).

Consumer groups have not worked in isolation. They have cooperated with disability-specific service agencies, government organizations, and other not-for-profit groups (Lord, 2010). The disability movement in Canada has increasingly transformed notions of disability issues, developed an alternative vision of services, and created innovative interventions operated by consumers.

Evolving Roles

The 1867 British North America Act delegated to the provinces responsibility for policy development related to housing, transportation, social supports, education, and other human services. Nevertheless, the federal government plays a significant role in cost sharing, standards setting, and programs for Aboriginal peoples. It also controls some accessible transportation and provides direct services such as income maintenance and employment programs. That said, the provinces and territories have the major role in many areas of disability policy. They develop social policies related to personal supports, barrier-free housing, accessible transportation, education, social assistance, employment training, and other community resources such as recreation. Government agencies, not-for-profits, and, increasingly, for-profit organizations implement the programs.

Many of these services are being eroded by reductions in government funding as a result of neoliberal policies and globalization. Another influence on services has been the devolution of responsibilities from the federal government to the provinces and then to the municipalities (Dunn, 2003). The result is increased disparities among the provinces (Dunn, 2003) and the emergence of private, for-profit disability agencies. Many of these agencies are more concerned with profits than with the empowerment of consumers (Lord & Hutchison, 2007).

Disability Policies and Programs

Disability Policies and Programs

This section discusses policy developments that enable Canadians with disabilities to live independently. Disability policies have evolved toward enabling consumers to participate fully in all aspects of community life and to take control over service delivery. This section discusses policies and programs related to housing, transportation, personal supports, income, education, employment, and community supports. A brief history of recent developments at the federal level provides an overall context for policy development in Canada.

The International Year of the Disabled Person in 1981 was a catalyst for the federal government to work with Canada's disability community to identify and take action on outstanding issues. The Special Parliamentary Committee on the Disabled and Handicapped (1981) documented, in a report titled *Obstacles*, the major barriers confronting people with disabilities in Canada. *Obstacles* listed 130 recommendations for action by federal government departments. A follow-up report in December 1981 recommended action on issues related to Aboriginal peoples.

In 1982, physical and mental disabilities were included under Section 15 of the Canadian Charter of Rights and Freedoms—the first instance of a national constitution referring specifically to individuals with disabilities. The UN declared 1983–92 the Decade of Disabled Persons. It was not until 1985, however, that Prime Minister Brian Mulroney agreed to recognize that decade in Canada. That same year, a Sub-Committee on Equality of Rights produced a report, *Equality for All*, that highlighted the delays in implementing *Obstacles*. The same report recommended establishing a permanent Parliamentary Committee to deal with disability issues. The federal government designated the Secretary of State as the Minister Responsible for the Status of Disabled Persons and established a Status of Disabled Persons Secretariat to plan federal initiatives. It also expanded its Court Challenges program to fund litigation dealing with equality rights under the new Charter. In 1987 the work of the Special Parliamentary Committee culminated in the establishment of the Standing Committee on Human Rights and the Status of Disabled Persons (Secretary of State, 1991).

The Standing Committee produced a report in 1990, *A Consensus for Action: The Economic Integration of Disabled Persons*, which urged the federal government to make the economic integration of Canadians with disabilities a national priority; to ensure more responsible policy, legislation, and regulations; to pursue employment equity provisions; and to develop a federal–provincial–municipal plan for consultation with consumers. It documented the major limitations of the federal government's efforts and the frustration of consumers at delays in fulfilling ten-year-old promises. In 1991 the federal government announced a $158 million National Strategy for the Integration of Persons with Disabilities over a five-year period (Secretary of State, 1991).

Disability Policies and Programs

In 1992 the federal, provincial, and territorial governments produced *Pathways to Integration,* better known as *Mainstream 92,* as the final report on their collaborative review of services. The Standing Committee on Human Rights and the Status of Disabled Persons continued to focus on employment issues. It also produced *Completing the Circle* (1993a), a report outlining issues related to Aboriginal people with disabilities; as well as *The Grand Design* (1993b), which argued for better programs and services. But these reports did not lead to much concrete action, and consumers became increasingly bitter (Council of Canadians with Disabilities, 1996). Their demands led to the creation of a Task Force on Disability Issues in 1996. Its report, *Equal Citizenship for Canadians with Disabilities: The Will to Act,* incorporated many of the recommendations of the consumer movement (Federal Task Force on Disability Issues, 1996). It proposed that disability considerations be incorporated into mainstream policies and programs. In 1998 the federal, provincial, and territorial ministers responsible for social services produced a report, *In Unison: A Canadian Approach to Disability Issues,* which emphasized a collective approach. The same ministers signed the Unison Accord, which proposed services that are accessible and portable and that focus on the individual. Despite all these reports and efforts, Canadians with disabilities still confront discrimination and multiple barriers.

Disability rights organizations continued to advocate for action on the Unison Accord, including funding for programs promoting disability inclusion. Frustrated with the pace of change, they issued *A Call for Action* in 2005. This proposal urged new investment in disability-related supports by all governments to break the cycle of exclusion and poverty confronting Canadians with disabilities (Council of Canadians with Disabilities, 2005). In 2010 the Government of Canada ratified the UN Convention on the Rights of Persons with Disabilities (Council of Canadians with Disabilities, 2010).

Housing

Government policies and programs at all levels have had a major impact on improving housing for people with disabilities. Barrier-free housing helps people with disabilities get in and out of their homes and use bathrooms, kitchens, and bedrooms independently. It also provides assistance for individuals with visual, hearing, and developmental disabilities. These aids include audio signals in elevators, tactile and colour-contrasting cues where useful, visual alarms for fires, and easy-to-read signs. While housing is a provincial and territorial responsibility, the federal government's National Research Council develops national building codes approximately every five years. Since 1965 it has included some barrier-free standards as advisory standards for provincial and territorial governments. A separate section for barrier-free standards (s. 3.7) was added to the code in 1985 but does not include universal design standards that would ensure that all units can be easily adapted to individual needs. Such standards would require adjustable counters and bathrooms large enough for wheelchairs, making all housing more inclusive (Dunn, 2003).

The provinces and territories usually revise their building codes every five years and, when they do, incorporate many of the federal provisions. Eight of the thirteen provinces and territories have building codes with accessibility regulations. These apply to new apartment buildings and to those being substantially renovated but do not include single-family homes or existing apartments. While provincial and territorial codes have improved, most do not go as far as the United States' Fair Housing Act Amendment, which includes universal features in all apartments units. Instead, a specific percentage of units—often 5 percent—is usually required to be accessible (Dunn, 2003).

Housing adaptation programs make existing housing more accessible. The federal government's role, designated in the National Housing Act, is carried out by the Canada Mortgage and Housing Corporation (CMHC). Its national Residential Rehabilitation Assistance Program (RRAP), launched in 1973 as a home improvement program, was expanded in 1981 to include grants and loans to adapt existing housing. In 1986 the program became the Residential Rehabilitation Assistance Program for Persons with Disabilities [RRAP-D]. In 1992, the CMHC introduced Housing Assistance for Seniors' Independence to fund minor modifications of seniors' homes.

Seven provinces and territories developed housing adaptation programs, and ten had home improvement programs, most of which included funding for modifications. The most extensive were in Ontario and Quebec, but Ontario ended its program in 1993. Funding for programs in other provinces was reduced. Of the programs still available, many provide limited funding for only a small number of home modifications (Dunn, 2003).

Canadians with disabilities confront other issues related to housing. CMHC has reduced or eliminated programs to make housing more affordable. Funds for the Rent Supplement and Non-Profit Housing Programs were reduced in the early 1990s. In 1996, CMHC curtailed funding for new social housing. Many provinces and territories took over the administration of federal co-op and not-for-profit housing. In 1997 the Ontario government devolved social housing to municipal control. Recent federal initiatives have not substantially increased the supply of affordable housing. Not surprisingly, with governments cutting social housing programs, many more people with disabilities have become homeless, including many consumer/survivors. Many emergency hostels are inaccessible and unsafe. People living in boarding homes or group homes are usually not covered by landlord and tenant legislation (Carpenter, 2001; Nelson, 2006).

Transportation

Jurisdictional issues related to accessible transportation are complex. Generally, if a public carrier crosses borders between provinces or territories, it comes under the responsibility of the federal government. The provinces and territories have jurisdiction over ferries, local trains, commuter buses, buses crossing municipal boundaries, and traffic rules. The municipalities generally have responsibility for taxis, municipal buses, subways, and light-rail transit, and specialized parallel transportation. Many municipal services receive provincial funding.

Nine provinces established funding for specialized parallel transportation in the late 1970s and early 1980s. The exception, Prince Edward Island, offered not-for-profit accessible bus services in its major communities. The territories have not provided specialized transportation because many communities are not serviced by roads. Provincial expenditures substantially increased for specialized transportation during the Decade of Disabled Persons, but later, both eligibility and funding were restricted.

During the Decade, most provinces and territories launched programs to help taxi companies purchase accessible taxis. These increased consumer control over the timing of rides and reduced the stigma associated with segregated transit. Surprisingly few provinces offer funding to modify consumers' automobiles unless they qualify for specific vocational rehabilitation or workers' compensation. Under pressure from consumer groups, many provinces introduced policies emphasizing various transportation services that give consumers flexibility. Accessible buses, subways, and trains began to receive funding by the end of the Decade, and some municipalities introduced low-floor buses.

Still, many trains and buses continue to be inaccessible. The older Toronto and Montreal subways offer poor accessibility, and bus and train stations are often inaccessible to people with mobility, visual, and/or hearing disabilities. As a result, many people cannot travel freely in Canada. Baker (2005) found that mandatory rather than voluntary government action was critical in making transportation more accessible. In fact, since the federal government adopted the voluntary approach in the mid-1990s, the state of accessible federal transportation has moved backwards.

The Americans with Disabilities Act, passed by the U.S. congress in 1990, offered a different approach to regulating accessible transportation and promoting inclusion (Dunn, 2003). It required all new private and public buses, train and bus stations, and rapid and light-rail trains to be accessible. All communities with conventional transportation were required to provide a specialized parallel system to serve eligible people, and bus and rail companies were required to install devices for individuals with hearing limitations.

Personal Supports

Social policies related to personal supports are complex and confusing in Canada: there are multiple levels of jurisdiction; people with different disabilities or ages may fall under different government departments or multiple ones; and these arrangements change constantly. Furthermore, there are no agreed-upon definitions of personal supports. These may include home health care, homemaker services, attendant services, respite for caregivers, technical aids and equipment, skills training, home support workers, and community living skills coaches. Torjman (2007) raises fundamental concerns about the system of personal supports—concerns that include disparities in their availability, high costs for users, and complicated eligibility rules. Personal support services are rarely portable, which makes it difficult for consumers to travel or to move. Many services are based on a medical model that fails to respond to individual needs and that fosters dependency (Yoshida et al., 2006).

While the provinces and territories have responsibility for personal supports, the federal government plays a role through cost sharing as well as through its responsibility for "Status Indians." Today, the federal government funds many personal support services through the Canada Health and Social Transfer. Provincial and territorial departments of health and community services provide support services either directly or through indirect channels, which can include purchased services, direct cash assistance, vouchers, and/or tax provisions that offset expenses. Municipalities often help deliver and pay for these supports. Commercial agencies such as insurance organizations also play a funding role. Generally, not-for-profit agencies actually provide the services (Dunn, 2003).

Many provinces developed home support policies and programs in the early 1970s, primarily for seniors. During the Decade of Disabled Persons, these programs were expanded to other groups. By the end of the decade, all provinces and territories were offering some form of personal supports; they were also coordinating services through a single entry point, providing cross-disability supports, and decentralizing community services. However, reduced funding in the 1990s and 2000s did not keep pace with demand—this at a time when the population was aging and more people were living independently (Dunn, 2003). Prince (2005) points out that there is still not a national strategy of disabilities supports in Canada.

Some provinces and territories have developed innovative programs, which include individualized funding. These programs provide money directly to consumers to obtain the supports they require. They enable consumers to hire, fire, and direct their support workers. Often less expensive, individualized funding has been adopted in most provinces and territories on a limited scale. Consumer organizations, such as the Independent Living and Resource Centres in Winnipeg and Toronto, have worked with government departments to administer individualized funding programs. They also teach consumers how to manage their own services. Micro-boards are an innovation developed in British Columbia for individuals with developmental disabilities. These are not-for-profit organizations of five to eight unpaid members contracted by the government to provide circles of support and to oversee individualized funding. Despite these innovations, many consumers in Canada have overwhelming problems simply obtaining basic personal supports (Dunn, 2003; Lord & Hutchison, 2007; Torjman, 2007).

Income

Many Canadians with disabilities are poor. Furthermore, many of them face extraordinary costs associated with having a disability. Many cannot find paid employment because of work-related barriers, leaving them dependent on Canada's disability income security system. This system is not based on need. Rather, the amount of money a person receives depends on how she or he became disabled. A hierarchy of programs, from private pensions to welfare assistance, has evolved in a haphazard and piecemeal fashion. It is not integrated, coordinated, comprehensive, or fair (Council of Canadians with Disabilities, 2005).

Dunn (2003) describes the various income programs for people with disabilities, which include personal injury awards through the courts, insurance programs, and non-insurance supports. The two key public insurance programs are the Canada/Quebec Pension Plan and the various provincially administered workers' compensation schemes. Workers' compensation protects workers and their families from wage loss due to occupational injury or disease. The Canada/Quebec Pension Plan, established in 1966, is a social insurance plan for retired people and for workers with severe and permanent disabilities. These two public insurance programs are available only to those with an earnings record. People who have not worked must rely on non-insurance supports such as welfare. Welfare provides assistance significantly below Statistics Canada's poverty line. It is stigmatizing and often has built-in disincentives to work.

Mendelson and colleagues (2010) have proposed reforming the social insurance system to create a new basic income program for people with disabilities. This would entail a refundable and more comprehensive Disability Tax Credit as well as expanded disability supports. These proposals focus on the need for a more systematic program, one that covers all people regardless of earning status or extent of disability. Many consumer groups have argued for a comprehensive income program for all Canadians in need (Council of Canadians with Disabilities, 2005).

Education

From special segregated classes for a few people grew the concept of inclusive, integrated education for many. The steps toward deinstitutionalization in the 1950s and 1960s, along with parental pressure, led to segregated special education for children with disabilities in schools. These parallel services proliferated in the 1970s and 1980s. In the 1980s, parents began advocating for integrated education for their children, since their children were often labelled and isolated in segregated school systems. In contrast, children in integrated schools developed skills, friendships, and communication abilities (Reid & Knight, 2006).

Education is a provincial and territorial responsibility with the federal government playing an important role in education for Aboriginal peoples. However, a dramatic shift occurred in 1982, when the Charter of Rights and Freedoms was entrenched in the Canadian constitution. The Charter's equality rights section provided an effective tool for parents' lobbying and litigation against segregated education (Learning Disability Association of Canada, 2002). Nevertheless, the needs of many children with disabilities have not been accommodated, especially with recent cuts to education. There is considerable variation across Canada in inclusive education.

Porter (2001) points out that successful inclusive education depends on a number of factors. Schools must have effective mechanisms for including parents in decision making and problem solving regarding their children's education. Children must be accepted as having a rightful place in the school. Supports, such as development and planning time, must be offered to teachers. Also, students may need accessible school facilities, computer-aided technologies and other devices, tutorial and interpreter support, and therapeutic services. Classroom instruction needs to accommodate different learning styles. Also, teachers, families, and students must be committed to inclusion for it to be effective. Unfortunately, many students continue to face multiple barriers in the educational system.

Inclusive post-secondary education is an increasing priority in Canada. This is reflected in the growth of Accessible Learning Centres, along with personal supports. Funding for post-secondary education comes from both federal and provincial sources. But with funding cuts to colleges and universities, many supports for students with disabilities have decreased while tuition fees have increased. Post-secondary students who are disabled continue to face multiple barriers. Many cannot obtain adequate funding, and many colleges and universities are not physically accessible or lack technology for individuals with hearing or visual disabilities. Often there is inadequate funding for sign language interpreters in classrooms. Often as well, faculty are not trained or sensitized. Without these supports, many students do not complete their studies, and even when they do, they are unable to find meaningful employment upon graduation (Canadian Centre on Disability Studies, 2004; Dunn et al. 2007).

Employment

Around one million working-age Canadians with disabilities are unemployed or out of the labour force. The cost of lost productivity is estimated at $35 to $38 billion annually (Crawford, 2005). Consumers argue for meaningful, decent-paying jobs in the regular labour force rather than employment in demeaning sheltered workshops (Council of Canadians with Disabilities, 2007).

Disability Policies and Programs

Human rights legislation has not been very effective in addressing employment discrimination. Consumers have difficulty obtaining employment-related supports such as aids and devices, home supports, transportation, and adaptations to the workplace. Individuals often do not have equal access to training and education. The current system of funding and service delivery is complex, fragmented, and piecemeal. Those who become employed have problems obtaining additional income to meet their disability-related costs.

Policy initiatives have been developed to address some of these issues. The Canadian Human Rights Act and all provincial/territorial human rights acts prohibit discrimination in employment on the basis of disability. Some human rights legislation includes "duty to accommodate"—that is, employers are required to modify a job or workplace. In 1997, the federal government replaced a thirty-five-year-old program called Vocational Rehabilitation of Disabled Persons with one called Employability Assistance for People with Disabilities (EAPD). The name reflects a stronger emphasis on employability. The federal government contributes 50 percent of the costs up to a maximum; the provinces and territories administer the services and tailor programs to local needs.

The unemployment and underemployment rate of Canadians with disabilities remains extremely high. A number of additional policies are required to support people in meaningful employment. Social security programs must eliminate disincentives, and people must get adequate income supports, education, housing, transportation, personal supports, and aids and devices (Lord & Hutchison, 2007; Neufeldt, 2006). Without these, many people will continue to confront barriers that prevent them from entering the economic mainstream of Canadian society.

Other Community Resources

Other community resources enable Canadians with disabilities to live independently. Social policies related to health care are critical. Fortunately, Canada has a universal health care policy. However, cutbacks to preventative services and drug and prescription programs have eroded the system of personal supports. Funding from the health care system has been used to establish innovative services, but this often perpetuates a traditional medical model. Many consumers feel oppressed by government institutions, hospitals, and rehabilitation services. The plight of psychiatric consumer/survivors in these institutions has been well documented: these people have been stripped of their identity and have lost control over their lives (Capponi, 2008; Nelson, 2006; Nelson, Lord, & Ochocka, 2001).

Other aspects of community life, such as leisure activities, have tended to be segregated, but there is movement toward more integrated community activities (Smith et al., 2005). For example, libraries are becoming more accessible to people with visual disabilities through large-text formats and

Braille. Movies and theatres are offering technology for those with hearing disabilities. Nevertheless, consumers continue to confront multiple barriers in the community.

Conclusions and Future Directions

Many social policies and programs were developed for Canadians with disabilities during the Decade of Disabled Persons. The budgets of some of these programs enjoyed substantial increases in the 1980s, but by the 1990s, many gains were being eroded as a result of funding reductions. The federal government diluted national standards and downloaded services to the provinces and territories—and in turn to the municipalities—thus creating a patchwork of services across Canada. As a result, some regions have few services and others have none. Also, many programs are based on a medical model that categorizes and stigmatizes people.

Despite these barriers, a new concept of services is emerging in Canada—one that is based on choice, flexibility, and consumer control. Consumers have lobbied for this paradigm shift. They have advocated for universal adaptable housing features that can meet everyone's needs. Transportation policies are slowly moving from specialized, separate transit systems to a family of accessible transportation that allows consumers more choice. Direct, individualized funding programs are giving consumers more control, choice, and flexibility over personal supports. Integrated education and community resources are increasingly available. Moving these from small-scale initiatives to large-scale programs is, however, a challenge.

As part of its British legacy, Canada inherited a model of social policy that provides for a comprehensive social welfare safety net. Yet this model is crumbling because of funding reductions. In contrast, the United States has developed civil rights laws, such as the Fair Housing Act Amendment and the Americans with Disability Act, that offer promising examples for Canada. The Canadian disability movement is increasingly emphasizing national coordinated policies and human rights legislation.

Frustrated over the lack of action, the Council of Canadians with Disabilities (2007) proposed a *National Action Plan on Disability*. This report outlined a comprehensive pan-Canadian approach that would build provisions for individuals with disabilities into mainstream policies and programs. The CCD advocated for a joint federal–provincial–territorial effort to create comprehensive disability standards across Canada and called on the federal government to use a disability policy lens when developing future laws, policies, programs, and human rights regulations. This plan highlights the need for the federal government to fulfill its commitment to Aboriginal people with disabilities. The report recommends the development of a federal Disability Act, one that would include the following: the availability of comprehensive disability supports throughout the country; the alleviation of poverty for persons with disabilities and their families; greater labour market integration; and access, inclusion, and full citizenship of Canadians with disabilities. This plan also emphasizes the need to implement these new policy directions with concrete enabling legislation and adequate funding.

Consumer groups have advocated for more comprehensive disability policies at the provincial/territorial level as well. One proposal has been to develop a Canadians with Disabilities Act in each province and territory similar to the AODA. This would require each jurisdiction to identify existing barriers and design timely plans to reduce them.

Future policies must involve all levels of government and guarantee citizenship rights with national standards. Policies must be comprehensive and responsive to individual needs, must support Aboriginal control of their programs, and must ensure consumer control, choice, and flexibility. Also essential is consistent enforcement of the legislation. Only through this multi-pronged approach will Canada create an environment in which all citizens can live independently.

References

AODA Committee. (2005). *Accessibility for Ontarians with Disability Act.* Toronto: Author.

Armitage, A. (2003). *Social welfare in Canada revisited.* Toronto, ON: Oxford University Press.

Baker, D. (2005). *Moving backwards: Canada's state of transportation accessibility in an integrated approach.* Winnipeg, MB: Council of Canadians with Disabilities.

Barile, M. (2000). Understanding the personal and political role of multiple minority status. *Disability Studies Quarterly, 20*(2), 123–128.

Barnes, C., & Mercer, G. (2010). *Exploring disability.* Cambridge, UK: Polity Press.

Beachell, L. (2011). *CCD annual report.* Winnipeg, MB: Council of Canadians with Disabilities.

Bramham, D. (2011, May 30). Evidence rules leave disabled Canadian girls open to sex abuse. *Vancouver Sun,* p. 1.

Canadian Centre on Disability Studies. (2004). *Students with disabilities: Transitions from post-secondary education to work.* Winnipeg, MB: Author.

Capponi, P. (2008). *The corpse will keep.* Toronto, ON: HarperCollins.

Carpenter, S. (2001). Housing blues from institutions to community. *CAILC New Bulletin, 6*(1), 10–13.

Carpenter, S., Estey, S., & Rioux. M. (2010). Disability rights: A call to arms. *Abilities.* Toronto, ON: Canadian Abilities Foundation.

Council of Canadians with Disabilities. (1996). *CCD's final presentation to the Task Force on Disability.* Winnipeg, MB: Author.

Council of Canadians with Disabilities. (2005). *A call for action.* Winnipeg, MB: Author.

Council of Canadians with Disabilities. (2007). *From vision to action building: Building an inclusive and accessible Canada: A national action plan.* Winnipeg, MB: Author.

References Council of Canadians with Disabilities. (2010). *Canada ratifies United Nations Convention on the Rights of Persons with Disabilities.* Winnipeg, MB: Author.

Crawford, C. (2005). *Breaking the mold: Furthering the employment of people with disabilities through new policies, programs, and financing arrangements.* Toronto, ON: Roehrer Institute.

Crawford, C. (2010). *Disabling poverty and enabling citizenship.* Winnipeg, MB: Council of Canadians with Disabilities.

Davis, L. (Ed.). (2010). *The disability studies reader.* Toronto, ON: Routledge.

Denton, L. (2000). From human care to prevention. *Canadian Journal of Community Mental Health, 19*(2), 127–134.

Dunn, P. (2003). The evolution of disability policies in Canada. *International Journal of Rehabilitation Research, 25*(3), 215–224.

Dunn, P. Hanes, R., Hardie, S. Leslie, D., & MacDonald, J. (2008). Best practices in promoting disability inclusion within Canadian Schools of Social Work. *Disability Studies Quarterly, 28*(1), 1–10.

Durst, D., & Bluechardt, M. (2004). Aboriginal people with disabilities: A vacuum in public policy. *SIPP Briefing Note,* (6), 1–7. Regina, SK: Saskatchewan Institute in Public Policy.

Durst, D., South, S., & Bluechardt, M. (2006). Urban First Nations peoples with disabilities speak out. *Journal of Aboriginal Health,* (September), 34–43.

Elias, B., & Demas, D. (2001). *A profile of Manitoba First Nations people with a disability.* Winnipeg, MB: Assembly of Manitoba Chiefs.

Enns, H., & Neufeldt, A. (2003). *In pursuit of equal participation: Canada and disability at home and abroad.* Concord, ON: Captus Press.

Ethno-Racial People with Disabilities Coalition of Ontario. (2000). *Three lives: A journey out of darkness.* Toronto, ON: Fireweed Media Productions.

Everett, B. (2000). *A fragile revolution: Consumers and psychiatric survivors confronting the power of the mental health system.* Waterloo, ON: Wilfrid Laurier University Press.

Federal Task Force on Disability Issues. (1996). *Equal citizenship of Canadians with disabilities: The will to act.* Ottawa, ON: Minister of Public Works and Government Services Canada.

Hanes, R. (2010). Social work with persons with disabilities. In S. Hick (Ed.), *Social work in Canada: An introduction* (pp. 217–234). Toronto, ON: Thompson Educational Publishing.

Hiranandani, V. (2005). Towards a critical theory of disability in social work. *Critical Social Work, 6*(1), 1–6.

Human Resources Development Canada. (1998). *In unison: A Canadian approach to disability issues.* Ottawa, ON: Author. Retrieved from http://www.socialunion.gc.ca/pwd/unison/approach_e.html.

Human Resources and Skills Development Canada. (2007). *Aboriginal people with disabilities. Advancing the inclusion of people with disabilities.* Ottawa, ON: Human Resources and Skills Development Canada.

Hutchison, P., Pedlar, A., Dunn, P., & Lord, J. (2000). The impact of Independent Living Resource Centres. *International Journal of Rehabilitation Research,* 23(2), 61–74.

Learning Disability Association of Canada. (2002). *Learning disabilities and the law.* Ottawa, ON: Author.

Lord, J. (2000). Is that all there is? Searching for citizenship in the midst of services. *Canadian Journal of Community Mental Health, 19*(2), 165–169.

Lord, J. (2010). *Impact: Changing the way we view disability: The history, perspective, and vision of the Independent Living Movement in Canada.* Ottawa, ON: Independent Living Canada.

Lord, J., & Hutchison, P. (2007). *Pathways to inclusion: Building a new story with people and communities.* Toronto, ON: Captus Press.

Lord, J., Snow, J., & Dingwall, C. (2005). *Building a new story: Transforming disability supports and policies.* Toronto, ON: Individualized Funding Coalition of Ontario.

McKnight, J., & Block, P. (2010). *The abundant community.* San Francisco, CA: Berrett-Koehler Publishers.

McRuer, R., & Berube, M. (2006). *Crip theory: Cultural signs of queerness and disability.* New York: NYU Press.

Mendelson, M., Battle, K., Torjman, S., & Lightman, E. (2010). *A basic income plan for Canadians with severe disabilities.* Ottawa, ON: Caledon Institute for Social Policy.

Miceli M. (2010). The disavowal of the body as a source of inquiry in critical disability studies: The Return of impairment? *Critical Disability Discourse, 2,* 1–14.

Morris, J. (2001). Impairment and disability: Constructing an ethics of care that promotes human rights. *Hypatia, 16*(4), 1–16.

Nelson, G. (2006). Mental health policies in Canada. In A. Westhues (Ed.), *Canadian social policy: Issues and perspectives* (4th ed.) (pp. 245–266). Waterloo, ON: Wilfrid Laurier University Press.

Nelson, G., Lord, J., & Ochocka, J. (2001). *Shifting the paradigm in community mental health: Towards empowerment and community.* Toronto, ON: University of Toronto Press.

Neufeldt, A. (2006). *Re-imaging disability employment supports.* Third International Forum on Disability Management. Brisbane, Australia.

Pedlar, A., Haworth, L., Hutchison, P., Taylor, A., & Dunn, P. (1999). *A textured life: Empowerment and adults with developmental disabilities.* Waterloo, ON: Wilfrid Laurier University Press.

Peters, Y. (2004). *Twenty years of litigating for disability equality rights: Has it made a difference?* Winnipeg, MB: Council of Canadians with Disabilities.

Pfeiffer, D. (2003). The origins of independent living. *Ragged Edge.* July, 1–2.

Porter, G. (2001). *Disability and education: Towards an inclusive approach.* Washington, DC: Inter-American Development Bank.

Pothier, D., & Delvin, R. (Eds.). (2006). *Critical disability theory: Essays in philosophy, politics, policym and law.* Vancouver, BC: UBC Press.

Prince, M. (2005). *A national strategy for disability supports.* Kingston, ON: Faculty of Health Sciences, Queen's University.

Reid, D. K., & Knight, M.G. (2006). Disability justifies exclusion of minority students: A critical history grounded in disability studies. *Educational Researcher, 35,* 18–23.

Rioux, M., & Prince, M. (2002). The Canadian political landscape of disability: Policy perspectives, social statuses, interest groups, and rights movement. In A. Puttee (Ed.), *Federalism, democracy, and disability policy in Canada* (pp. 11–28). Montreal, QC, and Kingston, ON: McGill-Queen's University Press.

Secretary of State. (1991). *The national strategy for the integration of persons with disabilities.* Ottawa, ON: Supply and Services Canada.

Smith, R., Kennedy, D., Youngkhill, L., & Hutchison, P. (2005). *Inclusive and special recreation.* Toronto, ON: McGraw-Hill.

Special Parliamentary Committee on the Disabled and the Handicapped. (1981). *Obstacles.* Ottawa, ON: Minister of Supply and Services Canada.

Standing Committee on Human Rights and the Status of Disabled Persons. (1990). *A consensus for action: The economic integration of disabled persons.* Ottawa, ON: Minister of Supply and Services Canada.

Standing Committee on Human Rights and the Status of Disabled Persons. (1993a). *Completing the circle.* Ottawa, ON: Minister of Supply and Services Canada.

Standing Committee on Human Rights and the Status of Disabled Persons. (1993b). *The grand design.* Ottawa, ON: Minister of Supply and Services Canada.

Statistics Canada. (2006). *Disability rates for Canada.* Ottawa, ON: Ministry of Industry, Science and Technology.

Stienstra, D. (2002) *Intersections: Disability and race / ethnicity / heritage language / religion.* Winnipeg, MB: Canadian Centre on Disability Studies.

Torjman, S. (2007). *Five-point plan for reforming disability supports.* Ottawa, ON: Caledon Institute.

Walters, T. (2010). *Independent Living Canada Annual Report.* Ottawa, ON: Independent Living Canada.

Wendell, S. (2006). Towards a feminist theory of disability. In L. David (Ed.), *The disability studies reader* (pp. 243–256). Toronto, ON: Routledge.

Wharf, B., & McKenzie, B. (2010). *Connecting policy to practice in human services* (3rd ed.). Toronto, ON: Oxford University Press.

Yoshida, K., Willi, V., Parker, I., & Locker, D. (2006). The Emergence of self-managed attendant services in Ontario. In M.A. McColl & L. Jongbloed (Eds.), *Disability and social policy in Canada* (pp. 315–336). Toronto, ON: Captus Press.

Additional Resources

Access for All http://still.my.revolution.tao.ca/radical
Alliance for Equality of Blind Canadians http://www.blindcanadians.ca
ARCH Disability Law Centre http://www.archdisabilitylaw.ca
Canadian Association of Community Living (CACL) http://www.cacl.ca
Canadian Association of the Deaf (CAD) http://www.cad.ca
Canadian Centre on Disability Studies (CCDS) http://disabilitystudies.ca
Canadian Council of the Blind (CCB) http://www.ccbnational.net
Canadian Hard of Hearing Association (CHHA) http://www.chha.ca
Canadian Mental Health Association (CMHA) http://www.cmha.ca
Canadian National Institute for the Blind (CNIB) http://www.cnib.ca
Confédération des Organismes de Personnes Handicapées du Québec (COPHAN) http://www.cophan.org
Council of Canadians with Disabilities (CCD) http://www.ccdonline.ca
Disabled People's International http://www.dpi.org
DisAbled Women's Network of Canada (DAWN-RAFH) http://www.dawncanada.net
Disability-Related Policy in Canada http://www.disabilitypolicy.ca/index_english.php

Additional Resources

Ethno-Racial People with Disabilities Coalition of Ontario http://www.ryerson.ca/erdco

Independent Living Canada (ILC) http://www.ilcanada.ca

Learning Disabilities Association of Canada (LDAC) http://www.ldac-taac.ca

National Aboriginal Network on Disability (NAND) http://www.schoolnet.ca/aboriginal/health-e.html

National Education Association of Disabled Students (NEADS) http://www.neads.ca

National Federation of the Blind Advocates for Equality (NFBAE) http://www.nfbae.ca

National Network for Mental Health (NNMH) http://www.nnmh.ca

Office for Disability Issues (ODI) in HRSDC http://www.hrsdc.gc.ca/eng/disability_issues

People First of Canada http://www.peoplefirstofcanada.ca

Roeher Institute http://www.roeher.ca

Caring and Aging

Examining Policy Inequities

15

Sheila Neysmith

As people age, the quality of their lives is affected by a range of social policies. In Canada, as in many other countries, finding ways of meeting the forecasted health care needs of old people has taken centre stage as *the* policy concern of an aging population. It is anticipated that this demographic phenomenon will make heavy demands on the health care system, necessitating a growth in services that will be costly. On the one hand, the Canadian population is aging, albeit still quite young compared to those of European countries. On the other hand, on a global scale Canada could be categorized as one of a handful of privileged nations that can meaningfully consider options that affect the quality-of-life possibilities of its aging citizens.

The causal link between an aging population and rising health costs has been repeatedly challenged by research (e.g., Evans et al., 2001; Gilleard & Higgs, 1998; Hollander & Chappell, 2007; Robertson, 1997), but this is routinely ignored as correlations between health cost drivers and age-related utilization data are proclaimed as "obvious." The power of this demographic crisis discourse remains quite unabated and seems to reappear in a new guise as soon as an old one is discredited. In recent years its new name is the "Boomer Tsunami." If one must use geological analogies, a glacier would be more accurate. There is nothing unexpected or overwhelming about the aging of the Canadian population. Its profile has been known for decades. Just as surely, we can predict that by 2031 the last of the baby boomers will have moved into the 65-plus cohort and that by the year 2051 those over 65 will comprise about 25 percent of the population, with many more proportionately over 80 (Statistics Canada 2005a). What policies we put in place will result from political choices we make, not demographic imperatives. Understanding the relationship between an aging population, the distribution of caring responsibilities, and health costs—the focus of this chapter—demands a willingness to engage with research and policy debates that open up rather than foreclose options.

The shape and content of the health care literature reflect the influence of professions and organizations that are powerful players in—and thus definers of knowledge about—the health care services used by elderly people. In the last edition of this book I argued that policy discussions tend to position old women in particular—because of their higher morbidity and longevity rates—as a caring problem (Gibson, 1996), a problem that will get worse and that will be costly to address. This, unfortunately, has not changed; and meanwhile, attempts to address "the problem" have given rise to a focus on the older person's responsibility for maintaining a healthy lifestyle. Later in the chapter I consider some of the implications of this. An aging nation does present different policy challenges than that of a demographically young nation. Whether this translates into a "caring problem" depends on how this demographic fact is incorporated into social policy.

Older people will continue to suffer from more chronic conditions than younger people, a fact that often translates into people needing help with some of the activities of daily living. An important policy issue then is how to ensure that the resources, and types and amounts of services needed, are available and can be provided in an equitable way (Deber, Hollander, & Jacobs 2008). The complexity of meeting this policy objective cannot be reduced to media sound bites which assert that Canadians are committed to universal health care or that seniors want to remain in their own homes. Equally concerning are statements, such as those made by the major political parties before the federal election of May 2011, about maintaining an annual 6 percent increase to provincial health care budgets after the current accord expires in 2014. Such declarations gloss over important controversies about what types of services are required in order to meet the needs of an aging population, where responsibility lies for guaranteeing these, and how accessible they are to a diverse population (Kittay, Jennings, & Wasunna 2005). At present, it is families, not the health care system, that do the lion's share of caring for relatives who are in need of daily assistance. We know that this proves costly to many women as they age; yet our social policies and health care services seem unable to ameliorate, let alone eliminate, these costs. In many cases it seems that existing policies actually perpetuate inequities (Ferraro & Shippee, 2009; Grenier, 2005).

The population of older Canadians, like that of younger age cohorts, is marked by diversity. Figures available from Statistics Canada (2005b) confirm that this diversity will increase dramatically in the next decade. For instance, nationally, 96 percent of the visible minority population now live in metropolitan areas compared to 68 percent for the total population. This has implications for service structures in cities such as Toronto, Vancouver, Winnipeg, and Halifax. However, social disparities also travel along axes of diversity such as gender, class, ethnoracial differences, ability, and sexuality, to name but those most visible. These differences are as important as age in determining how social policies affect the quality of people's lives as they age (see Dilworth-Anderson, Williams, & Gibson, 2002, for a twenty-year review of these issues in caregiving research).

In the following pages, I look at how several key concepts are used in defining the "caring problem." This will be followed by a consideration of some of the stakeholders in long-term care policy. The next section assesses several existing programs. In the final part of the chapter I step back to ponder what it is that Canadians envision for their own aging as members of our society. The chapter closes with a few reflections on future Canadian social policy directions that could ensure that groups of aging citizens are not excluded.

The Power of Concepts in Defining Reality

Language is important—it shapes our thoughts and communicates meaning. Concepts and theories used in social policy are not neutral. They emphasize what is important to consider, and consequently what can be ignored. For instance, what is often called "long-term care" policy varies across provinces, and policy statements are littered with ambiguous references to health, community, and caring. Long-term care policy is usually seen as part of health care policy. Although the concept of health seems to be used in a very broad sense in policy statements such as the preamble to the Canada Health Act of 1985 (R.S.C. 1985, c. C-6), when operationalized in terms of services covered, it is narrowed to hospitals, physician fees, drugs, and lab tests. This effectively means that most of the services needed by elderly people living in the community are excluded. Similarly, policy concepts such as community care, managed care, and the mixed economy of care reverberate with service delivery implications; yet most actual care occurs in people's homes, delivered informally by family members, where the minimal formal services that are available are not covered by the CHA. Finally, "caring" is a word that carries positive overtones, but it also is used ambiguously. One is never sure exactly what it covers, so its meaning needs to be investigated in each setting. The considerable feminist literature on the topic of caring defines the concept as the physical, mental, and emotional activities involved in looking after, responding to, and supporting others (see, for example, Kittay et al., 2005; Neysmith, 2000; Tronto, 1993). It includes both paid and unpaid work.

Another much-used yet ephemeral policy concept is that of community. The term will probably always be ambiguous; the challenge is to determine how the idea is being employed today in long-term care policy. The concept of community-based care both captures a range of services that exist and expresses a policy goal for what we would like to exist. Not surprisingly, once we start to operationalize it, we discover some very contradictory ideas. The term seems to invoke a nostalgia for simpler times, reflecting idealizations of what family and community were like in some imagined past. However, there is an alternative discourse that points out the exclusionary practices in many communities. The challenge is around how to build alliances that recognize differences but that can also deal with conflicts as part of the process of pursuing desired policy goals (McBride, 2005).

The Power of Concepts in Defining Reality

Canadian civil society at any given historical moment is made up of individuals who belong to multiple communities, but these memberships also change over a life course. The question is, "What ideas of community inform our discussions of community-based care?" As programs based on universal entitlements are cut back, services get more and more targeted. As publicly funded services shrink, market-based substitutes expand to fill the void but are available only to those who have the resources to purchase them. With this in mind, I want to consider some of the assumptions behind the concept of "community" that are being enacted on the long-term care policy/program stage at this particular historical hour.

The drama is supposedly about providing services that can help people remain engaged in the life of their families and communities even as physical abilities decline. The plot line, however, is unclear. Indeed, the players seem at points to be reading from different scripts. In the current production, the character of "client" has disappeared. The "consumer/customer" has taken her place. Rather oddly, sometimes this role is played by an old person, but very often "family" is the designated substitute. Either way, these actors speak quietly. Indeed, their microphone seems to have been usurped by service providers and industry reps, who march around the stage loudly proclaiming "consumer choice" and "customer satisfaction." There is also a phantom on stage called "taxpayer," whose spirit is invoked to justify claims of service misuse and/or calls for tax breaks. At times this chorus line is so loud one can hardly make out the dialogue, let alone follow the story. Hovering in the wings is a tattered character called "citizen," who can be most charitably defined as having an identity crisis. When she or he occasionally says something, there is silence for an instant, and then the chatter continues as if "citizen" had never spoken. It is worth stopping to consider what is going on here.

Community-based care policy is ambiguous because contradictory language and concepts are at play. The market language of consumer/customer/taxpayer is about choice and purchase power, not need and access, which is the language of citizen-based claims. In an earlier edition of this book, I wrote: "It is ironic that in the mixed economy of care models (Baldock, 1997; Evers, 1993) operating across countries today, if choice exists at any point it is where a designated access agency tenders contracts to provide services. An old woman, or family member, gets little choice—they receive service from a designated provider. Granted, for those with sufficient resources, there is the option to purchase from commercial firms, if these exist where one lives. Like all market transactions, however, it is a case of 'buyer beware.'" In the intervening years these trends have intensified. In Ontario, for instance, for-profit organizations provided 18 percent of home nursing services before contract bidding was introduced in 1997. By 2001, this had increased to 48 percent (Ontario Health Coalition [OHC], 2005). In 2011 there continues to be consolidation of community-based services as both for-profit organizations and not-for-profit ones try to develop some efficiencies of scale in an increasingly competitive market where yearly allowable cost increases are minimal but reporting demands are high. In this environment the survival rate of small organizations seems increasingly unlikely in the years ahead. Across the country there are provincial variations in the funding, organization, and delivery of home care services. Deber, Hollander, and Jacobs (2008) analyze some of the incentives and disincentives built into the mixed funding models used in various Canadian jurisdictions. Firbank (2011) presents an instructive case study of the Quebec situation, where the contracting out of services is an established practice, as it is in other provinces. In Quebec, however, a dominant policy frame exists that centres responsibility in government to fund and provide home care. Thus contracting out results in quite different outcomes than in provinces where government has not assumed such a responsibility.

In sum, receiving services in one's own home does not mean that one is part of a community or that the services are developed by or in a community, yet the use of the term carries both these overtones. Ambiguous and contradictory concepts are not just the result of fuzzy policy thinking or poor program planning. They exist because there are competing priorities among long-term care policy players.

Who Are the Stakeholders in the "Caring Problem"?

Who Are the Stakeholders in the "Caring Problem"?

A quick tabulation suggests that the stakeholder list would include hospitals, home care agencies, federal and provincial governments, businesses, families, and old people themselves. Equally important to recognize is that some of these players are more powerful than others and that there are tensions between and among them: family, state, market, and voluntary sectors as service providers; cash and services as modes of delivery; carer and person cared for as persons involved in a relationship; caring responsibilities and the demands of paid work done by women and men; and nation-states as importers and exporters of caring labour in a growing global care chain (Browne & Braun, 2008; Ehrenreich & Hochschild, 2003).

It seems obvious to claim that the quality of life of elderly persons is the primary policy concern because they are the ones experiencing the conditions that give rise to the above policy. It can be argued, however, that old persons are the weakest stakeholder because the problem is in fact a creation of the health care system. The discourse casts the former as needy and resource users; the latter are positioned as service providers with limited resources who are being inundated by ever-increasing demands. In this scenario, the old person is depicted as a dependant rather than as a senior citizen with attendant entitlements. The image projected is usually that of a poor old woman. As I have argued elsewhere, aging is a gendered process, so women experience old age differently than do men. One of these differences

Who Are the Stakeholders in the "Caring Problem"?

is that old women inhabit an aging body in a culture that devalues both old age and women. To be old, non-white, disabled, or female is not only to be different but also to be inferior (Neysmith & McAdam 1999; Shildrick 1997; Twigg 2009). The implications of this for the well-being of women as they age have not received a lot of attention in gerontology. Certainly, much has been written about the state of the aging female body. Professional concerns connect the deteriorating condition of this body to service use implications. That is, the effects of physical frailty on an elderly person's ability to perform certain tasks are not taken up in policy discourse as problematic because they are a threat to a person's sense of identity, nor are they seen as an indicator that the health care system is failing to meet need. Rather, persons are categorized as "at risk," bearing warning signs of potential demands on service budgets. Ironically, research has consistently demonstrated that these are in fact poor predictors of service use and that it is the presence or absence of informal carers that is most critical (Mitchell, Roos, & Shapiro, 2005, p. 66).

Chronic conditions seen as manageable at home assume that there is a family member who will be able to provide most of the care and manage what limited community services are available. In this version of community-based services, the old person and her or his family are considered a service unit for assessment-of-service purposes. In other words, what an old person needs is conflated with what family can provide at the point of assessment. Front line workers are aware of this dynamic but see few options except to factor in family caring potential as they ration the very limited services available.

No matter how understandable, given front line realities, such practices are built on dangerous assumptions. First, there is no evidence that family members can provide the type of care delivered by a qualified nursing assistant or home care worker. This off-loading onto families also results in services being moved off the public stage and rendered invisible by relocating them in the private sphere of family responsibility. The item is effectively removed from public scrutiny. Second, as is well documented in the caring literature (Hooyman & Gonyea, 1995; Neysmith, 2000; Neysmith & Reitsma-Street, 2009), the emotional, mental, and physical costs to both parties are ignored. The social construction of aging as a problem of physical deterioration ignores the other dimensions that make up what is commonly referred to as "quality of life." In a synthesis of the extensive literature in the area, Kelley-Gillespie (2009) posited six domains of well-being: social, physical, psychological, cognitive, spiritual, and environmental. Most of these dimensions are ignored as physical well-being is prioritized.

Similarly, the mental health of women as they age has been associated with the stress and financial implications of caring across the life cycle. Milne and Williams (2000), in a wide-ranging assessment of what literature is available, concluded that social inequality was a powerful but much neglected determiner of the mental health of aging women. This earlier analytical thread has received important impetus with Ferraro and Shippee's (2009, pp. 334–36) articulation of the five axioms of cumulative inequality within theories of aging. In summary, these are:

1. Social systems generate inequality, which is manifested over the life course through demographic and developmental processes.
2. Disadvantage increases exposure to risk, but advantage increases exposure to opportunity.
3. Life course trajectories are shaped by the accumulation of risk, available resources, and human agency.
4. Perceptions of life trajectories influence subsequent trajectories.
5. Cumulative inequality may lead to premature mortality; therefore, nonrandom selection may give the appearance of decreasing inequality later in life.

In conclusion, health care research and aging theory need to be monitored to ensure knowledge is generated that can inform the articulation of policy goals which can promote the quality of life of an aging population and which are not undercut by short-term health care crises.

What Approaches Have Been Tried to Address the "Caring Problem"?

Policies can be thought of as providing resources directly in the form of services or indirectly through the tax system. In this section, four policy approaches tried in Canada, two of each type, are briefly discussed (Neysmith, 2005). These are home care, caregiver payment schemes, caregiver tax credits, and compassionate leave. The discussion comes with a major caveat, however. Since kin provide most of the care to people as they age, the programs discussed in the following paragraphs are only minor players in accomplishing the task of caring for people who need help with the activities of daily living, even though, as players, they seem to occupy centre stage. Furthermore, while each province has some form of community-based care legislation, Canada does not have a national home and community care program like that, for example, which exists in Australia—a country with many similar state structures (Neysmith, 1995). Consequently, there is not the same guarantee of funding as exists for hospitals and physician fees, which are covered by the Canada Health Act (1985).

It is important to note, however, that there continue to be calls for a national policy. At the time of writing the most recent one was in the form of a Senate report, *Canada's Aging Population: Seizing the Opportunity*, released in April 2009. Its findings support recommendations made by earlier reports. It called on the federal government to provide leadership and coordination in policy areas such as a National Integrated Care Initiative, a National Caregiver Strategy, and a National Pharmacare Program. It also called for federal transfers to address the needs of provinces with the highest proportion of the aging population. These recommendations were based on widespread consultations. After the release of the report, Senator Carstairs, who chaired the committee, assumed responsibility for taking the report and its recommendations on the road—and she did so tirelessly for two years. It is telling that in the spring of 2011 she announced that she was retiring because she "was tired." Challenging inequitable policies decade after decade, like living with them, has a negative cumulative effect!

As it stands, federal funding continues to come via the Canada Health Transfer (CHT), an amendment to the Federal Provincial Fiscal Arrangements Act in 2004 that imposes few restrictions on provinces as to how the funds are to be allocated among competing health care priorities and this is exactly what happens. For instance, Ontario in 2007 introduced an *Aging at Home Strategy* (Ontario, 2007). Initially, community consultations resulted in a range of innovative community-based projects designed to support frail elderly persons in the community. Over its life course of four years, however, that strategy's priorities changed—projects increasingly were funded on the basis of how well they addressed overcrowding in hospital emergency rooms by reducing emergency use by those 65 and older and/or by facilitating hospitals' chronic care patients' return home more quickly (commonly referred to as the ER/ALC problem). At the policy level, once again, community care was expected to solve a hospital problem—despite the disproportionate weighting of resources to the latter (Williams et al., 2009).

In most provinces, public agencies are not the providers of services; rather, regional bodies are mandated to oversee the contracting out of service delivery to competing not-for-profit and for-profit home and public sector care providers. I will go no further on the problems of this model; considerable ink has been spilled on it already (Aronson & Neysmith, 1997, 2006; Canadian Association of Retired Persons, 1999; Chester, Hughes, & Challis 2010; Light, 2001; Ontario Health Coalition, 2005; Williams et al., 1999). What is important is that this model of health care funding and delivery, along with the discourse of scarce resources that accompanies it, is the context in which case managers are deciding how to ration their very tight budgets. One consequence is that assessments of need in practice take into account whether clients can obtain additional services from commercial home care services, and that this reinforces gender and class inequities. This trend is also troubling because pay levels, as well as the conditions of employment and training of personal support workers (PSWs), continue to be poorly regulated (Aronson, Denton, & Zeytinoglu, 2004). Using Canadian data, Denton, Zeytinoglu, and Davies (2002) have documented how working conditions negatively affect the mental health of visiting home care workers. Armstrong (2009) found that in Canadian long-term-care institutions, many of the problems that care workers identified stemmed from understaffing. Residents, for example, often became violent toward care providers because they were frustrated beyond endurance with the lack of care. The daily supportive care provided by personal support workers is the backbone of the chronic care an aging population needs. This lack of attention to labour force issues across sectors does not bode well for the realization of policies that can address Canada's "caring problem."

What Approaches Have Been Tried to Address the "Caring Problem"?

The existence of respite services is one of the few concrete indicators of recognition of who is doing most of the caring work. Respite relieves caregivers by providing them with temporary relief through in-home or out-of-home care. Understanding what respite is and a commitment to providing it—because it is the one service consistently requested by users—does not mean that there is agreement on what is meant by the call for respite. The pressing question is why carers are experiencing burden to the point that they need it. Respite may provide relief, but perhaps prevention should be the focus of our inquiries. Thus, it is important to know under what conditions the cry for respite arises. What does respite mean to users, providers, and policy makers? How important is respite compared to other services on the highly political health care priority list? These questions are not directly answered in the available research, but studies can throw light on how we might start to address them.

Those who are employed to do caring work—that is, formal care providers—are not calling for respite. While the disparities among the salaries and working conditions of doctors, nurses, social workers, and home care workers are great, respite is built into their work—that is, into the institutional structures of work schedules, benefits, vacations, and so on. Not so for those who do most of the caring work: family members. Study after study shows that kin carers do not want out, they want some relief! Respite is one word used to describe services that might address this well-documented need; but does the word challenge assumptions around kin-based care that make respite necessary? The current concept of respite puts it in the same type of service model as food banks and shelters. They are necessary to the survival of users, but at the same time their use casts a stigma: it implies a weakness on the part of users and questions their ability to cope. Thus respite is a good temporary response but in and of itself will not address the basic issue. If caring labour needs such services, then it indicates a problem, not the answer—much as food banks and shelters indicate failures of policy, not individuals or families. Now, we can confine ourselves to the equivalent of building more shelters and developing more food banks, or we can ask the policy question: How do we eliminate the need for respite?

Another approach to increasing the supply of caring labour is the development of carer allowances, which are available to relatives in a number of countries. This policy option is not well developed in Canada (Keefe & Rajnovich, 2007). This attempt to undergird the care provided by kin is fraught with dubious outcomes for many women. Its merits continue to be debated in the international literature, so it seems prudent to post huge "Proceed

With Caution" signs along this policy road (for an assessment of various approaches to paying for informal care in European countries, see Ungerson, 2004; Ungerson & Yeandle, 2007). The money available is usually more of a compensation (allowance) rather than payment for work done. Kin carers cannot negotiate pay scales or working conditions. Perhaps most worrisome are the types of differences between women who use such programs and those who do not. For instance, Janice Keefe in Nova Scotia has undertaken a series of studies that compare those who use carer allowances with those who use home care services (Keefe & Fancey, 1997; Keefe & Rajnovich, 2007). The former are non-urban, and they live in areas where services are scarce and where unemployment is high. Thus, any choices that such programs might theoretically make available come up against the stark reality that these women are making decisions under conditions where few options in fact exist. Geographical variation is just one of many aspects to consider when examining what is happening to elderly people and their families in the mixed economy of care.

Turning to the tax system as a possible avenue for increasing the resources available to old people and their families, the Caregiver Tax Credit is the most visible. Introduced in 1998, the 2011 credit is $4,282, which reduces federal income tax by a maximum of $642. However, you must live in the same residence as the person you are caring for, that person must be a direct relative, and it does not apply if the dependent person is not defined as low income. The credit has numerous shortcomings, the most obvious of which are that the amount is low; it does not reflect the amount of work done; and it is of no value if the caregiver is not employed, if his or her income is just over the allowed amount (often the case where elderly spouses provide care), or if the elderly person needing care does not live in the home of the caregiver—the norm for many Canadian households. Minor modifications in criteria to qualifiy for tax credits and/or benefits across provinces constantly occur but their impact on the costs of caring labour carried out by family members is minimal. For an estimate of these proportional costs, see Leong et al. (2007) .

Another tax route policy introduced in 2004 is Compassionate Care Leave (Human Resources and Skills Development Canada, 2005). This provides employees with up to six weeks of leave from their job with benefits protected. To qualify, the employee must be in a job covered by Employment Insurance and have at least 600 hours of earnings. A person must obtain a certificate from a physician stating that the individual needing care—who must be a direct family member—is at risk of death within twenty-six weeks. This policy had a very low take-up rate in the year following its introduction. In fact, only 5 to 6 percent of those expected to use it did so. One immediate problem was the restrictive definition of who was eligible. Another was the reluctance by physicians to "certify" the life expectancy of a patient. One can imagine that family members were equally unwilling to hear such predictions.

Developing Policy That Recognizes Caring Labour

I do not want to leave this examination of efforts taken to address the "caring problem" without mentioning one other sector that appears in policy documents—the volunteer. A discourse on volunteering emerged in the 1990s that could not have been imagined during the decades that marked the reign of the welfare state (Hughes, 1998). At that time the word "volunteer" was avoided because it conjured up images of charity that were quite at odds with ideas about citizen entitlements and state obligations; yet today volunteers have become players in a wide array of social programs. At least at the level of official policy, their presence is articulated as essential to the achievement of both program and organizational goals. When positioned as citizens whose voices are critical for ensuring that services reflect community concerns, volunteers are indeed key policy players. The contributions that seniors make as volunteers have been noted in many policy documents (Chappell & Prince, 1997). They do indeed contribute, but people volunteer for many reasons. The question is, "How is the discourse on volunteering developing in a rhetoric of scarce resources?" A pressing concern is the implications of this renewed emphasis on volunteerism in a hollowed-out welfare state. The labour of volunteers is also becoming increasingly essential to the capacity of organizations to carry out their mandates. Thus, we can add volunteers to the for-profit and not-for-profit organizations, families, and public services that make up the mixed company of players who deliver home care. In summary, we cannot avoid the paid/unpaid labour dilemma by reinventing the volunteer.

These sketches of what is happening to different sectors of the caring labour force together offer a picture that formal and informal carers have much to be concerned about. In the mixed economy of care that characterizes what we call community care policy today, the much discussed restructuring of health care is not resulting in the transfer of resources to home care—rather, it is resulting in the transfer of *costs*. Furthermore, as costs are jettisoned from acute care budgets, they land in the community, where women as aging citizens, as home care workers, and as family members pick up the responsibilities with no say as to the terms and conditions under which caring is done.

Developing Policy That Recognizes Caring Labour

Several issues are shaping Canada's "caring problem," and some of them are more obvious than others. It is obvious that family-based caring is not recognized as labour and that when such labour is done by non-kin, a low value is ascribed to it. On the one hand, we talk about old people who need care as users or consumers (or sometimes even customers); on the other, we refer to family carers as service providers. The former take, the latter give. In such a scenario the actors are positioned in ways that guarantee conflict, guilt, and resentment. The setting is disempowering for all. What are the possibilities if we change the script? Let me suggest that perhaps the problem in this policy drama is its underlying principle of independence (Plath, 2009), which steers the audience toward the conclusion that if people acted responsibly, they would "age successfully" and not be in their current situation. The implication is that basically, they are responsible for needing help now, or put more bluntly, that they are to blame for needing care. Physically they did not take care of themselves, or socially they did not stay engaged, or economically they did not save, or they made poor choices (Rozanova, 2010). Two related assumptions underpin this image of what successful aging entails that need to be interrogated: the ideal of independence and the ethic of individual responsibility. Feminist scholarship has exposed how dependency and dependency care are invisible because of the private/public split in Western thought (Folbre, 2008; Hamington & Miller, 2006; Held, 2006). The independent individual is at the centre of liberal concepts of the citizen, with entitlements, rights, and claims for equitable treatment (Ellis, 2004; Nelson, 2006; Nelson & England, 2002). If humans were assumed to be interdependent, then relationships of various types would have to be built into theories that underpin ethical codes, family and community relationships, and most of our health care, political, economic, and other social institutions. If interdependence and shared responsibility were central to social policy, then very different debates would ensue about how responsibility (rather than blame) is to be equitably distributed across different sectors of society, across nation-states and over time. Considering all these dimensions is beyond the scope of this chapter, but they are fundamental to fair and equitable long-term-care policies. (This broader debate is approached somewhat differently across disciplines but underpins feminist theories about "care." An accessible summary continues to be Kittay and colleagues (2005), but see also Adam and Groves (2011).)

Certainly many aspects of social life are organized without regard to the caring responsibilities that citizens carry. Employment practices do not build in caring as a normal and expected responsibility of adults, a responsibility that requires work schedules that accommodate the demands of caring (Howell, 2007; Kershaw, 2006; Lewis & Guillari, 2005). Most jobs are regulated by employment standards and minimum wage schedules; many also have pension benefits and supplementary health insurance. Some unions and progressive employers have even brought in family care benefits, but these are concessions from the "normality" of paid employment. They are defined as fringe benefits, which suggests that they are not central to paid employment, even though the demands made on the employee may be anything but fringe-like in their impact. Of course, for those who provide unpaid care, this is not even regarded as work. Thus, those family members who take up the responsibility of providing care suffer the economic consequences of doing so. Behind this is the continued existence of a framework that separates the public and the private lives of citizens. The assumption that family life and its responsibilities are a private matter is rooted in 19th-century industrial models yet continues to dominate policy thinking at the beginning of the 21st century.

Developing Policy That Recognizes Caring Labour

It might help shake up assumptions if we asked ourselves how long-term-care programs would be described if we took out all references to family (read primarily women) providing care. One approach to crossing the public/private divide that is so costly to women is to ungender caring labour and institutionalize what Nancy Fraser (1997), an American political scientist, terms a universal caregiver model. Such a model would assume that all adults carry caring responsibilities; the ebb and flow of these may change over the life cycle of individuals, but caring responsibilities are a social given. Under such a model, employment policies and job descriptions would have caring-related rights and benefits that complement the health and pension benefits of today. Promotion ladders that do not allow for caring responsibilities could be challenged as discriminatory. Doing so is pivotal if women's citizenship claims are to be realized. This will happen only if caring for others is seen as central to the lives of all citizens, as central as holding down a paid job, participating in community affairs, paying taxes, and being a consumer (Feinberg & Whitlatch, 1998; Neysmith et al., 2009).

Such an orientation would also force us to recognize that quality control cannot be guaranteed when care is assumed to be provided by family members, so we would have to figure out how to ensure that neither party is forced into provider or receiver roles against their wishes. At the least, such a stance would be reassuring to that 25 percent of the elderly population with no spouse or children, for whom kin-based care is a myth. I am not saying this would be easy. What I am saying is that we would be preoccupied with a different set of issues. Such a discussion is important because it will affect the hard choices that all of us have to make regarding what to support, what to steer away from, and what coalitions to participate in.

Although feminist debates about how to conceptualize as well as promote citizenship have consistently highlighted the deleterious effects of the split between private and public spheres, in the 1990s the issue took on a certain edge as neoliberalism began to equate citizenship rights with ideas of choice—in particular, choice in the marketplace (for a synopsis of some of the arguments, see Lister, 1997, 2007). The new citizen became the consumer of goods and services in one domain and the taxpayer in another. Such a rendition, which permeates professional as well as market and government programs, restricts our thinking about alternatives. Totally absent from this discourse is an awareness of how exclusionary such talk is. One needs time and money to be both consumer and taxpayer. If this is what it takes to be a citizen, then those who are carrying out caring responsibilities lack the coinage to be citizen-like. The exclusionary circle is now complete. Policies that emphasize the centrality of choice are a bad joke if your only option is sole responsibility.

Conclusion

The analysis I have presented is premised on the assumption that citizenship debates are critical to the well-being of carers. However, it is not caring that is the problem; rather, it is that caring takes place in a society where inequities of gender, class, race, and ability—to name but those highlighted in this chapter—play themselves out to the advantage of some and the oppression of others. Through the caring labour that they do, women make major contributions to their communities as surely as they do in the labour market and within their families (Neysmith & Reitsma-Street, 2009). Any discourse can be picked up in ways that reinforce oppression rather than promote equity. Discussions about connecting caring labour to citizenship claims are as susceptible to this as any other policy discussion. This threat notwithstanding, avoidance would be costly. Not conceptualizing caring work in terms of contributions to the community, and ultimately to the nation, reinforces its invisibility while leaving intact gendered definitions of who are "contributing" members to their society, what qualifies as work, and, ultimately, who is entitled to make claims as citizens. The result is the reinforcement of social exclusion (Craig, 2004).

In this chapter I have attempted to articulate another way of thinking about "the caring problem." Yes, this is visionary; but having a vision is essential to protesting the discriminatory effects of policies. Responses that resources are scarce are not responses. Resources are always scarce; decisions around priorities need to be debated. If we are silent, the process of marginalizing those who provide informal care—those who do 80 percent of the work—will increase even more. That process will not cease because we stop naming it. The work to be done is daunting. It entails ongoing contestation of definitions as well as coalition building with groups of people all of whom come with shifting alliances and unequal power. However, these are the daily ingredients of social change work. For those who wish to engage, I would argue that the caring labour done by women is as legitimate a basis for claiming social entitlements as that of individuals who currently are enshrined in images of the rights-bearing taxpayer or the sovereign consumer.

References

Adam, B., & Groves, C. (2011). Futures tended: Care and future-oriented responsibility. *Bulletin of Science, Technology, and Society, 31*(1), 17–27. doi:10.1177/0270467610391237

Armstrong, P. (2009). Long-term care problems: Both residents and care providers denied fair treatment. Retrieved from http://www.policyalternatives.org

Aronson, J., Denton, M., & Zeytinoglu, I. (2004). Market-modelled home care in Ontario: Deteriorating working conditions and dwindling community capacity. *Canadian Public Policy, 30*(1), 111–125. Retrieved from http://economics.ca/cgi/jab?journal=cpp&article=v30n1p0111

References

Aronson, J., & Neysmith, S. (1997). The retreat of the state and long-term care provision: Implications for frail elderly people, unpaid family carers, and paid home care workers. *Studies in Political Economy, 53*, 37–66.

Aronson, J., & Neysmith, S. (2006). Obscuring the costs of home care: Restructuring at work. *Work, Employment, and Society, 20*, 27–45. doi: 10.1177/0950017006061272

Baldock, J. (1997). Social care in old age: More than a funding problem. *Social Policy and Administration, 31*(1), 73–89. doi: 10.1111/1467-9515.00039

Browne, C. V., & Braun, K. L. (2008). Globalization, women's migration, and the long-term-care workforce. *Gerontologist, 48*(1), 16–24. doi: 10.1093/geront/48.1.16

Canada. Senate Special Committee on Aging. (2009). *Canada's Aging Population: Seizing the Opportunity.* Retrieved from http://www.parl.gc.ca/Content/SEN/Committee/402/agei/subsite/Aging_Report_Home-e.htm

Canada Health Act, R.S.C. 1985, c. C-6. Retrieved from http://www.laws.justice.gc.ca/en/C-6

Canadian Association of Retired Persons. (1999). *Putting a face on home care.* Kingston, ON: Queen's Health Policy Research Unit, Queen's University.

Chappell, N.L., & Prince, M. (1997). Reasons why Canadian seniors volunteer. *Canadian Journal on Aging / La Revue canadienne du vieillissement, 16*(2), 336–353. doi: 10.1017/S0714980800014380

Chester, H., Hughes, J., & Challis, D. (2010). Patterns of commissioning, contracting, and care management in social care services for older people in England. *British Journal of Social Work, 40*, 2523–2537. doi: 10.1093/bjsw/bcq044

Craig, G. (2004). Citizenship, exclusion, and older people. *Journal of Social Policy, 33*(1), 95–114. doi: 10.1017/S0047279403007207

Deber, R., Hollander, M., & Jacobs, P. (2008). Models of funding and reimbursement in health care: A conceptual framework. *Canadian Public Administration / Administration Publique du Canada, 51*(3), 381–405. doi: 10.1111/j.1754-7121.2008.00030.x

Denton, M., Zeytinoglu, I.U., & Davies, S. (2002). Working in clients' homes: The impact on the mental health and well-being of visiting home care workers. *Home Health Care Services Quarterly, 21*(1), 1–27.

Dilworth-Anderson, P., Williams, I.C., & Gibson, B.E. (2002). Issues of race, ethnicity, and culture in caregiving research: A 20-year review (1980–2000). *The Gerontologist, 42*(2), 237–272.

Ehrenreich, B., & Hochschild, A.R. (Eds.). (2003). *Global woman: Nannies, maids, and sex workers in the new economy.* New York, NY: Metropolitan Books.

Ellis, K. (2004). Dependency, justice, and the ethic of care. In H. Dean (Ed.), *The ethics welfare: Human rights, dependency and responsibility* (pp. 29–48). Bristol, UK: Policy Press.

Evans, R., McGrail, K.M., Morgan, S., Barer, M., & Hertzman, C. (2001). Apocalypse no: Population aging and the future of health care systems. *Canadian Journal on Aging*, 20(suppl. 1), 160–191.

Evers, A. (1993). The welfare mix approach: Understanding the pluralism of welfare systems. In A. Evers & I. Svetlik (Eds.), *Balancing pluralism: New welfare mixes in care for the elderly* (pp. 3–31). Aldershot, UK: Avebury.

Federal Provincial Fiscal Arrangements Act, R.S.C. 1985, c. F-8. Retrieved from http://www.laws.justice.gc.ca/en/F-8

References Feinberg, L.F., & Whitlatch, C. (1998). Family caregivers and in-home respite options: The consumer-directed versus agency-based experience. *Journal of Gerontological Social Work, 30*(3/4), 9–28.

Ferraro, K., & Shippee, T. (2009). Aging and cumulative inequality: How does inequality get under the skin? *The Gerontologist, 49(3),* 333–343. doi: 10.1093/geront/gnp034

Firbank, O. (2011). Framing home-care policy: A case study of reforms in a Canadian jurisdiction. *Journal of Aging Studies,* 25, 34–44. doi: 10.1016/j.jaging.2010.08.009

Folbre, N. (2008). Reforming care. *Politics and Society, 36*(3), 373–387. doi: 10.1177/0032329208320567

Fraser, N. (1997). *Justice interruptus: Critical reflections on the "postsocialist" condition.* New York, NY: Routledge.

Gibson, D. (1996). Broken down by age and gender: The "problem of old women" redefined. *Gender and Society, 10*(4), 433–448. doi: 10.1177/089124396010004005

Gilleard, C., & Higgs, P. (1998). Old people as users and consumers of healthcare: A third age rhetoric for a fourth age reality? *Ageing and Society, 18*(2), 233–248.

Grenier, A.M. (2005). The contextual and social locations of older women's experiences of disability and decline. *Journal of Aging Studies, 19,* 131–146. doi: 10.1016/j.jaging.2004.07.003

Hamington, M., & Miller, D. (Eds.). (2006). *Socializing care: feminist ethics and public issues.* Lanham, MD: Rowman and Littlefield Publishers.

Held, V. (2006) The ethics of care: Personal, political, and global. Oxford, UK: Oxford University Press.

Hollander, M., & Chappell, N. (2007). A comparative analysis of costs to government for home care and long-term residential care services, standardized for client needs. *Canadian Journal on Aging / La Revue canadienne du vieillissement,* 26 (sup. 1), 149–161. doi: 10.1353/cja.2008.0018

Hooyman, N.R., & Gonyea, J. (1995). *Feminist perspectives on family care: Policies for gender justice.* Thousand Oaks, CA: Sage Publications.

Howell, J. (2007). Gender and civil society: Time for cross-border dialogue. *Social Politics: International Studies in Gender, State & Society, 14*(4), 415–436. doi: 10.1093/sp/jxm023

Hughes, G. (Ed.). (1998). *Imagining welfare futures.* London, UK: Routledge and Open University.

Human Resources and Skills Development Canada. (2005). Employment Insurance (EI) Compassionate Care Benefits. Retrieved from http://www.hrsdc.gc.ca/en/ei/types/compassionate_care.shtml

Keefe, J., & Fancey, P. (1997). Financial compensation for home help services: Examining differences among program recipients. *Canadian Journal on Aging, 16*(2), 254–278. http://proquest.umi.com.remote.libproxy.wlu.ca/pqdlink?did=705624001&sid=4&Fmt=1&clientId=27850&RQT=309&VName=PQD

Keefe, J., & Rajnovich, B. (2007). To pay or not to pay: Examining underlying principles in the debate on financial support for family caregivers. *Canadian Journal on Aging / La Revue canadienne du vieillissement,* 26(sup. 1), 77–90. doi: 10.1353/cja.2008.0022

Kelley-Gillespie, N. (2009). An integrated conceptual model of quality of life for older adults based on a synthesis of the literature. *Applied Research Quality Life*, (4), 259–282. doi: 10.1007/s11482-009-9075-9

Kershaw, P. (2006). *Carefair: Rethinking the responsibilities and rights of citizenship*. Vancouver, BC: UBC Press.

Kittay, E.F., Jennings, B., & Wasunna, A.A. (2005). Dependency, difference, and the global ethic of long-term care. *Journal of Political Philosophy, 13*(4), 443–469.

Leong V., Guerrier, D., Coxford, R. & Coyte, P. (2007). The magnitude, share and determinants of private costs incurred by clients (and their caregivers) of in-home publicly financed care. *Healthcare Policy* 3(1), 2–19.

Lewis, J., & Guillari, S. (2005). The Adult Worker Model family, gender equality and care: The search for new policy principles and the possibilities and problems of a capabilities approach. *Economy and Society, 34*(1), 76–104. doi: 10.1080/0308514042000329342

Light, D.W. (2001) Managed competition, governmentality, and institutional response in the United Kingdom. *Social Science and Medicine, 52*, 1167–1181. doi: 10.1016/S0277-9536(00)00237-9

Lister, R. (1997). Citizenship: Towards a feminist synthesis. *Feminist Review, 57*, 28–48.

Lister, R. (2007). Inclusive citizenship: Realizing the potential. *Citizenship Studies, 11*(1), 49–61. http://hdl.handle.net/2134/2524

McBride, K.D. (2005). *Collective dreams: Political imagination and community*. University Park, PA: Penn State University Press.

Milne, A., & Williams, J. (2000). Meeting the mental health needs of older women: Taking social inequity into account. *Ageing and Society, 20*(6), 699–723.

Mitchell, L., Roos, N.P., & Shapiro, E. (2005). Patterns in home care use in Manitoba. *Canadian Journal on Aging, 24*(suppl. 1), 59–68. http://proquest.umi.com.remote.libproxy.wlu.ca/pqdlink?did=861463881&sid=3&Fmt=2&clientId=27850&RQT=309&VName=PQD

Nelson, J.A. (2006). Can we talk? Feminist economics in dialogue with theorists. *Signs: Journal of Women in Culture and Society, 31*(4), 1051–1074.

Nelson, J., & England P. (2002) Feminist philosophies of love and work. *Hypatia, 17*(1), 1–18. doi: 10.1111/j.1527-2001.2002.tb00762.x

Neysmith, S. (1995). Would a national information system promote the development of a Canadian home and community care policy? An examination of the Australian experience. *Canadian Public Policy, 21*(2), 159–173. http://www.jstor.org/stable/3551591

Neysmith, S. (Ed.). (2000). *Restructuring caring labour: Discourse, state practice and everyday life*. Toronto, ON: Oxford University Press.

Neysmith, S. (2005, May). Promoting equity: Funding mechanisms are important. Keynote address to the Taiwan/Canadian Symposium on Women and Family Care. Taipei, Taiwan.

Neysmith, S., & McAdam, M. (1999). Controversial concepts. In S. Neysmith (Ed.), *Critical issues for future social work practice with aging persons* (pp. 1–26). New York, NY: Columbia University Press.

Neysmith, S., & Reitsma-Street. M. (2009). The provisioning responsibilities of older women. *Journal of Aging Studies, 23*(3/4), 236–244. doi: 10.1016/j.jaging.2008.03.001

References Neysmith, S., Reitsma-Street, M., Baker Collins, S., & Porter, E. (2009). A study of women's provisioning: Implications for social provisions. In M.G. Cohen & J. Pulkingham (Eds.), *Public policy for women: The state, income security, and labour market issues* (pp. 94–113). Toronto, ON: University of Toronto Press.

Ontario. Ministry of Health and Long-Term Care. (2007, August 28). McGuinty government transforming community living to help seniors live independently at home: Aging at Home Strategy http://www.health.gov.on.ca/english/media/news_releases/archives/nr_07/aug/nr_20070828_3.html

Ontario Health Coalition. (2005). *Market competition in Ontario's home care system: Lessons and consequences*. Toronto, ON: Author.

Plath, D. (2009). International policy perspectives on independence in old age. *Journal of Aging and Social Policy*, 21, 209–223. doi: 10.1080/08959420902733173

Robertson, A. (1997). Beyond apocalyptic demography: Toward a moral economy of independence. *Ageing and Society, 17*(4), 425–446.

Rozanova, J. (2010) Discourse of successful aging in the *Globe and Mail:* Insights from critical gerontology. *Journal of Aging Studies, 24*, 213–222. doi: 10.1016/j.jaging.2010.05.001

Shildrick, M. (1997). *Leaky bodies and boundaries: Feminism, postmodernism, and (bio)ethics*. New York, NY: Routledge.

Statistics Canada. (2005a). *Population projections for Canada, provinces, and territories*. Retrieved from http://www.fedpubs.com/subject/demog/popproj.htm

Statistics Canada. (2005b). *Population projections of visible minority groups, Canada, provinces, and regions 2001–2017*. Catalogue no. 91-541-X1E. Ottawa: Supply and Services Canada. http://dsp-psd.pwgsc.gc.ca/Collection/Statcan/91-541-X/91-541-XIE.html

Tronto, J.C. (1993). *Moral boundaries: A political argument for an ethic of care*. New York, NY: Routledge.

Twigg, J. (2009). Clothing, identity, and the embodiment of age. In J. Powell & T. Gilbert (Eds.), *Aging and identity: A postmodern dialogue* (pp. 93–104). New York, NY: Nova Science Publishers.

Ungerson, C. (2004). Whose empowerment and independence? A cross-national perspective on "cash for care" schemes. *Ageing and Society, 24*, 189–212. doi: 10.1017/S0144686X03001508

Ungerson, C., & Yeandle, S. (Eds.). (2007). *Cash for care in developed welfare states*. Houndmills, UK: Palgrave Macmillan.

Williams, P., Barnsley, J., Leggat, S., Deber, R., & Baranek, P. (1999). Long-term care goes to market: Managed competition and Ontario's reform of community-based services. *Canadian Journal on Aging, 18*(2), 125–153. http://proquest.umi.com.remote.libproxy.wlu.ca/pqdlink?did=413302701&sid=1&Fmt=1&clientId=27850&RQT=309&VName=PQD

Williams, P.A., Lum, J., Deber, R., Montgomery, R., Kuluski, K., Peckham, A., ... Zhu, L. (2009). Aging at home: Integrating community-based care for older persons. *Healthcare Papers: New Models for the New Healthcare, 10*(1), 8–21.

Toward Inclusion of Lesbian, Gay, and Bisexual People

Social Policy Changes in Relation to Sexual Orientation

16

Brian O'Neill

One of the most striking social changes in Canada and much of the world over the past three decades has been the increased acceptance of lesbian, gay, and bisexual (LGB) people, and the decrease in discrimination based on sexual orientation. This change, though contentious and hotly debated, represents a shift in Canadian values evident in social policies at various levels. Four developments have been pivotal: changes to the Criminal Code in 1969 that decriminalized certain sexual acts that were prosecuted mainly against same-sex couples; declassification of homosexuality as a mental disorder by the American Psychiatric Association (APA) in 1973; recognition of the rights of LGB people under the 1982 Canadian Charter of Rights and Freedoms and federal and provincial human rights codes beginning in the late 1970s; and increased awareness of human service needs related to same-sex sexual orientation, due in part to the advent of the HIV/AIDS pandemic in the 1980s. This chapter first discusses heterosexism (Eldridge & Johnson, 2011), a set of discourses that generate and provide rationales for the oppression encountered by LGB people. It then introduces concepts related to sexual orientation and highlights features of gay and lesbian communities. The remainder of the chapter traces changes in public policies relevant to same-sex sexual orientation and identifies directions for future development.

Heterosexism

Historically, the response in Canada to same-sex sexual orientation has been shaped by heterosexism. Analogous to racism and sexism, modern heterosexism is "an ideological system that denies, denigrates, stigmatizes or segregates any nonheterosexual form of behavior, identity, relationship, or community" (Walls, 2008, pp. 27–28). As with other oppressive belief systems (Thompson, 2011), heterosexism is reproduced at the structural, cultural, and personal levels, privileging those who conform to the dominant sexual orientation, heterosexuality, and disadvantaging those who show signs of same-sex sexual orientation. At the structural level, heterosexism entails "the continued promotion by the major institutions of society of a heterosexual lifestyle while simultaneously subordinating any other lifestyles" (Neisen, 1990, p. 25). Heterosexist discourses in legislation, education, and health and social care have transmitted negative stereotypes of gay men and lesbians as dangerous sex offenders, threats to the family, and mentally ill (Fish, 2008; Herek, 2002). Positive stereotypes often reproduced in popular media—for example, that gay men are highly artistic and emotionally caring, and lesbians aggressive and athletic—also further the "othering" of LGB people by highlighting attributes that are inconsistent with traditional gender role definitions (Walls, 2008). Because heterosexuality has been presented as natural and universal, oppression related to sexual orientation has until recently been widely supported at least tacitly, and, for the most part, gone unrecognized. However, the emergence of gay and lesbian communities, and challenges to heterosexism by members of these communities and their allies, have led to social changes reflected in legislation, organizational policies, and public attitudes.

The term "homophobia," coined by Weinberg in 1972 to identify the irrational fear of people who have same-sex sexual orientation, is commonly used to refer to prejudice at the personal level against gay men and lesbians. The term is not used in this chapter in that way because to do so obscures the systemic nature of oppression based on sexual orientation, creating the impression that discrimination against LGB people is related solely to individuals' attitudes and psychological problems (Herek, 2009).

Intersection of Heterosexism with Racism and Other Oppressive Ideologies

It is an oversimplification to assume that LGB people are subject only to heterosexism. The intersectional model (Beck et al., 2002; Davis, 2008) recognizes that any one person may have more than one social location and that forms of exclusion based on race, ethnicity, class, gender, sexuality, age, and ability may interact, producing complex and harsh experiences of oppression. Thus, LGB people who are members of groups marginalized on the basis of differences other than sexuality may be simultaneously ostracized within LGB communities as well as the other communities they belong to (O'Neill, 2010).

In the past, some North American Aboriginal societies had more complex understandings of gender and sexual roles, accepting and honouring people who did not conform strictly to the gender binary (Brotman et al., 2002a). However, in large part due to colonialism, many First Nations communities incorporated the heterosexist values that informed the dominant culture. Thus Aboriginal people today who experience same-sex attraction may encounter marginalization within their indigenous communities as well as the dominant culture. The term "two-spirit" has been adopted by many Aboriginal people as a culturally appropriate way to identify their multifaceted gender and sexual identities (Cameron, 2005) and to gain acceptance within their communities (Gilley, 2010).

Same-Sex Sexual Orientation

Gender, Sexuality, and Identity

Terms related to gender and sexuality are often confused despite their distinct meanings (Todd, 2010). "Gender identity" is the sex that individuals believe they are—usually male or female—based on their primary physical sex characteristics. "Gender roles" are behaviours deemed appropriate for each sex, and vary across cultures. They may be defined loosely or rigidly, and they extend to all areas of life, including not only speech and behavioural mannerisms, but also choices of occupation, family roles, and sexual partners. Heterosexism shapes gender roles in our culture to exclude same-sex sexual behaviour. Despite stereotypes to the contrary, most gay men think of themselves as male and most lesbians consider themselves to be female. It is transgender persons who have gender identities different than those ascribed to them based on their physical characteristics—for instance, people with male genitalia who consider themselves to be female (Hines, 2007). Transgender individuals may have either heterosexual or same-sex sexual orientation. Policies specifically focused on transgender people are not addressed in this chapter because the oppression they may encounter is primarily related to their gender identity and to the performance of gender roles, although it is often expressed in anti-gay language.

The commonsense understanding of "sexual orientation" in the northern European traditions that have shaped the dominant cultures of Canada is that heterosexuality refers to attraction between males and females, homosexuality to attraction between members of the same sex, and bisexuality to attraction to people of both sexes (Lee, 2008). In other cultural contexts, attribution of sexual orientation may also be based on the age and roles of participants in addition to their gender (Elliston, 2005). It has been argued that for women, gender is not as important a factor in determining sexual attraction as it is for men (Bailey, 2009).

Same-Sex Sexual Orientation

It is an oversimplification to assume that sexual orientation is a clear-cut and stable trait. Kinsey's pioneering investigations of sexuality suggested that 5 to 10 percent of males (Kinsey, Pomeroy, & Martin, 1948), and 3 to 5 percent of females (Kinsey, Pomeroy, Martin, & Gebhard, 1955), participate in sex primarily with members of their own sex for a period of three or more years during their adult lives. In addition, an equal number of people have same-sex attractions that they do not act on, have erotic attraction and experiences with people of both sexes, or experience changes in the focus of their sexuality during their lives (Savin-Williams, 2009).

Theories about the causes of variation in sexual orientation abound. Some explanations focus on biological factors such as differences in brain structure, prenatal hormonal influences, and genetic heredity (Bailey, Dunne, & Martin, 2000). There is some empirical support for these propositions, but it is not conclusive. A second set of theories points to social environmental influences. For instance, some interpretations of psychoanalytic theory hold that same-sex sexual orientation is an aberration in psychosexual development due to deficiencies in parent–child relationships (Drescher, 2002). Yet a third line of thinking holds that sexuality is socially constructed; influenced by cultural values and circumstances, people have the potential for sexual involvement with others regardless of sex, and may or may not identify as gay, lesbian, or bisexual (Savin-Williams, 2009; Vance, 2005). The fact that some people who have previously been exclusively heterosexual participate in sexual behaviour with members of their own sex when in sex-segregated environments or when they meet a particular individual supports the argument that human sexuality is extremely flexible (Diamond, 2003). However, there is no evidence supporting claims that sexual orientation can be changed by means of behavioural, psychological, or other forms of therapy.

Studies based on samples of LGB people drawn from non-clinical populations provided evidence that same-sex sexual orientation in and of itself was not pathological, a finding that supported the removal of homosexuality from the listing of mental disorders (Minton, 2002). However, there is evidence that LGB individuals have higher rates of mental health problems related to the stress and lack of social support they experience living in a heterosexist environment (Cochran, Sullivan, & Mays, 2003; Meyer, 2003; Omoto & Kurtzman, 2006; Parks & Hughes, 2007). Although this research adds to knowledge about LGB people, it does not shed much light on the lives of those who have some degree of same-sex sexual orientation but do not identify as LGB, or who are unwilling to come out.

Identities Based on Sexual Orientation

The terms "sexual identity" and "sexual orientation" are often used interchangeably in referring to sexual attraction and behaviour. Although there is evidence of same-sex sexual behaviour in numerous cultures throughout history (Churchill, 1967; Crompton, 2003), until relatively recently, having particular sexual interests, whatever their cause, was not necessarily the basis for ascribing identity. Rather, sexual contact with another person of the same sex has had diverse meanings across time and in various social contexts. In some cultures, it was considered simply to be a behaviour, though often censured; for instance, in Europe during the Middle Ages, same-sex sexuality may have been disapproved of as immoral in much the same way that heterosexual adultery was, but not seen as a marker of identity. In contrast, in certain cultures, same-sex activity was a highly valued aspect of the process of taking on an adult identity, although not necessarily seen as erotic or an identity in and of itself (Elliston, 2005). As noted earlier, in some cultures sexual identity may be defined more in terms of roles played in sexual encounters than the genders of the people involved.

Gay and Lesbian Communities

Until the Kinsey studies, it was thought that same-sex sexual orientation was relatively rare because its expression was largely covert due to its stigmatization. It was not until the late 19th century that the concept of homosexuality as a defining characteristic of identity appeared, primarily within medical discourse, and that people who were attracted to others of their own sex came to be known as homosexual and labelled mentally ill (Weeks, 2001). In reaction to the creation of the "homosexual" as a stigmatized category of person, during the second half of the 20th century people who were sexually attracted to members of their own sex began to define themselves as gay, lesbian, or bisexual, but gave these identities a positive connotation (Altman, 2001). Although the term "gay" may be applied to both men and women, recently it has come to be understood more narrowly as referring specifically to males who are sexually attracted to males, while the term "lesbian" is used in relation to attraction between females. However, there is evidence that identifying as gay or lesbian can be highly influenced by affectional bonds (that is, one can "fall in love" with someone of either sex) (Diamond, 2003) and that how one self-identifies may change during one's life (Diamond, 2005).

The process of becoming aware of and disclosing one's gay, lesbian, or bisexual identity is referred to as "coming out" (Cox et al., 2011). There are differences related to gender, age, and culture in the way that coming out occurs (Rosario, Schrimshaw, & Hunter, 2011). Modern research indicates that a lower proportion of respondents identify as LGB than would have been predicted by Kinsey's studies of sexual behaviour. For example, American studies found that approximately 4 percent of respondents identified themselves as LGB (Gates 2006; Hawkins & Stackhouse, 2004), while Statistics Canada in 2003 and 2005 found that only 1.9 percent of respondents claimed to be LGB (Statistics Canada, 2008). These findings need to be understood taking into account that the number of people who come out is smaller than those who experience same-sex sexual orientation, in part because of fear of discrimination, but also because not all people who are attracted to or participate in sex with members of their own sex identify as gay, lesbian, or bisexual. Nevertheless, there is still a significant segment of the population that identifies as LGB, and sizable communities have emerged around the world, exerting considerable influence on the development of social policies, particularly in Canada.

Gay and Lesbian Communities

There are well-developed but largely unrecognized social networks among people who are attracted to members of their own sex throughout rural Canada (Warner, 2002). However, it is the communities that have developed in the centres of large Canadian cities, in part due to migration from rural and suburban areas, that have shaped public images of gay and lesbian people.

These communities originated primarily around commercial establishments catering to gay men, such as bars, baths, and restaurants, but over time they came to include organizations focusing on the needs of both men and women. In gay and lesbian communities are found businesses that provide various products and services, as well as newspapers and magazines, cultural organizations, religious groups, sports and recreational clubs, political associations and social change movements, support groups for youth and seniors, and health care and counselling services. The advent of HIV in the 1980s stimulated the development of AIDS service organizations based largely in gay communities (Roy & Cain, 2001). In addition to participating in communities dominated by gay men, lesbians have developed separate communities in the context of the women's movement (Gilmore & Kaminski, 2007). No comparable bisexual communities have emerged.

Media coverage has contributed to a distorted image of gay and lesbian populations. In current movies and television shows, gay men and (to a lesser extent) lesbians are portrayed as relatively wealthy, youthful, white, middle class, and able-bodied (e.g., Mitchell, 2005). In reality, there is diversity within the LGB population with respect to race/ethnicity, age, social class, physical and intellectual ability, and religion, and many lesbians and gay men care for their children as well as support aging parents (Taylor & Ristock, 2011). Members of various ethnic minority groups and religions as well as people with disabilities have organized to counter discrimination against them within LGB communities (Warner, 2002).

Canadian Acceptance of LGB People

Individuals' opinions about sexual orientation are correlated with their social locations and belief systems (Herek, 2009). In general, prejudice toward gays and lesbians is associated with being male, older, less educated, and living in a rural area. Negative beliefs are also stronger among those who have authoritarian personalities, hold conservative religious beliefs, and support traditional gender roles. In contrast, attitudes are more positive among those who have had personal contact with gay men and lesbians. In 1975 only 28 percent of Canadians were accepting of same-sex sexual orientation (Bibby, 1995). However, since 1980, attitudes have consistently become more positive (Andersen & Fetner, 2008). For instance, a 2011 national survey indicated that 83 percent of respondents believed that the lives of LGB people were "just as valid as those of heterosexual people" (Todd, 2011). In part this change may be related to greater familiarity with same-sex issues due to LGB activism, more people coming out, and the HIV/AIDS epidemic.

Canadian Social Policies

Public policy in Canada has evolved from outright denunciation of same-sex sexual behaviour, to requirements for tolerance of differences in sexual orientation, to the current recognition of the equality rights of LGB people. Given the diverse meanings of sexual behaviour and identity, and the lack of a value consensus in relation to human sexuality, developing social policies relevant to sexual orientation is a challenge. This section of the chapter discusses key changes in legislation, professional guidelines, and organizational policies that have reduced the stigmatization of same-sex sexual orientation and increased the accessibility and responsiveness of human services.

Criminal and Immigration Law

Historically, the most direct and wide-reaching expression of heterosexism was in criminal laws. Although the criminalization of same-sex sexuality has decreased, sexual activity between people of the same sex is still an offence in more than 76 countries around the world (Bruce-Jones & Itaborahy, 2011). The death penalty continues to be the punishment in five countries. When it was passed in 1892, Canada's Criminal Code included gross indecency and anal intercourse as sexual offences (Kimmel & Robinson, 2001). These offences were prosecuted primarily against men who had consenting sex with men, and repeated conviction could lead to being declared a dangerous sexual offender and indefinite incarceration. In 1969 the Criminal Code was amended to allow these acts between married couples and consenting adults in private. Subsequently, in 1988, the offence of gross indecency was deleted from the Code and the age of consent for anal intercourse was lowered to eighteen.

Another significant expression of heterosexism in federal law was found in the Immigration Act, which barred LGB people from entering Canada (Willms, 2005). Although this provision was dropped in 1977, Canadian residents were unable to sponsor their same-sex partners as immigrants whereas those in male–female relationships were able to do so. In 2002 the Immigration Act was replaced by the Immigration and Refugee Protection Act (Bill C-11), with regulations allowing sponsorship of same-sex partners. In addition, individuals who claim to have been persecuted on the basis of their sexual orientation are admitted as refugees under the act. This practice is consistent with the interpretation of the UN High Commissioner for Refugees, which recognizes gay men and lesbians as social groups that can suffer persecution (United Nations, 2011).

The heterosexist provisions of the Criminal Code and the Immigration Act continue to influence discourse about sexual orientation even though for the most part they have been repealed. The impression persists among many that same-sex sexuality is illicit and that gay men and lesbians are somewhat disreputable. This perception subtly shapes the administration of justice, so that gay men and lesbians are treated more harshly than heterosexuals (MacDougall, 2004). Nevertheless, the most serious implication of the stigmatization of same-sex sexual orientation is that it provides a rationale for discrimination and violence perpetrated against those perceived to be gay or lesbian (Lyons, 2006; Plumm et al., 2010). Data from Canadian police forces indicate that in 2009, hate crimes related to sexual orientation comprised 13 percent of all those reported and were the most violent of all incidents recorded (Dauvergne & Brennan, 2011). The positive evolution in public values, however, is evident in the addition to the Criminal Code in 1995 of stiffer sentences for hate crimes, including those committed against gay men and lesbians.

Psychiatric Classification

After its decriminalization, the declassification of homosexuality as a mental disorder was the next significant step in the evolution of policies regarding same-sex sexual orientation. With the development of psychiatry in the late 19th century, homosexuality had come to be considered a mental illness (Drescher, 2010). This theory was buttressed by research conducted largely on samples drawn from mentally ill and incarcerated populations and informed by the assumption that same-sex sexual orientation was a problem in itself. However, studies conducted in the latter half of the 20th century with appropriate research designs did not detect any differences in mental health or cognitive abilities related to sexual orientation (e.g., Hooker, 1957). Nevertheless, homosexuality remained classified as a disorder by the APA until 1973 (Silverstein, 2009) and by the World Health Organization until 1991. This designation guided the provision of mental health services in Canada, with serious repercussions for clients as well as care providers. Clients who revealed their same-sex sexual orientation were diagnosed as mentally ill and often subjected to abusive and ineffective interventions aimed at changing their sexuality. Furthermore, health and social service workers who were gay or lesbian were reluctant to reveal their sexual orientation, depriving clients of the benefits of their knowledge and experience.

Although no longer endorsed by professional bodies, the psychiatric classification of homosexuality continues to shape the perception of same-sex sexual orientation as an illness. Influenced by the previous criminalization of same-sex sexual behaviour and by the more recent advent of HIV/AIDS, LGB people are frequently portrayed in popular culture as strange, dangerous, and contaminated. Nevertheless, the declassification of homosexuality as a mental illness allowed for the possibility of the development of health and social services that could be supportive to gay and lesbian people. Despite this development, some service providers have continued to hold negative beliefs regarding same-sex sexual orientation (Bowers, Plummer, &

Minichiello, 2005; Brotman, Ryan, Jalbert, & Rowe, 2002b; Burch, 2008), and this has contributed to the lack of accessibility and responsiveness of services.

Human Rights Legislation and the Charter

Following the achievement of changes in the Criminal Code, and the recognition by mental health professionals that homosexuality is not a psychiatric illness, the focus of Canadian gay and lesbian activism turned to gaining protection from discrimination through the inclusion of sexual orientation in human rights codes. Human rights legislation identifies grounds on which discrimination is prohibited in areas such as housing, services, employment, and membership in organizations, and applies in both the public and the private sphere (Nierobisz, Searl, & Theroux, 2008). In addition to harassment and violence, people perceived to be gay or lesbian have frequently encountered discrimination in areas addressed by human rights legislation (Warner, 2002). As a result of a concerted campaign of political action and court challenges, sexual orientation was added to the Quebec Charter of Human Rights and Freedoms in 1977 and subsequently incorporated into all other provincial and territorial human rights codes (Nierobisz et al., 2008). Furthermore, the Canadian Human Rights Act was amended in 1996 to include protection for gays and lesbians. In contrast, sexual orientation discrimination is proscribed in only 54 of the 192 members of the UN (Bruce-Jones & Itaborahy, 2011) and is not addressed in the Universal Declaration of Human Rights.

With discrimination on the basis of sexual orientation prohibited by human rights laws, the achievement of full equality became the focus of attention. The Charter of Rights and Freedoms (the Charter), part of the 1982 Canadian constitution, addresses the right of Canadians to equal treatment by public services, regardless of ethnicity, gender, or other differences (Nierobisz et al., 2008). After the introduction of the Charter, gay men and lesbians successfully mounted court challenges to policies that denied same-sex partners access to public services such as benefits under the Old Age Security Act. As a result, although it does not refer explicitly to sexual orientation, since 1996 the Charter has been interpreted by the Supreme Court as applying to sexual orientation. These developments have had far-reaching implications for the legal recognition of same-sex couples as well as for policies regarding employment benefits, pensions, taxes, inheritance, and family life. In 2000 the federal government passed the Modernization of Benefits and Obligations Act (Bill C-23), requiring that federal laws apply equally to both same-sex and heterosexual common-law couples. Provincial governments amended their laws similarly.

One of the most contentious developments related to sexual orientation were legal changes allowing same-sex couples to marry. The federal law restricting the right to marry to male–female couples was struck down in a British Columbia court in 2003 (Nierobisz et al., 2008) and subsequently in most other provincial courts. Although national polls indicated that a majority of Canadians supported same-sex marriage (EGALE, 2004), there was vigorous debate across the country. In 2005 the Canadian Parliament passed the Civil Marriage Act (Bill C-38), which omitted reference to the sex of individuals, effectively making same-sex marriages lawful in all provinces and territories.

Despite these successes in the courts and legislatures, some gay men and lesbians have reservations about being included in policies that formerly applied only to heterosexuals (Mule, 2010; Taylor & Ristock, 2011). They fear that inclusion of gay and lesbian people in mainstream social institutions may reinforce the status quo rather than advance social changes in relation to sexuality and gender—changes that have been goals of the gay liberation and feminist movements. For instance, the achievement of same-sex spousal benefits privileges only those involved in long-term relationships, particularly if they are in higher tax brackets. In addition, there are concerns about same-sex couples being able to marry, given that this institution has historically been an unequal relationship, usually benefiting the male partner at the expense of the woman. In any case, a significant implication of the recognition of the rights of LGB people to equal treatment is that human services are required to provide services that are accessible and appropriate regardless of sexual orientation.

Impact of HIV/AIDS

A major impetus to addressing issues related to same-sex sexual orientation in human service policies has been the HIV/AIDS epidemic. Although the rate of infection among men who have sex with men declined during the 1990s, this group still accounts for 68 percent of Canadian AIDS cases (Public Health Agency of Canada, 2010). Thus, health and social services have been called on to respond to the needs of gay and bisexual men, and their families and friends. The epidemic also had a positive impact on LGB communities because it stimulated the development of community-based AIDS service organizations (Cain, 2002). The need to develop policies for the prevention of HIV infection and to address the complex medical and social needs of those already living with the disease forced mainstream services to address issues related to same-sex sexual orientation in more supportive ways. One of the barriers to accessing services for people with HIV/AIDS is the shame attached to the disease because of its association with same-sex sexuality (Poindexter, 2007), a stigma some agencies have attempted to avoid by downplaying their connections to the gay community.

Policies of Social Services and Professional Education

Policies of Social Services and Professional Education

In addition to having the range of health and social service needs experienced across the general population, people with same-sex sexual orientation may have issues related to the discrimination and harassment they may experience. One of the more severe concerns is that LGB people are at higher risk of physical violence (Statistics Canada, 2010) and sexual coercion (Kuyper & Vanwesenbeeck, 2011) than heterosexuals. Some youths and seniors fear rejection in school and in long-term-care settings should they reveal their sexual orientation, and many of those who do, experience bullying and isolation (Addis et al., 2009; Dysart-Gale, 2010; Smith et al., 2010; Stein, Beckerman, & Sherman, 2010). There is evidence that in coping with the stress of heterosexism, LGB people are vulnerable to various mental health problems, including depression, anxiety, and substance misuse (Adams, Braun, & McCreanor, 2010; Cochran et al., 2003). The scarce research on bisexuals suggests that in addition to sharing many of the health and social issues of gay and lesbian people, they experience exclusion not only by heterosexuals, but also by lesbian and gay people (Oswalt, 2009). Many LGB people need the help of social workers and other professionals in integrating their sexuality into their lives, developing a positive identity, and establishing supportive relationships (Mallon, 2008; Morrow & Messinger, 2006). Despite the progressive policy developments described earlier in relation to same-sex sexual orientation, heterosexism continues to present barriers to accessing services that respond adequately to these needs.

A lingering effect of the history of criminalization and pathologization of same-sex sexuality is that health and social services are slow to respond to the rights of gay people to equitable services (Mule, 2005). Although agency policies proscribe direct discrimination on the basis of sexual orientation, for the most part they do not provide services that support the lives of LGB people. The intent of this omission may be to provide services equally to all (Brotman et al., 2002b); however, another purpose may be to avoid the controversy that officially addressing gay and lesbian issues could provoke. Unfortunately, because of the pervasiveness of heterosexism, the effect is to silence discussion of sexual orientation, thereby impeding the development of accessible and responsive programs and leaving decisions regarding service delivery to individual workers. This approach may not only prevent clients from receiving adequate service, but also leave workers without guidance and support in their practice.

When differences of sexual orientation are not comprehensively addressed throughout organizational policies, heterosexist assumptions subtly shape practices (Daley, 2006). Most health and social services do not gather information regarding the sexual orientation of clients. However, even if they do, in the absence of official statements affirming respect for LGB people, clients may not feel safe enough to reveal their sexual orientation, withholding information that could be crucial in their care (Brotman et al., 2002b). The result is that agencies remain for the most part unaware of the presence of people who are oriented to their own sex in the populations they serve and do not recognize their unique needs. For example, the presupposition that battering occurs only in male–female relationships may contribute to services being unresponsive to the needs of those abused by same-sex partners (Merrill & Wolfe, 2000); lack of acknowledgment of same-sex relationships by health care providers may result in exclusion of the partners of LGB patients from involvement in their care (Killian, 2010).

The absence of affirmative policies leaves undisturbed the lack of awareness of the influence of heterosexism on deficiencies in the knowledge and attitudes of many helping professionals (Brotman et al., 2002b). Although there is evidence that inclusion of issues of sexual orientation in professional education has improved the quality of services to gay and lesbian clients (Eubanks-Carter, Burckell, & Goldfried, 2005), there are still educational policy and curriculum gaps in this area. Similar to the policies of many service providers, while the Canadian Association for Social Work Education (CASWE, 2011) prohibits discrimination on the basis of sexual orientation, it does not specify that content regarding heterosexism and same-sex sexual orientation must be included in curricula.

The first step in addressing the lack of attention to sexual orientation in mainstream social services is to acknowledge that LGB people are among the clients of the agency (Mule, 2005). Subsequently, queer people can be involved in the systematic review and development of policies to comprehensively address issues related to sexual orientation. It would be particularly effective for non-gay community organizations that focus on countering discrimination to join with gay and lesbian organizations in addressing heterosexism.

Conclusion

This overview of social policy developments in Canada relevant to sexual orientation reveals a steady movement toward respect for LGB people and recognition of their rights to equitable access to social resources. This trend is consistent with Canadian ideals regarding acceptance of diversity and the attainment of social justice. It seems inevitable that the process will continue and that social institutions will become more fully responsive to the needs of LGB people. Given changes at the legislative level, the focus now shifts to challenging heterosexism at the program level. Health and social services will need to systematically examine their policies and practices to determine how they subtly silence, ignore, and disadvantage people who are oriented to members of their own sex. This process will require openness, sensitivity, and courage, as addressing issues related to sexuality touches on strongly held values that are integral to identity. At the same time, it needs to be recognized that heterosexism is but one oppressive ideology. To successfully advance social justice, policies at each level simultaneously need to address the expression of all forms of marginalization.

References

Adams, J., Braun, V., & McCreanor, T. (2010). A critical analysis of gay men's health policy documents. *Gay and Lesbian Issues and Psychology Review, 6*(1), 42–59. Retrieved from http://www.groups.psychology.org.au/glip/glip_review

Addis, S., Davies, M., Greene, G., MacBride-Stewart, S., & Shepherd, M. (2009). The health, social care, and housing needs of lesbian, gay, bisexual, and transgender older people: A review of the literature. *Health and Social Care in the Community, 17*(6), 647–658. doi: 10.1111/j.1365-2524.2009.00866.x

Altman, D. (2001). Gay/lesbian movements. *International Encyclopedia of the Social and Behavioral Sciences* (pp. 5895–5899). Retrieved from http://www.sciencedirect.com/science/referenceworks

Andersen, R., & Fetner, T. (2008). Cohort differences in tolerance of homosexuality: Attitudinal change in Canada and the United States, 1981–2000. *Public Opinion Quarterly, 72*(2), 311–330. doi: 10.1093/poq/nfn017

Bailey, J.M. (2009). What is sexual orientation and do women have one? In D.A. Hope (Ed.), *Contemporary perspectives on lesbian, gay and bisexual identities* (pp. 43–63). New York, NY: Springer. doi:10.1007/978-0-387-09556-1_3

Bailey, J.M., Dunne, M.P., & Martin, N.G. (2000). Genetic and environmental influences on sexual orientation and its correlates in an Australian twin sample. *Journal of Personality and Social Psychology, 78*(3), 524–536. doi:10.1037/0022-3514.78.3.524

Beck, E., Williams, I., Hope, L., & Park., W. (2002). An intersectional model: Exploring gender with ethnic and cultural diversity. *Journal of Ethnic and Cultural Diversity in Social Work, 10*(4), 63–80. doi:10.1300/J051v10n04_04

Bibby, R. (1995). The Bibby report: Social trends Canadian style. Toronto, ON: Stoddart.

Bowers, R., Plummer, D., & Minichiello, V. (2005). Homophobia in counselling practice. *International Journal for the Advancement of Counselling, 27*(3), 471–489. doi: 10.1007/s10447-005-8207-7

Brotman, S., Ryan, B, Jalbert, Y., & Rowe, B. (2002a). Reclaiming space-regaining health: The health care experiences of two-spirited people in Canada. *Journal of Gay and Lesbian Social Services, 14*(1), 67–87. doi: 10.1300/J041v14n01_04

Brotman, S., Ryan, B., Jalbert, Y., & Rowe, B. (2002b). The impact of coming out on health and health care access: The experiences of gay, lesbian, bisexual, and two-spirited people. *Journal of Health and Social Policy, 15*(1), 1–29. doi: 10.1300/J045v15n01_01

Bruce-Jones, E., & Itaborahy, L.P. (2011). *State-sponsored homophobia: A world survey of laws criminalizing same-sex sexual acts between consenting adults.* International Lesbian, Gay, Bisexual, Trans and Intersex Association (ILGA). Retrieved from http://old.ilga.org/Statehomophobia/ILGA_State_Sponsored_Homophobia_2011.pdf

References

Burch, A. (2008). Health care providers' knowledge, attitudes, and self-efficacy for working with patients with spinal cord injury who have diverse sexual orientations. *Physical Therapy, 88*(2), 191–198. doi: 10.2522/ptj.20060188

Cain, R. (2002). Devoting ourselves, devouring each other: Tension in community-based AIDS work. *Journal of Progressive Human Services, 13*(1), 93–113. doi: 10.1300/J059v13n01_06

Cameron, M. (2005). Two-spirited Aboriginal people: Continuing cultural appropriation by non-Aboriginal society. *Canadian Woman Studies, 24*(2/3), 123–127. Retrieved from https://pi.library.yorku.ca/ojs/index.php/cws

Canadian Association for Social Work Education (CASWE). (2011). Revised Standards of Accreditation. Retrieved from http://www.caswe-acfts.ca

Churchill, W. (1967). *Homosexual behavior among males: A cross-cultural and cross-species investigation.* New York, NY: Hawthorn Books.

Cochran, S.D., Sullivan, J.G., & Mays, V.M. (2003). Prevalence of mental disorders, psychological distress, and mental health services use among lesbian, gay, and bisexual adults in the United States. *Journal of Consulting and Clinical Psychology, 71*(1), 53–61. doi: 10.1037/0022-006X.71.1.53

Cox, N., Dewaele, A., van Houtte, M., & Vincke, J. (2011). Stress-related growth, coming out, and internalized homonegativity in lesbian, gay, and bisexual youth. An examination of stress-related growth within the minority stress model. *Journal of Homosexuality, 58*(1), 117–137. doi: 10.1080/00918369.2011.533631

Crompton, L. (2003). *Homosexuality and civilization.* Cambridge, MA: Harvard University Press.

Daley, A. (2006). Lesbian and gay health issues: OUTside of Canada's health policy. *Critical Social Policy, 26*, 794–816. doi: 10.1177/0261018306068474

Dauvergne, M., & Brennan, S. (2011, June 7). Police-reported hate crime in Canada. Juristat Article. Retrieved from http://www.statcan.gc.ca/pub/85-002-x/2011001/article/11469-eng.pdf

Davis, K. (2008). Intersectionality as buzzword: A sociology of science perspective on what makes a feminist theory successful. *Feminist Theory, 9*(1), 67–85. doi: 10.1177/1464700108086364

Diamond, L.M. (2003). What does sexual orientation orient? A biobehavioral model distinguishing romantic love and sexual desire. *Psychological Review, 110*(1), 173–192. doi: 10.1037/0033-295X.110.1.173

Diamond, L. M. (2005). A new view of lesbian subtypes: Stable versus fluid identity trajectories over an 8-year period. *Psychology of Women Quarterly, 29*, 119–128. doi:10.1111/j.1471-6402.2005.00174.x

Drescher, J. (2002). Causes and becauses: On etiological theories of homosexuality. *Annual of Psychoanalysis, 30*, 57–68. Retrieved from http://web.ebscohost.com.ezproxy.library.ubc.ca/ehost/pdfviewer/pdfviewer?vid=4&hid=25&sid=d1486e7f-34dd-4290-be4d-d2311908a198%40sessionmgr14

Drescher, J. (2010). Queer diagnoses: Parallels and contrasts in the history of homosexuality, gender variance, and the Diagnostic and Statistical Manual. *Archives of Sexual Behavior, 39*, 427–460. doi: 10.1007/s10508-009-9531-5

Dysart-Gale, D. (2010). Social justice and social determinants of health: Lesbian, gay, bisexual, transgendered, intersexed, and queer youth in Canada. *Journal of Child and Adolescent Psychiatric Nursing, 23*(1), 23–28. doi: 10.1111/j.1744-6171.2009.00213.x

References

EGALE. (2004, July 1). Survey finds huge increase in support for equal marriage. Retrieved from http://www.egale.ca/index.asp?lang=E&menu=30&item=1055

Eldridge, J., & Johnson, P. (2011). The relationship between old-fashioned and modern heterosexism to social dominance orientation and structural violence. *Journal of Homosexuality, 58*, 382–401. doi: 10.1080/00918369.2011.546734

Elliston, D.A. (2005). Erotic anthropology: "Ritualized homosexuality" in Melanesia and beyond. In J. Robertson (Ed.), *Same-sex cultures and sexualities: An anthropological reader* (pp. 91–115). Malden, MA: Blackwell Publishing.

Eubanks-Carter, C., Burckell, L.A., & Goldfried, M.R. (2005). Enhancing therapeutic effectiveness with lesbian, gay, and bisexual clients. *Clinical Psychology: Science and Practice, 12*(1), 1–18. doi: 10.1093/clipsy.bpi001

Fish, J. (2008). Far from mundane: Theorising heterosexism for social work education. *Social Work Education, 27*(2), 182–193. doi: 10.1080/02615470701709667

Gates, G.J. (2006). *Same-sex couples and the gay, lesbian, and bisexual population: New estimates from the American Community Survey*. Los Angeles, CA: Williams Institute, UCLA School of Law.

Gilley, B.J. (2010). Native sexual inequalities: American Indian cultural conservative homophobia and the problem of tradition. *Sexualities, 13*(1), 47–68. doi: 10.1177/1363460709346114.

Gilmore, S., & Kaminski, E. (2007). A part and apart: Lesbian and straight feminist activists negotiate identity in a second-wave organization. *Journal of the History of Sexuality, 16*(1), 95–113. doi: 10.1353/sex.2007.0038

Hawkins, R., & Stackhouse, W. (2004). U.S.A. adults: Homoerotic, homosexual, and bisexual behaviors. In R.T. Francour & R.J. Noonan (Eds.), *Continuum complete international encyclopedia of sexuality*. Retrieved from http://www.kinseyinstitute.org.

Herek, G.M. (2002). Gender gaps in public opinion about lesbians and gay men. *Public Opinion Quarterly, 66*, 40–66. doi: 10.1086/338409

Herek, G.M. (2009). Sexual stigma and sexual prejudice in the United States: A conceptual framework. In D.A. Hope (Ed.), *Contemporary perspectives on lesbian, gay, and bisexual identities* (pp. 65–111). New York, NY: Springer.

Hines, S. (2007). *Transforming gender: Transgender practices of identity, intimacy, and care.* Bristol, UK: Policy Press.

Hooker, E. (1957). The adjustment of the male overt homosexual. *Journal of Projective Techniques, 21*, 18–31. doi: 10.1080/08853126.1957.10380742

Killian, M.L. (2010). The political is personal: Relationship recognition policies in the United States and their impact on services for LGBT people. *Journal of Gay and Lesbian Social Services, 22*, 9–21. doi: 10.1080/10538720903332149

Kimmel, D., & Robinson, D.J. (2001). Sex, crime, pathology: Homosexuality and Criminal Code reform in Canada, 1949–1969. *Canadian Journal of Law and Society, 16*(1), 147–165. Retrieved from: http://www.utpjournals.com/cjls/CJLS-161.html

Kinsey, A.C., Pomeroy, W.B., & Martin, C.E. (1948). *Sexual behavior in the human male.* Philadelphia, PA: W.B. Sanders.

Kinsey, A.C., Pomeroy, W.B., Martin, C.E., & Gebhard, P. (1955). *Sexual behavior in the human female.* Philadelphia, PA: W.B. Sanders.

Kuyper, L., & Vanwesenbeeck, I. (2011). Examining sexual health differences between lesbian, gay, bisexual, and heterosexual adults: The role of sociodemographics, sexual behavior characteristics, and minority stress. *Journal of Sex Research, 48*(2–3), 263–274. doi: 10.1080/00224491003654473

Lee, J.A. (2008). Homosexuality. In *The Canadian encyclopedia,* J.H. Marsh (Ed.). Retrieved from http://thecanadianencyclopedia.com

Lyons, C.J. (2006). Stigma or sympathy? Attributions of fault to hate crime victims and offenders. *Social Psychology Quarterly, 69*(1), 39–59. doi: 10.1177/019027250606900104

MacDougall, B. (2004). Continuum of homophobic expression in Canadian law. In E. Ceccherini (Ed.), *Sexual orientation in Canadian law* (pp. 153–178). Milan, Italy: Giuffre Editore.

Mallon, G.P. (2008). *Social work practice with lesbian, gay, bisexual, and transgender people* (2nd ed.). New York: NY: Routledge.

Merrill, G.S., & Wolfe, V.A. (2000). Battered gay men: An exploration of abuse, help seeking, and why they stay. *Journal of Homosexuality, 39*(2), 1–30. doi: 10.1300/J082v39n02_01

Meyer, I.H. (2003). Prejudice, social stress, and mental health in lesbian, gay, and bisexual populations: Conceptual issues and research evidence. *Psychological Bulletin, 129*(5), 674–697. doi: 10.1037/0033-2909.129.5.674

Minton, H.J.L. (2002). *Departing from deviance: A history of homosexual rights and emancipatory science in America.* Chicago, IL: University of Chicago Press.

Mitchell, D. (2005). Producing containment: The rhetorical construction of difference in Will & Grace. *Journal of Popular Culture, 38*(6), 1050–1068. doi: 10.1111/j.1540-5931.2005.00175.x

Morrow, D.F., & Messinger, L. (2006). *Sexual orientation and gender expression in social work practice: Working with gay, lesbian, bisexual, and transgender people.* New York, NY: Columbia University Press.

Mule, N. (2005). Beyond words in health and well-being policy: Sexual orientation—from inclusion to infusion. *Canadian Review of Social Policy, 55,* 79–98. doi: 10.1186/1475-9276-8-18

Mule, N. (2010). Same-sex marriage and Canadian relationship recognition—One step forward, two steps back: A critical liberationist perspective. *Journal of Gay and Lesbian Social Services, 22,* 74–90. doi: 10.1080/10538720903332354

Neisen, J.H. (1990). Heterosexism: Redefining homophobia for the 1990s. *Journal of Gay and Lesbian Psychotherapy, 1*(3), 21–35. Doi: 10.1300/J236v01n03_02

Nierobisz, A., Searl, M., & Theroux, C. (2008). *Human rights commissions and public policy: The role of the Canadian Human Rights Commission in advancing sexual orientation equality rights in Canada.* Ottawa, ON: Canadian Human Rights Commission. doi: 10.1111/j.1754–7121.2008.00017.x

Omoto, A.M., & Kurtzman, H.S. (2006). *Sexual orientation and mental health: Examining identity and development in lesbian, gay, and bisexual people.* Washington, DC: American Psychological Association.

O'Neill, B.J. (2010). Settlement experiences of lesbian, gay, and bisexual newcomers in BC. *Canadian Social Work, 12*(1), 24–31.

Oswalt, S.B. (2009). Don't forget the "B": Considering bisexual students and their specific health needs. *Journal of American College Health, 57*(5), 557–561. doi: 10.3200/JACH.57.5.557-560

References

Parks, C.A., & Hughes, T.L. (2007). Age differences in lesbian identity development and drinking. *Substance Use and Misuse, 42,* 361–380. doi: 10.1080/10826080601142097

Plumm, K.M., Terrance, C.A., Henderson, V.R., & Ellingson, H. (2010). Victim blame in a hate crime motivated by sexual orientation. *Journal of Homosexuality, 57,* 267–286. doi: 10.1080/00918360903489101

Poindexter, C.C. (2007). Management successes and struggles for AIDS service organizations. *Administration in Social Work, 31*(3), 5–28. doi: 10.1300/J147v31n03_02

Public Health Agency of Canada. (2010, July). HIV/AIDS Epi Updates. Retrieved from http://www.phac-aspc.gc.ca

Rosario, M., Schrimshaw, E.E., & Hunter, J. (2011). Different patterns of sexual identity development over time: Implications for the psychological adjustment of lesbian, gay, and bisexual youths. *Journal of Sex Research, 48*(1), 3–15. doi: 10.1080/00224490903331067

Roy, C.M., & Cain, R. (2001). The involvement of people living with HIV/AIDS in community-based organizations: Contributions and constraints. *AIDS Care, 13*(4), 421–432. doi: 10.1080/09540120120057950

Savin-Williams, R.C. (2009). How many gays are there? It depends. In D.A. Hope (Ed.), *Contemporary perspectives on lesbian, gay, and bisexual identities* (pp. 5–41). New York, NY: Springer.

Silverstein, C. (2009). The implications of removing homosexuality for the DSM as a mental disorder. *Archives of Sexual Behavior, 38,* 161–163. doi: 10.1007/s10508-008-9442-x

Smith, L.A., McCaslin, R., Chang, J., Martinez, P., & McGrew, P. (2010). Assessing the needs of older gay, lesbian, bisexual, and transgender people: A service-learning and agency partnership approach. *Journal of Gerontological Social Work, 53,* 387–401. doi: 10.1080/01634372.2010.486433

Statistics Canada. (2008, March 19). Study: Health care use among gay, lesbian, and bisexual Canadians. *The Daily.* Retrieved from http://www.statcan.gc.ca/daily-quotidien/080319/dq080319b-eng.htm

Statistics Canada. (2010, June 14). Police-reported hate crimes. *The Daily.* Retrieved from http://www.statcan.gc.ca/daily-quotidien/100614/dq100614b-eng.htm

Stein, G.L., Beckerman, N.L., & Sherman, P.A. (2010). Lesbian and gay elders and long-term care: Identifying the unique psychoscocial perspectives and challenges. *Journal of Gerontological Social Work, 53,* 421–435. doi: 10.1080/01634372.2010.486433

Taylor, C., & Ristock, J. (2011). LGBTQ families in Canada: Private lives and public discourse. In N. Mandell & A. Duffy (Eds.), *Canadian families: Diversity, conflict, and change* (4th ed.) (pp. 125–163). Toronto, ON: Nelson Education.

Thompson, N. (2011). Promoting equality. *Working with diversity and difference* (3rd ed.). Basingstoke, UK: Palgrave Macmillan.

Todd, D. (2011, June 30). A true north guide to Canadian values. *Vancouver Sun* (pp. A8–A9).

Todd, S. (2010). Social work and sexual and gender diversity. In S.F. Hick (Ed.), *Social work in Canada: An introduction* (3rd ed.) (pp. 298–308). Toronto, ON: Thompson Educational Publishing.

References

United Nations. (2011, April). Tackling discrimination on grounds of sexual orientation and gender identity. Retrieved from http://www.ohchr.org

Vance, C.S. (2005). Anthropology rediscovers sexuality: A theoretical comment. In J. Robertson (Ed.), *Same-sex cultures and sexualities: An anthropological reader* (pp. 15–32). Malden, MA: Blackwell Publishing.

Walls, N.E. (2008). Toward a multidimensional understanding of heterosexism: The changing nature of prejudice. *Journal of Homosexuality,* 55(1), 20–70. doi: 10.1080/00918360802129287

Warner, T. (2002). *Never going back: A history of queer activism in Canada.* Toronto, ON: University of Toronto Press.

Weeks, J. (2001). Sexual orientation: Historical and social construction. *International Encyclopedia of the Social and Behavioral Sciences* (pp. 13998–14002). Retrieved from http://www.sciencedirect.com/science/referenceworks

Weinberg, G.H. (1972). *Society and the healthy homosexual.* New York, NY: St. Martin's Press.

Willms, M. (2005). Canadian immigration law and same-sex partners. *Canadian Issues,* (Spring), 17–20. Retrieved from http://canada.metropolis.net/pdfs/CITC_Spring_05_EN.pdf

Immigration and Refugee Policy in Canada

Past, Present, and Future

17

Usha George

Canada is one of the few countries in the world that has an active immigrant and refugee admission policy and program. Even before 1860, when figures on immigration became available, immigrants and refugees from different countries made Canada their home. The numbers of newcomers and source countries have depended on the immigration policies and practices in effect at particular times. Immigration has become an enduring feature of Canada's policy milieu; however, this does not imply that immigration is an uncontested topic in Canada. As Freeman (1995) points out, in liberal democracies such as Canada, the political economy model of policy making, with a constitution based on individual rights, competitive party systems, and periodic elections, influences the direction of immigration policy.

The inevitable question is: Why immigration? The question can be answered at a general theoretical level or by examining factors specific to Canada. At the theoretical level, push-and-pull factors can explain immigration. Push factors operate when individuals decide to leave their country of origin because of worsening economic conditions, including high levels of unemployment. Pull factors operate when individuals are attracted to a country because of the opportunities it offers for economic betterment and social mobility. The distinction between push and pull factors is not always clear (Isajiw, 1999).

There are two further explanations specific to the Canadian situation. First, Canada's natural population growth "has declined steadily in recent decades from 3 percent in the 1950s to less than 1 percent in the late 1990s" (Knowles, 2000, p. 4). The main reasons for the decline in population growth are the drop in the fertility rate as a result of women entering the workforce, and the growing tendency for couples to have fewer children or none at all. The fertility rate declined from 4 children per woman in 1959 to less than 2 per woman by 1998. As Knowles (2000, p. 4) has observed, "should this low fertility rate continue—and all the indications are that it will—immigration will become essential for this country's healthy growth and even, perhaps, for its survival."

Second, there is the need for skilled labour. In fact, early immigration was spurred by the demand for labour to build railways and to support industries such as mining, fishing, and forestry. As the supply of manual labour from the United States and Europe began to dwindle in the 1880s, more than 1,500 labourers were recruited from China to lay track for the Canadian Pacific Railway (Bolaria & Li, 1988; Henry et al., 2005). Recent years have seen an increase in labour migration around the world, and this is expected to further increase in the future (International Organization for Migration, 2010). In recent times, the need for skilled labour for Canada's expanding industrial and high-tech fields has been well recognized.

This chapter provides a brief overview of Canada's immigration and refugee policy and practice. The first section defines key terms such as "immigrant," "refugee," and "newcomer." The next section provides a brief overview of the history of immigration in Canada, followed by an examination of the provisions in the current Immigration Act, which came into effect in 2002. To illustrate the workings of the Immigration Act, a summary of the annual plan for 2010–2011 follows, along with an analysis of the directions of immigration and refugee policy in Canada. Recent developments in immigration and refugee programs and policies are discussed. The final section briefly reviews the impact of Canadian immigration policy.

The term "immigrant" generally refers to anyone from another country who is legally admitted to live in a country. In Canada, these individuals are also called permanent residents or landed immigrants. Landed immigrants can apply to become Canadian citizens after three years. Canadian citizenship is granted to any landed immigrant, provided the person meets residency requirements, has no criminal record, and passes a simple citizenship test. A landed immigrant is entitled to all the privileges of a citizen except the right to vote in provincial and federal elections; however, once a citizen, regardless of the country of origin, a person is entitled to all rights and privileges.

In practice, however, immigrants experience landed immigrant status and citizenship differently because of discrimination and prejudice in Canadian society. While each group of immigrants has its own experiences of discrimination and prejudice, individuals from visible minority backgrounds generally continue to be perceived as immigrants, regardless of their length of stay in Canada. A great deal of scholarship has developed around the notion of the "social construction of immigrants and refugees." Li (1997) refers to this as "benchmarking," as the term "immigrant" is used as a folk, bureaucratic, and analytical concept.

As Isajiw (1999, p. 71) observes, "refugees are people who have to leave a country because they are denied a human existence and are accepted by another country on account of this country's humane or humanitarian concerns." These refugees are also called convention refugees, as per the United Nations Convention Relating to the Status of Refugees, 1951, to which Canada is a signatory. Two distinct groups of refugees are recognized in Canadian policy and practice circles: sponsored refugees, and asylum seekers or refugee claimants. Sponsored refugees can be sponsored either privately or by government. Privately sponsored refugees are those sponsored by religious or other not-for-profit groups. Once in Canada, sponsored refugees receive landed immigrant status and all related entitlements. Asylum seekers or refugee claimants, in contrast, are individuals who arrive in Canada as visitors and who apply for refugee status for fear of persecution in their country of origin. Asylum seekers must undergo a lengthy process of hearings and appeals with the Immigration and Refugee Board (IRB). Once accepted by the IRB, these individuals acquire the status of convention refugees, but they have to go through the immigration process to become landed immigrants. Canada's domestic law integrates its international obligations by stipulating that convention refugees legally in Canada cannot be deported unless they pose a threat to national security or commit a serious crime (Christensen, 1999).

In recent times, the term "newcomer," which does not distinguish individuals on the basis of their legal status, has been used by academic, bureaucratic, and social service communities because it is considered more inclusive. This term distinguishes individuals based on their length of time in Canada—a distinction that serves an instrumental purpose for the federal Department of Citizenship and Immigration settlement services, which are generally available to landed immigrants who have been in the country for less than five years. Service providers, however, contend that the term "newcomer" masks the ongoing problems faced by immigrants in general, regardless of the length of their stay in Canada. Discrimination in employment, stereotyping faced by visible minorities, and family and youth issues faced by second-generation immigrants are examples of such problems.

Another important term in Canadian immigration policy is "family class." Generally, family-class or family-related immigrants are those who migrate to another country to join immediate relatives. Family-class relatives may include lineal relatives such as spouses, parents, children, and grandparents, as well as lateral relatives such as brothers, sisters, and uncles (Isajiw, 1999). Although historically, Canadian immigration policy and practice have allowed a mix of lineal and lateral relatives, the current policy restricts family class to lineal relatives.

History of Canadian Immigration Policy and Practice

Canadian immigration policy and practice have attracted a great deal of scholarly attention. Bolaria and Li (1988) examine the experiences of different visible minority ethnic groups in Canadian society in terms of Canada's attempts at capital accumulation for the development of a capitalist state.[1] Other scholars have divided the history of Canadian immigration into stages or phases, often based on history (Isajiw, 1999) or major policy changes (Abu-Laban, 1998; Christensen, 1999; Green & Green 1996; Henry et al., 2005; Knowles, 2000).

History of Canadian Immmigration Policy and Practice

While Canada has had immigration laws since 1869, the first specifically named Immigration Act, of 1906, established formal policies and gave the federal government power over national borders (Knowles, 2000). The period between the two world wars was one of immigration restriction and reduction. The Canadian government took specific measures to prevent immigration from non-European countries and to limit the arrival of the families of the immigrants already here. Concerns about the ethnic composition of the Canadian population were foremost in the minds of policy makers. The continuation of the Head Tax for the Chinese, the limitation of Japanese immigration to 400 per year, the introduction of the "continuous passage" rule for immigration from India, and restrictions on black immigration are all examples of how policy makers handled such concerns. At the end of the Second World War there was large-scale immigrant and refugee movement to Canada; however, the restrictions on Asian immigration remained, for it was believed that large-scale immigration from the Orient would alter the "fundamental composition" of the Canadian population (Isajiw, 1999).

Government policy began to change during the first half of the 1960s, signalling an approaching end to nationality-based immigration, although Caucasian immigrants continued to be preferred. For example, in 1961, British immigration was only 17 percent of the total immigration for the year; by 1966, it had risen to 37 percent (Isajiw, 1999). The number of immigrants from other ethnic groups, including Asian and black, also increased during this period.

The White Paper on immigration, released in 1966, formed the basis for the new immigration regulations of 1967 (Isajiw, 1999). Through regulatory changes, racial discrimination was eliminated as the basis for selecting immigrants; in addition, a point system was introduced in an attempt to bring fairness to the immigration process, as well as to meet the needs of the country. Under the new merit-point structure, applicants in the category of "independent immigrants" were to be assessed on the basis of a number of characteristics, each of which was assigned a range of merit points. The characteristics included education and training; personal qualities such as adaptability, motivation, and initiative; demand for the individual's occupation in Canada; occupational skill; arranged employment; knowledge of English or French; relatives in Canada; and employment opportunities in the area of destination (Isajiw, 1999). Beginning in 1968, the ethnic composition of immigrants changed as a result of this non-racist immigration policy. The years 1968 to 1976 "represented the reversal of the proportion of the white to non-white immigrants to Canada" (Isajiw, 1999, p. 85). Furthermore, Canada's endorsement of the UN Convention on Refugees in 1970 led to refugees from Czechoslovakia, Tibet, Uganda, Chile, Vietnam, and Cambodia being admitted to Canada.

The volume of immigration became more of a concern in 1974; that year, Canada had one of the largest influxes in the postwar period. A government study of immigration—the Green Paper on immigration—was tabled in the House of Commons and became the Immigration Act of 1976, which took effect in 1978. The changes introduced by the new legislation grew out of a number of factors: internal pressure for a multiculturalism policy that would recognize Canada's racial and ethnic diversity; increasing politicization and mobilization of minority immigrant groups demanding a fair immigration policy; pressure by human rights activists; pressure from the international community to eliminate open racism; and, most important, economic need. With European immigration dwindling, the shortage of highly educated and skilled workers was a major government concern (Henry et al., 2000).

Bill C-11 The Immigration and Refugee Protection Act, 2002

The 1976 act was "framework" legislation—in other words, it included only the main provisions and left most of the details to regulations. The Immigration Act and Regulations were based on fundamental principles such as non-discrimination; family reunion; humanitarian concern for refugees; and the promotion of Canada's social, economic, demographic, and cultural goals (Citizenship and Immigration Canada, 2001a). Major features of the act included these: it linked immigration to economic conditions and demographic needs; and it required the Minister of Immigration to announce annual immigration plans, which would estimate the number of immigrants Canada could absorb comfortably each year. These plans were to be presented to Parliament after mandatory consultations with the provincial and territorial governments and the private and voluntary sectors. The act also stipulated four basic categories of individuals eligible for landed immigrant status: (1) family class; (2) humanitarian class, consisting of refugees as defined by the 1951 UN Convention and also of displaced persons who did not qualify as refugees under the UN definition; (3) independent class, selected on the basis of the point system; and (4) assisted relatives—that is, distant relatives sponsored by a family member in Canada and who met some of the selection criteria of the independent class (Knowles, 2000). The act also established the Immigration and Refugee Board and required immigrants and visitors to obtain visas from abroad. And it protected the civil rights of immigrants and visitors through a quasi-judicial tribunal and provided short-term alternatives to permanent deportation for cases involving violation of the immigration law (CIC, 2001a).

Bill C-11: The Immigration and Refugee Protection Act, 2002

In 1994 the federal government held public consultations to decide future directions for immigration and refugee policy. A non-partisan advisory group set up by the federal government reviewed legislation, programs, and policies relating to immigrants and refugees. In 1998 the group produced a report titled *Not Just Numbers: A Canadian Framework for Future Immigration*. That report, with its 172 recommendations, was to form the basis for a new immigration law, replacing the 1978 Immigration Act. On 13 June 2001, the House of Commons passed the Act Respecting Immigration to Canada

Bill C-11 The Immigration and Refugee Protection Act, 2002

and the Granting of Refugee Protection to Persons Who Are Displaced, Persecuted or in Danger.

The new act, much like its predecessor, is framework legislation; but it also incorporates some core principles previously intended to be included in the regulations. These include the principles of equality and freedom from discrimination; of detaining a minor child only as a last resort and in the "best interests of the child"; and of equality of status for both official languages. The act specifies separate objectives for immigration and refugee admission (ss. 3.1 and 3.2). The act and its regulations include provisions regarding consultations with provinces, the volume and selection criteria of immigrants, the definition and processing of refugees, sponsorship rights, fees, and appeals and deportation. Although it does not specify each covenant to which Canada has subscribed, the act does refer to the Canadian Charter of Rights and Freedoms and states that immigration policy must fulfill Canada's international legal obligations. These obligations include the Convention on the Rights of the Child, the Convention Relating to the Status of Refugees, the Convention Against Torture, the Convention on the Reduction of Statelessness, and the Declaration of the Rights and the Duties of Man.

The act recognizes three categories of foreign nationals for permanent resident status: family class; economic class, to be selected on the basis of each applicant's ability to become economically self-sufficient in Canada; and convention refugees, who may be selected before they have entered Canada or after they have arrived. The act establishes family class for the first time, and parents are now included in the definition of family class. Family class also includes common-law and same-sex partners. The act also broadens the definition of "dependent child" from under age nineteen to under age twenty-two.

The government can now collect from a sponsor the amount of social assistance given to a sponsored family member. The length of the sponsorship requirement has been reduced from ten to three years for spouses and common-law partners, both opposite- and same-sex. The age at which Canadian citizens and permanent residents can sponsor has been reduced from nineteen to eighteen. The act has also created an in-Canada landing class for sponsored spouses and partners of both immigrants and refugees, and it exempts sponsored spouses, partners, and dependent children from inadmissibility on the basis of excessive demand on health and social services. Family reunification provisions are mostly left to regulations (Canadian Council for Refugees, 2001, p. 48). Sponsorship obligations have been strengthened for individuals who default on court-ordered child support payments. Also, individuals who have been convicted of domestic abuse and who have not demonstrated rehabilitation do not have sponsorship privileges. Except in cases of disability, individuals on social assistance do not have sponsorship privileges. Through legislative provisions, the act strengthens the federal government's ability to recover the cost of social assistance in cases of sponsorship default.

Bill C-11 The Immigration and Refugee Protection Act, 2002

The act establishes criteria for permanent residents. Permanent residents have to meet the physical residency requirement of being present in Canada for a cumulative period of two years for every five working years. Exceptions are allowed for individuals who have to spend time outside Canada to accompany a Canadian citizen or work for a Canadian company, or for humanitarian reasons. Every permanent resident is to have a fraud-resistant permanent resident card. Loss-of-status cases can present an oral appeal to the Immigration and Refugee Board (CIC, 2001b).

With regard to selecting skilled workers in the economic class, perhaps one of the act's most unique features is its movement away from an occupation-based model to one that is based on flexible and transferable skills. The proposed human capital model replaces the "general occupation" list and "intended occupation" concept. Education and knowledge of an official language are given more weight; however, language facility is not a bar to admission. An in-Canada landing class has been created for temporary workers, including recent graduates who have a permanent job offer and have been working in Canada. The temporary worker program will be expanded to meet the immediate needs of employers. With regard to the investor and entrepreneur programs, the act proposes to establish objective criteria for assessing business experience and for establishing a net worth for entrepreneurs (CIC, 2001b).

The act defines two classes of refugees: convention refugees and people in need of protection. The act proposes to strengthen refugee protection and overseas resettlement by ensuring that people in need of urgent protection are brought to Canada within days and by pursuing agreements with non-governmental organizations to locate and pre-screen refugee applications in areas where refugees are most in need of protection. It also proposes to amend the criteria for claimants' ability to establish themselves in Canada to include social as well as economic factors. To facilitate family reunification of refugees, overseas families (including extended family members) are to be processed as a unit whenever possible. Dependants of a refugee, whether they live in Canada or abroad, will be processed as part of the same application within one year of the refugee's obtaining permanent status. Another feature of the act is its provision for faster and fairer refugee processing inland. Referral to the Immigration and Refugee Board is to be made within three working days, with single interviewers supported by paper appeal being the norm. A single hearing is to examine all risk grounds, such as the Geneva Convention, the Convention Against Torture, and the risk of cruel and unusual punishment. The waiting period for landing in Canada for undocumented refugees, who are unable to obtain documents from their country of origin, has been reduced from five to three years. A security check is to be initiated when a person makes a refugee claim; merit will be

Table 17.1 Permanent Residents by Immigrant Category and Sex, 2008–2009, by %

	Family class	Economic class	Protected persons	Other	All classes
Males	60	48	48	53	52
Females	40	52	52	47	0

Source: CIC (2010b). Annual report to Parliament on immigration, 2010. Retrieved from http://www.cic.gc.ca/english/resources/publications/index.asp.

determined by an independent adjudicator. Perhaps the most controversial provisions of the act concern enforcement: the act increases penalties for existing offences and creates a new offence for human trafficking. The penalty for migrant smuggling and trafficking is life in prison.

Critiques of the Immigration and Refugee Protection Act, 2002

Many organizations, such as Amnesty International, the Canadian Bar Association, the Canadian Council for Refugees, the Maytree Foundation, and the UN High Commissioner for Refugees, along with provincial and citywide advocacy groups, have raised significant concerns about the new act. Criticisms of the two documents leading to the new Immigration Act (Bill C-11 and its precursor Bill C-31) can be grouped into three main areas: the framework legislation's lack of transparency; human rights; and class and gender concerns.

Lack of Transparency

Like previous ones, the current act is framework legislation, in that many important details are left to regulations, which are constantly changing. This means that Citizenship and Immigration Canada (CIC) can implement immigration policy changes without having to face the House of Commons or public scrutiny. This latitude allows the government to say one thing but, in effect, do another (Green & Green, 1996). Although it is recognized that this structure allows the system to be more flexible and responsive, such wide powers of discretion are seen as problematic (Amnesty International, 2001; Canadian Council for Refugees, 2001; Maytree Foundation, 2001). For example, family unification provisions, the selection of independent immigrants, and the definitions of terms such as "international rights" and "terrorism" are all left to regulations; this has serious implications for many individuals and families.

Human Rights and Humanitarian Concerns

The potential for human rights abuses is evident in the tone and substance of the act and is a major concern for many (Amnesty International, 2001; Canadian Council for Refugees, 2001; Maytree Foundation, 2001; United

Annual Immigration Plans

Nations High Commissioner for Refugees [UNHCR], 2001). The act has expanded the powers of immigration officers and is more restrictive toward asylum seekers and permanent residents. Overall, the act emphasizes economic objectives. Admissibility criteria—such as the ability to settle, find work, and become independent—are also applied to refugees (Hyndman, 1999). Similarly, the act's emphasis on finding refugees resettlement close to their own country reflects more of a political strategy to reduce the numbers of refugees who are asylum seekers in Canada (UNHCR, 2001) than a commitment to social justice.

Class and Gender Issues

The class and gender biases in the 1976 Immigration and Refugee Act received much attention (Bolaria & Li, 1988; Boyd, 1995; Das Gupta, 1994). Similar observations have been made of the new Immigration Act and the consultations that preceded it. Since 1976, the Canadian government has held consultations with various stakeholders to determine immigration policy. However, even though the government espouses democratic ideals, the framing of questions and issues in immigration consultations reaffirms sexist and racist ideology (Thobani, 2000). The requirement for official language competence for independent immigrants is bound to have a gendered impact (Hyndman, 1999). The relative positioning of the family class and the independent immigrants in relation to the latter's potential for self-sufficiency is seen as "a new problematization of the immigrant family. More specifically, because immigrant women typically come under the family class, the plan also reflects a problematization of immigrant women" (Abu-Laban, 1998, p. 200). The act will have differential negative consequences for women and racialized minorities (Canadian Council for Refugees, 2001). Bill C-11 Immigrant and Refugee Protection Act (IRPA) became law on 28 June 2002.

Annual Immigration Plans 2010–2011

The Report on Plans and Priorities (CIC, 2009a) for the year 2010–11 lists the long-term outcomes that the CIC hopes to achieve through its strategic plans. Each strategic outcome has accompanying program activities and subactivities chalked out. The strategic outcomes are as follows:

- Migration that significantly benefits Canada's economic, social and cultural development, while protecting the health, safety, and security of Canadians
- International recognition and acceptance of the principles of managed migration consistent with Canada's broader foreign policy agenda, and protection of refugees in Canada
- Successful integration of newcomers into society and promotion of Canadian Citizenship. (CIC, 2009a, p. 8)

Annual Immigration Plans

Table 17.2 Immigration Overview: Permanent and Temporary Residents

Category	2000	2001	2002	2003	2004	2005	2006	2007	2008	2009
ECONOMIC CLASS										
Skilled workers–p.a.*	52,120	58,911	52,974	45,377	47,894	52,269	44,161	41,251	43,360	40,735
Skilled workers–s.d.**	66,468	78,323	69,756	59,847	65,557	77,969	61,783	56,601	60,374	55,227
Canadian experience class–p.a.*										1,775
Canadian experience class–s.d.**										770
Entrepreneurs–p.a.*	1,658	1,608	1,176	781	668	750	820	581	446	372
Entrepreneurs–s.d.**	4,529	4,479	3,302	2,197	1,800	2,098	2,273	1,579	1,255	943
Self-employed–p.a.*	795	705	636	446	366	302	320	203	164	179
Self-employed–s.d.**	1,732	1,451	1,271	981	824	714	632	373	341	358
Investors–p.a.*	1,390	1,768	1,234	972	1,671	2,591	2,201	2,025	2,832	2,872
Investors–s.d.**	3,561	4,574	3,402	2,723	4,428	7,020	5,830	5,420	7,370	7,435
Provincial/territorial nominees–p.a.*	368	410	680	1,417	2,086	2,643	4,672	6,329	8,343	11,801
Provincial/territorial nominees–s.d.**	884	864	1,447	3,001	4,162	5,404	8,664	10,765	14,075	18,577
Live-in caregivers–p.a.*	1,759	1,874	1,521	2,230	2,496	3,063	3,547	3,433	6,157	6,273
Live-in caregivers–s.d.**	1,023	753	464	1,074	1,796	1,489	3,348	2,684	4,354	6,181
Total Economic Immigrants	**136,287**	**155,720**	**137,863**	**121,046**	**133,748**	**156,312**	**138,251**	**131,244**	**149,071**	**153,498**
FAMILY CLASS										
Spouses and partners	36,814	39,402	34,197	39,676	44,218	45,448	45,303	44,912	44,204	43,894
Sons and daughters	3,951	3,932	3,645	3,618	3,037	3,232	3,191	3,338	3,255	3,027
Parents and grandparents	17,771	21,341	22,244	19,385	12,733	12,475	20,005	15,813	16,599	17,179
Others	2,080	2,119	2,205	2,438	2,278	2,209	2,016	2,179	1,519	1,100
Total Family Class	**60,616**	**66,794**	**62,291**	**65,117**	**62,266**	**63,364**	**70,515**	**66,242**	**65,577**	**65,200**
REFUGEES										
Government-assisted refugees	10,669	8,697	7,505	7,508	7,411	7,424	7,326	7,573	7,295	7,425
Privately sponsored refugees	2,933	3,576	3,043	3,252	3,116	2,976	3,337	3,588	3,512	5,036
Refugees landed in Canada	12,993	11,897	10,546	11,264	15,901	19,935	15,884	11,696	6,994	7,204
Refugee dependants	3,497	3,749	4,021	3,960	6,259	5,441	5,952	5,098	4,059	3,181
Total Refugees	**30,092**	**27,919**	**25,115**	**25,984**	**32,687**	**35,776**	**32,499**	**27,955**	**21,860**	**22,846**
OTHER IMMIGRANTS										
Retirees, DROC and PDRCC***	460	206	–	79	53	20	23	15	2	6
Temporary resident permit holders	0	0	–	97	148	123	136	107	113	106
H and C**** cases	0	0	619	2,375	2,984	3,110	4,312	4,346	3,452	3,142
Other H and C cases outside the family class / Public policy	0	0	3,026	6,649	3,939	3,534	5,904	6,844	7,170	7,380
Total Other Immigrants	**460**	**206**	**3,780**	**9,200**	**7,124**	**6,787**	**10,375**	**11,312**	**10,737**	**10,634**
Category not stated	0	1	0	1	0	2	2	1	2	1
Total	**227,455**	**250,640**	**229,049**	**221,348**	**235,825**	**262,241**	**251,642**	**236,754**	**247,247**	**252,179**

*p.a. = principal applicants **s.d. = spouses and dependants *** Deferred removal orders and post-determination refugee claimants in Canada
**** Humanitarian and Compassionate

Source: CIC (2010b). Facts and figures 2009—Permanent and temporary residents. http://www.cic.gc.ca/english/resources/statistics/facts2009/permanent/02.asp.

Annual Immigration Plans

Table 17.3 Immigration Level Plan 2011

IMMIGRANT CATEGORY	2011 PLAN TARGET RANGES Low	High
ECONOMIC CLASS		
Federally selected economic class*	**74,000**	**80,400**
Principal applicants†	33,200	36,600
Spouses and dependants†	40,800	43,800
Provincially selected economic class*	**76,600**	**80,900**
Principal applicants†	31,900	33,800
Spouses and dependants†	44,700	47,100
Provincial nominee program	**42,000**	**45,000**
Principal applicants†	17,500	18,800
Spouses and dependants†	24,500	26,200
Quebec-selected skilled workers and business	**34,600**	**35,900**
Principal applicants†	14,400	15,000
Spouses and dependants†	20,200	20,900
Subtotal economic class—principal applicants	**65,100**	**70,400**
Subtotal economic class—spouses and dependants	**85,500**	**90,900**
TOTAL ECONOMIC CLASS	**150,600**	**161,300**
FAMILY CLASS		
Spouses, partners, and children	**45,500**	**48,000**
Parents and grandparents	**13,000**	**17,500**
TOTAL FAMILY CLASS	**58,500**	**65,500**
PROTECTED PERSONS		
Government-assisted refugees	**7,400**	**8,000**
Privately sponsored refugees	**3,800**	**6,000**
Protected persons in Canada	**8,200**	**10,500**
Dependants abroad of protected persons in Canada	**3,800**	**4,500**
OTHER		
Humanitarian and compassionate grounds / public policy	**7,600**	**9,000**
Permit holders	**100**	**200**
TOTAL OTHER	**7,700**	**9,200**
TOTAL	**240,000**	**265,000**

Source: Citizenship and Immigration Canada (CIC). (2010a). Annual report to Parliament on immigration, 2010. Retrieved from http://www.cic.gc.ca/english/resources/publications/index.asp.

* This year admission projections for economic immigration are being presented based on selecting and/or nominating jurisdiction because the direct involvement of provinces and territories in economic immigration has grown. Under the Canada–Quebec Accord Relating to Immigration and Temporary Admission of Aliens, the Government of Quebec has responsibility for selecting immigrants destined to its province, and other jurisdictions participating in the Provincial Nominee Program have the responsibility to nominate foreign nationals for permanent resident status.

† The number of principal applicants and spouses and dependants is estimated based on historical averages, and is included for illustrative purposes only.

The strategic plans will be carried out through activities of the Immigration Program, Refugee Program, Temporary Worker Program, Citizenship Program, and Integration Program as well as through Canada's role in international migration and protection.

Table 17.2 provides the number of permanent residents by category from 2000–2009 and Table 17.3 provides details of the immigration plan for 2011.

Recent Developments

Since the transfer of enforcement and intelligence functions from CIC to the newly created Canada Border Services Agency (CBSA) in 2003, CIC has developed new vision and mission statements that provide the basis for an integrated package of programs and services. CIC's activities are to be guided by the three strategic outcomes listed above.

On 29 December 2004, Canada implemented the Safe Third Country Agreement with the United States. This agreement stipulates that refugee claimants must request asylum in the first safe country they arrive in. This agreement applies to refugee claims made at land borders. Refugee claimants accessing Canada from the Canada–U.S. land border are not eligible for a refugee determination hearing with the IRB unless they qualify for an exception. Implementation of this agreement has reduced the number of land border refugee claims by 40 percent (Canadian Council for Refugees, 2005).

In pursuance of the successful integration of newcomers to the Canadian labour market and society, all settlement programs have been strengthened. In addition, a coordinated strategy to integrate foreign-trained Canadians and immigrants into the Canadian labour market was developed in 2004 as part of a government-wide initiative focusing on four areas: foreign credential assessment and recognition, enhanced language training and bridge-to-work initiatives, labour market information, and research.

In April 2005 the Minister of Citizenship and Immigration announced a tripling of the target for parents and grandparents to 18,000 admissions per year to address the backlog within the system. In 2010, however, the Harper government has gone full circle by reducing the number of parent and grandparent sponsorships allowed while increasing the number of sponsorships for spouses and children (CIC, 2010a).

In the past few years there has been a clear shift toward prioritizing occupation-specific migration. In 2008, CIC announced its Action Plan for Faster Immigration, which proposed changes to the Federal Skilled Worker Program (FSWP). Persons were now eligible to apply for immigration under the FSWP only if they met one of these three criteria: they had arranged an offer of employment; they had been living in Canada legally for the past year as either a foreign worker or an international student; or, they had at least one year of work experience in one of the thirty-eight occupations shortlisted by

Recent Developments

the CIC. Changes were also announced to the work permits available to international students who had completed their education in a Canadian university, allowing them to obtain open work permits under the Post-Graduation Work Permit Program, even without a job offer and with no restrictions on the type of employment. In addition, the duration of the work permit was extended from one to two years, then three years across the country (CIC, 2008).

In 2010, CIC announced further changes to the policy, reducing the number of in-demand occupations to twenty-nine. Under the new changes, to be eligible to apply for the FSWP, the applicant must either have a job offer in hand or must be trained and experienced in one of the twenty-nine in-demand occupations. Furthermore, CIC has set limits on the number of applications to be processed under each occupational category (CIC, 2010c). Proposed changes to the FSWP in 2011 include redirecting points from those allotted to the number of years of work experience to those allotted to official language proficiency and to younger age workers. The proposed changes also encourage the immigration of skilled tradespeople by lowering the number of years of education required to claim points as a skilled worker (CIC, 2011a).

While the Citizenship Act required immigration applicants to have language proficiency in one of Canada's two official languages, ascertaining that the applicant met this requirement had long been done through interactions with CIC officials. In 2010, CIC announced that language proficiency would from now on be assessed through a uniform language screening tool (CIC, 2010d) administered by designated language testing agencies.

In 2009, CIC announced a modernized approach to settlement programs. This was to be an outcomes-based approach that integrated previously separate funding programs—Language Instruction for Newcomers to Canada (LINC), the Host Program, and the Immigrant Settlement and Adaptation Program (ISAP)—into one cohesive program (CIC, 2009b). As has been mentioned before, the Immigration Act is a framework document with regulations that specify how it must be implemented. This flexibility allows the government to make changes to its programs as and when required.

Since April, 2011 regulatory improvements have been made to the Temporary Foreign Worker Program. For example, there are now stricter assessments of the genuineness of employment offers. There is also a two-year period of ineligibility for employers who default on their commitments relating to wages and working conditions, and a four-year upper limit of time for some categories of temporary workers (CIC, 2011b).

Impact of Immigration Policies: 1967 to Present

Impact of Immigration Policies: 1967 to Present

Overall, Canadian society has experienced three major trends in relation to the post-1967 changes to immigration policies. The first is the continuous increases in the diversity of the population due to immigration from non-traditional source countries. The second is that immigration is recognized more and more as the primary source of labour supply in Canada. The third, although not attributable to immigration policy per se, is the growing social inequality between newcomers and native-born Canadians.

Increasing Diversity

Although the elimination of racist immigration policies in 1967 resulted in increased immigration from non-traditional source countries, the introduction of three immigrant classes in 1993 spurred even further growth in inflows from non-European nations (Isajiw, 1999). The 2006 Canadian census reported more than 200 ethnic groups in Canada. Non-indigenous ethnic groups reported in this census included older immigrant groups such as Irish, German, Italian, Chinese, Ukrainian, Dutch, Polish, and East Indian, as well as newer ethnic groups such as Montserratan (from the Caribbean) and Chadian, Gabonese, Gambian, and Zambian (from Africa). An estimated 5,068,100 individuals reported belonging to the visible minority population; that is 16.2 percent of the total Canadian population. It is anticipated that by 2017 the visible minority population will have grown to one-fifth of the total population. South Asians, followed by Chinese, were the largest visible minority groups in Canada in 2006.

Religious affiliations have also changed over time. Prior to 1961, 83.5 percent of immigrants belonged to a Christian denomination; by the period 1991–2001, this was the case for only 45.3 percent, reflecting increases in admissions of those reporting Muslim, Hindu, Buddhist, and Sikh religious affiliations, as well as for those reporting no religious affiliation (Statistics Canada, 2003).

Primary Source of Labour Supply

Historically, immigration has been the key source for meeting labour needs in Canadian society. More recently, labour shortages have been identified as a major business constraint. Labour shortages are likely to become a challenge as baby boomers retire over the next two decades. It is predicted that without immigration, the size of the Canadian labour force will decline. It is estimated that by 2017, immigration will account for *all* the net growth in the labour force.

Growing Social Inequality

Growing Social Inequality

Inequality between newcomer and Canadian-born populations is evident in a number of spheres, including employment, housing, civic and political participation and representation, and access to human services. These inequalities in access and outcomes exist in areas related to primary settlement needs; thus, they impede the ability of newcomers to integrate successfully into Canadian society. Although racism is difficult to measure, many scholars assert that disparate outcomes in spheres such as those outlined above are evidence of pervasive racial discrimination in Canadian society (Castles, 1997; Henry & Tator, 2005; Kunz, Milan, & Schetagne, 2000; Ornstein, 2000).

A number of studies have documented racial prejudice and employment disparities in Canada (Boyd, 1995; Galabuzi, 2001; Li, 1997; Reitz & Breton, 1994, quoted in Reitz, 2004). Income disparities between newcomers and the native-born have increased now that more and more newcomers belong to non-dominant racial groups (Jackson & Smith, 2002). This has led to the phenomenon of racialized poverty. Earnings differentials between visible minority newcomers and white Canadian-born citizens because of unrecognized credentials, and direct discrimination toward the former (Harvey, Siu, & Reil, 1999; Ornstein, 2000), cost the Canadian economy about $55 billion a year (Reitz, cited in Siddiqui, 2001) and create a highly stratified society. The average newly arrived male immigrant earned roughly 80 percent of the average native-born salary in 1980; by 2000, he earned only 60 percent (Reitz, 2004). A recent report (Block & Galabuzi, 2011) that used the 2006 Census data to compare the earnings of racialized and non-racialized workers found that racialized persons earned less than non-racialized persons and that these discrepancies were worse for women than for men. Racialized Canadians earn 81.4 cents for every dollar earned by non-racialized men. Racialized men were 28 percent more likely to be unemployed than non-racialized men despite their willingness to work, while racialized women were 48 percent more likely to be unemployed than non-racialized men.

The systemic barriers associated with credential evaluation and licensing for trades and occupations are well documented (Basran & Zong, 1998; Brouwer, 1999; Calleja, 2000; George, Chaze, Brennenstuhl, & Fuller-Thomson, 2011). Newcomers to Canada have higher levels of education on average than Canadian-born citizens, yet they find it more difficult to land jobs (Badets & Howatson-Leo, 1999; McDonald & Worswick, 1997). Research also suggests that visible minority status may continue to have differential income outcomes for second-generation immigrant men (Palameta, 2007). It is argued that the barriers to employment for newcomers, such as the requirement for Canadian employment experience and the non-recognition of foreign credentials and experience, can be directly attributed to racism and/or other forms of discrimination (Cabral, 2000; Galabuzi, 2001; Henry & Tator, 2005; Integrated Settlement Planning Research Consortium, 2000).

Growing Social Inequality

There is evidence that newcomers to Canada face numerous barriers to housing in the private *and* social housing markets (Housing New Canadians, n.d.), with many disadvantaged in the housing market on the basis of race, ethnicity, class, and/or gender (Murdie et al., 1999). Newcomers often reside in the least desirable housing units in the least desirable areas (Sparks & Wolfson, 2001) and are increasingly overrepresented in Toronto's high-poverty neighbourhoods. In 1980, 24.4 percent of low-income neighbourhood residents were recent immigrants, whereas by 2000, 39.1 percent were recent immigrants (United Way of Greater Toronto & Canadian Council on Social Development, 2004). Furthermore, "visible minorities" often reside in unsafe, rundown buildings yet typically pay nearly the same amount for housing as their neighbours with higher incomes and better housing (Ornstein, 2000).

Newcomers are increasingly represented in the category of "absolute homelessness" (i.e., residing outdoors and using community shelters) (Ballay & Bulthuis, 2004, p. 119). In Toronto in 1999, refugees comprised 24 percent of families requiring emergency shelter (City of Toronto, 2001a, cited in Ballay & Bulthuis, 2004) and 23 percent of singles who used a shelter more than five times in the year (City of Toronto, 2001b, cited in Ballay & Bulthuis, 2004, p. 120). In 2001, 800 refugee claimants were accommodated in Toronto's shelters at any given point (City of Toronto, 2001a, cited in Ballay & Bulthuis, 2004).

Although civic and political participation is an integral component of democracy, proportionate representation of diversity remains lacking in Canada's political life (Biles & Tolley, 2004). The proportionality index for "visible minorities" on Toronto's municipal council is 0.3 (Bird, 2004); this means they are represented at only one-third of the level required for proportionate representation. The proportionality index for "visible minorities" in the federal House of Commons is slightly higher, at 0.4. However, defining political participation as only participation in electoral and party politics excludes numerous other forms of political activism, such as involvement in social and protest movements, trade unions, and "homeland politics" (Stasiulis, 1994, cited in Stasilius 1997, p. 1). Newcomers also participate politically through a large number of organizations, agencies, and coalitions aimed at improving their chances for success, as well as through charitable giving and volunteering.

Newcomers underutilize human services due to lack of access to appropriate programs and services (Henry & Tator, 2005). Lack of access for members of non-dominant racial and cultural groups is caused by lack of information about the services, unavailability of services, service providers' lack of knowledge of the linguistic and cultural needs of different groups, and inappropriate service models. A number of studies have demonstrated the existence of barriers to services for newcomers (Neufeld et al., 2002; Reitz, 1995, cited in George & Ramkissoon, 1998; Truelove, 2000).

Employment-oriented disparities appear to have received the most attention thus far, and within this area, initiatives have been developed occurred for foreign-trained professionals. Broadly, programs and initiatives for foreign-trained professionals can be categorized as providing the following: information; assessment of international credentials and/or work experience; specialized advisement and/or counselling; bridging; coordination and/or integration of service provision; policy advocacy; and employer incentives. In April 2005 the federal government launched the Internationally Trained Workers Initiative, which encompasses the Integration of Internationally Trained Health Professionals program; the Foreign Credential Recognition (FCR) program; the Going to Canada Immigration Internet Portal; and Enhanced Language Training (ELT) and Bridge to Work (CIC, 2005). The Government of Ontario has introduced a plan to speed the entry of internationally trained professionals and tradespeople into the labour market (Ontario Ministry of Training, Colleges, and Universities, 2005). This plan focuses on making information on Ontario's labour market needs and the criteria for licensure, registration, or certification available to prospective immigrants; expanding access to higher-level language training; offering an assessment service that evaluates international credentials and compares them with those earned in Ontario; increasing skill upgrading opportunities; and increasing opportunities to gain the equivalent of Canadian work experience.

Conclusion

The success of the immigration and refugee program should not be judged only by the achievement of annual immigration targets. Although there is no overall evaluation of Canadian immigration policy, academic and practice communities have consistently raised critical issues. Some of the academic debates centre on questions such as the annual number of immigrant and refugee admissions; the proportions of family, economic, and refugee classes admitted; and immigration's role in economic growth (DeVoretz, 1995). Immigrant and refugee advocates have raised concerns about issues such as landing fees, the criminalization of racial minorities, processing delays, and the lack of access to trades and professions for newcomers.

This chapter might have been titled "Social Policy in Relation to Newcomers to Canada" rather than "Immigration and Refugee Policy in Canada," because while the current immigration and refugee policy enables Canada to meet its overall goal of population growth, there is a major policy vacuum concerning the adaptation and integration of newcomers to Canada. As economic goals are high on the agenda for immigration, an important question is whether immigrants to Canada, especially those in the economic class, have adequate opportunities to become fully contributing members of Canadian society. Reitz (1998) argues that four institutions—immigration,

References labour market structure, educational institutions, and the welfare state—should work together to form an institutional approach to immigration and immigrant adjustment in Canada.

Note

1 The term "visible minorities" is defined in the Employment Equity Act (1995) as "persons, other than Aboriginal peoples, who are non-Caucasian in race or non-white in colour."

References

Abu-Laban, Y. (1998). Welcome/stay out: The contradiction of Canadian integration and immigration policies at the millennium. *Canadian Ethnic Studies, 30*(3), 190–211. Retrieved from http://findarticles.com/p/articles/mi_hb039/is_3_30/ai_n28722750

Amnesty International. (2001). Brief on Bill C-11: An act respecting immigration to Canada and the granting of refugee protection to persons who are displaced, persecuted or in danger. Retrieved from http://www.amnesty.ca/Refugee/Bill_C-11.pdf

Badets, J., & Howatson-Leo, L. (1999). Recent immigrants in the workforce. *Canadian Social Trends, 52,* 16–22. Retrieved from http://www.statcan.gc.ca/bsolc/olc-cel/olc-cel?catno=11-008-X19980044420&lang=eng

Ballay, P., & Bulthuis, M. (2004). The changing portrait of homelessness. In C. Andrew (Ed.), *Our diverse cities, 1* (pp. 119–123). Ottawa, ON: Metropolis Institute. Retrieved from http://canada.metropolis.net/research-policy/cities/publication/diverse_cite_magazine_e.pdf

Basran, G., & Zong, L. (1998). Devaluation of foreign credentials as perceived by visible minority professional immigrants. *Canadian Ethnic Studies, 30*(3), 6–23. Retrieved from http://findarticles.com/p/articles/mi_hb039/is_3_30/ai_n28722742/?tag=content;col1

Biles, J., & Tolley, E. (2004). Getting seats at the table(s): The political participation of newcomers and minorities in Ottawa. In C. Andrew (Ed.), *Our diverse cities, 1* (pp. 174–179). Ottawa, ON: Metropolis Institute.

Bird, K. (2004). Obstacles to ethnic minority representation in local government in Canada. In C. Andrew (Ed.), *Our Diverse Cities, 1* (pp.182–186). Ottawa, ON: Metropolis Institute. Retrieved from http://canada.metropolis.net/research-policy/cities/publication/diverse_cite_magazine_e.pdf

Block, S., and Galabuzi, G. (2011). Canada's Colour Coded Labour Market: The gap for racialized workers. Toronto: Canadian Centre for Policy Alternatives and Wellesley Institute. Retrieved from http://www.wellesleyinstitute.com/new_notable/canadas-colour-coded-labour-market-the-gap-for-racialized-workers

Bolaria, B.S., & Li, P.S. (1988). *Racial oppression in Canada* (2nd Ed.). Toronto, ON: Garamond Press.

Boyd, M. (1995). Immigrant women: Language and socio-economic inequalities and language issues. In S.S. Halli, F. Trovato, & L. Driedger (Eds.), *Ethnic demography: Canadian immigrant, racial, and cultural variations* (pp. 275–296). Ottawa, ON: Carleton University Press.

References

Brouwer, A. (1999). Immigrants need not apply. Ottawa, ON: Caledon Institute of Social Policy. Retrieved from http://maytree.com/PDF_Files/summary immigrantsneednotapply1999.pdf

Cabral, V. (2000). Settlement services for newcomers and access to family services. Toronto, ON: Integrated Settlement Planning Research Project and the Multicultural Coalition for Access to Family Services. Retrieved from http://atwork.settlement.org/downloads/Access_Family_Services.pdf

Calleja, D. (2000). Right skills, wrong country: Why is Canada making it next to impossible for talented newcomers to practice in their fields of expertise? *Canadian Business, 73*(12), 34–39.

Canadian Council for Refugees. (2001). Bill C-11 brief. Retrieved from http://ccrweb .ca/c11brief.PDF

Canadian Council for Refugees. (2005). Closing the front door on refugees: report on the first year of the safe third country agreement. Retrieved from http://ccrweb.ca/closingdoordec05.pdf

Castles, S. (1997, June). Globalization and migration. Some pressing contradictions. Keynote address presented at the UNESCO-MOST Intergovernmental Council, Paris. Retrieved from http://www.unesco.org/most/igc97cas.htm

Christensen, C.P. (1999). Immigrant minorities in Canada. In J.C. Turner & F.J. Turner (Eds.), *Canadian social welfare* (pp. 179–212). Scarborough, ON: Allyn and Bacon.

Citizenship and Immigration Canada (CIC). (2011a). Backgrounder: Proposed changes to the federal skilled worker programs. Retrieved from http://www.cic.gc.ca/english/department/media/backgrounders/2011/2011-02-17a.asp

Citizenship and Immigration Canada (CIC). (2011b). News release: New rules to strengthen the Temporary Foreign Worker Program. Retrieved from http://www.cic.gc.ca/english/department/media/releases/2011/2011-03-24a.asp

Citizenship and Immigration Canada (CIC). (2010a). Annual report to Parliament on immigration, 2010. Retrieved from http://www.cic.gc.ca/english/resources/publications/annual-report2010/index.asp

Citizenship and Immigration Canada (CIC). (2010c). Government of Canada will welcome more economic immigrants in 2010. News Release. Retrieved from http://www.cic.gc.ca/english/department/media/releases/2010/2010-06-26.asp

Citizenship and Immigration Canada (CIC). (2010d). Implementation of the new language screening tool in the citizenship process: Operational bulletin 246. Retrieved from http://www.cic.gc.ca/english/resources/manuals/bulletins/2010/ob246.asp

Citizenship and Immigration Canada (CIC). (2009a). Reports on Plans and Priorities for 2010–2011. Retrieved from http://www.tbs-sct.gc.ca/rpp/2010-2011/inst/imc/imc-eng.pdf

Citizenship and Immigration Canada (CIC). (2009b). Settlement Program implementation of the Modernized Approach. Retrieved from http://atwork.settlement.org/downloads/atwork/CIC_Modernized_Approach_SPOs.pdf

Citizenship and Immigration Canada (CIC). (2008). Backgrounder: Action Plan for Faster Immigration: Ministerial Instructions. Retrieved from http://www.cic.gc.ca/english/department/media/backgrounders/2008/2008-11-28.asp

References

Citizenship and Immigration Canada (CIC). (2005, April 25). Government of Canada announces internationally trained workers initiative. News Release. Retrieved from www.cic.gc.ca/English/press/05/0513-e.html

Citizenship and Immigration Canada. (CIC) (2001a). Appendix B: Immigrant arrivals, 2000. 2001 Annual Immigration Plan. Ottawa, ON: Minister of Public Works and Government Services Canada.

Citizenship and Immigration Canada. (2001b). Immigration and Refugee Protection Act Introduced. News release. Retrieved from http://www.cic.gc.ca/english/press/01/0103-pre.html

Das Gupta, T. (1994). Political economy of gender, race, and class: Looking at South Asian women in Canada. *Canadian Ethnic Studies, 26*(1), 70–71.

DeVoretz, D.J. (1995). *Diminishing returns: The economics of Canada's recent immigration policy.* Ottawa, ON: C.D. Howe Institute.

Freeman, G.P. (1995). Modes of immigration politics in liberal democratic states. *International Migration Review, 29*(4), 881–903. Retrieved from http://www.jstor.org/stable/2547729

Galabuzi, G.E. (2001). *Canada's creeping economic apartheid: The economic segregation and social marginalization of racialized groups.* Toronto, ON: Centre for Social Justice and Foundation for Research and Education.

George, U., Chaze, F., Brennenstuhl, S., & Fuller-Thomson, E. (2011) Looking for work but nothings seems to work: The job search strategies of internationally trained engineers in Canada. *Journal of International Migration and Integration,* doi: 10.1007/s12134-011-0197-1.

George, U., & Ramkissoon, S. (1998). Race, gender, and class: Interlocking oppressions in the lives of South Asian women in Canada. *Affilia, 13*(1), 102–119. doi: 10.1177/088610999801300106

Green, A., & Green, D. (1996). The economic goals of Canada's immigration policy, past and present. Research on Immigration and Integration in the Metropolis, Working Paper Series, no. 96-04. Burnaby, BC: Simon Fraser University. Retrieved from http://www.jstor.org/stable/3552422

Harvey, E.B., Siu, B., & Reil, K.D.V. (1999). Ethnocultural groups, period of immigration, and socioeconomic situation. *Canadian Ethnic Studies, 31*(3), 94–103.

Henry, F., Tator, C., Mattis, W., & Rees, T. (2000). *The colour of democracy: Racism in Canadian society* (2nd ed.). Toronto, ON: Harcourt Canada.

Henry, F., & Tator, C. (with Mattis, W., & Rees, T.) (2005). *The colour of democracy: Racism in Canadian society* (3rd ed.). Toronto: Thomson Canada.

Housing New Canadians. (n.d.). Introduction: Research theme #1: The "housing trajectory" of newcomers. Retrieved from http://www.hnc.utoronto.ca/intro/theme1.htm

Hyndman, J. (1999). Gender and Canadian immigration policy: A current snapshot. *Canadian Woman Studies, 19*(3), 6–10.

Integrated Settlement Planning Research Consortium. (2000). Re-Visioning the newcomer: Settlement support system. Toronto, ON: Author. Retrieved from http://atwork.settlement.org/downloads/newcomer_settlement_support_system.pdf

International Organization for Migration (2010). World migration report 2010: The future of migration building capacities for change. Geneva, Switzerland:

International Organization for Migration. Retrieved from http://publications .iom .int/bookstore/free/WMR_2010_ENGLISH.pdf

Isajiw, W.W. (1999). *Understanding diversity: Ethnicity and race in the Canadian context.* Toronto, ON: Thompson Educational Publishing.

Jackson, A., & Smith, E. (2002). Does a rising tide lifts all boats? Recent immigrants in the economic recovery. *Horizons, 5*(2), 1–30. Retrieved from http://www .ccsd.ca/pubs/2002/risingtide/risingtide.pdf

Knowles, V. (2000). Forging our legacy: Canadian citizenship and immigration, 1900–1977. Ottawa, ON: Public Works and Government Services Canada. Retrieved from http://www.cic.gc.ca/english/resources/publications/legacy/index.asp

Kunz, J.L., Milan, A., & Schetagne, S. (2000). Unequal access: A Canadian profile on racial differences in education, employment and income. (Report prepared for the Canadian Race Relations Foundation by the Canadian Council on Social Development). Retrieved from http://atwork.settlement.org/downloads/Unequal_Access.pdf

Li, P.S. (1997). Biases in benchmarking immigrants. In B. Abu-Laban & T.M. Derwing (Eds.), *Responding to diversity in the metropolis: Building an inclusive research agenda* (pp. 112–118). Proceedings of the First Metropolis National Conference on Immigration. Edmonton, AB: Prairie Centre of Excellence for Research on Immigration and Integration.

Maytree Foundation. (2001). Brief to the Standing Committee on Citizenship and Immigration regarding Bill C-11, Immigration and Refugee Protection Act. Retrieved from http://maytree.com/PDF_Files/summarybriefc-11immigration andrefugeeprotectionact2001.pdf

McDonald, J.T., & Worswick, C. (1997). Unemployment incidence of immigrant men in Canada. *Canadian Public Policy, 23*(4), 353–373. Retrieved from http://qed.econ.queensu.ca/pub/cpp/Dec97/Wors.pdf

Murdie, R.A., Chambon, A.S., Hulchanski, J.D., & Teixeira, C. (1999). *Differential incorporation and housing trajectories of recent immigrant households: Towards a conceptual framework.* Toronto, ON: Canada: Housing New Canadians Research Working Group.

Neufeld, A., Harrison, M.J., Stewart, M.J., Hughes, K.D., & Spitzer, D. (2002). Immigrant women: Making connections to community resources for support in family care giving. *Qualitative Health Research, 12*(6), 751–768. doi: 10.1177/104973230201200603

Ontario Ministry of Training, Colleges, and Universities. (2005). Opening doors: An investment in prosperity. Retrieved from http://www.edu.gov.on.ca/eng/document/reports/getresults/index.html

Ornstein, M. (2000). *Single and multi-dimensional disadvantage. Ethno-racial inequality in the City of Toronto; An analysis of the 1996 census.* Prepared for the Access and Equity Unit, Strategic and Corporate Policy Division. Toronto, ON.

Palameta, B. (2007). Economic integration of immigrant's children. Statistics Canada. Cat. No. 75-001-XIE. Retrieved from http://www.statcan.gc.ca/pub/75-001-x/2007110/article/10372-eng.htm

Reitz, J.G. (2004). Canada: Immigration and nation-building in the transition to a knowledge economy. In W.A. Cornelius, T. Tsuda, P.L. Martin, & J.F. Hollifield (Eds.), *Controlling immigration: A global perspective* (pp. 97–133). Stanford, CA: Stanford University Press.

Siddiqui, H. (2001, January 14). Immigrants subsidize us by $55 billion per year. *Toronto Star*, A13.

Sparks, R.J., & Wolfson, W.G. (2001). Settlement in the workplace: The settlement needs of employed newcomers. Toronto, ON: COSTI Immigrant Services. Retrieved from http://atwork.settlement.org/downloads/Settlement_in_the_Workplace.pdf

Stasiulis, D.K. (1997, November). Participation by immigrants, ethnocultural/visible minorities in the Canadian political process. Paper presented at the Second National Metropolis Conference. Montreal, QC. Retrieved from http://canada.metropolis.net/events/civic/dstasiulis_e.html

Statistics Canada. (2003). *Religions in Canada* (2001 Census: analysis series. Catalogue no. 96F0030SIE2001015). Ottawa, ON: Minister of Industry.

Thobani, S. (2000). Closing ranks: Racism and sexism in Canada's immigration policy. *Race and Class, 42*(1), 35–55. doi: 10.1177/030639600128968009

Truelove, M. (2000). Services for immigrant women: An evaluation of locations. *Canadian Geographer, 44*(2), 135–151. doi: 10.1111/j.1541-0064.2000.tb00698.x

United Nations High Commissioner for Refugees (UNHCR). (2001, March 5). Comments on Bill C-11: An Act respecting immigration to Canada and the granting of refugee protection to persons who are displaced, persecuted, or in danger. Submission to House of Commons Standing Committee on Citizenship and Immigration. Retrieved from http://ccrweb.ca/c11hcr.PDF

United Way of Greater Toronto and Canadian Council on Social Development. (2004). Poverty by postal code: The geography of neighbourhood poverty: City of Toronto, 1981–2001. Retrieved from http://www.unitedwaytoronto.com/who_we_help/pdfs/PovertybyPostalCodeFinal.pdf

Additional Resources

Canadian Council for Refugees http://www.web.net/~ccr

CERIS http://www.ceris.metropolis.net

Citizenship and Immigration Canada http://www.cic.gc.ca

Maytree Foundation http://www.maytree.com

Ontario Ministry of Citizenship http://www.gov.on.ca/mczcr

Driedger, L. (1996), *Multi-ethnic Canada: Identities and inequalities* (Toronto, ON: Oxford University Press)

Housing Policy

18

Jill G. Grant and Tonya Munro

Housing policy has concrete effects on the homes available to people whose incomes do not allow them to meet their needs in the market. The Canadian Housing and Renewal Association (CHRA, 2009) contends that those most negatively impacted by the current system include Aboriginal households, female-led single-parent families, single persons, youth, people with disabilities, new immigrants, and seniors. There simply is not enough low-rent housing to meet the demand; indeed, in Ontario alone, 124,032 people are on waiting lists for social housing (Schuk, 2009). Canadians who are affected by social barriers and those who experience marginalization are the same people who are most likely to be affected by an inadequate supply of affordable and safe housing (Dunn et al., 2006).

Safe, secure, adequate, and affordable housing is a social determinant of health. Krieger and Higgins (2002) outline the infectious and chronic diseases that substandard housing can cause or exacerbate. For example, the presence of mould can cause or aggravate asthma and other respiratory conditions; poor ventilation can lead to high levels of exposure to toxic substances, levels that in turn lead to respiratory and other illnesses, sometimes shortening life expectancy. In addition, they note that issues like faulty wiring and insecure construction are common causes of injury and are often found in the rental homes that are most affordable for those with low incomes. From an ecological perspective, Krieger and Higgins discuss the deleterious health, psychological, and social impacts of living in neighbourhoods that are unkempt, that have poor maintenance, and/or that are replete with abandoned housing. They found that living in isolation, surrounded by empty or deteriorating housing, can lead to depression and anxiety. Dunn and colleagues (2006) also note that parental stress, which can be a result of living in substandard or insecure housing, has negative impacts on child health. Frankish, Hwang, and Quantz (2005), after reviewing the literature on homelessness and health status, conclude that there is a direct relationship between homelessness and poor physical and mental health; furthermore, poor health status may increase the risk of being homeless.

In the most extreme cases, a lack of affordable, safe housing leads to homelessness. Homelessness is a pressing issue in Canada (Frankish et al.,

2005; Shapcott, 2001). It is a difficult status to measure. Some researchers include hidden or concealed homelessness in their count—that is, people may sleep at friends' or family members' homes or in temporary shelters; others include only those currently with no housing—that is, absolute homelessness (Echenberg & Jensen, 2008; Frankish, Hwang, & Quantz, 2005). Echenberg and Jensen report that, while the National Secretariat on Homelessness estimates that 150,000 Canadians are homeless, the number is widely considered to be higher because official counts normally can only include absolute homelessness measured through shelter use and street living. In addition, the Canadian Mortgage and Housing Corporation (CMHC) and Indian and Northern Affairs Canada (INAC) (2004) estimate that 16 percent of non-Aboriginal Canadians and 25 percent of Aboriginals face core housing need. Core housing need refers to a situation where one's home is inadequate (needing major repairs) or unsuitable (not created for the number of inhabitants).

Lack of affordable housing is the principal cause of homelessness in Canada (Hartman, 2000; Hulchanski, 2002; Sewell, 1994; Shapcott, 2001). People who are at high risk of homelessness often feel neither safe nor stable in their homes and may fear being victimized by crime. They may be embarrassed to invite family or friends over, or their residence may lack room for privacy of self or belongings, with many living in shared dwellings (Anucha, 2010). Thus, individuals can be considered to be "housed" yet still consider themselves to be homeless.

For all of the reasons outlined above, housing policy is a social justice issue. Such policies can reduce or exacerbate differences in the ability of low-income Canadians to find housing that enhances their physical and mental well-being, and also ensure that all Canadians live in physical surroundings that support a quality of life that the majority of Canadians would consider acceptable.

History of Housing Policy in Canada

Prior to 1935, there were only intermittent pockets of federal and provincial government involvement in the provision of housing, generally in response to an economic, natural, or industrial crisis. Housing was understood to be a responsibility of the market, not the public sector (Sewell, 1994). The first government foray into housing policy was generated by the horrific Halifax Explosion of 1917, which left 6,000 people completely homeless and many more with homes requiring major repairs (Rose, 1980). The magnitude of the need for housing, and the immediacy of the need for a response, drew the provincial and federal governments to enter new terrain for social policy in Canada.

The Dominion Housing Act (DHA), passed by the federal government in 1935, marked the reluctant acknowledgment that housing Canadians was

History of Housing Policy in Canada

not an issue that could be left solely to the market. The act was significant in that it created the provision for joint lending by the federal government and financial institutions and ensured the availability of low-interest loans (Sayegh, 1987; Sewell, 1994). The amount of the mortgage possible increased from 50 to 60 percent of the cost of the home (the amount typically approved by financial institutions at the time) to 80 to 90 percent for eligible applicants, making homeownership more affordable for lower-income Canadians. When the act was renamed the National Housing Act (NHA) in 1938, the federal government retained its provisions that made homeownership more affordable. Subsequent amendments to the act set the term of the mortgage at twenty years and gave borrowers the right to repay on the anniversary date. In 1954, joint lending was replaced with government-insured loans in an attempt to draw more private lenders into the market and to make mortgages available for the many new families that were being formed in the postwar years (Hulchanski, 2002). But it was not until 1969 that the term of the loan and the interest rates could be negotiated, thus being set by the market—practices that prevail to this day and that make homeownership more precarious than it is when mortgages are of twenty or more years' duration at a fixed rate (Orr, 2000).

While the primary goal of housing policy in Canada appears to have been to make homeownership more affordable and more secure, the federal government has also made a number of policy provisions for social housing. Social housing, according to Hulchanski (2002, pp. 8–9), includes "non-market housing that is owned and managed by government, non-profits or non-equity co-operatives." Provisions of the 1938 NHA made funds available to the provinces to build low-cost rental housing, though no units were actually built under this provision (Hulchanski, 2002; Sewell, 1994). The Federal/Provincial Public Housing Program, created through an amendment to the act in 1949, drew the provinces to begin providing public housing, with rent geared to income (Orr, 2000). As in other areas of social policy where the federal government assumed a role in service delivery, a constitutional challenge to the provision for federal/provincial joint ownership of public housing projects soon followed. It was argued that municipal affairs and land development were provincial responsibilities and that the federal government had infringed on the provinces' domain by requiring a partnership with the provinces for the development of public housing. A subsequent amendment to the NHA in 1964 limited the federal role in social housing to making funds available for its development (Orr, 2000). By 1974, further amendments to the act required that all new subsidized housing was to be built by cooperatives, not-for-profit organizations, or municipalities (Sayegh, 1987).

This role clarification was followed by a period during which the federal government committed itself to develop policy that not only increased the supply of housing but also addressed the state of repair and adequacy of

History of Housing Policy in Canada

existing housing stock. "Adequacy" here related to concerns about neighbourhood safety as well as the housing units themselves. Programs that were introduced included an assisted homeownership program, a neighbourhood improvement program, a housing rehabilitation program, a municipal land assembly program, a Native housing program, and a new not-for-profit and co-op housing program (Hulchanski, 2002). The words of the former urban affairs minister, Ron Basford, capture the goal of the Trudeau government, then in power, with respect to housing policy: "When we talk about the subject of housing, we are talking about an elemental human need—the need for shelter, for physical and emotional comfort in that shelter ... Society and government obviously have an obligation to assure that these basic needs of shelter are met" (Hulchanski, 2009, p. 3).

Basford's vision was that housing should go beyond the simple provision of shelter to provide people with a home. A home, for us—as it appears to have been for him—represents a place where people feel safe and secure and that is adequate for their needs as well as affordable.

Initiatives were also put in place to address the housing needs of one of Canada's most marginalized groups—Aboriginal people. Under the 1876 Indian Act, the federal government carries responsibility for the health, education, and welfare of on-reserve Aboriginal people. Housing falls within the definition of "welfare." In 1973, funding was extended to cover the development of housing for off-reserve Aboriginals. While initially this funding was limited to not-for-profit and co-op housing, pressure from advocacy groups led the federal government to designate and operate 400 social housing units a year for Aboriginals living off-reserve (CMHC & INAC, 2004).

After the virtual elimination of federal support for housing in the 1990s and in some cases the transfer of responsibility from provinces to municipalities, federal and provincial support for housing slowly began to be reinstated in the early 2000s. One initiative was the 2005 partnership among the Province of Ontario, municipalities, and the federal government (through the CMHC, the organization created in 1946 to administer the NHA) that produced the largest housing project in Canadian history. This partnership had four aspects: Rental and Supportive Housing, Homeownership, Northern Housing, and Housing Allowances. This partnership ended in 2008, and task groups have since been developed to create a long-term housing plan for Ontario (CMHC, 2011).

Another example of a recommitment to social housing policy is the federal Homelessness Partnering Strategy, which is intended to help communities reduce homelessness through a $1.9 billion initiative over five years (2009–14). The strategy provides a mix of homeless assistance services and transitional and supportive housing. Praised by the UN as an international best practice, this affordable housing initiative has resulted in the creation of 27,000 units of non-market housing since 2001 (CHRA, 2009). The initiative is community-driven, enabling local groups to determine their own

History of Housing Policy in Canada

needs and to develop appropriate projects based on those needs (Human Resources and Skills Development Canada [HRSDC], 2011). Consistent with Vaillancourt's conceptualization of a new social democracy (Chapter 7), this initiative represents a substantive shift toward collaboration among local governments, private companies, community groups, and others to work together on housing-related issues and to create new capacity at the local level (CHRAP, 2009).

Despite evidence of the federal government's new contributions to funding for social housing, a closer inspection reveals that much of its program funding in recent years has been used for repairs and improvements to energy efficiency in existing housing units rather than for the development of new social housing units (CMHC, 2009). Most of the funding continues to go to homeowners rather than to reducing the waiting lists for subsidized rental homes. Hulchanski (2007) notes that the CMHC reported that more homeowners were helped through mortgage insurance in 2005 (746,157) than through all the social housing units funded in the past thirty-five years (633,300) (2007). Statistics such as these have led him to conclude that, just as in the pre–Second World War period, we are again living in a time during which policy is being shaped by a belief that the market can take care of housing Canadians (Hulchanski, 2002). He concludes as well that the net effect of our housing policy is that "Canada's housing system is now the most private-sector market-based of any Western nation, including the United States, where intervention on behalf of homeowners is extensive" (Hulchanski, 2002, p. 8).

A summary of the policy initiatives reviewed in this section is displayed in Figure 18.1, a timeline of highlights in the development of Canadian social housing policy.

Figure 18.1 Timeline of Canadian Housing Policy

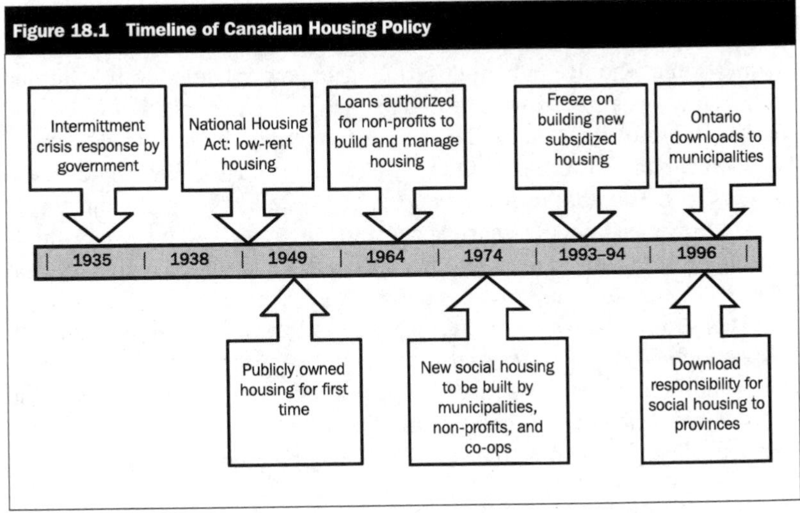

Canadian Housing Policy Themes

Understanding the Changes

Carroll and Jones (2000) suggest that policy changes and policy decision making occur not as isolated incidents but in a context of multiple policy networks. They argue that policy changes in three main ways: inertia, innovation, and convergence. In relation to Canadian housing policy, inertia refers to policies that have been inherited from previous governments and that are sometimes even rolled back. Innovation happens when individuals operating in a creative environment are willing to develop and try out new ideas. Convergence refers to policies that result from societies becoming similar and creating parallel structures and policies. They describe the period 1968–78 as a time of innovation in Canadian housing policy, and 1978–94 as a period of convergence, but with the beginning stages of inertia starting to appear as early as 1986. The year 1994 is described as a time of total inertia in social housing policy. Carroll and Jones suggest that there have been some new and innovative approaches to housing in the 2000s but that these efforts are scattered, with many networks developed being unravelled.

Canadian Housing Policy Themes

Four themes appear to be emphasized in the above review of Canadian housing policy: privileging ownership, housing as an economic stimulant, policy responses to need, and policy decisions based on political expediency.

Privileging Ownership

From its inception, Canadian housing policy has been consistent in its privileging of homeownership over home rentals (Purdy & Kwak, 2007; Sereacki, 2007). Sereacki asserts that this focus on ownership over rental support is a fundamental flaw of our system. Hulchanski (2007) argues that Canada actually has a two-tiered system of housing, with ownership (high-end renters and some who live in cooperative housing are included in this tier) as the primary system, and with those who live in the lower half of the rental market and impoverished rural owners belonging to the secondary system. In this secondary sector, housing is of poor quality. He differentiates these systems by noting that those in the primary system receive benefits in the form of universal benefits (mortgage insurance programs and government-sponsored mortgage lending systems), while those in the secondary system receive benefits (if at all) on a selective basis. In addition, the neighbourhoods of those in the primary system tend to have better community services. Hulchanski also notes that those in the secondary system have little political influence, whereas those in the primary system have considerable political influence during political elections and in decision-making processes at all levels of government.

As noted in Figure 18.1, the DHA provided assistance for those purchasing homes by providing loans in partnership with financial institutions and by reducing interest rates for mortgages. Dalton (2009) documents the increase in homeownership after the Second World War, largely a result of policies to support the building and purchasing of homes. According to Rose (1980), this focus on ownership continued into the 1960s, throughout which time the federal government made it a priority for every family to own a home. Perhaps the more recent decision to download responsibility for social housing also reflects a desire to discourage rental housing (Sereacki, 2007). In the same vein, in 2008 the First Nations Market Housing Fund was established to help First Nations community members qualify for loans to purchase their own homes (Schuk, 2009).

Despite its focus on ownership, housing policy has always had provisions for social rental housing. Yet from the 1930s to the 1960s, very few units of housing were developed for this purpose (Harris, 2000; Purdy & Kwak, 2007). This focus on support for homeownership to the detriment of support for rental housing has contributed to a marginalized—perhaps ghettoized—environment for those who are easily ignored, including sole support mothers, new Canadians, those with low income, and those with disabilities (Purdy & Kwak, 2007).

Gurney (1999) examined language and housing in Britain, noting that language is used to create divisions similar to those described by Hulchanski (2007) with regard to the two-tiered Canadian housing system. Gurney postulates that homeownership has been constructed as "normal" in Great Britain and that this normalization has created the narrative that homeowners' success in purchasing a home makes them more responsible citizens. Even the word "home" is used to refer to homeowners more often than to private and public renters. Conversely, the word "property" is far more often used when applied to public housing (Gurney, 1999). This use of language may serve to create renters as an out-group in our society. Hulchanski (2009) has noted a similar interesting linguistic contrast in Canada: when speaking about ownership, the word "home" is most often used, whereas "housing" is more commonly used when speaking about rentals. Harkening back to Basford's words at the beginning of the chapter, have we moved away from his recognition of the need for "physical and emotional comfort"? If the language is used as a measure, perhaps we have.

Housing as an Economic Stimulant

Postwar Canada experienced difficult economic times, as well as returning soldiers with few job prospects. The federal government used housing development as one means to address collective and individual economic challenges. In 1944 the NHA created War Time Housing Limited, which provided incentives for home building and homeownership for returning soldiers and their families. This same act was also intended to stimulate the postwar economic development by providing employment for these same soldiers (Sayegh, 1987).

Housing in Response to Need

Besides providing an economic stimulus, War Time Housing Limited was a response to the need for homes that had been created by the poverty generated by the Great Depression (Sayegh, 1987). Those most affected by the depression were living in poverty (Rose, 1980), and municipalities had limited resources to address their plight. These two factors combined to create a pressing need for federal intervention.

As noted above, advocacy groups were able to convince the federal government in 1996 to provide funding to Aboriginal reserves for the building of subsidized homes. The 2008 First Nations Market Housing Fund may be considered a response to need, but certainly one that privileges individual homeownership, which may not be culturally appropriate for all First Nations communities.

Political Motivations

In the second chapter of this text, Westhues describes the development and evolution of political policies as a complex process influenced by multiple interests and politically charged environments. Canadian social housing policy has reflected many shifts in focus, funding, and philosophy. One important reason for this variability in housing policy is the relatively frequent changes in the federal and provincial political parties in power. The interplay—both agreement and dissonance—among Canada's political parties has had a complex influence on social housing policies.

For example, in Ontario, under the New Democratic Party (NDP), and similar to postwar economic stimulus efforts, housing and job creation programs were connected through not-for-profit and cooperative rental projects. But these programs, which were almost identical to those the NDP had inherited from the Liberal government, were terminated by the Conservative government elected in 1995 (Carroll & Jones, 2000). Conversely, Hackworth (2008) argues that "centre-left" political parties (such as the Liberals in Canada) can be responsible for implementing and supporting "neoliberal" political policies such as rollbacks, maintaining the status quo, or even implementing rollout policies that may appear to be more representative of Conservative ideologies. For example, in 2003, Dalton McGuinty's Liberal government was elected in Ontario, seemingly as a rejection of the Mike Harris "Common Sense Revolution"; yet it took little action to change the neoliberal housing policies of the Conservative government.

Bryant (2004) notes that, even though neoliberal political ideology does not influence all areas of governance and policy in Canada, housing policy is especially impacted by this political ideology. Neoliberalism as a political ideology emphasizes individual responsibility and small government. Thus, free markets are rationalized as the only mechanism required to manage the distribution of society's resources. This system separates the "deserving" from the "undeserving" poor, viewing individuals as "responsible" for their own welfare and self-care (Edwards, 2009). Neoliberal ideologies have exerted great influence on housing policy in Canada, especially given that governments that represent neoliberal ideologies have been elected within the past two decades in Alberta and Ontario and, more recently, in British Columbia and Quebec (Bryant, 2004). The impacts on Canadian housing policy are clear. For example, in a study of social housing providers in Toronto, the providers stated that government ideology was blocking their ability to influence policy changes and that the current regime in Ontario was unresponsive to perspectives that did not concur with its own (Bryant, 2004).

Decision making based on political expediency and gain can be inferred throughout the history of Canadian housing policy. Citizen resistance to expanded public housing programs, for example, may help explain the ongoing privileging of homeownership in Canadian housing policy (Dalton, 2009). Another example of this phenomenon, Rose (1980) suggests, is that in 1973, a minority Liberal government, needing the support of the NDP to survive, amended the NHA so that it included funds for neighbourhood and home improvements. More recently, in 2004–5, when the federal Liberal minority government established new funding for housing initiatives, it was met with great political pressure, primarily from the Conservative opposition (Hulchanski, 2007).

Housing for All?

As mentioned earlier, the groups that face enormous social barriers in our society are the same groups that are challenged to find safe, secure, adequate, and affordable housing (Dunn et al., 2006). The next section explores the situation faced by four groups: First Nations, new Canadians, seniors, and individuals with mental health issues.

First Nations/Aboriginal Peoples

Aboriginals live in some of the worst conditions in Canada. Both on and off reserve, they are more likely than other Canadians to live in substandard housing (CMHC & INAC, 2004). This is particularly true in communities in rural and remote areas, where access to necessities that most Canadians take for granted can be extremely limited. As of 2002, for example, the National Aboriginal Health Organization noted that Indian and Northern Affairs Canada (INAC) acknowledged approximately 5,000 homes without access to safe water or sewage treatment (National Aboriginal Health Organization, 2002).

Even when the conditions are less severe, there is a deficit of appropriate housing for Aboriginals both on and off reserve. Indeed, CMHC and INAC (2004) estimate that 25 percent of off-reserve Aboriginals have a core housing need (i.e., their housing is neither adequate nor suitable) and that there is a shortage on reserves of 20,000 units. For members of Canada's First Nations, the most common barriers to finding a home are affordability and conditions of housing. Rural and remote communities, in particular, often do not have a housing market representing a range of options, so residents of these areas are greatly restricted in their choices of home.

The safe, secure, and adequate housing of community members in affordable homes is identified by First Nations communities as a pressing issue. Under the Urban Aboriginal Strategy pilot projects, eight communities have been funded to address their most important concerns. Four of those eight communities have chosen to address housing (National Aboriginal Health Organization, 2002).

New Canadians

When immigrants arrive in Canada, they are faced with the enormous task of building a new life. CMHC (2006) notes that citizenship starts with a secure home base; and that immigrants often start by finding a home, which then allows them to continue to create their lives, joining their new community and pursuing education, language study, training, and employment. However, newcomers to Canada, who often lack information and funds, often settle in declining neighbourhoods (Carter & Osborne, 2009), where rent may be less expensive, units may be more plentiful, and restrictions on tenants may be looser. The location and conditions of these neighbourhoods may create another barrier (among many) to a smooth transition to their new country.

Some subgroups of immigrants face additional barriers to suitable housing. Visible minorities often face discrimination when searching for a home (Carter & Osborne, 2009). The situation is especially difficult for refugees, who may not immediately qualify for any kind of support and who are often arriving in Canada after having spent time subsisting in refugee camps in their home country (Carter & Osborne, 2009).

Research demonstrates that refugee households are much more likely to experience crowding than households of other new Canadians. For example, in 2001, in both Montreal and Toronto, over 50 percent of refugees were living in crowded conditions, as compared to 16 to 30 percent of other new Canadians—of course, still a very high rate (CMHC, 2006), especially as compared to the 3.2 percent of Canadian-born individuals who live in crowded conditions (Health Co-Management Secretariat, n.d.). Crowded conditions are defined by the CMHC as situations where there is more than one person per room of the dwelling.

Seniors

As Canada's baby boomers continue to age, affordable housing for seniors requires increasing attention. The Aging and Homeless Project at the University of Toronto estimates that Canada may have 3,000 seniors who are homeless. The loss by many of high proportions of their retirement funds through the economic decline of 2008–10 may have put some seniors in an unexpectedly precarious financial situation.

As health conditions and mobility change, seniors may find their housing needs changing as well. Whether our society is equipped to deal with these changes will become increasingly apparent. It is important to remember that a wide variety of issues may impact the needs of older adults, including weather, proximity to family, availability of transportation, and accessibility of services and shopping (Wagner, Shubair, & Michalos, 2010; Wister & Gutman, 1997).

Subsidized housing organizations in many areas of Canada operate seniors-only buildings for those whose income is sufficiently low to qualify. CMHC also provides forgivable loans so that seniors are able to make home renovations that increase accessibility. Tenants whose landlords access these loans are protected from rent increases because of such improvements (CMHC, 2000). Similar to Grant and Westhues's (2010) research with individuals with mental health issues cited below, studies inquiring into seniors' preferences for housing highlight the importance of choice and of a wide range of options (CMHC, 2000; Wagner et al., 2010; Wister & Gutman, 1997). Unsurprisingly, seniors express a strong preference for remaining in their own home for as long as possible (Wagner et al., 2010).

In 1993, Haldeman and Wister identified three approaches to housing for seniors: institutions and homes built specifically for aging adults; housing alternatives, focusing on choice; and aging in place (staying in one's home with support for renovations and/or physical and emotional needs). The previously mentioned loans seem to address aging in place, and there appears to be a growing industry of regulated and non-regulated institutional care. However, it is apparent that the variety of alternatives may be lacking. As an illustration, two commonly available options (reverse mortgages, and garden homes or granny flats) only appeal to a small minority of seniors, according to the authors.

Individuals with Mental Health Issues

With the proliferation of deinstitutionalization of those with mental health issues, housing has become an important consideration for those who formerly would have been institutionalized (Capponi, 2003). The first residences provided for those leaving psychiatric institutions—mostly boarding homes with little support or programming (Carling, 1995; Marshall, 1982; Simmons, 1990)—were replaced or augmented by organizations providing an array of group homes combining structured programming with group living, often on a continuum of level of support (Nelson, Hall, & Forchuk, 2003). This residential continuum, criticized for its inflexibility and impermanence and for an erroneous assumption of linear recovery from mental health issues (Rog, 2004), started to be replaced in the 1980s by forms of supported housing that advocate increased integration into the community of those with mental health issues, increased normalization and permanency of housing, and greater choice in both housing and support models (Hopper & Barrow, 2003; Walker & Seasons, 2002).

Safe, secure, adequate, and affordable housing is recognized as one of the vital factors for recovery from mental health issues (Capponi, 2003; Rog, 2004). While adequate supply, quality, and affordability of housing for mental health consumer-survivors remain central concerns, there are increased choices for housing relative to the days of the residential continuum (Boydell et al., 1999). Limited research has been conducted comparing different models of supported/supportive housing, and the results have been inconsistent as to preferences and outcomes (Rog, 2004). Most recently, Grant and Westhues (2010) compared two models of mental health supported housing; they suggest that the inability to identify the best way to provide homes reflects that consumer choice is the vital factor.

Recommendations for Moving Forward

This chapter has explored housing policy in Canada, examining historical developments, changes, and attention to vulnerable groups. It is clear that homelessness and inadequate housing continue to be important challenges requiring action by many sectors. Focusing on homeownership to the detriment of affordable rentals, political agendas and changing political climates, and ongoing marginalization of our most vulnerable individuals, challenge the ability of our country to safely, securely, adequately, and affordably house all Canadians.

Sereacki (2007) has suggested some ways forward that merit our attention, focus, and resources. He maintains that social housing of the future will require collaborations among many stakeholders, including federal, provincial, and municipal governments as well as individual citizens, groups of citizens, and private business. He notes the importance of a long-term commitment to housing policy that is congruent to the overall direction of a government. Consistent with research related to both seniors and individuals with mental health issues, Sereacki also notes the importance of flexibility and a range of options, allowing for choice in homes.

In accordance with these priorities, Sereacki (2007) has developed a framework for evaluating housing development, in which he identifies guidelines that appear to provide important standards as we move forward. He suggests that housing partnerships must include the following: a clear framework and mandate (with timelines and specific goals); an effective partnership strategy that engages the community; and investment of resources.

Moskalyk (2008) discusses a recent housing strategy in Winnipeg that provides an example of possible outcomes from a creative public–private partnership that appears consistent with Sereacki's guidelines and that succeeds at recognizing housing as an integrative aspect of our social lives. Based on an American model, Housing Opportunity Partnership (HOP) is a not-for-profit inner-city housing revitalization program. It aims to refurbish and repair the housing stock in inner-city Winnipeg, with a focus on homeownership as a strategy for reducing crime and stabilizing neighbourhoods. Many residents in Winnipeg face inadequate housing, and Winnipeg is home to a large Aboriginal population, many of whom live in poverty and inadequate housing (Moskalyk, 2008). The program receives funding from all levels of government and partners with financial institutions and real estate advisory boards and committees. The primary focus of the program is to refurbish and repair vacant or rental homes and sell them to low- to moderate-income buyers who can take advantage of first-time home buyers' benefits.

This is one example of what may be our way forward in Canada. Although this partnership does focus on homeownership, it does so in such a way that individuals who would likely have difficulty in ever purchasing a home are able to do so with this program's support. We need creative partnerships such as HOP that recognize housing as Basford described it above—shelter and physical and emotional comfort—as a basic right for all Canadians, one that contributes to individual and collective health and well-being. Our history of privileging ownership over rental housing and of downloading responsibility for housing our citizens has worked against our attainment of Basford's vision. This is especially true of our most vulnerable people, who perhaps because of their marginalization have been easy to ignore. Recognizing the importance of creative and flexible solutions that engage communities, all levels of government, and businesses, and that are consistent with Sereacki's well-considered framework, may be what enables us to move beyond thinking of housing and shelter and toward thinking of the importance of a home for all Canadians.

References

Aging and Homeless Project. http://rgp.toronto.on.ca/aging_and_homelessness_project

Anucha, U. (2010). Housed but homeless? Negotiating everyday life in a shared housing program. *Families in Society, 91*(1), 67–75.

Bacher, J.C. (1993). *Keeping to the marketplace: The evolution of Canadian housing policy.* [Google Books version]. Retrieved from http://books.google.ca/books?id=MDftkd9FunQC&printsec=frontcover&dq=Bacher,John&sig=oi1ood1Cx6SoobMG3PDeYwo9qr4#v=onepage&q&f=false

References

Boydell, K.M., Gladstone, B.M., Crawford, E., & Trainor, J. (1999). Making do in the outside: Everyday life in the neighbourhoods of people with psychiatric disabilities. *Psychiatric Rehabilitation Journal, 23*(1), 11–18.

Bryant, T. (2004). How knowledge and political ideology affects rental housing policy in Ontario, Canada: Application of a knowledge paradigms framework of policy change. *Housing Studies, 19*(4), 635–651. doi: 10.1080/0267303042000222007

Canadian Housing and Renewal Association Policy. (2009). An affordable housing policy for Canada. Retrieved from http://www.chra-achru.ca/media/content/CHRA_Policy_Affordable_English.pdf

Canadian Mortgage and Housing Corporation (CMHC). (2011). Ontario's long-term affordable housing strategy. Retrieved from http://www.mah.gov.on.ca/Page9187.aspx

Canadian Mortgage and Housing Corporation (CMHC). (2009). Annual Report. Retrieved from http://www.cmhc.ca/ar-ra/2009/en/show/resoho.cfm

Canadian Mortgage and Housing Corporation (CMHC). (2006). The housing situation and needs of recent immigrants in the Montréal, Toronto, and Vancouver CMAs: An overview. Retrieved from http://www.cmhc-schl.gc.ca/odpub/pdf/65319.pdf?fr=1308442732927

Canadian Mortgage and Housing Corporation (CMHC). (2000). Supportive housing for seniors. Retrieved from http://www.cmhc-schl.gc.ca/odpub/pdf/65319.pdf?fr=1308442732927

Canadian Mortgage and Housing Corporation (CMHC). (1999). Documentation of best practices addressing homelessness. Retrieved from http://www.cmhc-schl.gc.ca/odpub/pdf/62406.pdf?fr=1317580002224

Canadian Mortgage and Housing Corporation (CMHC) and Indian and Northern Affairs Canada (INAC). (2004). Aboriginal housing background paper. Retrieved from http://www.aboriginalroundtable.ca/sect/hsng/bckpr/INAC_BgPaper_e.pdf

Capponi, P. (2003). *Beyond the crazy house.* Toronto, ON: Penguin Books.

Carling, P.J. (1995). *Return to community: Building support systems for people with psychiatric disabilities.* New York, NY: Guilford Press.

Carroll, B.W., & Jones, R.J.E. (2000). The road to innovation, convergence, or inertia: Devolution in housing policy in Canada. *Canadian Public Policy/Analyse de Politiques, 26*(3), 277–293. Retrieved from http://www.jstor.org/stable/3552401

Carter, T.S., & Osborne, J. (2009). Housing and neighbourhood challenges of refugee resettlement in declining inner city neighbourhoods: A Winnipeg case study. *Journal of Immigrant and Refugee Studies, 7*(3), 308–327. doi: 10.1080/94090315562150097

Dalton, T. (2009). Housing policy retrenchment: Australia and Canada compared. *Urban Studies, 46*(1), 63–91. doi: 10.1177/0042098008098637

Dunn, J.R., Hayes, M.V.J., Hulchanski, D., Hwang, S.W., & Potvin, L. (2006). Housing as a socio-economic determinant of health: Findings of a national needs, gaps, and opportunities assessment. *Canadian Journal of Public Health,* 97 (supp. 3), S11–S15.

Echenberg, H., & Jensen, H. (2008). Defining and enumerating homelessness in Canada. Government of Canada: Library of Parliament. Retrieved from http://www.parl.gc.ca/Content/LOP/ResearchPublications/prb0830-e.htm

References

Edwards, K. (2009). Disenfranchised not "deficient": How the (neoliberal) state disenfranchises young people. *Australian Journal of Social Issues, 44*(1), 23–37. Retrieved from http://search.ebscohost.com

Frankish, C.J., Hwang, S.W., & Quantz, D. (2005). Homelessness and health in Canada: Research lessons and priorities. *Canadian Journal of Public Health, 96*, S23. Retreived from http://journal.cpha.ca/index.php/cjph/article/download/1493/1682

Grant, J., & Westhues, A. (2010). Choice and outcome in mental health supported housing. *Psychiatric Rehabilitation Journal*, 33(3), 232–235.

Gurney, C.M. (1999). Pride and prejudice: Discourses of normalisation in public and private accounts of home ownership. *Housing Studies, 14*(2), 163–183. doi: 10.1080/02673039982902

Hackworth, J. (2008). The durability of roll-out neoliberalism under centre-left governance: The case of Ontario's social housing sector. *Studies in Political Economy, 81*, 8–26. Retrieved from http://spe.library.utoronto.ca/index.php/spe/issue/archive

Haldeman, V., & Wister, A. (1993). Environment and aging. *Journal of Canadian Studies, 28*(1), 30–43. Retrieved from http://search.ebscohost.com

Harris, R. (2000). More American than the United States: Housing in urban Canada in the twentieth century, *Journal of Urban History, 26*(4), 456–471. doi: 10.1177/009614420002600403

Hartman, D.W. (2000). Policy implications from the study of the homeless. *Sociological Practice, 2*(2), 57–76. Retrieved from http://resolver.scholarsportal.info

Health Co-Management Secretariat. (n.d.). Health determinants for First Nations in Alberta. Retrieved from http://report.hcom.ca/factors/housing/crowded-housing

Hopper, K. & Barrow, S.M. (2003). Two genealogies of supported housing and their implications for outcome assessment. *Psychiatric Services, 54*(1), 50–54.

Hulchanski, D. (2002). Housing policy for tomorrow's cities. Ottawa, ON: Canadian Policy Research Network. Retrieved from http://www.urbancentre.utoronto.ca/pdfs/elibrary/CPRNHousingPolicy.pdf

Hulchanski, J.D. (2007). Canada's dual housing policy: Assisting owners, neglecting renters. *Research Bulletin #38*. Centre for Urban and Community Studies, University of Toronto, Toronto, ON.

Hulchanski, J.D. (2009). Homelessness in Canada: Past, present, and future. Conference keynote address, Growing Home: Housing and Homelessness in Canada. University of Calgary, February 18, 2009.

Human Resources and Skills Development Canada (HRSDC). (n.d.). Homelessness Partnering Strategy. Retrieved from http://www.hrsdc.gc.ca/eng/homelessness/index.shtml

Krieger, J., & Higgins, J.L. (2002). Housing and health: Time again for public health action. *American Journal of Public Health, 92*(5), 758–768.

Marshall, J. (1982). *Madness*. Toronto, ON: Ontario Public Services Employees Union.

Moskalyk, A. (2008). The Role of public-private partnerships in funding social housing in Canada. Canadian Policy Research Networks Report. Ottawa, ON: Canadian Policy Research Networks. Retrieved from http://www.shscorp.ca/content/research/resources/DOCSCPRN_Alex_Moskalyk.pdf

References National Aboriginal Health Organization. (2002). Drinking water safety in Aboriginal communities in Canada. Retrieved from http://www.naho.ca/documents/naho/english/publications/ReB_water_safety.pdf

Nelson, G., Hall, G.B., & Forchuk, C. (2003). Current and preferred housing of psychiatric consumers/survivors. *Canadian Journal of Community Mental Health, 22*(1), 5–19.

Orr, S. (2000). A roof over our heads: Affordable housing and urban growth in Canada. Calgary, AB: Canada West Foundation. Retrieved from http://cwf.ca/pdf-docs/publications/September2000-A-Roof-Over-Our-Heads-Affordable-Housing-and-Urban-Growth-in-Western-Canada.pdf

Purdy, S., & Kwak, N.H. (2007). New perspectives on public housing histories in the Americas. *Journal of Urban History, 33*, 357–374. doi: 10.1177/0096144206297128

Rog, D.J. (2004). The evidence on supported housing. *Psychiatric Rehabilitation Journal, 27*(4), 334–344. Retrieved from http://search.ebscohost.com

Rose, A. (1980). *Canadian housing policies (1935–1980)*. Toronto, ON: Butterworths.

Sayegh, K.S. (1987). *Housing: A Canadian Perspective*. Ottawa, ON: ABCD-Academy Books.

Schuk, C. (2009). Overcoming challenges in centralized and decentralized housing models: Ontario and British Columbia compared. Canadian Policy Research Networks. Retrieved from http://www.cprn.org/doc.cfm?doc=2090&l=en

Sereacki, M.M. (2007). Fostering better integration and partnerships for housing in Canada: Lessons for creating a stronger policy model of governmental and community collaboration. Canadian Policy Research Networks. Retrieved from http://www.cprn.org/doc.cfm?doc=1782&l=en

Sewell, J. (1994). *Houses and homes: Housing for Canadians*. Toronto, ON: James Lorimer and Company.

Shapcott, M. (2001). The Ontario Alternative Budget 2001: Made-in-Ontario housing crisis. Ottawa, ON: Canadian Centre for Policy Alternatives. Retrieved from http://www.alexlaidlaw.coop/pdffiles/housing-crisis.pdf

Simmons, H.G. (1990). *Unbalanced: Mental health policy in Ontario, 1930–1989*. Toronto, ON: Wall and Thompson.

Wagner, S.L., Shubair, M.M., & Michalos, A.C. (2010). Surveying older adults' opinions on housing: Recommendations for policy. *Social Indicators Research, 99*, 405–412. doi: 10.1007/s11205-010-9588-5

Walker, R., & Seasons, M. (2002). Supported housing for people with serious mental illness: Resident perspectives on housing. *Canadian Journal of Community Mental Health, 21*(1), 137–151. Retrieved from http://cjcmh.metapress.com

Wister, A., & Gutman, G. (1997). Housing older Canadians. *Journal of Housing for the Elderly, 12*(1), 19–35. doi: 10.1300/J081v12n01_03

Canadian Health Care

Reclaiming Universal Legacies

19

Mike Burke and Susan Silver

Canada's national health care system, known as medicare, is a source of immense collective achievement. Unlike other facets of Canadian social policy, it sets out a vision of distributive justice based on the principle of "equity." Equity as a distributive principle requires that "need," not ability to pay, be the sole determinant of access and distribution of health services. Equity based on need alone means that no one has a prior entitlement based on status, wealth, race, or other social differences (Churchill, 1987, p. 94). Medicare escaped the "residual trap" (Taylor, 1978) that is characteristic of other social policy measures by adopting a universal, one-tier, publicly financed model of insurance covering hospital services and physician services for all Canadians, rich and poor alike. Though aggressively contested, the founding principle of "equity of access" has endured as a normative legacy in relation to "medically necessary" hospital services and doctor's services. Medicare has remained an egalitarian institution in an otherwise inegalitarian society.[1]

But while escaping this residual trap, we have not succeeded in quelling privatization pressures, which are inevitable in a nation that allows the private market, with its inherent inequities, to prevail as the dominant mechanism for allocating income and other scarce resources. These privatization pressures, while a mainstay of capitalist society, have been fuelled increasingly by the current neoliberal political climate. Neoliberalism, as a political ideology, calls for a profound reconfiguration of social welfare responsibilities among the public sector, the private sector, the family, and the not-for-profit sector (Burke, Mooers, & Shields, 2000). It seeks to minimize the social role of the state by recommodifying public services and, consequently, to expand the space available for the market provision of such services. It justifies this reconfiguration by an appeal to a narrow and distorted discourse of "efficiency" that equates efficiency with cutting public expenditures on social services.[2] In the case of health care, neoliberalism identifies efficiency as the predominant if not sole criterion of health policy evaluation, asserts that publicly funded systems of health care are inefficient by definition, and concludes that the state's role in health care must be severely curtailed in order to contain public costs. This definition of efficiency threatens to undermine the *quality* of our medicare system, disrupt considerations of equity, and exacerbate disparities in the health of Canadians.

These issues are critical, and the stakes are high for Canadians in general and for vulnerable populations that experience deepening health inequities. However, with total health care expenditures reaching an estimated $191.6 billion in 2010 (CIHI, 2010), proponents of privatization stand to achieve huge financial rewards. As expressed by an American health care firm, medicare is "one of the largest unopened oysters in the Canadian economy" (quoted in Canadian Centre for Policy Alternatives, 2000, p. 4).

These are the fundamental choices facing policy makers: Do we reaffirm and strengthen the public system and thereby the equity principle? Or do we seek to further accelerate the neoliberal program of privatization and the inevitable erosion of accessibility and quality? Yet the health care debate is not explicitly framed in terms of choices, but rather as a fiscal imperative obligating privatization.

This chapter begins with the assumption, borrowed from Richard Titmuss, that values are central to policy debates. Titmuss contends that "policy is all about values" (1974, p. 132), and he defines policy as the "principles that govern action directed towards given ends" (p. 23). He further argues that the goal of policy analysis is to "expose more clearly the value choices confronting society" (p. 136). Using this framework for policy analysis, this chapter examines the normative foundations or dominant values that framed the original intentions of medicare. It then reviews the program's early successes and the political shift from a concern with equity to a concern with cost control. Recent federal and provincial commissions and health policy initiatives are reviewed in relation to their contributions to the debate over the future of medicare. Three challenges to the normative foundations are then examined. These challenges—which are central to the neoliberal project—are as follows: (1) the retrenchment of the federal role in relation to national standards; (2) the privatization thrust, and with it the increasing commodification of health care services; and (3) the relegation of responsibility from the public sector to the family and the community. These challenges threaten to erode the normative foundations of medicare and to widen the gap between the "promise of citizenship and the reality of exclusion" (Galabuzi, 2004, p. 246) experienced by members of vulnerable populations such as racialized groups and immigrants.

Medicare's accomplishments extend far beyond the field of health care. Medicare is a beacon, a constant reminder of the possibilities of equality and inclusiveness in Canadian society. The ties that bind Canadians together are the shared and common experiences that result from a consistent interpretation of our fundamental national values. The chapter concludes with a rallying call to progressive social work activists to add their voices and values to the social policy debate, and to clearly articulate the normative possibilities of collective action.

Normative Policy Framework

A normative analysis attempts to expose and clarify the values that influence policy debates and policy outcomes (Titmuss, 1974). Values are conceptions of the desirable within every individual and society and serve as standards or normative criteria to guide action, attitudes, and judgments. A primary objective of a normative analysis is to clarify and understand the values that represent a nation's policy choices (Silver, 1993). Public policies, in this way, constitute choices among alternative normative intentions, among competing perceptions of the common good (Kronick, 1982). Normative choices are fundamentally distributive; they define what constitutes a "social" as opposed to a "private" good, and they set out the conditions of allocation.

Titmuss (1968) distinguished between residual/selective and institutional/universalist modes of distribution. Services delivered on a residual/selective basis almost always involve means tests that foster "both the sense of personal failure and the stigma of a public burden" (1968, p. 134). With residually delivered services or programs, state responsibility begins only when the private realms of the family and the market fail. In contrast, universalist services are distributed as a social right and are accessible to all citizens in a manner that does not involve any "humiliating loss of status, dignity or self respect" (1968, p. 129). There is no assumption of personal blame or failure. The service or program in question is considered an appropriate institutional (as opposed to residual) function of the state. Mediating this universalist discourse of institutional function, Ife (1997) has introduced a relativist understanding of need. In response to the postmodern critique of universalism, Ife offers a humanist vision in which social justice is both an expression of universal understandings of human rights and an endorsement of contextualized and culturally appropriate definitions of need (Ife, 1997, p. 126).

Esping-Andersen (1989) maintains that the essence of a welfare state is its capacity to grant "social rights"—that is, rights that are embedded in citizenship and distributed outside the market. "Decommodification" refers to the degree to which a service or basic good is detached from the market as the distributive mechanism. Social rights cease being commodities, thereby emancipating individuals from their market dependence (Esping-Andersen, 1989, p. 21). Commodification in health care refers generally to an increasing reliance on the market for either the financing or the delivery of health care (Offe, 1984; Esping-Anderson 1989).

With this framework, we now explore the normative foundations of medicare, specifically examining the social rights and allocative principles that were established.

Normative Foundations of Medicare

Normative Foundations of Medicare

Medicare originated with two pieces of legislation: the Hospital Insurance and Diagnostic Services Act of 1957, which insured hospital services, and the Medical Care Act of 1966, which insured doctors' services. Four federal–provincial cost-sharing conditions were imposed:

1. Universal coverage: every provincial resident must be covered under uniform terms and conditions.
2. Portability: all Canadians are entitled to receive health care services across Canada.
3. Comprehensiveness: all medially necessary hospital services and physician services are to be covered.
4. Public administration: each provincial plan must be publicly administered on a not-for-profit basis without the involvement of the private sector.[3]

By the end of 1971, every province had taken advantage of the federal cost-sharing incentive and close to 100 percent coverage had been attained in Canada.[4] The national plan was achieved by interlocking ten provincial plans, all of which shared certain features. Canadians were free to choose their own physician and hospital. There was no limit on the benefits payable as long as medical need had been determined. There were no limits on the number of days of hospital care or the number of visits to physicians. With respect to the scope of coverage, benefits were intended to be virtually complete. There was no distinction between basic and non-basic services; instead, all medically necessary physician and hospital services were covered by all provincial plans.

At the outset, physician and acute-care hospital services were the defining national aspects of our health care system. Specifically excluded from coverage were psychiatric hospitals, tuberculosis sanatoria, and institutions providing custodial care, such as nursing homes. These categories were excluded on the grounds that care in such hospitals was already being provided by the provinces, virtually without cost to provincial residents (LeClair, 1975). Other services not covered under the cost-sharing agreement were home care services, ambulances services, drugs administered outside hospitals, dentists, and any health care services not provided by physicians. These omissions have resulted in an overemphasis on doctors and hospitals, which in turn has resulted in a lack of comparable national standards across these other health care services.[5]

With medicare, a right to "medically necessary" health care services was established and medical services were "decommodified." Access to these services was determined solely on the basis of medical need and not on one's ability to pay. The doctor's office and the acute care hospital ward became "public" spaces where all Canadians shared common experiences of citizenship. Consequently, the principle of equal access became the normative foundation of medicare. That principle was further embedded by the stipulation that over 90 percent of residents must be covered by provincial plans and that each provincial plan was to operate on a not-for-profit basis, administered by a public agency. These two conditions essentially eliminated any incentives for private insurers and, with it, a private tier of coverage. Our one-tier system has successfully precluded an "exit option" for Canadians wishing to "jump the queue." The lack of an exit option requires that the system meet the expectations of *all* Canadians—a necessary prerequisite for high-quality public services.

Medicare also established a dynamic and often tense federal–provincial relationship that has remained a mainstay of ongoing health policy debates. Canadian constitutional practice has evolved to make the provision of health care services primarily a provincial responsibility. In addition, the constitution generated a fiscal imbalance, one in which the pre-eminent ability to raise money resided with the federal government whereas the significant obligations to spend money for health (and also for education and other social services) resided with the provincial governments (Van Loon & Whittington, 1971). Many provinces initially resisted or otherwise disagreed with trading their jurisdictional powers for federal funds. Through the federal conditional grant and the cost-sharing program, the federal government gained access to areas of health and social assistance. The degree of "shared" responsibility in medicare was unparalleled in Canadian social policy at the time.[6]

Much to the dismay of reluctant provincial governments and medical associations, the four program conditions for cost sharing resulted in a substantive set of national standards that were uniformly implemented across all provincial plans. The federal government's pivotal role as the guardian of national standards had been indelibly etched in the foundations of medicare.

Early Success

By the end of 1971, every province had been in medicare for at least one full year, and 100 percent coverage had been achieved in virtually every province. Around this same time, Canada was experiencing marked changes in many vital statistics. Before the introduction of the Hospital Insurance Program, Canada's infant mortality rate was around 40 percent higher than Australia's, 30 percent higher than England's, and 5 percent higher than that the United States'. By the end of 1971, Canada's infant mortality rate was almost identical to Australia's and England's and 10 percent lower than that of the United States. Also, maternal mortality rates dropped by one-third toward the end of 1971, with studies indicating that pregnant women were seeking medical attention a few months earlier than they had been (LeClair, 1975, p. 43).

With respect to utilization rates, hospital admission rates increased from 143.4 per 1,000 in the mid-1950s to 165.9 per 1,000 in 1970 (Taylor, 1987, p. 417). Because the hospital insurance program had been enacted ten years before the physicians' services insurance program, Canadians were by this time accustomed to using hospitals wherever possible. By the mid-1970s, Canada had the highest hospital admission rate in the world and was spending 60 percent of all health care expenditures on institutional care (Van Loon, 1978, p. 457).

Physician utilization patterns also reflected an initial spurt: a 4 percent increase within the first year of medicare (LeClair, 1975, p. 47). And by 1975 it had been recognized that adding a new physician to the system cost an additional $200,000 to $250,000 per year in health services utilization (Van Loon, 1978, p. 457).

By 1974, medicare had successfully replaced income-based access with needs-based access, with consumption patterns more closely aligned with health care risks (Manga, 1987). The association between income and health care utilization had been inversed, with the lowest-income groups consuming more than double the health care services of higher-income groups (National Council of Welfare, 1982, p. 23). By 1976, government spending on health services accounted for 7.2 percent ($7.1 billion, or $10.8 billion in current dollars as derived by CIHI) of Canada's GNP. At that time, the United States was spending 8.6 percent of GNP on health care, while England was spending 5.4 percent of GNP (Van Loon, 1978, p. 456).

In the wake of these early successes, the politics of medicare quickly moved from concerns about equal access to issues of cost containment. More recently, a social rights analysis has been eclipsed by a preoccupation with controlling and significantly reducing the public role in financing and delivering health care to Canadians. Next we examine more closely the current debate and the related challenges to medicare's normative legacies.

Current Challenges

Almost every day, Canadians are reminded of the health care system's fragility and warned about the pressure points that are destined to destroy it. Newspapers give prominence to stories about insured services being delisted; increasing numbers of private, for-profit clinics and hospitals; ever-growing waiting lists for medical treatment and diagnostic services; overcrowded emergency departments; escalating conflicts between health care providers and governments; shortages of nurses and physicians; shorter hospital stays coupled with decreasing home care budgets; increasing expectations that families and friends assume responsibility for care in the home; and the repeated posturing of federal and provincial governments, each accusing the other of funding shortfalls.

The debate on the future of health care in Canada has recently intensified. This is evident in the explosion of intergovernmental negotiations

Current Challenges

related to health, along with a proliferation of federal and provincial health reports. This debate revolves around two related issues: (1) securing and allocating sufficient resources to ensure the health care system's sustainability, and the respective roles of the public and private sectors in funding and delivering health care; and (2) constructing adequate and transparent mechanisms of public accountability, and the relative weight to be given to federal and provincial priorities in those mechanisms. The ongoing intergovernmental acrimony and deal making over the past decade can be understood in this context. The provinces have been struggling to recover the health funds lost in the initial cuts in the mid-1990s, and some of the problems that have delayed full intergovernmental agreement on health care have been related to sharp differences over the level of federal funding for health and the extent of federal control over accountability mechanisms.

Questions of sustainability and accountability also figure prominently in major federal and provincial reports on health care. In his interim report in February 2002, Roy Romanow noted that Canadians' concerns about the fiscal sustainability of health care were undermining public confidence in the system (Commission on the Future of Health Care in Canada, 2002a and 2002b). In November of the same year, he framed his final report with an expanded conceptualization of sustainability: "The changes I am proposing are intended to strengthen and modernize medicare, and place it on a more sustainable footing for the future" (Commission on the Future of Health Care in Canada, 2002c, p. 3). His final report calls for a strong federal role in a national, transparent, and accountable health care system. The same report recommends that a new "Canadian Health Covenant" be established, in part to clarify the responsibilities of governments in the funding and delivery of health care; that accountability be added as a sixth principle of the Canada Health Act; and that a new institutional means—the Health Council of Canada—be established to implement accountability (Commission on the Future of Health Care in Canada, 2002d).

In the context set by sustainability and federal–provincial disputes, the Canadian health care debate is being fuelled relentlessly by parallel forms of neoliberal welfare state dismantling. Three of these forms will be examined here: the decentralization of the federal system of government, the commodification of health care, and the relegation of health care. Taken together, these forms of dismantling constitute an unmistakable shift from collective to individual responsibility and from universal to residual modes of distribution, as health care increasingly becomes a private commodity.

Decentralization

The debate about the decentralization of the Canadian federation is tightly linked to the debate about national standards in social policy. Arguments for and against decentralization are often arguments about which level of government should take the primary fiscal and legislative responsibility for social policy. Although the provinces have primary constitutional jurisdiction for the general area of health care policy, the use of the federal spending power has long given Ottawa a large role in determining the resources available for health and in setting the broad conditions of health care provision.

After medicare was established in the 1960s, the use of the federal spending power in relation to national standards reached its pinnacle with the Canada Health Act (CHA), passed in 1984. The purpose of the CHA was to consolidate the Hospital Insurance and Diagnostic Services Act of 1957 with the Medical Care Act of 1966 and to define more precisely the terms and conditions according to which federal payments would continue to be made. The act reaffirmed the four program conditions that had been included in the Medical Care Act of 1966 and added a fifth: reasonable access. The most controversial aspect of the act pertained to Section 12(1), in which the conditions relating to the criterion of accessibility were specifically operationalized. The act stated that provincial plans "must provide for insured health services on uniform terms and conditions and on a basis that does not impede or preclude, either directly or indirectly whether by charges made to insured persons or otherwise the reasonable access to those services by insured persons."

For every dollar of extra-billing or hospital user fees, the federal government would withhold one dollar from its cash contribution. With the CHA, "equity of access" was affirmed as a national standard; with the elimination of user fees, the CHA succeeded in restricting efforts at privatizing physician and hospital services.

A decade later, the trend toward decentralization of power or "provincialism" was unmistakable and supported by both Ottawa and the provinces. The passage of the Canada Health and Social Transfer (CHST) in 1996 was a clear signal of this trend. The CHST consolidated funding into a single block transfer for health, post-secondary education, and social assistance and social services. According to Ottawa, one purpose of the fundamental restructuring of social policy arrangements embodied in the CHST was to decentralize power by providing provinces with "greater flexibility in determining priorities and in designing programs to meet local needs" (Canada, 1996, p. 10). Battle and Torjman regard the CHST as "a watershed in the history of Canadian social policy," one that consolidated "a withdrawal of both federal *dollars* and federal *presence* from the provincially run welfare, social services, postsecondary education and health programs that constitute a significant part of Canada's social security system" (Battle and Torjman, 1995, p. 1). They add that it represented a declining federal commitment to maintaining national standards in social policy.[7] Others have suggested that strengthening the federal presence is the only way to prevent the erosion of national standards in health care and other areas of social policy (Osberg, 1996; Begin, 1999; Silver, 1996; Barlow, 2002).

Current Challenges

The creation of the CHST, together with the announcement that Ottawa was decreasing federal transfer payments to the provinces by $7 billion over two years, underscored a key question in the decentralization debate: What is the appropriate federal–provincial balance between the level of responsibility for health care and the level of control over the fiscal resources necessary to *fund* health care?[8] From the moment the federal government announced the CHST cuts, provincial governments have been lobbying Ottawa to reverse them. As a result of this intense private bargaining and heated public disputation, Ottawa has regularly increased health funds to the provinces since 1996.

The Social Union Framework Agreement (SUFA) of February 1999 between the federal government, all provincial governments except Quebec, and the territories was in no small part about health care funding. SUFA was accompanied by a side agreement on health care that saw Ottawa increase CHST funding by $11.5 billion over five years (Canada, 1999a,1999b, 1999c, chap. 4). SUFA is also a prime example of the linkages between decentralized federalism and declining federal interest in maintaining national standards. In the agreement, Ottawa reconfirmed its policy not to introduce any new national initiatives in health care, post-secondary education, and social assistance without the agreement of a majority of provincial governments; recognized the provincial role in identifying the national priorities and objectives of such initiatives; and acknowledged the authority of the provinces and territories to determine the details of program design and mix.

SUFA evoked much negative comment from social policy advocates and other observers. Recalling the opposition to the CHST, critics noted that the Social Union discussions indicated a weakening of federal support for enforceable national standards in health care and social assistance. They also noted that the requirement to gain majority provincial support for new initiatives would probably prove to be an insurmountable obstacle to the creation of new programs in pharmacare, home care, and child care (PovNet, 1999; Walkom, 1999; Council of Canadians, 1999).

The three intergovernmental health agreements reached since 1999 have committed Ottawa to increase health funding by $23.4 billion over five years (2000), $34.8 billion over five years (2003), and $41.3 billion over ten years (2004) (Canadian Intergovernmental Conference Secretariat, 2000; Canada, 2003a, 2004a).[9] The 2003 accord also resulted in the creation of two new transfers, formed from the partition of the CHST: the Canada Health Transfer (CHT) for health, and the Canada Social Transfer (CST) for post-secondary education and social assistance and social services, including early childhood development (Canada, 2003b, p. 83). Establishing the CHT was consistent with the Romanow Commission's call for a separate transfer dedicated to health (Commission on the Future of Health Care in Canada, 2002d, p. 65).

Current Challenges

In his final report on Canadian health care in November 2002, Romanow stated that the "medicare bargain" had committed the federal government to provide a cash contribution equal to 25 percent of provincial/territorial expenditures on publicly insured health services. Yet he found that in fiscal year 2001–2, the federal cash share was only 18.7 percent of relevant provincial/territorial expenditures. To meet its commitment to pay a 25 percent share, Ottawa would have to spend an additional $15 billion between 2003 and 2006 (Commission on the Future of Health Care in Canada, 2002d, p. 64; 2002c). The Romanow Gap became the popular, but perhaps not the most illuminating, term used to describe this shortfall in federal funding of provincial/territorial health expenditures.[10] And a major part of provincial dissatisfaction with the 2003 health accord was that it did not provide sufficient federal funds to eliminate the gap (Laghi & McCarthy, 2003).

The 2004 Health Agreement closed the gap by providing additional federal funds—more money in fact than the Romanow Commission had recommended. Part of that funding included an annual 6 percent CHT escalator, of the kind Romanow had proposed, to ensure predictable growth in the federal share of provincial/territorial expenditures under the Canada Health Act. But if the funding gap disappeared, another Romanow Gap emerged in the accord's vague provisions on conditionality, accountability, and enforcement.

In an article published on the eve of the intergovernmental accord, Romanow warned of the need to address "unresolved obstacles to a truly renewed health care system" by developing clear accountability structures that would ensure additional monies were spent on effecting positive change in the system and by expanding coverage under the Canada Health Act (Romanow, 2004; Bueckert, 2004). It was in precisely these areas that the provisions of the 2004 health accord fell significantly short of the recommendations of the Romanow Commission.

On the question of accountability, the Romanow Commission envisioned a strong and vibrant Health Council playing a crucial role in (1) sustaining effective federal involvement in health care to ensure similar levels of quality and service around the country; and (2) developing a new approach to national leadership founded on the cooperation of federal, provincial, and territorial governments (Commission on the Future of Health Care in Canada, 2002d, chap. 2). The Health Council described in the 2003 and 2004 accords may prove to be that kind of institution, but the current prognosis is mixed. The Council has published much information that is vital to understanding the state of the Canadian health care system, including two progress reports on the implementation of the 2003 and 2004 health accords. But it is limited by the absence of councillors from Quebec and Alberta and by the imprecision of the two accords that established it. Generally, those accords prefer broad solutions and general guidelines to specific targets and take a weak and indirect definition of accountability that relies on information rather than enforcement.

The accord's separate and specific arrangements for Quebec, in which the Quebec government states that it will follow its own health plans and objectives in accordance with its fiscal capacity, may simply be an example of Ottawa's formal recognition of the need for "asymmetrical federalism" (Canada, 2004b). But such arrangements may also indicate the federal government's demonstrable lack of interest in enforcing national standards in health care.

If the 2004 accord fails to heed Romanow's warning on the need to develop meaningful structures of accountability and enforcement, it likewise fails to respond to his call for expanding health care coverage under the Canada Health Act. The final report of the Romanow Commission envisions a strengthened and modernized act, one that covers selected home care services and, eventually, prescription drugs. It also calls for clarification of the relationship between the act and diagnostic services to eliminate queue jumping and to prohibit user fees and extra-billing. The 2004 accord does not bring these health care sectors into medicare, nor does it attempt to modernize or expand the Canada Health Act in any way. As a result, the accord's provisions are not enforceable under the act and stand entirely outside its criteria and conditions.

In fact, the 2004 health accord signals a further retreat from federal enforcement of the Canada Health Act. The accord formalizes a 2002 intergovernmental agreement on how disputes under the act are to be avoided and resolved, an agreement that was itself a direct extension of the decentralizing trajectory of the 1999 Social Union Framework Agreement (Canada, 2002). At the heart of the dispute avoidance and resolution process is a commitment by the federal government to refrain from unilaterally enforcing the act's principles (Cohn, 2010, p. 5). While the accord may signal that federal funding for health care has recovered, it equally shows that federal influence or leadership in health has not.[11]

The 2004 intergovernmental agreement on health is an example of "decentralizing federalism": the absence of meaningful structures and processes of accountability, the lack of conditionality, and the failure to strengthen the Canada Health Act point to ineffective federal engagement and declining national standards. As Boismenu and Jenson suggest, though, this debate goes beyond the question of decentralizing power from Ottawa to the provinces:

> Despite often being presented in the language of "decentralizing federalism," and sometimes vaunted as a solution to the constitutional tangle of Quebec–Canada relations, the social union concept is more than that. The model of the social union involves decentralization to be sure. It is *not a shift within federalism* of decision-making power going from one level of government to the other, however. Rather, the power that

> is being decentralized is going from states to markets, and from public to private. The private sector, communities, families, and individuals are being exhorted to take more responsibility, as governments scale back their roles. At the same time ... the nine provinces acting together assert themselves as *co-managers* of the social union, seeking to establish institutional guarantees that they will be consulted and involved in Ottawa's actions in their areas of constitutional jurisdiction. (Boismenu & Jenson, 1998, pp. 60–61)

Commodification

This shift from states to markets and from public to private brings us to the second challenge to medicare, that of intensified commodification. In the process of commodification, health care service itself becomes a commodity—that is, it becomes a "unit of output" that is produced and packaged for sale in the sphere of capital accumulation (Leys, 2001, p. 84). The intricate and ever-changing mix of public and private principles in Canadian health insurance obscures some of the trends toward commodification (Naylor, 1986; Deber et al., 1998; Deber, 2000). But there are identifiable trends whose recognition is made easier by explicit comparisons that policy makers draw between the proper roles and responsibilities of the public and private sectors.

First, the discourse of health care reform is becoming increasingly characterized by the language, meanings, values, and assumptions of the market. Deber and colleagues capture the generality of, and tensions between, the old and new paradigms in health:

> In general, every industrialized country, with the exception of the United States, espouses the principle of universal health coverage for its people as a right of citizenship, rather than as a commodity to be bought and sold in the open market. Historically, principles of universality and equity of access have been the driving force behind decisions about financing health. These principles have recently been challenged as the general social and economic climate has turned to questions of efficiency and cost-effectiveness. (Deber et al., 1998, p. 504)

In the neoliberal conception of efficiency, to decrease waste and increase sustainability, public expenditures on social policy must be curtailed by expanding the role of the market and diminishing the role of the state.

Another example of commodification has been the process of "privatization by default" or "passive privatization," in which the private share of health care spending has been slowly creeping up over time, until very recently (Tholl, 1994, p.61). Almost every year from 1984 to 1997, private health spending increased faster than did public expenditure. In this period, the private share of health expenditures rose from under 24 percent to almost 30 percent. The discrepancy in public and private annual growth rates was particularly wide from 1992 to 1996, years in which governmental restraint measures held the average annual rate of growth of public health spending to only 0.6 percent, the lowest in 20 years. In the late 1990s, the situation was reversed, with public growth higher than private growth, reflecting particularly heavy governmental spending on capital projects and drugs. By 2002, private sector growth had recovered and the private share of spending stood at 30.3 percent (Canadian Institute for Health Information, 2001, 2004).

The commodification of health care is, however, a much more vigorous, explicit, and purposeful process than is suggested by the term "passive privatization." To be sure, the passive privatization of health care that characterized most of this period was partly the result of technological change: increasingly, health care was moving out of sectors dominated by public insurance, such as hospital and medical services, and into sectors in which private financing played a much larger role, such as home care and drug therapy outside hospitals. But this kind of privatization was not simply passive. It was also the result of proactive governmental decisions that constrained the growth of public health expenditures, removed health services from coverage under the public insurance plan, encouraged a kind of asymmetrical competition that marginalized not-for-profit health care providers and privileged for-profit providers, and failed to reinvest in community care the resources that had been saved by closing and restructuring hospitals (Fuller, 1998; Baranek, 2000; Browne, 2000; Tuohy, Flood, & Stabile, 2001; Epps & Flood, 2001).

Pat Armstrong (1997) uses the phrase "cascading privatization" to describe the process whereby decisions made by various health care players interact to reinforce the privatization of the heath care system: the federal government adopts the neoliberal project and slashes social spending; neoliberal provincial governments justify their own project of cutting costs, downloading services, and closing hospitals by pointing to federal cutbacks; the community health care sector, which remains seriously underresourced, is overwhelmed by the spiralling demands for its services; these engineered problems in the publicly funded system are used as evidence that medicare is not working and become a rationale for further privatization; the principle of universality is eroded as the wealthy pay for private health services; and the publicly funded system becomes increasingly vulnerable to additional privatization (CCPA, 2000; Browne, 2000).

Relegation

Relegating health care is a third challenge to medicare. Relegation refers to the direct or indirect transfer of responsibility for health care to the individual, family, and not-for-profit sector.[12] It involves shifting the provision and costs of care to family and friends, volunteer labour, and organizations that rely disproportionately on volunteer labour or that are otherwise in the not-for-profit sector.

Overcoming the Challenges

There is an observable trend toward relegating health care, with more and more patients receiving informal care at home from friends and relatives or in the community from volunteers and voluntary organizations (Armstrong & Armstrong, 1996). Governments certainly see relegation as an attractive policy option. For some years, the federal and provincial levels of government have been calling for increased voluntarism and developing initiatives to encourage donations and enhance the resources available to charitable organizations (Canada, 1997; Ontario, 1995).

Governments often use the progressive language of health promotion, community development, social empowerment, and mutual support to justify this shift in the responsibility for health care. But the predominant concerns of the neoliberal agenda in health care demand that relegation be used to contain or externalize costs. This view of the economic rationale for relegating health care is consistent with the conclusion of a recent study of home care in Ontario: it is likely that the "real driving force of the shift to home care has been governments' desire to reduce costs" (Browne, 2000, p. 82).[13] The transfer of funds to the family and community sector usually lags behind the transfer of responsibility. Governments are not generally willing to make a substantial financial commitment to home care and, consequently, have been reluctant to champion the 1997 recommendation of the National Forum on Health that home care be considered "an integral part of publicly funded health services" (National Forum on Health, 1997, p. 21).[14] And they have been equally reluctant to take up the more recent challenge of providing more-than-minimalist home care coverage that is adequate to meet social need (Health Council of Canada, 2008a, 2008b).

Overcoming the Challenges

Paradoxically, the pressure for privatization continues to grow in the face of overwhelming and incontrovertible evidence that undermines virtually all the assumptions and conclusions of privatized health care. This pressure increasingly comes in the form of concerns about the "sustainability crisis" or "unsustainability" of Canadian health care. Certainly, questions about medicare's sustainability are not new: as we mentioned earlier, the Romanow Commission was in part a response to such questions.[15] And the central tenets of the unsustainability thesis have not changed; they point toward the disproportionate growth of health care costs and how that growth "crowds out" or "squeezes out" public funding of other social programs. As one contemporary summary of the thesis put it:

> The essence of the non-sustainability argument is as follows: the costs of Medicare have been escalating at an alarming rate; cost pressures are only going to increase as our population continues to age; unless something drastic is done soon to slash the growth in health care costs, the system will bankrupt us.

Overcoming the Challenges

> The evidence offered for this position invariably begins with projections which purport to show that, if costs continue to escalate at current rates, Medicare will account for an unreasonable share of public spending or of government revenue or of Canada's GDP. "Unreasonable" is defined in this context as either resulting in unacceptable levels of taxation, or crowding out other important areas of public investment. (Mackenzie & Rachlis, 2010, 12)[16]

The unsustainability thesis has unquestionably experienced a sudden renaissance, with its proponents invigorated by two recent developments. Government spending initiatives to combat the 2008–9 recession led to renewed fears of heavy public debt loads and structural deficits; they also further highlighted the increasing weight of health care in public expenditures.[17] Another catalyst was the fast-approaching demise of the ten-year 2004 intergovernmental health accord—"Medicare as it is comes to an end on March 31, 2014"—and the realization that expenditures under the accord had not purchased sufficient reform of the health care system (Kent, 2011, p. 1).[18]

The renewed formulations of the unsustainability thesis have had social and political effects. Canadians are concerned about rising health care costs, and there is public anxiety about the unsustainability of the system. Partly in response to these popular attitudes, the Health Council of Canada initiated in early 2009 a conversation with Canadians about how to sustain public health care from a value-for-money perspective (Health Council of Canada, 2009).[19] And in January 2011, the Conference Board of Canada launched the Canadian Alliance for Sustainable Health Care, a five-year initiative to provide broad-based analysis and discussion of questions about sustainability (Conference Board of Canada, 2011).

The recent proliferation of analyses of the sustainability problem underscores how the debate about health care continues to be framed by the three neoliberal themes of decentralization, commodification, and relegation. Generally, calls for a more robust federal presence in health care come from opponents, not proponents, of the unsustainability thesis.[20] Skinner and Rovere (2011), enthusiastic advocates of the case for unsustainability, explicitly endorse the marginalization of Ottawa's role. They suggest that the Canada Health Act—the legislative cornerstone of federal involvement in the sector—be suspended for a five-year trial period to open space for provincial government intervention to secure fundamental reforms to health care financing and delivery. This proposal for radical decentralization of health care is buttressed by research suggesting that the intergovernmental institutions of the health sector embody a pan-Canadianism that necessarily undermines the value of "non-centralization" and that erodes the autonomy of provincial governments (Graefe & Bourns, 2009).

Not surprisingly, findings of unsustainability are often accompanied by prescriptions of commodification—that is, the solution to the unnatural and uncontrollable growth of health care costs is to destroy the government "monopoly" and open the sector to privatization by imposing market discipline and enhancing competition. For some, such as the Fraser Institute and the Organisation for Economic Co-operation and Development (OECD), commodification is an urgency, to be implemented in the short term to address the crisis (OECD, 2010b; Rovere & Skinner, 2010; Skinner & Rovere, 2008; Skinner & Rovere, 2011). For others, such as the TD Economics report on health care in Ontario, any explicit recommendation for a thoroughgoing increase in private funding of health care must be held in abeyance and preceded by small-scale privatization experiments, both to evaluate known risks to access and quality of care and to overcome the likely "political sensitivity" and popular resistance to such a fundamental change in a program as widely admired as medicare (Drummond & Burleton, 2010). For still others, the movement toward commodification is obscured by reassurances that "the path to sustainability" is neither "an ideological attack on the state" nor "about shrinking the role of the state." Such reassurances are, in the end, not very reassuring because that path does seem to involve reducing government to its "core business," shrinking its footprint, and "keeping taxation and public spending low" (Mowat Centre, 2010, pp. 3, 15, 17).[21]

The final neoliberal theme, relegation, is also evident in the new studies of heath care unsustainability. Part of the process of stripping down government to its core roles involves the transfer of erstwhile public responsibilities to not-for-profit organizations, the private sector, public–private partnerships, families, and individuals (Drummond & Burleton, 2010; Mowat Centre, 2010). It also involves redeploying economic incentives to make health care users accountable for their level of utilization (MacKinnon, 2004a, 2004b; Rovere, 2011), a proposal that will have the effect of making the sick pay for their ill health. And the new advocates of the sustainability crisis repeat an old theme by taking an individualized view of health promotion and prevention, in which they focus on changing individual lifestyles and risk behaviours to the relative neglect of action on the broader social determinants of health (Drummond & Burleton, 2010).[22]

Theses of the fiscal or financial or economic unsustainability of public health care in Canada are without substance. Virtually every element of the unsustainability case is flawed:[23]

- Medicare expenditures on hospitals and physicians are not spiralling out of control but have remained relatively stable over time, outside periods of recession. In fact, between 2000 and 2008, real annual growth in per capita health spending in Canada was below the OECD average. (OECD, 2010a)
- The illusion of out-of-control costs relative to GDP is largely a "denominator effect": health care costs as a percent of GDP will rise during periods of recession, even without any change in actual health care

Overcoming the Challenges

costs, because the denominator—GDP—declines; the health care share will remain higher than it would otherwise be if there were no full recovery from recession (Evans, 2007, p. 125).

- Similarly, the increasing weight of health care costs in provincial program spending is a result of changes to the denominator: cutbacks in federal transfers, provincial tax cutting policies, and provincial reductions in non-health program spending decreased the size of the denominator and created the impression of a sharp increase in health care costs (Canadian Doctors for Medicare, 2011, p. 3).
- A significant part of the increase in total health care expenditures is due to rising costs in the *non-medicare health sector,* for prescription drugs, for instance.[24]
- Contrary to what the unsustainability thesis suggests, the relative size of the public health care system in Canada is not large by international standards, but its private health sector is. In 2008, Canada ranked in the *bottom third* of twenty-six OECD countries on percentage of total health expenditures accounted for by the public sector. But it ranked in the *top third* on percentage of total health care spending financed by the private sector, and *third overall* on share of total health expenditures in private insurance (CIHI, 2010, pp. 65, 69–70).
- The aging of the population is only a moderate driver of the growth of health care costs and does not portend a crisis of sustainability. Claims that a "grey tsunami" will overwhelm the health care system have no substance.
- The hypothesis of "crowding out" is without empirical support: a study of provincial spending patterns between 1988–89 and 2003–4, designed specifically to test the crowding out proposition, concluded that "there is no evidence that increased provincial government health expenditures resulted in lower levels of spending on other categories of government provided goods and services" (Landon et al., 2006, p. 121).
- Single-payer universal health care systems help *control* costs, not expand them.
- Increasing the private share of health care financing, in the form of out-of-pocket payments or private health care insurance, will likely escalate the costs of care.
- Overall, then, "the claims of *economic* unsustainability appear from the data to be themselves wholly unsustainable" (Evans, 2007, p. 149).

There is a crisis of sustainability, but it is a *political* crisis, not an economic one. The appearance of crisis was created by the political choices of governments inspired or influenced by neoliberalism. Governments' active implementation of two of the defining characteristics of the neoliberal project—cutting social spending and reducing taxes—stands at the root of the manufactured crisis in health care, as suggested by the summary above.

Exaggerated assertions about the dire financial consequences of Canada's aging demographic profile or about the need for Canadians to choose some combination of drastic and unappealing actions—sharply increased taxes, higher individual payments for health, deep reductions in non-health public services, significantly deteriorating health care standards—contain a healthy element of "panic-mongering."[25] Such calls are part of a political campaign to weaken the strong popular support for publicly funded health care and to prepare the ideological ground for transformative change. Canadians are being led to believe that a crisis is coming that will require the dismantling of medicare.

As the absolute costs of health care rise (although nowhere near the level of crisis), there is a need for better public management of medicare to avoid waste and inappropriate care. Decisive government action is needed to bring about important changes in such areas as national pharmacare, primary care reform, and home care reform. These changes have great potential to save costs.[26] There also needs to be strong state support for initiatives to address the social determinants of health. Evidence from Canada and abroad points unequivocally to the deleterious health effects and high health care costs of poverty and income inequality; the same evidence shows that Canada lags behind other nations in addressing these social disparities (Mikkonen & Raphael, 2010; OECD, 2011; World Health Organization, 2008).[27] Instead of looking for ways to reduce to "core business," governments must begin to discover or rediscover their important social role, and promote a fair and progressive taxation system to ensure they have the resources to fulfill that role.

Recent calls for stronger federal leadership in health care (Kent, 2011; Mackenzie & Rachlis, 2010) may founder against the Harper government's ideological preference "to hollow out the redistributive role of the Canadian federal state" (Evans & Albo, 2008, p. 1). That government has recently strengthened its capacity to realize that preference through majority control of the House of Commons and the Senate. Advocates for progressive social change must be careful not to allow their demands for reform to become entangled in the discredited logic of "crowding out." If government action on combating poverty and income inequality is purchased from the health care budget, the health-enhancing effects of such action will be correspondingly weakened. There is a pressing need for simultaneous state action on health care and on the broader social determinants of health.[28]

The "unsustainability crisis" frames the health discourse in terms of monetary costs. Meanwhile, inequities in accessing the health care system and in health outcomes continue. Studies of income and health demonstrate that income continues to be associated with the use of health services (Asada &

Overcoming the Challenges

Kephart, 2007; Lightman, Michell, & Wilson, 2008; Wilkins et al., 2008). For example, Asada and Kephart (2007) found that people with lower incomes had less contact with general practitioners and with specialists, though once contact was established, visits to general practitioners were more frequent. Furthermore, individuals within the lowest quintile of income are 30 percent less likely to have a family physician than the average Canadian (Lightman et al., 2008, p. 18). And those in the lowest income category are five times more likely to report fair or poor health than Canadians in the highest income category (Frohlich, Ross, & Richmond, 2006, p. 134).

Mounting evidence of the disparities in health outcomes, disproportionately experienced by vulnerable and racialized populations (see Beiser & Stewart, 2005; Raphael, 2004; Galabuzi, 2004), further demonstrate what happens when an eroding public health care system runs up against a neoliberal social policy agenda. As examined by Galabuzi, "other determinants such as income, gender, race, immigrant status and geography increasingly define the translation of universality as unequally differentiated" (2004, p. 246). Groups particularly vulnerable to low health status include Aboriginal peoples, immigrants, refugees, the disabled, the poor, the homeless, and other groups in precarious life circumstances. For example, Aboriginal babies in Canada are three times more likely to die in their first year of life than non-Aboriginal babies (Beiser & Stewart, 2005, p. S4). Life expectancy for Aboriginal men is 67.1 years on-reserve and 72.1 years off-reserve, compared to 76 years for the general population (Frohlich et al., 2006, p. 133). Immigrants make up 18 percent of Canada's population but account for almost 60 percent of all cases of tuberculosis (Beiser, 2005, p. S32). One can only expect these disproportionate inequities to deepen with any further commodification of essential health services and the retrenchment of the welfare state.

Meeting these challenges to medicare and addressing growing health disparities will require health care analysts and social work activists to adopt an intersectionalities perspective, one that exposes the multiple and intersecting causes of health inequities (Hankivsky & Christoffersen, 2008). This analysis would interrogate the structural inequities both within medicare and across the broader range of health determinants, exposing the intersecting dynamics that create and sustain social inequities in health. Furthermore, activists need to do a better job at popular education that engages and mobilizes social constituencies in support of policies that prevent the further marginalization of various groups in Canadian society.

The battle for medicare and for the health of all Canadians will not be won in academic journals and books, although it may be lost there. It will be won by constructing a political coalition to oppose the disproportionate and debilitating political influence wielded by neoliberalism.

Notes

1 This conception of "equity" was formulated in Silver (1993).
2 This argument is based on the analysis in Burke (2000).
3 Reasonable access subsequently became the fifth independent program condition in the 1984 Canada Health Act.
4 When the program began on July 1, 1968, only Saskatchewan and British Columbia were operating schemes that were eligible for cost sharing.
5 The earlier proposals contained in the Heagerty report on Health Insurance in 1945 had included the full range of benefits such as dental, pharmaceuticals, and nursing services, but were then omitted, to be implemented in the next series of health care reforms, which, due to costs, never did materialize (Guest, 1985).
6 In contrast, with the Canada Assistance Plan, also passed in 1966, the federal government specified neither the precise eligibility conditions nor the level of benefits. Consequently, very little in the way of national standards of assistance has emerged. The amount of provincial discretion permitted by the legislation has resulted in a social assistance system that is extremely complex, treats similar cases of need differently, relies on an intrusive and stigmatizing determination of need, and sets assistance rates well below the most conservative poverty lines (National Council of Welfare, 1987, p. 7).
7 In recent budgets, Ottawa has increased the cash component of the CHST, but the money restored to health does not equal the money taken from health.
8 In the 1995 federal budget that announced the restructuring of social transfer payments, the CHST was originally called the Canada Social Transfer (CST).
9 CHST funding increases support not only for health but also for post-secondary education, social assistance, and social services.
10 Marchildon (2004b) notes how the term became embroiled in federal–provincial wrangling over health care funding and was (mis)used by both levels of government in ways that sowed confusion. This intergovernmental controversy over the nature of the Romanow Gap is a special case of what Boychuk has more generally termed the dysfunctional political dynamic of federal–provincial fiscal relations in health (Boychuk, 2004).
11 A point made by Mackenzie and Rachlis, who see Ottawa's waning influence as a result of its withdrawal from targeted health care funding and the damage done to its credibility by earlier unilateral cuts to provincial transfer payments (Mackenzie & Rachlis, 2010, p. 63).
12 This definition is similar to but broader than what Brodie calls refamilialization: "the growing consensus among policy-makers that families (whatever their form) should look after their own and that it is up to the neoliberal state to make sure that they do" (Brodie, 1996, 22–23).
13 The quoted phrase is emphasized in the original.
14 As health minister, Allan Rock showed a rhetorical commitment to home care and pharmacare but did not transform the rhetoric into public policy (Canada, 1998).
15 For an earlier statement of the sustainability problem, see Angus et al. (1995). Bayne and Associates (2008), for the Health Council of Canada, place the concern with sustainability in historical context.
16 Similarly, Mackinnon summarizes the unsustainability case as follows: "Health care costs are increasing at a faster rate than the revenue of any government in Canada, and the scramble by governments to fund health care means that other critical priorities are being underfunded" (MacKinnon, 2004b, p. 603; see also MacKinnon, 2004a).
17 This theme is evident in many recent analyses of unsustainability: Askari et al. (2010); Drummond & Burleton (2010); Mowat Centre (2010); Maioni (2010); and Mendelsohn, Hjartson, & Pearce (2010). Rovere and Skinner (2010) of the Fraser Institute also note that, in Ontario, the recession provides an opportunity to expand private sources of funding health care.

Notes

18 Two Health Council of Canada reports (2008b, 2011) on the progress made as a result of the 2003 and 2004 health accords show that there is considerable room for improvement across a whole range of health care initiatives.

19 The Health Council of Canada does believe that "a high-quality and sustainable health care system for all" is achievable (2009, p. 13).

20 Kent (2011) is an exception: he seems to accept the "facts" of unsustainability but argues that Ottawa should leverage its health care transfers to the provinces by attaching conditions that ensure reforms in the areas of health promotion and primary care delivery. Mendelsohn, Hjartson, and Pearce (2010) recommend that responsibility for a new national pharmaceutical plan be uploaded to the federal government, but see this uploading as a residual federal role in the context of Ottawa's shrinking fiscal responsibility for and intermittent and ineffective intervention in health care.

21 The Mowat Centre report is about fiscal responsibility, defined broadly, and not specific to health care. It does note, however, that "a focus on health care is essential" and that a "concerted effort to reduce the escalation of heath care spending will be imperative" (2010, pp. 23–24).

22 For an overview of the focus on lifestyle approaches in Canada, see Raphael (2008).

23 The analysis in this paragraph is taken from Evans (2004, 2007), Mackenzie and Rachlis (2010), Canadian Doctors for Medicare (2011), Lee (2007), Yalnizyan (2004), Boychuk (2004), and Marchildon (2004a). Also relevant is the debate about the "arithmetic of health care" that emerged in response to Janice MacKinnon's interventions (2004a, 2004b, 2005): see Kolkman (2005), Kalant (2005), McMurtry (2005), Dhalla (2007), and Béland (2007). Earlier studies contesting previous incarnations of the sustainability or fiscal crisis in health include Murnighan (2001), Friends of Medicare (2002), Deber et al. (1998), Evans et al. (2000), Rachlis et al. (2001), and Tuohy, Flood, & Stabile (2002).

24 Growth in drug spending has slowed considerably in recent years, although such spending remains an important overall driver of health care costs. One reason for the slowing of growth may be provincial government action on generic drug pricing (CIHI, 2011). The role of government in containing health care costs is addressed further in the body of the paper.

25 The quotation is from Evans (2010, n.p.). The list of drastic actions is from Dodge and Dion (2011). See also Mackenzie and Rachlis on Dodge's warning to the Liberal Party of Canada (2010, p. 68).

26 Gagnon (2010) says that creating a national universal drug plan offering first-dollar coverage could yield savings up to $10.7 billion per year. He also notes that "the only hindrance to establishing a fair, effective drug insurance program is political apathy, not economic cost restraints" (p. 11).

27 The Health Council of Canada (2010) notes that Canadian public policy on the determinants of health and health promotion is not as advanced as could be expected. Relatively weak income security policies have long been a feature of the welfare state in Canada (Tuohy, 1993). As an example of cost savings, Stanford (2010) notes the strong link between diabetes and poverty, with the incidence of diabetes twice as high among the poor as the wealthy, and estimates that state action to alleviate poverty could reduce the total direct health cost of diabetes by some $7 billion per year. A report by the Health Disparities Task Group (2004) suggests that some 20 percent of total health care costs are linked to income disparities.

28 That is, we need to resist taking positions like that of the Health Council of Canada (2010, pp. 6, 26), which explicitly cites the crowding out argument to endorse a refocusing of spending priorities away from direct health care toward the social determinants of health. While the health care status quo, with its disproportionately heavy investment in acute care and in treatment over prevention, is in need of reform, explicit calls for a movement of funds from one social spending envelope to another may well be self-defeating. As mentioned above, governments are much quicker in

heeding calls for social disinvestment than they are for reinvestment. And the council's reasoning here falls victim to the very compartmentalization it criticizes. To come to a full appreciation of government spending priorities and their relation to desirable public outcomes requires attention to all the fiscal envelopes, not just the social or health policy envelopes. It also requires a broader historical understanding of shifting patterns of government revenue and expenditure.

References

Armstrong, P. (1997, November). Privatization. Presentation to the Ontario Health Coalition, Toronto, Ontario.

Armstrong, P., & Armstrong, H. (1996). *Wasting away: The undermining of Canadian health care.* Toronto, ON: Oxford University Press.

Asada, Y., & Kephart, G. (2007). Equity in health services and intensity of use in Canada. *BMC Health Services Research, 7*(41), 87–101. doi: 10.1186/1472-6963-7-41

Askari, M., Barnett, R., Danforth, J., Matier, C., Recker, B., & Tapp, S. (2010, February). *Fiscal sustainability report.* Ottawa, ON: Office of the Parliamentary Budget Officer.

Baranek, P.M. (2000). Long term care reform in Ontario: The influence of ideas, institutions and interests on the public/private mix. (PhD dissertation). Department of Health Administration, Faculty of Medicine, University of Toronto, Toronto, ON.

Barlow, M. (2002). *Profit is not the cure.* Ottawa, ON: Council of Canadians.

Battle, K., & Torjman, S. (1995). *How finance re-formed social policy.* Ottawa, ON: Caledon Institute of Social Policy.

Bayne, L., & Associates (2008). Sustainability in public health care: What does it mean? Health Council of Canada.

Begin, M. (1999). *The future of Medicare: Recovering the Canada Health Act.* Ottawa, ON: Canadian Centre for Policy Alternatives.

Beiser, M. (2005). The health of immigrants and refugees in Canada. *Canadian Journal of Public Health: Reducing Health Disparities in Canada, 96*(March/April), S30–S44.

Beiser, M., & Stewart, M. (2005). Reducing health disparities. *Canadian Journal of Public Health: Reducing Health Disparities in Canada, 96*(March/April), S4–S5.

Béland, F. (2007). Arithmetic failure and the myth of the unsustainability of universal health insurance. *Canadian Medical Association Journal, 177*(1), 54–56. doi: 10.1503/cmaj.060930

Boismenu, G., & Jenson, J. (1998). A social union or a federal state? Competing visions of intergovernmental relations in the new Liberal era. In L.A. Pal (Ed.), *How Ottawa spends, 1998–99: Balancing act: The post-deficit mandate* (pp. 57–79). Toronto, ON: Oxford University Press.

Boychuk, G.W. (2004). The changing political and economic environment of health care. In G.P. Marchildon, T. McIntosh, & P.-G. Forest (Eds.), *The fiscal sustainability of health care in Canada: The Romanow papers, Volume 1* (pp. 320–339). Toronto, ON: University of Toronto Press.

Brodie, J. (1996). Canadian women, changing state forms, and public policy. In J. Brodie (Ed.), *Women and Canadian public policy* (pp. 1–28). Toronto, ON: Harcourt Brace Canada.

References

Browne, P.L. (2000). *Unsafe practices: Restructuring and privatization in Ontario health care.* Ottawa, ON: Canadian Centre for Policy Alternatives.

Bueckert, D. (2004, September 14). Romanow says health deal a huge mistake. Retrieved from http://cnews.canoe.ca

Burke, M. (2000). Efficiency and the erosion of health care in Canada. In M. Burke, C. Mooers, & J. Shields (Eds.), *Restructuring and resistance: Canadian public policy in an age of global capitalism* (pp. 178–193). Halifax, NS: Fernwood Publishing.

Burke, M., Mooers, C., & Shields, J. (2000). Critical perspectives on Canadian public policy. In M. Burke, C. Mooers, & J. Shields (Eds.), *Restructuring and resistance: Canadian public policy in an age of global capitalism* (pp. 11–23). Halifax, NS: Fernwood Publishing.

Canada. (1996). Renewing the Canadian federation: A progress report. Background document for the First Ministers' meeting, 20–21 June 1996.

Canada. (1997). Budget *1997*: Budget plan. Department of Finance. Ottawa, ON: Public Works and Government Services Canada.

Canada. (1998, February 4). Minister marks first anniversary of National Forum on Health report. *Health Canada* news release. Retrieved fromwww.hc-sc.gc.ca/english/media/releases/1998/98_07e.htm

Canada. (1999a, February 4) *A framework to improve the social union for Canadians.* Retrieved from http://www.socialunion.gc.ca/news/020499_e.html

Canada. (1999b). *The federal-provincial-territorial health care agreement.* 4 February. Retrieved from http://www.socialunion.gc.ca/ecd/ecd-back051203_e.html

Canada. (1999c). *Budget 1999.* Department of Finance. 16 February. Retrieved from http://www.fin.gc.ca/toc/1999/buddoclist99-eng.asp

Canada. (2002). *Canada Health Act Annual Report, 2001–2002.* Health Canada. Minister of Public Works and Government Services Canada.

Canada. (2003a). *2003 First Ministers' accord on health care renewal.* Health Canada. Retrieved from http://hc-sc.gc.ca/hcs-sss/delivery-prestation/fptcollab/2003accord/index-eng.php

Canada. (2003b). *Budget Plan 2003.* Department of Finance. Retrieved from http://www.fin.gc.ca/budtoc/2003/budlist-eng.asp

Canada. (2004a, September 16). *10-year plan to strengthen health care.* Health Canada. Retrieved from http://www.hc-sc.gc.ca/hcs-sss/delivery-prestation/fptcollab/2004-fmm-rpm/index-eng.php

Canada. (2004b, September 15). *Asymetrical* [*sic*] *federalism that respects Quebec's jurisdiction.* Retrieved from http://www.hc-sc.gc.ca/hcs-sss/delivery-prestation/fptcollab/2004-fmm-rpm/bg-fi_quebec-eng.php

Canadian Centre for Policy Alternatives (CCPA). (2000). *Health care, limited: The privatization of medicare.* Synthesis report prepared by the CCPA for the Council of Canadians. With guidance from CCPA research associates P. Armstrong, H. Armstrong, and C. Fuller, and in collaboration with the Canadian Health Coalition. Retrieved from http://www.policyalternatives.ca/publications/reports/health-care-limited

Canadian Doctors for Medicare. (2011). Neat, plausible, and wrong: The myth of health care unsustainability. Retrieved from http://www.canadiandoctorsformedicare.ca/health-care-sustainability.html

References

Canadian Institute for Health Information (CIHI). (2001). *National health expenditure trends, 1975–2010.*

Canadian Institute for Health Information (CIHI). (2004). *National health expenditure trends, 1975–2004.*

Canadian Institute for Health Information (CIHI). (2010). *National health expenditure trends, 1975 to 2010.* Retrieved from https://secure.cihi.ca/estore/productFamily.htm?pf=PFC1556&lang=en&media=0

Canadian Intergovernmental Conference Secretariat. (2000, September 11). News Release. First Ministers' Meeting: Communiqué on Health. Retrieved from http://www.scics.gc.ca/english/conferences.asp?x=1&a=viewdocument&id=1232

Churchill, L.R. (1987). *Rationing health care in America: Perceptions and principles of justice.* South Bend, IN: University of Notre Dame Press.

Cohn, D. (2010). Chaoulli five years on: All bark and no bite? Paper presented at the 2010 Annual Meeting of the Canadian Political Science Associations. Montreal, QC: Concordia University.

Commission on the Future of Health Care in Canada. (2002a). Statement by Roy J. Romanow, Q.C., Commissioner, on the release of the interim report of the Commission on the Future of Health Care in Canada at the National Press Theatre, Ottawa. 6 February.

Commission on the Future of Health Care in Canada. (Romanow report). (2002b). *Shape the future of health care. Interim report.* Retrieved from http://dsp-psd.pwgsc.gc.ca/Collection/CP32-76-2002E.pdf

Commission on the Future of Health Care in Canada. (2002c). Statement by Roy J. Romanow, Q.C., Commissioner, on the release of the final report of the Commission on the Future of Health Care in Canada at the National Press Theatre, Ottawa. 28 November.

Commission on the Future of Health Care in Canada. (Romanow Report). (2002d). *Building on values.* Final Report. Retrieved from http://dsp-psd.pwgsc.gc.ca/Collection/CP32-85-2002E.pdf

Conference Board of Canada. (2011). *The Canadian Alliance for Sustainable Health Care (CASHC).*

Council of Canadians. (1999). Power game. Five problems with the current social union talks. Retrieved from http://www.canadians.org/archive/documents/social_union.pdf

Deber R.B. (2000). Getting what we pay for: myths and realities about financing Canada's health care system. Health Law Canada, *21*(2), 9–56. Retrieved from http://www.utoronto.ca/hpme/dhr/pdf/atrevised3.pdf

Deber, R., Narine, L., Baranek, P., Sharpe, N., Duvalko, K.M., Zlotnik-Shaul, R., ... Williams, A.P. (1998). The public–private mix in health care. In National Forum on Health (Ed.), *Canada health action: Building on the legacy. Papers Commissioned by the National Forum on Health.* Vol. 4 (pp. 423–545). Sainte-Foy, QC: Editions MultiMondes.

Dhalla, I. (2007). Canada's health care system and the sustainability paradox. *Canadian Medical Association Journal,* 177:1 (July 3), 51–53. doi: 10.1503/cmaj.061064

Dodge, D.A., & Dion, R. (2011). Chronic healthcare spending disease: A macro diagnosis and prognosis. *C.D. Howe Institute Commentary: The Health Papers, 327* (April), 1–12. http://ssrn.com/abstract=1825363

References

Drummond, D., & Burleton, D. (2010). *Charting a path to sustainable health care in Ontario: 10 proposals to restrain cost growth without compromising quality of care.* TD Economics Special Reports. TD Bank Financial Group. Retrieved from http://www.td.com/economics/special/db0510_health_care.pdf

Epps, T., & Flood, C. (2001). *The implications of the NAFTA for Canada's health care system: Have we traded away the opportunity for innovative health care reform?* Working draft.

Esping-Andersen, G. (1989). The three political economies of the welfare state. *Canadian Review of Sociology and Anthropology, 26*(1), 10–35.

Evans, B., & Albo, G. (2008, September 5). Harper's bunker: The state, neoliberalism and the election. *The Bullet.* E-Bulletin no. 139. Retrieved from http://www.socialistproject.ca/bullet/bullet139.html

Evans, R.G., Barer, M.L., Lewis, S., Rachlis, M., & Stoddart, G.L. (2000). *Private highway, one-way street: The deklein and fall of Canadian Medicare?* Centre for Health Services and Policy Research, University of British Columbia. Retrieved from http://www.chspr.ubc.ca

Evans, R.G. (2004). Financing health care: Options, consequences, and objectives. In G.P. Marchildon, T. McIntosh, and P-G. Forest (Eds.), *The Fiscal sustainability of health care in Canada: The Romanow papers, Volume 1* (pp. 139–196). Toronto, ON: University of Toronto Press.

Evans, R.G. (2007). Economic myths and political realities: The inequality agenda and the sustainability of medicare. In B. Campbell & G. Marchildon (Eds.), *Medicare: Facts, muths, problems, promise* (pp. 113–155). Toronto, ON: James Lorimer and Company.

Evans, R.G. (2010). The "unsustainability myth": Don't believe claims medicare is becoming unaffordable. Canadian Centre for Policy Alternatives. Retrieved from http://www.policyalternatives.ca/publications/monitor/unsustainability-myth

Friends of Medicare. (2002, January 9). Real reform or road to ruin: Friends of Medicare analysis of the Premier's Health Advisory Council report. Retrieved from http://www.docstoc.com/docs/41238583/maz-fom

Frohlich, K.L., Ross N., & Richmond C. (2006). Health disparities in Canada today: some evidence and a theoretical framework. *Health Policy, 79*(2–3), 132–43. doi: 10.1016/j.healthpol.2005.12.010

Fuller, C. (1998). *Caring for profit: How corporations are taking over Canada's health care system.* Vancouver, BC: New Star Books.

Gagnon, M.A. With the assistance of G. Hébert. (2010). *The economic case for universal pharmacare: Costs and benefits of publicly funded drug coverage for all Canadians.* Canadian Centre for Policy Alternatives and Institut de recherche et d'informations socio-économiques. Retrieved from http://www.policyalternatives.ca/publications/reports/economic-case-universal-pharmacare

Galabuzi, G.E. (2004). Social exclusion. In D. Raphael (Ed.), *Social determinants of health: Canadian perspectives* (pp. 235–250). Toronto, ON: Canadian Scholars' Press.

Graefe, P., & Bourns, A. (2009). The gradual defederalization of Canadian health policy. *Publius: The journal of federalism, 39*(Winter), 187–209. doi: 10.1093/publius/pjn029

Guest, D. (1985) *The emergence of social security in Canada.* Vancouver, BC: UBC Press.

References Hankivsky, O., & Christoffersen, A. (2008). Intersectionality and the determinants of health: A Canadian perspective. *Critical Public Health, 18*(3), 271–283. doi: 10.1080/09581590802294296

Health Council of Canada. (2008a). Fixing the foundation: An update on primary health care and home care renewal in Canada. Retrieved from http://healthcouncilcanada.ca/docs/rpts/2008/phc/HCC_PHC_Main_web_E.pdf

Health Council of Canada. (2008b). Rekindling reform: Health care renewal in Canada, 2003–2008. Retrieved from http://healthcouncilcanada.ca/en/index.php?page=shop.product_details&flypage=shop.flypage&product_id=92&category_id=14&manufacturer_id=0&option=comvirtuemart&Itemid=170

Health Council of Canada. (2009). Value for money: Making Canadian health care stronger. Retrieved from http://www.healthcouncilcanada.ca/docs/rpts/2009/HCC_VFMReport_WEB.pdf

Health Council of Canada. (2010). Stepping it up: Moving the focus from health care in Canada to a healthier Canada. Retrieved from http://www.healthcouncilcanada.ca/docs/rpts/2010/promo/HealthPromo_appendicesDec2010.pdf

Health Council of Canada. (2011). Progress report 2011: Health care renewal in Canada. Retrieved from http://healthcouncilcanada.ca/en/index.php?page=shop.product_details&flypage=shop.flypage&product_id=137&category_id=16&manufacturer_id=0&option=com_virtuemart&Itemid=170

Health Disparities Task Group. (2004). *Reducing health disparities—roles of the health sector: Recommended policy directions and activities.* Federal/Provincial/Territorial Advisory Committee on Population Health and Health Security. Retrieved from http://www.phac-aspc.gc.ca/ph-sp/disparities/dr_policy-eng.php

Ife, J. (1997). *Rethinking social work.* Australia: Longman.

Kalant, N. (2005). More arithmetic of health care. *Canadian Medical Association Journal, 172*(6), 729. doi: 10.1503/cmaj.1041621

Kent. T. (2011). Health care in a renewed federalism. Ottawa, ON: Caledon Institute of Social Policy. Retrieved from http://www.caledoninst.org/Publications/PDF/932ENG.pdf

Kolkman, J.H. (2005). More arithmetic of health care. *Canadian Medical Association Journal, 172*(6), 729. doi: 10.1503/cmaj.1041622

Kronick, J. (1982). Public interest group participation in congressional hearings on nuclear power development. *Journal of Voluntary Action Research, 11,* 45–59. doi: 10.1177/089976408201100107

Laghi, B., & McCarthy, S. (2003, February 6). Premiers grumble, but PM gets deal on health. *Globe and Mail.* A1.

Landon, S., McMillan, M.L., Muralidharan, V., & Parsons, M. (2006). Does health-care spending crowd out other provincial government expenditures? *Canadian Public Policy, 32*(2), 121–141.

LeClair, M. (1975). The Canadian health care system. In A. Spyros (Ed.), *National health insurance: Can we learn from Canada*? (pp. 11–88). Malabar, FL: Krieger.

Lee, M. (2007). How sustainable is medicare? A closer look at aging, technology, and other cost drivers in Canada's health care system. Ottawa, ON: Canadian Centre for Policy Alternatives. Retrieved from http://www.policyalternatives.ca/publications/reports/how-sustainable-medicare

Leys, C. (2001). *Market-driven politics: Neo-liberal democracy and the public interest.* New York, NY: Verso.

Lightman, E., Mitchell, A., & Wilson, B. (2008). Poverty is making us sick: A comprehensive survey of income and health in Canada. Retrieved from http://wellesleyinstitute.com/files/povertyismakingussick.pdf

Mackenzie, H., & Rachlis, M. (2010). The sustainability of medicare. Ottawa, ON: Canadian Federation of Nurses Unions. Retrieved from http://www.nursesunions.ca/sites/default/files/Sustainability.web_.e.pdf

MacKinnon, J. (2004a). The arithmetic of health care. *Policy Matters, 5*(3), 1–28.

MacKinnon, J.C. (2004b) The arithmetic of health care. *Canadian Medical Association Journal, 171*(6), 603–604. doi: 10.1503/cmaj.1041224

MacKinnon, J. (2005). More arithmetic of health care. *Canadian Medical Association Journal, 172*(6), 730. doi: 10.1503/cmaj.1050015

Maioni, A. (2010). Health care funding: Needs and reality. *Policy Matters, 31*(5), 69–72.

Manga, P. (1984). Preserving Medicare: The Canada Health Act. *Perception, 70*, 12–15.

Marchildon, G.P. (2004a). The many worlds of fiscal sustainability. In G.P. Marchildon, T. McIntosh, & P-G. Forest (Eds.), *The fiscal sustainability of health care in Canada: The Romanow papers, Volume 1* (pp. 3–23). Toronto, ON: University of Toronto Press.

Marchildon, G.P. (2004b). Three choices for the future of Medicare. Ottawa, ON: Caledon Institute of Social Policy. Retrieved from http://www.caledoninst.org/Publications/PDF/466ENG.pdf

McMurtry, R.J. (2005). More arithmetic of health care. *Canadian Medical Association Journal, 172*(6), 730.

Mendelsohn, M., Hjartarson, J., & Pearce, J. (2010). Saving dollars and making sense: An agenda for a more efficient, effective, and accountable federation. Toronto, ON: Mowat Centre and School of Public Policy and Governance. University of Toronto.

Mikkonen, J., & Raphael, D. (2010). Social determinants of health: The Canadian facts. Toronto, ON: York University School of Health Policy and Management.

Mowat Centre. (2010). Shifting gears: Paths to fiscal sustainability in Canada. Toronto, ON: School of Public Policy and Governance, University of Toronto.

Murnighan, B. (2001). Selling Ontario's health care: The real story on government spending and public relations. Ontario Alternative Budget. Canadian Centre for Policy Alternatives. Retrieved from http://www.policyalternatives.ca/publications/reports/selling-ontarios-health-care

National Council of Welfare. (1987). *Welfare in Canada: The Tangled Safety Net.* Ottawa, ON: Supply and Services Canada.

National Council of Welfare. (1982). *Medicare: The public good and private practice.* Ottawa, ON: Supply and Services Canada.

National Forum on Health. (1997). Canada health action: Building on the legacy (Vol. 1: The final report of the National Forum on Health). Ottawa, ON: Minister of Public Works and Government Services.

Naylor, D.C. (1986). *Private practice, public payment: Canadian medicine and the politics of health insurance, 1911–1966.* Montreal, QC, and Kingston, ON: McGill-Queen's University Press.

References OECD (2010a). OECD Health Data 2010. Retrieved from http://www.oecd.org/document/56/0,3746,en_2649_34631_12968734_1_1_1_1,00.html

OECD (2010b). OECD Economic Surveys: Canada 2010. Retrieved from http://www.oecd.org/document/6/0,3746,en_2649_34569_45925432_1_1_1_1,00.html.

OECD (2011). Society at a glance 2011: OECD social indicators. Retrieved from http://www.oecd.org/searchResult/0,3400,en_2649_34569_1_1_1_1_1,00.html

Offe, C. (Ed.). (1984). *Contradictions of the welfare state.* Cambridge, MA: MIT Press.

Ontario. (1995). *1995* fiscal and economic statement. Toronto, ON: Queen's Printer for Ontario.

Osberg, L. (1996). The equity, efficiency and symbolism of national standards in an era of provincialism. Ottawa, ON: Caledon Institute of Social Policy.

PovNet. (1999). Social union framework heartless say social justice groups. PovNet social union press release and backgrounder. 4 February. Retrieved from http://www.povnet.web.net/socialunion.html

Raphael, D. (2004). Introduction to the social determinants of health. In D. Raphael (Ed.), *Social determinants of health: Canadian perspectives* (pp. 1–18). Toronto, ON: Canadian Scholars' Press.

Raphael, D. (2008). Grasping at straws: A recent history of health promotion in Canada. *Critical Public Health, 18*(4), 483–495. doi: 10.1080/09581590802443604

Romanow, R. (2004, September 13). Scrutiny is the best medicine. *Globe and Mail.* A15.

Rovere, M. (2011). Canada's health spending crisis. *Fraser Forum,* (May/June), 27–30. Retrieved from http://www.fraserinstitute.org/publicationdisplay.aspx?id=17532&terms=Canada%E2%80%99s+health+spending+crisis

Rovere, M., & Skinner, B.J. (2010). Health care at a crossroads. Will Ontario taxpayers continue to pay more and get less? Fraser Forum (February), 10–11. Retrieved from http://www.fraserinstitute.org/publicationdisplay .aspx?id=10758&terms=Health+care+at+a+crossroads

Silver, S. (1993). Universal health care: The Canadian definition. (PhD dissertation). Philadelphia, PA: Bryn Mawr College.

Silver, S. (1996). The struggle for national standards: Lessons from the federal role in health care. In J. Pulkingham & G. Ternowetsky (Eds.), *Remaking Canadian social policy: Social security in the late 1990s* (pp. 67–80). Halifax, NS: Fernwood Publishing.

Skinner, B.J., & Rovere, M. (2008). An unsustainable system. Fraser Forum (February), 30–32. Retrieved from http://www.fraserinstitute.org/publicationdisplay.aspx?id=10484&terms=An+unsustainable+

Skinner, B.J., & Rovere, M. (2011). Canada's medicare bubble: Is government health spending sustainable without user-based funding? Fraser Institute. Studies in health care policy. Retrieved from http://www.fraserinstitute.org/publicationdisplay.aspx?id=17414&terms=Canada%E2%80%99s+medicare+bubble

Stanford, J. (2010, December 8). To manage health costs, invest in social well-being. *Globe and Mail,* A23.

Taylor, M. (1987). *Health insurance and Canadian public policy: The seven decisions that created the Canadian health insurance system.* Montreal, QC, and Kingston, ON: McGill-Queen's University Press.

Tholl, W.G. (1994). Health care spending in Canada: Skating faster on thinner ice. In J. Blomqvist & D.M. Brown (Eds.), *Limits to care: Reforming Canada's health system in an age of restraint* (pp. 53–89). Toronto, ON: C.D. Howe Institute.

Titmuss, R. (1968). *Commitment to welfare*. London, UK: George Allen and Unwin.

Titmuss, R. (1974). *Social policy*. London, UK: George Allen and Unwin.

Tuohy, C. (1993). Social policy: Two worlds. In M. Atkinson (Ed.), *Governing Canada: Institutions and Public Policy* (pp. 275–305). Toronto, ON: Harcourt Brace Jovanovich.

Tuohy, C.H., Flood, C.M., & Stabile, M. (2001). How does private finance affect public health care systems? Marshalling evidence from OECD nations. Working paper. Retrieved from http://papers.ssrn.com/sol3/papers.cfm?abstract_id=1146608

Van Loon, R.J. (1978). From shared cost to block funding and beyond: The politics of health insurance in Canada. *Journal of Health Politics, Policy and Law, 2*(Winter), 454–478. doi: 10.1215/03616878-2-4-454

Van Loon, R., & Whittington, M. (1971). *The Canadian political system*. Toronto, ON: McGraw-Hill.

Walkom, T. (1999, February 9). Social union deal a step backward for Canadians. *Toronto Star*, A2.

Wilkins, R., Tjepkema, M., Mustard, C., & Choiniere, R. (2008). The Canadian census mortality follow-up study, 1991 through 2001. *Health Reports, 19*(3), 25–43.

World Health Organization (WHO). (2008). Closing the gap in a generation: Health equity through action on the social determinants of health. Final report of the Commission on Social Determinants. Geneva, Switzerland. Retrieved from http://www.who.int/social_determinants/thecommission/finalreport/en/index.html

Yalnizyan, A. (2004). Can we afford to sustain medicare? A strong role for federal government. Retrieved from http://www.policyalternatives.ca/publications/reports/can-we-afford-sustain-medicare-strong-role-federal-government

Additional Resources

Canadian Association for Community Care http://www.cacc-acssc.com/page2.html
Canadian Centre for Policy Alternatives http://www.policyalternatives.ca
Canadian Council on Social Development http://www.ccsd.ca
Canadian Health Coalition http://www.healthcoalition.ca
Canadian Home Care Association http://www.cdnhomecare.on.ca/e-index.htm
Canadian Institute for Health Information http://www.cihi.ca
Canadian Public Health Association http://www.cpha.ca/english/index.htm
Centre for the Study of Living Standards http://www.csls.ca
Health Action Lobby (HEAL) http://www.cna-nurses.ca/heal/healframe.htm
Health Canada http://www.hc-sc.gc.ca/english/
Tommy Douglas Research Institute http://www.tommydouglas.ca
World Health Organization http://www.who.int/home-page

Badgely, R., & Wolfe, S. (1967). *Doctor's strike*. Toronto, ON: Macmillan of Canada.

Begin, M. (1988). *Medicare: Canada's right to health*. Ottawa, ON: Optimum.

Evans, R., & Stoddart, G. (Ed.). (1986). *Medicare at maturity*. Calgary, AB: University of Calgary Press.

Additional Resources

Hall, E.M. (1980). Canada's national-provincial Health Insurance Program for the 1980s: A commitment for renewal. Ottawa, ON: Department of National Health and Welfare.

Lalonde, M. (1974). A new perspective on the health of Canadians. Ottawa, ON: Supplies and Services. National Council of Welfare. Retrieved from http://www.ncwcnbes.net.

National Council of Welfare. (1990). Health, health care, and Medicare. Ottawa, ON: Supply and Services.

Looking to the Future

Part IV

Social Service Workplaces

Reform Begins at Home

20

Anne Westhues

In the introduction to Chapter 1, I said that "social workers have a responsibility, as reflected in the Canadian Association of Social Workers *Code of Ethics* (2005), to advocate for social policies that 'uphold the right of people to have access to resources to meet basic human needs; that ensure fair and equitable access to public services and benefits; for equal treatment and protection under the law; to challenge injustices, especially those affecting the vulnerable and disadvantaged; and to promote social development and environmental management in the interests of all people' (CASW, 2005, p. 5)." Kaminski and Walmsley (1995) have argued that a commitment to advocacy is one attribute that may differentiate social work from other helping professions. In this final chapter I review what is meant by advocacy and discuss how professional associations may advocate for changes that promote greater access to social services for the most vulnerable Canadians.

Advocacy

The federal Voluntary Sector Task Force (Rektor, 2002, p. 1) defined advocacy as "the act of speaking or of disseminating information intended to influence individual behaviour or opinion, corporate conduct or public policy and law." Schneider and Lester (2001, p. 65), after a review of more than ninety definitions, proposed the following definition: "Social work advocacy is the exclusive and mutual representation of a client(s) or cause in a forum, attempting to systematically influence decision making in an unjust or unresponsive system(s)."

Advocacy in pursuit of policy changes on behalf of a specific client or individual is commonly called case advocacy. Case advocacy usually pursues a decision to allow a one-time exception to current policy. It may lead to cause advocacy, in which change is sought in operational, program, legislative, or strategic policy.

Cause advocacy addresses a "single issue, condition or problem that a number of people are interested in and support" (Schneider & Lester, 2001, p. 66). A distinction is sometimes made between cause advocacy that focuses on change within a single organization, and change that is intended to affect an entire service delivery system. Cause advocacy pursues change that will affect *all* the people using a service at a specific location (organization)—for example, all children at a particular elementary school, or all people using a particular counselling agency. It may also yield legislative or regulatory change that affects all people with a specific need within a defined jurisdiction—for example, all university students seeking financial assistance in Ontario, or all people seeking Employment Insurance benefits in Canada.

Following their exhaustive review of the literature, Schneider and Lester (2001, p. 59) argue that there are eleven dimensions of advocacy: pleading or speaking on behalf of; representing another; taking action; promoting change; accessing rights and benefits; serving as a partisan; demonstrating influence and political skills; securing social justice; empowering clients; identifying with the client; and using a legal basis. These descriptors are not mutually exclusive approaches to advocacy; two or more are often combined in any advocacy initiative. The dimensions are each decribed briefly below.

Pleading or speaking on behalf of means championing a case or a cause. Representing is more specific, referring to representation of an individual or group before decision-making authorities in social services, the courts, or other organizations that affect their well-being. Taking action means doing something to effect change; it is not enough to reflect on an issue and to be a silent supporter. The action may be case or cause oriented. Promoting change is about advocating for modifications to current policies that are understood to be in the best interests of a group, and so is cause-oriented. Acessing rights and benefits is about helping people obtain the services or opportunities to which they are entitled by current policy but which may have been denied. This type of advocacy is therefore case-based, but decisions may be made that result in policy change that then benefits others in similar circumstances. Serving as a partisan means taking a stand that is not neutral but that deliberately favours greater equity or social justice for a marginalized group. It carries the same meaning as Anne Bishop's (2002) "ally." Demonstrating influence and political skill addresses the need to understand the decision-making structures that must be engaged to effect change, and how to gain their attention. This aspect of advocacy is equally pertinent with case and cause advocacy. Securing social justice may be case or cause oriented and addresses issues of fairness in the distribution of resources and access to services. Empowerment is understood to be a benefit of advocacy that may accrue to individuals and to marginalized groups. Schneider and Lester (p. 63) tell us that for some people writing about advocacy, this intangible benefit is even more important that accessing rights or resources that have been withheld. Identifying with the client requires moving beyond partisanship to trying to understand the day-to-day experience of the individual who is being supported through advocacy. Finally, using a legal basis means utilizing legal structures such as the courts and quasi-legal appeal boards or tribunals (such as the Human Rights tribunal that Mullings critiques in Chapter 6) to effect change for individuals or groups.

Schneider and Lester (2001) distinguish advocacy from brokering, social reform, and social action. The broker's role is to facilitate a linkage with resources, not to make a case for access to them when it is not allowed by current policy. Social reformers focus solely on structural issues such as safer work conditions or creating equitable access to higher education for youth from all class backgrounds. Social work advocates may address these issues but will have identified them through their work with individual clients rather than through a commitment to an abstract value set or ideology. Schneider and Lester see advocacy as a specific form of socal action, once again emphasizing the centrality of representing a client or clients—a motivator that is not always present in social action.

Strategizing Advocacy

As discussed in Chapter 2, policy may be made at the international, federal, provincial, local, and organizational scales. Its purpose may be strategic (creating a vision and providing direction to policy developments), legislative (defining rights and eligibility for services), program (defining the expected goals and outcomes of a program), or operational (directives with respect to day-to-day operations of a program). Advocacy efforts may be directed to effect change at any of these scales/levels or purposes/domains. While social work advocacy is motivated by a concern about an individual service user, it may evolve into action that yields progressive change beyond a particular workplace or individual. The scale/level or purpose/domain that are the focus of change should be selected after systematic analysis of the issue and after setting clear goals about the desired change (Schneider & Lester, 2001; Kettner, Moroney, & Martin, 2008), as outlined in Chapter 3.

Kaminski and Walmsley (1995) also advise making an analysis of who is likely to support a proposed change and who is likely to oppose it. They recommend differentiating among the opponents, identifying those who are likely to be won over with collaborative strategies, those who may need the additional convincing of a campaign strategy, and those who are likely to engage in contest strategies, actively opposing the proposed change. Tactics associated with a collaborative strategy include conducting needs assessments and policy analyses about the issue, developing fact sheets and alternative proposals, creating task forces, conducting workshops, and maintaining onging communication with the opposition (Schneider & Lester, p. 129). Tactics associated with a campaign strategy include lobbying of decision makers, educating the public, engaging the media, launching letter-writing campaigns, and communicating with allies of the opposition (Schneider & Lester, p. 129). For a conflict strategy, the tactics escalate to include utilization of a negotiator or mediator; organizing demonstrations; coordinating boycotts, picket lines, strikes, and petitions; organizing civil disobedience and passive resistance; and arranging a media exposé (Schneider & Lester, p. 129).

Working with the Professional Associations

Saul Alinsky remains a legend as a community organizer and advocate for poor people. His *Reveille for Radicals* and *Rules for Radicals* continue to inspire advocates by setting out principles for confrontational but non-violent advocacy. His tactics focused on mobilizing large groups of people outside the system to draw attention to social injustices. Demonstrators at international meetings such as the G20 or the WTO tend to follow his principles in their fight against neoliberalism and economic globalization. The tactics of those working within the system, or through professional associations, tend to be more collaborative than confrontational.

Tactics utilized with case advocacy might include meeting with supervisors or managers, or holding a case conference with all the service providers for a particular service user. These actions might escalate to a letter-writing campaign, advertising through the media, or meeting with elected officials, but this would be uncommon for case advocacy.

Policy analysis can be an effective tactic when organizational, legislative, or regulatory change is sought. Allies may be sought among front line peers and among managers. In the case of voluntary organizations, board members may also be lobbied for support; and in the case of public sector organizations, support may be sought from elected officials. If a Consumer Advisory Committee exists, it may initiate many changes, or it may be engaged to support changes proposed by staff. Collaboration with advocacy groups outside the organization is a possible tactic if movement toward change is slow, or resisted, within the organization. Engagement with such groups needs to be carefully considered, however. Some organizations allow this level of politicization, while in others it will be discouraged or even lead to dismissal.

Working with the Professional Associations

The Canadian Association of Social Workers (CASW) was founded in 1926 (Foley, 2002). Nine provincial and one territorial association are affiliated with the national association. CASW's simply stated mission statement reflects a commitment to both the professional and the progressive perspectives: "CASW promotes the profession of social work in Canada and advances social justice (CASW 2010). The association's objects include the advancement of social justice, strengthening and promoting the social work profession, and supporting the regulatory and non-regulatory work of member organizations.

A review of the CASW website shows it to be engaged primarily in collaborative initiatives on social policy issues. It indicates that CASW holds membership in twenty-five national coalitions, which address issues ranging from women's rights to eradication of poverty, the rights of people with mental health issues, LGBT rights, and end-of-life care. These coalitions, and their respective mandates, are listed at the end of the chapter under Additional

Resources. Their websites are useful resources for becoming familiar with an issue, and for staying informed about what is happening with respect to advocacy and policy change.

Working with the Professional Associations

Also, a professional association exists in each province, and a northern association serves the three territories. While much of the advocacy of the provincial/territorial associations focuses on raising the profession's profile and advancing its interests, they also engage in cause advocacy. A review of these associations' websites shows that they are currently engaged in advocacy pertaining to the eradication of poverty, residential care for older adults, children's rights, equitable access to services for Aboriginal people, child protection, the adequacy of social assistance and employment insurance, and the retention of a universal health care program. The links for the provincial associations are provided under Additional Resources at the end of the chapter.

CASW Social Policy Principles

As part of its commitment to become more engaged in advocacy, in 2003 CASW selected the following principles to guide its analyses of federal social policy initiatives. This in turn may help stimulate the generation of policy alternatives.

Dignity and respect. Each individual has a right to self-fulfillment to the extent that the rights do not encroach on the right of others. To that end, social policy measures should intrude as little as possible on the choices that individuals make to realize their own personal life goals.

Equality. Because of the intrinsic worth of every human being, each person will be treated equally without unfair discrimination on the basis of disability, colour, social class, race, religion, language, political beliefs, sex, or sexual orientation.

Equity. Individuals and families are to be treated equally if they are in like circumstances; social inequalities are considered just to the extent that they result in compensating benefits for the least advantaged person in society.

Comprehensiveness. All persons in Canada are entitled to educational, health, and social services and social security on uniform terms and conditions in a manner that ensures a range of choice and that maximizes respect for the individual.

Quality services. Services are to be based on best practices and a participatory approach to their administration and improvement.

Constitutional integrity. Social programs are to be financed, regulated, and provided with full regard to the jurisdictional responsibility and competence of each level of government.

Subsidiarity. Social programs are to be provided at the lowest level of community possible unless it can be shown that they can be more effectively provided by higher levels of government.

Additional Resources

Social dialogue. Governments should take all necessary steps to encourage and facilitate extensive consultation with relative social partners in the development of social policies and programs.

Conclusion

The concluding statement of the CASW Social Policy Principles seems a fitting end to this chapter and to this book: "I am only one, but still I am one. I cannot do everything, but still I can do something. And because I cannot do everything I will not refuse to do the something that I can do."

References

Alinsky, S. (1969). *Reveille for radicals.* Chicago, IL: University of Chicago Press.

Alinsky, S. (1971). *Rules for radicals.* New York, NY: Random House.

Bishop. A. (2002). *Becoming an ally: Breaking the cycle of oppression* (2nd ed.). Halifax, NS: Fernwood Publishing.

Canadian Association of Social Workers. (2010). Mission Statement. Retrieved from http://www.casw-acts.ca/en/about-casw

Foley, J.M. (2002). Professional associations in Canada. In F.J. Turner (Ed.), *Social work practice: A Canadian perspective* (pp. 315–329). Toronto, ON: Prentice Hall.

Kaminski, L., & Walmsley, C. (1995). The advocacy brief: A guide for social workers. *The Social Worker, 63,* 53–58.

Kettner, P., Moroney, R., & Martin, L. (2008). *Designing and managing programs: An effectiveness-based approach* (3rd ed.). Thousand Oaks, CA: Sage Publications.

Rektor, L. (2002). Advocacy: The sound of citizens' voices. Ottawa, ON: Voluntary Sector Initiative Secretariat. Retrieved from http://www.vsi-isbc.org/eng/policy/position_paper.cfm

Schneider, R.L., & Lester, L. (2001). *Social work advocacy.* Belmont, CA: Brookes/Cole.

Additional Resources

Professional Associations

Alberta College of Social Workers http://www.acsw.ab.ca

British Columbia Association of Social Workers http://www.bcasw.org/content/home.asp

Manitoba Institute of Registered Social Workers http://www.mirsw.mb.ca/main/about.htm

New Brunswick Association of Social Workers http://www.nbasw-atsnb.ca/home.php?lang=en

Newfoundland and Labrador Association of Social Workers http://www.nlasw.ca

Nova Scotia Association of Social Workers http://nsasw.org

Ontario Association of Social Workers http://oasw.org

Ordre des travailleurs sociaux et des therapeutes conjugaux et familiaux du Quebec http://www.optsq.org/fr/index.cfm?month=08-18-2011&suiv=01-01-2011

Prince Edward Island http://socialworkpei.ca/index.html

Saskatchewan Association of Social Workers http://www.sasw.ca/home.html
Association of Social Workers in Northern Canada http://www.socialworknorth.com

Advocacy Coalitions

Ad Hoc Coalition for Women's Equality and Human Rights http://www.womensequality.ca/index.html
The Ad Hoc Coalition for Women's Equality and Human Rights came together in 2006 to pressure the federal government and the opposition to commit to concrete and meaningful measures to advance women's equality in Canada.

Adoption Council of Canada (ACC) http://www.adoption.ca
The Adoption Council of Canada (ACC) is the umbrella organization for adoption in Canada. The ACC raises public awareness of adoption, promotes placement of waiting children, and stresses the importance of post-adoption services.

Campaign 2000 http://www.campaign2000.ca
Campaign 2000 is a non-partisan coalition of 19 national partners and a Canada-wide network of 33 community partners who are committed to securing the implementation of the 1989 federal all-party resolution "to seek to achieve the goal of eliminating poverty among Canadian children by the year 2000."

Canadian AIDS Treatment Information Exchange (CATIE) http://www.catie.ca
CATIE is a national, not-for-profit charity committed to improving the health and quality of life of all people living with HIV/AIDS in Canada by providing accessible, accurate, unbiased and timely treatment information to people living with HIV/AIDS and their caregiver, health care providers, and service organizations.

Canadian Alliance on Mental Illness and Mental Health http://www.camimh.ca
The Canadian Alliance on Mental Illness and Mental Health (CAMIMH), created in October 1998, calls for significantly increased attention to mental illness and mental health promotion at all levels of Canadian society and aims to put mental illness and mental health on the national health and social policy agendas.

The fifteen member organizations of the Canadian Alliance on Mental Illness and Mental Health (CAMIMH) represent all elements of the mental health continuum. Consumers and their families, researchers, and all manner of practitioners, including physicians, psychologists, and psychiatric nurses, are supporters of the alliance and its messages. Together, these organizations constitute a vibrant network of national, provincial, and local organizations that stretch from coast to coast.

Canadian Centre for Policy Alternatives http://www.policyalternatives.ca
The Canadian Centre for Policy Alternatives is a national, independent, non-partisan research institute concerned with local, national and international issues of social and economic justice. Founded in 1980, the CCPA is one of Canada's leading progressive voices in public policy debates.

The centre offers analysis and policy ideas to the media, the general public, social justice and labour organizations, academia, and government. The CCPA produces research studies, policy briefs, books, editorials and commentary, and other publications.

Additional Resources

Canadian Coalition for the Rights of Children http://www.rightsofchildren.ca
The Canadian Coalition for the Rights of Children (CCRC) brings together Canadian organizations and individuals who are concerned about the rights of children. The Convention on the Rights of the Child (CRC) is the guiding framework for all activities of the coalition.

Canadian Coalition for Seniors' Mental Health http://www.ccsmh.ca
Prompted by concern about inadequate services for the residents of long-term care facilities, a national symposium was held in April 28, 2002, with the goal of "improving the mental health of the elderly in long term care through education, advocacy and collaboration." A coalition was formed for the purpose of improving the mental health of seniors through a coordinated national strategy. The coalition's first priority is to focus on the unmet needs of seniors living in long-term care facilities.

Canadian Council on Social Development http://www.ccsd.ca
The mission of CCSD, a non-profit, non-governmental organization, is to develop and promote social policies that are inspired by social justice and equality. CCSD meets its mission through research, consultation, public education, and advocacy. Poverty, social inclusion, disability, cultural diversity, child well-being, employment, and housing are some of the issues that CCSD focuses on.

Canadian Mental Health Support Network http://www.cma.ca/cmhsn
CASW joined eleven organizations in the health care community to create the Canadian Mental Health Support Network (CMHSN). CMHSN came into being from a concern about the impact on Canadians of the tragic events that occurred in the USA September 11, 2001. Their Website contains resources for professionals and the public. A working group continues to meet and develop further resources for parents, caregivers and professionals.

Canadian Public Health Association—National Literacy and Health Program http://www.cpha.ca
The CPHA's National Literacy and Health Program promotes awareness among health professionals of the links between literacy and health. People with low literacy skills may not understand what health professionals tell them. They may not be able to read health information. Some may not use health services, except in an emergency. The National Literacy and Health Program is working in partnership with national health associations to raise awareness about literacy and health.

Child Care Advocacy Association of Canada (CCAAC) http://www.ccaac.ca/home.php
The Child Care Advocacy Association of Canada (CCAAC) is dedicated to promoting a publicly funded, inclusive, quality, not-for-profit child care system.

Coalition on Community Safety, Health and Well-being
The Coalition on Community Safety, Health, and Well-Being will seek broad support for crime prevention through social development as an approach to ensuring safe, healthy communities.

Dignity for All: The Campaign for a Poverty-Free Canada http://www.dignityforall.ca/en
The Dignity for All Campaign calls for vigorous and sustained action by the federal government to combat the structural causes of poverty in Canada.

The coalition, led by Canada Without Poverty and Citizens for Public Justice, is joined by diverse partners in mobilizing the multiyear, multipartner, non-partisan campaign, Dignity for All: The Campaign for a Poverty-Free Canada.

EGALE Canada http://www.egale.ca

EGALE advances equality and justice for lesbian, gay, bisexual, and transgendered people and their families across Canada.

G7 (Group of 7 Health Professions)

G7 is a group of national health care professional associations who formed a partnership to work collaboratively on health initiatives with a view to broadening policy initiatives beyond traditional health care providers. Along with the CASW, members of the G7 include the Canadian Association of Speech Language Pathologists and Audiologists, Canadian Pharmacists Association, Canadian Occupational Therapy Association, Canadian Psychologists Association, Canadian Physiotherapy Association, and Dietitians of Canada.

Health Action Lobby http://www.healthactionlobby.ca

The Health Action Lobby (HEAL) is concerned about the direction and sustainability of the health care system and public policy in Canada. It is seeking to understand better the potential impact that changes to intergovernmental transfers will have on the health care delivery system, health insurance programs, and the health of Canadians.

Mental Health Table for Regulated Health Professionals

The Mental Health Table for Regulated Health Professionals is a grouping of national health professional organizations for the purpose of identifying problems common to health professional communities, undertaking actions on key strategies to transform mental health care delivery, and responding collectively to and working collaboratively with the Mental Health Commission of Canada.

National Alliance for Children and Youth http://www.nationalchildrensalliance.com

The Children's Alliance provides a forum for a group of national organizations with an interest in the well-being of children. The group aims to work cooperatively to devise strategies to promote a national children;s agenda, and to respond to concerns and issues affecting children and their families.

National Coalition on Housing and Homelessness http://www.povnet.org

The mission of the National Coalition on Housing and Homelessness is to support a new dedicated federal social housing program. This mission is based on the belief that it is time for the federal government to take action to deliver housing that low income Canadians can afford.

National Initiative for the Care of the Elderly (NICE) http://www.nicenet.ca

NICE is a national network of researchers and practitioners involved in the care of older adults that is mandated to disseminate research and best practice knowledge among interdisciplinary practitioners and academia regarding the care to the elderly.

Promoting Relationships and Eliminating Violence Network (PREVNET) http://www.prevnet.ca

PREVNET is a national partnership of university researchers and national non-governmental organizations that is mandated to create sociocultural change in Canada by reducing the negative use of power and aggression in relationships.

PREVNET is interested in creating a national strategy to address bullying problems and promote healthy relationships among children.

Quality End-of-Life Care Coalition

The Quality End-of-Life Care Coalition supports implementation of the June 2000 Senate report *Quality End-of-Life Care: The Right of Every Canadian*. The coalition represents a broad cross-section of stakeholders who wish to be part of the process of creating a national strategy for end-of-life care and who have a great deal to contribute on behalf of the millions of Canadians they represent.

The Canadian Hospice Palliative Care Association has been designated as its secretariat.

Contact person: Sharon Baxter, e-mail: sbaxter@scohs.on.ca

Repeal 43 Committee http://www.repeal43.org/index.html

The Repeal 43 Committee is a national, voluntary committee formed in 1994 to advocate repeal of Section 43 of the Criminal Code of Canada, which is a defence to assault that justifies violence against children by teachers and parents in the name of correction.

Contributors

Mike Burke is an Associate Professor in the Department of Politics and School of Public Administration at Ryerson University, where he teaches research methods and Canadian politics. His research interests and publications are in the areas of Canadian health care policy, labour market inequality, welfare state development, trade unions, and conflict and peace in Ireland.

Marilyn Callahan is Professor Emerita in the School of Social Work at the University of Victoria. She has an abiding interest in how child welfare discourses and services affect the lives of children, their mothers, and families, and has published widely in this area. Her most recent book, with Karen Swift, is *At Risk: Social Justice in Child Welfare and Other Human Services.*

Peter A. Dunn is an associate professor in the Faculty of Social Work at Wilfrid Laurier University. He has been involved in disability research dealing with barrier-free housing, issues confronting seniors with disabilities, the development of government independent living policies, the impact of independent living and resource centres, and the empowerment of adults with developmental disabilities. More recently he undertook a national survey related to disability policies and practices of Canadian Schools of Social Work with the Disability Caucus of the Canadian Association of Schools of Social Work. At present, Dr. Dunn is coordinating the quantitative component of a CURA-funded project related to the social exclusion of lone mothers in Canada.

Patricia M. Evans is a Professor Emerita from the School of Social Work, Carleton University. Her research and writing explores the ways that social policies reflect, reinforce, and redress inequalities, such as those arising from a gendered division of labour. Income security programs that have specific impacts on women's paid and unpaid work (such as workfare and parental benefits) are an important focus of her work.

Judy Finlay is Associate Professor, School of Child and Youth Care at Ryerson University. She is also Co-chair and a founding member of Mamow

Sha-way-gi-kay-win: North-South Partnership for Children. Judy is the former Child Advocate for the Province of Ontario (1991–2007). She has worked for more than three decades in the fields of child welfare and children's mental health. She began her career as a group home operator with a children's aid society, was a co-founder of the Women's Community House in London, Ontario, was a member of a crisis unit with a community police force, the Clinical Director for a regional children's mental health centre in Northern Ontario, and an Executive Director for an inpatient/outpatient children's mental health centre in eastern Ontario. Her current research interests include the social determinants of health in remote northern First Nations communities, kids crossing from care to custody, and the role of youth engagement and citizenship.

Usha George is a Professor and Dean of Ryerson University's Faculty of Community Services. Her scholarship focuses on social work with diverse communities, and her research interests are in the areas of newcomer settlement and adaptation, organization and delivery of settlement services, and community work with marginalized communities. She has completed research projects on the settlement and adaptation issues of various immigrant communities in Ontario. Her interests also include international social work, and she is currently involved in research projects in India.

Jill G. Grant is Assistant Professor in the School of Social Work at the University of Windsor, where she teaches and conducts research in the areas of mental health services, generalist practice, and relationships between service users and service providers. After working in supportive housing with individuals with mental health issues and with women leaving prison, she developed a particular interest in increasing the possibility for everyone to have a home.

Garson Hunter is an Associate Professor of Social Work at the University of Regina. He has taught courses in direct social work practice, social policy, research methods, and field education, and has published on welfare and child poverty. Currently he is researching with intravenous drug users around issues of poverty and harm reduction strategies.

Carol Kenny-Scherber is a Senior Policy Adviser with the Ontario government who has worked in five different ministries during the twenty-seven years of her social work career. The focus of most of her work has been on education, training, and employment policy.

Iara Lessa is an Associate Professor at the Ryerson University School of Social Work. Her research interests are broadly focused on social policy, gender, and immigration. In the past, her research activities have explored the effects of contemporary Canadian policy on the lives and situations of certain groups such as immigrants and single mothers. She is currently participating in the development of various activities and tools to increase gender equity in Brazil's programs addressing occupational health and safety and food security.

Delores V. Mullings is an Associate Professor at Memorial University of Newfoundland and Labrador in the Faculty of Social Work. Her research interests and writing currently focus on older immigrants, foster mothering, and issues of race and racism in Canadian social policy.

Tonya Munro is a doctoral student in Social Work at the University of Windsor. She currently teaches at the undergraduate level in the area of social welfare and social policy. Her research interests include the following: leadership in social work, discourse analysis as a practice intervention (especially in supervision), the social construction of mental illness and its social impacts, supported housing, and the strengths and needs of adults with autism and their families.

Geoffrey Nelson, a community psychologist, is Professor of Psychology at Wilfrid Laurier University. He served as the senior editor of *Canadian Journal of Community Mental Health.* Together with the Canadian Mental Health Association–Waterloo Region Branch, he received the Harry V. McNeill Award for Innovation in Community Mental Health from the American Psychological Foundation in 1999.

Sheila Neysmith is a Professor in the Faculty of Social Work, University of Toronto. She is known internationally for her research and writing on social policy issues important to women, in particular how home care services, unpaid work, and caring labour affect the quality of women's lives as they age. She is co-editor of *Women's Caring: Feminist Perspectives on Social Welfare,* 2nd ed. (Oxford UP, 1998); editor of *Critical Issues for Future Social Work Practice with Aging Persons* (Columbia UP, 1999); and *Restructuring Caring Labour: Discourse, State Practice, and Everyday Life* (Oxford UP, 2000). Her most recent books are *Telling Tales: Living the Effects of Public Policy* (Fernwood, 2005), co-authored with Bezanson and O'Connell, and *Beyond Caring Labour to Provisioning Work* (U of Toronto P, 2012), co-authored with Reitsma-Street, Porter, and Baker Collins.

Brian O'Neill obtained his MSW from Carleton University in 1971, and subsequently worked in child welfare management in Toronto until 1988. He received his PhD from Wilfrid Laurier University in 1994, after conducting a study of Canadian social work education from the standpoint of gay men. He is currently an Associate Professor at the University of British Columbia School of Social Work and Family Studies in Vancouver, where he teaches interprofessional practice in relation to HIV/AIDS, research design, and social service management. His current research focuses primarily on issues in social service policy and management for gay men and lesbians.

Malcolm A. Saulis was born on the Tobique Indian reserve. He is a Malicite Indian of the Negoot-gook tribe. He was educated at St. Thomas University in Fredericton, New Brunswick, where he received a BA Honours degree in Psychology. He went on to get an MSW at Wilfrid Laurier University. He sought guidance from his elders to determine where he should put his efforts to better the reality of First Nations peoples, and was told to work in making communities better places to live. He subsequently dedicated his life to making the reality of First Nations better, primarily through community-based university educational processes. He has helped communities develop programs, services, and institutions in health, child welfare, restorative justice, education, and social policy. He has consulted with government departments on various social development areas. He is a trained Traditional Circle keeper and works extensively in holistic healing processes.

Susan Silver is an Associate Professor in the School of Social Work at Ryerson University. She teaches courses on research methods, program evaluation, social welfare policy, and critical social work practice. She has conducted a number of research studies exploring issues of access and inclusion in relation to health care, employment, and income security. Her current interests and projects include critical spatiality and transformative pedagogy.

Karen Swift is a Professor in the School of Social Work at York University. She is the author of *Manufacturing "Bad Mothers": A Critical Perspective on Child Neglect*, and co-author of *At Risk: Social Justice in Child Welfare and Other Human Services*. She has also written numerous articles and book chapters on child welfare issues, especially as they relate to women. She also publishes on issues of social policy related to the effects of globalizing economies on the work of women. Her current research project, funded by the Social Sciences and Humanities Research Council, focuses on risk and risk assessment in child welfare.

Yves Vaillancourt is adjunct professor in the School of Social Work of the Université du Québec à Montreal, where he is a member of LAREPPS (Laboratoire de recherche sur les pratiques et les politiques sociales), a research unit studying social policy and social practices, and of CRISES, a research centre on social innovations. The founding editor of *Nouvelles pratiques sociales*, Vaillancourt has written extensively in the area of social policy and social economy. He has worked on the history of Canadian social policy, federal–provincial relations, home care services, social housing, and services for elderly and handicapped persons. He is a member of CURA (Community University Research Alliance), managed by the Council of Canadians with Disabilities and working on the theme "Disabling Poverty and Enabling Citizenship." He is active in the GESQ (Groupe d'économie solidaire au Québec), working to bridge with Latin American Social and Solidarity Economic networks.

Fay Weller worked at a senior level in government for over ten years and is currently a PhD candidate at the University of Victoria as well as a community activist on Gabriola Island. Her research interests include social change, climate change, community governance, and alternatives to current economic systems. Her publications have focused on contradictions in the child welfare system, community governance, and alternative community spaces.

Anne Westhues is a Professor in the Faculty of Social Work at Wilfrid Laurier University, where she taught research, social policy, and community practice. Her research interests include evaluation of policy and practice, social and strategic planning, and evidence-based practice. Her publications include articles on adoption (international adoption, disclosure, disruption, and reunions), family violence (elder abuse and prevention of wife assault), and planning (conceptualizations of social planning, human resources study of the profession of social work).

Brian Wharf was Professor Emeritus at the University of Victoria. During his career at this university, he was Director of the School of Social Work, Dean of the Faculty of Human and Social Development, Professor in the Graduate Multidisciplinary Program focused on connecting policy and practice, and Acting Director of the School of Public Administration. His research interests focused on connecting policy with practice and on community and child welfare. This focus is reflected in two recent books: *Community Work Approaches to Child Welfare* (Broadview Press, 2002), and *Connecting Policy and Practice*, 3rd ed. (Oxford UP, 2010), with Brad McKenzie.

Joan Wharf Higgins is a Professor in the School of Exercise Science, Physical & Health Education and a Canada Research Chair in Health and Society at the University of Victoria. She has degrees in Leisure Studies (BA), Adult Health and Fitness (MA), and Health Promotion (PhD). Joan's research and teaching interests include planning and evaluation, social marketing, community and population health, and participatory action research methodologies.

Author Index

Subject Index